W9-DDQ-524

21st Century Edition

ENCYCLOPEDIA OF
BODYBUILDING
THE COMPLETE A–Z BOOK ON MUSCLE BUILDING

Robert Kennedy

Published by Robert Kennedy Publishing

5775 McLaughlin Road

Mississauga, ON

L5R 3P7 Canada

Visit us at www.emusclemag.com

Encyclopedia of Bodybuilding

Art Directors: Alex Waddell and Jason Branidis

Editor: Wendy Morley

Proofreader: Jacqui Hartley

Library and Archives Canada Cataloguing in Publication

Kennedy, Robert, 1938-

    The encyclopedia of bodybuilding : the complete A-Z book on muscle building / Robert Kennedy. -- 21st century ed.

Includes index.

ISBN 978-1-55210-051-6

    1. Bodybuilding. I. Title.

GV546.5.K454 2008   613.7'13   C2008-904637-4

10 9 8 7 6 5 4 3 2 1

Distributed in Canada by

NBN (National Book Network)

67 Mowat Avenue, Suite 241

Toronto, ON

M6K 3E3

Distributed in USA by

NBN (National Book Network)

15200 NBN Way

Blue Ridge Summit, PA

17214

Printed in Canada.

Robert Kennedy Publishing Book Department

Art Director: Gabriella Caruso Marques

Managing Editor: Wendy Morley

IMPORTANT

The information in this book reflects the author's experiences and opinions and is not intended to replace medical advice.

Before beginning this or any other nutritional or exercise regimen, consult your physician to be sure it is appropriate for you. Ask for a physical stress test.

"No matter how genetically gifted you are, it is unrealistic to expect to look like the pros in our magazine within a few months' time. Muscles like that take years of hard work and proper nutrition to develop."
– Editors of *MuscleMag International*

CONTENTS

Table of Contents

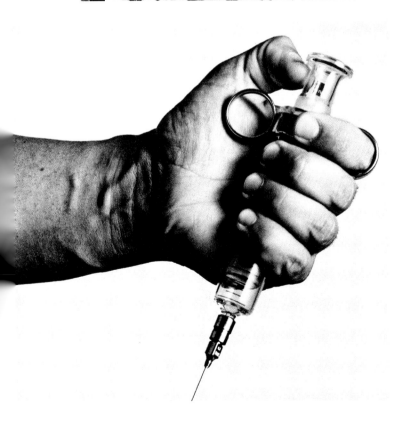

Preface

PREFACE

Has it really been 10 years since I published the first *MuscleMag International Encyclopedia of Bodybuilding*? Perhaps Einstein was right after all – time is relative. But one thing is for sure – it's been quite the 10 years!

It seemed that no sooner had the massive Brit, Dorian Yates, headed back to England with his sixth Mr. Olympia title when a relative unknown, Ronnie Coleman, started his record-tying run of eight Mr. Olympia wins. The big Texan was to continue the trend of ever-increasing physique size, carrying 290 pounds of ultra-striated beef into battle. With 2006 and 2007 winner Jay Cutler also tipping the scales in the 280+ pound range, the time seems near that the first 300 pounder will walk away with the sport's most coveted title.

Besides the escalating size, another revolution to come about during this time was in the training styles of most bodybuilders. Although a few bodybuilders still follow the traditional high-volume style of training made popular by Arnold Schwarzenegger back in the 1970s, most now follow the shorter, more intense form of training advocated by Dorian Yates.

And speaking of bodybuilding's most famous alumni, the lad from Austria has done quite well for himself since the first edition of this book. Not content to be the sport's No. 1 star and world's most successful actor, Arnold decided to throw his hat into the political arena. In typical Schwarzenegger fashion, he won the governorship of California in 2003. Many feel that with an amendment to the constitution (to allow those not born in the USA to run for the presidency) it's only a matter of time before Arnold flexes his way into the Oval Office.

While the popularity of both Arnold and male bodybuilding continues to climb, the same cannot be said for the female side of the sport. After starting with such promise in the early '80s and reaching very respectable heights, thanks in part to the great Cory Everson in the late '80s, the sport took a nosedive in the 1990s. Although numerous theories have been put forward as to why, the most prevalent is that bodybuilding fans – male and female – are just not interested in female physiques that would have won the Mr. America 40 or 50 years ago. Even the sport's top female title – the Ms. Olympia – is not immune, having nearly been cancelled on numerous occasions.

As female bodybuilding began its tumble, the new sports of women's fitness and figure took off. Displaying physiques hard and athletic yet still feminine, fitness and figure contestants have far exceeded their female bodybuilding counterparts in both popularity and prize money. Unless there's a change in the judging standards, this trend will no doubt continue.

One area that hasn't changed over the last 10 years is the popularity of food supplements. Creatine and whey protein are still the biggest sellers, but nipping at their heels are a whole host of others including nitric oxide, glutamine and the latest generation of fat-burners.

Related to the topic of supplements is the topic of performance-enhancing drugs. While at one time there was a definite distinction between the two, the supplement companies muddied the water in the late 1990s by releasing a new category of supplements called pro hormones. As the name suggests, pro hormones are not drugs in the classical sense, but can be converted to anabolic substances by the body. When baseball superstar Mark McGwire got caught with the pro hormone androstenedione in his locker, sales went through the roof. It was short-lived, however, as the U.S. government quickly added pro hormones to its list of banned substances. Thanks to the Anabolic Steroid Control Act of 1991 and subsequent modifications, possession of either steroids or pro hormones is now a felony in most states.

Yes it's been quite the 10 years. And that's why I felt it was time to overhaul an already great book and make it even better. How, you ask? Well for starters we give you new chapters. Each is jam-packed with the latest information on training, nutrition and recovery. And the chapters that feature the training routines of the top superstars are also brand new. You want to know how Jay Cutler built that incredible chest? Read on. Curious about how a 5'4" Lee Priest developed 22-inch arms? It's in here. Wonder how 280-pound Markus Ruhl created those yard-wide shoulders? It's just a few pages away. This book contains bodypart routines of just about every top bodybuilder competing today. And don't worry, I haven't forgot about the champions of the past. Immediately following the training routines of the current generation of stars I've included a chapter that looks at the workouts of such legends as Arnold Schwarzenegger, Lou Ferrigno, Dorian Yates, Lee Haney, Robby Robinson and Tom Platz.

So whip up your favorite protein shake, stretch out on the couch, sit back and enjoy.

INTRODUCTION

Introduction

"The beauty of bodybuilding is that anything can happen if you make it happen. By your own efforts you can add or subtract pounds of bodyweight. You can build your arms, shoulders, legs, chest and back. In doing so you can find pleasure in training that you might never have dreamed possible."

– Editorial in Musclemag International.

t's difficult to determine when exactly bodybuilding became a sport. It's like trying to determine which bodybuilding expert invented which training technique – ask three different people and you'll get three different answers. Before we dive into the heart of what makes bodybuilding such a fascinating sport, let's trace the sport's fascinating evolution.

GREEK AND ROMAN IDEALS

Many bodybuilding historians point us back to the ancient Greeks and Romans for a full understanding of the evolution of the sport. One of the top Hollywood movies of 2000 was *Gladiator*, staring Russell Crowe and bodybuilder Ralf Moeller. Beyond the epic's plots and subplots, one of the movie's underlying themes focused on the physical prowess of the gladiator. Sporting a physique that rivaled modern-day wrestlers and boxers, the Roman gladiator battled for the most valuable prize of all – his life! The Colosseum was no place for the meek, mild and underdeveloped. A gladiator's life literally depended on great physical condition and expert handling of an assortment of weapons.

For those who find the Roman form of entertainment too harsh, the ancient Greeks may be easier to understand. Instead of hacking one another to

Photo of Mike O'Hearn by Alex Ardenti

death for the amusement of the rich, the Greeks emphasized friendly competition among neighboring states. Rather than throw a spear to kill a lion or opponent, the Greeks would measure the distance it could be hurled. Instead of swinging a sword to disembowel, the Greeks had their competitors wrestle. Despite being abandoned for thousands of years, the Greek ideals of sport were revived in 1896 as the modern Olympics. The Greeks also referred to their athletes as "Olympians." Joe Weider honored these ancient Olympians by naming the top bodybuilding title the Mr. Olympia competition.

THE PHYSICAL CULTURISTS

"Strongest man" competitions go back centuries. While these individuals would never have won trophies in a future bodybuilding contest, they thrilled audiences with their great feats of physical strength, including hoisting large stones, tossing logs and the always-popular bending of iron bars. Don't be shocked if these feats of physical prowess seem familiar, as most are now regular parts of the Strongest Man in the World competitions.

One of the most important stages in physique devel-

opment took place in the mid 1800s as the Industrial Revolution began. Despite its numerous social benefits, the Industrial Revolution led to several health problems, including overcrowding and extreme pollution. One group of individuals, the Physical Culturists, recognized the dangers from these new technologies. These forerunners of modern-day lifestyle coaches were determined to improve the eating and exercise habits of 19th century Europe. They decided to promote one particular individual as the epitome of physical perfection and health. His name was Eugen Sandow. Unlike most of the other strongmen of the day, Sandow was also a showman and was devoted to physical appearance and health as much as he was to strength.

THE FIRST STAR OF BODYBUILDING

Given Sandow's reputation as both a great strongmen and showman, it's not surprising that an American promoter Florenz Ziegfeld (of the famous Ziegfeld Follies) also sought his talents. Ziegfeld was a promoter who knew how to please an audience and make money at the same time. When Ziegfeld heard of Sandow's success in

Europe, he convinced him to come to America. After nearly a century of Victorian repressiveness, American audiences were ready for something a little more risqué. With single-digit body fat levels and near-flawless proportions, Sandow awed audiences with his glass-booth posing exhibitions. Throughout the next couple of decades, Sandow became enormously wealthy simply by displaying his physique (covered by nothing but a fig leaf!). It wasn't long before young men everywhere wanted to look like Sandow. Contests were held regularly and sales of dumbells and barbells quickly increased. To honor Sandow's impact on physical development, in

1977 Joe Weider decided to present the winner of the annual Mr. Olympia title with a statue modeled after, and called, the Sandow.

A SPORT EMERGES

While Sandow was undoubtedly the top star of the early 20th century, other stars helped contribute to the birth of modern bodybuilding. In 1898, George Hackenschmidt ("the Russian Lion") won the Russian weightlifting championship. Beginning in 1903, Bernarr Macfadden held a series of contests to determine

America's Most Perfectly Developed Man. The first was held in New York's Madison Square Garden. Besides contests, Macfadden also founded the magazine *Physical Culture*, the forerunner to today's popular muscle magazines, which include *MuscleMag International*, *Flex*, and *Iron Man*.

Over the next couple of decades, Macfadden's contests grew in popularity and, unlike pure strength competitions, judged both strength and the quality of the competitor's physique. It was the 1921 contest that would introduce the world to an American icon. The winner that year was Angelo Siciliano (who later changed his name to Charles Atlas). He received $1,000 – an enormous sum in those days.

While other strongmen and "best physique" title winners gave exhibitions and lectures, it was Atlas who really turned bodybuilding into the money-making sport it became. He put together a series of training courses called Dynamic Tension – all targeted at the untapped market of teenage males. To get the attention he needed, Atlas cleverly placed a small ad in the back of popular comic books. The ad features a young skinny kid getting humiliated in front of a girl by a bully on a beach. The ad then shows the kid a couple of months later, much stronger and more muscular – and he easily drops the bully with one punch! Atlas' training course became so successful that by the mid 1970s over six million copies had been sold. Atlas knew how to connect with the teenager and for over 50 years the phrase "don't get sand kicked in your face," became the rally cry of American teenage males.

Atlas' success wasn't just due to his ability to market bodybuilding as a sport. His physique influenced an entire generation of followers. The irony is that Atlas built his physique lifting barbells and dumbells for "reps" and "sets." He may have built a financial empire selling Dynamic Tension, but he built his own body doing presses and curls.

One of the men influenced by Atlas was Siegmund Klein. Klein had that great combination of size, shape and definition. Klein also had a keen business sense, and was a successful gym owner and writer. Like those before him, Klein believed that physical appearance and health were just as crucial as pure physical strength.

Throughout the 1930s, physical culture contests continued to grow in popularity, and the term "bodybuilding" soon emerged. As a holdover from previous generations, competitors still had to perform some sort of physical act (usually involving strength or balance). As the quality of physiques improved, the need for physical demonstration began to fade into the background. In 1930, the first Mr. America contest was held. The competitors came from an assortment of athletic backgrounds, and it quickly became apparent that the weightlifters had the best physiques.

To many, the first true Mr. America was John Grimek, who won the title in 1940 and 1941. Unlike previous champions, John built his physique almost entirely with barbells and dumbells. Soon physical culture centers (now being called gyms) were packed with young bodybuilders trying to become the next John Grimek.

THE FIRST GENERATION OF SUPERSTARS

As John Grimek was turning heads with his near perfectly proportioned physique, another bodybuilder was also getting plenty of attention. Many consider Clancy Ross

I was there when this shot was taken, and those were not models. They were real girls who knew a good thing when they saw it!

the first massive bodybuilder. Unlike most of the other great champions of the day, including Grimek, whose focus was strength and Olympic weightlifting (the physique just happened to be a side effect), Ross relied almost solely on barbell and dumbell exercises for one purpose – to build his muscles to the maximum. In fact, Ross's workouts would fit right in at any bodybuilding gym today. With his broad shoulders tapering to a tiny waist, and low body fat revealing thick musculature, Ross could probably still hold his own in a modern city or state-level championship.

IN THE STEPS OF HERCULES

Ross and Grimek were undoubtedly two of the best-known stars among bodybuilders. But one person made the sport popular with the masses. His name was Steve Reeves, and until Arnold Schwarzenegger emerged decades later, he was the best-known bodybuilder to the general public. Many experts still consider Reeves's physique to be the epitome of the Greek ideals of proportion and development. After winning both the Mr. America and Mr. Universe titles, Reeves took his classic physique and manly good looks to Hollywood. Within a few years, he was one of Hollywood's biggest stars and made classic movies such as *Hercules* and *The Thief of Baghdad*.

THE '50s AND '60s

Many historians consider the 1950s a transition period in bodybuilding. Most of the first generation of stars had retired, went into the gym-owning business, or as in Reeves case, to acting. While the bodybuilders of the 1930s and 1940s stayed true to the Greek ideals of symmetry and proportion, the new bodybuilders believed "more is better." From America, such behemoths as Bill Pearl

Photo of Steve Reeves

> " There was no television to speak of until the 1950s and most people who lived in the Santa Monica area spent their weekends at the beach with their families. The place provided lots of free entertainment. So Muscle Beach took off again and became an even bigger attraction than in pre-war days."
>
> – George Coates, bodybuilding writer and historian

and Chuck Sipes thrilled audiences with their incredible size and strength. From England (via South Africa) came 6'2", 220-pound Reg Park. Park's awesome size would inspire a whole generation of bodybuilders, including a young boy in Graz, Austria – Arnold Schwarzenegger!

If the 1950s were a time of transition, the 1960s witnessed an explosion in the sport. Park and Pearl were still competitive, but a whole new generation of exciting bodybuilding personalities emerged. Some of the top bodybuilders of the 1960s included Dave Draper, Rick Wayne, Freddie Ortiz, Leroy Colbert, Frank Zane, Boyer Coe, Dennis Tinerino, Chet Yorton and Harold Poole.

BIRTH OF MR. OLYMPIA

By the 1960s, bodybuilding had reached a point where in any given year there could be two or three Mr. Americas and Mr. Universes. When you included the winners from previous years (not to mention the top stars from other countries) it's not surprising that a new debate emerged – which one was really the best bodybuilder alive? To answer that question, promoter and publisher Joe Weider created the Mr. Olympia contest, which would be open only to previous top title winners. The first two contests, the 1965 and 1966 Mr. Olympias, were won by California's Larry Scott. With his dark good looks and near perfect 20-inch arms, Larry became the idol of millions. He also came to symbolize the innocence of the sport in the 1960s.

When Larry retired from the sport (after acquiring small roles in numerous Hollywood movies), he was succeeded by The Myth – Sergio Oliva. Oliva defected to the U.S. while representing Cuba in weightlifting at the 1961 Pan American Games. Even by today's standards, Oliva was a muscle freak. His muscle density was about 20 years ahead of its time. In fact, those who never met him in person assumed he was just a "myth!"

Oliva dominated the Mr. Olympia from 1967 to 1969. He was so dominant that one year he was awarded the title because no one even dared to challenge him! By 1969, however, Oliva had a new challenger, and his name was Arnold Schwarzenegger.

THE AUSTRIAN OAK

Arnold's second place to Oliva at the 1969 Mr. Olympia contest launched the career of bodybuilding's most famous star. Starting with the 1965 Junior Mr. Europe title and continuing up until his first retirement in 1975, Arnold won six straight Mr. Olympia titles and five Mr. Universe titles. When he first landed in America from Australia in 1968, Arnold spoke little English and had no formal education. His 1968 defeat at the hands of a much smaller Frank Zane at the Mr. Universe contest would have shattered most, but not Arnold. Over the next few years he dropped his weight from a smooth 250 pounds to an ultra-hard 235 pounds and began his run for the coveted Mr. Olympia title. Arnold was so dominant during the early 1970s that fans debated only about who would win second place – Arnold was all but assured first place!

THE "PUMPING IRON" YEARS

Even though he was the dominant bodybuilding personality of the 1970s, a whole host of new and former stars were nipping at Arnold's heels. One of the best was Arnold's good friend from Europe, Franco Columbu. Standing a mere 5'5" tall, Franco proved that a short bodybuilder could defeat taller opponents. Like Arnold,

Franco established himself in Europe before emigrating to America. Once Arnold was settled in America, Franco decided to join him and quickly collected an impressive amount of victories, culminating with his 1976 Mr. Olympia win. What set Franco apart from other competitors was that he had one of the strongest physiques around. He won numerous powerlifting competitions and competed in a number of strongman championships.

Other bodybuilding stars of the early to mid '70s included Danny Padilla, Boyer Coe, Robby Robinson, Roy Callender, Mike Mentzer, Albert Beckles, Mike Katz and Ken Waller, but the biggest bodybuilder on the scene during the mid '70s was Lou Ferrigno. Lou stood 6'5" and weighed 260–270 pounds in contest shape. With his massive size and Mr. America and Mr. Universe wins he was expected to truly challenge for the Mr. Olympia, but opted instead to become a TV star, donning green body make-up and appearing each week as The Incredible Hulk.

One of the most significant events in bodybuilding's history took place in 1975 when two relatively unknown

> " With virtually no backing for promotion, the film *Pumping Iron* went on to be a smashing success. It quickly became the highest-grossing documentary in history, mostly because of the performance of its charismatic star, Arnold Schwarzenegger.
>
> – Nelson Montana, regular *MuscleMag International* contributor

filmmakers, George Butler and Jerome Gary, produced the ground-breaking documentary *Pumping Iron*. For nearly a year the two followed the training of the sport's top stars as they prepared for that year's Mr. Olympia and Mr. Universe contests. Although Arnold had decided to retire from the sport, appearing on the big screen was too enticing an opportunity to miss and he came back out of retirement. The documentary was based on the 1974 book of the same name that Butler had written with Charles Gaines. This famous documentary helped bring bodybuilding out of school gymnasiums and into large theater and concert venues. Besides Arnold, Ed Corney,

Photo (Clockwise from left) of Lou Ferrigno, Arnold Schwarzenegger & Franco Columbu, George Butler, Serge Nubret

Arnold Schwarzenegger
with friend and training
partner Franco Columbu

Lou Ferrigno

George Butler, director
of *Pumping Iron*

Serge
Nubret

PUMPING IRON

Arnold and Franco
flank Joe Gold

Robby Robinson, Mike Katz, Franco Columbu, Danny Padilla, Serge Nubret, Ken Waller, and Lou Ferrigno all appeared in the film.

Thanks to Arnold's on-screen charisma and the professionalism with which Gary and Butler portrayed bodybuilders, bodybuilding became solidified as a serious and legitimate sport.

THE ARRIVAL OF ONE ROBERT KENNEDY

It wasn't just European bodybuilding stars emigrating to North America in the 1960s and '70s. Despite securing a teaching position at a British arts college, I felt that life had more to offer and decided to pursue my dream of publishing a bodybuilding magazine. After leaving England for Canada, I realized that dream by publishing *MuscleMag International* – now one of the world's largest and most successful fitness magazines. I eventually expanded the *MuscleMag* empire to include five addition-

al magazines: *Reps!*, *Maximum Fitness*, *Curves*, *Oxygen* and *Clean Eating*; a book publishing division; and numerous *MuscleMag International* stores. I have also written over 50 bodybuilding and fitness-related books and hundreds of magazine articles. I always believed that bodybuilding is the best sport in the world, and I've devoted my career to proving it.

A NEW DIRECTION

After nearly ten years of dominance by Arnold and Sergio Oliva, the sport of bodybuilding took a new direction in 1977 when Frank Zane won the Mr. Olympia contest. Frank started his bodybuilding career in the 1960s (at the 1968 Mr. Universe he was one of the few to ever beat Arnold). Throughout the 1970s he established a reputation as one of the most symmetrical and proportionately balanced bodybuilders around. Early on Frank realized that his genetics would never allow him to build the same degree of mass as some of the other competitors, so he

The future governor of California and I talk bodybuilding.

Photo of Robert Kennedy and Arnold Schwarzenegger

took what he had and made the best of it. When the Greeks and Romans chiseled out statues of the perfect male physique it was Frank's they had in mind. With a posing routine to match his perfect proportions, Frank won the Mr. Olympia from 1977 to 1979.

"I'LL BE BACK!"

Although it would be four years before he uttered those immortal lines as The Terminator, Arnold Schwarzenegger caused quite the stir in the bodybuilding world when he came out of retirement to win the 1980 Mr. Olympia in Sydney, Australia. Arnold was training for his first major Hollywood movie at the time, *Conan the Barbarian*, and decided to step into the Olympia ring one more time. Most in the audience felt that Arnold shouldn't have won, as he was 10 to 15 pounds off his best weight. Conversely, some of his rivals, including Boyer Coe, Mike Mentzer and Chris Dickerson, were in the best shape of their lives. Regardless, Arnold was crowned Mr. Olympia for a record seventh time.

Arnold's 1980 win might have created controversy at the time, but it was Franco Columbu's win in 1981 that is still talked about. Franco was way off his 1976 form and didn't even appear well proportioned, having never really recovered from breaking his leg running with a refrigerator during a strongman competition. It didn't help Franco that four of the top bodybuilders in the world – Chris Dickerson, Danny Padilla, Roy Callender and Tom Platz – were in phenomenal shape. But Franco walked off with the Sandow trophy and was Mr. Olympia for the second time in his career.

After placing second to Arnold and Franco in 1980 and 1981, Chris Dickerson was all set to retire, but decided to give it one more try. His 1982 Mr. Olympia win was the crowning achievement in a successful career – a

Photo of Frank Zane

career that included being crowned the first African American Mr. America. Chris regularly trumped larger competitors by following Frank Zane's strategy of solid conditioning, superior proportions, and great posing routines.

The 1983 Mr. Olympia was won by Lebanon's Samir Bannout. Like Sergio, Arnold and Franco, Samir realized his future was in America, and with a near flawlessly proportioned physique, he captured the sport's top prize. The third-place finisher that year, Lee Haney, also deserves mention because the following year he began his record run of eight Mr. Olympia wins.

Like Oliva and Arnold before him, Atlanta's Lee Haney literally dwarfed the competition with his size. Weighing 250 pounds in contest shape, Lee first came to prominence when he won the 1982 Mr. America title. In 1984 he began his assault on Arnold's record seven Mr. Olympia wins. By 1991, with eight wins to his credit, Lee had established himself as the sport's new king.

Even though Haney won every Mr. Olympia between 1984 and 1991, he was pushed to the edge on three occasions by 185-pound Lee Labrada. Labrada was another refuge from Castro's Cuba. He was nicknamed "mass with class," with his perfect blend of shape, proportion and definition. Other bodybuilders who made bodybuilding exciting to watch in the 1980s included Gary Strydom, Vince Comerford, Mike Ashley, Berry DeMey and Mike Christian.

BRANCHING OUT IN THE 1980s

Besides the arrival of new stars in the 1980s, the decade also saw the bodybuilding tree branch out in many new directions. The first major change was the renaming of the bodybuilding titles by the sport's largest governing body, the International Federation of Bodybuilders (IFBB). The organizers decided to keep bodybuilding similar to other sports by calling the titles "championships." The former "titles" that became championships were the Los Angeles Championships, California Championships, National Championships and the World Championships. The only title that retained the "Mr." designation was the Mr. Olympia. Even the professional Mr. Universe changed names in 1989 when Arnold Schwarzenegger decided to team up with long-time friend Jim Lorimer. Recognizing the power of Arnold's name, the two decided to rename the Mr. Universe the Arnold Classic. While the Mr. Olympia is still the most prestigious title, the Arnold Classic draws larger crowds by making the event a weekend extravaganza of contests, fitness demonstrations and conferences. The show is held every spring in Columbus, Ohio.

Many of the smaller bodybuilding federations still use the old title names (the NABBA Mr. Universe being one) and most bodybuilders themselves still prefer the old names. There is just something mythical about being Mr. America or Mr. Universe that National or World Champion doesn't carry.

MS. OLYMPIA: THE WOMEN ARRIVE

Women had always been associated with men's bodybuilding but usually in an "eye-candy" role. Then in the late 1970s, Lisa Lyon arrived on the scene. Lyon demonstrated to women that they could use weight training to improve their health and appearance, without becoming too masculine. It wasn't long before the sport of women's bodybuilding became popular and female bodybuilders began making headlines alongside the men.

The biggest female star of the 1980s was Cory Everson, who won the Ms. Olympia title every year from 1984 to 1989. Cory combined femininity with good muscle size and definition. In many respects, Cory was the Arnold Schwarzenegger of women's bodybuilding – she helped bring female bodybuilding to the masses with her personality, books, videos and TV appearances. If Cory Everson was the Arnold of women's bodybuilding then

Six-time Ms. Olympia Cory Everson inspired millions of young women to hoist some iron.

Photo of Cory Everson

Lenda Murray was the Lee Haney. With eight Ms. Olympia titles to her credit, Lenda took female bodybuilding to the next level.

As expected, it wasn't long before women's bodybuilding began turning into a "more is better" contest. Where men's bodybuilding had had nearly three decades of drug-free competition (keeping in mind that anabolic steroids – the primary drugs used to build muscle mass – weren't even synthesized until the late 1950s), it took the women just a few years to dive into the murky world of performance enhancement. Soon the lineup in a top female bodybuilding contests began resembling a men's city championship! In fact, these days the great John Grimek or Steve Reeves wouldn't stand a chance of winning the *Ms.* Olympia contest!

Unlike men's contests, where attendance was solid, women's events starting suffering. At the heart of the matter was that the vast majority of women didn't want to look like the current generation of female bodybuilders. Men also did not find the massive physiques appealing to look at in a woman. In response to this, a new form of female competition emerged – fitness contests. Fitness contests require women to display strength and athletic agility with femininity.

If women's fitness has a drawback it's that the women who dominate tend to have gymnastic backgrounds. This is a big disadvantage to women with no such background because it's very difficult to learn advanced tumbling routines as an adult (most of the best gymnasts have been practicing since childhood). To give women with no gymnastics background an option to compete, the female figure contest was created. Such events require no posing routines or tumbling runs – instead the contest is judged almost entirely on the contestants' physical appearances just standing there and waking.

THE BRITISH INVASION

No sooner had Lee Haney contemplated retirement when the next bodybuilding superstar emerged on the scene. Britain's Dorain Yates pushed the size bar to yet another

level when he began his consecutive run of six Mr. Olympia titles in 1992. Packing 265 pounds of striated muscle on his frame, Yates was the largest Mr. Olympia ever. Like Arnold and Haney before him, he completely dominated the sport. He was also the first Mr. Olympia not based in the United States. Training out of Temple Gym in Birmingham, England, Yates preferred to keep a low profile and let his physique do the talking!

Other dominant bodybuilders of the 1990s included Paul Dillett, Lee Priest, Shawn Ray, Flex Wheeler, Nasser El Sonbaty, Aaron Baker, Vince Taylor, Chris Cormier, Kevin Lervone and Milos Sarcev.

Shawn Ray, one of the most popular bodybuilders ever.

Photo of Shawn Ray

BODYBUILDING MASTERS

There was a time that once an athlete retired, he or she pretty much faded into oblivion. But not anymore. Sports such as golf and tennis now have very lucrative masters divisions that rival the regular contest divisions. Tiger Woods may be the most famous golfer in the world, but the galleries are still packed when Jack Nicklaus, Gary Player and Arnold Palmer tee up. Likewise such tennis greats as John McEnroe and Jimmy Connors can still draw a crowd. To keep bodybuilding consistent with other sports, the IFBB inserted a masters division in 1994. Featuring such stars as Robby Robinson, Ed Corney, Danny Padilla, Boyer Coe, Chris Dickerson, Lou Ferrigno and Bill Grant, the event was a huge hit with audiences for the first few years it ran. Unfortunately, declining sponsorships and a low amount of competitor numbers led to the contest being canceled after the 2003 event.

KING RONNIE

There was nothing special about the ninth place finisher of the 1997 Mr. Olympia. To most in the audience, Ronnie Coleman seemed to be another journeyman bodybuilder whose claim to fame would be to merely crack the top ten. Few would have guessed that Ronnie

had other plans! Starting in 1998, Ronnie ran up an impressive record-tying eight Mr. Olympia titles. Weighing between 270 and 290 pounds in contest shape, Ronnie is definitely the largest Mr. Olympia in history and is considered by many to be the greatest. Right up until his defeat by Jay Cutler at the 2006 Mr. Olympia, many people still believed that Ronnie would win 10 or 12 straight Mr. Olympias.

After placing second to Ronnie on four different occasions, Jay Cutler finally did what many considered impossible by preventing Ronnie Coleman from winning his record ninth Mr. Olympia title in 2006. With Jay successfully defending his title in 2007 and Ronnie placing fourth, it appears the Cutler era has begun and as of this writing this there's no telling when it will end.

INTO THE FUTURE

With prize money for professional bodybuilding contests now in the hundreds of thousands of dollars, it's not surprising that every year more and more hungry young bodybuilders vie for the sport's top titles. Every year also brings larger and larger competitors, with the average weight of the Mr. Olympia winner increasing by about 10 pounds every decade. Just look at this timeline of comparisons:

1960s – Sergio Oliva: 230 pounds
1970s – Arnold Schwarzenegger: 240 pounds
1980s – Lee Haney: 250 pounds
1990s – Dorian Yates: 260 pounds
Present – Ronnie Coleman and Jay Cutler: 280+ pounds

City and state competitors are now stepping onstage weighing as much as Arnold and Sergio did at their best. Unless some new standards are adopted (highly unlikely given the bodybuilding public's fascination with mass) then it's only a matter of time before the first 300-pounder is awarded the famous Sandow statue. Ronnie Coleman won the Mr. Olympia one year at just under 290 pounds – nearly 100 pounds more than Frank Zane's competitive weight in the late 1970s.

Photo of Ronnie COleman by Irvin Gelb

2000s
RONNIE COLEMAN

2008
JAY CUTLER

At over 300 pounds in the off-season and 274 in contest shape, Jay Cutler knows the meaning of the word "massive."

WHY?

So just why are competitors weighing in heavier than ever before? Does it mean that today's bodybuilders are simply training harder than their counterparts? Probably not. No one trained harder than Arnold and the rest of the gang at the old Gold's Gym in Santa Monica, California during the early 1970s. However, today's bodybuilders are probably more knowledgeable than their forerunners. Like most sports, bodybuilding has evolved over the decades and the older practitioners keep passing their tips and secrets on to the next group of hungry competitors. The shelves of local bookstores are piled high with informative bodybuilding books. Glance at the magazine stand and you'll see dozens of top-quality magazines, jam packed with the latest information on training, nutrition and competition. Unlike in Arnold's time, today's young bodybuilder has an abundance of information at hand.

Besides knowledge, another factor to explain the increase in size is simply numbers. Far more people are hoisting iron today than 20 or 30 years ago. This makes it more likely that a person with good muscle-building genes will actually discover his aptidude in the gym.

A third explanation for why today's competitors are heavier is nutritional supplementation. Thirty years ago supplementation meant liver tablets, raw eggs and multivitamins. Today, bodybuilding supplement companies are worth billions of dollars. Moreover, supplements today offer bodybuilders hundreds of performance-enhancing products to choose from. From creatine and nitric oxide to glutamine and state-of-the-art whey protein, today's bodybuilders have it far better than their counterparts did 30 or 40 years ago.

We'd be remiss if we left out the pharmacological aspect to modern bodybuilding. Since the late 1950s when Dianabol, the first anabolic steroid, was created, bodybuilders have been steadily increasing the dosages and numbers of performance-enhancing drugs. There are drugs to build muscle and strength, drugs to strip away body fat, drugs to increase energy, drugs to reduce recovery time, drugs to increase blood volume, and to top it all off, drugs to combat the side effects of all these drugs!

While the top stars would probably still win without the pharmacology, they wouldn't be as massive as they are without the chemical assistance.

Thanks to such bodybuilding icons as Steve Reeves, Arnold and Lou Ferrigno, bodybuilding is now one of the most popular sports in the world. In terms of numbers, it rivals football (soccer), volleyball and tennis. In addition, competitors now have access to thousands of books and articles on training and technique.

While I can't make any promises that you'll win the next Mr. Olympia, I am confident that if you train hard, eat clean and maintain a healthy lifestyle, you'll build a body that will be the envy of everyone. And who knows? Maybe, just maybe, you are a future Mr. Olympia just waiting to become part of history. As you rise to fame, I'll be with you every step of the way.

LAYING THE GROUNDWORK

CHAPTER 1

The Sport of Bodybuilding

"I'm retiring from competition, but I'll never stop bodybuilding. It's the greatest sport."

– Arnold Schwarzenegger, in 1976, announcing his retirement from competition. Arnold was true to his word, as he still works out regularly and looks better than virtually every male half his age.

t doesn't receive the same coverage as such other mainstream sports as football, baseball and basketball, but by all definitions, bodybuilding is a sport. Compare bodybuilding to gymnastics and figure skating. Competitors in all three sports train hard, perform posing routines to music and demonstrate compulsory movements during competition. The rankings and placings in all three are determined by a panel of judges. The three sports are almost identical in organization, training and competition!

It took a long time for bodybuilding to become recognized as a legitimate sport, but thanks to the efforts of individuals such as Arnold Schwarzenegger, Joe and Ben Weider and perhaps me, (to mention just a few), bodybuilding is now one of the world's most popular sports. The top contests have prizes in the hundreds of thousands of dollars, and the Arnold Classic and Mr. Olympia contests receive regular TV coverage.

STEREOTYPES AND MYTHS

Most sports carry stereotypes and myths, but bodybuilding probably has more than any other. Bodybuilders put up with significant ridicule and false truths, whether from jealousy or ignorance, who knows? But as we'll learn, most myths have no scientific basis – in fact, most myths fall into the same category as ghosts, UFOs and the Loch Ness monster. Let's take a look at the most common.

The Posedown is always an exciting round for fans.

Photo by Garry Bartlett

IF YOU STOP TRAINING, IT ALL TURNS TO FAT

Out of all the false statements linked to bodybuilding, this is probably the most persistent. As bodybuilding great Franco Columbu said in one of his books: the most vocal critics of bodybuilders are usually built like laboratory flasks!

Muscle cannot turn into fat any more than fat can turn into muscle. They are two completely different biological entities. Muscle is healthy, vibrant, living tissue, and in general the more of it you have, the healthier you are overall. Fat, however, merely sits there as a stored source of energy in case one day the food supply is cut off. If not burnt, the storage pile just gets larger. If fat could turn to muscle, we would have a lot of Mr. Olympias out there, given the rate of obesity in western society!

We're not sure where this myth came from. It could be jealousy on the part of non-exercisers. Rather than pick up a barbell or go for a run, they sit back with their donuts and criticize those who take pride in keeping in shape. Of course, some bodybuilders and other strength athletes do gain weight as they get older or stop training. As we age, or as we lose muscle when we stop training, our metabolisms slow down and we don't need as many calories to survive. Unfortunately, many do not adjust their caloric intakes acccordingly. The end result is a build-up of fat, as it would be with anyone who consumes more food than their body needs. Football players and powerlifters are famous for this. During their competitive years, their huge appetites match their high-energy workouts. Unfortunately, when they retire they neglect to alter their diet, so excess calories get deposited around the midsection.

All I can say is trust me, your muscles won't turn to fat if you stop training. Assuming you adjust your caloric intake, you will simply lose the muscle tissue over time.

THEY'RE BIG, BUT NOT STRONG

Another myth based on ignorance. This myth is probably based on the fact that modern bodybuilders don't have to demonstrate feats of strength at contests (unlike their counterparts decades ago). To most audience members, today's bodybuilder simply steps onstage and flexes. Also, years ago, Olympic weightlifters and powerlifters would be seen on stage lifting heavy weights, but without the same degree of muscle mass as modern bodybuilders. Well, things have changed over the past couple of decades. Many powerlifters and Olympic lifters have physiques rivaling bodybuilders. And as for bodybuilders being weak – virtually the entire Mr. Olympia lineup can bench press 500+ pounds, curl 200+ pounds and squat 600+ pounds. Guys like Jay Cutler, Gustavo Badell, Ronnie Coleman, Mustafa Mohammad, Markus Ruhl and Toney Freeman work out with poundage the average strong man couldn't lift once, let alone for 10 reps or more! As we'll see later in the book, there is a direct relationship between strength and size. The bigger your muscles, the stronger you'll be. It also works the other way around; the stronger you are, the bigger you can build your muscles.

YOU'LL BE MUSCLE-BOUND

How often do you see some big bodybuilder playing a "heavy" on TV or in a movie, barely able to move himself, while some 150-pound main actor dances around him and kicks his ass?! It rarely works that way in real life, I assure you! In fact, bodybuilders are on average more flexible than non-bodybuilders, due to the nature of their training. But thanks to Hollywood, people perceive a bodybuilder as being some brainless deadweight who can't fight for himself. Most muscles work in pairs, and contracting one muscle tends to stretch the opposing muscle group. Unless you train with poor technique and only perform half movements, don't worry about becoming "muscle bound."

If you're still worried about increased muscle mass causing reduced flexibility, look no further than professional sports teams. For years, coaches forbade their athletes from going near the weight room for fear of reducing their flexibility. How things have changed!

Virtually every professional sports team has a strength-training coach these days. Boxers and hockey players spend as much time in the weightlifting gym as in the ring or on the ice.

Finally, take a look at the posing routines of current stars Melvin Anthony and Dexter Jackson, and 1990s star Flex Wheeler. Despite their massive muscle size, all three bodybuilders demonstrate flexibility that rivals gymnasts. Trust me – you won't become muscle-bound from bodybuilding.

David Henry's excellent flexibility and massive muscle size.

Photo of David Henry by Garry Bartlet

Photo (Top) of Mark Alvisi by Alex Ardenti

Wahlberg, Russell Crowe, The "Rock" and Matthew McConaughey, to name just a few) all sport great-looking physiques that women love. The fact that virtually all of these stars regularly take their shirts off in their movies shows just how important it is for an actor to have a muscular and conditioned body.

Of course, no amount of persuasion will change the mind of someone who stubbornly refuses to see reality. Still, if it's choice between the soft pudgy look and the hard muscular look, the vast majority of women will choose the latter!

I DON'T WANT TO LOOK LIKE A MAN: A WOMEN'S PERSPECTIVE

One of the first things personal trainers hear when they start working with women is the phrase "If I lift weights, I'll look like a guy!" For those women reading this book, let me assure you that you won't soon be stunt doubling for Arnold Schwarzenegger. Female body chemistry simply won't allow it. The extremely muscular physiques you see in female bodybuilding contests are the result of anabolic steroid use (synthetic versions of the male hormone testosterone) in combination with extreme weight training . No amount of weight training will make a female body look like a man's. It's just ain't gonna happen! What you can expect, however, is increased strength, increased muscle tone, decreased body fat, and a reduced risk of osteoporosis. There is nothing better a female could do for her physique than to weight train.

BODYBUILDING IS GROSS!

This is not so much a myth as it is a matter of opinion. It is true that a large segment of the general public finds the extreme ripped bodybuilding physique a turn off. Well, the same could also be said for gross obesity, or even the average overweight guy. While most women probably won't buckle at the knees at the sight of a 280-pound Mr. Olympia competitor, virtually all are very physically attracted to the muscular and balanced physiques in such magazines as *Reps!*, *Men's Health*, and *Maximum Fitness*. It is worth noting that most of the top Hollywood stars of the last 20 years (Arnold, Sylvester Stallone, Mark

CHAPTER 2

Gym Safety and Etiquette

"I told them the rules of my gym were strictly enforced. I read all the rules to them and explained that we didn't tolerate the breaking or even bending of the rules, and that we terminated many members for various infractions."

– Preston Rendell, Natural USA champion and gym owner

Before diving into the actual training principles and techniques that encompass the sport of bodybuilding, a discussion on safety and proper gym etiquette is required. This book has been written with your safety in mind. If you follow my directions properly, you should never experience an injury or life-threatening situation while training in the gym. But there is only so much I can tell you; ultimately your safety and conduct is in your own hands. Most gyms have the primary safety rules posted on the walls. Some of these rules are for safety, others for hygiene, others revolve around common courtesy. Please do your best to follow them. Here are the top rules for safety and gym etiquette:

"Many are guilty of complacency when it comes to a proper warmup – even me. Now that I am getting back to basics I urge you to do the same. Don't let an injury put you at a disadvantage and delay your gains. By planning ahead and taking the time to adequately prepare for training you won't need to take time off."

– John Rodrigues, *MuscleMag International* contributor

ALWAYS WARM UP

The vast majority of injuries are caused when people dive right into their maximum poundage before their muscles are properly warmed up. Think of your muscles as elastic bands. Elastic bands lose their flexibility when cooled. Conversely, they'll stretch better when warmed. Muscles behave in a similar manner. Do a short 5- to 10-minute cardio session

Photo of Pete Ciccone by Ralph DeHaan

to warm up the body in general and a few light warmup sets for each of the muscles you plan to train that day. Most importantly, never, ever start a workout with your heaviest weight!

WHERE POSSIBLE, USE A SPOTTER

For those not familiar with the term, a spotter is a friend, partner, or stranger for that matter, who stands behind you on exercises that could potentially leave you trapped under a barbell. People have been found dead in their basements, a barbell loaded with a couple of hundred pounds trapped across their necks. Exercises such as squats and bench presses should not be performed using heavy weight unless you have a trusted spotter behind

you. You probably won't need a spotter on most machine exercises as they're usually designed with safety in mind (the Smith machine being a possible exception). Likewise, dumbells are safe at any weight as they can be easily dropped if you run into trouble.

USE COLLARS ON YOUR BARBELL EXERCISES

You can think of collars as bolts or pins that lock the weight plates on the ends of a barbell as you lift and lower. Even with the best technique, you will normally have a slight tilt to the bar, at least during one part of any given exercise. If the bar tilts too much, the plates may slide off that side and then the bar will violently fall in the opposite direction (since that end is now heavier).

Depending on the weight and exercise, you could potentially break a wrist, or worse. For the sake of a few extra seconds, put a set of collars on the bar.

WHEN NECESSARY, USE A WEIGHTLIFTING BELT

You can consider a weightlifting belt as your shin guard or baseball glove. Other sports have protective gear, so why not bodybuilding? Certain exercises place tremendous stress on the spine. A wide (four to six inches) piece of leather will protect your lower back on such exercises as squats, deadlifts, and various pressing and rowing movements. However, don't use the belt on all exercises, or even on your light warmup sets – if you become dependent on it your lower back muscles will never strengthen. The belt should be used only as a protection device on risky exercises.

RETURN YOUR WEIGHTS TO THEIR PROPER RACKS

Nothing is more annoying than having to look all over the gym for a set of dumbells for your next set, except maybe when you have to take five minutes to strip a couple of hundred pounds off a leg press machine before you can use it. Putting back all the plates and dumbells ensures that other gym members won't have to waste time looking around the gym for them. There is also a more practical reason for putting your weights away – safety. Having weight plates or dumbells all over the floor is an accident waiting to happen. Someone could

easily trip and injure themselves. Most gym employees will enforce this rule, but why wait to be told? You're not a child anymore. Please take it upon yourself to clean up after your workout.

NEVER BE AFRAID TO ASK FOR ADVICE

As comprehensive as this book is, there will be times when you're unsure of an exercise. Most gym instructors are certified and know their stuff. Take advantage of their expertise anytime you have a bodybuilding-related question. If an instructor is not available, study some of the regular members. It won't be long before you spot who the experienced trainers are. Usually all it takes is once glance, but don't go by size alone – some average-sized individuals know more about bodybuilding than the 250-pounders. Watch for those with strict technique and confidence.

GOOD TECHNIQUE IS SUPERIOR

Perform all the exercises using proper form. While there are a few advanced bodybuilding techniques that involve what could be termed "loose training," in general using strict style is the best way to train, especially at the beginner or intermediate levels. It prevents injuries and will provide the most muscle gains from your training.

USE WEIGHT SUPPORTS AND RACKS WHERE NECESSARY

Most exercises can be performed with just the barbells or dumbells themselves. There are, however, a few that could leave you in a dangerous situation if you were to lose con-

DON'T THROW YOUR WEIGHT AROUND

Proper form is important when performing any exercise, but this holds especially true for biceps training, specifically in curling movements. Don't be one of those guys who boost the weight up from their hips. For a curl to be effective, the burden of the resistance must rest solely on your biceps. The key to proper form when curling is to pin your upper arms against your body while preventing yourself from leaning back.

Illustration by Mark Collins

trol. Two examples are the bench press and squat. At some point, everyone will attempt an extra rep on one of these exercises and fail. A proper squat or bench press rack has a series of pins or supports arranged at different levels to catch the weight if you can't return it to the starting position. Besides, it doesn't look cool when your face is lobster-red and your eyes are bulging out of your head because a couple of hundred pounds is lying across your spine or neck, so use the racks!

WIPE DOWN YOUR BENCH AFTER USE

Human sweat carries hundreds of germs. It's pretty disgusting to go to a bench or machine and see a layer of someone else's sweat dripping all over it! Most gyms have towels or paper towels available for wiping down equipment. Take a few seconds to wipe off your sweat when you're finished with that bench or piece of equipment. Laying your towel down before using the bench is also a great idea.

"Hey, you want to work up a sweat. Good for you. Just don't expect me to be thrilled about doing the backstroke in the pond you've just made when it's my turn to use the bench."

–Tom Schreck, *MuscleMag International* contributor

WEAR THE PROPER TRAINING ATTIRE

Some gyms can be very strict about attire, but most large fitness centers will leave it up to the members. If you're training in the summer and your gym is not air conditioned, wear something light, such as a T-shirt and pair of shorts. Conversely, if your gym is on the cool side, keep a sweatshirt on until your muscles are fully warmed up. In terms of footwear, always have a good pair of sneakers. Many exercises will place a great deal of stress on your ankles and you'll need solid support to protect the small muscles and bones in this region. Besides, a weight plate could slip out of your hand as you're putting it on the bar or weight rack. It would be great to have more between your foot and the plate than a sock!

NEVER STOP LEARNING

The fact that you're reading this book is a start. As in most sports, success in bodybuilding will require the application of new knowledge. Don't just learn a few exercises and think you know it all. Even the reigning Mr. Olympia is continually learning how to get the most out of his training or how to improve his diet. More knowledge will not only improve your health and physique, it will also help prevent injury. Most injuries are not caused by lifting too much weight, but by using improper technique – whether from ignorance or stupidity. Every month *MuscleMag International* hits the store shelves. Each issue is loaded with the latest pertinent information on training, nutrition, and supplementation. Even better – take out a subscription! Getting a subscription means you're guaranteed to always be informed!

EVEN THE GREATEST SEEK MEDICAL ADVICE!

No matter what shape you think you are in, we strongly urge you to get a physical. A physical will give you an indication of how physically conditioned you are, and you will discover any concerns you should be aware of. Your doctor will likely send you for some blood work. This is routine and will be a quick and relatively painless procedure. Getting your cholesterol and liver enzyme levels checked is the first step in determining how healthy you are. You should also get a physical stress test.

CHAPTER 3

Great Expectations

"Oddly enough, before he began training he showed signs of his eventual supremacy in competitive bodybuilding. He was thin and by anyone's standards quite average looking, yet he went on to redefine the limits of freaky musculature."

– Nelson Montana, *MuscleMag International* contributor, commenting on how average six-time Mr. Olympia, Dorian Yates, looked before he started training.

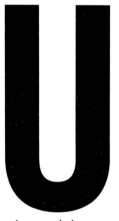

nlike most sports, where training tends to be generalized for everyone, bodybuilding programs can be tailored for an individual's genetic build and goals. If you're like most iron pumpers, improving your overall shape, appearance and health will be your primary goals. But as you begin seeing changes in your physique, you will start to feel great about how you look. Compliments and encouragement will begin to flood in. If you have the right genetics (more on that in a moment), train consistently and eat clean, there's a good chance you'll start seriously considering competing in a bodybuilding contest.

For other readers, perhaps your bodybuilding training will primarily be used to increase your performance in other sports. Athletes from wrestlers to boxers to tennis players and sprinters use bodybuilding exercises to reduce the risk of injury and improve their overall performance.

GENETICS – BLAME YOUR ANCESTORS

Change your exercises? Great. Alter your training schedule? Good idea. Tighten your eating practices or switch supplement brands? Go ahead! You can even change the color of your hair or skin. But there is nothing, absolutely nothing, you can do to alter your genes. From the moment of conception your DNA blueprint has been set and cannot be changed. Within a few months after you begin training you will quickly discover that certain muscle groups respond

> "No matter how genetically gifted you are, it is unrealistic to expect to look like the pros in our magazine within a few months' time. Muscles like that take years of hard work and proper nutrition to develop.
>
> – Editors of *MuscleMag International*

better than others. You may even notice that one side grows slightly faster than the other. Also, your chest may grow by simply looking at a barbell, while your back has to be pounded into growth.

Many bodybuilders have to accept that they have weak bodyparts. However, acceptance doesn't equate to

Photo of Darrem Charles by Irvin Gelb

giving up. It took Arnold Schwarzenegger over 10 years to bring his legs – his calves in particular – up to the superior level of his upper body. Don't let race influence your mindset either. While African Americans are generally considered to have poor genetics when it comes to building calves, some of the greatest calves of all time belong to such African American bodybuilders as Ronnie Coleman, Chris Dickerson, Vince Taylor and Dexter Jackson.

Everyone is different genetically. Just take a glance at the lineup of the most recent Mr. Olympia. Few bodybuilders can compare their front double biceps with Ronnie Coleman. Jay Cutler has brought his back up to the point that other bodybuilders pale in comparison in back shots. Lee Priest has more muscle on his 5'4" frame than many bodybuilders who are a foot taller. And while few would refer to Lee as symmetrical, or aesthetically pleasing, you can't deny that he has one awesome physique.

Conversely, Dexter Jackson has that Greek statue look. Even among these greats we have incredible diversity. Arnold Schwarzenegger's single double biceps pose (on the cover of his book *Education of a Bodybuilder*) has few equals. Franco Columbu's rear lat spread has yet to be duplicated. And when it comes to legs – Tom Platz was in a class by himself.

Genetics is the study of how traits are passed from one generation to the next. When relatives say you have your mom's eyes, or your dad's hair, they aren't trying to embarrass you – they are noticing inherited physical characteristics. Plenty of physical and personality traits become more and more visible as we age – some good, some bad. For example, cancer can "run" in some families. It doesn't mean that you'll definitely get cancer, but you will have a higher risk of developing it than someone whose family has no history of cancer.

GENETIC MARKER – BONE SIZE

Generally speaking, there is a direct relationship between skeleton size and muscle mass. A small-boned individual will have far more difficulty developing the same degree of muscle size as a larger-boned individual. A flip through a recent copy of *MuscleMag International* will confirm this. There may be a 20- or 30-pound difference in weight between two bodybuilders of the same height. Numerous bodybuilding authorities, including Robert Kennedy, have suggested that one of the best predictors of eventual arm size is wrist circumference. Generally speaking, you can expect to build your upper arms to about 10 inches larger than your wrist size. Keep in mind that this is adult wrist size, not teenage wrist size. If you're in your early to mid teens you still have many years of growth ahead of you, so don't let a seven-inch wrist depress you! By the time you're in your early 20s, it may be nine or ten inches in size. And even if it does max out at seven or eight inches, you could still develop large upper arms. A classic example of this is the great French bodybuilder and *Pumping Iron* star, Serge Nubret, who built 20+ inch arms with wrists measuring just seven inches.

I should add that there is an advantage to having small bones and joints. Nothing looks as impressive as large, full muscles separated by small joints. Extremely large-boned bodybuilders may have more muscle mass,

> **" The magic that is brought about by weight training never ceases to amaze me. I've seen fat guys lose all their flab and become ripped to shreds. Conversely, I've seen guys so thin that they had to move around in the shower to get wet who packed on so much muscle that they became in-demand subjects for the various bodybuilding mags.**
>
> – Editorial in *MuscleMag International*, discussing how a person can totally change his physique through weight training.

but they often appear blocky and chunky. Small-boned individuals tend to exhibit far better proportions and symmetry. Superstar Flex Wheeler built what many considered the greatest physique of all time and yet had a medium-sized bone structure at best.

Photo of Flex Wheeler by Robert Kennedy

NUMBER OF MUSCLE CELLS

As you are probably aware, muscles are made up of smaller subunits called muscle cells (more commonly called muscle fibers). It was once believed that individuals were born with a fixed number of muscle cells and that weight training simply enlarged them. Therefore, a person with 100 million cells in a given muscle would potentially be able to build more size than someone with 50 million cells. We all know guys who walk into a gym with muscular arms although they have never lifted a barbell in their lives. Such lucky individuals probably have an overabundance of muscle fibers in their arms – yet another blessing of good genetics! These are the guys who could one day grace the pages of *MuscleMag International* – assuming they train hard and eat plenty of clean food.

But as with wrist size, don't let this genetic variable curtail your hopes and dreams. Since the first edition of this book was written over 10 years ago, research has determined that weight training may be able to split muscle fibers, which can then enlarge.

HORMONALLY CHARGED

A third variable that can influence muscle size is hormone levels, testosterone in particular. I'll be saying more on hormones in the chapter on biology. Suffice it to say, individuals with naturally higher levels of the male hormone testosterone will probably build more muscle mass than someone with lower levels. Higher testosterone is one of the primary reasons that men on average are bigger and stronger than women.

Besides the physical advantages bestowed by testosterone, there is a psychological component. Higher testosterone levels have been linked to increased aggression levels (one reason why prison populations tend to be dominated by guys with high testosterone levels). Guys with super-charged hormone systems don't just work out with weights, they assault them! They can train for endless hours with energy and strength to spare. As expected, the greater the training intensity, the greater the increase in muscle strength and size.

But again, don't just give into genetics. Research indicates that natural testosterone levels can be elevated by doing basic multi-joint movements (called compound exercises) such as squats, deadlifts and bench presses. This is the reason why guys who do a lot of the heavy basic barbell exercises are much bigger and stronger than the guys who do a lot of machine and isolation movements.

A FINAL WORD

You've learned now that there is a genetic limit to how big and strong you'll get. One piece of potentially depressing news is that no matter how intensely you train, how clean your eating, or how many drugs you take, you'll still have a difficult time making it to the Mr. Olympia stage. If your natural bone structure dictates 170 pounds, then building a 250-pound ripped body is going to be challenge. However, everyone – and we mean everyone – can make tremendous gains in strength and size. Don't let anyone tell you otherwise! And you know what else? Who are we to say you'll never make it the Mr. Olympia stage without the right genetics?! Some of the top bodybuilders of all time won or came close to winning the Sandow statue without perfect genetics. There was nothing in the early pictures of guys like Franco Columbu, Frank Zane, Dexter Jackson, Dorian Yates or Lee Labrada to suggest bodybuilding superstardom. But they ultimately said: "To hell with genetics!" and went on to build incredible physiques. And so can you!

Photo of Mark Erpelding by Alex Ardenti

CHAPTER 4

All Shapes and Sizes

"When the shorter man builds quads that measure 25 to 28 inches around, they'll look astonishingly thick and muscular. A 6'4" man with the same quad size might be labeled 'chicken legs' in bodybuilding circles."

– Ron Harris, regular *MuscleMag International* contributor, commenting how genetics plays a role in a bodybuilder's appearance.

The next time you're in the gym, or at a shopping mall for that matter, take a close look at all the different body shapes and sizes. Although the general human population may seem extremely diverse, it's possible to group people according to common traits, the most common being skinny, fat and muscular. Probably the most popular method for classifying body types is Dr. William Sheldon's three-category somatotype system. Sheldon photographed over 46,000 men and women and discovered 88 distinct categories he called somatotypes. To keep things simple, he grouped all 88 into three major categories: endomorph, ectomorph and mesomorph.

Endomorphs tend to have more fat cells and large bones, and are usually short to medium in height. While building muscle is usually not a problem, losing body fat is. This is the most difficult group to classify. The person may truly be an ectomorph, but he or she could also be an ectomorph or mesomorph who is simply eating too much and doing little or no exercise.

Ectomorphs are often called "skinny" and tend to have long thin bones. Ectomorphs are lucky because they don't easily gain body fat. However, they have a difficult time building muscle and have to fight significantly for every ounce of muscle they gain.

Mesomorphs are the most blessed when it comes to bodybuilding. They usually have large bones and have no problem building muscle mass. Some mesomorphs gain fat easily, while others do not. Most of the competitors you see onstage at the Mr. Olympia contest are pure mesomorphs or mesomorphs blended with characteristics of one of the other two.

Few individuals fit precisely into any one of these categories – most are combinations of all three. To illustrate this, Sheldon created a scale to rank the dominance of each somatotype within each person. He came up with a scale that gives each somatotype a value from 1 to 7 with 7 being most dominant. For example, a person of ectomorphic 1, mesomorphic 5, and endomorphic 4, would be an endo-mesomorph. This person would gain muscle easily, but would also have trouble getting lean for a competition. Conversely, an ectomorphic 5, mesomorphic 3, and endomorphic 1, would be ecto-mesomorphic. For this individual, losing fat would not a problem, but gaining muscle would be.

Illustration by Eric Blais

ECTOMORPHS

Since ectomorphs are primarily concerned with gaining muscle mass, I suggest they keep their workouts short. The vast majority of exercises should be compound in nature (i.e. involving more than one joint and muscle group) and performed for no more than six to eight sets in total. Since losing fat is not really a problem, ectomorphs can take long rests between sets – at least one to two minutes. Cardio should also be kept to a minimum (no more than two or three 20-minute sessions per week) because any excess calories will be used for building muscle tissue, not for building body fat. A couple of cardio sessions will keep the heart and lungs in shape without interfering with recovery. When it comes to nutrition, ectomorphs are the luckiest of the three somatotypes because they can eat just about anything and get away with it. However, optimal muscle is built with optimal nutrition. You'll need protein for building muscle tissue and carbohydrates to supply energy. Don't forget good fats either, as they help with the recovery process as well as helping to maintain overall health.

ENDOMORPHS

Since they tend to gain fat easily, endomorphs should keep between-set rests to a minimum (about 20 to 30 seconds). As they gain muscle fairly easily, endomorphs can perform a combination of compound and isolation (single-joint – one-muscle) exercises. Cardio will play just as important a role for endomorphs as weight training, so a minimum of three 30-minute sessions should be performed per week, and you could easily go up to five or six sessions of 45 minutes. Adding in outdoor exercises such as cycling, hiking and tennis would also be a good idea.

Photo by (Left to right) Robert Reiff,
Irvin Gelb, Robert Reiff

Endomorphs will need to pay strict attention to their diets. Endomorphs are in many respects opposite to ectomorphs, and that means they store fat easily. All junk food will need to be avoided, especially deep-fried foods and simple sugars (i.e. fries, cakes, candies and most desserts).

MESOMORPHS

During World War II the bomber pilots had a "club" they referred to as the "lucky bastards club." To qualify for induction, a bomber crew had to survive between 25 and 35 missions (depending upon the year) over Germany. Well, mesomorphs are the lucky bastards of the bodybuilding world! They build the most muscle tissue of all three somatotypes and can drop their body fat levels as low as ectomorphs, provided they eat and train properly.

Mesomorphs have such fast recovery systems that they can endure very intense training sessions. They don't have to be as strict as endomorphs with their diets. However, to maximize their muscle gains they should eat highly nutritious meals containing good sources of protein, fresh fruits, vegetables and healthy fats.

SO WHAT AM I?

You're probably wondering by now which somatotype classification best describes your body. As you have discovered, classifying your body type does play a role in your eating and training. But let's face it – there is far more to bodybuilding than a grab bag of DNA! Dedication, passion, solid nutrition and strong training play the largest roles in building a great physique.

Photos by (Left to right) Irvin Gelb, Alex Ardenti; Robert Reiff

Remember: the greatest genetics in the world are useless if you don't train consistently and eat clean.

If you really want to label your body type, start by glancing in the mirror. Do you have nice wide shoulders that seemingly touch both sides of a doorframe, or are they narrow and sloped? Do you have large bones and joints, or are they small and frail? Consider your diet. Do you gain fat easily, or can you eat junk food every day and not gain an ounce, or something in between?

Although this book is primarily focused on bodybuilding, you can use body typing to help you choose sports and types of training. This doesn't mean that you avoid sports that are unsuited to your body type. It just helps you pick the sports or training that you may have more 'natural' success in. The following table lists common sports and the somatotypes that tend to dominate each. Keep in mind that I'm talking success at a very high level here. There are ectomorphs that make good wrestlers, and some great basketball players are more mesomorphic. Also, remember that one person is rarely a strict endomorph, mesomorph or ectomorph. Most people are a blend.

ENDOMORPH	MESOMORPH	ECTOMORPH
• Wrestling	• Judo	• High jumping
• Football	• Sprinting	• Triathlon
• Powerlifting	• Swimming	• Basketball
• Softball	• Rugby	• Volleyball
• Bodybuilding	• Bodybuilding	• Marathon running

While anyone can be a bodybuilder, an ectomorph would have a difficult time doing well in competition. If you are an ectomorph, however, you can still build your body a great degree, look amazing, feel great and perhaps get involved in personal training. *MuscleMag International* publisher Robert Kennedy is an ectomorph, and since beginning bodybuilding he has always looked incredible. Champion bodybuilders are normally mesomorphs and occasionally lean more to the endomorph category. Dorian Yates, Ronnie Coleman and Jay Cutler are primarily mesomorphs, but also have endomorph characteristics (all three

can weigh 30 or 40 pounds or more above their competition weight during off-season). Frank Zane is mainly mesomorph, but with ectomorph characteristics. Markus Ruhl and Mustafa Mohammad could be described as endo-mesomorphs or meso-endomorphs, depending on perspective. Both have incredible muscle mass but also tend to carry excess weight during the off-season. Even the great Arnold Schwarzenegger wasn't a pure mesomorph, with his tall frame and long limbs. In fact, Arnold has characteristics from all three somatotypes.

CONCLUSION

How genetics relates to bodybuilding is a complicated topic. You will never really know your genetic hold until you start training, and even then you'll never reach your maximum genetic potential. Guys like Arnold, Lee Haney, Dorian Yates and Ronnie Coleman, have come close, but all have areas they can (or could) improve upon. Also, individuals with seemingly inferior genetics do go on to win top bodybuilding titles. Conversely, others who were touted to be the next "Arnold" disappeared after a few short years.

Some of you will find your potential for bodybuilding is average. Some of you will have fantastic characteristics such as good size, great strength and a fast recovery system. At the same time, you'll also have some less-than-optimal traits like poor symmetry and an inability to get really defined and "hard." In terms of bodyparts, you may be able to compare your legs with state and national champions, yet your arms and chest could barely make it to the city level. You may have outstanding genetics which enable you to achieve success in other areas, such as your job, but those same traits may prevent you from training consistently. Or you might be prone to frequent injuries, tendonitis or weak joints.

So let's say that after a few years of training, you assess your potential as less than outstanding. Should you give up or cut back? No way! For one thing, your entire assessment might be wrong. How many potential Mr. Olympias gave up because they or someone else thought they had no future in the sport? Tons, we assure you! If you give up too soon, a vital part of your life will disappear. Your health will suffer, your social life will become reduced, and perhaps most importantly, you'll never know just how far you could have gone.

If you still think that your potential is limited in some way, the following guidelines will help you honestly assess it. And don't be surprised if you discover that you were wrong and that you have unlimited potential!

Don't make bodybuilding your entire life. Of all the bodybuilders training worldwide, only a small percentage will make their living from the sport. Even then, most of what they make comes from seminars and posing exhibitions, not prize money. There's probably nothing wrong with being obsessed with bodybuilding, but don't let that addiction keep you from enjoying other aspects of life. If you love reading about nutrition and anatomy then great.

> **"** Body-type training is important for a bodybuilder, especially in the beginning and intermediate stages. If the wrong approach is used, the lifter can actually hinder his progress instead of promoting it."
>
> – Dwayne Hines II, *MuscleMag International* contributor and author

Why not invest some of that energy into doing a personal-training course or nutrition degree? Completing some sort of education degree will not only help your bodybuilding, but also lead to greater financial rewards down the road.

Don't overtrain. Even though I'll discuss this in much more depth in a later chapter, a few words are needed now. You may love training, but the body can only endure so much before it reaches the point at which it can't fully recover between workouts. For the average person (who's not chemically enhanced!) three or four 45- to 60-minute workouts are more than adequate. As you'll learn later, it's better to undertrain than overtrain.

Mix it up. Unless your training routine keeps consistently bringing you results, change it up every four to six weeks. The body adapts very quickly, and often a lack of

progress is not so much a case of limited genetics as a lack of training variety.

Avoid drugs. While later in the book I'll be diving into the murky world of bodybuilding pharmacology, let's say right now that all the steroids in the world won't take you to the Mr. Olympia stage if you don't train hard, eat clean, and have the right genetics and the right attitude.

Learn as much as you can. Even if your genetics are limited, your potential to learn never is. Read and absorb everything about bodybuilding that you can get your hands on. This book is a start, but there are lots of others. Every month dozens of bodybuilding magazines hit the stands, each packed with training, nutrition, supplementation and recovery articles. You don't need to buy them all, but one or two a month won't break your budget and will allow you to learn a monumental amount. Most bodybuilders have a small library of books and magazines in their dens! A quick flip through one before a workout is bound to get the training juices flowing and provide important tips.

Train aggressively – but also wisely.

Photo of Ronny Rockel by Alex Ardenti

CHAPTER 5

Do You Have What It Takes?

"What the hell are you waiting for? Do you know that the number-one killer in America is heart disease? While you sit there considering whether or not to do anything about it, you are putting yourself more at risk."

– Frank Sepe, regular *MuscleMag International* columnist, responding to an overweight reader's question about whether he should start exercising.

While most readers will be content building a great-looking physique for its own sake, or maybe with entering a local bodybuilding competition, a few of you may be interested in dethroning Jay Cutler as Mr. Olympia! Greg Zulak, former *MuscleMag International* editor and current contributor, once compiled a list of physical and mental characteristics necessary to reach the top in our sport. Nearly every competitor at the international amateur and pro levels possess just about all of these characteristics. See how you stack up.

STRUCTURE AND FRAME

The ideal structure for a competitive bodybuilder is what's called the "X-frame." This means a bone structure with wide shoulders, narrow hips, bigger legs and a great V-taper. Bodybuilding greats like Ronnie Coleman, Mustafa Mohammad, Jay Cutler, Gustavo Badell, Victor Martinez and Dennis James, all have extremely wide shoulders. And while none will be accused of having small hips, they all have huge thighs and lats to balance the symmetry of their "X." Bodybuilders from the past whose bodies exemplified the X-frame include Arnold, Sergio Oliva, Lee Haney, Bill Pearl, Steve Reeves, Reg Park and Serge Nubret.

MUSCLE SHAPE

Despite what some magazine articles may claim, you can't really change a muscle's shape. Muscle shape is primarily genetic. Therefore, the best physiques tend to have muscles that already possess the right shape, and training simply enlarges the muscle. The best shapes are high, peaked biceps; long, full thighs; small, tight abdominals; low attaching and wide back muscles (primarily the lats); full shoulders with all three heads clearly developed and visible; full, diamond-shaped calves; and horseshoe-shaped triceps.

JOINT SIZE

Although bigger joints tend to mean more potential muscle mass, nothing looks as good as large muscles on small to medium-sized joints. Great examples of this include Serge Nubret, Flex Wheeler and Dexter Jackson.

MUSCLE SIZE AND MASS

While hardness and structure are relevant, bodybuilding is about muscles – strong, massive, powerful muscles! Granted, size is often related to height and bone structure, but few pro bodybuilders or top amateurs weigh less than 200 pounds in contest shape. Nearly every top bodybuilder has greater than 20-inch arms, 50-inch chest, 20-inch calves and 28-inch thighs. Competitors who possess this size in addition to an ultra-shredded look will usually place at or near the top.

Rest between sets to regain your strength.

Photo of Joel Stubbs by Robert Reiff

SYMMETRY, BALANCE AND PROPORTION

It's not enough to just have huge muscles; the muscle mass must be evenly spread over the body. From top to bottom and side to side, your body must be evenly balanced and proportioned. Your calves should not be noticeably larger or smaller than your neck or arms; your chest should not dwarf your back; your upper body should not make your legs look like stilts. Your ultimate goal is to have your body resemble a Greek statue. If you want to see what ideal proportion looks like, take a look at Dexter Jackson.

LONG MUSCLE BELLIES AND FULL MUSCLE INSERTIONS

As with joint size and muscle shape, these features are primarily dependent on your genetics. If you watch a bodybuilding contest or look at pictures, you'll notice that some competitors have muscles that run the full length of their bones, while others have noticeable gaps between the joint and the muscle belly. The biceps and triceps show great variation in this respect, and "high" lats and calves are not as coveted as "low" versions – in other words, it's preferable to have calves and lats with low insertions.

MUSCULAR DEFINITION

There was a time when the bodybuilder with the largest muscles would probably win any given contest, but not anymore. Today, bodybuilders are expected to carry as little body fat as possible. If your muscles don't display striations and cross-striations, you can kiss the winner's trophy goodbye! While genetics do play a role in achieving that "ripped" look, the primary variables for developing muscular definition are diet and cardio.

VASCULARITY

Vascularity refers to how well the veins stand out in bas-relief on your body. On some bodybuilders the veins will be closer to the surface, while on others they will be deeper. Vascularity is also related to body fat – the less fat on the body, the more the veins will stand out. Some bodybuilders have great vascularity year round, while others' veins won't start showing until the weeks leading up to a contest.

MUSCLE SEPARATION

As the term suggests, muscle separation refers to how well muscles are clearly separated from one another. It also refers to how clear the subunits of the muscles stand out from one another. For example, on some bodybuilders you can see the dividing line between both biceps heads. Having all four quadriceps heads separated is a must these days. The two pectoral (chest) muscles should be separated by a clear line, straight up the middle. To be really competitive, your muscles should not appear as one large lump of mass. Muscle separation is one of those areas where smaller bodybuilders can hold their own, and often beat, larger opponents.

MUSCLE DENSITY

You can tell the bodybuilders who blow their muscles up quickly with drugs and lift light weight for high-rep sets. They don't have that powerful, rugged look about them. Instead, they appear almost artifical. Only years of heavy training will give muscles that "dense" look.

HIGH ENERGY LEVELS

Building a good-looking physique takes at least a few months. A great one will require an investment of years of high-intensity workouts. Only those with the stamina and energy to endure such physical exertion will survive. A typical champion bodybuilder will train very hard, one to two hours a day four to six days a week. When you add in the four to six cardio sessions, you can see why this training is not for the lazy!

CONDITION YOUR MUSCLES

A muscular body burns more fat throughout the day. By increasing your metabolism through lifting weights regularly and eating smaller, more frequent meals, you'll continue to burn body fat long after you've left the gym. The increase in muscle will boost your metabolism, thereby increasing the amount of calories your body uses.

NATURAL STRENGTH

With one or two possible exceptions, all today's top bodybuilding stars are immensely strong. Guys like Jay Cutler, Ronnie Coleman, Mat DuVal and Mustafa Mohammad can each bench press over 400 pounds, squat over 500 pounds and barbell curl in excess of 200 pounds. If you find yourself holding your own with the strongest guys in your gym after a few months of training, you probably have the strength needed to build a large, muscular physique. Training will make you stronger, but those possessing natural strength from day one will usually progress the farthest in the sport.

A QUICK METABOLISM

One of the absolute musts of bodybuilding. A great-looking physique means being able to eat a lot of nutritious food and have the calories turned into muscle tissue, not fat. Some bodybuilders can eat in excess of 5,000 calories per day and still keep a six-pack set of abdominals. Others will get fat on 2,000 calories.

HIGH PAIN THRESHOLD

Weight training, especially the type required to build a large, muscular physique, is painful at times. Most, if not all, your sets should be carried through the pain barrier. Most of the top bodybuilding stars block the pain out (a few masochists actually enjoy it!) If stubbing your toe or pulling a band-aid off your skin hurts, forget about building a large, muscular physique! You won't survive the first training session!

Illustration by Mark Collins

WILLPOWER

Are you willing to make sacrifices to build a championship physique? Do you consistently find excuses to skip workouts? Would you prefer to hit the fast food-joint rather than broil some skinless chicken? Do you regularly get 8 to 10 hours sleep every night? With one or two exceptions, virtually all the top bodybuilders make bodybuilding a top priority. They are not lazy and they are extremely dedicated. This is how you absolutely must be if you want to reach the top.

POSITIVE MENTAL ATTITUDE

After Ronnie Coleman placed ninth at the 1997 Mr. Olympia, he didn't settle for merely cracking the top 10. Instead, he banished all negative thinking and set a new goal: to win the 1998 title. Then to show it was no fluke, he won the next seven! Likewise, Jay Cutler didn't give up after placing second to Ronnie Coleman on four different occasions. Determined to finally win the No. 1 spot, he found the positive energy needed to improve his physique and won the title in 2006 and 2007. If your goal is to someday win a major bodybuilding title, then you can't take a half-hearted approach and be defeated easily. There will be days when going to the gym is the last thing you want to do. But with the exception of when you are overtraining (more on this later in the book), you must kick yourself in the ass and hit the iron!

CHAPTER 6

The Dos & Don'ts of DOMS

"The funny thing about DOMS is that none of the muscles worked exhibit pain in the same way. It's not hard to tell you've had a great chest workout. All it takes is one arms-out stretch the next day and you'll be sore from sternum to armpit.

Likewise you may have trouble climbing a stairs two days after a leg workout. Then there is the back, and it may never really get sore."

– Editors of *MuscleMag International*, commenting on the differences among muscles with regards to DOMS.

You know the feeling. You get up in the morning and make that all-familiar arms-wide-open stretch and then it hits you: an intense, penetrating soreness. Then you say to yourself: "Oh yeah, that's right. I had a great chest workout yesterday." Unlike most people, however, who would be rushing to find their doctor's number, the serious iron-pumper in you actually welcomes the pain. In fact, no matter how intense or record-setting your workout, a lack of soreness the following day is not taken lightly. You begin to wonder if you're training hard enough. Perhaps you need to change your routine? Has your descent into old age begun?

No need to panic. While soreness is often associated with a great workout, it's not an absolute necessity. You don't need to be howling in pain. Some of the most massive bodybuilders around rarely get sore after their workouts.

Most people start experiencing soreness in the exercised muscles about 12 to 24 hours after their workout. Physiologists use the term "delayed onset muscle soreness," or DOMS, to describe this general condition. Some people may find that one or two muscles do not reach their full soreness until 48 hours later. The legs, particularly the calves, are well-known for this.

The intense burn you feel during exercise is caused by the buildup of lactic acid – one of the primary waste-products generated during anaerobic respiration. Originally, sports physiologists thought DOMS was just a continuation of the soreness that you feel during your workout. They assumed that the muscle soreness experienced over the next few days was a result of lactic acid remaining in the muscles. The most commonly held view now is DOMS is primarily caused by the micro-damage that occurs to muscle during high-intensity workouts, especially bodybuilding training. Negative repetitions, where you lower the weight in a slow and controlled manner, seem to magnify the degree of muscle soreness. Negatives apparently cause greater micro-trauma (damage at the muscle cellular level) than the positive, or lifting, part of the repetition. More reason to concentrate on negatives just as much as positives.

The type of pain you feel during and after a workout is different than the pain produced by an injury. You should try and develop the ability to recognize the difference between the good pain (i.e. soreness) from training and the bad pain associated with an injury. Unless the soreness is so extreme that it prevents you from doing normal day-to-day physical activity such as walking or stair climbing, then mild to moderate soreness is good pain. It's an indication that you had a great workout and that you trained hard enough to stimulate the muscles to new growth. A sharp pain that occurs on only one side of your body is surely an injury.

DOMS will be most pronounced in beginners, as their muscles are not used to strenuous exercise. With time their bodies will adapt to the workloads and the soreness will diminish with each respective workout. If you've been training for a while you can probably relate to this. The first few weeks were probably brutal but with time the intensity of the post-workout soreness is greatly diminished. Now, earlier I said that it wasn't necessary to be intensely sore following a workout, but if you follow the same workout month after month and experience virtually no soreness, odds are your body has gotten accustomed to your workout. You've reached a plateau and you'll

Photo of Leo Ingram by Paul Buceta

cease to make any strength or size gains until you change up your routine.

No matter how many years you've been working out, it's a good idea to change your exercise program every four to six weeks. Besides the increased enthusiasm that comes with a new training routine, you'll also experience an increase in soreness – in other words, your body is being forced to break down and build up new muscle tissue. The key to continued success is shocking your body with progressive overload. Every time you shock your body with a new exercise routine you can expect the soreness to return. You don't need to radically change your training routine. Even small changes can leave you feeling pretty sore. You can change the order of your workout, or the speed at which you perform the reps. You can use different exercises for the same bodypart, or you can increase or decrease the reps. Keep this in mind when designing your new program. Start out with a few simple changes and gradually increase the intensity.

Okay. So what if you're still sore from your previous workout? Should you still train the same muscles? If the soreness is mild, then go ahead and work right through it. In fact an extra shot of blood to the area will only speed up recovery and help eliminate the soreness. If, however, there is still a great deal of soreness remaining from the last training session, then the muscle has not completely recovered. Hitting it again before full recovery has taken place may push you into a state of overtraining. The end result could a loss of strength and size.

All right, let's say you have gone overboard and can hardly move because you're so sore. Is there anything you can do to alleviate the soreness? You betcha!

STRETCHING

Most of us know that stretching helps warm up muscles and is a great way to improve flexibility, but stretching is also an excellent way to reduce soreness. Stretching a muscle during or after a workout increases the transport of nutrients to the area and speeds up the removal of waste products. More nutrients and less metabolic waste helps quicken the body's repair processes.

CARDIO

Hop on a piece of cardio equipment after your workout. No need to do a full cardio session. Something in the order of five to ten minutes at low to moderate intensity would suffice. Try to pick a cardio machine that involves the muscles you trained that day. While all machines will bring in the legs, some of them also require the use of the upper body muscles (i.e. rower and crosstrainer). As with stretching, light cardio will help transport waste products away from the muscles and bring in extra nutrients.

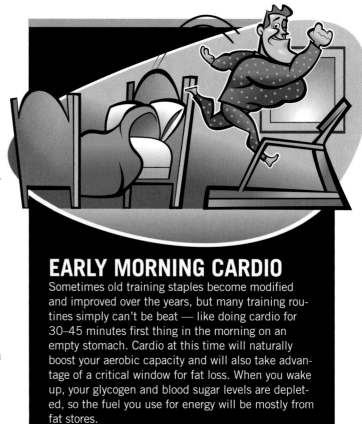

EARLY MORNING CARDIO

Sometimes old training staples become modified and improved over the years, but many training routines simply can't be beat — like doing cardio for 30–45 minutes first thing in the morning on an empty stomach. Cardio at this time will naturally boost your aerobic capacity and will also take advantage of a critical window for fat loss. When you wake up, your glycogen and blood sugar levels are depleted, so the fuel you use for energy will be mostly from fat stores.

MASSAGE

A final recommendation is to try massage. Athletes in the former Eastern Bloc countries used massage for decades to speed recovery and reduce post-exercise soreness. A good massage therapist uses different techniques to help remove metabolic waste products from the body and increase oxygen delivery to the area.

Some people just aren't satisfied unless they're sore the next day. Although in general increased soreness means more micro-damage and therefore more growth, this is not written in stone. So until we understand more about the whole process, it's probably adequate to say that mild to moderate soreness is preferred if we are looking for muscle growth.

Illustration by Mark Collins

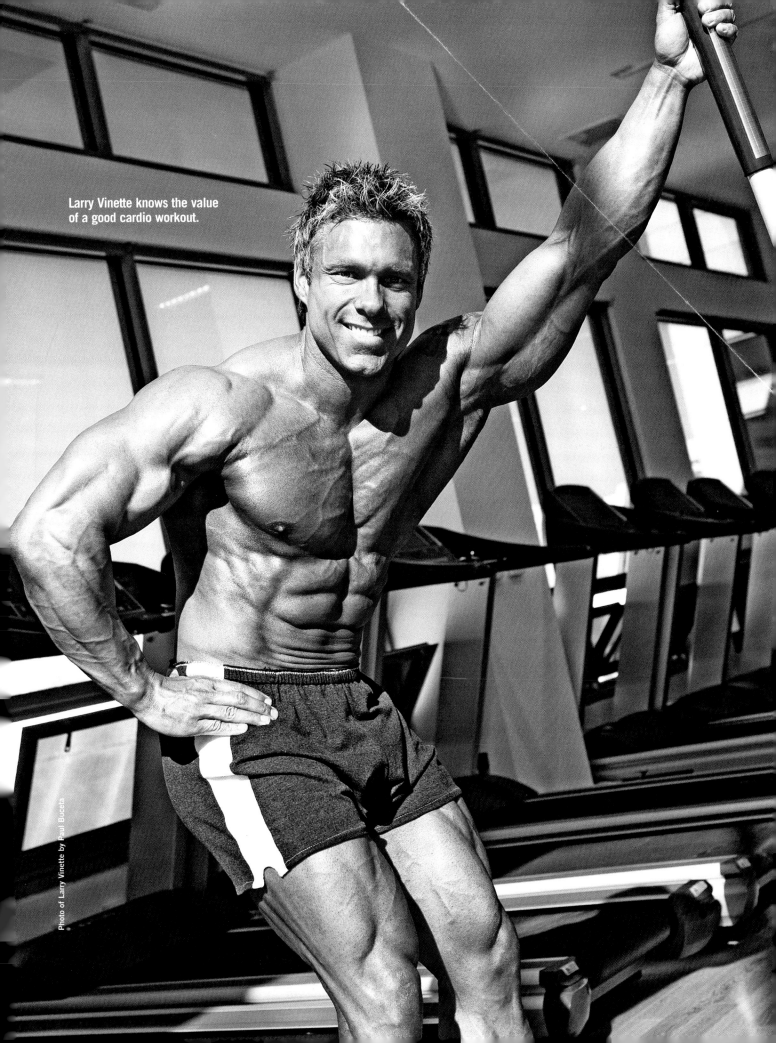

Larry Vinette knows the value of a good cardio workout.

CHAPTER 7

Bodybuilding 101: Reps

"No one knows why, but exercise physiologists have stated for years that the negative portion of an exercise movement produces more soreness and growth."

– Dr. Arthur Jones, Nautilus equipment inventor, giving his views on why negative training is just as important and positive training.

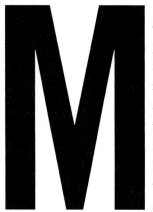

Most sports have their own language. Hockey players try to avoid "off-sides" and "icings;" football players try to make it to the "end-zone." If you're playing baseball, arriving "safe at home" is a high priority. Let's not forget the term "love" in tennis and the "natural high" of running. Bodybuilding also has its own unique language and terms, and before long you'll be well versed in the talk of supersets, pyramiding, and pre-exhaustion. This chapter details and explains each term associated with the sport of bodybuilding. After this chapter, you'll be totally fluent in bodybuildingese, even if you've never hit the gym!

REPS

Virtually every exercise and training routine relies on an understanding of this simple word. The word "rep" is an abbreviation of the word "repetition" and refers to one complete movement of an exercise. For example, curling a barbell up and then back down is one rep. With the exception of a few test lifts, bodybuilders rarely perform just one rep of an exercise. Instead, they perform a series of consecutive reps in a group or bunch, called a "set." The average number of reps in a set is 8 to 12, but this depends on such factors as the exercise itself, the goals of the trainer, the muscle group being worked, and the time of the year (i.e. off-season or pre-contest).

HOW MANY?

"So how do they train? With moderate weights, lots of sets and reps and they push at least one of those sets to near maximum effort. Ocassionally they will go real heavy, using low reps on presses or squats, but most sets involve a steady rhythmic motion of 10 to 12 reps. And invariably the set is stopped when it is obvious the bodybuilder could have squeezed out a couple of more reps."

– Editorial in *MuscleMag International*, on how most bodybuilders train in Venice, California.

Probably the most common question pro bodybuilders receive at seminars is: "How many reps should I perform?" Everyone wonders if there is some magical rep range that will produce the biggest and fastest gains in muscle size. It would be nice if you could plug your vital statistics into a computer and calculate that magical rep range, but it just doesn't work that way! For this reason, most bodybuilders will vary their rep ranges throughout the years. In fact many will alternate rep ranges during the same workout.

THE BIG THREE

Generally speaking, there are three broad rep ranges that bodybuilders follow throughout the year: ranges for building maximum strength, maximum size, and maintenance and conditioning.

If maximum strength is the goal, we recommend reps in the 3-to-5 range. This does not mean simply stopping at 3 to 5 reps, no matter how many you could have done, but rather using a weight that prevents you from achieving a higher number. Many bodybuilders follow this type of training for a few months during the off-season to maximize strength gains. Powerlifters tend to follow this pattern of reps for most of the year – even though they perform only single reps during competition.

If maximum muscle mass is the goal, then the accepted rep range is 8 to 12. Some bodybuilders find slightly lower ranges of 6 to 8 more productive. Others experi-

ence the best results by performing higher reps in the 15 to 20 range. For the most part, however, you probably can't go wrong keeping most of your exercises in the 8-to-12 zone. Unless otherwise stated, most of the exercise routines in this book are meant to be performed in the 8-to 12-rep range.

If general conditioning is the desired goal, then the 12–15 or sometimes 15–20 range is recommended. Many athletes and bodybuilders follow this range during their pre-contest phase of training as it burns slightly more calories, preserves muscle size and strength and reduces the risk of injury. (Higher reps require the use of lighter weights.)

> **"** If longevity is one of your goals, and if you want to avoid injuries, stick to strict form on 85 percent of your reps. Cheat only moderately and only when a muscle is really warmed up."
>
> – Greg Zulak, regular *MuscleMag International* contributor, offering advice on the importance of strict training.

STRICT STYLE IS KING

Back in the 1980s, an article titled "Strict Style is King" appeared in Joe Weider's magazine *Muscle and Fitness*. No truer words have been spoken in regard to bodybuilding training. With the possible exception of a few advanced training techniques, all reps should be performed in strict style. The two primary reasons for this are safety and effectiveness.

The safety aspect cannot be emphasized enough. Despite what most of the general pubic assumes, weight rarely causes injuries – bad technique does! An exercise using 10 pounds in poor style can do far more damage than one using 200 pounds in strict style. The body's joints, ligaments, tendons, etc., are not designed to be subjected to bouncing and jerking movements. Yet walk into any gym and you'll see guys bouncing bars off their chest, squatting up and down as fast as their legs can move them and jerking hundreds of pounds up with their lower backs. They may be able to lift more weight in this manner, but only because they are using their joints as elastic bands. Sooner or later something will give, and it's usually a ligament or tendon! While physiotherapists and

Arnold concentrated on every second of every rep.

orthopaedic surgeons may appreciate the business, body-building is meant to be safe. Always, and I repeat, always lift the weight in strict style.

Effectiveness is the second reason for using strict style on all your exercises. While it's not possible to completely isolate any given muscle group, you should always attempt to minimize the involvement of totally unrelated muscle groups. For example, working the triceps and front shoulders on the barbell bench press is acceptable, but arching your lower back and pushing with your thighs is not. Likewise, don't use your thighs and lower back to thrust the weight up during barbell curls. Remember that it's your muscles you want to pump up, not your ego!

During his *Pumping Iron* years, Arnold used 60- to 70-pound dumbells to train his biceps. While others were lobbing up 100-pounders by cheating with their other muscles and with momentum, Arnold was building two of the greatest arms of all time. Many people assumed that Arnold simply had better genetics or used a lot of drugs. However, the truth was that Arnold would perform each rep in a slow and controlled manner. He felt every rep in his biceps – not his lower back or thighs, like the guys who used to "swing." Most of today's champions follow Arnold's lead. You won't see Jay Cutler, Dexter Jackson or Melvin Anthony swinging and contorting their bodies just to lift the weight up. Each rep is performed in a deliberate and controlled fashion.

LESS AND LESS

As surprising as this may seem, most of today's body-building superstars are using less weight than they once did. Instead of 600-pound squats and 500-pound bench presses, most are using 405 to 500 on the squat and 315 to 405 on the bench press. A combination of injuries and learning how to use better technique led to a change in bodybuilding-training philosophy. Although most body-builders can still use huge poundage on their exercises, the majority opt for ultra-strict reps using a moderate amount of weight. Most bodybuilders find they get much better stimulation this way.

IT'S ALL RELATIVE

You'll eventually realize that "light" and "heavy" are relative terms and that you can make a weight feel light or heavy depending on technique and speed. A 30-pound dumbell can be made to feel like 50 or 60 pounds if lifted in a slow and controlled manner. Before moving on to the next topic, let us ask you this: If the vast majority of top bodybuilders use moderate weight on their exercises despite being strong enough to lift far more, why should you be any different?

FORCED REPS

One of the first advanced training techniques you will learn is called forced reps. Many bodybuilders discover this great muscle builder by accident. Forced reps are performed when, instead of stopping the set at the last possible rep, you have a partner or spotter assist you by providing just enough upward assistance to keep the bar or dumbells moving. The theory behind forced reps is fairly simple. Let's say you fail on the 10th rep of an exercise. Now you could terminate the set and take your normal rest period, or you could have someone help you, enabling you to squeeze out few additional reps. Forced reps is stimulate muscle fibers more intensely than if you stopped at failure. Most regular gym members know how to give a correct spot, so if you don't have a regular training partner, don't be shy about asking a stranger.

CONCLUSION

Reps are without a doubt the most important aspect of your bodybuilding training. To maximize your muscle and strength gains, you should experiment with various rep ranges to determine the range that works best for you, and remember to switch it up quite often. No two people respond the same and the best bodybuilders are those who frequently try different rep and weight combinations.

CHAPTER 8

Bodybuilding 101: Sets

"If you want bigger arms – squat. Squatting makes everything grow."

– Sergio Oliva, three-time Mr. Olympia, offering advice to beginners on the best way to increase their arm size.

f "rep" is the most common term in bodybuilding, then "set" is a close second. As explained earlier, you don't perform endless reps; you put them together in groups called sets. Now your first question is probably, "What is the most productive number of sets?" Ask two different bodybuilders and you'll probably get two different answers! As with reps, most bodybuilders experiment with different set numbers to determine which provides the best results.

Over the years two camps have evolved with regards to how many sets to perform: high intensity (or heavy duty), and the classical system. Most bodybuilders have tried the single-set, high-intensity system, but the classic multi-set system is still the most popular. In fact, as of this writing, no top bodybuilding champion has relied solely on the single-set system.

HIGH-INTENSITY, LOW-SET TRAINING

"A hard day of leg training is tough both physically and mentally. The enduring pain and suffering and the sheer magnitude of squatting thousands of pounds are gut wrenching, but they're also a bit like an endorphin after-party that makes showing up to the venue worth every penny of the admission price."
– Charles Glass, master trainer, commenting on the anguish and excitement of leg training.

The high-intensity system of training originated from the writings and works of Dr. Arthur Jones. Dr. Jones invented the Nautilus line of exercise equipment. Nautilus was the first serious challenger to the old Universal multi-stations found in many high school and college gyms. Jones decided to market

Photo of Mike Menxer

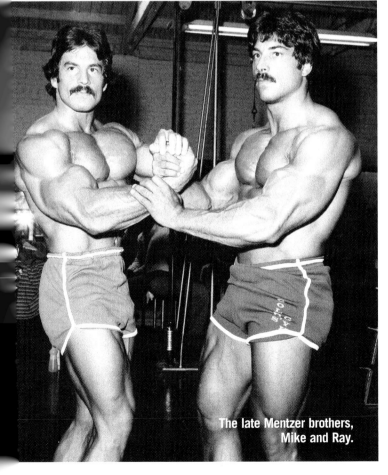

The late Mentzer brothers, Mike and Ray.

his equipment differently by claiming all one needed to do was to perform one set per muscle group on his eight to ten stations. Although Dr. Jones made millions selling Nautilus equipment in the '70s and '80s, this one-set-per-bodypart system didn't resonate with serious bodybuilders. It would take 1976 Mr. Universe winner, Mike Mentzer, to sell the high-intensity training principle to the masses. Mentzer was one of the top bodybuilders in the world and highly intelligent. With his great physique and strong presentation skills, Mike easily reframed Jones' ideas into his Heavy Duty system.

It's safe to say that Mike influenced millions with his writings right up until his untimely death in 2001.

Although he did use multiple sets for most of his training, six-time Mr. Olympia Dorian Yates was extremely influenced by Mentzer's writings. Dorain rarely did more than 6 to 8 sets for his largest muscle groups (as opposed to the 12 to 20 sets favoured by most other top bodybuilders).

Advocates of this system argue that all it takes to fully stimulate a muscle is one or two all-out high-intensity sets. Spending hours in the gym doing endless subpar sets is a waste of time. In fact it may lead to muscle loss as the human body can easily slip into a state of overtraining from such high-volume workouts. Dorian Yates probably put it best when he said: "Once a nail is driven into a wall, it's useless to keep hitting it – you'll only damage the wall!" The reality of high intensity or heavy duty is that few but the chemically enhanced or genetically blessed can handle such high-intensity training.

THE CLASSICAL, OR MULTI-SET, SYSTEM OF TRAINING

The classical system of training is by far the most popular style of training and has built more great physiques than all the other training styles combined. Starting with 1 or 2 sets per exercise, you gradually add sets and exercises until you're performing 3 to 5 sets of four or five exercises for the larger muscle groups. By the time most bodybuilders reach the advanced level of training, they are performing

20 to 25 sets for each of the large muscle groups such as the chest, back and thighs, and 12 to 15 for the smaller groups such as the biceps and triceps.

Bodybuilders who follow the classical system (this includes former greats Arnold, Oliva, Columbu and Haney and current stars like Coleman, Priest, Cutler and Badell) report that they needed to add sets and exercises in order to keep improving. Some critics have declared that these top bodybuilding pros are genetically blessed and would grow no matter which way they trained. This could be true to a certain extent, but there's no denying that the classical system has produced virtually every top pro and amateur bodybuilder of the last 60 to 70 years.

SO ... IS THERE A BEST SYSTEM?

"Most people's tolerance for excessive physical strain is not high enough and such training could lead to torn muscles and will lead to burnout. Call it by any name – stressed out muscle, extreme fatigue, sticking point, physical exhaustion, over tonus – whatever, it translates into zero muscle growth!"

– Editorial in *MuscleMag International*, on continuous high-intensity training.

By now you're probably wondering where to start. Given the solid reputation of the classical system, we suggest you start there. There is more to muscle growth than enlarging muscle fibers. You have to increase blood supply by stimulating the growth of new blood vessels. Unfortunately, the one-set system does a poor job of this. It's also not good for the joints because of the huge poundage that needs to be used (something Mentzer grudgingly admitted in later years).

Don't start out by doing 20 sets for each muscle group. For most beginners 2 or 3 sets of two exercises per muscle group is more than sufficient to adequately stimulate growth. Later in the book I'll go into more detail about the various types of training programs.

As time goes on you may want to experiment with the Heavy Duty style of training. Certainly if you're on the ectomorphic side, you may find that fewer but higher intensity sets may yield better results. Also keep in

Photo of Lee Priest by Paul Buceta

mind that the classical system requires enormous amounts of energy and hence food, to be effective. Many bodybuilders find 15 to 20 sets or more per bodypart just too draining.

HOW LONG DO I REST BETWEEN SETS?

The general answer to this question is: rest long enough to recover from the previous set, but not long enough to cool down. This normally works out to 45 to 60 seconds between sets. Powerlifters often rest two minutes or more between sets. Those weight training for general conditioning often rest less than 20 seconds (doing so keeps the heart rate elevated and provides a cardiovascular component to the workout).

TYPES OF SETS

"Forget the freaks. I want to help the millions who are less fortunate. To do that we must see how those with below-average genetics built their muscles. Better than

asking a top bodybuilder how to train, seek out a man who, because of his less-than-perfect genetics, had to discover the hard way what works and what doesn't."
– Editorial in *MuscleMag International* offering advice on who to ask for training advice.

There are a few different and challenging methods for completing your sets. Let's examine each in detail.

Straight Sets

This is the oldest style of training and is performed in a direct straightforward manner. In the purest sense, the same weight is used for the same number of sets and reps – for example, 3 sets of 12 reps using 225 pounds on the barbell bench press. The straight-set pattern is probably the most common training technique, and most of the advanced training techniques evolved from straight sets.

Pyramid Sets

If straight sets are the most common style of training, pyramid sets are a close second. Instead of using the same weight for the same number of sets and reps, the weight is increased with each successive set, while the number of reps is decreased. The top, or peak, of the pyramid is reached with the heaviest weight and fewest number of reps. The weight is then reduced and the number of reps increased. Essentially, you work your way up one side of the pyramid and down the other. Generally speaking, you perform the lighter sets for 15 to 20 reps, while the heaviest sets usually fall in the 6- to 8-rep range. One advantage of pyramid sets is that they allow the muscles to warm up fully before lifting the heaviest weight. This helps prevent injuries. It's also probably more effective. Think of muscles as engines – they work most efficiently after a good warmup.

An example of pyramid sets for barbell squats would look like this:

Photo of Monty Rogers by Robert Reiff

BARBELL SQUATS

SET	WEIGHT	REPS
1	135	20
2	225	15
3	315	10
4	404	6
5	315	10
6	225	12

Half Pyramids: Ascending and Descending Sets

You could also modify the full pyramid and do only one side. For example, you could slowly work your way up in weight and down in reps, finishing with the heaviest weight. Such sets are called ascending sets. Even more popular are descending sets. In this case, the heaviest weights are lifted first, and each successive set gets lighter. Bodybuilders usually prefer descending sets, as this allows them to lift heavier weights during the workout – ascending sets often tire the muscles out before the maximum weight is reached. While the debate continues as to whether or not reaching the maximum weight is absolutely necessary for growth, most bodybuilders still prefer to "max out."

If descending sets have a disadvantage it's that they increase the risk of injury. As we pointed out earlier, your muscles should be thoroughly warmed up before lifting heavy weights. The first set would be the heaviest set performed, meaning that the muscles would be cold while lifting the heavy weight. Since this is extremely dangerous, most bodybuilders perform a few very light, high-rep sets – just enough to get the blood flowing to the muscle. They don't count these sets because they are so light – they just call them warmup sets.

Here's an example of descending sets on the barbell curl:

BARBELL CURLS		
SET	WEIGHT	REPS
1	135	6–8
2	115	10–12
3	95	10–12
4	75	12–15

The best idea is to alternate between these types of workouts. Doing so will keep your muscles in a state of shock, which is just what you need to keep your muscles growing. Changing up your workouts will also prevent you from becoming easily bored.

Photo of Stan McQuay by Robert Reiff

No exercise builds biceps like the barbell curl.

CHAPTER 9

Bodybuilding 101: Just How Heavy?

"One of the differences between title winners and runners-up is that the title winners use weights as tools to build muscle, while the rest just heave the weight up any way they can."

– Editorial in *MuscleMag International*

big mistake made by novice and advanced bodybuilders alike is trying to use more weight than their muscles are capable of lifting.

You'll notice as you read through this book that I don't list how much weight to use in any of the exercises. That's because there is no way I can tell another person how much weight to use. I can advise you about the number of sets, reps, exercises, combinations, nutrition and even on how fast or slow to lift the weight. But there's no way I can tell you how many plates to put on that bar.

As a general guide, you should first determine how many reps you plan on performing. For example, let's say it's 10. Next, pick a weight that limits you to just 10 reps. Notice I said limits you to 10 reps. You don't just stop at 10 if you can manage 11 or 12 reps. If you can do 12 reps but you want to do only 10, then the weight is not heavy enough. There will be days that you'll be able to do those few extra reps; likewise, there'll be days when it will take every ounce of energy just to squeeze out those 8 or 9 reps. But as soon as performing more than 10 reps becomes the norm rather than the exception, add 5 or 10 pounds to the bar or machine. That is, if you have chosen 10 reps as your goal.

It won't be long before you'll be using different rep ranges in your workouts. You may think it will be difficult to keep adjusting the weight, but trust me, it's really not. Within a few workouts, you'll be adding and removing weight just to keep in your target rep range. Never sacrifice good form just to lift more weight. It's far safer and certainly more effective to lift 225 pounds on the bench press using good technique than to bounce 275 off your chest. Don't worry about the guy next to you either. So what if he's lifting 400 pounds? He certainly didn't start out lifting that weight. He had to work his way up over time, just like you. And just like him, if you keep working hard and lifting properly, you will soon be lifting 400 pounds – but you won't get there by trying to lift that weight before you're ready. Always try to "feel" the weight as you lift. If you can't feel the muscle being worked, you're either not using enough weight or you are relying on the smaller muscles to do most of the lifting.

Keep in mind that the terms "light," "heavy," "high," and "low" are relative terms. What's heavy for one person may be a light warmup weight for another. Likewise, some bodybuilders consider anything above 10 reps as high reps, while others think high-rep training starts at 20. Experiment with different rep and weight combinations to find what works best for you over time.

THE NEED FOR SPEED

Go into any gym and you'll see weights being thrown around in just about every conceivable manner. It's truly amazing that more people are not getting injured, considering what goes on daily in gyms. The human body was not designed to be jolted or jerked around in a rapid and abrupt manner – especially while supporting great poundage. Grabbing a bar and yanking it off the floor is not exercising using proper technique. Neither is bouncing up and down while doing squats. Both these movements could cause severe injury.

Severe injuries are also caused by placing too much stress on a muscle or joint in too short a period of time. For example, maybe your thighs can handle a 500-pound squat, but not if you subject your muscles to the entire

500 pounds in less than a second! Let's use the car analogy to illustrate: If you were driving along at 70 or 80 miles per hour without a seatbelt and suddenly hit a tree or another car, you'd probably go through the windshield. Why? Because your car went from 70 to 0 in less than a second, and your body just kept moving. If you'd had time to slowly reduce your speed and stop, you would have stayed in your seat and probably avoided the accident altogether. Well, the same applies to bodybuilding exercises – slow and controlled is the only way to do it.

TEMPO

Bodybuilders use the term "tempo" to describe rep speeds. While on average most bodybuilders use a two- to four-second tempo, you will see many different combinations. Many experts, including Charles Poliquin, don't look at reps as one unit, but rather as four distinct parts. Most people are aware of the raising (positive, or concentric)

Photo of James Lewis by Robert Reiff

and lowering (negative, or eccentric) sections of the rep, but often neglect the pausing section at the top and bottom. The reason for this is simple: stopping the weight for a split second makes the exercise more difficult and will probably demand that the individual lift less weight. But, as Poliquin and others have suggested, pausing helps take momentum out of the equation, helping recruit more muscle fibers. It's also safer because the soft ligament and cartilage tissues won't be used like springs.

Tempos can be written mathematically in the following manner:

EXERCISE	MUSCLE	WEIGHT	REPS	SETS	TEMPO
BARBELL PRESS	CHEST	185 lbs	10	3	2-1-2-1

In this example, the individual is lifting 185 pounds for 3 sets of 10 reps on the barbell bench press. The 2-1-2-1 tempo indicates that it takes two seconds to lift the weight, a one-second pause at the top, two seconds to lower the weight, and another one-second pause at the bottom.

The importance of repetition speed is debated, but not as hotly as it once was. The faster the reps, the lower the muscle tension – that much is true. Reduce your rep speed to a more controlled tempo and you increase the muscle tension. Developing muscle size is a matter of high muscle tension (coupled with progressive overload). The higher the tension, the more you'll grow. However, faster reps allow you to use more weight. More weight produces more growth. So which is better? The truth is, they both work. So use whichever speed works best for you.

THE ORDER OF THINGS

In general, most bodybuilders train the larger muscles first because they require more energy. The thighs, chest and back require considerably more energy to be stimulated than the biceps, triceps and shoulders. There's also a more practical reason for leaving the biceps and triceps until last. These smaller muscles are also used when training the larger muscles. The biceps are assisting muscles in upper back exercises. Likewise, the triceps come into play on most chest exercises. Training the smaller assisting muscles first would severely hinder your progress on your larger muscle groups, and make injury more likely. You may also want to train the shoulders after the chest or back, since the front and side shoulders are involved with chest training and the rear shoulders are involved with back training.

It probably doesn't matter what order you train chest and back if you're working both on the same day. Just make sure you don't fall prey to this dangerous mindset: "If I can't see it, it's not that important." In competition, you'll often see some amazing sets of pectorals. When the competitors turn around, it's an entirely different scene. Since the back muscles are harder to see, many bodybuilders don't train them with the same intensity as they do the chest. If your back development starts lagging behind that of your chest, use the "muscle-priority principle." This principle demands that as soon as you discover a muscle group lagging behind the others, you rearrange your program to train the lagging muscle group first. In other words, train your back before your chest. This way you will devote more energy to bring your lagging bodypart up to speed.

TRAINING TO FAILURE

Training to failure means terminating a set only after the muscle literally cannot contract for another rep. When you tried for one last rep, you failed. You'll sometimes hear advanced bodybuilders and writers saying you should train to failure on every set. In theory this sounds great and would make perfect sense if your recovery system could keep up. However, few but the genetically blessed or pharmacologically enhanced can endure training to total failure on every set. The average person would quickly become overtrained trying to work out this way. Their nervous systems would become so fatigued that even sub-intensity training would burn them out.

Training to failure causes significant damage to the muscle fibers. Training to failure on every set creates a situation wherein the individual's recovery system is not capable of regenerating before the next workout. In fact, they may actually experience a regression in muscle size and strength.

Two basic principles must be observed if you expect to keep progressing:

- **The muscles must be repeatedly subjected to increasing forms of physical stress.**
- **Sufficient rest time must be taken between workouts for full recovery to take place.**

If you repeatedly stress a given muscle to slightly greater physical loads from one workout to the next – progressive overload – the end result will be a larger, stronger muscle. But this can truly occur only if the muscle is allowed adequate recovery time between these workouts. If the stress is too great or the recovery period is too short, the muscle will not have time to rebuild the muscle fibers, and no improvement will occur. Training to failure on every set is simply too exhausting for most individuals. We suggest training to about 90- to 95-percent failure on most sets and leave complete failure training to the last one or two sets of a given exercise.

EVERY BREATH YOU TAKE

The most common practice is to inhale on the easy part of the movement (usually the lowering phase) and to exhale on the hardest part (usually the upward phase). In simple terms, you "blow the weight up." The advantage of this breathing pattern is that it helps with your training rhythm. For every rep you inhale and exhale once. This helps pace your training as it supplies the muscles with an adequate supply of oxygen.

Photo of Jorge Betancourt by Alex Ardenti

As your training experience advances, you'll discover that for some exercises it's just about impossible to breathe on every rep. The squat and leg press are two examples. Most bodybuilders hold their breathe for one or two reps on these exercises and are none the worse for it. In fact, on squats this is almost a necessity because the increased lung pressure provides extra support to the torso.

Our advice is to let the body breathe on its own. Odds are you'll find it easy to breathe on every rep for light warmup sets and to hold for one or two reps on heavier sets. Unless you find yourself holding for more than one or two reps, don't worry about it. Breathing is an involuntary physiological condition and the body should do an excellent job of regulating it on its own.

TRAINING FREQUENCY: HOW LONG BETWEEN WORKOUTS?

The amount of time needed to recover between workouts is influenced by many factors, including training intensity, sleep habits, nutrition and probably most importantly, genetics. For a beginner whose body is unaccustomed to intense exercise, a longer recovery period is required. On average, each muscle group should be given 48 to 72 hours of recovery between workouts. For a beginner, the best way to accomplish this is to train the whole body, using one exercise per bodypart for 2 or 3 sets total, every second day, for a maximum of three days per week. As conditioning levels improve, the number of workouts can be increased and the body may be "split." Instead of training the whole body during each workout, different muscle groups are trained on different days. The most popular version of this "split routine" is to train half the muscles on one day and the other half the next, taking a day of rest after these two workouts. This type of split has probably built more championship physiques than any other.

Illustration by Mark Collins

THE EVOLUTION OF TRAINING FREQUENCY AND RECOVERY

"Anyone who tries to tell you the one best way to train is a fool. There is no such thing. If you've been reading the magazines even for only a few months, you've already come across dozens of types of routines, systems of training and ways to manipulate rep tempo and technique. Our bodies are incredibly adaptive. Virtually any style of training will deliver results for a time."
– Ron Harris, regular *MuscleMag International* columnist, offering advice on the "best way" to train.

When guys such as Arnold, Dave Draper and Franco Columbu trained at Gold's Gym back in the early '70s, four-hour workouts and six-day splits were

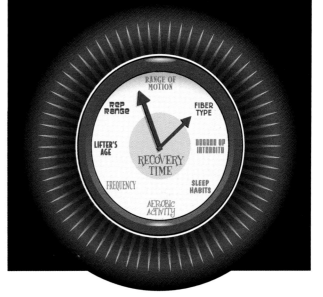

VARIABLES AFFECTING RECOVERY TIME

• Larger muscles take longer to recover than smaller muscles.
• In most cases, white (fast) muscle fibers take longer to recover than red (slow) muscle fibers.
• High-intensity, low-rep exercises with weights require more recuperation time than high-rep exercises.
• Full-range movements normally cause greater amounts of connective-tissue damage and require more recovery time than partial-movement exercises.
• Older lifters (35 to 40+ years) require more recuperation time than younger lifters.
• You can improve your recovery rate through good aerobic weight-training programs or hinder it by partaking in little or no aerobic efficiency training.

the norm. Anyone who trained fewer than five or six days a week was considered lazy or "recreational." Now, both scientific research and anecdotal evidence suggests that muscles take longer to recover than originally believed. It was such evidence that allowed Dr. Arthur Jones, Mike Mentzer and Dorian Yates to influence millions. Today's champions, such as Cutler, Coleman and Badell generally train four or five days a week for 60- to 90-minute sessions.

FACTORS THAT INFLUENCE MUSCLE RECOVERY

"To stay in an anabolic environment you have to get enough sleep – minimum eight hours a day. Sneaking a nap in there somewhere can help you reach this total. At one point in his amateur career Flex Wheeler slept sometimes 16 hours a day, and not coincidentally this period is when he made his most dramatic improvements in size and strength."
– Ron Harris, regular *MuscleMag International* contributor, commenting on the relationship between rest and recovery.

AMOUNT OF DAMAGE

Muscle growth can be considered a compensation process – damaged tissue becomes rebuilt into a slightly bigger, stronger version of itself. As stands to reason, the more damage inflicted, the more time is needed for rebuilding. Performing two or three 20-rep sets of squats using 100 pounds would place nowhere near the same demands on the recovery system that 315 pounds for 6 to 8 reps would for the same individual. So, in general, the more "heavy duty" your training, the more recovery time you need.

NUTRITION

Diet also plays a huge role in recovery time. Most experts agree that bodybuilders require more protein than sedentary individuals. When muscle tissue is being broken down and repaired, significant dietary protein is needed to aid this process. Besides protein, an individual needs to recharge his or her glycogen levels (the storage form of carbohydrate) between workouts. This is why bodybuilders who reduce their carbohydrate intake during the pre-contest phase often lapse into overtraining. Their bodies still need energy to function, and if the preferred source – carbohydrate – is not present, they will start burning the protein in muscle tissue for energy.

Photo of Benais Begovic by Irvin Gelb

Photo of Erik Seng by Irvin Gelb

ALL-IMPORTANT SLEEP

Sleep plays a vital role in the recovery process. Contrary to popular belief, muscles do not grow during the workout. Rather, recovery, and thus growth, takes place after you finish working out, and during sleep in particular. Sleep is such a vital component of health that humans spend about a third of their lives unconscious! Don't expect to maximize your bodybuilding gains if you regularly stay out until three in the morning. Sure the occasional Friday or Saturday night out is fine, but you will not recover (and thus grow) if you continually try to get by on three or four hours a night.

You may find it difficult to obtain eight hours of continuous sleep. Work, school or family responsibilities may interfere with sleep habits. However, keep in mind that two or three shorter sessions of sleep throughout the day yield nearly the same benefits as one longer session. So

even a couple of naps will improve your recovery.

Why is sleep so important? During sleep the body breaks down many of the fatigue toxins produced during exercise. For example, the stress hormone cortisol, released during intense training, is neutralized during sleep. It's also been proven that the greatest release of testosterone and growth hormone, two of the most powerful anabolic (muscle-building) hormones in the body, takes place during sleep.

Teenagers can't go wrong hitting the sack for a minimum of eight, and preferably10 or more hours. After all, not only are your muscles growing, but also your organs and bones. So the next time your mom says get to bed – listen to her! In fact, that goes for all readers!

CHAPTER 10

It's Time to Train

"I wanted to train when I was a teenager but I had no way to get to the gym. The closest gym was too far away for me to walk, so I waited until I got my driver's license to start training."

– Markus Ruhl, IFBB pro

So far I've talked a lot about what you need to do before you actually begin training. Now, I'm going to move into discussing training itself. One of the first decisions you'll have to make is where to work out. You have two choices: at home or at a fitness center or gym. Both have advantages and disadvantages.

HOME SWEET HOME

You'd be surprised where some of bodybuilding's greatest stars got their start. Many hoisted their first barbell in their basement on Christmas Day. The primary advantage of training at home is convenience. You can train pretty much any time you want. You don't have to worry about finding a parking space or waiting for equipment. However, training at home does has a few drawbacks. First, you'll have a limited amount of equipment. Unless you have deep pockets and a lot of space, you'll probably have access to only a few dumbells, a barbell and an adjustable bench. While this equipment is fine when you're starting out, your muscles will eventually need variety in order to keep growing. You also must consider safety. It won't be long before your strength will be enough to kill you. You'll be capable of lifting enough weight on exercises such as squats and bench presses that a slip-up could have grave consequences. Bodybuilders have been found dead in their basements with a loaded barbell across their necks. If you are going to be training heavy at home, make sure you're not alone when performing a heavy set of squats or bench presses. At a commercial gym or fitness center you are guaranteed to have a spotter or at least someone else around to keep an eye on you.

Another disadvantage to training at home is the lack of social contact. Unless you manage to convince a few buddies to train with you, you'll be working out alone most of the time. Not having a spotter affects your safety, but it also limits the amount of weight you can use. In addition, you won't have anyone around to motivate and push you. Unless you have incredible internal drive and motivation, you'll probably put the bar or dumbells down

> **Remember you don't have to move to L.A. Dorian Yates demolished all of the fancy Venice-based guys while training in a basement gym in Birmingham, England. The essential factor is the spirit, not always the location."**
>
> – Anita Ramsey, *MuscleMag International* contributor, on why it's not necessary to train in California to go all the way in the sport of bodybuilding.

once the muscle starts burning. Remember that it's those last couple of reps that really stimulate the muscles into new growth. There's nothing like having a training partner yelling at you to complete those painful, but highly productive, reps. He can even help you finish a couple extra. Even if you don't have a training partner, knowing other people might be looking at you often inspires you to squeeze out a few additional reps.

If you still decide to train at home, your first task will be setting up the training area. If you live in a house, the basement or garage often work best because they usually offer a large space that's removed from the general living area. This gives you room, privacy and prevents you from distracting other members of the household.

KEEP IT SIMPLE

To start your training you'll need some equipment. You can't go wrong by keeping it simple and buying a set of dumbells and an adjustable bench. The best dumbells are those that can be adjusted to change the weight or that will allow you to add and remove weight plates. A set of dumbells will allow you to train just about every muscle in

the body. In terms of the bench, definitely get one that adjusts everywhere from flat to a 90-degree incline, because it will allow you to vary the angle. You'll need this variety to hit the muscles from different angles. With time (and provided you have the room) you can add a barbell to your inventory. A barbell will allow you to perform the basic mass-builders such as squats, deadlifts and bench presses. With time, you'll want to consider adding a squat rack to your training room. This will almost certainly require a move to the basement or garage!

While a set of dumbells, a barbell and an adjustable bench limits you in terms of exercise variety, it does save you money. For less than $100 you can set up a small training area in your house or apartment. In fact, if you check around you might get the whole setup for less than $20. As soon as the last kid goes to college, many parents have a flea market to get rid of their children's weight sets. Alternatively, check out the paper – you never know what former bodybuilder might be selling off his workout gear!

THE GYM

"Always keep positive people around you … and make sure to have a game plan. Success in bodybuilding doesn't happen with a hit-and-miss attitude. Be precise in your plan, and then follow it."
– Will Harris, IFBB pro

Despite some of the advantages to working out at home, I feel that the gym is by far the best place to work out. Besides the huge assortment of equipment, you'll be surrounded by highly knowledgeable people. You'll get motivation, encouragement and variety, all in one spot. Of course working out at a commercial gym does have a few disadvantages.

The first disadvantage is commute time. It takes mere seconds to walk to your basement or bedroom, but unless you live within walking distance, it could take you 20 minutes or more to drive to the gym. Throw in the occasional weather delay or accident and you might waste an hour or two just going to and from the gym. All that extra driving will also mean extra money, given the price of gas these days!

While your home gym could be set up, at least in the

beginning, for $50, a gym membership will cost $40 to $50 per month (normally about $500 per year). Although this might feel like yet another extra bill, it's really not a huge amount to improve your health and appearance. What you get for that $500 is well worth it. Perhaps the biggest problem with training at a gym is that they can be really busy during peak times. Most people tend to work out in the evenings, and this means most gyms are overflowing between 5:00 and 7:00 p.m. One trip to the water fountain and you lose the squat rack. A quick chat to a friend and your dumbells have disappeared. Then you have the equipment hogs who are not satisfied until they've done no fewer than 20 sets.

Depending on how busy things are, you may not get to do one single exercise that you had planned in advance. Now, there's nothing wrong with occasionally modifying your training program – in fact times when you have to switch around your routine can be a blessing in disquise when it comes to growth – but if this situation becomes the norm, it's time to consider switching gyms or changing times. It won't take you long to determine which times are the worst when it comes to getting your workout completed.

Other factors to consider when choosing a gym include location, cost, hours of operation, clientele and equipment variety. You may be faced with a situation where cost or location prevents you from joining the gym of your choice. Consider all of these factors before you join any gym. You need to find the best one for you and your lifestyle, and it won't do you any good to join the perfect gym but find you can never get there.

THE BIG THREE

Gyms fall into three broad categories: health spas, hardcore gyms and middle-of-the-road fitness centers.

Health Spas

Considered the high-end of training establishments, health spas tend to cater to the wealthy and to business executives. Most health spas have a small weight-training area, a sauna, pool, cardio section, and a massage room. Health-

spa fees normally run from $1,000 to $2,000 dollars per year. Even if you can afford it, you have to ask yourself if you really belong there. Health spas tend to have very basic strength machines and often no free weights other than a few light dumbells. If you're planning on adding some serious strength and size to your physique, health spas won't give you the type and variety of equipment that you'll need. Finally – and this is probably the biggest drawback against health spas – the owners probably won't want you there! The last thing the owners and clientele of health spas want is some bodybuilder doing a heavy set of squats or deadlifts. Heaving, grunting, and sweating like that seems to offset the soft, relaxing atmosphere of the place. In their eyes you're nothing but a big intimidating musclehead and you're frightening away the regulars.

The Multipurpose Fitness Center

They go by many names, including health clubs, fitness centers and recreation centers. General fitness facilities such as the YMCA are middle-of-the-road training establishments that try to cater to everyone. In fact, the popularity of the general fitness industry has grown so much over the last couple of decades that many of the old hardcore gyms either closed down or decided to go mainstream. PowerHouse, World Gym and Gold's Gym all once catered exclusively to hardcore bodybuilders.

Most multipurpose fitness centers have a large floor area that contains hundreds of cardio and strength machines. You'll also find a good selection of free weights, along with squat racks and other equipment created for the bodybuilder. Many have a pool, indoor track and a couple of group fitness and spinning studios. Prices are reasonable and discounts are often given to teens, seniors and employees of corporations. The better fitness centers tend to be well-maintained and are constantly upgrading their equipment. Also, your membership card is usually accepted at any club that is part of that organization, no matter where it is – usually all over the city, often all over the country and sometimes even in other countries. This means that you can train at a different gym every day if you live in a large city.

Hardcore Gyms

"Hardcore is indeed a place, but don't try looking for it. The spot doesn't have a name and it doesn't have an address. You won't find it in the phone book, on the Internet, through a personal recommendation or with the right connections. Hardcore is in the heart. As long as you have an intense desire to train harder and heavier than you did the last time out – every time out – you're in the right place."
– Nelson Montana, regular *MuscleMag International* contributor, explaining how hardcore doesn't necessarily refer to a certain type of gym.

If your goal is serious weight training and bodybuilding, then hardcore gyms are probably your best bet. There'll be hundreds of dumbells and dozens of barbells and various racks to put them on. If you need to load the leg press up, no need to worry. There will be literally tons and tons of weight plates at your disposal.

Hardcore gyms like the original Gold's Gym in Venice, California and Temple Gym in Birmingham, England became world famous because of the champions that trained there. Even at your local hardcore gym, you'll probably be working out next to city and state champions. The person with the answer to just about any bodybuilding-related question is probably doing squats or bench presses a couple of feet away. Just try asking the typical health spa member how to improve your upper pectorals – their eyes might glaze over! Hardcore gyms offer a no-nonsense approach to bodybuilding at very affordable prices (usually in the range of $400 to $600 per year).

However, depending on you, your goals and your self confidence, the atmosphere can be pretty intense. It can be intimidating to begin your bodybuilding training using 90 pounds on the bench for your work set while the 250-pounder next to you is warming up with 225. Then there's the drug issue to be aware off. Many of the guys (and some of the "ladies") will be using steroids and other

Photo of Larry Vinette by Paul Buceta

performance-enhancing drugs. One of the side effects of these chemicals is attitude and irritability. Sometimes a glance is all it takes to set these individuals off. Also, unlike health spas, where clean clothes and showering are practically imposed upon members, the same cannot be said of hardcore gyms. Members at these gyms are totally into their workouts, and having a clean appearance or scent is just not a priority. Also, as you have probably already realized, hardcore gyms cater to just that – the hardcore. There are no idle exercisers at these places, so don't expect to have a chat between bodyparts. And be prepared to see nothing but massive physiques!

Finally, the location of hardcore gyms may be an issue. Hardcore gyms tend to be located either in rough city-center neighbourhoods or in industrial parks. Parking could be an issue, you could simply feel uncomfortable or you could in fact be unsafe.

Ultimately, where you decide to work out is your decision. One suggestion is to take a one-month membership at a couple of different gyms and see how it goes at each place. A month is usually enough time to determine such things as parking, commute time, equipment and atmosphere. It will also become apparent whether you like working out, period – bodybuilding either grabs you or not, and is not something that you'll stick with if you're just going through the motions.

THE GREAT OUTDOORS

Another possibility, if you are lucky enough to live or work near one, is an outdoor fitness center. Many larger gyms in warmer states like Florida and California have outdoor training areas. The weight pit on Venice Beach, California, is famous the world over. Bodybuilders have been training there since the '30s and '40s and it seems you haven't made it in the sport until you've done at least one photo shoot there!

Training outdoors offers numerous advantages. Even though the best gyms and fitness centers have air conditioning, it's still not the same as natural clean air. Training outdoors also offers those who train in non-air-condi-

tioned gyms a chance to train in a cooler environment on hot summer days. Hot, humid gyms can be brutal to train in and will drain even the most energetic trainers. If you're lucky enough to have access to an outdoor training area located on a beach, just think how much more fun it would be doing squats with the ocean in the background instead of a gray wall. The same applies to doing bench presses under a blue sky versus the ceiling. There's also something psychological about training outdoors, especially if it's on a public beach. Most trainers will do that extra rep or two if they know people are watching them. But you don't have to train at a beach. Why not bring your bench and dumbells into your own backyard, if you have one? Arnold and his friends would load up their cars with benches and weights and head to the woods. Here the future governor of California would squat until he could barely walk. Where there's a will, there's a way.

Training outside is great for motivation.

Do keep in mind if you're training outside that the sun can play havoc with your skin. Time passes very quickly while you're training under the sun. Before you know it you have been exposed to harmful rays for and hour or two. And don't let cloud cover mislead you – the sun's powerful rays easily penetrate clouds, and can cause just as much skin damage on cloudy days as it can on clear blue days. Always wear a good sunblock when training outdoors, and try to avoid training when the sun is at its highest peak (11:00 a.m. to 3:00 p.m. in most areas).

You'll also want to pay attention to your clothing when hoisting iron outdoors. Cotton is an excellent choice

Photo of Sean Glassman by Alex Ardenti

ing your workout. If you are sweating copious amounts, then eat a few salted nuts to replenish your sodium.

Don't neglect your warmup when training outdoors. You may feel that the warm air somehow takes the place of a warmup, but it's not that simple. A warmup raises your internal temperature, in addition to loosening the muscles and increasing blood flow to them.

You must also keep safety in mind when training under the sun. In extreme cases you could suffer from heat exhaustion (serious) or heat stroke (potentially deadly). If at any time you begin to feel lightheaded or dizzy, stop working out immediately and seek shade or go indoors. Take a few extra sips of water and lower your head to increase circulation to the brain. Before heading back to the weights, walk back and forth to determine whether or not you're fully recovered. If you still feel "off," let someone know (friend or staff member) and sit down. Don't risk turning heat exhaustion to deadly heat stroke for the sake of finishing a workout. Every bodybuilder who's had a severe injury has said he had warning signs that he ignored in order to finish his workout. Making that mistake could cost you dearly.

The issue of air quality must be discussed before we leave this topic. Even though the outdoor weight "pit" on Venice Beach is world famous with bodybuilders, there are days when no one should be training there. Large cities, including Los Angeles, are notorious for their high levels of smog. Industrial pollutants can cause everything from lung cancer to emphysema. During the hot summer months, air quality declines dramatically and as a result, many cities have smog alerts. Pay attention to these health warnings if you live in such an area. Even if you can tolerate the smell and don't fear the health consequences, the lack of fresh air will make your training more difficult.

After you finish working out, head to the showers. Besides cleaning off the dirt and sweat, a lukewarm shower helps lower the body's temperature. Resist the urge to take a cold shower, as the cold water could shock the warm muscles, causing them to cramp. And now you've finished your hot-weather workout, you can head off for an ice cream cone and a cold beer … naw, just kidding!

because it offers good absorption and ventilation. Lycra is also a good choice because it's light and allows sweat to evaporate quickly. A sweatband or bandana will help keep the sweat from your eyes, and a towel will come in handy for cleaning up after yourself.

Don't forget the issue of water loss either. The average adult male is estimated to lose 8 to 10 quarts of water per day through sweat. While this may occur only in extreme cases, training under the hot sun will inevitably cause your body to sweat large amounts of water to stay cool. Bring a water bottle and keep filling it up. Beware of salt loss, however, which can masquerade as dehydration. Electrolyte drinks (i.e. Gatorade) help with this, but beware of the sugar content. My advice is to primarily drink water dur-

CHAPTER 11

When and How Often

"Why on God's green earth are you weight training for two and a half hours per day? By following this routine you have a better chance of being struck by lightning or dating a supermodel than you do of being a top pro bodybuilder. It's great to be motivated and want to be the best bodybuilder in the world, but there is a fine line between intensity and stupidity."

– Frank Sepe, top bodybuilding writer and model, answering a beginner's question about whether two-and-a-half hours of training per day is too much.

When people ask me the best time to train, I usually tell them, "today!" The most important thing is not so much when you work out, but rather the fact that you work out regularly. Don't let anyone tell you that you must work out at sunrise, or in the evening. The best time to train is whenever you can fit it into your daily schedule.

That being said, researchers tell us that hormone levels usually peak in the early morning hours. Training at this time helps you take advantage of the body's natural rhythms. Also, you may have more energy because you're not drained from a stressful day at work or school. Of course hopping out of bed at sunrise to head to the gym is not for everyone. In fact, most people find that they need a couple of hours to "wake up" and then another couple of hours before they reach peak efficiency. This would move the time to late morning/early afternoon. But since this time is inconvenient for most people, they usually train between 3:00 and 5:00 p.m. (for students) or 5:00 and 7:00 p.m. (for workers).

If you're flexible with your time, even better – most gyms are open from 5 or 6 in the morning to 10 or 11 at night. A few gyms are even open 24 hours.

Training early in the morning or late at night allows you to avoid the crowds at peak times.

HOW OFTEN?

" Train three days per week and work your whole body each training session. Spend more time working your larger muscle groups such as your legs and back rather than your chest, arms and shoulders. Stick to basic exercises, keeping your sets at 3 or 4 and reps between 8 and 10 on the smaller muscle groups and 10 to 12 on the larger."

– Bill Pearl, bodybuilding legend, offering his views on the type of training program an ectomorphic beginner should follow.

Although telling you when to work out is rather easy, telling you how often is a bit more difficult. Generally speaking, you want to work the muscles hard enough to stimulate new growth, but not so hard that they won't recover before the next workout. Endless routine combinations will help you achieve growth. This book is designed to take you from the beginner level right up to the competitive levels of bodybuilding. Unfortunately, you can't skip the beginner and intermediate levels and go straight to pro-level training, because your recovery system is not yet capable of enduring heavy training intensity. Jay Cutler didn't start out by following a double-split, six-times-per-week training program! In fact, Jay and most of the other pros follow six-day splits only in the few months before a contest. The point, however, is that they started out small and eventually built up to their present training intensity. Here are the most popular split routines followed by bodybuilders. Later in the book we'll go into each in more detail.

THE WHOLE BODY – THREE TIMES PER WEEK

This is the routine most beginners start with, and it guarantees great results. You train the entire body during one

workout, and then take a day off from training. Do this three times a week, with a day off between each workout. The day off between workouts gives the body adequate time to repair itself before the next workout. On average it takes a muscle about 48 hours to recover from low- to medium-intensity workouts.

The primary disadvantage of this routine is that you'll only be able to do 2 or 3 sets for each muscle group. Trying to do more sets for each muscle group will leave you overtrained. Besides, trying to do 10 or 15 sets for every muscle group would take you three or four hours!

Photo of Bill Wilmore by Ralph DeHaan

FOUR DAYS PER WEEK – TWO ON, ONE OFF

The four-day-per-week split is probably the most common and effective routine for gaining muscle size and strength. The body is divided into two halves, with each half trained on one of two consecutive days. After one day of rest follow two more days of training. Unlike the full-body routine, where all the muscles must be trained during one workout, the four-day split allows you to do more for the muscles since you're training only half of them during any given workout. Instead of 2 or 3 sets of one exercise, you can do 3 or 4 sets of two, three or even four different exercises for each bodypart.

There are two different approaches to the four-day-split routine. You can train Monday and Tuesday, take Wednesday off, train Thursday and Friday, and take weekends off, or you can simply go two on, one off, regardless of what day of the week it happens to be. Many bodybuilders like to use the first approach, as it gives them the weekends off.

Some individuals have difficulty following this four-day split because they find training two days in a row too strenuous. For those who need that extra day's rest between workouts, a variation of the four-day split called the two-week split might be the solution.

TWO-WEEK-SPLIT ROUTINE

Just like the four-day split, you divide your training into two workouts. However, instead of training two days in a row, you train one day and take the next day off. While you can go one on, one off indefinitely, most bodybuilders do Day 1 on Monday and Friday and then Day 2 on Wednesday. The following week they perform Day 2 on

Monday and Friday and Day 1 on Wednesday. Basically you spread your training cycle over two weeks and perform each workout three times (twice in one week and once the next). See the example routine below of how this might work.

SIX-DAY-SPLIT ROUTINE

Eventually, most bodybuilders give the six-day split a try. As with the four-day split, you train different muscles on different days. In this situation, you divide your training into three separate workouts, perform them for three consecutive days and then take a day off. Some bodybuilders prefer to perform both three-day cycles back to back – six days in a row – and take the seventh day off.

The primary advantage of six-day splits is that you train only a couple of muscles each day. This means that you can train each muscle with extra sets and exercises. While it sounds great in theory, most bodybuilders find that they can endure training six out of seven days for only about two months. And I'm talking about the most experienced and genetically gifted bodybuilders out there. Most bodybuilders will limit this type of training to their pre-contest phase of training. They then switch back to a four- or five-day routine after the contest.

DOUBLE-SPLIT ROUTINE

The double-split routine is great for those who have less than 45 minutes to work out during each session, or for thpse who have plenty of time but prefer to concentrate on only one bodypart in a workout. You simply train twice a day, hitting one bodypart at a time. The advan-

EXAMPLE: TWO-WEEK-SPLIT ROUTINE

WEEK ONE	WEEK TWO
MONDAY: Chest, back, biceps	MONDAY: Legs, shoulders, triceps
WEDNESDAY: Legs, shoulders, triceps	WEDNESDAY: Chest, back, biceps
FRIDAY: Chest, back, biceps	FRIDAY: Legs, shoulders, triceps

Taking a day off in between each workout provides plenty of time for recovery. Many bodybuilders who had followed the four-day split found that when they switched to this routine, their strength and size gains increased dramatically.

tage to this is that you can devote all your energy to training just one muscle. You will be in and out, shower and all, in 30 to 45 minutes, or even less. Double-split routines can be incorporated into either four- or six-day splits, but most bodybuilders work it into the six-day split.

The primary disadvantage of double-split training is that most people either do not want to, or don't have enough time to work out twice a day. And don't forget that training twice each day can be hard on the recovery system. It's true that you're training only one muscle group for a short period of time, but you're still completing two workouts on the same day. If you were incorporating this into a six-day split it would mean 12 workouts per week. That's a lot of work.

ONE-MUSCLE-PER-DAY ROUTINE

The biggest obstacle most people face when trying to gain muscle size and strength is overtraining. For the average person not juiced up on performance-enhancing drugs, spending more than two hours in the gym for six or seven days a week is just not possible. In fact, it becomes counterproductive. Back in the 1960s, a few of the top bodybuilders at the time, including Mr. Universe Vic Downs, figured out a solution to this problem. Instead of multi-muscle sessions lasting two, three or four hours, you train just one muscle. Instead of pacing yourself for hours on end, you hit the muscle hard for 30 to 45 minutes and then leave the gym. The nice thing about the one-muscle-per-day routine is that it satisfies those who need to be in the gym every day, but at the same time it won't place too much of a demand on the body's recovery system. Such a routine also allows you to do multiple sets for that one muscle group. Instead of 10 to 12 sets, you could do 15 to 20. This lets you hit the muscle from just about every conceivable angle, which is great for lagging muscle groups.

One of the drawbacks to the one-muscle-per-day routine is that you can easily do 20 sets in 30 to 45 minutes. While the big muscles such as the chest, back and thighs

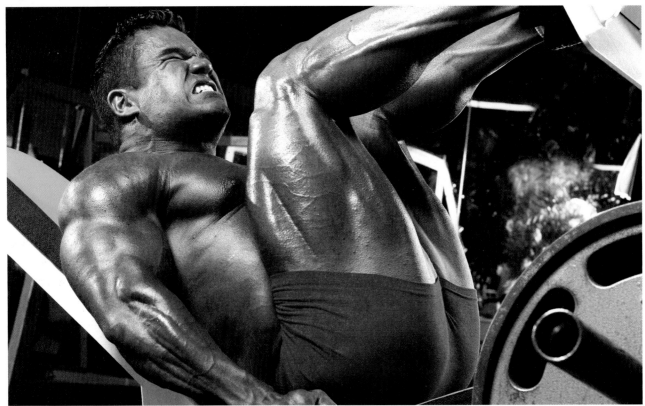

Photo of Troy Tate by Alex Ardenti

might be able to handle it, this many sets would be too much for the smaller supporting muscles such as the triceps and biceps.

Here is an example of the one-muscle-per-day routine:

SAMPLE ROUTINE

MONDAY	Legs
TUESDAY	Chest
WEDNESDAY	Back
THURSDAY	Shoulders
FRIDAY	Triceps
SATURDAY	Biceps

WORKOUT DURATION – HOW LONG?

There's a close relationship between workout length and type. If you follow the low-set, high-intensity style (i.e. Mike Mentzer's Heavy Duty program), you'll be in and out of the gym in under 20 minutes. Conversely, a 20-set per bodypart routine could have you hoisting iron for two hours. We feel that your workouts should take anywhere from 45 to 90 minutes (including cardio).

The topic of workout duration is always being debated. Some suggest that the human body has energy reserves for only about 60 minutes. Any longer and you're just going through the motions. There's also the argument that two- or three-hour workouts place an incredible strain on the recovery system. Some feel that they have not stimulated the muscle adequately enough after a short workout. There is also some merit to the argument that longer workouts do a much better job of stimulating the cardiovascular system. If you follow the high-volume style of training, give yourself 90 to 120 minutes. If high-intensity training is your preference, you should be spending anywhere from 30 to 45 minutes working out, and no longer.

CONCLUSION

I've just described to you the most common routines followed by bodybuilders. Later in the book I'll be showing you how to incorprate the various exercises into these routines. I strongly urge you to follow them as described. They have been arranged in ascending order of difficulty Don't make the mistake of jumping to Ronnie Coleman's or Jay Cutler's pre-contest six-day split routine. Not only do you not need it, but your system won't be able to handle it. As time goes on, such factors as time, goals and personal preference will let you decide what kind of split routine to follow.

Photos of Mark Dugdale by Robert Reiff

CHAPTER 12

Tips to Keep You Focused and Motivated

"Maintain a positive attitude and the long-term goals will take care of themselves."

– Arnold Schwarzenegger, on how to keep going over the long term.

Chances are you're fairly new to working out. And unfortunately, if you're like most North Americans, at least 50 percent of you will quit working out after the first month. By six months the number will have increased to about 75 percent. By the end of the year only about 10 percent of those who first began will still be hitting the gym on a regular basis. While the reasons are varied and mixed, most people who stop training do so because they become bored and unmotivated.

Well let's see if we can do something about that. Here are 12 tips to help keep you motivated and focused on your workouts. They're all easy to implement, free, and virtually guaranteed to work!

1 Get a workout buddy. There's nothing like a workout partner to kick your ass on those less-than-energetic days. Likewise, you can kick his (or hers!) on days he or she feels sluggish. A good training partner knows when to push you a little bit harder and when to give you slack. The two of you can have mini competitions. At the very least you'll have someone to keep you focused on training, and not worried about work or something distracting in your home life.

2 Fit yourself in. As crazy as it sounds, you may have to add your name to your day planner. If it takes making your workout one of your daily appointments, then so be it. The benefit of this is that it helps you balance your workouts with other daily activities such as family, work or school. You will be more successful and bound to stick with it if you make working out part of your lifestyle.

3 Pace yourself. Don't think that you're going to develop the body you want overnight. It probably took you years to get out of shape. A couple of weeks of all-out training will do nothing but make you incredibly stiff and sore, unwilling to work out and hating the sight of a dumbell or barbell. It's far better to train only two or three days a week year after year than to train seven days a week for one month and then quit because you're burned out. Remember, consistency is the key.

4 Rise and shine and work out! The last thing you may want to do bright and early in the morning is hit the gym. But if you find yourself going home after work or school and flopping on the couch, give it a try. By working out early in the morning you'll be sure of getting it done, you'll feel energized throughout the day, and your morning workout will prevent everything else in life from getting in the way of your all-important health and fitness goals.

5 The scale – who cares? Unless you have a huge amount of fat to lose, don't worry about your bodyweight. A ten-pound loss of fat and a ten-pound gain of muscle will make a huge difference in your appearance, clothes size and health,

Photos of David Rylah by Alex Ardenti

but the scales will show no change. Other than as a general guide for extremely overweight people, the scale is practically useless for measuring fitness success.

6 Pick a role model. There's nothing like having someone to look up to, to keep you focused on your goals. Literally millions of people look up to Arnold Schwarzenegger for this reason. From a naive 19-year-old who stepped off a plane in 1968 speaking no English to world's greatest bodybuilder, top Hollywood star and governor of California, Arnold knows a thing or two about motivation and staying focused. We're sure there are many "mini-Arnolds" in your life. They could be teachers, co-workers or someone in the gym who overcame horrendous odds to get where he is. On those days you don't feel like working out or doing that extra set, ask yourself what would your role model do? We thought so. Now do that extra set!

7 Keep track of your success. One of the best ways to know where you're going is to know where you've been. For a few dollars you can pick up a training journal and start recording such things as the amount of cardio, the exercises, the reps, sets and weight used on each exercise, and how you feel and why – were you up late the night before? Did you eat a heavy meal before coming to the gym? Forget to eat altogether? Periodically looking in your journal will give you plenty of insight. You can see how different exercises and routines affect you, and you can see just how far you've come. Your present warmup weights were once your workout weights. Those 20-minute cardio sessions two or three times per week have been replaced by

four 45-minute high-intensity workouts. So even if sometimes you feel you're going nowhere, your workout journal is telling you otherwise. Keep at it!

8 Get back on track. Missing a workout is not that big a deal. In fact, if you've been working out consistently an extra day off every month or so is recommended. But for many people, one day off becomes two days off, two becomes three, and before long they're skipping weeks on end. The gym becomes just a memory. This is similar to the dieter who, because she's eaten a cookie, eats the entire bag of cookies and a quart of chocolate ice cream. Setbacks and missed workouts are perfectly normal. But the quicker you get back on track, the quicker you will reach your fitness goals. Try to remember that health and fitness is not about being perfect. It is a way of life. Don't view your workouts as being all or none. Just be consistent.

Work hard in the gym, and then get out!

9 Evaluate your progress on a regular basis. If you don't check your progress regularly you'll be less inclined to push yourself and stay focused. For example, you may be lifting the same weight for the same number of reps month after month. If you're happy with the way you are and just want to maintain a reasonable level of fitness, then that's fine. But chances are you would like to actually improve – increase your strength, gain muscle mass, look better and have more energy. Unless you evaluate your strength, size and cardio levels on a regular basis, you won't feel inclined to push yourself.

10 Get to the gym! We all have days when we just don't want to work out. We'd sooner go home and lie back on the couch with a soda or beer. But don't. Force yourself to go to the gym. Tell yourself you will just do the first exercise then go home. Odds are that within the first 10 to 15 minutes you'll start feeling energized and have a great workout. Sometimes the days when you have the least energy to begin with end up being the days you have your best workouts. You'll feel especially great about it, because you had originally planned to skip the gym, remember?

11 Change it up. Nothing zaps motivation and drive like monotony. Doing the same routine over and over will leave even the most die-hard fitness fanatics bored. That's why you should change your training routine every month or so. The change doesn't have to be radical, either. Something as simple as increasing or decreasing the number of reps may boost your enthusiasm. Try changing the exercises on a regular basis as well. If you mainly use machines, then give free weights a try. If you always start your chest training with flat barbell presses, try doing incline dumbell or barbell presses. Or start with back instead of chest. Use the pre-exhaust system for a change. If you're really stuck in a rut, give your workout a total overhaul and combine the muscles into different groups. Usually do low reps and heavy weights? Try doing high reps with low weights. Do whatever it takes to get you back on track and focused.

Photos of David Rylah by Alex Ardenti

12 Take some planned time off. Even though earlier I said to force yourself to the gym, there will be times when taking a few days or even a whole week off is recommended. Often one of the major signs of overtraining is a decrease in training drive and motivation. In simple terms, your body is not getting a chance to fully recover before the next workout. Before long you're experiencing burnout. This is when the novice weight trainer is most likely to quit altogether. If you've been working out regularly for months on end, if you've tried all the other tips and nothing is helping, get out your calendar and block out one or two weeks to not train. Make sure to write the dates on a calendar, because randomly taking time off without a plan could turn into a permanent layoff. Unless you've really lost interest in training, a week or two off will have you chomping at the bit to get back to the gym, and if overtraining was indeed the cause of your motivation lapse, then you should come back stronger than ever.

CHAPTER 13

The Missed Workout

"One general rule most people have heard is that if you have a head cold you can work out, but if you're suffering below the neck you should not train. As anyone who has had the flu knows, your entire body aches, so training is pretty much out."

– Will Brink, regular *MuscleMag International* columnist, describing the differences between a head cold and a full-body flu.

t's inevitable. You will miss the occasional workout. If you train pretty consistently, don't worry about it – the extra day or two off will probably do you good! If on the other hand, you find yourself constantly missing workouts, you may want to re-evaluate your entire training philosophy.

There are numerous legitimate reasons for missing workouts. For example, if you're a full-time student, study time and exams will require missing workouts. During mid-terms or final exams, take two days off and devote yourself the books. Trust me – you won't lose muscle (the only size lost will be in your mind). Besides, scoring low on your exams will impact your life far more significantly than a couple of missed workouts.

Maybe you are no longer a student and are now a full-time business person. Staff meetings, business proposals, visiting clients and extra paperwork could all prevent you from hitting the gym. If you can foresee any of these delays, try rearranging your workouts ahead of time. For instance, if you know you're in for a late night at the office on Tuesday, change your split routine, go twice on Monday, or slip in for a quick workout over your lunch hour. If your job requires a lot of travel, you can manage because most hotels have fitness centers. If not, simply go to the nearest gym and pay a drop-in fee. If you're constantly traveling, check out the chapter "Bodybuilding on the Road," later in the book for some tips on keeping, and even improving, your physique with a demanding travel schedule.

There are also a number of personal reasons why you may need to miss workouts. If you have kids, a school play, track and field competition or soccer game will usually take precedence over your workout. Most parents know about these important activities in advance, so aim to work your schedule around them. If you have to stay home because your child is sick, then you'll just have to try to make up that workout the next day.

If you live in northern latitudes, severe weather may force you to miss the occasional workout. While most gyms try to stay open during rough weather, a severe snow storm may shut them down for a day or two. Even if the gym stays open, is a workout worth potentially getting stuck in the snow or getting into an accident because of freezing rain? We think not! It makes more sense to grab a set of dumbells left over from your home gym and perform a light modified workout at home. Besides, you can get creative during the bad weather, and stimulate your muscles in a totally different way than you do at the gym.

Speaking of weather, don't forget about the good ol' common cold that often comes along with it! It's bound to catch you at least once. Do yourself and the other gym members a favor and stay home to rest. Intense training will only weaken the body's ability to fight off the infection. You will also run the risk of developing pneumonia or bronchitis.

Transportation issues can also throw your training schedules off. If you drive an older car, you may find yourself hoisting a wrench on arm day instead of a dumbell! In case your car does break down, or you simply lose your ride, keep a copy of a bus schedule or the number of a taxi on hand. Buses are cheap, relatively clean and punctual, and go within one or two blocks of just about everywhere.

Sometimes financial issues can also interfere with training. Maybe you can't afford the gym on a monthly basis or are forced to consider dropping your membership because of the costs. Don't panic. As we discussed in Chapter 10, it is possible to build a great-looking physique at home. Also, don't underestimate the power of bodyweight exercises such as chin-ups, push-ups, sit-ups, dips between chairs, and one-legged squats and calf raises. If you are really creative and good with equipment, try building your own bench! That's right – actually build it. Just make sure it's stable and can take the weight – yours and the weight you'll be lifting. Some of the biggest and

Illustration by Mark Collins

STAY HOME

Most people nowadays don't have time to stay at home when they are sick. But research shows that going to work sick, even with a simple cold, can make you fatally ill. According to the health and attendance records of 10,000 British civil-service workers, 30 to 40 percent of those who continued to work when sick later suffered twice the rate of heart disease as those who stayed home. So next time you have a wicked case of the sniffles, grab the remote control and stay at home. A few days away from the gym won't kill your training goals, and the other weight trainers will thank you for not spreading the germs.

Source: *New York Post* Online

strongest guys around got started in garages using equipment built out of old car parts. The original Gold's Gym in Santa Monica, California, was filled with equipment built by Joe Gold himself.

The final reason why you may miss a workout is … because we highly recommend it!

Even with the best form and technique, the human body, particularly the tissues that surround the joints (i.e. cartilage, ligaments, tendons, etc.) can only endure so much. The vast majority of bodybuilders have nagging aches and pains. In fact, a large majority of them are probably overtrained. Yet they refuse to take the time to rest because they fear losing size and strength. The truth is, once you've been consistently training with progressive resistance for a while, you'd need to take a couple of months off before you would honestly experience any loss in strength and size (even if this does occur, you can regain it in a matter of weeks). It is during recovery time that your body recharges itself and makes the most gains (because it is getting a chance to rest). The time off will also increase your motivation. After a week's rest, you'll be attacking the weights with renewed vigor!

Regardless of why you miss a workout, maintaining the overall commitment is crucial. As long as you do this, a missed workout, or even a week or two off (in the case of overtraining), will not affect you long term.

CHAPTER 14

Equipment: Yours

"In most back exercises your grip will be your weak point, hindering you from lifting heavy weights the back can handle but the wrists and forearms can't. Straps definitely help you handle more weight in back exercises."

– Rahim Kassam, strength columnist in *MuscleMag International*

You'll need to buy a few items before beginning your quest to become a world-class bodybuilder. These items will increase the productivity of your workout and will cost you very little.

CLOTHING AND FOOTWEAR

Most gyms have dress codes, and while some are extreme (such as no hats, or no two-piece clothing), most certainly require a pair of shorts and a T-shirt. Few gyms allow guys to go topless – it's pretty disgusting having to wipe a large pool of sweat off a bench or machine before you use it. Besides, no one really wants to see your naked upper body, beautiful though it may be.

At times the gym temperature will be cool enough to wear a sweatshirt and track pants. Warmer clothing helps keep the muscles warm, soaks up more sweat and keeps the other competitors from knowing what shape you're in! During the summer months, or if your gym is already warm, throw on a tank top and pair of shorts. The bottom line is to dress according to the temperature and the dress code at you facility.

Footwear is a little easier. Nothing beats the sturdy ol' sneaker. You can head to the local department store and buy a pair of $20 specials or drop by a sports speciality store and pay $150 to $200 for a pair of top-of-the-line Nike or Adidas. While the cheapies may look as good as the more expensive brands, they usually won't offer the same support or last as long.

You may be tempted to go barefoot, but most gyms have rules against this.

For starters, it's not very hygienic. Also, it can be dangerous. You have no idea just what kind of damage a heavy dumbell or weight plate can do to an exposed foot. A sneaker may be the difference between a serious bruise and a broken foot. If your gym does allow you to remove your sneakers, limit it to such exercises as calf raises and chin-ups. Performing calf raises without sneakers will allow you to obtain a few extra degrees of movement at the top and bottom of the exercise. Barefoot chin-ups will give you a sense of freedom, and while the difference in weight may only be a pound, the feeling of lightness may enable you to squeeze out an extra rep or so.

HEADBAND

Even in the best air-conditioned gyms, you'll be sweating. Nothing is as irritating as sweat running into your eyes while you're trying to work out. The best solution is to wear a headband, do-rag, or bandana. You can spend $10 to $20 for a store-bought one, or go to a fabric store and buy enough material to make five or ten. Always check with your gym first to make sure they allow headbands. Most do, but a few of the larger fitness chains have a rule against them.

GLOVES

One of the first things those not used to manual labor or weightlifting will notice after a few workouts is blisters. After a short time the blisters will turn into dead skin that will start building up in layers, leading to the formation of

calluses. Calluses, while not the nicest thing to look at, are a preventative tool given to you by your body. The skin is the body's first line of defence against invading germs, and therefore the body makes darn sure that any damage to the skin is quickly repaired. Calluses prevent the skin from breaking in frequently chafed areas. If you have sensitive skin, need soft hands for your profession or just hate the look of calluses, for $15 to $20 you can buy a pair of gloves that protect your hands from chafing and callusing. Some have the fingers cut out to allow a better grip. Some bodybuilders use golf gloves instead. While thinner and not providing the same degree of protection as weightlifting gloves, they are a decent alternative. If gloves are not your style, then try holding a piece of sponge or rubber between your hands and the barbell.

Just remember that once you start wearing gloves, you're committed to them. My advice is to tough out the first few weeks and let the skin on your hands thicken. Not only will you have a better grip on the bar, you'll also be prepared for any odd job around the house that requires rough hands.

WRAPS

It won't take many workouts before you'll notice some bodybuilders wrapped up like Egyptian mummies! For some bodybuilders, it's preventative medicine, while for others it's to protect an injured joint. As you progress in your workouts, you may experience the occasional joint problem. In most cases you can train around the irritation, but you may need to go the wrap route on occasion.

Wraps are thin (two to three inches wide) pieces of cloth that are wrapped around the injured area to provide extra support and to keep the area warm. Most drugstores sell them for a few dollars.

Unfortunately, some bodybuilders abuse the procedure. Instead of wrapping only the injured or weak area, they wrap just about every joint. This not only restricts their range of movement (one of the negative aspects of wearing wraps), but also causes the joints to become dependent on the wraps. As you progressively increase the weights you use, your ligaments and tendons increase in strength alongside your muscles. If you wear wraps too much, your ligaments will not feel the need to strengthen.

Unless you have a serious injury, you shouldn't need to wear wraps this early in your training career. As your intensity increases, wrapping a joint may become necessary on heavy compound exercises such as squats and bench presses (the knees and elbows tend to be the most frequent joints that require wrapping), but do use wraps judiciously.

WEIGHTLIFTING BELTS

The weightlifting belt is another piece of equipment that has come to symbolize power and strength. Just think how many times you have seen some cartoon character wrap a belt around his waist, and then hoist a car or some other inhuman object. This symbolism has led to many a bodybuilder strapping on a belt before leaving the locker room and not taking it off until the end of the workout. In the "old" days, belts were used only on squats, deadlifts, rows and overhead presses. These days bodybuilders think they have to have one on constantly to be more powerful.

The purpose of a weightlifting belt is to provide additional support to the lower back when performing exercises that place extra stress on this region. The muscles and ligaments of the lower spine were not designed to endure the excessive stress from squats, deadlifts and rows. These movements place a tremendous amount of strain on the lower back, spinal erector muscles, ligaments and vertebrae.

The spine is also held upright by another force: intra-abdominal pressure, located below the diaphragm, and intra-thoracic pressure (ITP), located above the diaphragm. Both pressures are created by forceful contraction of the abdominals against the body's internal organs. Some physiologists estimate that these pressures can increase by a factor of 10 when lifting without a belt. A sturdy belt gives the abdominals something to push against.

As you might guess, wearing a belt continuously throughout every workout will keep your core muscles weak. It's best to wear a belt only on squats, deadlifts, overhead presses, rows and shrugs. The only time that you should wear a belt for the entire workout is if you have a lower-back injury.

Since weightlifting belts are popular, you will find them in numerous stores, from department stores to speciality stores. They range in price from about $25 to $75. If money is no object, you can go to a leather goods store and have one tailor made for you. While the price could be $100 or more, the extra cash will get you a finished product that will fit your physique perfectly and last forever. Belts come in several styles and generally range from four to six inches in width. They are usually secured around the waist in the same manner as a regular belt and are fastened with a buckle that could be one, two, three or four pronged.

There are three general sub-categories of belts and all three have their pros and cons. On one end, you have the stylish and colourful velcro-fastened belts that are not usually thick enough to provide much back support. I suggest avoiding these altogether. Then you have the thick, heavy-duty powerlifting belts that will literally support a ton of weight. Of course you'll pay more, and you should really ask yourself if you need half a cow wrapped around your waist at this stage! Somewhere in between are the middle-of-the road belts that cost $30 to $40 (as little as $10 to $20 on eBay) and were made famous by York and Weider. Given their low cost and solid support, you can't go wrong by purchasing one of these.

FOLLOW THESE TIPS SHOULD YOU DECIDE TO USE A BELT:

• Before buying a belt, try out a number of different styles and makes. The purpose of the belt is to provide lower-back support. It doesn't make sense to wear something that's stylish but doesn't really help. The best word to describe a good-fitting belt is "snug."

• Make sure the belt you buy is thick enough to provide good support. Some of those cheap velcro-fastened belts offer no more support than a towel wrapped around your waist!

• Always wear a belt on any heavy basic exercises that place pressure on the lower back. If you still have lower-back stress, you might want to give that exercise a pass. If more than one exercise causes lower-back discomfort, see a physician or chiropractor.

• Perform all your stretches and abdominal exercises without a belt. Wearing a belt not only restricts your range of motion, but the repetitive bending at the waist will cause the skin to chaff in that region.

• Don't become dependent on the belt! If you have a minor lower-back injury or your lower-back muscles are exceptionally tired one day, then perhaps you might want to wear the belt for the entire workout. But as soon as your back returns to normal, limit wearing it to the basic exercises.

• Strengthen your core muscles. Lower-back pain is often caused by weak abdominals, and lower-back injury is often caused by weak spinal erectors. Yet bodybuilders often ignore these two muscle groups. Having a strong core will make it less likely that you'll be sidelined by injury, and make it easier for you to use heavier weights – two ways a strong core will make you bigger!

Illustration by Mark Collins

WRIST STRAPS

Decades ago, powerlifters like the great Paul Anderson used wrist straps to help him deadlift thousands of pounds. It took bodybuilders some time to accept them, but now straps have become an integral part of the body-building workout.

Straps are short, narrow pieces of material (an average of two feet long by one to one and half inches wide) that are wrapped around the wrists and the barbell, or the handles of the machine being gripped. They are most commonly used on deadlifts, shrugs and rows because the forearm muscles are the "weak link" in the chain. Wrist straps enable you to subject the primary muscle to more weight than the forearms are capable of holding.

As with belts and wraps, the primary disadvantage of straps is that you can become dependent on them. If you use straps on just about every exercise, your forearm muscles and wrists will never develop their maximum gripping strength. Another drawback is improper use. Many bodybuilders experience severe wrist pain while using straps. While the weight being lifted could be the cause, it's more likely the position of the wrists relative to the hands. The wrist is really a meeting place between the forearm and hand bones. The radius and ulna forearm bones connect to the hand and finger bones by way of the small wrist bones. The most distinct features of this area are the two bony protrusions on the sides of the wrist. These two bumps play a huge role in proper usage of straps.

Many bodybuilders place the straps directly over the bumps, but this is not a good idea, as all the weight being lifted (which will probably be many hundreds of pounds) is then transmitted directly to the small wrist bones. These small structures are not designed to support that kind of weight and the result is often stretched ligaments, wrist pain and potentially broken bones. You also have to remember the main nerves for the hands run through the small wrist bones. Wearing straps improperly may cause nerve impingement; more commonly known as carpal tunnel syndrome. So what's the solution? Make sure that the straps are resting snugly around the bottom of your hand, missing the wrist altogether.

There are a number of different types of straps. Most cost about $15 to $20, but you could pay upwards of $40 to $50 for a top-end pair. Straps come in two styles. Some are simply straight pieces of material, while others have a loop at one end through which you feed the other end. Most bodybuilders prefer the loop variety for light exercises such as pulldowns and chin-ups, and the straight version for shrugs and deadlifts.

You could also easily make your own straps. Go into a fabric or hardware store and buy about six feet of tough woven or nylon material. Cut the straps into lengths of about 25 to 30 inches long and 1 1/2 to 2 inches wide. Anything less than 1 1/2 inches will cut into your wrists. Make sure to allow enough material to make the loop (if you are going to be making the loop variety). If you want extra strength and protection, cut the straps twice as wide and then fold in half and stitch. Make sure you use heavy thread and double stitching. Make sure the stitching is strong, especially if you make the loop variety.

Other sources of material include judo and karate belts and car seatbelts, which are all made of very strong material. The martial arts belts also have the benefit of softness. You may have to fold the car seatbelt in half to eliminate the sharp edge.

HEAD STRAPS

Some bodybuilders will develop large, powerful neck muscles simply by doing shoulder and back training. Others will need to hit the muscles directly if they want that no-neck look made famous by football players. A head strap is a harness that fits around the head. You then either hang weights from the end or attach it to a cable machine. Many of the older Universal leg curl/extension machines had such an attachment. If your gym doesn't have a harness you can go the wrist strap route and make

your own. Again, it's just a matter of picking up the material and doing a bit of stitching.

Besides appearance, strong neck muscles are an absolute must in sports like judo, wrestling, football, rugby and mixed martial arts. If your neck is undersized or you play any of these sports, invest in a neck harness and train your neck two or three times per week.

CHALK

Sweat can interfere with your grip on machine handles, bars and dumbells. Bodybuilders learned the value of chalk from powerlifters, Olympic lifters and gymnasts. Most sporting stores carry it and it's dirt cheap – less than $5 for a large block. Before you rush out and buy it, however, check your gym's policy. Many gyms won't allow it because it can make a mess. Other gyms allow it only in the free-weight area.

WATER BOTTLE

"Without adequate fluids, the body simply cannot convert carbs to energy efficiently. Since 70 percent of muscle tissue is water, it relies on consistent hydration to keep functioning, and when you're depleted of fluid, the muscle cells simply cannot load up with energy nutrients or amino acids."
– Jerry Kindela, *MuscleMag International* Group Editorial Director

It's amazing how many guys refuse to carry a water bottle and insist on drinking out of the water fountain. It's the old "water bottles are for wusses" mentality. Well, there's nothing wussy about catching someone else's flu or cold sore. Also, wusses rarely pass out from dehydration! You'll lose a quart or more of water through sweat during a typical workout and you'll want to replenish on a regular basis. For the sake of a few dollars, invest in a water bottle and try to consume at least one or two bottles per workout. Despite our land existence, we're still reliant on water for just about every metabolic function. Don't end up on the floor because of stubborn machismo!

Photo of Sagi Kalev by Irvin Gelb

Stay hydrated throughout your workout and beyond – your body needs water to function optimally.

CHAPTER 15

Equipment: The Gym's

"My buddy and I decided to check out Winston's Fitness Centre. When we walked in we were amazed. The place was full of weights and equipment ... I was struck dumb."

– Paul Dillett, champion IFBB bodybuilder

f you've never been in a large gym or fitness center before, day one will be an eye-opener. The days of old torn benches and a few rusty barbells are long gone. Instead the modern gym is filled with the latest in strength training and cardio equipment. The typical gym will have an inventory of equipment costing hundreds of thousands, and in many cases, millions of dollars. As I'll be looking at cardio training in greater detail later in the book, I'm going to devote this chapter to strength-training equipment.

Essentially, strength-training equipment can be divided into two primary categories – free weights and machines.

FREE WEIGHTS

Free weight is the term given to dumbells and barbells. The term "free" is used as there are no attached pulleys, cables, weight stacks or handles. Just a piece of iron with plates on each end. The free weight is the most basic form of bodybuilding equipment and, despite the advances made to weight-training machines, has built more great physiques than any other type of equipment.

Barbells

The barbell is probably the most recognizable piece of bodybuilding equipment, and various incarnations have been used for hundreds of years. Barbells are long (typically between four and seven feet) iron bars on which circular weight plates are placed on both ends. Olympic bars are the largest barbells and, at seven feet long and 45 pounds, are designed to support 1,000+ pounds. At each end of the bar is a thicker chrome-colored section called a sleeve, that allows the bar to rotate independent of the plates. This helps reduce the stress on the wrists.

The next time you see some Olympic lifter throwing 500 pounds over his head or some powerlifter squatting with 900 pounds, you can be sure he's using an Olympic bar. These bars are far too long to be used with arm exercises, so they tend to be used for training the larger muscles with such exercises as squats, deadlifts, presses and rows.

Besides the standard seven-foot Olympic bar, most gyms have shorter bars (four to six feet) that are more convenient for working the smaller muscles. To keep the plates from sliding off during exercise, a metal lock called a collar is secured to each end. Collars can either be the type tightened with a bolt, or simple spring collars.

Fixed Barbells

Your gym you may have a selection of fixed barbells. These short (four to five feet long) bars have the weights welded in position, so you simply grab the bar with the total weight you want to use. Most gyms have a full set of fixed bars ranging from 20 to 100–120 pounds, and these bars are stored in a special rack or stand. For both neatness, convenience and safety, gyms require that you return the bars to the rack when you're finished using them.

EZ-Curl Bars

Most gyms carry a variation of the barbell called an EZ-Curl bar. EZ-Curl bars are about three feet long, weigh about 20 to 25 pounds and have a double S-bend in the middle. Many bodybuilders find the EZ-Curl bars better to use that straight bars on arm exercises, as the curves allow the hands to rest in a more natural position throughout the movement, thereby allowing less stress on the wrists.

Weight Plates

Unless you're training light or warming up, bars are useless without extra weight on them. Weight plates are circular and designed to fit snugly over the ends of barbells. The standard gym plate is iron and ranges from 2.5 to 100 pounds in the following increments: 2.5, 5, 10, 25, 35, 45, 100.

No doubt some readers may be familiar with "plastic" plates. Many home gym sets by York and Weider come with weight plates made up of a hollow plastic shell filed with sand or cement. The nice thing about plastic plates is that they treat carpets and floors with more kindness than iron plates. Their chief disadvantage is their thickness, as they are at least twice as thick as an iron plate. This means you can't fit as many on the barbell and it won't be long before you'll outgrow them. In addition, if they drop on hard surfaces they can split, spilling the sand out and becoming unusable.

As with all small equipment, gyms will be diligent in requiring you to return the plates to their proper stands or racks when finished. Nothing is as dangerous as a couple of loose plates lying around the floor. Sooner or later someone is going to trip.

Dumbells

Contrary to popular belief, the name dumbell has nothing to do with being stupid. The original meaning of the word "dumb" was mute, or silent, and the word dumbbell literally means "silent bell."

Dumbells can be considered the little brothers of barbells. Dumbells are short (10 to 15 inches) bars that, like

Photo of Omar Deckard by Ralph DeHaan

barbells, can be used to train just about every muscle group. Unlike barbells, however, you usually hold one in each hand as opposed to using two hands to hold one bar. Like fixed barbell sets, most gyms have the plates on the dumbells welded in place. You simply grab the weight you wish to use. Virtually all gyms have the dumbells arranged in ascending order on racks located along by the mirrors – that is, if they've been put away properly. A typical dumbell set will range from 5 to 120 pounds, but gyms with larger and stronger trainers might have 150 or even 200 pounders kicking around. You don't realize what power is until you see some 280-pound bodybuilder banging out reps on presses with a pair of 150-pound dumbells.

The primary advantage of dumbells over barbells is that they allow you a greater range of motion on many exercises, including pressing movements. On such exercises as chest and shoulder presses the barbell will have to stop at the shoulders or chest but the dumbells, because they are shorter and held in each hand, can be lowered further, giving you an extra 10 to 20 degrees of motion. Many bodybuilders also find dumbells easier on the wrists as you can rotate the hands slightly inward or outward. Barbells force you to keep the hands and wrists locked in the one position. In addition, dumbells are safer, especially when you are working out alone. If you can't manage to complete a last rep on presses with dumbells, you simply drop them. If you can't manage the last rep with a barbell ... well, we've already told you about the dead bodybuilders in basements.

BENCHES

Although some exercises can be performed using just the barbell or dumbells, many exercises will need to be executed on some sort of bench. As there are numerous different types I'll discuss them separately.

Flat Bench

As the name suggests, flat benches are long, flat, and horizontal. They are supported by four legs and can be used to perform such exercises as flat dumbell presses, one-arm

rows and lying triceps extensions. While in some gyms the benches are bolted to the floors, most flat benches can be moved around. These benches will often have a rack attached for doing bench presses.

Incline Bench

To target the upper chest you'll need a bench that is tilted or inclined 30 to 45 degrees to the vertical. Most bodybuilders find that angles above 45 degrees tend to shift most of the stress to the front shoulders while angles less than 30 degrees target the lower chest to a greater degree. Besides chest, you can use an incline bench to work the biceps and triceps.

Decline Bench

Decline benches are just the opposite of incline benches and are primarily used to target the lower chest. They can also be used for training the abdominals, triceps, back and rear shoulders.

Vertical Bench

On some exercises such as shoulder presses and dumbell extensions for triceps, it's a good idea to brace your back against an upright surface. Most gyms have benches that are locked between 80 and 90 degrees. Resting your back against a vertical pad greatly reduces the stress on your lower back.

Adjustable Bench

Most gyms have adjustable benches that allow you to set the angle anywhere from 0 to 90 degrees. This allows bodybuilders to adjust the bench to suit the exercise. It also allows users to select the angle that feels best for them. While 0 (flat), 30, 45 and 90 degrees are the most popular angles for fixed benches, many bodybuilders prefer angles somewhere in between. We encourage you to experiment with different angles as time goes on – an angle that works for one bodybuilder maybe too steep or not steep enough for another.

Scott, or Preacher Bench

This was originally called the preacher bench, but when word got out that Larry Scott, bodybuilding's first Mr. Olympia, used it extensively to build his great set of biceps, the name Scott bench became common. The Scott bench is basically a pad set at 45 degrees. It often has an attached chair to sit on. By doing biceps curls on a 45-degree angle you can shift more of the stress to the lower biceps. Now, while you can't physically lengthen your biceps (length is genetically determined) you can give the lower biceps and upper forearms a thicker appearance. This helps fill in the gap between the upper and lower arms. Another advantage of Scott curls is that by sitting down and locking the upper arms on the pad, you can't swing the torso and cheat like you can on standing barbell curls. This also means you have to use less weight on Scott curls.

Abdominal Bench

An abdominal bench is basically a decline bench with double padded rollers at one end. Many have a short handle sticking out of the high end to hold on to and a pin or knob to adjust the height. Because of the angle, an abdominal bench allows you to place more stress on the abdominals. If you put your feet under the rollers you can perform situps and crunches to primarily target the upper abdominals. If you flip over and grab the handle with your hands and doing leg raises brings more lower abdominals into play. Both exercises can be made more difficult by increasing the angle of the bench.

Dipping Bar

While simple to look at, dipping bars are one of the most effective apparatus for working the chest, shoulders and triceps. The late Vince Gironda, the Iron Guru, said dips were the best chest exercise, period. Dipping bars can be parallel, like gymnastics bars, or V-shaped (coming closer together at one end). Performed with the body held vertical and elbows close to the sides, the exercise works primarily the triceps, while performing it while leaning forward with the elbows flared out makes it primarily a chest exercise.

Chin-Up Bar

Another oldie but goodie. A chin-up bar is simply a long overhead bar that allows you to pull yourself upwards. Basic bars are straight while the fancier ones may have numerous handles arranged at different angles. Chin-ups may have been a source of annoyance for you back in high school when the coach forced you to do so many chin-ups in a certain time period. Now that your bodybuilding training has begun let me be the first to tell you that chin-ups are one of the best, if not the best, back exercises in existence. Just about every top bodybuilding superstar includes chin-ups on back day.

Racks

Racks come in many sizes and shapes and have two primary functions – storage and assistance. Barbells and dumbells are not normally left lying around the floor or standing up in corners, but rather they are placed on racks to keep them out of the way and make them easy to find. Racks also come into play on exer-

cises where the muscle being targeted is capable of lifting much more weight than the muscles used to hoist the bar into position. It won't be long before you'll be performing squats with 300 pounds or more on your shoulders. As you can imagine, it's virtually impossible to hoist that amount of weight from the floor and place it on your shoulders. The easy solution is to place the bar on a rack at the desired height. Likewise, I don't think you'd want to lift a loaded bar from the floor and hold it above your chest for bench presses. Even if you did somehow manage to hoist it into the starting position and perform your set, just imagine trying to get back up off the bench holding a 300-pound bar.

Many racks also have safety catches or pins that allow you to rack the bar at a lower level if you can't return it to the starting height. This safety feature is an absolute must on such exercises as squats and bench presses.

Smith Machine

The Smith machine is a specialized machine that looks like a traditional barbell placed on a rack. But look closer and you'll see that the bar is attached to a straight vertical bar on each side and connected to the machine by a set of hooks. The primary benefit of the Smith machine is also its disadvantage – balance. Unlike a regular barbell, which you have to lift as well as balance, the Smith machine balances the bar for you. This makes it good for those with injuries, those new to the gym environment, and is safer for those working alone. The disadvantage of this, however, is that balancing the bar is a big part of the effectiveness of the exercise.

Another problem with the Smith machine is that most models force you to lift the bar in a straight line, whereas your body moves in a natural arc while performing presses. Forcing the body to move a bar in a straight line could cause undue stress on the joints and associated connective tissues.

The Arm Blaster

While he probably never used it as much as the photos might have suggested, the sight of Arnold blasting his 22-inch arms while wearing an Arm Blaster no doubt helped sell millions. An Arm Blaster is a short, two to three foot long, flat piece of curved metal (usually aluminium) that fits around the waist and is supported by a strap around the neck. By placing the elbows against the two ends, much of the cheating that bodybuilders are famous for while doing biceps curls are eliminated. While the apparatus doesn't really have any drawbacks, it never really caught on with bodybuilders.

EQUIPMENT – MACHINES

"I don't care for machines that start out with a fairly heavy weight, even before you add any plates. They can be downright dangerous. I wanted to do light leg presses so I put a 25-pound plate on each side. I didn't know the machine weighed 225 pounds, making my first set 275. It drove me into the floor like a guillotine."
– Bill Starr, regular *MuscleMag International* contributor and top strength coach

While barbells and dumbells are probably the oldest type of training equipment, machines have seen the greatest explosion in variety and numbers over the last couple of decades. Most machines have weight stacks made up of rectangular iron plates placed one on top of another. To select a weight you simply place a pin into the hole of the desired poundage. Most machines have the weight stacks attached to handles by way of cables and pulleys. In recent years some brands have adopted Kevlar belts in place of wire cables.

Machines come in two basic styles – individual and multi-station. Individual machines tend to work just one muscle, but with a bit of ingenuity bodybuilders have adapted them to train multiple muscles. Multi-stations have four, six, eight or more stations connected to a central frame, or core. The old Universal Gladiator is probably the oldest and most familiar multi-station around and most high school and college gyms have at least one of these units. While outdated by many of its younger rivals, it still finds its share of supporters.

There are literally hundreds of different machines that you can use to work the muscles. There's no way I

much stress on the lower back that you do with a squat. Leg presses also allow you to vary your foot position considerably. Doing so allows you to target different parts of the thighs, and is beneficial for reducing knee stress and glute involvement.

You may find a number of different variations of the leg press machine. Older models require you to lie on your back and push straight up. While very effective, this position is uncomfortable and can cause an enormous pressure buildup in the head. If you have high blood pressure or a history of stroke in your family I strongly suggest you avoid the vertical leg press.

The most common leg press these days is called the 45-degree leg press. Instead of pushing straight up, you lie back on a 45-degree pad and push a platform loaded with weight up on an angle. Such machines are designed to hold enormous loads of weight. If you're not already, it won't be long before you're using 500 pounds or more.

can cover them all here. Later in the book I'll be describing many of them as I explain the various exercises. For now I'll give you a brief description of a few of the better-known machines.

The other popular leg-press machine is called a lying, or horizontal leg press. This machine requires you to lie on your back and place your feet on a platform. From here you push with your legs, but instead of the platform moving away from you, you move away from the platform. Because most horizontal leg presses are stack loaded (you place a pin in a hole rather than put plates on the side), serious bodybuilders usually avoid them. Even if the stack holds 500 pounds, the mechanics of the machine will allow most serious bodybuilders to lift the entire stack within a short time of starting their training.

Lower Body

While the barbell squat is considered the best thigh exercise, there are a number of other machines that can effectively work the thighs. And even if you make squats the centerpiece of your workout, you'll need other movements to really hit the smaller muscles of the legs such as the calves and hamstrings.

Leg press: If squats are the No. 1 leg exercise then leg presses are a close second – and for many bodybuilders a safer way to train the legs. I'll be the first to admit that some individuals find the squat stressful on the knees and lower back, despite its many advantages. Others can easily perform the exercise, but get nothing more out of it than a large set of glutes (a large ass!).

Leg presses have two primary advantages over squats. You can go super heavy without placing anywhere near as

Hack machine: The hack machine, or "hack squat" will put a nice sweep to your outer thigh. The machine is angled slightly backwards. You lie back and rest your body against a long padded support. The weights are usually attached to the rear or sides.

Leg-extension machine: The leg extension machine consists of a chair with a long straight lever with one long or two short rollers attached. By sitting in the chair and placing your legs behind the rollers and lifting (extending) upward you can isolate the thighs. Although leg extensions are a great warmup or finishing exercise they won't build your thighs near as large or strong as squats or leg presses.

Leg-curl machine: Leg-curl machines are used to train primarily the hamstrings, but the glutes and calves do come into play. There are three primary types of leg-curl machines. The classic leg curl requires you to lie facedown on a long pad and rest your ankles under a set of padded rollers. You then curl the rollers up by bending at the knees. Older models of this machine were attached to the leg extension and the moving arm had both an upper and lower set of rollers. You simply sat on the end of the pad and used the lower rollers to perform extensions, and lay facedown and used the upper rollers to train the hamstrings.

In recent years the seated leg curl has grown in popularity. This machine looks very similar to the leg-extension machine, in that you sit in a chair. However, instead of placing your feet behind the rollers and pushing up, you place them on top of the rollers and curl down, or back towards your butt. The advantage of the seated leg curl is that it has an adjustable pad to keep you from sliding out of the chair. It also helps to prevent the cheating that can take place on lying leg curls by throwing your bodyweight into the exercise.

Standing leg curls require you to stand up and while your body is supported by one leg, you place the other leg in front of a padded roller and curl backward and upward.

Calf machines: Calf machines come in three basic styles. The standing calf machine consists of an upright frame with two horizontal pads that you step under and place on your shoulders. You stand on the edge of a platform and flex up and down at the ankle joint, targeting the upper calf muscle, the gastrocnemius.

Those who find the standing calf stressful on their lower back can use the leg-press machine. Instead of

standing up and resting the weight on your shoulders, you sit in a chair and place your toes at the bottom edge of the platform. Flex at the ankle joint, going right up on your toes and then bringing your heels down as far as possible. As your legs are kept straight at all times, the toe press primarily works the upper calf muscles.

To target the lower calves, use the seated calf machine. This machine consists of a small padded stool to sit on and an attached horizontal bar with a set of pads that rest on your knees. The movement is similar to standing calf raises and toe presses, in that you flex up and down at the ankles. However, since the knees are bent, most of the work is performed by the lower calf muscle (the soleus).

Upper Body

As with the legs, there are hundreds of exercise machines for the upper body. While some are virtually useless, many come close to duplicating the effectiveness of free weights.

Lat pulldown machine: The lat pulldown machine has been a staple in bodybuilding workouts since Universal put one on their multi-stations decades ago. While chin-ups get the nod for back-training effectiveness, pulldowns (which are just chin-ups in reverse – the bar comes down instead of you going up) are great for those not strong enough to lift their bodyweight, or for those who cannot get enough reps with bodyweight. The traditional version of the lat pulldown was to use a long straight bar and grab it with a wide grip. Nowadays dozens of different attachments can be hooked on to hit the lats (short for latissimus dorsi) from different angles. I should add that the lat pulldown machine probably gets as much use for training the triceps as it does for training the back muscles.

Pec-deck, or pec-flye machine: The pec-deck gets it name from the pectorals, or chest muscles. The original pec-deck was invented by Arthur Jones of Nautilus fame, but over the past couple of decades numerous versions have come on the scene. Some require you to place your forearms behind a set of pads and squeeze together, while others have handles for you to grab. While both these types of

machine are effective, you may notice a big difference in comfort from one to the other, particularly on the joints.

Lateral-raise machine: This machine consists of a padded stool to sit on and a small frame with two padded side arms to rest your forearms and elbows against. By raising the arms out and upward to shoulder height you can target the side, or medial, deltoid (shoulder) muscles. While the dumbell version of this exercise is probably more popular, the machine is actually more biomechanically correct. The resistance is kept more in line with the side shoulders when using the machine.

Biceps and triceps machines: Despite the variety of biceps and triceps machines (literally dozens) they don't seem to garner the same degree of attention as some of the chest, back and shoulder machines. It could be that most bodybuilders just prefer training their arms with free weights (is there anything any better than a basic barbell curl?), or it could be that machines don't seem to stress the arm muscles like some of the other upper-body machines stress the larger muscles. With the exception of triceps pushdowns on the lat machine and maybe cable curls on

a low-pulley machine, most arm machines just sit there looking cute but lonely!

TO USE OR NOT?

The issue of machines is one of the enduring, debates among bodybuilding experts. Many have a love 'em or hate 'em relationship. Others fall somewhere in the middle and use machines to supplement their free-weight programs. Machines do have some advantages over free weights. They are easier to set up, as all you really need to do is put a pin in a hole. Loading a leg press with 500+ pounds can be a workout in itself. Machines are also easier to use if you have an injury. And unlike barbells and dumbells, which need to be balanced as well as lifted, machines usually require you to simply lift the weight. Of course, this is also where critics condemn machines. By not having to balance the weight you are losing half the benefits of the exercise. The small muscles you use to stabilize and balance a barbell or dumbell are never fully utilized with machines. You will notice this weakness if you switch from machines to free weights doing the same exercise. The issue of symmetrical stress must not be forgotten, either. Many machines consist of one arm or lever that is lifted with two hands or legs. The problem with this is that the strong side of your body will do most of the lifting. The weaker side will never catch up if you only use such machines.

Of course, some exercises can only be performed using machines. The lat pulldown is one example. Until you can lift your bodyweight on the chin-up exercise you'll need to do pulldowns for lat width. Even then, you may find the lat pulldown does a better job of targeting the lats. With the possible exception of stiff-leg deadlifts there are not that many great free-weight hamstring exercises, whereas leg curls are great for targeting hamstrings. Calf training with free weights offers the same limitations.

Unless you honestly feel that you prefer to only use free weights, or conversely, injuries prevent you from using free weights, we suggest you incorporate a combination of machine and free-weight exercises into your training. Virtually every bodybuilding superstar does this, and so should you.

Photo of Franco Colombu

BOOK II

THE BODY YOU'RE BUILDING

CHAPTER 16

Bodybuilding Biology

"Most bodybuilders are focused on building bigger muscles, period! In fact, they should be focusing on building a big, proportionate, flexible, strong and healthy body."

– *MuscleMag International* editorial

t's been painted and sculpted for thousands of years. Poets write about it and people routinely spend thousands of dollars trying to perfect it. The human body has been called everything from a work of art to an incredible machine. As a bodybuilder your goal is to improve both its appearance and health, not to mention its strength.

In many respects the human body is like an internal combustion engine. Both need fuel to supply energy and both give off waste products. Both need constant maintenance and both eventually wear out – much more quickly if not properly cared for. The following discussion of muscle anatomy and physiology may bring back memories of high school biology. In fact you may still be in high school. That's fine, as there's nothing like practical application to help you remember something.

MUSCLES

The human skeleton is covered by approximately 650 muscles, which create the distinct contours and shape of the human body. Anatomists disagree on the exact number of muscles. The main area of controversy concerns whether certain muscles are one unit or two units working together. (Clearly we did not evolve to please anatomists.) It is generally accepted, however, that there are at least 630 muscles in the human body. By contracting and relaxing, these muscles produce movement.

Although bodybuilding helps strengthen bones, ligaments and tendons, it is the muscles that receive the greatest benefit from this sport. The words bodybuilding and muscles go hand in hand. Muscles show the results of your labor. You don't ask a person to show you his Achilles' tendon – you ask to see his

Biceps
Bis
To flex (curl) the forearms at the elbow.

Latissimus Dorsi
Lats (back)
To draw the arms back toward the dorsal region.

Abdominals
Abs
To bend the body at the waist and stabilize it when walking or standing.

Pectorals
Pecs
To draw the arms forward toward the center of the body.

Quadriceps
Quads (front thigh)
To extend the lower leg at the knee joint.

Photo of Mark Dugdale by Robert Reiff

biceps. Muscles are the symbol of strength, even though strength relies on tendon power and leverage as much as muscle power. The associated ligaments and tendons are forgotten in the excitement – until you pull one.

There are three types of muscle tissue: cardiac, smooth and skeletal. From a bodybuilding standpoint we are concerned with the third type, so we will be brief when describing the first two.

Cardiac muscle is found only in the heart. Its main function is to force blood through the body's arteries, veins and capillaries. Smooth muscle makes up the walls of such internal hollow organs as the small and large intestines, the respiratory tract, and most of the reproductive system.

Skeletal muscle acquired its name because, for the most part, it is attached to the body's skeleton. This type of muscle is often said to be striated because of the alternating dark and light areas. (Smooth muscle is nonstriated, while cardiac muscle is finely striated.) Unlike smooth and cardiac muscle, which contracts involuntarily (i.e. you have no direct control over it), skeletal muscle contracts voluntarily in most cases. This means you can contract skeletal muscle whenever you want.

Skeletal muscles are covered and held together by fibrous connective tissue called fascia. Fascia can be divided into two types – superficial and deep. Deep fascia is composed of layers of dense connective tissue and is found between individual muscles and groups of muscles. As does superficial fascia, deep fascia contains an assortment of nerves, blood vessels and lymph vessels.

FUNCTION

Skeletal muscle has three main functions – movement, heat production and posture. In normal day-to-day activities (standing, walking, sitting, etc.) the contracting and relaxing of muscles produces much of the heat responsible for maintaining the body's internal temperature (average of 98.6 degrees Fahrenheit, 37 degrees Celsius). Even holding normal posture is a function of skeletal muscle. This is most obvious in people with lower-back injuries. The muscles of the lower back, called the spinal erectors,

help keep the body in an upright position. If they become injured or even just tired, the person will start to slouch, having great difficulty sitting or standing upright.

STRUCTURE

Skeletal muscle is composed of long muscle cells called muscle fibers. These fibers give skeletal muscle its striated look. Muscle fibers are composed of smaller fibers called myofibrils, which in turn can be broken down into myofilaments. The muscle fibers are supplied with blood by a network of capillaries, small blood vessels that branch off from larger arteries. Capillaries serve two main functions: They bring oxygen and nutrient-rich blood to the muscles, and at the same time they remove the waste products of metabolism.

Muscle contraction is under the control of the central nervous system and follows an all-or-none principle. As this book is not a biophysiology text, I will not go into great detail here. Suffice it to say that for a given muscle fiber to contract, it needs a certain amount of stimulus. When this stimulus is received, the muscle fiber in question fires (neurophysiological jargon for contracts) to its full extent. A smaller stimulus does not produce a smaller contraction of the muscle fiber. Once the minimum stimulus needed is received, the particular muscle fiber contracts fully. Keep in mind, however, that one muscle is made up of perhaps half a million individual muscle fibers.

If the stimulus is spread over a large area (i.e. the whole muscle), all the necessary muscle fibers will fully contract. The strength of the muscle contraction is based on the number of fibers contracting, not the intensity of each fiber. Lifting a 20-pound dumbell will cause more fibers to contract than lifting a 10-pound dumbell. The individual muscle fibers, however, are contracting with the same intensity.

MUSCLE CONTRACTION

Muscles become shorter when contracted and lengthen when relaxed. This action enables us to lift and hold objects, walk, breathe and perform many other activi-

Triceps
Tris
To extend the forearms at the elbow joint.

Trapezius
Traps
To elevate, rotate and retract the scapulae (shoulder blades).

Erector Spinae
Lower Back
To hold the body erect, and flex the spine.

Gastrocnemius
Calves
To flex the foot at the ankle joint (primarily when the knee is straight).

Deltoids
Delts (shoulders)
To elevate and rotate the arms.

Gluteals
Glutes
To extend the leg at the hip joint.

Biceps Femoris
Hamstrings (rear thigh)
To flex the lower leg at the knee joint.

Soleus
Lower Calves
To flex the foot at the ankle joint (primarily when the knee is bent).

Photo of Mark Dugdale by Robert Reiff

ties that involve movement. While you are likely aware of this concept, you may not understand the actual mechanisms involved.

Scientists explain the shortening of muscles with the "sliding-filament" theory. Basically the theory states that muscle fibers contain two major proteins called actin and myosin, which are arranged in cylindrical bundles. When a muscle contracts, the ends of the myosin attach to the actin molecules of adjacent fibers. The myosin then undergoes a conformational change, resulting in the end of the fiber bending. This pulls on the actin fiber. Once the myosin filament completes this change, it detaches itself from the actin fiber and straightens out. The whole process then repeats in a kind of "leap frog" manner, with adjacent fibers sliding past one another. In order for this process to work most effectively, sufficient quantities of calcium, sodium and tropomyosin must be present. Most of these are supplied in the diet, so it's obvious why nutrition plays such an integral part of muscle contraction and growth.

ISOTONIC VERSUS ISOMETRIC

Muscle contraction falls into two broad categories. The first, isotonic, is what comes to mind when we think of muscle contraction. It involves a shortening and thickening of the muscle. Just about all bodybuilding exercises involve isotonic contractions.

The second type of contraction is called isometric. Earlier in the book I talked about Charles Atlas' training courses from the 1940s and 1950s. These exercises were based heavily on isometric contraction. Unlike isotonic contractions, isometric contractions don't involve a shortening of the muscle. To get an idea of an isometric contraction, forcefully push the heels of your hands together. While the muscles are tight and tense, they are not changing in size. You can get the same effect holding a barbell. Grab a bar and prepare to do a standing barbell curl. Before the bar moves up, the muscles are in use but are not changing in length. This is an isometric contraction. As soon as you start moving the bar, the biceps muscles short-

en and bunch up (get thicker), and when you move the bar they lengthen again. This is an isotonic contraction. Both types of contractions require energy and produce heat. Most body movements are a combination of the two, although some are predominantly one or the other. Walking is mainly isotonic, whereas standing is primarily isometric.

For bodybuilding purposes isotonic movements are, by far, the most effective. There is a limit to what isometrics can accomplish. They are probably useful only when access to weights is impossible, such as when you're on the road. Some bodybuilders find that isometric (often called isotension) exercises add that extra bit of hardness when they're preparing for a contest, but from a mass-gaining point of view, sticking with basic isotonic exercises is your best bet.

FIBER TYPES

Muscle fibers can be divided into two broad categories – fast-twitch and slow-twitch. The ratio of slow- to fast-twitch muscle fibers is determined by genetics, and doesn't change much over a lifetime. (Recent research suggests that it might be possible to transform one into the other.)

FAST-TWITCH MUSCLE FIBER

Fast-twitch muscle fibers are adapted for rapid short-duration contraction. For example, the small muscles controlling the eyes and fingers are adapted for very quick movements, but they have a very short duration. Try blinking your eyes very fast for a sustained period of time. You'll find that after a short time they tire to the point that you can hardly move them. The reason? These muscles have a reduced amount of myoglobin, an oxygen-binding protein that speeds up the rate of oxygen movement into a muscle fiber. Fast-twitch muscle also has fewer capillaries than slow-twitch muscle. This means a slower rate of nutrient replenishment. The shortage of capillaries and myoglobin means a reduced number of red blood cells, giving the muscle a pale color. Such muscles are called white muscle.

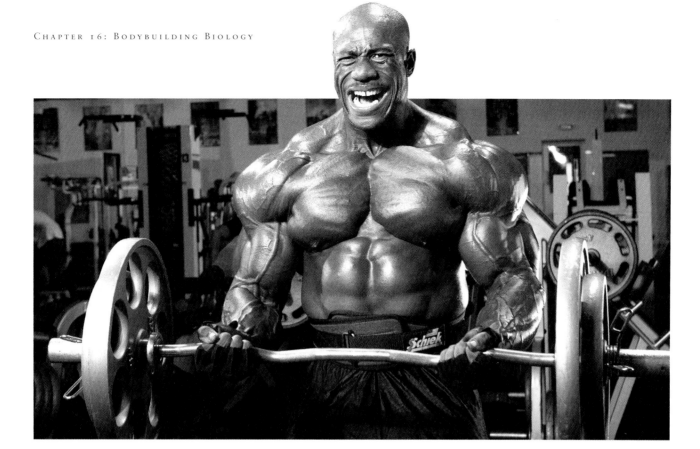

Photo of Joel Stubbs by Robert Reiff

SLOW-TWITCH MUSCLE FIBER

Areas of the body that need prolonged, steady contractions are controlled by slow-twitch muscle fibers. Slow-twitch muscle fibers don't tire as easily as fast-twitch. For example, the spinal erectors of the back, which keep us upright all day, are primarily composed of slow-twitch muscle fibers. Unlike fast-twitch, slow-twitch muscle fibers have a large capillary network and increased amounts of myoglobin. The increased myoglobin gives the muscle a reddish color. The most easily visible examples of red and white muscle tissue are in poultry (chicken, turkey, duck, etc.). What we refer to as white meat and dark meat are in reality fast-twitch and slow-twitch muscle fibers.

So what does this distinction mean for bodybuilding? For starters, most of the body's main muscle groups are predominantly fast- or slow-twitch. This means that each muscle group will respond differently to varied rep ranges. In general, bodybuilders find that calves and forearms respond best to high reps (20 plus), whereas other muscles such as those of the chest and back seem to require lower reps (8 to 10). Of course, some bodybuilders find heavy weight and low reps (6 to 8) to be the most effective combination for the calves, and others find high reps optimal for chest.

An individual with a predominance of slow-twitch muscle fibers would need to include a high number of sets and reps to adequately stimulate his or her muscles. Conversely, someone with a proportionately high number of fast-twitch muscle fibers would probably respond better to heavier weights and lower reps.

The latest research suggests that fast-twitch muscle fibers contract twice as quickly (it takes about one millisecond for a muscle fiber to contract) and are 10 times stronger than slow-twitch muscle fibers. They respond best to workouts involving 2 to 6 sets of 4 to 6 reps. The sets should be performed with the maximum amount of weight that can be handled for the given number of reps, the sixth rep being the last that could be completed. Slow-twitch muscle fibers were found to respond most effectively to a high-set (8 to 10), high-rep (12 to 20) routine.

The average untrained person has muscles with a 50:50 fast-twitch to slow-twitch ratio. In top athletes, however, we find a different ratio. This is partly because athletes excel at sports their bodies have an aptitude for, and partly because their muscles respond to the specialized demands placed on them. In simple terms, the body adapts to the type of stress endured (e.g. long-distance running versus weight training). The ratio of the two contributes to success in the athlete's chosen sport. Muscle biopsies on marathon runners reveal muscles with as high as 90-percent slow-twitch muscle fiber. For bodybuilders the ratio is reversed – red muscle fibers account for 80 percent of the muscle. The high percentage of red fibers can be explained by the type of workouts performed. Slow and continuous exercises with moderate to heavy weights (average rep range of 8 to 12) stimulate the production of red muscle fibers.

As for the white muscle fiber, recent studies suggest that it can be converted into red muscle fiber. This change results from slow and steady contractions over time. It's believed that the type of nerve impulse determines the ratio of fast-twitch to slow-twitch (white to red) muscle fibers. However, even top bodybuilders display much variation in their muscle composition. Some have ratios in favor of fast-twitch, others in favor of slow-twitch. Through trial and error each individual has determined which type of training works best for him. Unless your ratio is extreme – a rare phenomenon for the average person – you can make great progress no matter which type of muscle fiber predominates. To take full advantage of both slow- and fast-twitch muscle fibers, bodybuilders generally alternate rep ranges (6 to 8 versus 12 to 15). This way, no matter what the individual fiber ratio, you can be sure your muscles are being fully stimulated.

MUSCLES – HOW THEY WORK

Skeletal muscles produce movement by pulling on tendons, which in turn pull on the connecting bone. Most muscles pass across a joint and are attached to both bones that form the joint. When a muscle contracts, one of the attached bones remains stationary while the other moves along with the contraction. For convenience we say that the muscle section attached to the stationary bone is called the origin, and the point of muscle attachment on the moving bone is called the insertion. Keep in mind that origin and insertion are relative terms, and can be reversed depending on the action involved. Contrary to popular

belief, muscles can only pull, not push. Even though many exercises are considered "pushing" movements, the muscle being worked is actually pulling the associated bone. When you're performing triceps extensions, the triceps muscle is contracting and pulling the forearm to an extended position, yet most bodybuilders refer to triceps extensions (as well as any other triceps exercise for that matter) as a pushing movement. Similarly the bench press, while commonly called a pushing exercise, causes the chest muscles to contract, pulling the arms toward the center of the body.

The human body evolved such that many of the major muscle groups work in opposing pairs. Triceps and biceps provide a classic example. Contracting the biceps draws the forearm toward the upper arm, whereas contracting the triceps extends the forearm away from the upper arm and back to its original extended position.

To further enhance your bodybuilding biology vocabulary, the muscle that contracts to produce a desired movement is called the agonist. The muscle that produces the opposite movement is called the antagonist. English majors will recognize the terms from studying novels, the protagonist being the central character, while his or her opponent is the antagonist. When the agonist (e.g. biceps) is contracting, the antagonist (triceps) is relaxed. As with insertions and origins, an agonist in one movement may be an antagonist in another.

Bodybuilders often replace the words agonist and antagonist with flexor and extensor. Contraction of the biceps bends, or flexes, the elbow bringing the lower and upper arm bones closer together. Conversely, contracting the triceps extends the elbow joint, drawing the bones away from one another, increasing the angle. Bodybuilders use the terms "flexing" and "extending" to describe the function of the muscle rather than the joint, so therefore you "flex" the biceps and "extend" the triceps.

Most complex exercise movements are the result of many muscles working together. For example, the bench press is considered a chest exercise, but the shoulders and triceps also receive a great deal of stimulation. In fact, some trainers find the bench press a poor exercise for the

BICEPS

TRICEPS

QUADRICEPS

Photos of Troy Alves, Desmond Miller and Peter Putnam by Jason Mathas, Ralph DeHaan and Irvin Gelb

chest. Instead of great pecs, they end up with well-developed front deltoids or triceps. There is nothing wrong with this. It just means you have to start doing other exercises to work your chest, and make sure to work your rear delts to keep up with the front.

In the bench press the chest muscles (pectorals) are called the primary movers, and the deltoids and triceps are referred to as secondary movers. Aside from secondary movers, other muscles also assist the primary movers. The back muscles (latissimus dorsi) help stabilize the body. Though they are not directly involved in moving the weight, they nevertheless assist the primary movers.

NAMING

The name of a muscle typically tells us something about its structure, location, size or function. Shape is described in such muscles as the trapezius, deltoid or gracilis. The corresponding shapes are trapezoidal, triangular and slender, respectively. Gluteus maximus and gluteus minimus, the muscles that make up the buttocks region, are two names that indicate relative sizes.

Such terms as supraspinatus and infraspinatus indicate relative position – supra indicating above the spine of the scapula, and infra below the spine of the scapula. Familiar to most bodybuilders are the latissimus dorsi. They are named as such to indicate that they are found laterally on the body toward the dorsal, or back region. (Just remember where a shark's dorsal fin is located.) Likewise the rectus abdominis is a straight muscle located in the abdominal region.

Some muscles are named according to their number of "heads." The head is defined as the expanded, rounded surface, or belly, of a muscle. The biceps muscle has two heads, hence the prefix bi. The triceps has three heads, and the front thigh muscle, called the quadriceps, has four heads.

Muscles can also be named according to the direction of their fibers – transverse (across) and obliques (slanted). They indicate the direction of the muscle fibers with respect to the structures to which they are attached.

CHAPTER 17

The Pump

"Ve vant to pump you up!"

– Hans and Franz, those endearing characters with that familiar Austrian accent, from *SNL*.

ince I just discussed muscle anatomy and physiology, it only makes sense to take a look at a unique bodybuilding term – the pump. Considered by some athletes to be almost sexual in nature, the pump is conceivably the most desired sensation of hard-training bodybuilders. After a couple of sets of an exercise the muscle becomes engorged with blood. It swells, the veins stand out and the owner begins to feel that on any day of the week he could match physiques with Arnold Schwarzenegger!

The pump is caused by blood rushing into the muscle faster than the circulatory system can remove it. Many bodybuilders assess the quality of their workout by the level of pump. If the worked muscle does not pump to any degree, the individual often feels the workout was wasted.

The level of pump varies among individuals and also within one individual. You may get an incredible pump from one set on one day, while on another day no amount of exercise will bring on the desired feeling. In addition, it's possible to fully pump the muscle only to lose the pump with continued exercise. When you begin to lose the pump, stop exercising that particular muscle. The idea is to become so in tune with your body that you know exactly the maximum number of sets to perform without losing the pump.

Is a good pump necessary? Although it's not a prerequisite for growth, the general consensus is that the better the pump, the greater the development. A good pump signifies that the muscle in question is receiving a good blood supply. Also, the speed at which a muscle pumps up is indicative of its neuromus-

Photo of Arnold Schwarzenegger

cular pathway. There is a definite relationship among supply, nerve transmission and muscle growth. In short, the better the blood, supply to a muscle, the better it pumps, and the faster it grows. The important aspect is not so much the blood but rather what it carries. As the body's chief transport medium, blood brings to the muscles all the nutrients and oxygen needed for growth and repair. At the same time blood removes such metabolic wastes as carbon dioxide and lactic acid. An increased blood supply also means the establishment of more blood vessels.

If you need more convincing, ask yourself this question: "What are my best bodyparts?" Chances are your best muscle groups are those that pump up the fastest and to the greatest extent. On the flipside of the coin, those muscles that lag behind probably pump up little or not at all.

Achieving a proper pump requires intense, heavy training, not endless sets of reps using light weight. Such training strategies as Vince Gironda's 6 sets of 6 reps with 30 seconds rest between sets, and Dorian Yates' high-intensity training (a modification of Mike Mentzer's heavy-duty system) are great ways to achieve the maximum pump in the shortest time.

What happens if you fail to achieve a pump or it's much smaller than usual? Such a failure is caused by one of several factors. All the training in the world will not produce a pump if there is no glycogen in your muscles. A flat look to the muscles and a failure to achieve a pump are caused by insufficient glycogen storage. You need more carbs such as sweet potatoes and oatmeal.

Another reason for a less-than-adequate pump is overtraining. Doing 20 or 30 sets per bodypart is the surest way to hold yourself back and in many cases reverse your progress. There is no way your recovery system can restock the body's muscles with glycogen if you follow such a routine. Why do sprinters have huge muscular thighs while marathon runners have long slender thighs? Sprinters concentrate on doing the maximum amount of work in the shortest time. Marathon runners, on the other hand, expend so much energy over such a long time that their systems (particularly their muscles) never get a chance to totally recover. The same principle holds true for bodybuilders. Spend hours on the stationary bike or performing endless high-rep sets, and the muscles cannot help but take on a stringy appearance. There is a fine line between not enough and too much.

If you're eating properly and not overtraining, the lack of a pump is due to some other cause. How long do you rest between sets? Anything over two minutes is way too much. Most bodybuilders find 45 seconds to a minute to be the best rest interval. If you can operate on less rest – say, 30 seconds or so – you most certainly will achieve a pump, as long as you're getting 6 reps per set.

Other training techniques that almost guarantee a pump are supersets, trisets and giant sets. All of these training practices ensure much work being done in a short time – the perfect conditions for a great pump.

While achieving a pump is not an absolute necessity, it is one of the most frequently used benchmarks for measuring the adequacy of a workout. Make a habit of leaving the gym with a muscle-busting pump, and there can be but one outcome – growth.

CHAPTER 18

Exercise and Adaptation

"Thirty years ago Arthur Jones, the near-eccentric all-around entrepreneurial wizard and inventor of the Nautilus machine wrote: 'Make an exercise harder and you make it better.' He was right. As long as you avoid injury, eat correctly and rest appropriately, anything that makes an exercise more difficult causes the muscles to undergo more stress, creating the potential for more growth."

– Editors of *MuscleMag International*, reiterating advice that Dr. Arthur Jones was preaching nearly 40 years ago.

Unlike a machine, which cannot repair itself, the human body is continuously modifying its physiology. If a harmful organism invades, antibodies and white blood cells rush to the body's defense. A small skin abrasion is repaired in a few days, and muscle growth follows a similar pattern.

Many people refer to bodybuilding as progressive resistance training. This is an apt description, as your goal is to gradually increase the amount of weight lifted in each exercise. Contrary to what many believe, muscles do not grow during training. Think of exercise as a type of message. By working out you are ordering your muscles to get bigger and stronger. With time you have to send stronger messages (heavier weight) to get the same effect.

Adaptation is defined as a change in response to a stimulus. Let's see how this definition applies to bodybuilding. When you perform an intense set of curls, after a given number of reps the biceps become fatigued. Over the next couple of days the body repairs the damage. (This term does not imply that the

Photo of David Hughes by Robert Reiff

muscle itself has been injured, only that some muscle tissue has been broken down.) Repair involves the use of building blocks called amino acids (more on these in the nutrition chapter). The body combines the amino acids into protein which is then integrated into muscle tissue.

An interesting fact about the recuperation process is that the body doesn't repair the muscle as it was. Instead it goes a step further, making the muscle slightly larger and stronger. In effect, your body is saying: "Whoa, that was a great deal of stress. I need to make that muscle stronger so next time it can handle that stress better." Once the extra muscle tissue has been built, you can see that your body will handle that weight quite well. To keep the muscle growing, the amount of weight lifted must be gradually (gradually!) increased. That way, your body is always trying to deal with increased loads by adding a little more muscle tissue.

Most muscle growth is the result of what's called hypertrophy – the increase in diameter of existing muscle

cells. In addition, the muscles' blood supply and number of mitochondria (energy-producing organelles) is increased. Of course the opposite can also occur. If a muscle is not regularly exercised, or if there has been some sort of nerve damage, it begins to shrink. This process is called muscular atrophy. A good example of atrophy can be seen in astronauts who spend long periods of time in orbit. The reduced gravity means their muscles don't have to work as hard and they lose muscle mass.

At one time it was believed that hypertrophy was the only mechanism by which muscles grew, but the evidence is mounting that intense forms of exercise – particularly weight training – can cause individual muscle fibers to split. Each part of a split cell will become a cell on its own, and increase to normal cellular size. This is welcome news for those who weren't blessed genetically with a larger number of muscle fibers to begin with. As Jeff Goldblum said in the movie *Jurassic Park*, "Nature always finds a way."

ASSOCIATED STRUCTURES

Tendons

Muscles are not attached directly to bones or other muscles. They are connected by a tough cord of connective tissue called a tendon. A tendon may connect a muscle to another muscle, or a muscle to a bone. The thickest tendon in the human body is the Achilles' tendon. It attaches the calf muscle to the heel bone. From a bodybuilding perspective, the biceps tendon, which connects the biceps to the radius bone of the forearm, is probably the most familiar. Tendons add length and thickness to muscles and are especially important in reducing muscle strain.

Ligaments

Bones are held together by fibrous connective tissue called ligaments. Varying in shape and even strength, depending on their location and function, most ligaments are considered inelastic, yet they are pliable enough to permit movement. Ligaments tend to tear rather than stretch, but because of their strength they can withstand a great amount of stress. When they do tear, the condition is marked by intense pain and swelling. Surgery is often needed to correct the problem.

Cartilage

Cartilage is a specialized type of connective tissue and can be called the shock absorbers of the body. Its main function is to prevent bones from rubbing against one another within a joint. With time, disease or injury, cartilage tissue may become damaged, resulting in reduced movement and pain.

One of the most frequent sports injuries is torn knee cartilage. When this happens the cartilage may become lodged between the upper (femur) and lower (tibia) leg bones, causing the joint to lock. The patient of 20 years ago could look forward to many months of therapy and pain after surgery. Recent advances in arthroscopic surgery have cut the recovery time in half. Using microscopic tools, surgeons can repair the damaged cartilage and allow movement much sooner, preventing the surrounding muscles from atrophying.

As with other sports, the most common bodybuilding injuries concern the knee region. Bouncing at the bottom of the squat does not make for a great set of thighs. Neither does forcefully locking out in the leg extension. These motions both lead to damaged knees. Remember to always perform the movements in a nice, slow and controlled manner.

Bursae and Tendon Sheaths

Two other structures associated with muscles and joints are bursae and tendon sheaths. Bursae are flattened sacs filled with synovial fluid. They are found wherever it is necessary to eliminate the friction that occurs when a muscle or tendon rubs against another muscle, tendon or bone. Bursae also cushion certain muscles and facilitate the movement of muscles over bony surfaces. A modification of bursae is tendon sheaths – long cylindrical sacs filled with synovial fluid that surround long tendons. Tendon sheaths allow tendons to slide easily. They are found in areas where the tendons are under constant movement and friction such as your wrists, fingers and palms.

Weight training and other intense forms of exercise can cause muscle fibers to split. As the cell numbers grow, so do your muscles.

CHAPTER 19

The Cardiovascular System

"If you want to become a great bodybuilder, then cardiovascular exercise must be a part of your off-season and precontest training regimen."

– Frank Sepe, popular model and longtime *MuscleMag International* columnist.

The cardiovascular system is composed of the heart, blood vessels and blood. The heart is shaped like a blunt cone and is about the size of a clenched fist. In males it weighs about 300 grams, in females about 250 grams. Because of its importance, the heart is one of the first organs to begin functioning in a developing embryo, about four weeks after conception.

The heart is divided into four chambers – two entering chambers called the atria and two pumping chambers called the ventricles. Because of this unique arrangement, the heart can be considered a double pump. The oxygen-depleted blood from the body's tissues returns to the right atrium and is then pumped by the right ventricle into the lungs where oxygen and carbon dioxide are exchanged. The newly oxygenated blood returns to the heart at the left atrium. From there it is pumped by the powerful left ventricle to the rest of the body.

BLOOD VESSELS

Although the heart is the center of the cardiovascular system, it's the affiliated blood vessels that carry the blood throughout the body. There are three types of blood vessels – arteries, veins and capillaries. While all three carry blood, each has a different task.

Arteries carry blood away from the heart. Because of this function, arterial walls are very elastic and can expand in relation to the blood being pushed by the contracting ventricles. You can feel this sensation the next time you perform a heavy set of squats. Place your fingers on your wrist and notice the pulsations just below the skin surface. Each pulse corresponds to one beat of the heart. We commonly refer to this rate as the pulse, though in fact we are measuring heart rate.

Veins return blood to the heart. They are more flexible than arteries because they have thinner walls, and will collapse if blood pressure is not maintained. The speed of blood traveling through veins is much slower than through arteries.

Capillaries are microscopic blood vessels which serve as exchange points among arteries, veins, and the body's tissues. Their small size and large numbers mean an enormous amount of surface area for the exchange of gases, nutrients and waste products. To give an idea of the amount of surface area involved, if the capillaries of the body were connected end to end, the resulting chain would stretch 100,000 kilometers. Perhaps more revealing is the fact that for every pound of fat lost, the heart has 1700 fewer kilometers to pump blood through.

BLOOD

The main purpose of all this plumbing is to provide a highway for the body's blood supply. Blood makes up about 8 percent of the bodyweight of an average male, translating into a volume of about five to six liters. It consists of a liquid part, called plasma, and a solid part, called formed elements. The formed elements include red blood cells, white blood cells and platelets.

As blood circulates throughout the body, tissues are continuously adding their waste products, secretions and metabolites. Simultaneously, the body's tissues remove vital nutrients, oxygen, hormones and other important substances from the blood.

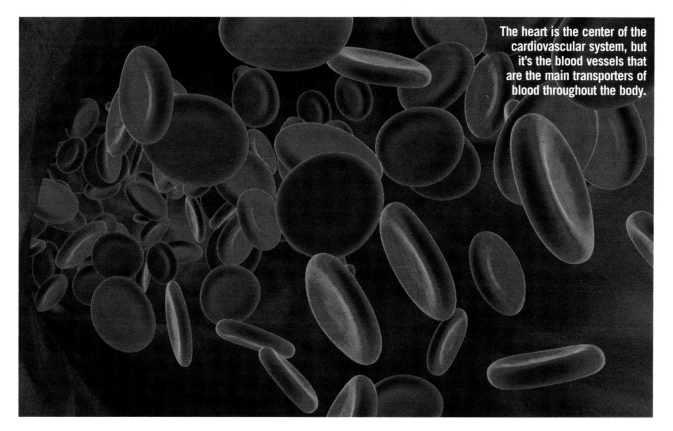

The heart is the center of the cardiovascular system, but it's the blood vessels that are the main transporters of blood throughout the body.

In summary, blood serves the following functions: It transports oxygen from the lungs to the body tissues, and transports the resulting waste products of cellular metabolism from the body's tissues to the various filtration organs. These include the liver, kidneys and sweat glands.

BLOOD REGULATES THE FOLLOWING:

- Blood-clotting to stop bleeding.
- Body temperature, by increasing or decreasing blood flow to the skin.
- Acid-base balance (pH) through the distribution of buffers.
- The amount of water and electrolytes in body fluids.

Blood protects against harmful microorganisms and other dangerous substances by transporting white blood cells, proteins and antibodies to the site or sites of infection.

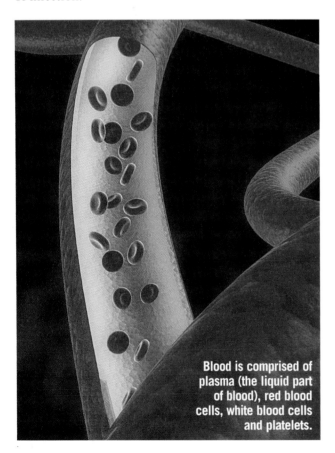

Blood is comprised of plasma (the liquid part of blood), red blood cells, white blood cells and platelets.

THE COMPONENTS OF BLOOD

Plasma — This is the liquid part of blood, which is comprised of 90 percent water, 7 percent proteins, and 3 percent dissolved substances such as amino acids, glucose, enzymes, hormones, electrolytes, wastes and nutrients.

Red blood cells (RBCs) — These make up half the volume of the blood. They are shaped like a flat donut with an indentation rather than a hole in the middle. There are about 25 trillion RBCs in the human body at a density of six million for every cubic millimeter of blood. Virtually the entire weight of the RBC is composed of an oxygen-attracting globular protein called haemoglobin. Since part of the haemoglobin molecule contains iron, the RBC has a reddish color – hence the name red blood cell. The main function of RBCs is to transport oxygen from the lungs to the body's tissues. At the same time waste gases such as carbon dioxide are transported to the lungs where they are exhaled.

White blood cells (WBCs) — These serve as scavengers. They destroy microorganisms at infection sites, help remove foreign molecules, and remove debris that results from dead or injured tissue cells. In adults there are between 4,000 and 11,000 WBCs per cubic millimeter of blood. This number may increase to 25,000 or more in times of infection.

Platelets — These are dynamically shaped blood cells whose main function is to start the intricate process of blood-clotting. Roughly 200 billion platelets are produced by the body every day, each with a life span of only seven to eight days. When a blood vessel is injured, platelets immediately move to the injured area and begin to clump together. They release a chemical called serotonin, a blood-vessel constrictor. If the cut is small, the platelet plug will prevent blood loss. If the cut is considerable, platelets begin the process of blood-clotting. We will not look at this mechanism here. Suffice it to say there are numerous steps, resulting in a fibrous net which entangles escaping blood cells, forming a clot. After a few hours the clot begins to dry out, and a solid barrier is left. After a few days the dried-out clot (a scab) falls off, exposing the repaired underlying tissue.

LYMPHATIC SYSTEM

In addition to the blood circulatory system, we have a subsystem called the lymphatic system. Its three main functions are:

- Collection and return of interstitial fluid to the blood.
- Contribution to the immune system's fight against invading organisms.
- Absorption of lipids from the digestive tract.

The lymphatic system is similar to the cardiovascular system in that it has a network of transport vessels and associated fluid. The fluid, called lymph, is a clear liquid that serves as the system's transport medium. At regular intervals lymph vessels are organized into small masses of tissue called lymph nodules (nodes). The tonsils and adenoids are two such examples. The thymus gland and spleen are also part of the lymph system. You're probably aware that it's possible to survive without parts of the lymph system (spleen and tonsils). If these become infected and have to be removed, other parts of the body take over and perform the same functions.

HOW IT WORKS

As with the cardiovascular system, the lymph vessels terminate at the body's tissues with a network of capillaries. Interstitial fluid enters the capillaries and is passed on to larger vessels called lymphatics. This fluid is then carried by way of the lymphatics to the various lymph nodes. Here it is filtered to remove bacteria and other harmful matter. Afterward the fluid re-enters the circulatory system by way of the subclavian veins found in the shoulder region.

Unlike the cardiovascular system, the lymph system does not have a pumping muscle like the heart. Instead, the walls of the lymph vessels pulsate, pushing the fluid along. Valves within the vessels prevent the lymph from flowing backward. The rate of flow is increased when anything compresses body tissue. When muscles contract or arteries pulsate, the increased pressure on the lymph vessels enhances the flow of lymph fluid.

Bodybuilders and other hard-training athletes may periodically notice a swelling of the lymph nodes, particularly in the neck, groin and armpit regions. This can be a sign of overtraining. The increased stress placed on the body taxes the lymph system to the limit. The swelling is the result of a buildup of fluid containing the byproducts of exercise. The lymph system will cleanse itself of such metabolic debris after a few days, and the swelling will go down. Of course, if you keep overstressing the body with a twice-a-day, six-day-a-week program, this process will be impeded. We'll take a more detailed look at overtraining later in the book.

Overtraining can lead to swollen lymph nodes. Swelling in the neck, groin and armpits are an indication that the body is under increased stress.

Photo of Phil Heath by Ralph DeHaan

CHAPTER 20

Skin — The First Line Of Defense

"He made an amateur's mistake of coming in too light."

– Garry Bartlett, *MuscleMag International* correspondent, discussing why one favored bodybuilder did not place well in a contest.

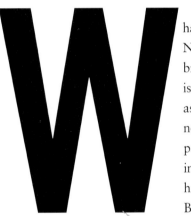

What's the largest organ in the human body? No, it's not the liver. Nor is it the heart or brain. Give up? The body's largest organ is the skin. Most people don't think of it as an organ because it's neither internal nor fixed in its shape. It's not a neat little package like a kidney. It measures approximately 20 square feet in surface area and has an average thickness of 2 millimeters. Because of its importance to the body, the skin receives roughly one-third of all circulated blood.

The skin is the body's first line of defense against invading organisms. Long before the immune system comes into play, harmful pathogens have to contend with this protective outer covering. Germs make their way into the body at breaks or tears in this layer. Take a look the next time you receive a small cut. First the area takes on a reddish color. Soon white blood cells rush to the area and attack the invaders. (This mass of white blood cells creates what is commonly called pus). In all but the most extreme cases the condition clears up within a few days.

Besides protecting, the skin helps regulate body temperature. On hot summer days millions of sweat glands release water, the evaporation of which cools the body. Make sure you consume sufficient water during long, hot training sessions. Failure to do so could lead to heat exhaustion or heat stroke.

Two characteristics of the skin are important to body-builders: color and thickness. The darker-tanned competitor will have an advantage over his lighter opponent. For this reason bodybuilders will spend many hours working on their tans prior to a contest. Tanning also tightens the skin, making it hug the body's contours. (For the full discussion of this topic, see the section on competition.)

Skin thickness also plays an important role in the success of a bodybuilder. Thick skin obscures muscle separation and striations. Rapid weight fluctuations (bulking up) can lead to baggy skin or stretch marks, both of which detract from the final product – a contest-winning physique. Perhaps a book shouldn't be judged by its cover, but a great physique will be. Proper skin care is an integral part of modern bodybuilding. Don't make the mistake of neglecting your cover!

Many bodybuilders spend hours trying to achieve the darkest tan possible to get a competitive edge over their opponents.

Photo (Top) of JC Ballivian by Ralph DeHaan
Photo (Bottom) of Branch Warren by Irvin Gelb

CHAPTER 21

The Nervous System

"A warmup set not only helps you to literally warm up your muscle, it also helps open the neuropathways – very important for optimizing muscle performance."

– Editorial in *MuscleMag International*

n order to maintain homeostasis (a fancy term that means internal balance with respect to outside factors), the body is constantly reacting and adjusting to the external environment. Such changes are detected and conveyed via nerves to the spinal cord and brain. Here the messages are analyzed, combined, compared and coordinated by a process called integration. After being sorted out, messages are conveyed by nerves to the body's various target organs, of which glands and muscles are two of the most prominent. Once stimulated, muscles contract or relax, and glands release their products (called hormones).

Your nervous system can be called the "first and last" system of the body. It is the first system to develop in an embryo, and in general the last system to shut down when you die.

The nervous system can be subdivided into the central, autonomic and the peripheral nervous systems. The central nervous system (CNS) consists of the brain and spinal cord, which are protected by the skull and vertebral column. The CNS may be thought of as the body's principal control center. Here messages are received, sorted, interpreted and relayed to and from all parts of the body.

The peripheral nervous system (PNS) consists of nerve cells and their associated fibers, emerging from and going to the CNS. The PNS serves as an intermediary between the body's muscles and organs and the CNS.

The autonomic nervous system controls the body's smooth muscles, glands and organs. As the name implies, the autonomic system controls the involuntary target organs – organs you have no direct control over. You have no authority over your digestion rate – except through drug use – and although you can change your heart rate, this is an indirect action.

The nervous system conducts messages with nerve impulses. These are electro-chemical changes set up between adjacent nerve cells. These chemical changes are under the control of specific ions (charged atoms), the most common being sodium, potassium and calcium. The presence or absence of one or more of these ions sets up different electrical charges between adjacent nerve cells. These electrical differences (called potential gradients) cause the nerve cell to "fire," the result being a nerve impulse.

Another name for these ions is electrolytes. Many bodybuilders consume electrolyte drinks to replenish their supply of these important substances, which are lost in sweat during an intense workout. For proper biochemical functioning, electrolyte levels must be in balance. Too much sodium, for example, causes the body to dehydrate. Too little interferes with the nervous and muscular systems. During a contest bodybuilders often have troubles with muscles cramping. These cramps are caused by an improper electrolytic balance, frequently brought on by diuretics (more on this in the competition and nutrition sections).

From a bodybuilding perspective, it's probably the spinal cord that causes the most problems. Even with good form and proper warmups, sooner or later many bodybuilders develop a bad back. Most injuries are minor and consist of slight muscle strains to the spinal erectors. Reducing the weight or changing exercises should address the problem. In a few cases, however, the underlying problem is within the spinal column itself. This is a much more serious situation, so at the slightest hint of such an injury, stop your training and see your physician. To give some idea of why back injuries are so common, let's take a closer look at the back's structure.

THE VERTEBRAL COLUMN

Thirty-one pairs of spinal nerves exit the spinal cord through the associated spinal bones called vertebrae. The great number of articulating vertebrae gives the spine tremendous flexibility. If the spine consisted of only one or two bones, such simple movements as bending over or sitting down would be almost impossible.

Each vertebra has a pencil-sized hole in the middle which houses and protects the spinal cord. Unfortunately, with improper exercise technique or too much weight, damage is often done to the spinal area, particularly the lower spinal region.

Of all the exercises that may injure the lower back, perhaps none does so more frequently than the squat. The human spine was not designed to support hundreds of pounds of weight. Some medical experts argue that it does a poor job of supporting even bodyweight, given the number of bad backs diagnosed each year. One theory for this is that human brains outstripped human physiology. In short, humans stood up too quickly. We are walking around with a spinal design that would probably be more suited to walking on all fours. Whether or not you agree with this theory, few would argue that spinal injuries are to be avoided at all costs. Later in the text I'll look at injuries in more detail, and offer ways to avoid or treat them.

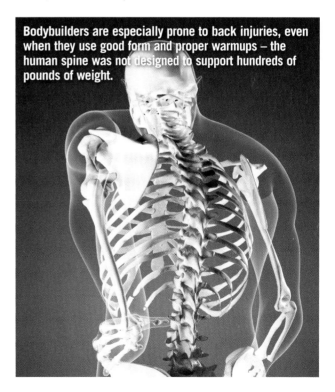

Bodybuilders are especially prone to back injuries, even when they use good form and proper warmups – the human spine was not designed to support hundreds of pounds of weight.

CHAPTER 22

The Endocrine System

"The main effects of growth hormone are stimulation of bone growth, anabolic effect in the muscles, conservation of protein and carbohydrates, and lipolysis, i.e. mobilization of fat for energy."

– Ori Hofmekler, *MuscleMag International* contributor

The endocrine system works with the nervous system to maintain the body's internal balance. It is, in other words, a regulatory system. Regulation can take two forms: monitoring and adjusting internal physiological mechanisms, and adapting the body to external stimuli. The endocrine system carries out these important functions by use of chemical messengers called hormones. By definition a hormone is a chemical substance that is produced in one part of the body and travels by way of the bloodstream to another area where it carries out its action. Bodybuilders will be interested to know that hormones are either protein or steroid in nature.

Hormone production and release are controlled by various parts of the brain. Among these areas are the hypothalamus, and anterior and posterior pituitaries. These activation centers stimulate the various endocrine glands that are located throughout the body. Everything from excretion to digestion to sleep and sex drive is controlled by hormones. For the purposes of this book it's not necessary to go into great detail. To give the reader a basic understanding of endocrinology (the study of hormones), I shall look at one hormone, testosterone, and its implications for bodybuilders.

Testosterone is produced by the testes of sexually mature males. It's often called "the male hormone," but this term is misleading as females also have testosterone circulating in their bodies. Conversely, the hormone estrogen, often referred to as "the female hormone," is also found in males. It's the relative concentrations of both that have given rise to the descriptions male and female.

Photo of Elle Patille and Larry Vinette by Paul Buceta

Testosterone and estrogen are present in both men and women – it's the relative amounts that differentiate "male" and "female."

Through a number of intermediate steps, testosterone is produced from the precursor, cholesterol. (Yes, there is a use for it after all, but don't consciously try to include it in your diet as you will get all you need, even if you cut down on high-cholesterol food.)

Testosterone has numerous functions, among which are deepening of the voice, growth of pubic hair, increased muscle size and strength, and sperm production. This is the hormone that causes males to be, on average, larger and stronger than females. Even among males there is much variation. Ectomorphs tend to have low levels and are usually underweight, timid and nervous. Nervousness could possibly reduce testosterone levels, so it's difficult to say which is the cause and which is the effect.

Mesomorphs have bloodstreams loaded with testosterone. The result – low bodyfat level, a skele-ton covered with muscle (or great potential for it), and a tendency towards increased aggression. The high levels of circulating hormone produce rapid muscular weight gains, and at the same time keep bodyfat percentage to a minimum.

Endomorphs fall somewhere in between. They have good muscle size, but they are also inclined to carry excess fat. The most recent research suggests that regular exercise (including bodybuilding) increases the production of testosterone. Naturally there is an upper limit. Train too hard for too long and you'll overtax the body's recovery system. To combat stress, the body reduces testosterone production and increases cortisol production. Cortisol has the opposite effect of testosterone, as it reduces muscle mass. This is why I keep stressing the perils of overtraining throughout the book.

Photo of Gunter Schlierkamp, Dexter Jackson and Jay Cutler by Raymond Cassar

READY, SET, GO!

CHAPTER 23

The Warmup

"It's just common sense. You need to prepare the joints and muscles for the heavy work to come. By doing light stretching and warmup sets, you loosen tight muscles, lubricate the joints, tendons, and ligaments, and warm up the area by bringing blood into the muscles."

– Greg Zulak, regular *MuscleMag International* contributor, commenting on the importance of warming up before a heavy training session.

> " In a cold gym your body needs more time to warm up and your muscles quickly cool between sets. A cold environment carries an increased risk of injury, especially when you are lifting heavy weights."
>
> – Dr. Nick Evans, *MuscleMag International* columnist.

t's amazing the number of bodybuilders who head straight for the squat or bench-press rack without a warmup. Their muscles are "cold" and not prepared to become subjected to hundreds of pounds of stress. No matter how pressed for time you are, don't plunge headfirst into a workout without properly warming up. A good warmup will accomplish the following:

• Help prevent injuries.
• Increase the removal of lactic acid and other waste products of exercise.
• Increase the efficiency of contracting muscles.
• Increase neuromuscular coordination.
• Improve the coordination of muscles.
• Increase heart rate, speeding up blood circulation.
• Increase the delivery of oxygen to the muscles.
• Increase the body's cooling mechanisms.
• Increase the muscles' range of motion.
• Mentally prepare you for the workout.

A proper warmup should prepare your muscles for the work ahead without draining your energy reserves.

WALKING A FINE LINE

There is a fine line between a warmup that adequately prepares the muscles and one that reduces your training intensity. A good warmup should increase your heart rate, produce a light sweat, increase your body temperature and loosen up the muscles. On the other hand the warmup shouldn't drain your energy reserves to the point that you can't complete the desired number of sets and reps with maximum weight. Here are a few guidelines:

- Modify the warmup so it increases body temperature and produces sweat, but does not deplete your energy level or cause fatigue.
- Include stretching exercises to help loosen muscles.
- Include lighter versions of the exercises you'll be doing in your workout to prepare your muscles for more intense training.
- Stop the warmup after about 10 minutes.

Generally speaking, warmups can be divided into three categories, or phases.

PHASE ONE

Phase One can be considered a full-body warmup. Even if you are only planning to work one part of your body, say chest or back, your heart and lungs play a major role, and you want them operating at peak efficiency. For most bodybuilders, five to ten minutes will be a sufficient warmup. There's no need to pedal the Tour de France! A few minutes on the bike will get the heart and lungs pumping and will ensure the muscles will receive sufficient amounts of oxygen and nutrients. Other machines you can use are the treadmill, rower (called an ergometer), and StairMaster. If cardio machines are not your thing, try skipping rope, doing a quick jog up and down your street, or running up and down a few flights of stairs. Any of these activities will prepare your body's major systems for the work ahead.

PHASE TWO

The second phase of your warmup should focus on preparing the muscles for injury prevention and efficient functioning. Probably the best form of exercise for doing this is stretching. Stretching is one of those activities that can be performed before, during and after your workout. It both warm ups the muscles and relaxes them after a workout. It also increases blood flow to the muscles and speeds up the removal of waste products. Ideally, you should stretch the whole body, but if you can't, perform a few light stretches for the muscles that you will be training that day. I'll deal with stretching in greater detail later in the book.

PHASE THREE

The third phase focuses on performing a few light sets of a given exercise before moving to your heaviest weight. If you're working up to 200 pounds on the bench press, start off with just the bar and do 15 to 20 reps. Then put 100 to 120 pounds on and do 10 to 12 reps. You could then go to your top weight of 200 pounds on the next set, or you could do a third warmup set with about 150 to 160 pounds. Always do at least two good warmup sets before lifting your heaviest weight. In fact, you may need to do three or four warmup sets once you can manage 400 pounds or more. No matter how strong you become, you're still at risk for injury. In fact, the stronger you get the higher the risk, because of the huge poundage you end up using. So far you may have been skipping warmup sets with no ill effects. However, I warn you that one of these days you could be repping out when rrrrrriiiiiippppppp! There you go – a massive tear has occurred that could require surgery and many months of therapy. It has happened to some of the top pros, so it could certainly happen to you.

CONCLUSION

On average, your warmup – both cardiovascular and muscular – should take no more than 15 to 20 minutes. This is long enough to prepare your body for more intense training without depleting your energy reserves too much. For those who consider 15 to 20 minutes too long, look at it this way: investing this small amount of time could prevent months of potential grief and misery – not to mention muscle atrophy.

Photo of Greg Jones by Robert Reiff

By warming up for 15 to 20 minutes, you decrease the risk for injury and increase the muscles' ability to function efficiently.

CHAPTER 24

Record Keeping and Evaluation

"With just a flick of a few pages I can see what weights, sets and reps I was using seven weeks ago or seven years ago."

– Tosca Reno, well-respected fitness and nutrition expert and author of *The Eat-Clean Diet* series.

There's an old saying in bodybuilding: You can keep following a training routine as long as you're getting results. But as soon as it ceases to be effective, you should switch to something new.

If you're eating correctly, training progressively and getting adequate rest, then you should be continuously increasing your muscle size and strength. If this is not the case, then something's wrong. In order to solve a problem you must first identify its source. Now's the time to sit down and evaluate your entire training philosophy.

During this time, it's very beneficial to have training records to refer to. Training records can then help you answer such questions as: "Am I including enough variety in my training?" "Are my protein and carb intakes adequate?" "Do I get enough rest between workouts for full recovery?" It's very difficult to answer these questions if you don't have notes or records to refer back to. Only by reviewing all aspects of your training can you objectively identify the problem and take steps to fix it.

Bodybuilders use three primary types of records: written notes, photographs, and tape measurements. You can use one or all three to chart your progress and ensure your training is yielding results. One of the best ways to know where you're going is to know where you have been!

Keeping a training journal will help you track your progress and motivate you to reach your goals in the gym.

Photo of Tomm Voss by Robert Reiff

TRAINING JOURNAL

Most top amateur and professional athletes keep training journals. Why should bodybuilders be any different? You can look back every couple of weeks and see how things are progressing. You can see what's working and what's not. A training journal also serves as a source of motivation because you'll have proof of the progress you're making (besides your physique of course). What can be better than finding out that over the past two months you've increased your bench press by 50 percent?

Your training journal can be a cheap spiral-bound notebook or an expensive executive-style day planner. You can also buy specially designed record books through the various muscle magazines, including *MuscleMag International*. Not sure exactly what you should be recording? To start, record the date; time of the workout; the exercises performed; number of sets, reps, weights; and the amount of cardio. If you really want to get detailed you could also include how much sleep you got the night before; what you ate that day; any supplements you used; and how you felt before, during and after the exercises. You may even want to write down daily activities that at first don't seem to be relevant. For example, perhaps after reviewing your notes you discovered that your worst leg workouts always seem to follow your late shift. You can use this insight to redesign your workouts. No doubt you will find other patterns emerging as you analyze the data you've collected over the months and years.

Like most professions, bodybuilding has its own form of shorthand. The general format is to list, from left to right, the exercise name, weight, and number of reps. Here's a typical example for three working sets of the bench press. (We do not normally write down the warmup sets, but you can if you like.)

THREE WORKING SETS FOR THE BENCH PRESS

Flat Bench Press: 200 X 10, 200 X 8, 200 X 6

In this example, after an initial warmup the individual performed three sets of flat bench presses using 200 pounds. The number of reps decreased with each successive set. If you were to perform the same number of reps for each set using the same weight, it would look something like the breakdown below:

Flat Bench Press: 200 X 8 X 8 X 8 or even simpler:
Flat Bench Press: 200 X 8 X 3

You should always record the date of the workout somewhere on the page. This way you can find the exact time you are looking for. You may also want to list the exercises down the page in the order you performed them, as their order can also be relevant to your progress.

PHOTOGRAPHS

No doubt you've heard the saying "a picture is worth a thousand words." Well, in the bodybuilder's case, this is certainly true. Numbers in a book will be useful, but to really capture the look of your physique you need a photo. I should warn you that your first photo shoot will probably depress you. Once you get to the point where you are receiving lots of compliments on your physique from your gym buddy, girlfriend or the photographer, you'll probably start comparing your photos to the ones in *MuscleMag International*. Don't bother. Odds are your photos won't measure up to what we present every month. For one thing, top magazines use professional photographers who have expensive equipment and perfect lighting conditions. Besides, a couple

> " Jay Cutler and Milos Sarcev are two friends that come to mind when I think of smart career moves. They truly do have a good work ethic embedded in them. They both show up on time and will continue shooting until I'm the one who can't take it anymore."
>
> – Alex Ardenti,
> top physique and swimsuit photographer

of months (or even years) of training won't turn your physique into what you see in the magazines. However, you can figure out how to get there if you analyze your photos seriously and use them to determine your weak areas. One close look and you should be able to see which areas of your body need work.

Photo of Jay Cutler by Ralph DeHaan

EVERY ANGLE

You may flex a mighty set of pecs in the mirror, but how does your back stack up? Unless you set up multiple mirrors, you won't be able to see it. However, a couple of photos will show you what you need to know. Photos enable you to objectively scrutinize your physique. They are also a great way to track your progress over time. Again, the first set probably won't flatter you, but the next set in a couple of months will show the fruits of your labor. You'll be able to clearly see the progress you are making. (I'll be saying a lot more on photography in the section on competition).

TAKING MEASUREMENTS

Unless you are one of those genetically blessed individuals, odds are you won't see huge changes in your measurements on a month-to-month basis. If you do decide to throw a tape around your muscles, do so only every four to six months (even then the changes may be slight). The average hardworking, properly eating natural bodybuilder (as opposed to someone using large amounts of anabolic steroids or other performance-enhancing drug) can expect to gain about 10 to maybe 15 pounds of muscle per year. You may gain a little more in your first year, but for most that'll be about one pound a month, or a quarter pound per week. Now, all this muscle won't be going to your biceps – it will be evenly distributed over your entire body.

Photo of Scott Peckham

If you gain this much muscle, you can expect to gain about an inch on your arms and a couple of inches around your chest in a year. Now this doesn't seem like much, but it means that those average-looking 15-inch arms could be 20-inch guns in five years. As the years go by, you'll gain less and less in overall size. This is because most bodybuilders gain about 90 percent of their total muscle mass in the first five years of training. Yes, there will be exceptions to this rule. For example, the bodybuilders you see in books and magazines were almost invariably the exceptions.

Muscle hardness, quality, and separation make plenty of impact on the judges these days, perhaps even more than sheer size. However, bodybuilders do like to compare statistics. If you decide to see how you stack up, grab a fabric measuring tape and wrap it around the middle of the flexed muscle. If you want a "true" measurement, take the measurement before your workout, because the muscle will fill up with blood and be larger after the workout. If you want, you can take measurements of your muscle relaxed before and relaxed after, and flexed before and flexed after. Bodybuilders normally measure the biceps (really the total upper arm); chest (really chest and back); waist, neck, legs (thighs); and calves.

CONCLUSION

Besides all the reasons just discussed, there is a final, though less obvious, reason for keeping a detailed record of your progress. If you have that great combination of training drive, genetics and competitive spirit, sooner or later you may be placing high or even winning some big contests. When that happens, it won't be long before you catch the keen eye of *MuscleMag International*'s art and editorial team. Virtually every superstar bodybuilder, from John Grimek and Steve Reeves to Jay Cutler and Ronnie Coleman has been featured in the muscle magazines over the years. A record of your early years makes great reading and will act as inspiration for the next generation of bodybuilders. So get out the camera, pen and paper, and start recording now!

CHAPTER 25

Stretch for Success and Injury Prevention

"Stretching enables you to build bigger muscles because it stretches the fascia, a protective sheath of connective tissue that envelops the muscle. When the fascia is stretched, the muscle underneath has more room to grow."

– Muscle Bites, a monthly feature in *MuscleMag International*

tretching is one of the most basic physical acts. Everyone, from a baby to a senior citizen, can enjoy a good stretch. The first thing many of us do upon waking is stretch our arms high above our head. It feels good while we're doing it and we feel more refreshed afterward. Unfortunately, stretching is probably the most neglected component in health and fitness. During exercise you contract, or shorten, your muscles. This constant shortening causes the muscles to become very tight. Just take a moment and clench your fist. That is similar to what happens to the contracted muscle – it becomes tight and rigid, feeling cramped and "heavy." Now open your hand and stretch out the fingers. Doesn't that feel good? So why do so many of us skip stretching? Oh, maybe we think we're too busy, or we just don't consider it important ... after all, you don't stretch to build muscle, do you? But as we'll learn, stretching offers bodybuilders numerous benefits.

WHAT TO STRETCH

First let's discuss what exactly is being stretched. For bodybuilders trying to add size and prevent injury, two types of tissue should be stretched on a regular basis: the fascia and the tendons and ligaments. While all are connective tissue, the fas-

cia is more elastic in nature and should get the majority of your attention, especially as it relates to muscle growth. Stretching the tendons and ligaments is also important, however, and has a vital role in promoting strength gains.

Fascia is the protective sheath, or covering, that surrounds muscles. As people age, the soft texture of the fascia begins to harden and takes on the feel of an outer shell. Under certain circumstances, this could restrict muscle growth. Stretching helps keep the fascia soft and supple, allowing the growing muscle to expand. Think of a balloon. New balloons are more difficult to blow up because the rubber is tough. Repeatedly blowing up the balloon softens the rubber, making it easier to stretch and blow up.

Stretching the tendons will allow you to perform additional reps. Attached to the ends of tendons are small receptors called golgi tendon organs (GTOs). You can think of GTOs as circuit breakers that act as safety switches. When a muscle is stretched beyond a certain point, the GTO fires and shuts the muscle down to prevent further contractions. If the GTOs didn't exist you could easily tear a muscle or tendon from its attachment. You may have experienced this phenomenon: you're repping out on dumbell presses when your pecs just give out, with

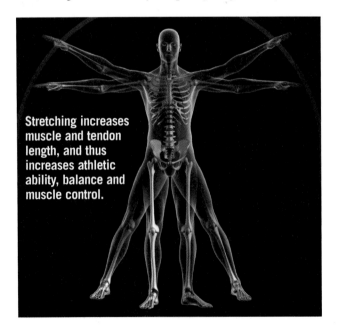

Stretching increases muscle and tendon length, and thus increases athletic ability, balance and muscle control.

little or no warning. You may be sure you have the strength to force out a few extra reps, but the muscle just won't contract.

BENEFITS OF STRETCHING
Decreased Risk of Injury

A regular stretching program helps increase the length of muscles and tendons. This not only reduces muscle tension, but also increases their overall contractile range, which in turn makes them less susceptible to injury. By increasing the muscles' contractile range, in other words, the range of motion around a joint, we increase the distance our limbs can move before muscle or tendon damage occurs. For example, the muscles and tendons in the back of our thighs are put under great stress when we kick a soccer ball. It only makes sense that the more flexible and pliable those muscles are, the further our leg can travel forward, thus decreasing the chance of injury.

Increased Muscle and Athletic Ability

There is a myth that stretching too much will decrease joint stability and muscle power. This is absolutely untrue! By increasing muscle and tendon length, you are increasing the distance over which the muscles are able to contract. This results in a potential increase to the muscles' strength and power. You'll have actually increased you athletic ability, balancing ability, and muscle control.

Reduced Muscle Soreness

Before long you'll start experiencing tightness and soreness in your muscles the day after your workout, if you haven't already. Walking up a set of stairs the day after leg training may be very painful indeed! The muscle soreness that follows strenuous physical activity is usually referred to as post-exercise muscle soreness or delayed onset muscle soreness (DOMS). This discomfort is the result of micro tears (minute tears within the muscle fibers), and a buildup of

Muscle fatigue, and the lack of motivation that comes with it, can be reduced through regular stretching.

metabolic waste products, particularly lactic acid. Stretching helps alleviate this soreness by lengthening the individual muscle fibers, increasing blood and nutrient delivery to the muscles, and removing waste products.

Reduced Antagonistic Pressure

Muscle fatigue is a major problem experienced by those who exercise regularly. It results in a decrease in both physical and mental performance. But increased flexibility through stretching can help reduce the effects of fatigue by taking pressure off the muscles being exercised. Most muscles in the body have an opposite or opposing muscle. When these opposing muscles (called antagonists) are more flexible, the working muscles (called agonists) do not have to exert as much force against the opposing muscles. Each movement of the working muscles actually takes less effort.

Mentally Relaxing and Rewarding

With all the attention on the physical components of exercise, we often neglect the mental components. People who regularly stretch are more likely to feel good about themselves. This leads to a boost in self-confidence, which in turn helps enhance physical performance and motivate the individual to participate in regular exercise.

Stretching is beneficial before, during and after your workout – it takes minimal energy so it won't negatively affect your training.

Photo of Will Harris by Robert Reiff

WHEN TO STRETCH?

Before

Stretching before a workout helps prepare the muscles for the work to follow. It loosens the muscles and increases the blood flow to the area, allowing for more efficient nutrient and oxygen delivery. Stretching also helps remove lactic acid – one of the primary causes of post-workout soreness. Just remember that it's not a good idea to engage in rigorous stretching the moment you walk in the gym. Cold muscles do not stretch well. Do a light warmup first and then proceed to your stretches.

During

The primary benefit of stretching during a weight-training workout is that it saves you time. While you are taking your minute or so rest between sets, add in a stretch for that particular muscle group. Don't worry about it affecting your training, as stretching takes little energy to perform. It will keep the muscles limber and help remove lactic acid and deliver nutrients. And you'll save 10 to 15 minutes at the end of your workout.

After

Most people stretch at the end of their workouts because the muscles are fully warmed up and can endure more vigorous stretching. The muscles will also be full of lactic acid and other metabolic wastes that must be removed. Stretching greatly facilitates this removal process. Also, stretching is relaxing and calming, making it an ideal way to finish off a good workout.

TYPES OF STRETCHING

Passive Stretching

Passive stretching is often referred to as "static stretching," and is the type we most often think of. A passive stretch is one in which you hold the stretched position for 15 to 30 seconds. Slow, relaxed static stretching can relieve spasms in muscles that are healing after an injury. It also relaxes your body after a workout. I suggest that you save the static stretches until after your workout. Your muscles will be fully warmed up and it will be easier to hold the positions.

Isometric Stretching

Isometric stretching is a type of passive stretching that involves using the resistance of other muscle groups, a partner or a stationary object. The stretching positions are held for a much longer time than with passive stretching because the ultimate aim is to improve overall flexibility and strength.

An example of a partner-assisted stretch would be holding your leg up high and having your partner push it toward you while you try to force it back down to the ground. An example of using a stationary object would be the wall stretch for shoulders. You place your hand against a doorway or beam and then push forward leading with your shoulder.

Ballistic Stretching

Ballistic stretching uses the weight and momentum of a moving body to force the muscle beyond its normal range of motion. Essentially, you are bouncing into (or out of) the stretched position, using the stretched muscles as springs that pull you out of the stretched position. This type of stretching is really only useful for high performance athletes, because the risk of injury is too great for most people. It doesn't allow your muscles to adjust to the stretched position and relax. Instead, it may cause them to tighten up even more. Unless you are in excellent physical shape to begin with or play intense sports (hockey, rugby, basketball, etc.), avoid ballistic stretching.

Dynamic Stretching

Dynamic stretching involves gradually increasing the distance and speed of a muscle's range of motion. Please don't confuse dynamic stretching with ballistic stretching. Dynamic stretching consists of controlled movements that take you to the very limits of your range of motion. Ballistic stretches involve trying to force a muscle beyond its natural range of motion. In dynamic stretching there are no bouncing or sudden movements. A good example of dynamic stretching would be slow, controlled leg swings, arm swings or torso twists.

Using a variety of stretching techniques will help you improve your overall flexibility and strength.

Photo of Sagi Kalev by Irvin Gelb

COMMON STRETCHES

Hamstring Stretch

Sit on the floor and place the leg you wish to stretch straight out in front of you. Then bend the other leg alongside to make a triangle with your legs. With a straight back and straight knee, bend from your hips, and reach for the toe of your straight leg with both hands and hold for 20 seconds.

Lying Hamstring Stretch

Lie on your back and pull your leg in toward your chest. Clasp both hands behind your knee. Slowly extend the leg up. Try to straighten your knee as much as possible. Gently pull your (straight) leg toward your chest, and wrap your hands around your ankle. Hold for 10 seconds and then try to bring the leg further in toward your chest. Hold for another 10 seconds. Repeat with other leg.

Achilles' Stretch

Stand facing a wall with one leg in front of the other. Your front knee is bent and your hands are on the wall. Your back leg is straight and your heel is held flat on the floor. Lean toward the front knee, keeping the back foot and heel flat. Hold for 15 to 20 seconds. Relax. Repeat with the other leg.

Quadriceps Stretch

Stand leaning against a wall or other upright with one hand. Wrap your other hand around the ankle and pull the heel to the butt, feeling the stretch in the top of the leg. Try to keep your knees together. Concentrate on pulling the heel into the butt. To maximize the stretch, tuck your pelvis in and gently push your hips out.

Groin Stretch

Sit on the floor. Put the soles of your feet together, with your knees as close to the ground as possible and pointed outward. Grasp your ankles, pull in toward your groin and hold that position for a count of 10. Relax and repeat three times.

Spread Groin Stretch

Begin in a seated position with your legs spread apart, feet facing directly forward. Try to reach the inside of your ankles. Bend forward from the hips, keeping your knees straight. Hold until you feel tightness on the inside of your legs. Relax and repeat.

Calf Stretch

Get into a push-up position, but put one knee on the ground. Put your weight on the toes of your other foot and then push the heel down until you feel a slight pull. Hold that position for a count of 10. Relax and repeat three times with each leg.

Back Stretch

Lie on your back, grasp your legs behind your knees

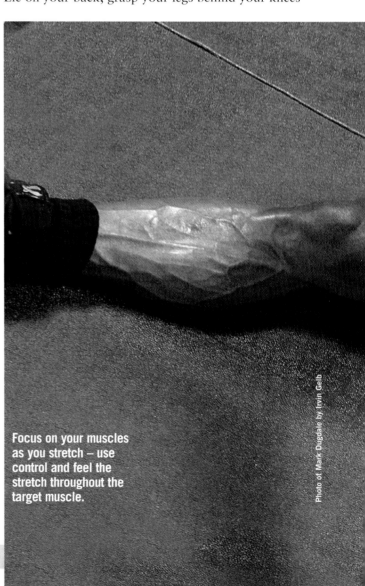

Focus on your muscles as you stretch – use control and feel the stretch throughout the target muscle.

and pull toward your chest, lifting your butt off the ground. Keeping your other leg straight and your head on the ground, hold this position for a count of 10. Repeat three times with each leg.

Chest Stretch

Grab a stationary upright with one hand, and with your arm locked out straight, gently turn away. Hold for a count of 10 and then switch arms.

Shoulder Stretch #1

Move one shoulder toward the other, keeping your arm parallel to the floor. Grasp the elbow of that arm with your other hand and gently pull toward your opposite shoulder. Hold for a count of 10. Repeat three times with each arm.

Shoulder Stretch #2

Interlace your fingers above your head, palms facing up. Push your arms up and back gently. Hold for 15 seconds.

Biceps Stretch

Place your hand on a wall. Lean forward with your feet positioned slightly away from the wall. Hold for 10 seconds. Repeat on the other arm. Alternate the stretch on each arm three times.

Triceps Stretch

Take one arm overhead and bend it at the elbow. Standing as straight as possible, gently press down on the elbow with your other hand until you feel a stretch at the back of your upper arm.

CHAPTER 26

Beginner Guidelines and Goals

"First and foremost you must set goals that are in accordance with the correct skill level. Overestimating your abilities is one of the biggest mistakes in bodybuilding, because this is a sport whose athletes are susceptible to macho attitudes. Setting goals too high will shake your confidence for future outings and paint your bodybuilding experience with negative brush strokes."

– Charles Glass, pro bodybuilding coach and trainer, offering beginners some great advice on goal setting.

Hopefully you won't skip this section and go straight to the intermediate or advanced training chapters. You might be tempted, but here's why you shouldn't: There's an old saying that a house is only as good as its foundation. Well, truer words have never been spoken in terms of bodybuilding. Out of all the levels of training, the beginning level is by far the most important. It's at this level that you'll learn the fundamentals and lay the groundwork for the rest of your bodybuilding life. Without first learning the basics, you'll never achieve the success you want – whether for you that means simply having a great body or winning the Sandow. Furthermore, skipping the basics could set you up for a future injury.

> "Nothing is more ridiculous than a beginner doing sets of cable crossovers while ignoring bench presses, incline presses and dips, or doing cable curls and concentration curls while ignoring heavy barbell and dumbell curls. For the first two years of training, beginners should be doing nothing but the 'hard' exercises. Forget about the isolation, icing-on-the-cake stuff."
>
> – Greg Zulak, long-time bodybuilding writer and expert, giving good advice to beginner bodybuilders.

weight after quitting smoking do so because they eat (often junk) every time they want a cigarette. For the teenagers reading this, smoking doesn't make you look "older." You simply look like a teenager smoking a cigarette! However, if you keep smoking you'll look older before your time. Smoking causes wrinkles and it gives a gray pallor to the skin. Don't let peer pressure get to you either – it takes more maturity to say no to smoking than it does to light up. Smoking will likely shorten your life, as each cigarette contains hundreds of chemicals, some of which have been linked to cancer, stroke, and heart disease. Most smokers eventually develop chronic lung disease. Even if you somehow escape the more serious side effects of smoking, you'll still be slowing down your recovery abilities. Your body's oxygen levels are decreased a great deal by smoking, which seriously affects your ability to exercise. Need I go on?

Keep your alcohol consumption low to moderate. There's no way you'll be able to drink heavy three or four nights per week and still have the energy for intense training. Alcohol takes water and oxygen to metabolize – two of the most important compounds necessary in training and recovery. It also affects your energy the next day. One or two beers or glasses of wine a couple of times a week probably will not hurt you, but don't abuse the bottle – no matter what your age. Not only will it slow down your progress and probably lead to serious side effects down the road, it also makes you store fat more easily. In addition, because alcohol decreases your inhibitions, it makes you less likely to stick to your diet.

Photo of Hidetada Yamagishi by Jason Mathas

For beginners, a key factor for success is setting realistic goals. Don't expect to see results overnight.

Photo of Ronnie Coleman by Raymond Cassar

BEGINNERS' GOALS

One of the first questions you should ask yourself is why you began training in the first place. Developing a Mr. Olympia-sized physique might be the furthest thing from your mind. You'll be happy with changing your waist-chest differential by a few inches each way. Well, many pros said the same thing and before long, a few inches became many inches. Once you develop a muscular 45-inch chest, it won't be long before you'll start eyeing the 50-inch barrier. And those 18-inch arms will just have to be pushed to 20 inches! This is what makes bodybuilding such an exciting sport – you can tailor your workouts to suit your individual goals.

Perhaps you have set the bar at the top rung. A chest measurement anywhere in the 40s just won't satisfy you. You won't stop until you have over 50 inches of armor plating hanging off your ribcage. There's nothing wrong with this, but don't start off performing workouts designed for existing 50-inch chests. Put it this way – you don't learn how to ride a bike by hopping on a Harley-Davidson or learn to fly in the cockpit of a 747. Bodybuilding is no different. You start out by performing straight sets and eventually graduate to more advanced training techniques.

STARTING OUT

Enough talk. Let's start building you some serious muscle tissue! Your primary goal at this level is to lay down a good foundation. Nothing fancy here – just basic exercises. Over the next few months you'll gradually prepare your body for more advanced training. It's imperative that you follow the advice put forward in this chapter. It takes your muscles a while to be ready for advanced training, and it takes your tendons and ligaments even longer. And if you think it would be a drag to be off for a few weeks with a damaged muscle, then remember that tendons and ligaments take far longer to heal – and some never do.

Don't go adding extra sets or exercises or skip the section all together. You may look at Ronnie Coleman's biceps and figure that the shortest route to a pair of similar-sized arms is by following his arm routine. Not a chance! Ronnie didn't start out by following his current biceps' program. He slowly worked up to it over the years. Also keep in mind that a lot of the programs you see in the magazines are really pre-contest training programs. Most of the stars follow significantly reduced training routines during the off-season – if you want to progress you must do the same.

Your beginning bodybuilding program should be performed three times per week on alternate days. If you're like most people this will be Monday, Wednesday, and Friday, but the body doesn't know the days of the week. You can work out on any three nonconsecutive days.

Your goal is to train the entire body during each workout, performing one exercise per muscle group for 3 sets of 10 to 12 reps per set. After a couple of weeks, you'll be easily performing 12 reps with your starting weight. Well done – you're on your way and your muscles are getting stronger. Now add five pounds to the bar or machine and keep going. Another week or two and this will start feeling light. Keep with this pattern as long as you keep getting stronger while maintaining solid technique. There will be the occasional week or two of little-to-no strength gain, but overall you'll be adding weight to the bar every couple of weeks. Now you're probably beginning to see why weight lifting is called "progressive resistance training" – because you increase the resistance progressively over time.

Photo of Chad Ray Martin by Irvin Gelb

COMPOUND VS. ISOLATION EXERCISES

Generally speaking, bodybuilding exercises can be broken down into two categories – isolation and compound movements. As the name suggests, isolation exercises tend to only work one muscle group. They involve just one joint. Isolation exercises make great warmup, finishing, and pre-contest exercise, but they are close to useless for increasing strength and size. Compound exercises, on the other hand, involve movement around two or more joints and stimulate more than one muscle group at a time. Compound exercises allow you to lift considerably more weight than isolation movements and are thus more effective for building muscle strength and size. For example, while dumbell flyes work the chest, dumbell or barbell presses work the chest, shoulders and triceps. Likewise, squats and leg presses do a far better job of building your thigh muscles than leg extensions.

The exercises I have chosen are all compound exercises. They are among the best for beginning bodybuilders who are trying to lay down a solid strength and size foundation. In time you will add isolation exercises to your routine to help refine the new muscle mass.

Photos of Ben Pakulski

Arnold illustrates just how impressive a large ribcage looks in a side pose.

to 240 or 250 pounds during the off-season and then, about three months before the contest, try to diet the excess fat off. Unfortunately, much of the weight gained in the off-season would be fat rather than muscle. Shedding the excess fat was difficult and the frequent large changes in overall body size often left the individual with stretched and loose skin.

Bulking up was all the rage in the '60s and '70s, but with the ultra-ripped look that began to emerge in the late '70s and early '80s, most bodybuilders abandoned the practice. Obtaining this new defined, cut look is almost impossible if you have 30 or 40 pounds to lose. In addition, since guest posing and advertising contracts are their main means of support, many bodybuilders need to be within 10 to 15 pounds of their competitive weight all year round.

So, does bulking up still have a place? Could it work for you? Well that depends on your somatotype. Endomorphs should not try to bulk up. They have enough problems trying to stay lean under normal circumstances. Mesomorphs may benefit from the practice, but why spend months of the year carrying excess body fat? You'll probably have no trouble gaining muscle mass without fat, by simply eating properly. Besides, let's not forget the health consequences of carrying extra body fat. In fact, before fat starts accumulating on the outside of the body, it has already started forming around the internal organs. Unless you're a mesomorph with ectomorph characteristics (i.e. very lean, with trouble gaining muscle mass) you should pass on bulking up. About the only group that might benefit from this practice is ectomorphs. Ectomorphs have to fight for every ounce of muscle they gain and the extra calories will help create muscle. Ultimately, the decision to try bulking up is yours. If you're an ectomorph, go for it and see what happens.

RIBCAGE EXPANSION

While most bodybuilders focus on building the pectoral (chest muscles), few realize that it is possible to enlarge their chest measurement in another way. The chest mus-

Not counting getting changed and bathroom breaks, your workout should last no more than 45 to 60 minutes. If you must chat and socialize, try to limit it to one or two minutes. Better yet, leave it until after your workout. However, much of what you'll learn about bodybuilding will be from more experienced bodybuilders. By all means strike up conversations with these individuals. The solution to a problem you have may be standing a few feet away at the gym. Just remember that the majority of your time in the gym should be spent training – not talking.

To bulk up or not to bulk up – that is the question! If you are under 40 years old you may never have heard of this term! It's seldom used today, but there was a time when "bulking up" was one of the most common terms in bodybuilding. Bulking up meant to eat everything in sight and train very heavy, all in an effort to gain as much weight and size as possible. If a bodybuilder wanted to weigh 200 pounds in contest shape, he would "bulk up"

cles don't just hang in space, but rest on top of the ribcage. The ribcage is essentially a box-like structure composed of ribs attached to the sternum. While genetics dictate the size of this frame, you can enlarge it to some degree by stretching the cartilage that attaches the ribs to the sternum. If you are past your 20s, you will experience less success in this area than if you're in your teens. This is because the cartilage holding the ribs to the sternum starts losing its pliability in the early to mid 20s. It doesn't mean a 30-year-old can't expand his ribcage – he can. He'll just need to work harder at it.

There are a number of reasons for enlarging the ribcage. The obvious one is cosmetic. A larger ribcage gives you a larger chest measurement. All other things being equal, the bodybuilder with the largest ribcage will look more impressive in side poses.

A second reason to enlarge your ribcage is structural. Let's say you do have the potential to build Schwarzenegger-sized pecs. You'll need a large, strong ribcage to support them on. A larger set of chest muscles on a small ribcage could throw off your center of gravity and cause lower-back problems. A final reason for ribcage expansion is health. Regular breathing squats will do wonders for your heart and lungs. A larger ribcage will also help your internal organs.

To effectively stretch the ribcage you must approach it from two angles. The first is from the inside. Every time you inhale, you stretch the ribcage cartilage. Breathing squats are like regular squats, but the amount of weight lifted is secondary. However, since the exercises are so similar, I suggest you perform breathing squats on the same day as your regular leg workout. With breathing squats you use light weight and perform 25 to 30 reps instead of using heavier weight for 6 to 12 reps. As you perform the squats, concentrate on inhaling and exhaling as deeply as you can.

Your next step is to perform an exercise to stretch the rib cartilage from the outside. Probably the best exercise for this is dumbell pullovers. There are two variations of this exercise. You can lie lengthwise on the bench as you normally would, or you can lie across the bench. I suggest

the latter, as it allows you to drop your hips and shoulders and really stretch the ribcage. The other way prevents you from getting the full range of motion.

As with breathing squats, the emphasis with this exercise is on breathing deeply and stretching, not seeing how much weight you can lift. (For a full description of both exercises, see the exercise descriptions in Appendix Two). While you can perform the exercises on separate days, most bodybuilders find they get better results by working them together. Perform one set of breathing squats and then immediately perform a set of cross-bench pullovers. I also suggest performing the exercises toward the end of your workout. Doing them early could reduce the amount of weight you can lift on your other exercises.

Photo of Mark Erpelding by Alex Ardenti

BEGINNER ROUTINES

Okay, now let's start pumping iron. Here are five excellent routines to start you on your way. At first glance, they may seem simple and elementary, and in some respects they are. But don't forget that at this stage your muscles are not ready for more intense routines. More importantly, you don't need anything more challenging than this. In fact, a number of top bodybuilders follow such basic routines in the off-season when trying to gain muscle mass, so don't think that they are too simple to be productive. The late, great Mike Mentzer was fond of saying that the average beginner "would grow simply by putting the weights away." Just about anything you do at this stage is going to produce fantastic gains in strength and size. Why risk injury or extreme soreness from an advanced routine, when one of the routines listed here will produce the same results?

Speaking of injury, you'll notice two exercises listed here that you'll rarely see in other books and magazine articles. Internal and external shoulder rotations probably won't win you any bodybuilding contests, but they will help keep your shoulders in good health. Most shoulder injuries are not centered on the large outer deltoid muscles, but the smaller underlying rotator cuff. One of the most common injuries is a rotator cuff tear. Unfortunately once you tear it, surgery may not even

restore it properly, and you may be permanently prevented from working your upper body properly. The rotator cuff is actually a group of four muscles and their tendons. They wrap around the front, back and top of the shoulder joint. Bodybuilders and powerlifters frequently develop problems in that region from the years of heavy pressing movements. The best way of treating a rotator cuff tear is preventing it in the first place. Do shoulder rotations as a simple exercise involving very light weight. You should perform a few sets of these important exercises before any shoulder or chest exercises.

Perform one of the following routines three times per week, making sure to give yourself a rest day in between. You'll notice that I've suggested slightly higher rep ranges. This is for two reasons. First, higher reps help prepare the muscles for more intense training down the road. Second, higher reps means using lighter weights, thus reducing the risk of injuries. After a couple of months under your belt, you can increase the weight and lower the reps from 12 to 15 to about 8 to 10. I don't suggest using heavy weight and low reps (4 to 6) until you've been training for at least six months, you've have given your tendons and muscles a chance to strengthen and get accustomed to weight training. Remember this vital rule: Train the muscles and not the ego!

ROUTINE A

EXERCISE	SETS	REPS
Squats	3	12–15
Leg Curls	3	12–15
Standing Calf Raises	3	15–20
Flat Barbell Presses	3	12–15
Chin-Ups	3	12–15
Front Barbell Presses	3	12–15
Triceps Pushdowns	3	12–15
Barbell Curls	3	12–15
External Rotations	2	15–20
Internal Rotations	2	15–20
Crunches	3	15–20

ROUTINE B

EXERCISE	SETS	REPS
Leg Presses	3	12–15
Leg Curls	3	12–15
Standing Calf Raises	3	15–20
Incline Barbell Presses	3	12–15
Front Pulldowns	3	12–15
Wide-Grip Upright Rows	3	12–15
Lying Triceps Extensions	3	12–15
Standing Dumbell Curls	3	12–15
External Rotations	2	15–20
Internal Rotations	2	15–20
Leg Raises	3	15–20

ROUTINE C

EXERCISE	SETS	REPS
Squats	3	12–15
Stiff-Leg Deadlifts	3	12–15
Toe Presses	3	15–20
Flat Dumbell Presses	3	12–15
Seated Pulley Rows	3	12–15
Front Barbell Presses	3	12–15
Seated Dumbell Extensions	3	12–15
Seated Dumbell Curls	3	12–15
External Rotations	2	15–20
Internal Rotations	2	15–20
Reverse Crunches	3	15–20

ROUTINE D

EXERCISE	SETS	REPS
Leg Presses	3	12–15
Leg Curls	3	12–15
Standing Calf Raises	3	15–20
Dips	3	12–15
One-Arm Dumbell Rows	3	12–15
Dumbell Shoulder Presses	3	12–15
Narrow-Grip Presses	3	12–15
Reverse Curls	3	12–15
External Rotations	2	15–20
Internal Rotations	2	15–20
Leg Raises	3	15–20

ROUTINE E

EXERCISE	SETS	REPS
Squats	3	12–15
Stiff-Leg Deadlifts	3	12–15
Standing Calf Raises	3	15–20
Incline Dumbell Presses	3	12–15
Barbell Rows	3	12–15
Front Barbell Presses	3	12–15
Bench Dips	3	12–15
Preacher Curls	3	12–15
External Rotations	2	15–20
Internal Rotations	2	15–20
Crunches	3	15–20

ROUTINE F

EXERCISE	SETS	REPS
Leg Presses	3	12–15
Leg Curls	3	12–15
Seated Calf Raises	3	15–20
Incline Bench Presses	3	12–15
Front Lat Pulldowns	3	12–15
Wide-Grip Upright Rows	3	12–15
Triceps Pushdowns	3	12–15
EZ-Bar Curls	3	12–15
External Rotations	2	15–20
Internal Rotations	2	15–20
Reverse Crunches	3	15–20

Photo of King Kamali by Paull

PRINCIPLES OF NUTRITION

CHAPTER 27

Nutrition 101: The Basic Food Groups

"Genes may have something to do with it, but the culprit is more often bad dietary habits that may have been passed on from one generation to the next. Growing up with people who inhale junk food and fried foods, who slather butter, heavy sauces and mayonnaise on any good food choices, makes it more likely that you will follow in their fatty footsteps."

– Ron Harris, regular *MuscleMag International* contributor, commenting on the real reason for today's increased waistlines.

Some of the most important components for building muscle include intense training, great genetics, supplements and attitude. Yet probably the most important component of all – food – is also the most overlooked. You can work out all you want and even possess Cutler-sized genes, but you won't gain an ounce of new muscle tissue if you don't consume the right nutrients.

There's nothing earth shattering about bodybuilding nutrition. You simply take in slightly more quality calories than your body uses each day. Notice I said "slightly" and "quality." I don't mean gulping down everything in sight. And all calories are not created equal. If your body requires 2500 calories per day, both to carry out it's normal day-to-day functions and gain new muscle weight, and you eat four bags of potato chips and six candy bars, then I guess you're taking in enough calories to gain weight. But how much of this will be new, lean, hard muscle tissue? Not much. The majority will be deposited around your waist and internal organs as fat. Junk food is composed of what nutritionists call empty calories. These foods simply do not provide the vital nutrients needed to build new muscle tissue.

THE FOOD GROUPS

Dairy

This group contains everything from milk to cheese to yogurt to cream. Although ice cream also fits in here, it's a treat you should limit to perhaps once a week and in small amounts. Dairy products are very nutrient dense. The foods in the dairy group are high in vitamins A and D, riboflavin, calcium, phosphorous, fats, and protein. While they contain valuable nutrients (protein, vitamins and minerals) dairy products can also be high in undesirables (saturated fat and simple sugar). Low-fat dairy products are available, but there are good reasons to limit their intake, as we'll learn later.

Fruits and Vegetables

Nothing fancy here. Most vegetables consist of the roots, stalks and leaves of the plant. Fruit, on the other hand, is the fleshy, pulpy part of the plant that surrounds the seeds. Many foods considered vegetables such as tomatoes, squash, peppers and cucumbers, are actually fruits. No matter what your definition of fruits and vegetables, they are among nature's greatest foods. They are loaded with fiber, vitamins, minerals, and good healthy carbohydrates. Your goal is to eat anywhere from four to six servings per day.

Protein

This group can be considered the "body-building" group, because it contains all the high-protein foods such as meat, poultry, fish, beans and nuts. Besides being high in protein, sources in this group tend to be high in iron and B vitamins.

Grains

This group contains whole grains, breads, cereals, flour, pasta, cornmeal, oatmeal, and all the other grain products. This group is high in such nutrients as B vitamins, iron, fiber, and complex carbohydrates.

Photo of Mark Erpelding by Alex Ardenti

> "Some nutrition gurus will tell you that eating anything at all will boost your metabolic rate – it's called digestion. Yet of the three macronutrients, protein boosts that rate the most – up to 200 calories per day – since it requires a great deal of energy to digest and absorb."
>
> – Jerry Kindela, group editorial director of Robert Kennedy Publishing and *MuscleMag International* contributor

Oils and Fats

This group contains all the edible animal and plant oils, butter, margarine, honey and fats. Like the dairy group, this group is a mixed bag. While the good fats are vital for optimum health, the saturated fats and especially trans fats should be avoided if possible. Even the good fats can pack fat around your waist if consumed in excess.

Ultra Crap

While you need to consume foods from all the other groups to maintain good health and build superior muscle, items from this group should be kept to a minimum or eliminated altogether. The ultra-crap group contains such villains as candy bars, potato chips, refined sugar and flour, candy, processed meat, donuts, cakes, pastries, soft drinks, and deep-fried anything! These foods are all considered low-density because they contain a low percentage of good nutrients in relation to their high calorie content. Also included in this group is alcohol. If your sport is sumo wrestling then perhaps you can feast from this food group. But if it's a lean and muscular physique you're after, you should avoid these foods entirely!

CHAPTER 28

The Nutrient Groups

"From chicken breasts to oatmeal to donuts, every food you eat should serve your physique goal."

– Steven Stiefel, bodybuilding writer, journalist and photographer

he primary nutrients found in food are protein, fats, carbohydrates, vitamins, minerals, fiber and water. Though the vast majority of foods contain several of these nutrients, very few foods contain them all, and virtually no food contains them all in ample quantities. This is why you must consume a wide variety of food. And that's why nutritionists keep talking about "well-balanced" diets.

PROTEIN

Given the large amount of protein that bodybuilders eat, it's surprising how little they know about this potent muscle-builder. Proteins are extremely large molecules made up of smaller subunits called polypeptide chains. Polypeptide chains in turn are made up of even smaller units called amino acids. Structurally, amino acids contain both a carboxyl (acid) group (COOH) and an amino group (NH_2) attached to a central carbon atom, normally a hydrocarbon. A hydrogen atom and another side group will also be attached to the carbon atom. The general molecular formula for a typical amino acid is as follows:

$$
\begin{array}{c}
H \\
| \\
COOH - CH - NH_2 \\
| \\
R
\end{array}
$$

There are approximately 20 amino acids in the human body that make up protein (although some biochemists suggest anywhere from 22 to 26) and they all have unique chemical characteristics. The exact amino acid content and the sequence of the amino acids in the chain determines each protein's characteristics and what it will be used for. Besides building muscle, protein is used as a structural component in red blood cells, antibodies, and hormones.

The human body can manufacture 11 of the 20 amino acids; the others must be supplied completely by your diet. Failure to obtain even one of these "essential amino acids" can lead to degradation of the body's protein-based tissues, including organs, muscles, and enzymes. And unlike fats and carbohydrates, the human body does not store excess amino acids for later use. They must be consumed in our food every day. The essential amino acids are: phenylalanine, valine, threonine, tryptophan, isoleucine, methionine, histidine, leucine, and lysine. In addition, the amino acids arginine, cysteine, glycine, glutamine and tyrosine are all considered conditionally essential amino acids – our bodies create them, but under certain circumstances, such as during times of stress or healing, we cannot create enough. Remember that bodybuilding puts our bodies in a constant state of repair, so we need to make sure we get enough of these conditionally essential amino acids.

The amino acids that can be synthesized by the body are considered nonessential and include alanine, asparagine, cysteine, glutamate, proline, serine and tyrosine.

Complete and Incomplete

"When you blend several protein foods, the biological pattern of the amino acid content is boosted. It's comparable to the strong man who helps the weak one. Together they can accomplish efforts that singly might be difficult. The weaker amino acid of one food becomes naturally enriched and fortified when it is eaten together with a stronger amino acid from another food."
– Carlson Wade, author of *Miracle Protein*

Protein sources can also be classified based on their amino acid makeup. Animal sources contain all the amino acids and are termed complete. Most plant sources are deficient in one or more of the amino acids and are called incomplete. This is why vegetarians must consume a wide range of plant sources to obtain all the amino acids in sufficient quantities.

Photo by Alex Ardenti

Animal sources are considered complete proteins. By consuming meat, you're getting all the amino acids.

How much?

For many years nutritionists and other interested parties have debated the amount of protein humans require. This argument has been revived in recent years because of the success of many high-protein weight-loss diets. The current DRI (Dietary Reference Intake) is 0.8 grams per kilogram of bodyweight per day. However, for decades bodybuilders and other athletes have ignored this recommendation and consumed protein in far greater amounts. Quality scientific research now backs up the bodybuilders by demonstrating that these recommendations are inadequate for those involved in high-intensity sports.

Individuals engaged in sports such as bodybuilding, powerlifting, football, rugby or wrestling may find that consuming only the DRI is slowing their recovery times and limiting their muscle growth. It is generally accepted that endurance athletes should consume 1.2 to 1.4 grams per kilogram of bodyweight per day. Strength and bodybuilding athletes need at least 1.4 to 1.8 grams per kilogram of bodyweight per day. However, bodybuilding experts maintain that the optimal amount is 1 gram per pound of bodyweight per day.

Is too much protein dangerous?

Bodybuilders and other athletes have been following high-protein diets for decades. When protein supplements first became available in the 1940s, bodybuilders were the first in line to use them. Since then the traditional bodybuilder has been consuming an average of 1 gram of protein per pound of bodyweight per day. For a 200-pounder that's 200 grams of protein – far more than the average person consumes. Given this, it's not surprising that many in the medical community question this practice and even condemn it. The main argument is that excess protein places tremendous stress on the liver and kidneys because these organs need to work overtime to filter and excrete the waste products generated by protein metabolism. There is no question that individuals who consume excess protein will need to take in a lot of extra water to help digest it and wash away any extra protein circulating in the blood, but if you do consume enough water you should not have a problem in this regard.

Some nutritionists argue that excess protein is simply a waste of money. They say all the protein a bodybuilder needs can be supplied by a regular diet, and those who consume extra protein are simply being misled by supplement-industry marketing. They argue that those who feel extra protein is making a difference are actually driven by the placebo effect. (The placebo effect simply means that a person's belief in a drug can take the place of any actual biochemical effect produced by the drug. So the belief that extra protein increases muscle size causes the muscle to grow, not the extra protein.)

Given that the scientific research is mixed (some studies suggest that athletes benefit from extra protein while other studies show no relationship), we may have to rely more on anecdotal evidence for an answer. Millions of bodybuilders and other athletes have been following high-protein diets for over 50 years. Bodybuilders are all about effects – if something doesn't work, they don't do it – period. If the extra protein really did not make a difference, then bodybuilders would have stopped using it years ago, just as they have with countless other "miracle" supplements.

Unless you have a pre-existing medical condition that limits your protein consumption, we suggest keeping your protein intake somewhere in the .5 to 1 gram per pound of bodyweight range. It has worked for millions of others, so why not you?

> "Never skip breakfast, arguably the most important meal of the day, especially when you want to hype your metabolism and keep losing fat."
>
> – Jerry Kindela, *MuscleMag* Group Editorial Director

SIX ARE BETTER THAN THREE

The biggest animals on the planet spend virtually their entire waking existence eating. Their bodies are continuously being infused with mass-building nutrients. As a bodybuilder, you should be doing something similar. To allow your body to actually absorb and use all the calories you ingest, you must reduce your meal size, but increase your meal frequency. Dividing your calories into smaller, more frequent portions allows the food to be absorbed and utilized more efficiently. If you are one of those "skip breakfast, eat a small lunch, and then a huge supper" types, stop right now! Instead, start viewing your meals not as breakfast, lunch, and supper, but rather as meal 1, meal 2, meal 3, etc. In other words, try to eat six small meals spread out evenly during the day. Every two to three hours eat something small, but nutritious. This ensures that your body always has nutrients on hand for repair and growth.

You should make sure to have some sort of protein at every meal, and optimally that protein should be from animal sources. Soy and plant protein sources such as quinoa have their place, but the truth is that getting enough protein for muscle building is not easy without meat, fish, or at least eggs. That being said, a couple of the top bodybuilders have been vegetarian – Bill Pearl comes to mind – but even they ate eggs and milk products. To maximize your muscle-building potential, you should get most of your protein from such sources as whey, casein (cottage cheese), eggs, beef, poultry, and fish.

FAT – THE GOOD AND THE BAD

Of all the nutrient groups, none have seen such a dramatic turnaround in consumers' minds as fats. Granted, the human body has always depended on certain fats for optimum health. However, the media hype around fat has tarnished the reputation of this vital compound in the eyes of the public. Fats are just as important for health as protein and carbohydrates. Also, despite their name, fats actually play a role in fat loss. Yes, you read correctly! The much-misaligned fat nutrient can actually help you drop body fat and get leaner.

Biochemically, fats are concentrated sources of energy that contain 9 calories per gram versus 4 calories per gram for both protein and carbohydrates. Fats can be divided into a number of different categories, but saturated and unsaturated are the two primary distinctions. Without

Photo of Chris Jalali by Robert Reiff

"Many hardgainers fall short in their total caloric intake because they don't consume enough fat in their diets. However, as we should all know by now, all fats are not created equal. You want to stay away from saturated and trans fats found in prepared foods such as cheese, fatty cuts of meat, sauces, ice cream, donuts, and french fries, but you do want the essential fatty acids (EFAs) found in foods such as salmon, raw nuts, and flaxseed oil."

– Ron Harris, regular *MuscleMag International* contributor

The human body needs certain fats to maintain good health. It's important, however, to be able to distinguish the "good" from the "bad."

going into too much biochemistry, suffice it to say that the terms saturated and unsaturated refer to the number of hydrogen atoms connected (called bonded) to the central carbon atoms. Saturated fats have the full compliment of hydrogen atoms while unsaturated are lacking. Given that hydrogen is nature's simplest atom you wouldn't think that a few less or more of them would make much of a difference. But it makes a huge difference.

Saturated fats are commonly called "bad" fats, but

the word evil is more appropriate! Saturated fats tend to be solid at room temperature. Because the body doesn't digest them easily, they tend to get deposited along arterial walls. It's saturated fat that causes heart disease, stroke, and certain cancers. Your goal should be to keep saturated fat to a minimum. Closely related to saturated fats are trans, or hydrogenated fats. If saturated fat should be kept to a minimum, trans fats should be avoided entirely. This fat mutation is the result of 20th century food processing. As these fats rarely occur in nature, the human body doesn't have the enzymes necessary to break them down. As bad as saturated fat is for increasing the risk of heart disease and stroke, trans and hydrogenated fats are among the greatest health destroyers. Do everything in your power to eliminate them from your diet. No exceptions.

Unsaturated fats are commonly called "good" fats, and can be divided into monounsaturated and polyunsaturated. Unlike their saturated cousins, these fats are vital to life. Unsaturated fats are usually liquid at room temperature and used for metabolic processes such as transporting vitamins A, D, E and K, maintaining cell membranes, maintaining health of skin, eyes and hair, lowering cholesterol levels and serving as a source of energy. They are also used in the manufacturing of some hormones.

Receiving a lot of press these days is the polyunsaturated group referred to as essential fatty acids (EFAs). Essential fatty acids are polyunsaturated fatty acids that the human body requires for optimum health. Like essential amino acids, they cannot be synthesized by the body (except omega-9 in limited quantities) and therefore have to be acquired in the diet. The two most important EFAs are omega-3 and omega-6. Omega-3 fatty acids have a special bond called a "double bond" in the third carbon position from the naming end (hence the use of "3" in their name. Omega-6 fatty acids have their first double

> "If you want to keep shedding adipose tissue, you can't allow the body to get contented with the status quo. Just as you manipulate growth with training adjustment, you should do the same with carb manipulation. Keep the metabolic furnace revved by consuming sweet potatoes, brown rice and yams."
>
> – Jerry Kindela, *MuscleMag* Group Editorial Director

bond in the sixth carbon position from the naming end (hence the "6" designation). It's especially important to make sure you get plenty of omega-3 fats in your diet, as the average healthy North American diet provides plenty (perhaps too much) of the omega-6 fat.

Foods containing high amounts of omega-3 fatty acids include salmon, halibut, sardines, albacore, trout, herring, walnut, flaxseed, hemp seed, chia seed and canola oil. Other foods that contain omega-3 fatty acids in lesser quantities include shrimp, clams, catfish, cod, tuna and spinach. Examples of foods rich in omega-6 fatty acids include whole grains, corn, safflower, sunflower, soybean and cottonseed oil.

EFAs offer numerous health benefits for the human body and help control and regulate an amazing number of metabolic processes. Essential fatty acids help regulate the fluidity of cell membranes and improve their "gate-keeping" abilities by helping keep toxins out and bring nutrients in. Essential fatty acids also influence the activation of cell genes, and help produce eicosanoids. These hormone-like compounds play a role in helping reduce inflammation in the body. They also help keep blood from clotting internally, and help keep the blood vessels dilated (open). Finally, a diet rich in EFAs can be helpful in preventing many diseases including cancer and heart disease.

Fat Storage – A Mixed Bag

As most people are aware, fat – whether good or bad – will be stored if not used immediately as an energy source. While large amounts of fat are undesirable from both a health and physical-appearance point of view, small amounts of stored fat are useful. Stored fat is a readily available source of energy. If carbohydrate levels are low, stored fat can be used as a backup energy source. It also plays a role in cushioning the internal organs against injury

Illustration by Mark Collins

from blows. Finally, fat helps prevent heat loss through the skin (one of the reasons marine mammals have thick layers of fat, called blubber, beneath their skins).

CARBOHYDRATES

The true energy generators of the human body are carbohydrates, or "carbs." Carbs get their name from their chemical makeup of just carbon (C), hydrogen (H), and oxygen (O). The most familiar carbs are sugars, starches, and cellulose. The most common sugar molecule in the human body is glucose. In fact, the liver converts most other simple sugars into glucose.

There are two major types of carbohydrates: simple and complex.

Simple carbohydrates are also called simple sugars and

THE IMPORTANCE OF CARBS

If you are serious about having a hardcore physique you must learn about nutrition. Carbs are the body's primary source of energy. Without enough carbs you can forget going heavy and you'll never have a rock-hard body. The glycogen your body produces from carbs is stored in your muscles. If your carb level is too low, your body must turn to protein as an energy source. Without adequate protein you can't grow. End of story. Carbs also provide glucose to fuel your brain with energy. Carbohydrate intake affects your brain's performance, your mood and personality. You may find it helpful to obtain a chart that lists the glycemic index of foods and then eat carbs that rate very low.

occur in foods such as candies, cookies and cakes. In fact, just about any food that contains refined sugars (such as the white sugar you find in a sugar dish) can be considered a simple sugar food. Simple sugars also occur in more nutritious foods such as milk, fruit and some vegetables. Hopefully, most readers are aware that it makes far more sense to obtain simple sugars from fruits and vegetables than from sodas and candy! Fruits and vegetables provide you with more than sugar – they'll be giving you vitamins, minerals and fiber. That extra-large slice of cake does not provide these nutrients.

Complex carbohydrates take longer than simple sugars for the body to break down. Unrefined grains are loaded with valuable nutrients such as vitamins, minerals, and fiber (which helps your digestive system work better, as well as help you feel full, making you less likely to overeat). Have you ever noticed that a bowl of hearty oatmeal makes you feel full, while a sugary cereal with the same number of calories leaves you wanting more? Most vegetables are also good sources of complex carbs.

As soon as you eat carbohydrates, the body starts breaking them down into simple sugars. These sugars are then absorbed into the bloodstream. As the sugar level rises in your body, the pancreas releases a hormone called insulin. Insulin transports the sugar from the blood into the cells, where it's used as a source of energy. If this process moves quickly – as it usually does with simple sugars – you're more likely to feel hungry that much sooner. Complex carbs (i.e. whole grains), however, take much longer to break down and you won't experience those hunger cravings as quickly. Complex carbohydrates give you energy over a longer period of time.

Besides their relationship to energy, complex carbs are healthier. As you just read, simple sugars cause a rapid rise in insulin (called an insulin spike). Over time, this extra stress on the pancreas can lead to diabetes. Diabetes is caused by an insufficient production of insulin or an inability of the body's insulin receptors to interact with the hormone. In either case, the end result could be multiple medical problems including obesity, cardiovascular disease, reduced circulation in the extremities (often leading to amputation), and blindness. Although the primary

A bodybuilder's diet needs all the macronutrients — not just protein. Experiment with herbs and spices to keep it interesting.

focus of this chapter is on eating for bodybuilding purposes, you're also improving your overall health by restricting your intake of simple sugars. Eating complex carbohydrates – whole grains such as brown rice, quinoa, wheat berries, oats, barley; whole wheat breads and pastas; and most vegetables, including potatoes and sweet potatoes – is guaranteed to have you looking and feeling great.

VITAMINS

Much of the early information about vitamins comes from the research on diseases, including scurvy and beriberi. Scurvy probably killed more sailors than any enemy gun action. It was a Scottish surgeon by the name of James Lind who discovered that the disease could be prevented by citrus fruits, including limes (this is where the popular nickname for British sailors, "Limey," came from).

While Lind knew that something in citrus fruit was helping prevent the condition, it would be over one hundred years before the first vitamins were isolated. The father of vitamin research is considered to be Casimir Funk, a Polish biochemist studying the malnutrition disease beriberi, in London. Funk found he could prevent the disease by administering a powerful compound isolated from rice. Given that the compound was an amine (organic compound containing nitrogen), and vital to life, he coined the term "vit amine" or vitamine. Later, as similar compounds were discovered that were not amines, the final "e" was dropped and the present term "vitamin" was adopted.

Vitamins can be defined as inorganic compounds that are necessary for growth, health and normal metabolism. They may act as enzymes (substances that speed up or slow down chemical reactions) or as essential components of hormones.

Vitamins can be divided into two categories: fat-solu-

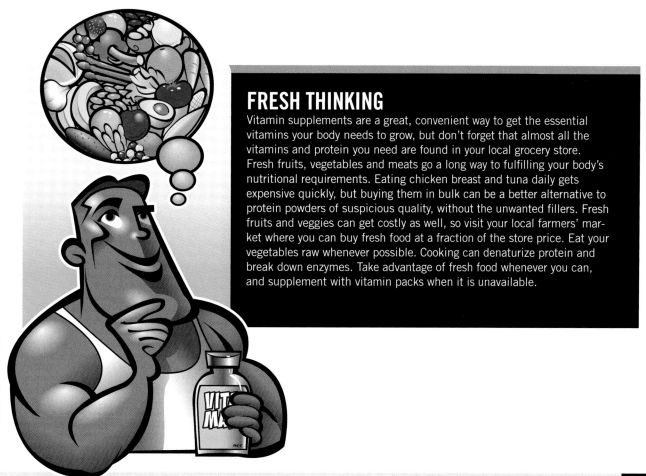

FRESH THINKING

Vitamin supplements are a great, convenient way to get the essential vitamins your body needs to grow, but don't forget that almost all the vitamins and protein you need are found in your local grocery store. Fresh fruits, vegetables and meats go a long way to fulfilling your body's nutritional requirements. Eating chicken breast and tuna daily gets expensive quickly, but buying them in bulk can be a better alternative to protein powders of suspicious quality, without the unwanted fillers. Fresh fruits and veggies can get costly as well, so visit your local farmers' market where you can buy fresh food at a fraction of the store price. Eat your vegetables raw whenever possible. Cooking can denature protein and break down enzymes. Take advantage of fresh food whenever you can, and supplement with vitamin packs when it is unavailable.

Illustration by Mark Collins

PRIMARY FAT-SOLUBLE VITAMINS

VITAMIN	NATURAL SOURCE	FUNCTION	DRI*
A	Liver, sweet potatoes	Vision	900 mcg
D	Fish oil, egg yolk	Bone growth & repair	5 mcg
E	Sunflower seeds, almonds	Fights free radicals	15 mcg
K	Green vegetables	Blood clotting	120 mcg

*DRI is Daily Recommended Intake for men 19–50. Institute of Medicine. http://www.iom.edu/Object.File/Master/21/372/0.pdf. 27 March 2008
*http://www.health.gov/dietaryguidelines/dga2005/document/html/appendix B.htm. 27 March 2008

PRIMARY WATER-SOLUBLE VITAMINS

VITAMIN	NATURAL SOURCE	FUNCTION	DRI*
B-1	Whole grain cereals, liver	Carbohydrate metabolism	1.2 mg
B-2	Milk, nuts	Red blood cell formation	1.3 mg
B-3	Liver, whole grains	Reduces cholesterol	16 mg
B-5	Whole grains, eggs	Fights free radicals	5 mg
B-6	Liver, oatmeal	Strengthens immune system	1.3 mg
B-9	Wheat germ, greens, vegetables	Red blood cell formation	400 mg
B-12	Shellfish, liver, eggs	Carbohydrate metabolism	2.4 mcg
C	Citrus fruits, greens, vegetables	Strengthens immune system	90 mg

*DRI is Daily Recommended Intake for men 19–50. Institute of Medicine. http://www.iom.edu/Object.File/Master/21/372/0.pdf. 27 March 2008
*http://www.health.gov/dietaryguidelines/dga2005/document/html/appendix B.htm. 27 March 2008

ble and water-soluble.

Fat-Soluble Vitamins

Fat-soluble vitamins are named as such because they dissolve in dietary fat. When excess amounts are consumed in the diet and not used right away, they are stored as body fat for later use. Of course this storage can be a double-edged sword. Some of the fat-soluble vitamins can be toxic to the body, particularly the liver, in excessive amounts. Too much vitamin D has even been linked to heart disease and kidney stones.

Water-Soluble Vitamins

Unlike fat-soluble vitamins, water-soluble vitamins cannot be stored in the body to any great extent and must be consumed in the diet on a daily basis. Under certain circumstances that are stressful on our bodies such as illness, injury, disease and intense exercise, individuals may have difficulty obtaining adequate amounts in their diet. In this case a vitamin supplement may be necessary.

MINERALS AND TRACE ELEMENTS

The terms mineral and trace element are really just different names for the same substances. Biochemists and nutri-

> In order to build muscle and gain strength you must take in all the needed minerals and not just those that receive media attention like calcium and iron. I suspect one of the reasons minerals are not as popular as vitamins or the more trendy products on the market is because they are relatively inexpensive."
>
> – Bill Starr, regular *MuscleMag International* contributor

tionists use the term mineral if the body needs more than 100 mg (milligrams) of a particular element each day. If less is required, the term trace element is used. Both minerals and trace elements can be defined as inorganic substances that the body needs for growth, maintenance, and repair. They are also used for nerve conduction, heart rate regulation, and water conservation. Because minerals and trace elements are only needed in very small amounts, deficiencies in Western society are very rare. Possible exceptions include athletes who train in hot weather, those suffering from wasting diseases and women with heavy menstrual periods.

FIBER

Fiber is one of those catch-all terms, in this case used to describe plant material that can't be digested by the body. Most fiber comes from the tougher parts of plants, including stems, roots, seeds, and leaves. The primary component of most fibrous compounds is cellulose. Fiber passes through the gastrointestinal tract mostly undigested until it reaches the large intestine, where it helps to form stool and maintain regularity. Dietary fiber plays an important role in the prevention of many diseases, including colon cancer. A high-fiber diet has also been proven to help people lose weight. Since the fiber takes longer to move through the digestive system, you feel satisfied longer and thus do not overeat. As well, soluble fiber fills up with water and makes you feel full.

For superior health, people should get 25 to 30 grams of fiber each day. The best sources of fiber include whole grains, vegetables, fruit, nuts, seeds and beans. This is yet another reason to avoid processed food – the fiber has been removed from most processed foods.

SALT

Salt is a compound made from two elements, sodium and chlorine. Salt is a mixed bag when it comes to nutrients. On one hand, it's vital for metabolic processes such as nerve conduction, muscle contraction, and water regulation. On the other hand, excessive amounts can cause heart disease and kidney problems. However, most individuals won't need to make a conscious effort to consume salt – they'll get more than they need in their diets. Just two slices of bread supplies the body's daily salt requirements. In general, your goal is to try to reduce your salt intake.

WATER

In many respects, water is probably the most important single nutrient. You could live for only a few days at most without water. Water is a major component of every cell and makes up about two-thirds of the mass of the human body. It forms most of the volume of human blood, serves as the medium for virtually all chemical reactions, is essential for digestion, helps regulate body heat and plays a major role in waste excretion.

A typical person will lose about two liters of water every day through waste excretion and sweating – more if involved in intense exercise or working outdoors in hot weather. It's for this reason that water should be consumed on a regular basis. Start with six to eight glasses a day and add more when needed. During a typical workout, you should try to sip and drink at least one liter. Try taking a sip of water after every set of an exercise.

> **Not only is it a key nutrient that is crucial to good health, but when included as part of a clean protein and complex carb-rich diet, fiber can help bodybuilders both stay lean and build fat-free mass."**
>
> – S.J. Wells, *MuscleMag International* contributor

CHAPTER 29

Cholesterol

"Cholesterol plays a vital role in bodily functions. Every cell in the human body contains and requires cholesterol for life. If the AHA (American Heart Association) keeps lowering the level considered to be a normal blood cholesterol level, the incidence of heart attacks won't even matter because life itself will cease without an adequate supply of essential cholesterol."

– Dr. Melvin Anchell, offering his views on the AHA's stance with regards to what's considered normal cholesterol levels.

Cholesterol is another food ingredient that gets more than its fair share of bad press. Biochemically, cholesterol is a steroid-based molecule related to fat. Despite what you sometimes hear, cholesterol is needed in small amounts for good health. It is a major structural component of many body tissues, including the cardiovascular and nervous systems. It's also used in the synthesis of many of the sex and adrenal hormones, as well as some digestive enzymes.

There are two primary forms of cholesterol: high-density lipoprotein (HDL) and low-density lipoprotein (LDL). From a health point of view, your goal is to keep HDL levels high and LDL levels low. LDLs tend to be sticky in texture and attach more easily to arterial walls, causing blockages. If the blocked arteries happen to be located in the heart, the end result could be a heart attack. Blocked arteries in limbs can lead to cell death, gangrene, and eventually amputation. Evolution has decided that HDLs should be used to combat the destructive LDLs. HDLs attach to and carry away LDLs before they have a chance to build up on arterial walls. HDLs also carry extra cholesterol to the liver, where it is converted to bile salts and excreted.

Most readers are probably aware of the risk factors that negatively impact cholesterol. While you have little control over genetics, such lifestyle factors as smoking, drinking, nutrition, and exercise can be controlled. Quit smoking (or never start), reduce your alcohol consumption, cut down on saturated and trans fat, and start exercising – including cardio (hopefully you're already way ahead on this one!).

CHOLESTEROL BLOOD TESTS

Even if you're following this advice it's a good idea to have regular blood tests performed to check your cholesterol levels. Now you probably think that a blood test for cholesterol would simply tell you how much cholesterol is in your body. Well it does, but doctors actually use several measurements to deduce your risk of developing cardiovascular disease.

The three measurements are:

LDL cholesterol

HDL cholesterol

Total cholesterol

The first thing I should tell you is that total cholesterol doesn't simply mean LDL cholesterol plus HDL cholesterol. There are additional types of cholesterol, but I really don't need to discuss them here.

Cholesterol is measured as milligrams of cholesterol per deciliter of blood. Medical types have abbreviated it as mg/dL. In some cases only your total cholesterol will be measured, other times you will get results for all three. With regards to total cholesterol, here is a general guide:

Less than 200 mg/dL	Optimal
200–239 mg/dL	Borderline high
240 mg/dL and above	Too high

The values for HDL cholesterol are as follows:

Less than 40 mg/dL	Too low
More than 40 mg/dL	Desirable
Above 60 mg/dL	Optimal

If you are 20 years or older and have no signs of heart disease, the values for LDL cholesterol are as follows:

Less than 100 mg/dL	Optimal
100–129 mg/dL	Near optimal
130–159 mg/dL	Borderline high
160–189 mg/dL	High
190 mg/dL and above	Extremely high

Your doctor may give you these cholesterol values as a ratio of total cholesterol to HDL cholesterol. This is calculated by dividing your total cholesterol by your HDL cholesterol. According to the American Heart Association (AHA), the ratio should be below 5:1. A ratio of 3.5:1 is considered optimal.

So, you should not simply keep track of your cholesterol levels, but you should also do everything in your power to keep your LDL levels low and HDL levels high.

FOODS TO HELP LOWER CHOLESTEROL

Most of us probably realize that fried foods, ice cream, and fatty red meats raise cholesterol levels. Well here's some great news. There are actually foods you can add to your diet to reduce your cholesterol levels. Researchers have discovered that some foods, particularly deep sea fish, oatmeal, walnuts, and foods high in plant sterols, can help regulate your cholesterol. Research has also revealed that a diet combining some of these foods may be just as effective at reducing cholesterol as cholesterol-lowering drugs (particularly LDL or "bad" cholesterol).

In no particular order, here are some superfoods that will help keep your arteries cholesterol free for decades to come!

Oatmeal and Other Fibrous Foods

Besides tasting great and being a staple breakfast food, oatmeal is loaded with soluble fiber. Soluble fiber has been shown to reduce LDL, the "bad" cholesterol. Soluble fiber is also found the following foods: brussels sprouts, pears, apples and prunes.

Some fibers – especially the gel-like soluble fiber – binds bile (which also contains cholesterol) and free cho-

Nuts

For years nuts have had a bad reputation because they are high in fat. However, most nuts, especially almonds and walnuts, have high amounts of monounsaturated or polyunsaturated fats – the "good" fats. These fats actually help to lower cholesterol levels. Researchers at Loma Linda University discovered that a diet fortified with pecans not only lowered total and LDL cholesterol significantly, but also helped keep levels of HDL high. Other studies, such as those studying Mediterranean-style diets high in walnuts, also demonstrated the cholesterol-lowering abilities of nuts. The evidence is in, so don't be afraid to go nuts on a regular basis!

Fruits and Vegetables

While some of the foods on this list may surprise you, most readers are probably aware of the numerous health benefits of fruits and vegetables. Fresh fruits and vegetables such as apples, pears, citrus fruit, berries, green leafy vegetables and yams are high in soluble fiber and pectin. Both have shown to be beneficial in reducing cholesterol levels. Try to have at least five servings a day for the full benefits.

lesterol so the body can excrete it faster, thereby reducing its absorption in the intestines. You don't need to eat whopping amounts either – just five to ten grams of soluble fiber a day decreases your LDL cholesterol by about 5 percent. One cup of cooked oatmeal provides you with a solid 4 grams of fiber.

Soy Protein

Don't worry guys, soy protein won't make you grow breasts, but it just may keep you from developing heart disease. The cholesterol-reducing abilities of soy protein was confirmed when the FDA approved the health claim for soy's capability to reduce the risk of heart disease. For optimum effect, it is recommended that you consume at least four servings of about 6 to 6.5 grams of soy protein per day, totaling 25 to 26 grams. Since the health benefits claims and FDA endorsement, many supplement manufacturers have introduced soy drinks and protein bars containing 10 to 20 grams of soy protein.

Flaxseed Oil

Flaxseed oil is high in alpha-linolenic acid (a polyunsaturated fat), which has been proven to lower cholesterol. Studies show that flaxseed helps lower total and LDL cholesterol levels. Other research has revealed that another ingredient in flaxseed, omega-3 fatty acid, may also help lower blood triglyceride levels and blood pressure. It may also keep blood platelets from becoming sticky and adhering to arterial walls. So if you're already using flaxseed and/or flaxseed oil, keep doing so. If not, head to the supplement store right now. Make sure to buy whole seeds, then grind it at home and keep it in the fridge to avoid rancidity.

Olive Oil

There are centuries of evidence showing that people who follow Mediterranean diets have a low occurrence of heart attacks. One of the reasons is the high amounts of olive oil in such diets. Olive oil contains large amounts of monounsaturated fats and studies have shown that it can lower both LDL and total blood cholesterol levels. There is also evidence to suggest that olive oil reduces the clotting ability of blood; not to the point that it's dangerous, but to the extent that it helps prevent buildup on the arterial walls. So even if you can't afford that trip to Italy or Spain, place a bottle of olive oil on your kitchen table.

Fish

Studies from the 1970s showed that the Greenland Inuit had lower rates of heart disease than any other ethnic group living in the area. After analyzing the data, the researchers came to the conclusion that the diet of the Inuit – specifically fish, seal and whale meat – was the cause. Fish oil and sea mammals contain high amounts of omega-3 polyunsaturated fatty acids that make the blood more slippery and less likely to clot. Omega-3 fatty acids also seem to lower total and LDL cholesterol levels. The best sources of fish are salmon, herring, trout and sardines.

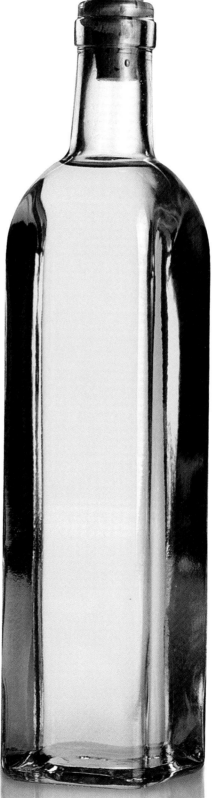

CHAPTER 30

Digestion

"Learn to chew and spend more time masticating your food. You cannot expect to zoom through a 30-minute meal in just eight minutes! Body processes cannot be rushed."

– Editorial in *MuscleMag International*

Bodybuilders are often knowledgeable about carbohydrates, fats and proteins, but they should also understand what happens to food after it has entered their digestive system. Because the vast majority of foods are too large to be absorbed across the plasma membranes of the cells, the food must be broken down first, both chemically and mechanically. This process is called digestion.

What follows is a very technical discussion of digestion and metabolism. Outside of a biology or medical textbook one would not normally encounter such detail. My logic for adopting this approach was to ensure that you, the bodybuilder, would be fully informed as to how your digestive system works. Understanding this process empowers you to make better decisions regarding diet and the use, or nonuse, of supplements.

Mechanical digestion consists of various movements that aid chemical digestion. Food must be broken down by the teeth before it can be swallowed. The smooth muscles of the stomach and small intestine then churn the food so it is thoroughly mixed with the enzymes that catalyze the reactions.

Chemical digestion is a series of catabolic (decomposition) reactions that break down the large carbohydrate, lipid and protein molecules of food into smaller molecules. These products of digestion are small enough to pass through the walls of the digestive organs, into the blood and lymph capillaries, and finally into the body's cells.

The digestive system is divided into two main sections: the gastrointestinal tract (GI), also referred to as the alimentary canal, and the accessory organs. The

GI is made up of the mouth, pharynx, esophagus, stomach, small intestine and large intestine. The GI tract holds the food from the time it is eaten until it is prepared for excretion. Muscular contractions in the walls of the GI tract break down the food physically by churning it. Secretions produced by cells along the GI tract break down the food chemically.

The accessory organs include the teeth, tongue, salivary glands, liver, gallbladder, pancreas and appendix. Teeth aid in the physical breakdown of food. With the exception of the tongue, the accessory organs lie outside the GI tract, and produce or store secretions that aid the chemical breakdown of food. These secretions are released into the tract through ducts.

DIGESTION – BY LOCATION

The Mouth

For the most part digestion in the mouth is done by the salivary glands, teeth and tongue. The salivary glands produce most of the saliva, with the buccal glands of the mucus membranes that line the mouth producing the remainder. Saliva is a fluid continuously secreted by glands in or near the mouth. Saliva is secreted to keep the mucous membranes of the mouth moist. When food enters the mouth, secretion increases so saliva can lubricate, dissolve and chemically break down the food. Through chewing, the teeth tear the food apart and mix it with saliva. Saliva is 99.5 percent water and 0.5 percent solutes. These include salts (chlorides, bicarbonates, and phosphates of sodium and potassium); mucin; the bacteriolytic enzyme lysozyme; and the digestive enzyme amylase.

The water in saliva provides a medium for dissolving foods so they can be tasted and so digestive reactions can be carried out. The chlorides in the saliva activate the amylase. The bicarbonates and phosphates buffer chemicals that enter the mouth and keep the saliva at a slightly acidic pH of 6.35 to 6.85. Mucin is a protein that forms mucus when dissolved in water. Mucus lubricates the food so it can be easily turned in the mouth, formed into a ball, or bolus, and swallowed. The enzyme lysozyme destroys bacteria, thereby protecting the mucus membrane from infection and the teeth from decay. The enzyme salivary amylase initiates the breakdown of polysaccharides (carbohydrates); this is the only chemical digestion that occurs in the mouth. The function of salivary amylase is to break the chemical bonds between some of the monosaccharides that make up the polysaccharides called dextrins. In time the enzyme can further break down the dextrins into disaccharide maltose, but the food is usually swallowed so quickly that only 3 to 5 percent of the dextrins are broken down in the mouth. The salivary amylase continues to act on the polysaccharides in the stomach for another 15 to 30 minutes until stomach acids inactivate the enzyme.

Before we go any further, consider what you've just read. When bodybuilding contests became popular decades ago, judges used to inspect the contestants' teeth! Perhaps it wasn't such a silly concept after all. What's the point of buying expensive foods and supplements if you can't digest them properly? Just as an army marches on its stomach, the

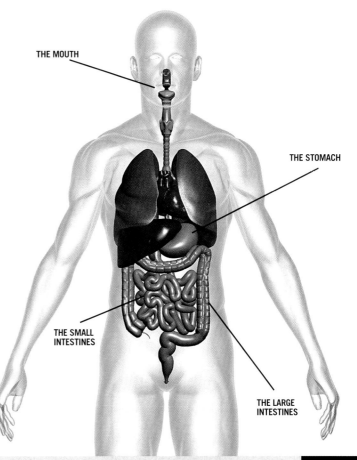

THE MOUTH

THE STOMACH

THE SMALL INTESTINES

THE LARGE INTESTINES

most important muscles in bodybuilding are found in the digestive tract. Before you work them out, see your dentist.

After being chewed, food is swallowed (deglutition) and travels down the esophagus (a muscular, collapsible tube located behind the trachea). The food is pushed down by muscular contractions in a process called peristalsis. It then passes through the inferior part of the esophagus, called the gastroesophageal sphincter (a sphincter is an opening that has a thick circle of muscle around it), into the stomach.

The Stomach

A few minutes after food enters the stomach, peristaltic movements ripple across the stomach every 15 to 25 seconds except for in a part of the stomach called the fundus, which acts as a storage area. Here foods may sit for an hour or more with only salivary digestion continuing. In the rest of the stomach the movements, or mixing waves, churn the food with the gastric secretions, producing a thin liquid called chyme.

The main chemical activity of the stomach is to begin the breakdown of proteins. This is accomplished by the gastric juice, which is made up by the enzymes pepsin and rennin, and hydrochloric acid (HCl). Pepsin breaks certain peptide bonds between the amino acids that make up proteins. Hence a protein chain of many amino acids is broken down into fragments of amino acids. Long fragments are called proteoses and short fragments are called peptones.

Rennin helps solidify casein, a milk protein. Thus it can be held in the stomach long enough for pepsin to break it down. Pepsin is most effective in the acidic environment of the stomach (pH of 1). The HCl in the gastric juice ensures an acidic medium.

A less important enzyme is gastric lipase. This enzyme breaks down the butterfat molecules in milk. Because this enzyme works best at a pH of 5 to 6, adults rely on an enzyme in the small intestine to digest fats.

The stomach releases its contents into the duodenum two to six hours after ingestion. Food rich in carbohydrates leaves the stomach in a short period of time. Protein-rich foods are slower, and fatty foods are the slowest of all to be emptied out. The stomach is impermeable to the passage of most materials into the blood (with the exception of some water, salts, certain drugs and alcohol), so most substances are not absorbed until they reach the small intestine.

The Small Intestine

Chemical digestion in the small intestine depends not only on its own secretions but also on the activities of three organs outside the GI tract: the liver, gallbladder and pancreas.

Carbohydrates in the form of dextrins are reduced to disaccharide maltose by the enzyme pancreatic amylase. Two other disaccharides, sucrose and lactose, are also reduced. The enzyme sucrase splits sucrose into a molecule of fructose and a molecule of glucose. Lactose is reduced to a molecule of glucose and a molecule of galactose by the enzyme lactase. And the enzyme maltase splits maltose into two molecules of glucose.

Proteins that may have escaped reduction in the stomach are dealt with in the small intestine. The pancreatic enzymes trypsin and chymotrypsin digest intact proteins into proteoses and peptones, and break them into dipeptides (containing only two amino acids), and divide some of the dipeptides into single amino acids. The enzyme carboxypeptidase reduces whole or partly digested proteins to amino acids. Any remaining dipeptides are reduced to single amino acids by a group of enzymes given the collective name erepsin.

Fats are digested in the small intestine. Bile salts break down the globules of fat into droplets (emulsification) so the fat-splitting enzyme can attack the fat molecules. Then the enzyme pancreatic lipase hydrolyzes each fat molecule into fatty acids, glycerol and glycerides.

Mechanical digestion consists of three distinct peristaltic movements, which serve to mix the chyme with the digestive juices and move the entire mixture further down the GI tract.

The products of digestion are now ready for absorption. The monosaccharides and amino acids are absorbed into the blood capillaries of the villi and transported via the bloodstream to the liver. Fatty acids, glycerol and glycerides are surrounded by bile salts to form water-soluble particles called micelles, which are then absorbed into the intestinal epithelial cells. The fat molecules are resynthesized. These molecules, together with small amounts of cholesterol and phospholipids, are organized into protein-coated fat droplets called chylomicrons. The protein coat prevents the chylomicrons from sticking to each other and to the walls of the lymphatic and circulatory system. Transported by these two systems, the chylomicrons reach the liver.

The Large Intestine

Digestion is almost complete by the time the chyme reaches the large intestine. Bacterial action results in the synthesis of vitamin K and some of the B vitamins. Any remaining proteins and amino acids are broken down by bacteria into simpler substances: fatty acids, hydrogen sulfide, skatole and indole. Together with intestinal water, some of it is absorbed. What is left is passed out of the body.

METABOLISM

Growth is an adaptively regulated process in which anabolism predominates over catabolism. For bodybuilding this means the building up of protein into the permanent muscle mass of the bodybuilder. The passing of digestive products from the GI tract to the circulatory and lymphatic systems makes these products available to be incorporated into the living tissues of the body. But these products will also be used for maintenance, stored as energy reserves, or burned off immediately to satisfy present energy demands. A simple meal initiates a complex sequence of events that are all compounded by the body's need to maintain an internal balance, called homeostasis. Life depends on the composition of body fluids remaining, within very narrow boundaries. The flood of lymph and blood with the products of digestion provides counter to this principle. Thus the body uses hormones such as insulin and human growth hormone (HGH) to restore normalcy.

The point here is that just because you consume a high-quality supplement does not mean you will see a corresponding increase in muscle mass. The body has its own agenda. Those multivitamins and carbohydrates will have their fates

decided at the cellular level. The only certainty is that we can artificially shift the odds in favor of greater muscle mass by consuming high-quality foods and supplements while creating a metabolic demand through heavy exercise.

Metabolism of Fat

The metabolism of fat is controlled partly by hormones from the pituitary and adrenal glands, and partly by sex hormones. Any severe disturbance of liver function results in the almost complete absence of fat from the usual adipose tissues. This indicates that the fat must be acted upon in some way by the liver before it can be stored or metabolized.

Gluconeogenesis

Current research has demonstrated that in addition to carbohydrates and fats, amino acids can contribute to energy metabolism. During periods of exercise, hormones called glucocorticoids are released from the adrenal glands located on top of the kidneys. These hormones cause the body to remove amino acids from muscle tissue.

Glucocorticoids work with other hormones in promoting normal metabolism. Their role is to make sure enough energy is provided. They increase the rate at which amino acids are removed from cells and transported to the liver. These amino acids may be synthesized into new proteins, such as the enzymes needed for metabolic reactions. If the body's reserves of glycogen or fat are low, the liver may convert amino acids to glucose. This process is called gluconeogenesis.

Photo of Leo Ingram by Paul Buceta

CHAPTER 31

Nutrition 201

"Your daily nutrition will dictate the extent of your muscle growth. Everything you eat and drink affects your body. The most important thing to remember is that food is your friend. Be sure you're eating six meals a day. Each meal should be high in protein, high in complex carbs and low in fat."

– Editors of *MuscleMag International*, outlining the importance of good nutrition to bodybuilding success.

You'd be amazed at the number of people who have no idea how to buy and prepare food. Nutrition is very important for both bodybuilding and health purposes. Moreover, there's nothing like a well-prepared, great-tasting and nutritious meal – especially after a tough workout.

OUTFITTING YOUR KITCHEN

In many respects, your kitchen is like the gym – it contains a lot of equipment for building things. At the gym, it's your muscles being built, but in the kitchen you are creating meals to support your muscles. If you are serious about bodybuilding, you'll need certain helpful appliances to outfit your kitchen. These include a fridge, freezer, stove (or hotplate and small toaster oven), blender (or food processor), and microwave oven.

The fridge and freezer are your two primary storage appliances. Short-term items will be stored in the fridge, and the long-term items should be placed in the freezer. Don't just randomly toss things in the fridge and freezer. Organize it like a filing cabinet. Divide your fridge and freezer into sections and group the foods into categories such as meats, fish, breads, vegetables and fruits. If you're using plastic containers, label each so you don't need to go opening and closing them every time you're looking for a particular food item.

DREADED LEFTOVERS

Bodybuilders who cook for themselves may go overboard with their portions by cooking too much at one time. Although cooking in volume can be a great time saver, it can also lead to the temptation to pile up your plate with more than you need. This increases the risk of putting on unnecessary body fat. Research has shown that people eat more than they need when extra helpings are available. If you cook in batches to save time, pack up the extra meals in freezer-safe containers and put them away before you sit down to eat.

This will save you time and minimize the risk of contamination due to increased air exposure.

Here are some other tips:

• Remove as much air as possible when you place food in freezer bags. Trapped air absorbs flavor from food, and also contains moisture that will form frost that can destroy flavor and transfer odors to other foods.

• Try to seal freezer bags and containers as airtight as possible. This prevents moisture from leaking in and out. You can also use freezer tape to keep the bags/containers even more secure.

• Try not to over pack your freezer. Having space around food allows for a more even freezing.

• While heat will usually kill germs, extreme cold may not. It may just put them in hibernation. Therefore, always wash your hands thoroughly before and after handling food that is to be frozen.

• Don't use metal to wrap acidic foods, as the acid could leech metal into the food. Some metals are toxic to humans even in low concentrations.

• Date and label all containers. This way you know what it is and more importantly, how old it is. Chomping down into a piece of meat or fish dating from the Reagan administration is not a good idea!

Even in a deep freeze most foods are only good for three months to one year.

Here's a rough guide for some common foods:

FOOD	TIME IN FREEZER
Stews	6 months
Meat and poultry	3 to 6 months
Soups	6 months
Fish	3 to 6 months
Sandwiches	1 to 2 months
Vegetables	3 to 6 months

THE MICROWAVE OVEN

In many respects, the microwave is your best friend. You'll use it to heat your food. Notice I said heat and not cook. Yes you can cook with a microwave, but cooking with a conventional oven is almost foolproof. Microwave cooking needs to be much more precise. A few extra minutes in a regular oven will probably not make much difference to your food item, but it could ruin the food entirely in a microwave.

Microwave ovens work by converting electrical energy into microwave energy that is directed at the food. Water molecules in the food absorb this energy and then begin to vibrate – up to 2.45 billion vibrations per second! Such high vibrations cause a lot of friction inside of the food and this leads to heat. This heat then cooks the food. That's why they say microwaves cook food from the inside out.

There are dos and don'ts with regards to what you can put in the microwave. The best containers to use are glass and ceramic. Many plastics leach dangerous chemicals when heated, so make sure plastic container says "microwave safe" before using — or even better, avoid plastic altogether. Under no circumstances should you place metal or metal wrap in your microwave. The end result will be an electrical storm in your kitchen! You should even check to make sure that your glassware is microwave-friendly. Most manufacturers place warning print on the bottom saying if their product is compatible or not.

Also, don't put airtight containers or bags in the microwave. As the food heats up it will increase the air pressure inside the bag or container. If this pressure is not released slowly, it will build up and the bag or container will explode. At the very least, you'll have a mess to clean up, but you might also have a destroyed kitchen on your hands. I should also add that some foods may act like airtight containers. The biggest culprits are eggs, which have been known to exhibit grenade-like properties when cooked in microwaves. The worst thing about eggs is that they might explode after you remove them from the microwave, causing eye injuries or severe burns. While a black eye from a fistfight may be a badge of honor, being taken out by an egg is just downright embarrassing.

Make sure if you're heating up food in a plate or bowl to cover lightly with another plate. This allows air to escape, but prevents food exploding all over the inside of your microwave. This is especially important when heating up food containing beans or peas.

Consult your microwave oven's manual for precise heat times and power settings for different foods. It will give you recommendations as to what power setting to use for each type of food and how long to warm it.

TOO COOK OR NOT TO COOK?

While most bodybuilding magazines are a treasure trove of nutrition articles, occasionally an article will creep in that is just out to lunch (no pun intended)! For example, some articles actually promote the benefits of eating raw meat or fish. Yes it's true that cooking will reduce the nutritional content of meat and fish by some degree. But cooking does more than just make meat and fish more palatable – it also kills the germs. Perhaps the single biggest advancement in preventative medicine was the discovery of fire because it made eating meat safe. The occasional meal of sushi in a respectable restaurant is probably relatively safe, but if you get into a habit of eating raw meat (and this includes eggs), sooner or later you'll develop a case of salmonella poisoning, contract a tapeworm, or suffer the consequences of some new, undetected virus. Besides, contrary to popular belief, raw eggs have considerably less bioavailable protein. In fact, a raw egg has a BV of only 51, whereas a cooked egg has a BV of 91.

Although I strongly urge you to cook all your meat and fish, most raw vegetables are fine. There are very few bacte-

ria and other germs in plant foods that are harmful to humans. This means that you can eat them raw. It's still a good idea to give everything a good wash before eating it, but there's no need to leech most of the nutrients out by boiling vegetables in hot water. If you have a hard time digesting vegetables or simply prefer them to have a softer texture, simply steam them. Doing so preserves most of the nutrients while still maintaining taste. Roasted veggies are great, too.

If the idea of whole vegetables and fruits is still distasteful to you, try cutting them into medium-sized chunks and tossing them into a blender. There are endless amounts of delicious shake recipes that can be made with fruits and vegetables. Later in the chapter on supplements, I'll give you some recipes.

COOKING OILS

Quick question: what do you think is the best oil to use for cooking? Is it olive, canola or soybean? Or is it corn, peanut or sunflower? How about just plain ol' butter? While personal taste plays a major role, there are a few points that need to be considered.

Cooking

The first thing to understand is that cooking at high temperatures can damage oils. Ironically, the more omega-3 fatty acids in the oil, the less suitable it is for cooking. The heat not only breaks down the fatty acids, it also converts them into harmful substances. This is why hydrogenated oils are often used for cooking. Since they have already been "damaged" by previous chemical processing, they are less likely to be further damaged by heat. Oils that are high in saturated fats or monounsaturates (peanut and olive) are usually the most stable when heated.

To preserve the health benefits and the flavor of unrefined oils, try the "wet-sauté" technique practiced by gourmet chefs around the world. Add about a quarter-cup of water to a frying pan and heat to just below boiling point. Then add the food and cook it for a few minutes before adding the oil. Wet-sautéing shortens the time the oil is in contact with the hot pan, allowing you to use more flavorful oils. Stirring frequently helps, too. Never heat oils to the smoking point, because this damages their fatty acid content and destroys their taste.

Storing

If you buy your oil in large quantities, store it in dark bottles. Clear plastic or glass bottles easily allow light to penetrate the oil. A chemical process called oxidizing, similar to rusting on metals, then occurs. If the oil comes in a clear bottle, either transfer it to a dark bottle or wrap it with a dark covering. Also, try to keep the lid on tightly between uses because contact with air will also affect the quality of the oil. It's better to buy oil in small quantities. Although this may be slightly more expensive, it will ensure that you'll use it before it spoils. You should also store oil in a cool, dark place. Most cooking oils spoil when exposed to warm temperatures, so they need to be refrigerated if you are not going to use them right away. The notable exception to this is olive oil, which need not be refrigerated because it is high in both oleic acid and antioxidants, which slow the spoiling process.

Organic?

If you can afford it, paying extra for organic oils is definitely worthwhile. Many oils come from plants that are heavily sprayed with herbicides and pesticides. As most herbicides and pesticides are fat-soluble, the chemicals concentrate in the oil portion of the plant. One of the safest oils is extra virgin oil, which is not refined or deodorized, and may even be organically grown.

Labeling woes

The already negligent food-labeling laws are especially careless when it comes to oils. Avoid any oil simply labeled "vegetable oil." You have every right to know which vegetables they are talking about. The same warning goes for "all-purpose" vegetable oils. Chances are that the manufacturer simply added inexpensive, highly processed oils such as cottonseed oil to top up the bottle. You should also be aware that most labels do not list the types of fatty acids the oil contains (i.e. the amounts of omega-3 and omega-6). The label should state whether the oil was chemically extracted or mechanically pressed. Obviously you should look for mechanically extracted oils, but as this method is usually more expensive to produce, most manufacturers opt for the chemical process. If the oil is pressed, the label will say it, so if it doesn't, assume the worst.

The best?

Now that you have a basic understanding of cooking oils, the next step is to choose one. As I said earlier, personal preference will play a role in regards to taste. Unless you have a specific medical issue, you can't go wrong with any of the following choices: peanut oil, high oleic sunflower oil, high oleic safflower oil, sesame oil and olive oil.

Here are a few simple suggestions when it comes to buying and using cooking oils:

- As all oils have about 120 calories per tablespoon (no matter whether they're "good" or "bad"), use as little as possible. Oil is a fat, and at 9 calories per gram it does contribute to obesity.
- Oils high in monounsaturated fats such as olive and canola may actually benefit your heart and arteries. If you have heart disease in your family or have it yourself, choose these oils first.
- If you're looking for that extra pinch of flavor, select a stronger-flavored oil such as sesame or walnut. However, use these flavored oils in salad dressings instead of cooking, or add them just at the last moment of cooking because most do not tolerate heat well.

CHAPTER 32

Nutrition 301

"Stick to the aisles around the perimeter of the grocery store. That's where you'll find healthy produce and fresh meats. The inside aisles are where you'll find the prepared, pre-packaged foods that destroy your clean-eating ambitions."

– Tosca Reno, nutrition expert and author of *The Eat-Clean Diet* series

Before looking at how to buy and store various foods, let's spend a few moments on hygiene. If asked what the dirtiest room in their house or apartment is, most people would say the bathroom. But they'd be wrong. The dirtiest place by far is the kitchen. All those microscopic (and not so microscopic) particles of food serve as a perfect breeding ground for bacteria. Yet it's amazing how people who are experts on nutrition pay little or no attention to cleanliness during food preparation. A bad case of food poisoning can easily put you on your squat-enlarged glutes for a few days. Here are a few tips to avoid becoming ill:

- Scrub your sink with a mixture of hot water, vinegar and baking soda each day, or even bleach if you are so inclined.
- Regularly wipe down your countertops, stovetops and table, preferably with vinegar.
- Have a supply of cloths or rags around and wash them often.
- Before using a sponge or cloth that's been sitting around, throw it in the microwave for 60 seconds. That kills the bacteria.
- Keep separate cutting boards for meat, bread and vegetables, and wash them thoroughly after every use – especially the one for meat.
- Clean your fridge at least once a week.
- If you're in doubt as to how long something's been in the fridge, chuck it out. Better safe than sorry. Keep a little masking tape on hand and write the date on everything you keep in the fridge to help out with storage length.

- Avoid putting the mail or newspapers on the table or countertop. Just think about how many people handled those items.
- When freezing food, seal it in an airtight container and label with the date.
- Always wash your hands thoroughly before and after handling food.

VEGETABLES

If you haven't done so already, gradually modify your diet so vegetables (and fruits) make up about 70 to 80 percent of it, volume-wise. Vegetables are one of nature's perfect foods, being cholesterol- and fat-free (not counting nuts), and high in complex carbohydrates, minerals and vitamins. While "meat and potatoes" may help you gain muscle mass, this limited diet won't keep you healthy.

Buying Fresh Vegetables

You may think it's only a matter of filling your basket with random vegetables, but unfortunately it isn't that easy! Here are some dos and don'ts of vegetable selection:

- Do your best to buy only ripe fresh vegetables. Unlike fruits, vegetables won't ripen in storage. The taste will be poor and the nutritional value will be inferior if veggies are not ripe.
- Avoid bruised and damaged vegetables. Most will be lacking in nutrients and won't keep as long.
- Try to buy vegetables that have deep green, red, yellow and orange colors – even purple! A rainbow of veggies each day ensures that you are getting an array of vitamins and minerals, including antioxidants.
- Vegetables should be firm, not soft and mushy. If they're mushy now, what will they be like after cooking and storage?
- Try to avoid vegetables that are beginning to sprout. In many cases the sprouting sections contain poisonous chemicals.
- Buy dried vegetables (legumes)
- Buy in bulk, as the price is much cheaper.

- Always inspect for insect holes and other pest-related damage.
- Try to buy legumes in uniform size, as different-sized legumes have different cooking times.

Storing Vegetables

- Don't keep potatoes in the refrigerator. The cool temperature can actually convert potato starch into sugar. Not only will the taste change, but the color will darken as well.
- Never store potatoes and onions together because the onions will cause the potatoes to sprout faster. Conversely, the onions will absorb moisture from the potatoes and become moldy. The only time to combine these two vegetables is when cooking.
- Store potatoes in paper bags, as this allows for air circulation and prevents the light from turning the potatoes green. Store the onions in a loose net, as this allows for air circulation.

Clean food preparation is just as important as clean eating.

Fruits and vegatables offer numerous health benefits. If raw veggies aren't your thing, experiment with various cooking methods to suit your tastes.

Photo of Larry Vinette by Paul Buceta

- Wash all flower and stemmed vegetables (e.g. broccoli) as soon as you bring them home from the store, and then put them in non-airtight plastic bags and refrigerate. This helps keep them fresh and crisp.
- Try to consume most vegetables within a week of purchase, and potatoes and onions within three weeks.

Storing Dried Vegetables

It's best to transfer these legumes to ceramic or glass containers such as mason jars, and then store them in a cool, dry place – a cupboard should be fine. This helps keep the contents fresh and safe from insects.

Cooking Vegetables

Many people don't like eating vegetables because they are bland and squishy. But this is only if they are cooked incorrectly.

Ironically, the most common cooking technique is also the worst. Boiling vegetables and then pouring the water down the drain leaves behind a soft blob of pulp that may contain less than 10 percent of its original nutrients. If you must boil vegetables, do so for only a few minutes to soften them slightly. Don't put your vegetables on at the same time as your meat because animal products need far longer cooking times. When your meat or poultry is about 5 minutes from cooked, add your vegetables to boiling water.

A superior way to cook vegetables is to steam them. This preserves most of the nutrients and crispness. But they can still be pretty bland. Here are some other ways to cook vegetables that will soon have you loving the taste:

Grilling
Roasting
Stir-frying
Adding sautéed onions, garlic and spices
Adding them to soups, stews and curries

One of my favorite vegetables is fresh spinach wilted in a pan with a spoonful of chopped garlic, a sprinkling of sea salt and a half lemon squeezed in.

BUYING AND STORING FRUITS

Given their importance to the human diet, it's not surprising that fruits can be purchased fresh, frozen, canned or dried. The quality of fresh fruits depends on how mature and ripe they are. There is, however, a distinction between the two terms. Mature means a fruit has reached its full size. Ripe fruit is ready to eat. Most fruits are picked when mature but not ripe. They are then allowed to ripen in transit or at the supermarket (for example, green bananas turn yellow after a few days on store shelves). Immature fruit is smaller than normal, poor in color and usually tough to eat. As they'll never ripen properly, I suggest saving your money.

Citrus fruits and grapes are two of the few fruits that are picked after they ripen. While you may see green oranges on store shelves, don't worry. A combination of warm weather and bright store lights has brought some of the chlorophyll back to the orange skin. This process is called regreening and the oranges are just as fresh and ripe as their orange-colored neighbors.

Every now and then you'll see a sale on overripe or damaged fruit. While the price may be right, the taste is usually off, the texture is lacking (soft and mushy) and the nutrient value is decreased. Unless you're buying for cooking purposes and can use the fruit immediately, you won't save any money because you'll end up simply throwing it out.

Buying Fresh Fruit

- Squeeze the fruit gently. It should give slightly, indicating ripeness, but should not be too soft or mushy.
- Try to select fruit that is firm and plump. Avoid any fruit that is overly soft, hard or dried out.
- Look for fruit with the correct shape. Deformed-looking fruits often have an "off" taste.
- Fruit that is heavy for its size is usually full of juice.
- Ripe fruit should have a sweet, distinct smell, especially tropical fruits such as mangoes. If the fruit doesn't smell right, avoid it.

Storing Fresh Fruit

- Try to consume all fresh fruit within one week.
- Most fruits with skins (i.e. mango, banana, orange, apple) will store fine at room temperature for a few days. Keep them in the refrigerator if you think they won't be eaten within four or five days, and yes, that includes bananas! While banana skin can turn black in the fridge, the fruit inside is fine.
- Unripe fruit can be ripened at room temperature by placing it inside a brown paper bag.
- Most berries and cherries don't last long, so keep weeding out the spoiled ones and keep them refrigerated in an airtight container.
- Fruit that is cut should be sprinkled with lemon juice, wrapped in plastic and placed in an airtight container.
- When bananas are ripe they have a balance of starch and sugar, but when overripe the starches convert to sugars, so be careful not to eat too many.
- Wash all fruit as soon as you arrive home. While some fruit is picked by machine, much of what you buy has been hand-picked in third-world countries – and this means not only dirt, but also fungicides, herbicides and pesticides, some of which are not even allowed in this country anymore. Washing also helps flush out insect remains, including dead insects and egg sacks.
- Don't neglect the less familiar fruit. While the big three – oranges, apples, and bananas – are nutritious, some of the lesser-known fruits are even more so. And you will experience some unique flavors and textures. Try lychee and mangosteen from the Far East, kiwi from New Zealand, and of course, mangoes and papaya from the tropics. Want an amazing taste with color to match? Try a dragonfruit. Expensive, but delicious.

Frozen Fruit

Frozen fruit is a good alternative to fresh fruit, but keep in mind that not all fruits freeze well. When water freezes it expands and often ruptures the cell walls that give the fruit form and structure. Thus, when you thaw it out you're often left with mush. Try serving your frozen fruit chilled to help it keep some of its form, or use it in smoothies. Thawed berries are great to add to your morning oatmeal or for cooking, as well. When buying frozen fruit:

- Make sure the package is frozen solid.
- Don't buy it if the package has a buildup of ice. This could mean that it was frozen, thawed and refrozen.
- Don't buy the fruit if the package has any openings or is damaged.
- If freezing your own fruit, remember to use airtight containers, try to get as much air out as possible, and label and date it. A great way to freeze your own fruit (and vegetables) is to cut it into small pieces or use small fruits such as berries, put it into a Ziploc bag, close the bag around a straw and then suck out the air. Close completely the instant you bring out the straw.

Canned Fruit

Always buy fresh or frozen before canned, but sometimes this is not possible. If buying canned fruit, look for fruit

Photo by Jason Mathas

packed in water or its own juices. Avoid anything with added sugar. Tinned fruit should contain the same number of calories per gram or ounce as fresh fruit.

Dried Fruit

Dried fruits are usually dried in the sun or by mechanical means and are a good occasional alternative to fresh fruit. While not as high in nutrients as fresh or frozen fruit, they are cheaper when bought in bulk. It generally takes several pounds of fresh fruit to make one pound of dried. The big disadvantage to dried fruit is that the sugar is much more concentrated than in fresh fruit. If you eat to your fill, you may be taking in many times the number of sugar calories.

Buying dried fruit

- Don't buy dried fruit that has any evidence of insects or foreign material.
- The fruit should be of uniform color (unless it's a mixed variety, of course). Dried fruit of varying color often means the fruit is of different ages and/or quality.
- Even though it's dried, it should still be soft and liable. Dried fruit that is completely dried out is usually old.

Storing Dried Fruit

- Keep in a cool, dry place.
- Once opened, keep in an airtight container and refrigerate.

BUYING AND STORING GRAIN PRODUCTS

Grain products are made from the seeds of cereal grasses such as barley, oats, rye, corn, rice and wheat. The seed itself consists of three parts. The outer covering is called bran and is rich in fiber and the B vitamins. Most of the seed is rich in protein and starch. The sprouting section inside the seed is rich in oils, fats, minerals and B vitamins. When whole grains are processed, the germ and bran are removed so most of the nutrients are lost. This is why white flour is then artificially enriched and fortified with

additional nutrients. The whole grain products that you buy in stores may also have nutrients added, but they have not been processed to the same degree. Bodybuilder or not, you should try to only eat whole grain products and avoid the processed grains as much as possible.

Pasta is a grain product. Most pasta noodles, including macaroni products, are made with white flour, egg solids and water. Pasta should not be eaten too often as it does not offer the same nutrition as other less-processed grain items, and you should always purchase whole grain pasta. Brown rice pasta is a great alternative.

The breakfast cereal aisle is a real minefield, offering everything from the healthiest rolled oats to the okay shredded wheat to the avoid-at-all-costs sugar-filled brands. And cereal companies are notorious for convincing us that cereal made of white flour and covered in icing is actually healthy because they include the word "wholesome" somewhere on the box. Don't be fooled. Read every label. If you're serious about building a great-looking and healthy physique, eat cereals made with whole grains and without all the added junk.

Breads can be made of whole grains, but bread is a manufactured food and should not make up too large a part of your diet. It's easy to have a sandwich for every meal, but is this really offering you the most nutrition, and therefore the best physique? Nope. Try to get most of your grains from the actual grain: brown rice, whole barley, wheat berries, oats, etc.

With regards to storing grain products, follow the guidelines outlined for dried vegetables. The main difference is that you should refrigerate grain products if you plan on storing them for a long period of time. The oils in whole grains can turn rancid at room temperature.

BUYING MEAT

Meat is primarily the muscle portion of the animal. In a manner of speaking, you're eating another animal's muscle to build your own muscle. Besides muscle, meat also consists of fat, connective tissue, and bone. Beef, lamb and veal are graded in both the U.S. and Canada and then stamped.

Don't worry about the stamp because it's harmless vegetable dye. The ironic part about meat grades is that the top grades are actually the worst in terms of health. The three grades in order of price are prime, choice and select. Prime grades contain the most marble (a polite way of saying fat) and are the juiciest. Choice grades are leaner than prime but still contain fat. Select cuts contain little marble and are less moist. As a bodybuilder trying to build muscle and keep fat levels to a minimum, try to stick to select cuts of meat. Not only are they cheaper, they are healthier and better for your physique.

Pork comes from young pigs and is so uniform in nature that it is not usually sold in grades. Once the excess visible fat has been trimmed away, it is an excellent source of animal protein. This is not to say that sausages, ham and bacon are good choices. They tend to be very fatty and contain nitrites and other additives, along with excessive salt.

Besides the meat from animal muscle, you can also buy organ meat (i.e. liver, heart, etc). Liver is an excellent source of vitamins, minerals and protein. It's also one of the cheapest cuts of meat available. If liver is not to your liking, try beef heart. Stuff the heart and bake it like a chicken. It tastes fantastic and heart muscle tissue is one of the best protein sources available.

Storing Meat

- Use fresh meat within two days or freeze it.
- Store meat in the coldest part of your fridge or freezer.
- If it is properly prepackaged, store as it is.
- If it's in butcher paper, rinse with water and store in plastic.
- Label and date the meat so you know what it is and how old it is.
- Try to let the meat defrost in the fridge. Defrosting at room temperature can cause the outside to spoil before the inside is thawed out.
- If any meat product has brown spots, a slippery feel to it or any unnatural odor – chuck it. Better to spend a few dollars on a fresh piece of meat than to end up with food poisoning.

BUYING AND STORING POULTRY

Poultry is a broad term for such food birds as chicken, turkey, ducks and geese. As a bodybuilder you may want to avoid geese and ducks, as they tend to have a very high fat content. The occasional meal during the off-season is fine, but most store-bought geese and ducks have been "fattened" for flavor. I should note that if you are an ectomorph you may need the extra fat from foods such as this in order to boost your caloric level and gain muscle.

Like meat, poultry is classified according to tenderness. Think of tenderness as another name for fat content. In order of highest fat content of fowl you have broiler, roaster, capon and stewing. While considered the worst classification, stewing fowl is the meatiest and contains the least amount of fat. Luckily, it's also the cheapest. Don't worry about tenderness because if you cook it properly it will be soft enough. When buying poultry, it's more economical to buy large birds. You'll not only get more servings, but also more lean meat in proportion to fat and bone.

Store poultry following the same guidelines for storing meat. However, you should keep eggs in their original cartons as they can absorb odors from other foods.

BUYING AND STORING FISH AND SHELLFISH

Although they tend to place third on the popularity list behind red meat and poultry, fish and shellfish are low in calories, great sources of healthy unsaturated fats and high in protein. Fatty fish include trout, salmon, mackerel and herring. The fats offered by these fish are the good unsaturated kind and, believe it or not, even fatty fish are lower in fat calories than most red meats and poultry. Lean fish include cod, pollock, haddock, turbot, perch and tuna.

Buying Fresh Fish

- Check to see that the fish is fresh and firm by squeezing.
- The eyes should be clear and bulging, not glazed and sunken.
- The skin should be bright and shiny.

- The gills should be red and relatively dry, not brown and slimy.
- The fish should have no odor or smell only slightly fishy. If a fish has a strong pungent smell, avoid it.
- If the fish has not being cleaned and gutted, have them do it at the store or do it yourself immediately after getting home. Do not freeze ungutted, uncleaned fish.
- If eating fresh fish, rinse it, wrap it in plastic and refrigerate it immediately when you get home. Eat it within two days, and preferably within one.
- If you don't like the smell of cooked fish, try adding lemon. Also, vinegar makes an excellent cleaning agent for removing the fish smell from your hands.

Buying Frozen Fish

- Buy only fish frozen in an airtight bag or container.
- There should be little or no detectable odor.
- The fish should be uniform in color. Avoid fish that has light or dark blotches or patches.

Canned Fish

Fish is an excellent source of protein and has contributed to some great physiques in bodybuilding. But don't just stop at tuna. How about salmon? Salmon has a milder taste than tuna and is much higher in unsaturated fats.

When buying canned fish always look for fish packed in water, not oil. Oil is high in fat and usually loaded with salt. As a safety precaution, rinse the top of the can with boiling water before opening. This way, if the lid falls in when you open it, you won't contaminate the fish. If you don't use all of the tin's contents, transfer it to an airtight container and refrigerate. Don't refrigerate in the open tin. As with meat and poultry, try to eat it within two to three days.

Shellfish

Shellfish can be generally divided into two broad categories: molluscs, which have two single-piece shells, and crustaceans, arthropods with a segmented outer covering, antennae, and eyes on stalks. They actually look like giant insects. In fact, carpenter insects are indeed crustaceans – but you probably wouldn't want to eat those. Examples of molluscs include oysters, clams, mussels and scallops. Common crustaceans include crab, shrimp, lobster and crayfish.

Don't get too fond of raw shellfish – particularly molluscs. Molluscs belong to a class of animals that biologists commonly call filter feeders. Basically, they hang out on the sea bottom, suck in water and trap tiny food particles in mucus. If the oyster bed happens to be located next to a sewage outlet the whole oyster population may be contaminated with any number of toxic agents. Under no circumstances should you eat raw oysters or any other mollusc. The restaurant may be truthful in saying that they came from a safe area, but what about all the marine parasites that could be present? Treat shellfish as you would red meat and poultry, and cook it.

Buying Shellfish

- When buying lobster, pick it up by its body and watch the tail. If the tail curls under the body it's healthy. If the tail just hangs there, the lobster is either dead or dying.
- Molluscs shells should be tightly closed. If they are open even a little, toss them out.
- Fresh scallops should be creamy colored and smell slightly sweet.
- Live crabs should be just that – alive and very active. Stay away from the lethargic members in the tank!
- Fresh shrimp should have little or no odor, and when uncooked should not have even a hint of pink color.
- Eat all fresh shellfish within a couple of days and freeze any leftovers in an airtight container.

CHAPTER 33

White Death – Avoiding the Insulin Spike

"Forget anything made with white (read processed) flour. Largely without nutritive value and high on the glycemic index scale, this stuff is likely to add to your waistline. When grabbing bread, cereal, rice or pasta, pick whole-grain versions every time. Whole grains are low in fat and high in fiber and complex carbohydrates – they convert to long-term energy."

– S.J. Wells, *MuscleMag International* contributor

Arnold Schwarzenegger once referred to white bread as "white death." He could also have included white sugar and white rice, as these three make up the deadly trio that destroys most diets and adds inches to the midsection. While fat often takes the bad rap – sometimes with good reason – the real bad guys are these three types of foods that often slip under the dietary radar. Why are white sugar, white rice and white bread so bad for the diet? Well, these food items are converted to glucose at a rapid rate. In other words, they have a high glycemic index. This rapid conversion in turn causes the body to release large amounts of insulin to handle the wave of glucose. Over time this often-repeated process causes the body to start to respond sluggishly. Insulin promotes the formation of fat, technically known as lipogenesis. While you might be targeting dietary fat, body fat is sneaking in the backdoor via refined carbs.

Refined carbs and sugars (refined is a polite way of saying leached, bleached and chemically destroyed), particularly the white variety, hurt the body in more

White bread has a high glycemic index and therefore promotes fat storage.

Whole grain bread is high in fiber and full of nutirents to promote health.

ways than one. One problem is that these types of foods have had the fiber removed. A carbohydrate source lacking fiber becomes an insulin bomb, an unnatural creation that makes the body highly susceptible to fat storage.

Unfortunately, most foods today have had most of their fiber and other nutrients removed. The food item in its natural state is good for the body, but once the nutrients are removed the product becomes basically worthless for health purposes. Why would the manufacturing industries remove the nutrients and create an unnatural substitute? One of the main reasons is extended shelf life for the product. The concern of the food industry is not your health but their bottom line, which is increased when a product can stay on the shelf for longer periods of time. The refining process, however, yields a food item that is virtually worthless. The original food item might have been highly nutritious but the processed end result is not. Whole wheat flour is good; white flour is not. Brown rice is a good food choice; refined white rice is not. Generally, when a food item is artificially white it has had all of the good nutrients removed through various refining processes. Rice is polished and flour is degerminated and bleached. The end result is food that is very high on the glycemic index. Did you know that white bread normally has a higher glycemic index rating than pure sugar? That is because all fiber and nutrients have been removed. Over the past century, artificial, sugary, starchy items that offer no nutrition have replaced good healthy food. Is it any wonder that our society is becoming ever more obese?

Another area of concern is what we drink. White sugar shows up in drinks, but so do other problematic additions. Soft drinks and most fruit drinks have refined concentrated sweeteners added in abundance. Look at the label of almost any juice or fruit drink and you will find

EASE UP ON THE SPORTS DRINKS

Sports drinks may be refreshing after a hard workout, but according to a recent study they decay your pearly whites 11 times more than sugary soft drinks. What to do if you don't want to give them up altogether? Chug them down. Severe enamel erosion occurs when you sip the drink for hours on end, such as when you're working on your computer or driving. It is also recommended that you rinse with water after drinking any sugary drink to flush away the "sugar bunnies."

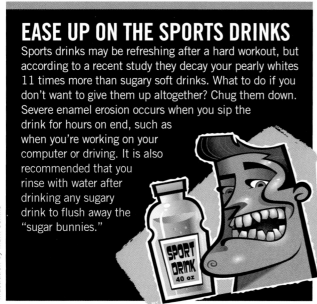

Illustration by Mark Collins

that corn syrup or a similar sweetener has been added. White sugar and its cousins such as corn sweeteners blast blood-sugar levels into the stratosphere. To make matters worse, these drinks typically contain no fiber, protein, fat or any other metabolic brake. If you drink any of these items on a habitual basis it should be no surprise why you struggle with body fat. Bodybuilders are not immune from such problems. If your diet consists of bodybuilder-typical fare such as egg whites and protein drinks mixed in fruit juice, you may also be tiptoeing the line to a low-fiber, high-insulin problem. This is particularly true if you tend to cheat on your diet a little too frequently. Have a slice of cake at the office party? That is one of the worst possible choices you can make as white cake with frosting ranks at the very top of carb density charts (almost pure refined carbs and sugar and a carb density rating of 74). Another frequent culprit in the diet is bread. Do you have a bagel on a frequent basis? They are very high in carbs of the refined variety. Many bodybuilders pat themselves on the back for avoiding fat, however, most types of bread should be avoided just as assiduously. You will have to work at it to avoid it. The color alone is not enough. While it is true that white bread is basically worthless in the area of nutrition, all white bread is not white. Some white bread has been colored brown to make it appear as though it is not white bread – but guess what? It is really white bread with artificial color added.

Bread doesn't have to be white to be highly refined. Many "wheat" breads and "multigrain" breads sound healthful, but the first and main ingredient is the same enriched wheat flour used in white bread, with a smattering of added grains and color to give the bread a slightly different texture and look than white bread. The key to the type of bread you are looking at is not in the color, but in the ingredients. This means examining the label of every bread item you plan to purchase.

The presence of whole grains makes all the difference. The label on Pepperidge Farm's 9-Grain Natural Whole Grain Bread shows that the first ingredient is 100 percent whole wheat flour, and each slice packs three grams of fiber. If you know how to read the package, picking the most nutritious bread isn't hard. Make sure the first ingredient contains the word whole – either whole wheat or another whole grain. The first ingredient in Arnold's Real Jewish Rye Bread, for instance, is enriched wheat flour – refined rye flour is the third ingredient, and a slice contains less than one gram of fiber. But the first ingredient in Baker's Whole Grain Rye is whole rye, and each slice has nearly five grams of fiber.

If you want to give your diet a real boost, avoid the whites – white sugar, white rice, and white bread (and derivatives) as much as possible. It isn't enough to simply aim at lowering fat in the diet. Refined sugars and carbs are a worse obstacle and need to be eliminated from your menu. So if you're stuck at the 15 percent body fat level or more and can't understand why you can't drop lower, try dropping out the whites and watch what happens.

A muscular, lean, healthy physique is dependent upon many factors – a key one being avoiding all food products that contain refined carbs.

Photo of Lou Joseph by Jason Breeze

CHAPTER 34

The Importance of Breakfast

"The best breakfast contains more than just complex carbohydrates. If you consume a protein drink along with your carbs, you'll not only enhance glycogen storage but you'll also have insurance against any breakdown of structural protein that occurs when aerobic intensity gets to be a bit much."

– Kevin Kolodziejski, *Musclemag International* contributor, discussing why a good breakfast should contain more than just carbs.

If you regularly skip breakfast, break that habit right now! Breakfast is not just another meal – it is the meal. In fact, the word itself reveals its importance. It's the first meal to "break the fast." After three or more hours between dinner and bedtime, and then at least six hours of sleep, your body is craving nutrients. This would be an ideal time to have some protein mixed with some carbs. You need this right now, because the instant you wake up, your brain needs fuel. And your brain burns almost nothing but carbohydrates as a fuel source. (It also burns a very small amount of fat.) If you don't get some carbs into your system first thing, you run the risk of forcing your body to convert the amino acids from your muscles to carbs for use as a fuel source. Can't handle a full breakfast first thing? At least have a scoop of protein powder with a banana or strawberries mixed in a blender. Have the shake and then wait a few minutes. By then you may be able to eat a little more solid food.

After your protein shake you can start thinking about breakfast. You can't go wrong with oatmeal or other nutrient-rich hot cereals. Add some diced fruit, nuts, seeds or cinnamon. Speaking of fruit, nothing adds some spice to breakfast like a mixed salad of chopped fresh pineapple, watermelon or cantaloupe.

Another breakfast favorite is eggs. Eggs have gotten a bad reputation over the years, but they are again being accepted as one of nature's perfect foods that won't increase your risk of cardiovascular disease. However, if you have a genetic predisposition to developing high cholesterol and heart disease, avoid eating too many yolks.

There are literally hundreds of ways to prepare eggs. Just pay attention to how you cook them. Frying eggs in a cup of lard or butter made from hydrogenated vegetable oil is not conducive to bodybuilding, or general health. If you must fry them, use a small amount of non-hydrogenated oil, or a squirt of cooking spray in a nonstick pan.

If you have a good appetite you can add a slice or two of toast to your breakfast. Just make sure the bread is whole grain and not covered in high-fat butter or sugar-loaded jam. Smoked fish is popular for breakfast throughout northern Europe, including Great Britain. They're also a source of inexpensive quality protein, often costing less than a buck for a small serving. Buy them packed in water or tomato sauce rather than oil.

Since breakfast is the most important meal of the day, you want to make a special effort to get some high-class muscle-building nutrients into your system. Whole grain hot or cold cereals are great for complex carbs. Add in some eggs or smoked fish for protein and healthy fats and a piece or two of fruit and you're setting the stage for a day of building quality muscle.

I suggest you go out and pick up a good cookbook. Some of the best cookbooks are for diabetics; these will show you how to prepare great-tasting, low-fat, high-protein and complex-carb dishes. Two of the best are *Muscle Meals: A Cookbook to Build Muscle and Lose Fat*, by John Romano, and *The Eat-Clean Diet Cookbook: Great-Tasting Recipes That Keep You Lean*, by Tosca Reno. You can buy both at better bookstores, online at Amazon.com, or through the pages of *MuscleMag International* magazine.

For now, here are some recipes to get you started:

EGG-WHITE OMELET WITH VEGETABLE-CHEDDAR FILLING
Cooking Time: 4 to 5 minutes
Preparation Time: 10 minutes

INGREDIENTS
3   large egg whites, 1 yolk
1   teaspoon water
2   teaspoons chopped fresh dill (optional)
1/8 teaspoon salt
1/8 teaspoon freshly ground pepper
1/2 cup loosely packed, chopped fresh spinach
1   plum tomato, chopped
2   tablespoons shredded nonfat cheddar cheese
Vegetable cooking spray

DIRECTIONS
1. Whisk egg whites, water, dill (if using), salt and pepper together.

2. Lightly coat an omelet pan or small skillet with cooking spray and heat over medium heat for 1 minute. Pour egg mixture into pan and cook until eggs begin to set on bottom.

3. Spread spinach, tomato and cheese over half of omelet, leaving a 1/2-inch border. Lift up side of omelet with a spatula and fold over filling. Cook 2 minutes. Slide omelet onto a serving plate and garnish.

SERVES: 1

Per serving: Calories 110, fat 0.5 g, saturated fat 0 g, cholesterol 3 mg, sodium 906 mg, carbohydrates 8 g, fiber 1 g, protein 18 g.

BLUEBERRY YOGURT CRUNCH

Total Time: 5 minutes

INGREDIENTS
1   container (8 ounces) nonfat vanilla yogurt
1/2 cup blueberries
1/4 cup bran cereal

DIRECTIONS
1. Combine all ingredients in a bowl. Serve immediately.

SERVES: 1

Per serving: Calories 190, fat 1 g, saturated fat 0 g, cholesterol 5 mg, sodium 250 mg, carbohydrates 44 g, fiber 11 g, protein 8 g.

ZESTY CHEDDAR-ASPARAGUS QUICHE

Cooking Time: 45 minutes
Preparation Time: 25 minutes

INGREDIENTS
1   tablespoon breadcrumbs
8   ounces small all-purpose potatoes, peeled
    and very thinly sliced
2   teaspoons olive oil
1   pound asparagus, trimmed
1/2 teaspoon salt, divided
3/4 cup shredded reduced-fat sharp cheddar cheese
3   scallions, sliced
1   can (12 ounces) evaporated fat-free milk
2   large eggs
2   large egg whites
2   teaspoons butter, melted
1   teaspoon dry mustard
1/4 teaspoon freshly ground pepper

DIRECTIONS
1. Heat oven to 400° F. Coat a 9-inch pie plate with vegetable cooking spray and sprinkle with breadcrumbs. Beginning in center, arrange potato slices in slightly overlapping circles up to rim. Lightly brush with olive oil and press down gently. Bake 10 minutes.

2. Set 8 to 12 asparagus spears aside. Cut remaining spears into 1-inch pieces.

3. Sprinkle crust with 1/4 teaspoon salt and 1/4 cup cheddar. Cover with asparagus pieces, then sprinkle with scallions and another 1/4 cup cheese. Arrange whole asparagus spears on top.

4. Beat evaporated milk, eggs, egg whites, butter, mustard, pepper and remaining 1/4 teaspoon salt in a medium bowl. Pour into pie plate and sprinkle with remaining cheddar. Bake until a knife inserted in center comes out clean, for about 35 minutes.

5. Divide into 6 slices. One serving equals 1 slice.

SERVES: 6

Per serving: Calories 200, fat 8 g, saturated fat 3.5 g, cholesterol 86 mg, sodium 316 mg, carbohydrates 20 g, fiber 2 g, protein 13 g.

SILVER-DOLLAR PANCAKES

Cooking Time: 5 minutes per batch
Preparation Time: 15 minutes

INGREDIENTS

1/2 cup whole grain flour
1 heaping teaspoon Sucanat, honey or agave nectar
1/4 teaspoon baking soda
3/4 cup buttermilk
1 tablespoon vegetable oil
1 large egg
1/2 teaspoon vanilla extract

DIRECTIONS

1. Whisk flour, sugar and baking soda together in a medium bowl. Make a well in center. Whisk buttermilk, oil, egg and vanilla together in another bowl until blended. Pour into well and blend just until moistened. Let stand 5 minutes.

2. Coat a large nonstick skillet with cooking spray and place over medium heat until hot but not smoking.

3. For each pancake, pour 1 tablespoon batter into skillet. Cook until bubbles appear all over the cakes, about 3 minutes. Turn and cook until undersides are golden, about 1 to 2 minutes more.

SERVES: 4 (makes 16 pancakes)

Per serving: Calories 130, fat 5.5 g, saturated fat 1 g, cholesterol 55 mg, sodium 341 mg, carbohydrates 16 g, fiber 0 g, protein 5 g.

QUICK FRENCH TOAST

Total Time: 10 minutes

INGREDIENTS

1 large egg
1/2 teaspoon vanilla extract
1/4 teaspoon cinnamon
2 teaspoons Sucanat, honey or agave nectar
1 tablespoon skim milk
1 slice whole grain bread

DIRECTIONS

1. Place all ingredients except bread in a shallow bowl and whisk well until combined.

2. Pour egg mixture into a shallow bowl. Place bread in egg mixture and soak, turning once.

3. Coat a nonstick skillet with cooking spray and heat over medium heat. Place bread in skillet and pour any remaining egg mixture over bread. Cook until browned on bottom, then turn over to brown other side.

SERVES: 1

Per serving: Calories 160, fat 6 g, saturated fat 2 g, cholesterol 215 mg, sodium 200 mg, carbohydrates 14 g, fiber 0 g, protein 9 g.

CHAPTER 35

Lunch

"Clean eating means eating every two or three hours. Skipping a meal will cause your body to catabolize its hard-earned muscle."

– Editorial in *MuscleMag International*

A s your second primary meal of the day you should put some effort into making your lunches both tasty and nutritious. To make your life as simple as possible, try preparing your lunch the night before. Store it in the refrigerator and then bring it with you the next day. Don't forget to add variety to your lunches. A sandwich is fine sometimes, but why not add a piece of fruit? How about a variety of raw vegetables such as carrots, tomato and celery? And why limit yourself to sandwiches? Bring soups, stews, stir-fried chicken with rice and vegetables. Most workplaces have refrigerators and microwaves available for employee use. Since when does lunch have to be cold and bland? Use the staff lunchroom to reheat or to even cook your lunches. Try to make meals that store conveniently, do not spoil quickly, and that can retain their flavor when sealed in plastic bags or containers.

Try these tips:

- Cold meats are quick and great sources of protein for sandwiches. Try to eat meat you cook yourself rather than cold cuts, which normally contain tons of sugar and preservatives.
- Use fat-free dressings or salsas on tuna and other tinned seafood to give it some much-needed substance and flavoring. Tuna may taste like cardboard on its own, but with the right ingredients, its less than stellar taste can be masked.
- Be creative with your spreads. Mayo and butter will do nothing for your physique. Try spreading your breads with hummus, bean dip or tzatziki

Your lunch is only as good as you make it. Break away from the sandwich trend and be creative, choosing a variety of nutrient-packed foods.

Photo of Sean Glassman by Alex Ardenti

sauce made with yogurt. These choices not only lower your sandwich's fat content, they also give your nutrition a boost.

• Use whole grain pita, tortilla and breads rather than white.

• Dried fruit is good in moderation. Yes it's high in concentrated sugar, but it contains lots of vitamins, minerals and fiber. Mix it with some raw almonds for a nutrition boost – but watch the portion sizes. If you're trying to gain weight you can eat up to a half cup throughout the day, but if you're trying to lose you probably want to skip it altogether.

• Bring a portable cooler. There are tons of choices these days, and if you don't have access to a fridge, a cooler will allow you far more options.

• When bringing salads, keep the dressing in a separate container and don't add it until you're ready to eat. Veggies soaked in dressing for too long lose their structure and taste.

• Pick up some sandwich-sized containers if you bring sandwiches to work. This prevents unnecessary litter and helps prevent your lunch from falling apart.

• Think outside the lunch box. Be creative. Your lunch options are limited only by your own imagination. There's no reason not to have jerk chicken with rice and peas. Or baked potato with pepper steak left over from the night before. Sandwiches are convenient but often short on nutrition, and when you're trying to build muscle, you need your food to be as nutrition packed as you can get it.

CHAPTER 36

Main Courses

"Each of your six meals a day should be of moderate size and high nutrition."

– Editorial in *MuscleMag International*

lthough you should be eating four to six small to medium meals a day instead of two or three large ones, I understand that traditional socializing and work/ school circumstances may lead to a larger meal in the evening. This is fine as long as the meal is nutritious and not loaded with empty calories (and as long as you don't go back for seconds or thirds!). The following recipes are easy to prepare, loaded with muscle-building nutrients and tasty, too.

STIR-FRIED CHICKEN WITH SNOW PEAS AND BABY CORN

INGREDIENTS
4   teaspoons reduced-sodium soy sauce, divided
4   teaspoons dark sesame oil, divided
1   tablespoon rice wine, dry sherry or rice vinegar
1   pound chicken breasts, skinned and boned, cut into one-inch cubes
1/2 cup chicken stock or low-sodium chicken broth mixed with
2   teaspoons cornstarch
1   tablespoon vegetable oil
1   tablespoon minced fresh ginger
1   tablespoon minced garlic
4   green onions, white part only, sliced
2   cups snow peas, trimmed
1   can (14 ounces) baby corn, drained and rinsed

DIRECTIONS
1. In a medium-sized bowl, mix 2 teaspoons each of the soy sauce and sesame oil with the wine. Add the chicken and let marinate for 30 minutes. In a small bowl, combine the stock-cornstarch mixture with the remaining 2 teaspoons each of soy sauce and sesame oil.

2. In a 12-inch nonstick skillet, heat the vegetable oil over medium-high heat. Add the ginger, garlic and green onions, and stir-fry for 30 seconds. Add the chicken and stir-fry for about 2 minutes or until no longer pink on the outside. Add the snow peas and corn and stir-fry 2 minutes more.

3. Add the cornstarch-stock mixture to the skillet, lower the heat and simmer, stirring for 2 to 3 minutes or until the sauce is slightly thickened and the juices run clear, not pink, when the chicken is pricked with a fork.

SERVES: 4

Per serving: Calories 302, saturated fat 2 g, total fat 11 g, protein 31 g, carbohydrates 23 g, fiber 2 g, sodium 536 mg, cholesterol 66 mg.

GRILLED JALAPENO CHICKEN WRAPS

INGREDIENTS
1   pound boneless, skinless chicken breasts
1   tablespoon garlic powder
1   tablespoon onion powder
1   tablespoon pepper
2   teaspoons seasoned salt
1   teaspoon paprika
1   small onion, cut into strips
15 jalapeño peppers, halved and seeded (When cutting or seeding hot peppers, use rubber or plastic gloves to protect your hands. Avoid touching your face.)
1   pound sliced bacon, halved width-wise
Low-fat blue cheese or ranch salad dressing

DIRECTIONS
1. Cut chicken into 1 1/2-inch strips.

2. In a large resealable plastic bag combine the garlic powder, onion powder, pepper, seasoned salt and paprika. Add chicken and shake to coat.

3. Place a chicken and onion strip in each jalapeño half. Wrap each with a piece of bacon and secure with toothpicks.

4. Grill, uncovered, over indirect medium heat for 18 to 20 minutes, turning once, or until chicken juices run clear and bacon is crisp. Serve with low-fat blue cheese or ranch dressing.

MAKES: 2 1/2 dozen

CURRIED CHICKEN AND APPLE SANDWICH

Total Time: 20 minutes

INGREDIENTS

1/4   cup reduced-calorie mayonnaise
1/4   cup plain low-fat yogurt
3/4   teaspoon curry powder, or to taste
1/8   teaspoon salt
1/8   teaspoon chili or cayenne pepper
1   garlic clove, minced
2   cups diced cooked chicken or turkey (8 ounces)
5   scallions, including tops, sliced
1   large green or red bell pepper, cored, seeded and chopped
1   small Golden or Red Delicious apple, cored and diced (1 cup)
2   tablespoons minced fresh cilantro or 2 tablespoons minced
4   whole wheat pita rounds, halved
Fresh parsley combined with 3/4 teaspoon dried cilantro
Several dark green lettuce leaves

DIRECTIONS

1. Whisk together mayonnaise, yogurt, curry powder, salt, ground red pepper and garlic in a medium bowl. Stir in diced meat, scallions, bell pepper, apple and cilantro.

2. Tuck lettuce leaves into each pita half, then stuff with filling. Cover with plastic wrap and chill until ready to serve.

SERVES: 4

Per sandwich: Calories 280, fat 7 g, saturated fat 1 g, cholesterol 54 mg, sodium 337 mg, carbohydrates 30 g, fiber 2 g, protein 23 g.

BEEF VEGETABLE STIR-FRY

Cooking Time: 15 minutes
Preparation Time: 10 minutes

INGREDIENTS

2   teaspoons cornstarch, divided into 1/2 teaspoon portions
4   tablespoons reduced-sodium soy sauce, divided
1   pound beef sirloin steak, cut into 2-inch strips
2   medium green peppers, cut into strips
2   medium onions, thinly sliced
1   tablespoon canola oil
1/2   pound sliced fresh mushrooms

DIRECTIONS

1. In a large bowl, combine cornstarch and 2 tablespoons soy sauce until smooth. Add beef; stir to coat.

2. In a large skillet or wok, stir-fry the green peppers and onions in oil for 3 minutes; add beef. Cook and stir for 3 minutes.

3. Add mushrooms. Cook and stir for 3 to 5 minutes or until vegetables are tender and meat is no longer pink.

4. Stir in remaining soy sauce.

SERVES: 4

Per serving: Calories 254, fat 9 g, saturated fat 3 g, cholesterol 63 mg, sodium 658 mg, carbohydrates 17 g, fiber 3 g, protein 26 g.

BEEF OR LAMB SHISH KABOBS

Cooking Time: 10 minutes
Preparation Time: 1 hour

INGREDIENTS
1/4 cup dry red wine
2 scallions, chopped
2 tablespoons balsamic vinegar
1 tablespoon minced fresh rosemary or 1/2 teaspoon dried rosemary, crumbled
2 tablespoons olive oil
2 tablespoons water
2 cloves garlic, crushed
1/2 teaspoon salt
1/2 teaspoon black pepper
1 pound boneless beef chuck or leg of lamb, cut into 1 1/4-inch cubes

DIRECTIONS
1. In a large, self-sealing plastic bag, mix together all ingredients except beef. Add beef, seal, turn to coat and refrigerate at least four hours or preferably overnight.

2. Preheat the grill or broiler. Pat beef dry and thread on four skewers, spacing evenly.

3. Grill kabobs over medium-hot coals for 10 to 12 minutes for medium-rare to medium, basting frequently with the marinade and turning once. Or broil four inches from the heat for 10 to 15 minutes for medium-rare.

SERVES: 4

Per serving: Calories 277, saturated fat 5 g, total fat 17 g, cholesterol 82 mg, sodium 1085 mg, carbohydrates 3 g, fiber 0 g, protein 26 g.

BEEF, TURKEY AND MASHED POTATO PIE

Cooking Time: 1 hour
Preparation Time: 30 minutes

INGREDIENTS
1 pound lean ground beef
8 ounces lean ground turkey
1 tablespoon olive or canola oil
2 large onion, coarsely chopped
2 cloves garlic, finely chopped
2 large carrots, coarsely chopped
1 can (28 ounces) crushed tomatoes
1/2 teaspoon dried thyme
1/8 teaspoon each salt and pepper
2 pounds sweet or all-purpose potatoes or rutabaga, peeled and sliced 1/2-inch thick
1/4 cup 1% low-fat milk
2 tablespoons chopped parsley

DIRECTIONS
1. Heat a Dutch oven over moderately high heat until hot. Add the beef and turkey and sauté, stirring frequently, about 7 minutes or until the meat is no longer pink and has released its juices. Remove from heat and spoon the meat into a sieve set over a bowl. Allow all the fat to drain from the meat for at least 10 minutes.

2. Meanwhile, in the Dutch oven, heat the oil over moderately high heat. Add the onions, garlic and carrots and sauté about 10 minutes or until softened and golden brown. Return the meat to the pan.

3. Stir in the crushed tomatoes, thyme, salt and pepper and bring to a boil. Cover and simmer, stirring occasionally, about 25 minutes or until a rich stew has formed.

4. Preheat the oven to 400° F. Meanwhile, simmer sweet potatoes in a pan of boiling water about 10 minutes or until tender. Drain, return to the saucepan, and mash them with the milk until smooth. Stir in the chopped parsley.

5. Transfer the meat mixture to a 13 x 9 x 2-inch baking dish and smooth out to an even layer.

6. Spread the mashed sweet potatoes over the meat and smooth the surface with a spatula. Bake 12 to 15 minutes or until heated through and bubbling around the edges.

SERVES: 6

Per serving: Calories 393, saturated fat 2 g, total fat 7 g, cholesterol 68 mg, sodium 360 mg, carbohydrates 52 g, fiber 8 g protein 31 g.

SWEET-AND-SOUR SKEWERED SHRIMP

Cooking Time: 10 minutes
Preparation Time: 15 minutes

INGREDIENTS

1/2 cup barbecue sauce
1/4 cup lemon juice
1/4 cup pineapple preserves
4   teaspoons soy sauce
1/2 teaspoon ground ginger
30   uncooked large shrimp (about 2 pounds)
1/2 pound fresh mushrooms, halved
1 to 2 large green peppers, cut into 1-inch pieces

DIRECTIONS

1. In a small saucepan, combine the first five ingredients. Bring to a boil over medium heat, stirring frequently.

2. Remove from the heat; cool. Set aside 1/2 cup for basting. Place remaining sauce and shrimp in a glass or ceramic bowl, covered, in the fridge for 30 minutes.

3. Drain and discard marinade. Alternate the shrimp, green peppers and mushrooms on each of six metal or soaked wooden skewers.

4. Grill, uncovered, over medium-high heat for 2 minutes on each side. Turn and brush with reserved sauce. Continue grilling for 4 to 8 minutes or until shrimp turns pink, turning and basting several times.

SERVES: 6

GRILLED SALMON STEAKS

INGREDIENTS

2   tablespoons white wine vinegar
2   tablespoons honey, Sucanat or agave nectar
1   tablespoon dill
3/4 teaspoon salt
4   salmon steaks (1-inch thick)
1/8 to 1/4 teaspoon pepper

Mustard Dill Sauce
3   tablespoons mayonnaise
3   tablespoons Dijon mustard
3   tablespoons dillweed
1   tablespoon sugar
4   teaspoons white wine vinegar
1/4 teaspoon pepper

DIRECTIONS

1. Combine the first five ingredients in a glass or ceramic dish. Add salmon. Turn to coat. Cover and refrigerate for 1 hour, turning occasionally.

2. In a small bowl, combine the sauce ingredients; cover and refrigerate. Drain salmon, discarding marinade.

3. Coat grill rack with cooking spray before starting the grill.

4. Grill salmon, covered, over medium-high heat for 5 minutes. Turn; grill 7 to 9 minutes longer or until fish flakes easily with a fork. Serve with the mustard dill sauce.

SERVES: 4

TUNA AND TOMATO PIZZA

Cooking Time: 10 minutes
Preparation Time: 15 minutes

INGREDIENTS

2   teaspoons olive oil, divided
1   onion, finely chopped
1   can (14 1/2 ounces) chopped tomatoes
1/2   teaspoon dried oregano
2   ready-made pizza crusts, about 8 1/4 ounces each
2   tablespoons tomato puree
1   can (7 ounces) tuna in spring water, drained and flaked
4   teaspoons capers
8   black olives, pitted and sliced
Salt and pepper
Fresh basil leaves to garnish
Pinch of sugar

DIRECTIONS

1. Preheat the oven to 425° F.

2. Heat 1 teaspoon of the oil in a small saucepan, add the onion, and cook over medium heat until softened, about 4 minutes. Add the tomatoes, their juice, oregano and sugar. Season with salt and pepper to taste, and simmer for 10 minutes, stirring occasionally.

3. Put the pizza crusts on two baking sheets. Spread 1 tablespoon of tomato puree over each crust. Spoon the tomato sauce over the pizzas, then add the tuna. Sprinkle with the capers and sliced olives, and drizzle the remaining olive oil over top.

4. Bake the pizzas until the crusts are crisp and golden, about 10 minutes. Sprinkle with torn basil leaves and serve immediately.

SERVES: 4

Per serving: Calories 449, fat 4 g, saturated fat 0 g, cholesterol 13 mg, sodium 740 mg, carbohydrates 80 g, fiber 7 g, protein 22 g.

SOUTHERN SEAFOOD GUMBO

Cooking Time: 35 minutes
Preparation Time: 25 minutes

INGREDIENTS

1   medium onion, chopped
2   celery ribs with leaves, chopped
1   medium green pepper, chopped
3   garlic cloves, minced
1   tablespoon olive oil
1   bottle (46 ounces) spicy V8 juice
1   can (14 1/2 ounces) diced tomatoes, not drained
1/4   teaspoon chili or cayenne pepper
1   package (16 ounces) frozen sliced okra, thawed
1   pound catfish fillets, cut into 3/4-inch cubes
3/4   pound uncooked medium shrimp, peeled and de-veined
3   cups cooked long-grain rice

DIRECTIONS

1. In a large saucepan, sauté the onion, celery, green pepper and garlic in oil until tender. Stir in the V8 juice, tomatoes and chili pepper; bring to a boil. Reduce heat; cover and simmer for 10 minutes.

2. Stir in okra and catfish; cook 8 minutes longer. Add the shrimp; cook about 7 minutes longer or until shrimp turn pink. Place rice in individual serving bowls; top with gumbo.

SERVES: 12

Per serving (1 cup gumbo with 1/4 cup rice)**:** Calories 180, fat 5 g, saturated fat 1 g, cholesterol 60 mg, sodium 512 mg, carbohydrates 22 g, fiber 3 g, protein 14 g .

PORK CHOPS STUFFED WITH APPLES AND PEARS

Cooking Time: 1 1/2 hours
Preparation Time: 20 minutes

INGREDIENTS

2   teaspoons olive or canola oil
2   leeks or 1 small onion, trimmed and sliced
2   tart apples, peeled, cored and diced
1   ripe pear, cored and diced
1/2 teaspoon dried sage
3/4 cup unsweetened apple juice
1/4 cup chicken stock
1/2 teaspoon finely grated orange zest
6   pork loin chops with bone, 1 inch thick (about 8 ounces each) vegetable oil cooking spray

DIRECTIONS

1. Preheat the oven to 350° F.

2. In a saucepan, heat the oil over moderate heat. Add leeks and sauté 3 to 4 minutes or until softened and lightly browned. Add the apples, pear and sage. Sauté about 3 minutes. Stir in 1/2 cup apple juice and the stock. Bring to a boil, reduce heat and simmer, uncovered, about 2 minutes or until the fruit is slightly soft.

3. Drain the fruit mixture, reserving the liquid in the saucepan. Allow the fruit to cool slightly. Stir the orange zest into the fruit mixture.

4. Trim all the fat from the pork chops. Make a horizontal slit into the side of each chop until the knife blade reaches the bone. Move the knife back and forth to make a pocket about three inches long, taking care not to go through to the outside of the meat at any point. Stuff the fruit mixture into the pockets.

4. Coat a nonstick pan with cooking spray, add three chops, and cook on medium-high heat for 2 minutes on each side or until browned. Repeat with second batch.

5. Place the stuffed chops in a nonstick roasting pan, add the remaining apple juice and roast about 1 hour or until tender and the internal temperature of the meat is 170° F. Transfer the chops to a platter and cover with aluminum foil to keep them warm.

6. Spoon off most of the fat from the roasting pan. Stir in the reserved fruit poaching liquid and place over moderate heat. Bring to a boil, reduce heat and simmer, stirring to loosen the brown bits on the pan, about 3 minutes or until a rich sauce forms. Ladle overtop the chops on each plate.

SERVES: 6

Per serving: Calories 384, saturated fat 5 g, total fat 15 g, cholesterol 113 mg, sodium 133 mg, carbohydrates 21 g, fiber 3 g, protein 40 g.

MARINATED PORK ROAST

Cooking Time: 50 minutes plus standing time
Preparation Time: 10 minutes plus marinating time

INGREDIENTS

1/4 cup reduced-sodium soy sauce
1/4 cup grated onion
1   tablespoon canola oil
1   teaspoon lemon juice
3   garlic cloves, minced
3/4 teaspoon ground ginger
1   boneless whole pork loin roast (2 1/2 pounds)
1/4 cup white wine or chicken broth
1/4 cup honey
1   tablespoon brown sugar

DIRECTIONS

1. Combine the first six ingredients in a large glass or ceramic dish. Add pork roast and turn to coat. Refrigerate for 8 hours or preferably overnight, turning several times.

2. Drain and discard marinade. Place roast on a rack in a shallow, foil-lined roasting pan. Bake, uncovered, at 350° F for 25 minutes.

3. In a small bowl, combine the wine or broth and honey. Brush half over the meat. Bake 15 minutes longer. Brush with remaining honey mixture. Bake 10 to 20 minutes longer or until a meat thermometer reads 160° F. Let stand for 10 minutes before slicing.

SERVES: 9

Per serving (3-ounce serving)**:** Calories 227, total fat 9 g, saturated fat 3 g, cholesterol 70 mg, sodium 195 mg, carbohydrate 10 g, fiber trace, protein 25 g.

A great cookbook will help you add variety and new tastes to your regular menu.

CHAPTER 37

Snacks

"Forget the disgusting junk food available in every grocery store and restaurant on the planet. Learn to eat clean from now on. Be very selective and enjoy lean meats, fish, poultry, brown rice, whole grains, yams, nuts, oatmeal, fresh fruits and salads. These will give you lasting health and vitality."

– Editorial in *MuscleMag International*, discussing the importance of healthy eating.

While I suggest that you view all six meals as equal, you may find that meals 1, 3 and 5 will be more traditional in nature (breakfast, lunch and supper) because that's simply the way the world is set up. Meals 2, 4 and possibly 6, could be termed snacks. However, I don't mean snacking in the traditional sense! A snack is not a bag of potato chips, chocolate bar or bowl of high-fat ice cream. Your snacks should supplement your bodybuilding goals, not destroy them. If you eat garbage like this you might as well throw your bodybuilding dreams out the window. Healthy snacking will keep your energy level high and keep your body infused with muscle-building nutrients.

The key is to pay close attention to what you eat. Stuffing your face with a large order of fries between lunch and supper may give you a temporary boost, but a snack this high in fat and calories is doing nothing for muscle-tissue repair. And I think you already know what it will do to your midsection! Let's put it this way – six-pack abs are not built with foods from the deep fryer!

To keep your energy level high and to avoid gaining fat, steer clear of foods with a lot of simple carbohydrates (sugars) such as candy bars or soda. Instead, go for foods that contain complex carbohydrates, such as whole grain breads and cereals. Combine these foods with protein-rich items such as natural nut butter or low-fat yogurt or cottage cheese.

SO JUST WHAT IS A HEALTHY SNACK?

Selecting healthy snacks means shopping smarter. Always be wary of the health claims on food labels. Just because something is labeled "all natural" doesn't necessarily mean it's nutritious. For example, all-natural juice drinks or sodas can still be loaded with sugar. And despite being "natural," sugar will still lead to extra fat around your waist.

Another great example is the granola bar. Although granola bars can contain a certain amount of vitamins and nutrients, many brands also contain tons of sugar and a great deal of fat, including the artery-clogging trans and saturated fat.

> "Unfortunately the stuff is everywhere. If you care at all about your waist, you should treat trans fat like it's a rattlesnake and stay far away."
>
> – Dwayne Hines II, author and regular *MuscleMag International* contributor, commenting on the evils of trans fat.

Many are no better than a typical candy bar. Always read the Nutrition Facts label on the package to be sure just what you're putting into your body.

Always be skeptical of foods that claim they are "low-fat." When manufacturers lower the fat content, they often compensate by adding loads of sugar. Many low-fat foods have as many calories as their full-fat counterparts – and often with less nutrition.

In addition, always read the ingredients section on the package. The nutrition label is usually in a table and lists common items such as saturated and trans fat, cholesterol, carbohydrate, protein, and total calories per serving. The ingredients section is usually in small print and is located in the corner. Even though the table may say zero for trans and saturated fat, the ingredients section may say "made with hydrogenated vegetable oil." If you see the words "hydrogenated" or "partially hydrogenated," place the item back on the shelf and move on. As I discussed earlier, hydrogenated fats and oils rarely exist in nature and therefore the human body didn't evolve the enzymes necessary to digest them. Instead of being broken down and used for constructive metabolic activities such as growth, repair and energy production, they get deposited on your artery walls or fat cells and cause heart disease.

Here are a few words to look out for:

Triglycerides: contain, in varying proportions, three groups of fatty acids – saturated, monounsaturated, and polyunsaturated.

Saturated Fats: these fats tend to be solid at room temperature and are the only fatty acids that raise blood cholesterol levels. Animal fats are usually saturated, with the exception of fish. Such foods as butter, meat and high-fat dairy are all especially high in saturated fat.

SNACK ON SUNFLOWER SEEDS

Sunflower seeds contain a good fat that we need in our diet: linoleic acid. Your body can't make this essential fatty acid and yet requires it to help synthesize other fats. Linoleic acid is great for your heart. In a study, those who had the highest intakes of linoleic acid had a 23 percent lower risk of heart disease than those with the lowest intakes. To get more in your diet, add two or three tablespoons of these seeds to low-fat granola, trail mix or hot cereal.

Illustration by Mark Collins

Monounsaturated and polyunsaturated Fats: these tend to be liquid at room temperature and don't raise blood cholesterol levels. These fats are actually essential for health. The best sources are olive and canola oils, nuts, seeds and fish.

Trans Fat: these fats rarely occur in nature and are the result of hydrogenation of vegetable oils. The human body has no ability to digest trans fats and therefore they should be eliminated from the diet entirely.

Cholesterol: is an essential fat found in food and also synthesized by the liver. Too much dietary intake may raise blood cholesterol levels, and lead to heart disease. Cholesterol is transported through the bloodstream by lipoproteins.

HDL's: (High-Density Lipoproteins) are called "good" because they move cholesterol away from artery walls and back to the liver.

LDL's: (Low-Density Lipoproteins) are called "bad" because they keep cholesterol circulating in the blood, causing the arteries to become clogged with deposits.

Low-carb, low-fat, omega this, omega that. Every year or two some valid health information is hijacked by marketers bent on parting you from your money. Snack food is more susceptible to this than others – marketers know you really do want to eat junk food. If they can convince you it's healthy, you'll buy food you otherwise wouldn't. So they put things on the label such as "trans fat-free," "high in omega-3," "low-carb," "good source of antioxidants," or "sugar free." Know that junk food is junk food. Just because they added omega-3, or that research shows chocolate to be high in antioxidants doesn't mean you should be eating it. Chocolate may be high in antioxidants, but guess what? Fruits and vegetables are higher.

Here are some tips to help you with your snacking:

Be conscious of marketing strategies that try to label junk food as having healthy ingredients.

1 OUT OF SIGHT, OUT OF MIND

Resisting that Snickers bar or bag of spicy potato chips in the cupboard during a snack attack could prove impossible. If you have to get up and drive to the store to buy it, you have a much better chance at resisting. Go through your cupboards and toss any junk food. Your shelf space should be stocked with healthy and nutritious foods, not waist-enlarging junk food! When you go grocery shopping, make sure to eat before you leave. That way you'll be less tempted by restricted goodies. Read a bodybuilding mag such as *MuscleMag International* before you set out. This will bring your goals to the front of your mind, helping to keep temptation at bay.

2 DON'T FORGET YOUR DRINKS

Just because it's a liquid doesn't mean it can't be a snack. In fact, liquid snacks are very convenient. Protein shakes provide your body with 20 to 30 grams of muscle-building protein and energy. Add some fruit and yogurt or skim milk and you have a complete meal for a snack.

Photo of Mark Alvisi by Alex Ardenti

3 SNACKING FOR TWO

Instead of meeting your buddy for coffee or a beer, meet for a protein shake. Keep each other up to date on supplements, bodybuilding progress and any interesting new exercises you've found.

4 CLOSE AT HAND

Keep healthy snacks stashed all over the place: in a desk drawer at work, your briefcase, your locker or your gym bag. If you have healthy snacks readily available when the munchies hit, you'll be far less likely to rush out to the coffee truck or the corner store for a candy bar or bag of nachos.

EXAMPLES OF GOOD MUSCLE-BUILDING SNACKS

- Whole grain wrap with natural peanut butter and a banana rolled up inside
- Celery sticks with peanut butter and raisins on top
- Whole grain bread or rice cakes with natural nut butter and a glass of milk
- Low-fat cheese cubes
- Hardboiled eggs
- Yogurt mixed with fruit and nuts
- Cottage cheese mixed with fruit and nuts
- Cottage cheese mixed with tuna and salsa
- Trail mix (stick to a handful)
- Nuts (ditto)
- rutides such as carrot sticks, broccoli or cauliflower florets, cherry tomatoes, etc., served with hummus or yogurt tzatziki
- Half of a turkey or tuna sandwich on whole wheat bread
- Yogurt and granola
- Leftover chicken or turkey (great to eat cold)
- Healthy fiber-rich or grain cereal (great to eat dry from a baggie)
- Half a large whole wheat bagel with light cream cheese
- Apples, bananas, oranges, strawberries, grapes, other berries and fruit
- Fruit smoothie in a thermos
- Low-fat muffin
- Low-fat granola bars without the added sugars
- Nutritional supplement bars (Be careful. Make sure they are not over 200 calories, have fewer than 7 grams of fat, and carry significant nutrients without excess or artificial sugar.)

Photo of Mike O'Hearn by Robert Reiff

There are numerous healthy snacks that will keep your muscle-building goals on track. Plan ahead to avoid junk food cravings.

CHAPTER 38

Supplements

"Many of the speakers displayed an extreme level of bias and rhetoric, and attempted to convince the audience that supplement use by athletes is cheating of a comparable nature to the use of anabolic steroids. Of course none of them presented data to support these claims."

–Will Brink, regular *MuscleMag International* columnist, commenting on a U.S. government-sponsored conference that he attended.

Bodybuilders have been using supplements since the 1940s. However, since the first edition of this book hit the stands in 1997 there has been a virtual explosion in the number of bodybuilding supplements available. But which one is right for you? Are there some you shouldn't even think about taking? Are the marketing claims simply sales gimmicks? To help you shift through the myths and realities of supplements, I'm going to scrutinize some of the most popular supplements available these days.

BUYER AND USER BEWARE

Before getting into the individual supplements, I need to say a few words on the supplement industry in general. When an industry is worth billions of dollars annually, manufacturers and "experts" crawl out of the woodwork. Now combine this with the fact that the supplement industry is poorly regulated and you can just imagine the number of unqualified manufacturers and experts out there.

The bigger companies such as EAS, Twin Lab, MuscleTech, ProLab and Weider are tried and true, reliable, and have too much to lose to mess around with their products. However, you really have to be wary when it comes to products from the new companies that emerge almost weekly. If you're lucky

Do your research when it comes to supplements. Every bodybuilder is different and it's important to find the right supplements for you.

Photo of Brad Castleburt by Robert Reiff

size difference, bodily functions, or reactions with medications. Before taking any supplement, it's a good idea to get some blood work done to establish baseline values for cholesterol, enzymes, and blood cell counts. It also wouldn't hurt to have a discussion with a knowledgeable doctor or pharmacist. I say "knowledgeable" because unfortunately most doctors and pharmacists know little or nothing about food supplements beyond multivitamins.

If you do decide to use any of the following supplements or others, pay close attention to any signs and signals your body may give you. If any supplement causes diarrhea, nausea or cramping, stop taking it immediately. Likewise, any nervousness or heart irregularities are cause for concern. Go see your doctor immediately should any of these symptoms occur.

CREATINE

Since its first mass production in the early '90s, creatine has vaulted to and stayed at the top of the supplement charts. While small numbers of elite athletes used creatine in the mid '60s, these days everyone from pro athletes to weekend warriors and everyone in between seems to be on the creatine bandwagon. Unfortunately the combination of creatine's rapid rise in popularity and the public's lack of knowledge has lead to numerous myths and misunderstandings about its effectiveness and safety.

Background

you might simply buy a worthless product that does nothing except deplete your bank account. But you also run the risk of consuming ingredients that could truly damage your health.

Besides recognizing the uncertainty of ingredients, you have to understand that there is a fine line between a supplement and a drug. By definition, a drug is a compound that exerts a physiological or psychological effect or change within the human body. If they work as claimed, then by definition supplements are in fact drugs. Now, the pharmaceutical industry is very well regulated, and this is one of the reasons you need a doctor's prescription to buy drugs. But you can buy all the supplements you want if you have the cash. So you are, in effect, buying drugs without a prescription. And even if the supplement in question is tested and safe, they may react differently in different people – whether that's because of

Creatine was first identified in 1838 by the French chemist Chevreul. In 1847, another scientist, Lieberg, concluded that the accumulation of creatine in the body is directly involved in supplying muscles with short-term energy. The investigation of creatine supplementation began in the early 1900s using creatine extracted from meats. But it wasn't until the early 1960s that synthetic creatine production began. Former Eastern Bloc countries started using it for power sports, including weightlifting and track and field. Reports have circulated that several British Olympic athletes were supplementing with creatine before the 1992 Olympic games in Barcelona. The Olympic

Photo of Marl Erpelding by Irvin Gelb

games in Atlanta were jokingly referred to "The Creatine Games" because a number of athletes supplementing with creatine were awarded gold medals.

To date, dozens of highly credible scientific research articles have been published about creatine in various sports and medical journals. In addition, a number of papers have been presented at various meetings such as the National Strength and Conditioning Association's Creatine Symposium. As of this publication, creatine is one of the most extensively studied nutritional sports supplements available to today's athletes. It's also one of the few supplements that does what the manufacturers claim and in a relatively safe manner.

ATP – The Energy Powerhouse

To fully understand creatine, we need to begin with adenosine triphosphate (ATP). ATP is the fuel used by the body for muscle contraction. From getting out of bed in the morning to those 300-pound bench presses later in the day, ATP is responsible for all the muscle action we take for granted. But our muscles have limited stores of ATP available. Therefore our bodies must continually synthesize it.

The Big Three

The body utilizes three different mechanisms to manufacture ATP:

- Creatine kinase (anaerobic)
- Glycolysis (anaerobic)
- Oxidative phosphorylation (aerobic)

The initial and most effective method is creatine kinase, which utilizes a non-oxygen dependent process that is responsible for all maximal or near-maximal muscle contractions. Creatine kinase rapidly converts the initial stores of ATP to energy, and is responsible for any high-intensity, short-duration activity such as sprinting, jumping or lifting weights. As ATP is used, it loses a phosphate molecule and becomes adenosine diphosphate (ADP), which is useless until it can be converted back into ATP. This is where creatine comes in. Creatine is initially stored in the muscle as creatine phosphate. As creatine phosphate, it can "donate"

its phosphate group to ADP, thus converting it back into ATP, which is then available as a fuel source. This process is continuously occurring, with ADP converting to ATP, and ATP breaking down into ADP + a single phosphate group.

Glycolysis, the second mechanism for producing ATP, is less efficient than the creatine kinase pathway. During glycolysis, a glucose molecule is broken down into two pyruvic acid molecules, yielding two ATP molecules in the process. Glycolysis, however, requires more steps than creatine kinase, and thus results in a slower yield of ATP. Even though glycolysis provides the energy to perform intense exercise, it has two important consequences. First, it consumes large amounts of nutrient fuel to yield the ATP molecules. This, in turn, rapidly depletes the muscle's glycogen stores. Second, the end product of anaerobic glycolysis is lactic acid. Lactic acid is one of the causes of that soreness you feel during and after an intense workout. The lactic acid buildup is also one of the reasons you fatigue after 60 to 90 minutes of exercise.

The third mechanism for ATP production is called oxidative phosphorylation. This is an aerobic process fueled by glucose or fatty acids, depending on the duration and intensity of the activity. Of the three, this is the slowest process for producing ATP because of the high number of steps involved, and because of its dependency on a constant supply of oxygen. Oxidative phosphorylation sometimes works in conjunction with glycolysis. The type and duration of the exercise dictates which of these energy processes will be used in greater amounts.

Don't let all this biochemistry frighten you. What's important to remember is that in the short term, anaerobic exercise is enhanced with creatine supplementation, which in turn provides the increased supply of creatine phosphate molecules needed to convert ADP back into ATP. Also, by increasing the body's store of creatine phosphate, creatine supplementation prolongs the creatine kinase process. This delays the need for the oxidative phosphorylation and glycolysis pathways, which, as we saw earlier, are slower and less efficient. In the research to date, creatine supplementation has not been shown to enhance aerobic activities.

Creatine Usage

Despite what some supplement manufacturers would have you believe, creatine is naturally synthesized in the liver, pancreas and kidneys from the precursor amino acids: arginine, glycine and methionone. Dietary creatine is also available in meats and fish, but creatine content depletes rapidly when foods are cooked. One pound of raw, red meat offers approximately 2 grams of creatine.

Most people, however, store only about 60 to 80 percent of their potential creatine levels. Supplementing with creatine enables individuals to elevate their creatine stores an average of 30 percent. This additional creatine gives the body the necessary ingredients to reproduce more ATP during the creatine kinase process and to ultimately generate more work. At its simplest: more work equals more muscle stimulation and more muscle stimulation equals greater muscle size. Creatine does for the bodybuilder what carbohydrate loading does for the long-distance runner: it provides more energy-producing materials, which enables more work to be generated.

Proper Dosage

The key to proper creatine usage is to find the lowest dosage that supplies the maximum benefit. Currently no optimal dosage amount has been determined. However, there is a huge volume of anecdotal evidence. One of the most popular ways to go about creatine taking is to complete a loading phase, which consists of taking approximately 5 grams of creatine, three to four times a day, for a period of five to seven days. This is followed by a maintenance phase, which consists of taking 2 to 5 grams per day thereafter. Some suggest that the loading phase is unnecessary, wasteful and simply a ply by manufacturers to get bodybuilders to buy more of their product. They state that an individual who starts supplementing with only the maintenance phase (2 to 5 grams/day) will have the same muscle saturation in three weeks as the individual who loads.

Creatine absorption is enhanced when combined with a substance such as dextrose, which increases insulin levels. You can take creatine with juice or any other high sim-ple-sugar beverage. Ingesting creatine with a meal will provide the same effect, as food causes increased insulin production. Some studies have also shown that worked muscles will absorb more creatine than non-worked muscles. It follows that taking creatine directly after a workout may make some sense, although evidence to support this is not conclusive. Many bodybuilders take creatine with their pre-workout meal and then again after their workout with fruit juice or other high-sugar drink

Side Effects

Over that last couple of years, creatine has been getting a lot of bad press. The media maligning of this popular sports supplement has been a surprise to many athletes and coaches, because it is known with relative certainty that creatine can indeed help improve muscular strength and size in a variety of different athletes (including football players, bodybuilders, weightlifters, swimmers, and cyclists).

The heart of the bad press concerns creatine's alleged side effects, including muscle, tendon and ligament strains. In theory, creatine can improve the explosive energy production of muscle cells without actually fortifying the mechanical strength of a muscle, its attached tendons or the ligaments holding together the joints across which muscles and tendons act. As a result, the theory goes, the unusually powerful contractions produced in creatine-loaded muscles might literally tear the muscle cells and/or their associated connective tissues.

Anecdotally, athletes using creatine do appear to have increased incidences of strain. However, I must point out that no carefully controlled scientific study has linked creatine supplementation with a heightened risk of muscle or connective-tissue damage. In addition, linking two events together – increases in creatine loading with apparent increases in injuries – does not mean that one causes the other. Perhaps the athletes who are likely to use creatine are also more likely to push themselves to the extreme, risking injury.

Some reported deaths of wrestlers brought creatine a heap of bad press in the late 1990s. The fact that the wrestlers were taking diuretics and engaging in other risky

Photo of Brad Castleburt by Robert Reiff

weight-loss practices was quietly ignored by the media. Instead, the press focused exclusively creatine, making it the scapegoat.

Most of the side effects associated with creatine use, such as stomach cramping and diarrhea are dosage related. Most users who experience these side effects are taking 10 grams or more all at once, instead of taking smaller amounts spread throughout the day, as recommended. No substantiated reports of serious side effects from creatine have occurred despite over 12 years of mainstream usage. Whether long-term side effects from this natural compound occur years down the road remains to be seen.

PROTEIN

Until creatine came on the scene in the early 1990s, protein supplements were by far the most popular ergogenic aids used by bodybuilders. Protein supplements go back to the 1940s. In a manner of speaking, they were considered the steroids of their day. Protein supplements were

even given out as prizes in bodybuilding contests. Despite the arrival of creatine, protein supplements are still among the most popular muscle-building supplements. As a result, the modern bodybuilder has a bewildering assortment of protein products and brands to choose from.

Protein Sources

Although there are hundreds of protein products to choose from, most can be subdivided into three categories: whey, milk and egg, and soy.

Whey

Whey is one of the two major proteins found in cow's milk, the other being casein. About 20 percent of milk protein is whey. Whey is considered superior to most other protein sources because of its digestibility, bioavailability (the ease with which the body uses it), and high concentrations of such proven muscle-builders as branched-chain amino acids and glutamine. From a practical point of view, it mixes more easily than others, and doesn't seem to cause the bloating and gastrointestinal discomfort that other protein sources are known for.

Milk and Egg

A short time ago we would have said that milk and egg sources were inferior to whey, but this is no longer the case. Refinement techniques have closed the gap to the point that you're really not missing much if you opt for milk and egg over whey. Really the only respect in which whey is still far superior is in its ease of mixing. Most milk-and-egg products still need to be mixed in a blender. Whey, on the other hand, can be mixed with a few swirls of a spoon. Milk-and-egg protein may also cause gastrointestinal problems for some individuals. Many whey products have the lactose and other gastro-upsetting culprits removed. However, most people now consider the newer milk-and-egg products just as effective for bodybuilding and muscle-building as whey sources.

Soy

As with milk-and-egg proteins, soy has gotten a new lease on life. Soy is one of the few plant sources that contain all the amino acids (most plant sources are deficient in one or more amino acids). For this reason, it's considered a complete protein. However, compared to high-end sources such as whey, soy falls a little short. It doesn't mix as well, and its taste is slightly bitter. Still, it has its health benefits, including helping to lower cholesterol and reduce heart disease.

Protein Preparation Techniques

Have you ever wondered about the fancy jargon used by supplement advertisers and bodybuilding magazines when they describe protein supplements? Terms like "concentrate," "isolate" and "microfiltration," are used to manipulate you into separating you from your hard-earned cash. Well, I'm here to help you cut through much of the crap and make you a more informed consumer!

Soy, Whey or Egg Protein "CONCENTRATE"

This usually refers to a protein supplement source that has been concentrated through high-heat drying (dehydration), filtration, or acid extraction to reduce the original to a more concentrated protein source. This is the least-expensive method of protein extraction. Unfortunately, other substances such as lactose, fat, and some other impurities are also concentrated with it. It is usually 60 to 70 percent protein by dry weight.

Soy or Whey Protein "ISOLATES"

Protein isolates are created by using a "wash," which might be alcohol, water or ionization. The objective is to separate the protein from the carbohydrates and fats. The water method is the least expensive, while the ionization technique is the most-expensive method (many believe it's also the most beneficial). Additional filtration techniques then purify the protein isolate even further. The alcohol method is rarely used for soy protein isolates because the alcohol either destroys or removes the beneficial "isoflavones" you keep reading about. Most manufacturers use water separation techniques to prepare soy protein isolates.

Microfiltration and Cross Microfiltration

These terms describe the type of filter used to further refine and separate unwanted substances from, the concentrated protein. Nothing mystical involved!

Ion Exchange

Most molecules possess either a negative or positive charge. This fact can be taken advantage of to extract or separate the protein molecules from most of the other substances in the source. It is primarily used in preparing whey protein isolates.

Hydrolyzed Protein

Hydrolysis is a preparation technique involving the addition of water molecules to protein sources to help break

GET YOUR POST-WORKOUT PROTEIN

If you want larger muscles, consuming protein after a heavy weight-training session is important for muscle growth and repair. However, you can benefit from protein even when you exercise at a low intensity, according to Kristine Clark, PhD., RD, director of sports nutrition and assistant professor of nutrition science at Penn State University. "But protein alone does not appear to aid recovery," she says. "If total caloric intake is insufficient, protein after exercise will not benefit recovery. The best kinds of protein after exercise are complete proteins – those that contain all essential amino acids. Complete proteins are found in any form of food derived from animal sources and in soy. Aim for 20 to 30 grams of protein after your workout."

GREAT WORKOUT!

Illustration by Mark Collins

them down into smaller molecules called peptides. Peptides are chains of two to five amino acids (the building blocks of protein), which are theoretically absorbed by the body more quickly than protein. As this is the most expensive approach it rarely appears on protein supplement labels. For marketing purposes, some companies will add just enough to get it on the label in an attempt to make their product look better. Unless you have digestive problems or are hospitalized, there is little benefit to forking out extra cash for expensive hydrolyzed protein supplements.

> " Another shake you had better be consuming on a regular basis if lean muscle gain is your goal is the post-workout shake. Your body is in a highly anabolic state immediately after a workout and in a unique position to suck up nutrients."
>
> – Ron Harris, regular *MuscleMag International* contributor

Methods for Measuring Protein Sources

Since biochemists love classifying and measuring molecular compounds, it's not surprising that protein has been given plenty of attention. Here are some of the more common terms you'll see in biochemistry and nutrition journals. These terms are also frequently used by supplement manufacturers to try and hype their product.

PER (Protein Efficiency Ratio)

This is an old (read: outdated) method of measuring protein quality based on the growth rate of young rats using various protein combinations. Initially, egg protein with a PER of 2.5 was considered an excellent standard to compare other proteins against. Later, casein (milk protein) with a PER of 3.0 started being used. The drawback with the PER method is that it gives too much importance to the essential amino acid methionine. Methionine is highly valuable to hair development in rats – something most humans are not too worried about.

NPU (Net Protein Utilization)

This is another outdated and now seldom-used measure to reflect the value of protein foods. It is basically the amount of protein that a given food makes available to your body based on digestibility and the amino acid com-

position. A value of 100 indicates that every gram of protein eaten would be used to produce lean tissue. The highest NPU is egg protein, with a score of 94.

BV (Biological Value)

Also outdated, the BV scale is still used. This system evaluates protein based on the amount of nitrogen retained by the body after absorption of a given protein source. Again the egg is the standard and the highest value possible is 100, even though some supplement companies try to tell you that their products score higher.

PDCAAS (Protein Digestibility Corrected Amino Acid Score)

While a mouthful to say, this protein quality system is considered to be most reliable. The highest score is 1.0 and this is given to any protein source considered complete for use by the human body. Soy protein isolates, egg white, whey protein isolates and casein proteins supplements all score 1.0 on this test. For comparison, such food sources as beef and beans scored 0.92 and 0.68, respectively.

Do I Need a Protein Supplement?

Supplement manufacturers have made billions from sales of protein to bodybuilders. In fact, much of the Weider empire was built from selling protein supplements to aspiring Schwarzeneggers. But how much protein is too much? Critics have argued for decades that an excessive amount of protein is not only unnecessary, but also potentially dangerous. They argue that bodybuilders and other strength athletes only need the RDA of .8 grams per kilogram of bodyweight to make all the gains they want; that any excess will simply be converted to fat. Some claim that extra protein places too much stress on the kidneys. However, the studies they use to support this claim involve patients with pre-existing kidney problems. To date there are few, if any, peer-reviewed studies linking the effect of high-protein diets on kidney health in bodybuilders.

So How Much?

Although I can't tell you precisely how much protein to use I am convinced that the RDA of .8 grams per pound of bodyweight is indeed too low for any athlete – but especially bodybuilders. (And just about every bodybuilder and bodybuilding expert I know agrees.) Based on this value an 80-kilogram man (about 176 pounds) would require only 64 grams of protein per day. This might be adequate if our 176-pounder was sedentary during the day and stretched in front of the TV at night. But if this individual is performing four or five weight-training sessions and three or four cardio sessions per week, he or she will need more. The value that gets quoted most often by bodybuilders and in the bodybuilding literature is one gram per pound of bodyweight per day. Some supplement manufacturers and 300-pound bodybuilders suggest higher – 2 to 3 grams per pound of bodyweight, but this is probably overkill. My advice is to try and obtain most of your protein from natural food sources such as meat, fish and chicken, and then add one or two protein shakes per day.

How to Mix a Protein Drink

You'd think that mixing a protein drink would be simple, but you'd be amazed at how many people screw it up! First you have to understand that you're trying to build quality lean muscle, not just body mass. Before you begin experimenting, read protein supplement labels carefully. Many cheaper brands are loaded with sugar and inferior protein sources. Stick to a reputable brand such as MuscleTech, Twin Lab, or EAS.

If you don't have one already, you'll need to buy a blender. While most of the better protein powders can be mixed with just a spoon, a blender will allow you to jazz things up by adding in fruit, peanut butter, and yogurt.

You'll probably be tempted to take double or triple the recommended amount of protein, but there's no need. The human body can only use about 20 to 30 grams of protein at any given time (about the amount that one

scoop of protein plus milk will provide). Taking two or three times the serving size could give you gas, nausea or digestive problems. Besides, the excess will just get deposited around your waistline.

What else can you add? The options are almost endless. While juice and water make decent mixing mediums, most bodybuilders prefer milk. Unless you're lactose intolerant, milk is an excellent source of protein, carbohydrates and calcium, and it makes your protein shake taste more like a milkshake … never a bad thing! For extra nutrients and taste, add in some fruit such as banana, strawberries, berries or kiwi. A tablespoon or two of peanut butter makes another great addition (natural peanut butter, not the commercial brands loaded with trans fats and sugar). You can add oatmeal, flaxseed or other high-fiber, high-nutrition choices. Blend first on medium to chop the solid ingredients, then switch to high speed to liquefy.

If you are lactose intolerant, you may be able to use yogurt. Yogurt is a milk product, but can usually be tolerated by those who cannot digest lactose. Special bacteria in the yogurt break down much of the lactose. One type of bacteria, called lactobacillus acidophilus, also implants in the intestine and produces some of the B vitamins. Yogurt is an excellent source of protein, minerals and carbohydrates. It has even been linked to lowered cholesterol levels and increased longevity. Again, I'm talking about natural yogurt. Look for plain, low-fat yogurt with live bacterial cultures and no fillers.

AMINO ACIDS

Amino acids are the building blocks of protein and muscle tissue. Consuming amino acids instead of protein seems to make more sense. Already in digested form, (you digest protein down to the various amino acids) they place less stress on the liver and kidneys. Amino acids are directly absorbed into the bloodstream.

As sensible as this appears it may be misleading. First of all, scientists are not sure in what proportions the amino acids are best consumed. Second, as there are 20 to 22 amino acids, you'd have to consume this many differ-

Your health is of utmost importance, so be wary of the cheaper supplements. Spending a bit more money is well worth it to ensure your're getting quality products.

Photo of Joey Gloor by Irvin Gelb

ent supplements. Third, since they need to undergo a more extensive production process, amino acid supplements are much more expensive. Finally and most importantly, there is both scientific and anecdotal evidence to suggest that large amounts of some amino acids may be harmful – either by themselves or when combined with other amino acids or supplements.

Many people argue if you are eating enough high-quality protein in the form of food, then amino acid supplements are not necessary and simply a waste of money. Furthermore, it seems that our society is becoming increasingly dependent upon pills as quick-fix solutions to everything. Combine that with a "more-is-more" mentality and you have problems. The common painkiller Aspirin® is a perfect example. One or two Aspirin® might cure your headache, but 100 will not cure it faster. In fact, this amount of drug will probably kill you. The same might apply to amino acids. Your body evolved to remove the amino acids it needs from food in a slow and controlled manner. The digestive process can be called selective absorption. The body breaks down food at its own pace, removing what it needs when it needs it. Jumping over much of the digestive process does not mean you're making things more efficient. In fact, you may overload your system and throw off the balance of crucial metabolic reactions, endangering your health.

Are They Helpful?

Of course there is an opposing argument. Proponents of amino acid supplementation point out that ample research proves bodybuilders can use amino acid supplements without risk of injury. In fact, some experts suggest that they are an absolute must to maximize strength and size gains. The theory is that since muscle growth is heavily dependent on nitrogen balance, it stands to reason that nitrogen-based compounds, such as amino acids, will make a huge difference. For those not familiar with the concept, biochemists use nitrogen balance to measure, among other things, the potential for muscle growth. Positive nitrogen balance means the amount of nitrogen being taken in from protein and amino acids should be

greater than the amount of nitrogen waste being excreted. This is the state necessary for amino acids and protein to be converted into new muscle tissue. Conversely, negative nitrogen balance indicates that more nitrogen is being excreted than taken in. In such states, the body will not only have difficulty building new muscle tissue, it may start burning existing muscle tissue. While a high-protein diet should ensure a state of positive nitrogen balance, amino acid supplements guarantee it.

What Now?

Taking high dosages of individual amino acids has become less popular over the past decade or so. Most bodybuilders report that the costs just didn't match the results.

Here are some of the amino acids and their reported effects:

AMINO ACID	EFFECT
Serine	helps energy production
Alanine	improves glycogen storage
Arginine	helps growth-hormone release
Proline	aids tissue repair
Leucine	necessary in the manufacturing of other components in the body
Taurine	counters the effects caused by human aging
Glutamine	increases nitrogen retention; boosts the immune system
Histidine	needed for protein synthesis
Tryptophan	induces sleep

Branched-Chain Amino Acids – BCAAs

One group of amino acids deserves special mention because of their popularity among athletes. The branched-chain amino acids (leucine, isoleucine, and valine) are named as such because of their molecular structure, which has side groups or "branches" attached. BCAAs are among the fastest-absorbed amino acids. Upwards of 70 percent of the amino acids processed by the liver and released into the bloodstream are believed to be BCAAs. Within about three hours of eating a high-protein meal, anywhere from 50 to 90 percent of the amino acids taken in by muscle tissue are BCAAs. Muscle cells have an affinity for BCAAs. Many physiologists postulate that after muscle cells take in BCAAs, the body creates an increase in the absorption of other amino acids to keep things in balance. As leucine stimulates insulin release, the end result is an increase in amino acid transport and muscle-tissue synthesis. It's because of this that many promoters of BCAAs consider them anabolic compounds.

The average dosage suggested for BCAAs is 1 to 4 grams taken 60 to 90 minutes after your workout.

L-Glutamine

Of all the amino acids that can be taken separately, none come close to generating the potential of L-glutamine. (Don't let the "L" confuse you – many molecules exist in two forms that are mirror images of one another. Chemists use "L" and "R" to denote left- or right-hand orientation.) L-glutamine is classified as a "semi-essential" or "conditionally essential" amino acid. Under normal circumstances the body can synthesize sufficient L-glutamine from other amino acids to meet physiological demands, but under some conditions the body cannot do so.

Recently, L-glutamine has come to be regarded as one of the most important of the amino acids when the body is subjected to stress such as trauma (including surgical trauma), cancer, burns and … intense exercise! Under these conditions, L-glutamine becomes an essential amino acid, and it is therefore very important to consume sufficient amounts to meet the increased physiological demands created by these situations.

L-glutamine is primarily synthesized and stored in skeletal muscle. A closely related amino acid, L-glutamate, is converted to L-glutamine in a reaction catalyzed by the enzyme glutamine synthase. This reaction requires ammonia, ATP and magnesium.

L-glutamine is a very versatile amino acid and participates in many reactions in the body. It is important in the regulation of acid-base balance and allows the kidneys to excrete high-acid urine, thus protecting the body against acidosis.

For bodybuilders, glutamine's primary benefit is to keep the body in positive nitrogen balance, as discussed earlier. One simple way to determine if the body is in a state of negative nitrogen balance is to use your nose. Yes that's right, take a good sniff! If the body is breaking down muscle tissue to be used as a fuel source, one of the byproducts is ammonia. There is no mistaking the smell of ammonia. Next time you see a triathlete or marathon runner at the gym, just keep your nose open as you walk by. Chances are you'll detect the distinct smell of ammonia in their sweat. You'll even smell it near pre-contest bodybuilders, as they are often in a catabolic, muscle-wasting state.

Bodybuilder or not, everyone wants to remain healthy, and besides being a necessity in muscle building, glutamine is also a primary ingredient in many of the immune system's potent germ fighters. Such immune-system cells as monocytes, lymphocytes, and neutrophils are enhanced with glutamine supplementation. As long periods of intense exercise can depress the immune system, athletes would be wise to supplement with glutamine. The fact that the amino acid also boosts muscle-tissue synthesis is a bonus.

The normal dosage of glutamine taken by bodybuilders and other athletes is 5 to 10 grams per day. As

GLUTAMINE AFTER TRAINING

The body can produce glutamine on its own, but sometimes this essential amino acid is needed in greater amounts than the body has the ability to produce. If you are training hardcore, taking L-glutamine can help increase protein synthesis, regulate blood sugar, accelerate recovery time and enhance immune function. It is suggested that you take 5 grams immediately post-workout to aid recovery and decrease soreness, and another 5 grams six hours later.

WHEW!

GLUTAMINE SUPPLEMENT

Illustration by Mark Collins

Certain supplements are more beneficial when taken either pre- or post-workout. Pay attention to optimal dosages and suggested timings.

Photo of Benais Begovic by Robert Reiff

with creatine supplementation, it makes more sense to take smaller amounts more frequently.

MCT OIL – MEDIUM CHAIN TRIGLYCERIDES

MCT oil is another of those supplements that seems to have had its day. When the first edition of this book came out, MCT oils ranked right up there with protein and creatine as a must-use supplement. But, like many supplements that fell short of their promises, MCT oil is no longer a favorite with bodybuilders.

As the name suggests, MCTs are medium-length fatty acid molecules believed to act like carbohydrates as an

> **Dave ended up shitting his pants for two days and then was taken to hospital for two days' observation. He was in a bad way for two weeks because he failed to read the label."**
>
> – Marc Rainbow, IFBB pro, telling of the time a gym member drank a bottle of MCT oil all at once in an attempt to increase his energy level.

energy source. They seem to play a role in fat metabolism by speeding up an individual's metabolic rate, thus causing body fat to be utilized faster. MCTs also produce a compound called ketones that can also be used as an energy source. Many bodybuilders on pre-contest diets find that MCTs suppress their appetites and help them preserve muscle tissue.

The anecdotal evidence from bodybuilders is that MCT oils are just not that effective. In addition, large amounts of MCT oils can interfere with the absorption of fat-soluble vitamins A, D, E and K. Those suffering from diabetes should avoid MCT oils because of their ability to increase ketone levels (a common side effect of diabetes). An individual with diabetes taking MCT oil runs the risk of developing acidosis – a condition in which the body's blood becomes too acidic in nature, causing life-threatening problems.

CHROMIUM PICOLINATE

Chromium is a naturally occurring mineral found in such foods as meat, poultry, fish and whole grain breads. The FDA recommends a daily chromium intake of approximately 130 micrograms. Combining chromium with picolinic acid simply aids in efficient chromium absorption – this combined form is the most popular form found in supplements.

Bodybuilders use chromium picolinate primarily as a fat-burning agent. Some experts go as far as to claim that this supplement can literally melt fat, drastically reduce appetite and increase metabolism. Chromium is also believed to improve carbohydrate and fat metabolism. Most of chromium's effects appear related to its ability to make the body more sensitive to the hormone insulin. The exact mechanism by which chromium improves insulin efficiency is currently unclear. It has been suggested that chromium somehow works to increase sensitivity of insulin receptors. There seems to be some merit to this theory, as a number of medications used to treat diabetes are based on chromium.

I caution you, however, because research still hasn't determined the exact mechanism of chromium picolinate as it relates to fat loss. One claim is that improved insulin efficiency causes an increase in the production of seratonin, which subsequently reduces appetite. Another theory is that chromium can regulate the fat-production processes in the body, preventing excess fat from forming.

The reaction among bodybuilders has been mixed. Some swear by chromium's fat-burning effects; others consider it worthless. Since it's not that expensive and relatively safe, you may want to give it a try – just don't expect any dramatic results.

ZMA

ZMA is the name given to a patented mineral formula containing 30 milligrams of zinc and 450 milligrams of magnesium along with 11 milligrams of vitamin B-6. Balco Labs was the original developer. If this name sounds familiar it's because Balco Labs was made famous when it was raided by federal agents in September of 2006. The owner of the lab was charged with selling designer steroids to some of the world's top athletes.

Balco observed that athletes often had mineral deficiencies, including zinc and magnesium. Zinc plays a major role in testosterone production and magnesium helps oxygenate muscle tissue. It stands to reason that deficiencies in either can severely hamper muscle-building abilities. According to Balco, multivitamins that contain identical amounts of these minerals will not cure the deficiency for athletes, but taking the minerals separately in their ZMA product can, because of the theory of competing nutrients. If you take these products on their own they do not compete with other minerals in your body and therefore you can use more of them.

Many bodybuilders supplementing with ZMA have reported that they sleep better. The importance of regular sleep for building muscle was discussed earlier and needs to be re-emphasized. Sleep is a time when many anabolic hormones (including testosterone and growth hormone) are released in greater concentrations. Sleep is also the time when muscle tissue is built and repaired. To support their claims, Balco released the results of several studies that revealed testosterone increases of about 30 percent and strength increases 2.5 times greater than placebo groups. The main criticism of these studies was that the test subjects were athletes on high-protein diets. Increased protein intake and high-intensity exercise are likely two major contributing factors to their results. Besides, Balco Labs basically provided performance-enhancing drugs to top athletes in exchange for ZMA endorsements. Barry Bonds went so far as to attribute his dramatic physique transformation to ZMA. That makes their claims a little less believable.

PROHORMONES

Prohormones remained largely unknown to the general public until 1998, when a reporter spotted androstenedione in the locker of home-run slugger Mark McGwire. Suddenly, young athletes everywhere were desperate for this new wonder supplement. The fact that McGwire broke Roger Maris' record of most home runs in a single season that year sent sales through the roof.

In some respects, prohormones are a direct result of the reclassification of anabolic steroids as illegal substances back in 1990. Recognizing that many former steroid users would be looking for a legal alternative supplement, manufacturers began hiring biochemists to synthesize a new class of supplements that possessed steroid-like effects without side effects or legal issues. Thus, the prohormone was born. While the effectiveness and safety of prohormones has been debated since their first use in bodybuilding, there is no argument about their current status – they are illegal! In 2004 the Anabolic Control Act was amended to include prohormones as illegal substances. Essentially, this act means that possession of either steroids or prohormones could land you some serious jail time. It's not worth the risk of using prohormones. Still tempted? Well, look at it this way – where would you rather pump iron? The local gym or the prison courtyard?

Breaking it Down

For those not familiar with prohormones and the terms commonly used to describe them, let's begin with a brief overview.

Using androstenedione as an example, we see that it is a molecule very similar to testosterone, the principal male sex hormone. The primary difference is that where testosterone has a hydroxyl group (hydrogen and oxygen bonded together and written as –OH) in a specific position, androstenedione has a keto group (carbon and oxygen bonded by a double bond; C=O). Simply put, androstenedione is one step away from testosterone. This makes it a "precursor" or a "pro" (coming before) hormone.

The body can convert androstenedione to testosterone (and vice versa) by use of a specific enzyme that is present

in the body in fairly large amounts. Oral androstenedione supplementation very briefly increases blood levels of testosterone. It is this ability to act as a direct hormonal predecessor of testosterone that makes it attractive to bodybuilders and other athletes. But while androstenedione is a precursor of testosterone it is also, unfortunately, a precursor of estrone, one of the estrogenic hormones. As such, it can have adverse estrogenic effects similar to those of anabolic steroids, such as gynecomastia (feminized swelling of the nipples). Also, testosterone not only converts to estrone, but to a potent androgenic compound known as dihydrotestosterone (DHT). Increased DHT levels will sometimes lead to hair and skin problems.

Other variations of androstenedione are available including 4-androstendiol (4-AD) and 5-androstenediol (5-AD), which differ chemically by the position of the chemical double bond in the steroid molecule (hence the "4" and "5" designations). Like androstenedione, they also have both androgenic and estrogenic activity (but in the case of 4-androstendiol, the estrogenic conversion is indirect).

Another group of prohormones called "norandro" products are precursors of a compound called nortestosterone, also called nandrolone. Nandrolone is a sex hormone found in certain animals including horses. It also makes up half of the popular anabolic steroid nandrolone deconate (also known as deca-durabolin).

Nadrolone exhibits a higher anabolic (tissue-building) activity in humans in relation to its androgenic activity than does testosterone. Since nandrolone metabolizes to a weaker compound than testosterone does, called dihydronandrolone, precursors of nandrolone are much less likely than testosterone to cause hair, skin and other androgenic problems. Available variations are 19-nor-4-androstenedione (19-nordione), 19-nor-4-androstenediol and 19-nor-5-androstenediol (19-nordiols) (once again the numbers indicating the relative positions of the primary bonds in the molecule).

Photo of Chris Jalali by Robert Reiff

TRIBULUS TERRESTRIS

The herb Tribulus terrestris (also known as puncture vine) first gained prominence as a "secret weapon" employed by Bulgarian weightlifters. Tribulus terrestris is supposed to have many metabolic properties including increasing muscle growth, improving sex drive, and "boosting" male performance in the bedroom. There are also reports that Tribulus terrestris can treat colic pains, lower blood pressure and reduce your cholesterol levels.

Mechanism of Action

Tribulus is believed to work by increasing the body's levels of luteinizing hormone (LH), produced by the body's pituitary gland. LH in turn stimulates the testes to boost production of testosterone. It's commonly known that testosterone improves the body's ability to build muscle mass and strength. That's why synthetic testosterone and related supplements (in the form of anabolic steroids) are so popular. It should be emphasized, however, that Tribulus is not a hormone supplement or prohormone. Because it works by increasing the body's natural production levels of testosterone, it works only within the body's natural limits to help men achieve their strength and muscular potential. Tribulus will not cause the body to indefinitely produce more and more testosterone, but rather it balances natural hormone levels. As with any supplement, Tribulus is no quick-fix miracle product. It will only help to improve strength in conjunction with an exercise program that places the muscles under strain and then allows them to recover. Anecdotal evidence suggests that the best dosage is 750 to 1,500 milligrams per day. As of this publication, Tribulus terrestris is legal and doesn't fall under the Anabolic Control Act.

EPHEDRINE, EPHEDRA AND MA HUANG

These terms are all used to refer to the same substance derived from the ephedra plant. Other common names for a beverage made from these plants are whorehouse tea and Mormon tea. Ephedra is a shrub-like plant found in

Photo of Lind Walter by Irvin Gelb

desert regions in central Asia and other parts of the world. The dried greens of the plant are used medicinally. The primary ingredient in ephedra is a stimulant called ephedrine, an FDA-regulated drug found in many over-the-counter asthma medications.

Biochemically, ephedrine is what's known as a beta agonist. This means it stimulates beta receptors in the sympathetic nervous system (the "flight-fight" system). Ephedrine is used by bodybuilders and other athletes for two primary reasons: for fat loss through thermogenesis and as a stimulant.

Thermogenesis is the process of fat loss whereby the body's temperature (particularly the temperature of fat cells) is elevated slightly. Increased body temperature makes fat deposits more susceptible to burning as a fuel source during periods of aerobic activity.

As a stimulant, ephedrine ranks somewhere between caffeine and amphetamine. Unlike most over-the-counter supplements that claim to provide more energy, ephedrine is actually very effective. In fact, it's so effective at boosting performance that most sports organizations have banned its use. Ephedrine's close cousin, pseudoephedrine, which is not as powerful, is also banned. A number of prominent athletes – including Canadian Olympic rower Silken Laumann – have failed drug tests after using over-the-counter cold medications that contain pseudoephedrine to combat the drowsy-inducing effects of some of the other ingredients. The amount of pseudoephedrine present in these common medications is certainly not enough to give the athlete any performance boost. Yet, athletes who have used them failed the test and were disqualified from competition. This illustrates how serious sports organizations are about eliminating drug use in sports.

The ECA Stack

Bodybuilders have discovered that combining caffeine, aspirin and ephedrine is probably the most effective over-the-counter fat-loss and stimulant combination available. Although its effectiveness is not fully understood, it is believed that taking all three drugs together produces a synergistic effect. In other words, when the drugs are combined together, they magnify one another's effects. Instead of 2+2=4, 2+2=6, 8, 10 or more. The same parallel can be seen with bodybuilding drugs. Separately, steroids, growth hormone and insulin produce amazing effects. However, when all three are stacked together the end result is a line-up of 280-pound freaks with 2 percent body fat!

Side Effects

In recent years, there has been an attack on ephedrine-based products by both the media and legislators. While still legally available, ephedrine products must now not contain more than 8 milligrams per tablet.

Much of the anti-ephedrine hysteria is based on a few cases where people died while using the supplement. In virtually all the cases, the individuals either had pre-existing heart problems or were taking megadoses of the drug. However, humans are, well, human, and just as with protein powder or amino acids many people will think if some is good, more is better, despite the warnings on the box – which they probably didn't read anyway. The other problem is that people often don't know they have a pre-existing medical condition until something happens … such as dying.

So is ephedrine dangerous? Virtually every drug is dangerous if abused or if the individual has pre-existing health issues. Ephedrine is no different. When used properly by healthy individuals, it is probably the most effective stimulant and fat-loss compound available.

NITRIC OXIDE

Nitric oxide has become extremely popular in bodybuilding circles. Nitric oxide is a free-form gas produced by the body to help cells communicate with each other. At the molecular level, it's composed of the amino acid arginine, chemically connected to the compound alpha-ketoglutarate (itself synthesized from the amino acids ornithine and glutamine). Nitric oxide is produced within the flat endothelial cells that line the inside of blood vessels. When endothelial cells are stimulated – for example, during muscle contraction – nitric oxide is synthesized and released.

Once released, nitric oxide diffuses across the endothelial cell membrane into the adjacent smooth muscle tissue of the blood vessels, causing them to relax and widen (a process called vasodilation).

Bodybuilders have added nitric oxide to their kitbags for two reasons: To boost recovery and to reduce joint and muscle pain. Nitric oxide increases blood flow, and many bodybuilders believe increased blood flow delivers more nutrients to the muscle cells, thus helping them grow during the adaptation and recovery phase. The anti-inflammation properties of nitric acid are also valued, since intense training is hard on the joints and muscles.

Nitric Oxide Supplements and Side Effects

It may surprise you to learn that most nitric oxide supplements don't contain nitric oxide. Instead, they contain the precursor, arginine. Now, the body evolved to use amino acids in proportion and balance, as earlier discussed, and the long-term risks associated with high dosages of individual amino acids are unknown. Many users have reported experiencing nausea and diarrhea when supplementing with more than 5 to 10 grams of arginine per day.

ESSENTIAL FATTY ACIDS (EFAs)

Essential fatty acids (EFAs) are a paradox in the nutrition field. We are continuously bombarded with information about the evils of fat. Yet, as discussed earlier, some fats are just as vital to health as protein, vitamins and carbohydrates. And to really confuse the issue, EFAs can actually help you lose body fat!

Biochemically, EFAs are long-chain polyunsaturated fatty acids derived from linolenic, linoleic, and oleic acids. Humans cannot synthesize these, so they must therefore be obtained through diet. Omega-3 and omega-6 are the two most important fatty acids to get through diet. The third, omega-9, is considered non-essential because the body can manufacture a modest amount on its own, provided the other essential EFAs are present.

EFAs support the cardiovascular, reproductive, immune and nervous systems. The human body needs

A contest-winning physique is a testament to dedicated training, proper nutrition, and educated supplementation.

Photo of Jorge Betancourt by Alex Ardenti

EFAs to manufacture and repair cell membranes, enabling the cells to obtain optimum nutrition and expel harmful waste products.

Not eating enough EFAs is a leading cause of hardening of the arteries, abnormal blood-clot formation, coronary heart disease, high cholesterol, and high blood pressure. EFAs, unsaturated fats, are utilized as building materials for cell membranes in all cells in the body. Without them, the body has to use other fats, such as saturated fats, which over time can lead to blocked arteries. EFAs also produce prostaglandins, hormone-like elements required for energy metabolism, and for cardiovascular and immune system health.

The relationship between EFAs and fat loss is both ironic and true. Essential fats help us keep slim by acting like the hormones that increase fat-burning and decrease fat production in the body. They shift the body from carbohydrate-burning mode to fat-burning mode. Only the essential fats, especially omega-3, accomplish these func-

tions. By comparison, saturated fats (and some monounsaturated fats) do not increase fat-burning and can lead to increased body fats.

YOHIMBINE TOPICAL CREAM – A NEW TAKE ON SPOT REDUCTION

Much as we may wish it wasn't true, we can't spot reduce, or tell the body which specific fat deposits to take. This aspect of dieting and exercising is frustrating because we all have a place or two where the fat likes to settle – normally around the middle: waist and hips. Most people will find that fat-loss techniques such as calorie reduction and cardio will leave them ripped in the upper body. But getting a six-pack set of abs and for women, reducing the hips, can take an almost superhuman effort. Since nobody wants to work hard to achieve their goals, the industry has seen a boom in miracle fat-loss products. Just one swipe of this cream and your hips will dramatically be reduced! Yeah right!

Photo of Armon Abidi by Alex Ardenti

The latest supplement to be making its rounds in the competitive bodybuilding arena is yohimbine topical cream. But before looking at how yohimbine works I need to look briefly at the adrenogenic system.

The Role of Receptors

There are two types of adrenergic receptors: alpha and beta. There are also subtypes of each, and depending on which are activated, lipolysis (breakdown of fat) can be either promoted or impeded.

Most readers are probably familiar with the beta receptors. These can be further subdivided into beta-1, -2 and -3 receptors. It is through these receptors that drugs such as the popular ephedrine/caffeine/Aspirin® stack and Clenbuterol exert their effects. While Clenbuterol directly stimulates beta-2 receptors, ephedrine promotes its effects by stimulating the release of norepinephrine (NE) – the body's primary endogenous thermogenic hormone. Unlike Clenbuterol, NE is not limited to binding to beta-2 receptors. Besides binding to the beta-2 receptor, it also binds to both alpha receptors as well as the beta-1 and -3 receptors. Its binding to the alpha-2 receptor is relevant to the role of yohimbine, so that is where I'll now focus my attention.

The Norepinephrine and Alpha-2-Receptor Relationship

When alpha-2 receptors are stimulated, NE release is inhibited. NE is nonselective for receptors and will bind to most of them, including alpha-2 receptors. By binding to this receptor, NE acts as its own negative feedback signal. In simple terms, it shuts off its own release. You can probably gather why this is not productive for fat loss. To further confuse the issue, alpha-2 receptors are activated at lower NE levels than the beta receptors. Thus, thermogenesis is pretty much always turned off, particularly in areas with high alpha-2 densities.

Most people realize that men and women store body fat in different areas. However, most do not realize the underlying biochemical reason. Basically, females tend to have a large number of alpha-2 receptors and few beta receptors in the hips, thighs and butt. Men, however, have this receptor distribution in the midsection. With exercise or the use of the popular ephedrine/caffeine stack, NE levels can be increased to a point where the alpha-2 induced inhibition fat-breakdown is partially overcome. But even then, the alpha-2 receptors are still trying to shut off the fat breakdown process.

How Does Yohimbine Work?

Yohimbine is a selective alpha-2 antagonist. This means it can short-circuit the feedback loop where NE binds to alpha-2 receptors, shutting down the fat-breakdown process.

A second, more indirect mechanism by which yohimbine can aid fat loss is by increasing peripheral blood flow to the target areas. Adipose tissue (body fat) is known to have poor vascularity. When triglycerides and other fats are broken down during lipolysis, they must also be transported away from the fat cell or they risk being reincorporated into adipose tissue. Although beta-receptor stimulation increases vasodilation (opening of the blood vessels), it does not increase it enough to remove all of the free fatty acids released during lipolysis. Contributing further to the problem is that NE also stimulates alpha-1 and -2 receptors, and this causes vasoconstriction (a decrease in blood flow). Therefore, increasing the amount of yohimbine to an area would be expected to increase blood flow and thus increase the disposal of the various breakdown products of fat lipolysis.

Now you may think the easiest way to do this is by taking yohimbine in pill form or injecting it directly into the blood stream. Unfortunately, to do this with pills or any other method that results in high levels in the blood also means that there will be high levels in the heart and central nervous system. This leads to unpleasant and dangerous side effects such as tachycardia (irregular heart rate), high blood pressure, and anxiety. One way to get around all this is by using transdermal delivery.

Transdermal – The Straight-In Approach

As the name implies, transdermal delivery means just that – across the dermis, or skin. You may be familiar with popular transdermal drugs such as anti-smoking and anti-seasickness patches that are placed on the shoulders or behind the ear. These drugs go directly into the blood stream. Yohimbine fat-loss creams work in a similar manner – the cream is applied directly to the area holding the extra fat and it immediately goes to work. Fat breakdown is increased through the escalating NE efficiency (interfering with the feedback loop) and through the increasing blood flow to the fat deposits.

Side Effects

Although rare, side effects from yohimbine creams can occur. Most are related to the stimulation of the adrenogenic system. These include loss of appetite, dizziness, hand tremors, and excessive sweating. Keep in mind that, as with most drugs, the risk of side effects can be reduced by not abusing the product. For topical creams, we suggest using it for only six to eight weeks. Also, rely on common sense – if you start experiencing severe side effects like a hand tremor or irregular heartbeat, simply stop using the drug immediately!

GREENS: BE SURE TO EAT YOUR VEGETABLES!

We all know that fruits and vegetables are good for us. Most of us had our mothers threaten to take away our desserts if we didn't eat our veggies! Now doctors, nutritionists and other healthcare professionals push the same information on us.

Unfortunately, most of us consume only a fraction of the fruits and vegetables we all know we should. In fact, on average we are consuming only a third of the recommended daily intake suggested by nutritionists. It's difficult trying to eat five to ten servings of vegetables with our hectic lives and our impatient attitude. It's seems easier to chose fast-food.

But by not eating sufficient amounts of fruits and veggies we are placing ourselves at risk for cancer, heart disease, rapid aging, memory impairment, acid alkaline imbalance and many other conditions too numerous to list here. Including a nutrient-rich "greens" supplement as part of your daily diet does not make up for this lack, but

it can act as an insurance policy and provide most of the protective power of fresh fruits and veggies.

Green Food Supplements as Antioxidants

Extreme stress triggers such as environmental toxins, dietary imbalances and job-related stress, all contribute to an excessive production of what are called free radicals. Free-radical production is a natural process that occurs in all of us. The difference lies in how many we produce and more importantly, how effectively our bodies can neutralize them. Free radicals are atoms, usually oxygen, that have lost a smaller subunit called an electron. That loss makes them unstable, so they try to take electrons from other molecules within the body. It is this "kidnapping" of electrons that causes damage at the cellular level. Unless neutralized, excessive free radicals can speed up the aging process, disrupt immune function, and cause genetic mutations in cells that can then become cancerous. In fact, free radicals have been implicated in many common diseases.

Thankfully the body has evolved substances to neutralize free radicals. They are called antioxidants, and they help protect cells from the destructive nature of free radicals. Common sense should tell you that consumption of antioxidant-rich foods and supplements is critical. Well

Photo of Katsumi Ishimura by Paula Crane

guess what, fruits and vegetables, especially bright and colorful varieties, are loaded with antioxidants!

Maintaining a Healthy Acid/Alkaline Balance

The foods we consume also have an impact on the delicate balance of acids and bases (alkalines) in our bodies. Foods such as meat, sugar, alcohol, coffee and table salt, and factors such as stress and disease tend to increase the level of acidity within our bodies. By contrast, fruits, vegetables, herbs and spices are acid neutralizing, which means they help to bring our systems back into balance.

Food is the best source of antioxidants and acid-neutralizing compounds. However, if you do not eat enough fruits and vegetables, a quality greens food supplement can help. Greens supplements are composed of super green foods such as wheat grass, barley grass, alfalfa, chlorella, spirulina and other valuable plant extracts. Green food supplements typically come in both powder and capsule form. The powder can be added to juice or water and is best taken first thing in the morning. If you have never taken a greens supplement before, the rich green color of the drink may throw you off, but the deepness of the color is a great indication of the nutrients it provides. Some studies have revealed that the antioxidant capacity of land and sea vegetables and herbs is actually greater when properly dried and powdered, offering more than in its original raw form. This is because much of the volume of the plant is made up of water and when the water is removed properly, the nutrient value is not only maintained, but also concentrated.

VITAMIN AND MINERAL SUPPLEMENTS

It's safe to declare that the good ol' multivitamin is the most popular food supplement used by the general public. It seems just about everyone is taking a one-a-day multivitamin. While it probably makes sense from a general health perspective, there is considerable debate as to whether or not extra vitamins and minerals boost exercise performance. On one hand, you have coaches, magazines and even the media, saying that hard-training athletes need extra

vitamins and minerals. On the other side, you have nutritionists and researchers saying that good eating practices will supply more than enough vitamins and minerals.

Unlike protein, for which there is some evidence to suggest that hard-training athletes need more – no such evidence exists regarding vitamins and minerals. The few studies that did reveal boosted performance focused only on individuals who were deficient in one or more vitamins or minerals to begin with.

While some evidence suggests that female athletes who have heavy menstrual periods may need extra iron, most people don't need to mega dose on vitamins and minerals. In fact, as mentioned earlier, some vitamins and minerals are toxic in high dosages.

The best way to determine whether or not you need a multivitamin is to critique your diet. Are you getting the right number of servings per day? Do you eat plenty of fruits, but not nearly the same amount of vegetables? Supplements should be just that – an addition to a diet that is lacking in something. Take vitamin and mineral supplements only if you really feel you need to.

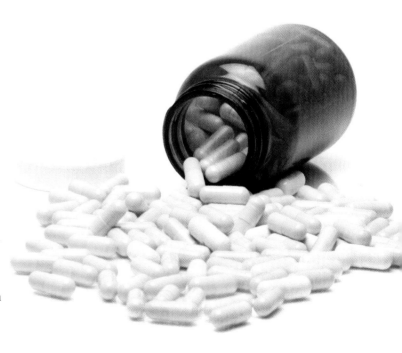

Photo by Paul Buceta

Photo of Quincy Taylor by Raymond Cassar

INTERMEDIATE-LEVEL CONCERNS

CHAPTER 39

Size or Shape? – The Chicken & Egg Dilemma

"A four-inch chest gain is great, but a four-inch waist gain at the same time is not at all acceptable."

– Frank Sepe, top bodybuilding model and columnist for *MuscleMag International*, clearing up some confusion about size and shape.

> **"** Reeves' training sometimes ran counter to the traditional wisdom of the day. He was known to downsize a muscle – or simply neglect training it – if it didn't complement adjacent muscles."
>
> – Michael J. De Persis, *MuscleMag International* contributor, commenting on how the great Steve Reeves always tried to keep his muscles in perfect proportion.

The irony about the never-ending size-and-shape debate is that there really shouldn't be any debate at all. Shape and size are interrelated; you can't really have one without the other. Besides, shape really means two things: the shape of the individual muscles and the overall shape of the body. You can't do much to change the shape of your muscles, because muscle shape is primarily a result of genetics. Fortunately, you have more flexibility when it comes to changing your overall body shape. As soon as you begin building size you automatically change the shape of your body. But you want to ensure that the shape you are building is appealing – you must build muscle evenly. Building the largest body may be your goal, but a preferable goal might be to build the most perfectly proportioned body. Always keep track of which exercises you're doing, why you're doing them, which muscles are responding and which ones are lagging behind and need more work. This is the only way to shape the body properly.

The shape of your muscles is primarily determined by genetic makeup. By training, you build size and thus change your overall body shape.

Photo of Dexter Jackson and Phil Heath by Irvin Gelb

If your goal is to eventually compete in bodybuilding contests you should concentrate on shaping your body from the very beginning. Now by this we don't mean limiting yourself to isolation exercises. Instead, use basic compound movements to put mass where it belongs. Compound movements also give your physique great-looking proportions, because they work more than one muscle at a time.

It's amazing what a bit of creative training can do for a physique. Just take a look at Dexter Jackson or Victor Martinez. While neither has the mass of Jay Cutler or Ronnie Coleman, they can hold their own in competition because they've paid careful attention to their proportions. By following this philosophy, guys such as Zane, Shawn Ray, and Lee Labrada beat competitors who outweighed them by 30 or 40 pounds. But the big guys wouldn't shine without proportion, either. Guys like Oliva, Arnold, Haney, Yates, Coleman and Cutler all have had (or have) well-proportioned bodies with muscle mass distributed evenly over their bodies.

TRAINING IMPLICATIONS

"You cannot build a good physique using just a few movements. It's impossible. Just think for a moment. How can an individual build a balanced physique when typically his workout routine includes 15 sets of bench presses, 10 sets of shoulder presses, 5 squats, even fewer back movements, and probably no forearm, calf, or abdominal work."
– The late Vince Gironda, the Iron Guru, commenting on where most bodybuilders go wrong in their training.

So what does all this mean for your training? Despite what some experts may tell you, all exercises are mass-builders – no exceptions. Yes it's true that some exercises are better than others for building mass (bench presses, squats, barbell curls, etc.), but even the so-called shaping exercises (side laterals, dumbell flyes, concentration curls, and leg extensions) will stimulate muscle growth – just not to the same extent as the basic compound movements. Your shape comes from where the muscle mass is added. Side laterals, for example, shape the shoulders by building the side shoulder. Dumbell flyes build the outer

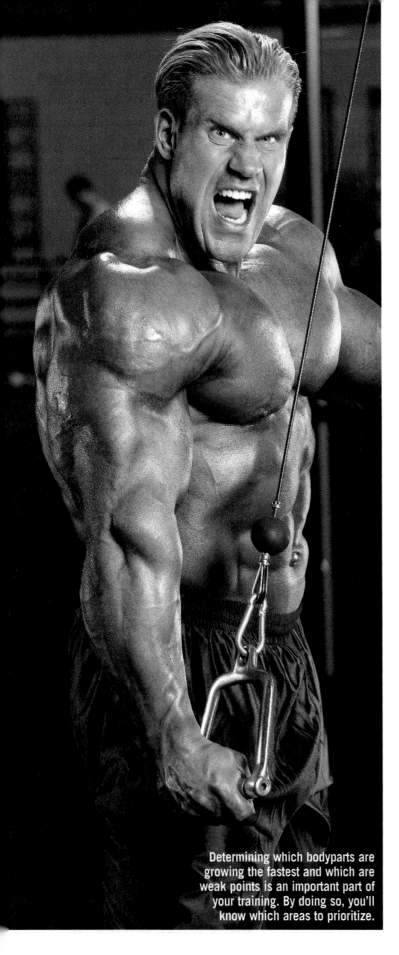

Determining which bodyparts are growing the fastest and which are weak points is an important part of your training. By doing so, you'll know which areas to prioritize.

regions of the chest muscles. The flat barbell bench press is great for building the lower and outer chest, but eventually you'll probably need to do more incline presses and flyes to balance out the upper chest. In fact, sticking to the bench press is a pitfall of many bodybuilders. The bench is great for beginners because it stimulates many different muscles of the upper body including the shoulders and triceps. But many bodybuilders let their egos take over and begin to focus on "how much they can bench" rather than if the exercise is producing results. Because they are using whatever means necessary to push the weight up, you'll often see their front delts take over from their chest in development.

One of the worst things you can do is to become set in your ways. You'll have to follow a program to begin with, but if a certain exercise is not increasing the size of the targeted muscle and adding to the shape of your body, get rid of it. Even bodybuilders who seem to grow by looking at weights must constantly modify their training routines to keep their physiques balanced and in proportion.

TRAINING GUIDELINES

Your first step to fantastic, huge, perfect proportions might surprise you, but it will guarantee results: Read. Read as many books as you can on anatomy and physiology. Try a used bookstore as you'll probably pick up university and college textbooks for a few dollars. Don't forget the monthly magazines such as *MuscleMag International* and *Reps!* Remember there is no such thing as too much knowledge.

The next step is to listen to your body. If you've said it's leg day but your legs are still aching from the last workout, then work out a different bodypart. And just because the bench press is a great chest exercise for some doesn't necessarily mean it will put Cutler-sized pecs on you. For some people the bench press does very little for chest development because their front delts and pecs take over. You must learn what works for you and trust your training judgment.

Photo of Jay Cutler

Besides your own judgment, it never hurts to get a second and even third opinion. While your friends are a good place to start, keep in mind they may hide their negative opinions – or they may just not know about bodybuilding physiques. If you know a few competitive bodybuilders or, better still, bodybuilding judges, ask them to give you an honest appraisal of your physique. Now be warned – you may get a brutally honest opinion. And that's what you want. Just remember that honest comments will do more for your physique than the classic: "You look great." Bodybuilding judges will not judge you on how you look relative to Joe Couch Potato, they will be comparing you to the best onstage with you.

GIVE PRIORITY WHERE IT'S DUE

Another strategy is to pay close attention to your bodyparts to determine which are growing the fastest and which are lagging behind. As soon as you notice weak points, modify your training routine to give them priority. Start training them first in your workout when your energy reserves are highest. Don't be afraid to perform a few extra sets and reps for these slackers, either. In order to balance out a physique it's sometimes necessary to deliberately slow down the progress of fast-growing muscles so the slow-growers catch up. If your back is weak and your chest is strong, then train your back first and give it lots of sets. Meanwhile, train only enough chest to keep up what mass you have. You can even do the same within one bodypart. For example, if your upper chest starts lagging behind your lower chest, back off on your flat presses and flyes and increase your inclines.

The same logic applies to legs. Early in your training career you can begin every leg workout with squats, but if you're like most bodybuilders, eventually your thighs and glutes will start overpowering your hamstrings. Stiff-leg deadlifts and leg curls might not give you the same degree of satisfaction as squats do, but they'll balance the back of your upper legs with the front. And believe me, no one can win a competition at any level with flat hamstrings, no matter how great their quads are.

STRIKE A BALANCE

Another mistake many bodybuilders make is training bodyparts that respond quickly because they enjoy seeing the results while ignoring bodyparts that don't respond well or that they can't see. But just because you can build certain areas to a huge size doesn't necessarily mean you should. Men are notorious for building biceps and not triceps, chest and not back, quads and not hamstrings, and even upper body but not lower body. This is like walking around with a rat's nest at the back of your head thinking that because you look fine in the mirror there's no problem. You may not have a 360-degree view of yourself, but others do, so make sure you look balanced from every perspective.

Most people seem to have an easy time building their upper muscles and a hard time building their "lowers." You likely have a better-developed upper quad than lower, and the same goes for your biceps. On the other hand, your upper chest development probably pales in comparison to your lower chest. A great-looking physique requires a balance between your "uppers" and "lowers" – especially the upper and lower chest, upper and lower biceps, upper and lower quads, upper and lower abs, and upper and lower back.

Finally, for complete development you need to remember that the muscles have two main parts: the large muscle belly, and the end regions, which are called origins and insertions. Squats will do a great job of building the center thighs and glutes, but you'll probably need to perform extensions and leg presses to fill in the thighs closer to the knee. The standing barbell curl is probably the best exercise for building the belly of the biceps. However, to really fill in the lower biceps and brachialis (the muscle that connects the upper arm to the forearm) you'll have to incorporate preacher curls and reverse curls into your arm training. Generally speaking, basic compound exercises are best for the larger belly of the muscle and isolation exercises work for the origins and insertions.

BE A MASTER OF ILLUSION

Just as a ripped 180-pound bodybuilder will appear larger than a smooth 220-pounder, so too can you use illusion to maximize your physical appearance. Hopefully by now you are beginning to see that muscle size, shape, proportion and symmetry are not purely the result of genetics; how you train is a huge factor. Intelligent training allows you to improve your symmetry by emphasizing weak areas and de-emphasizing fast-growing areas. Even with limited genetic ability you can turn mediocrity into greatness. You may never carry the Olympia-sized mass of a Jay Cutler, Ronnie Coleman or Gustavo Badell, but there's no reason you can't develop an eye-catching physique.

For thousands of years magicians have used illusion to make people see what wasn't there. From a bodybuilding perspective, illusion can be a genetically challenged competitor's best friend. Although structural weaknesses cannot be totally hidden or eliminated, with creative training they can be minimized or disguised.

The best example in bodybuilding is the illusion of shoulder width. There is little you can do to widen your bone structure. (You can "stretch out" your clavicles if you are under 30. More on that later.) Yet with a bit of creativity you can make your shoulders appear a couple of inches wider. By adding just an inch to each shoulder, your shoulders appear two inches wider. At the same time, you can use a combination of diet and cardio to reduce your midsection by another two or three inches. The final effect of all this is a four- to five-inch increase in the appearance of your shoulder width. Besides the extra couple of inches on your shoulders, you've dramatically enhanced your V-taper by shrinking your waist a few inches.

Let's continue your transformation by balancing out those legs of yours. First, add in some leg extensions and presses to increase the size of your lower quads. Then by adding in seated calf raises to work your lower calves, you create the illusion that you have long full calves.

You can carry out similar changes to the upper body. You'll do preacher curls to bring out the lower biceps and dips to emphasize the lower and outer chest. By building the lower and outer chest you emphasize the line that separates the chest from the abdominals. This gives the pecs an armor-plate look and also creates the illusion of upper-body width. If your arms appear as two straight sticks, you can overcome this by emphasizing the side (lateral) triceps. This makes you look as if you have two hams hanging from your shoulders.

The average bodybuilder can expect to make noticeable changes in as little as four to six months. Within half a year you'll actually start looking like a bodybuilder. Another six months and you might be ready for your first bodybuilding contest. Another year or two and it might be the state or regionals. Don't let your current appearance deflate your confidence.

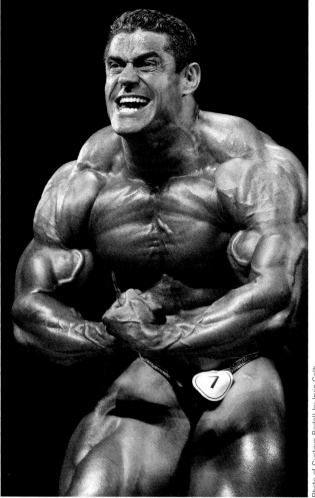

Photo of Gustavo Badell by Irvin Gelb

Photo of Victor Martinez by Irvin Gelb

36

Bodybuilding isn't magic, but it does involve the power of illusion. Certain exercises will help minimize specific structural weaknesses.

EXERCISES FOR SHAPE AND ILLUSION

Now that you know the importance of building size in the right places, let's look at some of the best exercises for developing symmetry and proportion, and ways to create illusion.

Upper Chest: Although it is a great exercise, the flat barbell press doesn't do a very good job of filling in the upper chest. The best exercises for this are incline presses using barbells, dumbells, or the Smith machine. Once you have a decent amount of muscle mass in the upper chest, start adding incline dumbell flyes to your routine to give the upper chest a good stretch and to help fill in the area where the front shoulders join the chest. You may have to experiment with the angle on the bench. Most bodybuilders find that angles between 20 and 30 degrees work best, but others need to go even shallower – say to 10 or 15 degrees. Other may need to go higher – somewhere between 30 and 45.

Outer Chest: To really create the illusion of chest and torso width, try dips. Most gyms have parallel dipping bars but you may have access to bars that form a V. Try both and see which feels the most comfortable, particularly on the shoulder joint. When doing dips for the chest, always lean forward and keep the elbows flared wide. Narrow upright dips tend to put most of the stress on the triceps. Flat and decline flyes are great for building the outer chest and for carving that clean line that separates the chest from the torso.

Lateral Head of the Triceps: To hit the outer or lateral head of the triceps, try triceps pushdowns with your elbows held wide (that is, not tucked close to the sides like traditional pushdowns). Also, try performing the exercise with a rope instead of a metal attachment. The rope allows you to flare your hands out at the bottom of the exercise. Another great way to target the outer triceps is to perform lying dumbell extensions by lowering to the opposite side of the body rather than to the ears.

Lower Triceps: While there is no way to lengthen short triceps, you can create the illusion of length by building the lower end of the long head. One of the best exercises for doing this is the lying EZ-bar extension, again with the elbows flared wider than normal. Another lower-triceps builder is one-arm cable pulldowns with the hand supinated (facing upwards).

Lower Biceps: Nothing looks as impressive as a front double biceps pose that shows no gap or space between the upper forearm and lower biceps. Unfortunately, biceps length is primarily genetic. But, as you're learning, you can create the illusion of increased length by targeting the lower biceps. And without a doubt the No. 1 exercise for hitting the lower biceps is the preacher, or Scott, curl. You can use the straight or EZ-curl bar, dumbells or a cable machine for this exercise. Try them all. After preacher curls, the hammer curl and Zottman curl will also help fill in the gap by beefing up the upper forearms and brachialis.

Side Shoulders: By far the best way to widen the shoulders (at least in terms of muscle mass) is to increase the size of your side shoulders. The best exercise for doing this is the side dumbell raise (also called a lateral raise). For variety, try performing the exercise with one or two arms at a time. You can also do the exercise on a cable pulley machine or side raise machine. Other great side shoulder exercises are medium- or wide-grip upright rows.

Rear Shoulders: Nothing adds power to the physique and impressiveness to back poses like a well-developed set of rear shoulders. Just take a look at the rear deltoids on such current champions as Victor Martinez, Dexter Jackson, Jay Cutler, Toney Freeman and Gustavo Badell. Without rear delts, your coconuts will be a half shell! The best exercise to target the rear deltoids is the bent-over lateral raise. You can perform this exercise either standing up and bent over at the waist, or sitting down on the end of a flat bench. If you find the exercise stressful on the lower back, try performing it lying facedown on a 20- to 30-degree inclined bench. As with dumbell side raises, you can also perform bent-over lateral raises using a cable pulley machine. Another great rear shoulder exercise is the reverse pec-deck.

Lower Lats: When it comes to full back development, few bodybuilders come close to Jay Cutler and Ronnie Coleman in back poses. (Although Franco Columbu and Dorian Yates in their day would beg to differ!) True back impressiveness is heavily dependent upon genetics; where your lats attach to the torso can make or break most back poses. Those with the best lat spreads have lats that attach down low, and their lats have that broad, sweeping manta-ray look. Conversely, those with high lats have a large gap between their lats and waist.

While you can't shift the lat attachments, you can emphasize the lower lats and create the illusion of lower lat attachments. Instead of performing front pulldowns with a wide, palms facing forward grip, grab the bar with a shoulder-width grip, palms facing towards you (called a reverse grip). You can make the same modification on chin-ups. Barbell rows can also be performed this way. But keep in mind that this grip places more stress on the biceps than a wider grip does. You'll eventually reach a point where the back muscles will be capable of lifting much more weight than what the biceps can safely handle (six-time Mr. Olympia Dorian Yates found this out the hard way when he tore one of his biceps while reverse barbell rowing with over 350 pounds). One way to help take your biceps out of the equation is to use Flexsolate lifting straps.

Serratus: While bulging biceps are a dime a dozen in gyms and on bodybuilding stages, there's just something about a well-developed set of serratus that gives the physique a truly polished look. Besides adding a finishing touch to your physique, a well-developed set of serratus will give you more stability on such exercises as squats and bench presses. One of the best exercises for working the serratus is the cross-bench dumbell pullover. Other great exercises include narrow reverse-grip pulldowns and chin-ups, and straight-arm pushdowns. But diet is just as important to the serratus as any exercise. This is one of those muscles that simply disappears under a layer of fat.

Upper Thighs or "Thigh-Rods": These are the chords of muscle located at the top of the thighs that go right up under the posing trunks. Probably the best exercise to bring them out is the lying leg extension. As many gyms don't have this variation of the leg extension, you can try sissy squats and lunges. Also, practice contracting your thighs hard between sets.

Lower Thighs: The best exercise for bringing out the lower thigh muscles is the leg extension, but make sure you lock completely out at the top of the exercise. Other great lower thigh-builders are sissy squats, front squats, hack and Smith-machine squats. The vastus medialis, or teardrop, is stressed mainly in the top half of the squat, whereas the whole quad is stressed evenly at the bottom. So do your full squats, but if you need to bring out your teardrop then do a set of half squats as well.

Lower Calves: Most people who are considered to have weak calves have a gastrocnemius that attaches high on the leg. To help camouflage this deficiency you should spend extra time working on the low calf muscles (called the soleus). By building this smaller muscle you can make it appear as if your calves are longer and fuller than they really are. The best exercise for this is the seated calf raise machine, but most calf exercises done with the knees bent will shift most of the stress from the upper to the lower calves.

CHAPTER 40

Intermediate-Level Training

"No painting or sculpture is ever judged solely on how big it is, any more than a piece of music is judged only on how long it takes to play. Size alone just won't cut it. Why should you be any different?"

– *MuscleMag International*'s editor-in-chief, commenting on the state of bodybuilding in which size, above all else, seems to be vogue.

While it's difficult to determine precisely when one becomes an intermediate-level bodybuilder, the general opinion is that once you've completed four to six months of regular and consistent training you may consider yourself intermediate.

Initially, one exercise per bodypart produced good results. However, by now your muscles have adapted to that workload, developing the strength and conditioning to handle more intense workouts. You might add more sets and more exercises. The core of your workouts will still be basic compound exercises, but you'll now start adding some isolation exercises (the exception to this will be back training because most exercises are compound movements). Up until now you have been working your full body three days a week. The incorporation of these extra exercises into your program will mean splitting your workouts.

Different exercise positions and variations will recruit different muscle fibers, allowing you to maximize mass and shape.

INTERMEDIATE TRAINING ROUTINES
Four-Day Splits

"You must realize that no single exercise will work an entire muscle. Different exercise positions bring different muscle fibers into play. Therefore, mass and shape are both best built by doing a number of exercises for each muscle group."

– Editorial in *MuscleMag International*

Photo of Armin Scholz by Robert Reiff

I've listed the following routines as Day 1: Monday and Thursday, and Day 2: Tuesday and Friday; you can perform them on a two-days-on/one-day-off or one-day-on/one-day-off schedule. You can even alternate these in a two-week program. No matter what version you follow, simply perform the opposite workout from the previous day's training. And make sure to take your days off! The body needs rest in order to build muscle. Please see exercise descriptions in Appendix Two for details.

Training splits aren't set in stone – adjust your program and find a split that works best for your bodybuilding goals.

ROUTINE (1a)

Monday-Thursday

EXERCISE	SETS	REPS
Flat Bench Presses	3	8–12
Incline Flyes	3	8–12
Chin-Ups	3	8–12
One-Arm Rows	3	8–12
Barbell Curls	3	8–12
Concentration Curls	3	8–12
External Rotations/Internal Rotations	2 each	15–20
Crunches	3	15–20
Leg Raises	3	15–12

ROUTINE (1b)

Tuesday-Friday

EXERCISE	SETS	REPS
Squats	3	8–12
Leg Extensions	3	8–12
Leg Curls	3	8–12
Standing Calf Raises	3	15–20
Seated Calf Raises	3	15–20
Shoulder Presses	3	8–12
Lateral Raises	3	8–12
Bench Dips	3	8–12
One-Arm Reverse-Grip Pushdowns	3	8–12

ROUTINE (2a)

Monday-Thursday

EXERCISE	SETS	REPS
Incline Bench Presses	3	8–12
Flat Flyes	3	8–12
Barbell Rows	3	8–12
Lat Pulldowns	3	8–12
Dumbell Curls	3	8–12
Preacher Curls	3	8–12
External Rotations	2	15–20
Internal Rotations	2	15–20
Crunches	3	15–20
Reverse Crunches	3	15–20

ROUTINE (2b)

Tuesday-Friday

EXERCISE	SETS	REPS
Leg Presses	3	8–12
Hack Squats	3	8–12
Lying Leg Curls	3	8–12
Toe Presses	3	15–20
Seated Calf Raises	3	15–20
Front Barbell Presses	3	8–12
Bent-Over Laterals	3	8–12
Barbell Shrugs	3	8–12
Lying Extensions	3	8–12
Dumbell Extensions	3	8–12

ROUTINE (3a)

Monday-Thursday

EXERCISE	SETS	REPS
Flat Dumbell Presses	3	8–12
Incline Flyes	3	8–12
Military Presses	3	8–12
Lateral Raises	3	8–12
Upright Rows	3	8–12
Upright Dips	3	8–12
One-Arm Reverse-Grip Pushdowns	3	8–12
External Rotations/Internal Rotations	2 each	15–20
Swiss-Ball Crunches	3	15–20
Ball Passes (with partner)	3	15–12

ROUTINE (3b)

Tuesday-Friday

EXERCISE	SETS	REPS
Squats	3	8–12
Hack Squats	3	8–12
Stiff-Leg Deadlifts	3	8–12
Standing Calf Raises	3	15–20
Seated Calf Raises	3	15–20
T-Bar Rows	3	8–12
Seated Cable Rows	3	8–12
Barbell Curls	3	8–12
Dumbell Curls	3	8–12
Bench Dips	3	8–12

ROUTINE (4a)

Monday-Thursday

EXERCISE	SETS	REPS
Dips	3	8–12
Incline Dumbell Presses	3	8–12
Front Barbell Presses	3	8–12
Lateral Raises	3	8–12
Narrow-Grip Bench Presses	3	8–12
Triceps Pushdowns	3	8–12
External Rotations/Internal Rotations	2 each	15–20
Roman-Chair Sit-Ups	3	15–20
Swiss-Ball Crunches	3	15–20

ROUTINE (4b)

Tuesday-Friday

EXERCISE	SETS	REPS
Leg Presses	3	8–12
Leg Extensions	3	8–12
Seated Leg Curls	3	8–12
Standing Calf Raises	3	8–12
Toe Presses	3	15–20
Chin-Ups	3	8–12
Seated Pulley Rows	3	8–12
Seated Incline Dumbell Curls	2	8–12
Standing Cable Curls	3	8–12

ROUTINE (5a)

Monday-Thursday

EXERCISE	SETS	REPS
Squats	3	8–12
Leg Extensions	3	8–12
Lying Leg Curls	3	8–12
Standing/Seated Calf Raises	3 each	15–20
Flat Bench Presses	3	8–12
Incline Dumbell Flyes	3	8–12
Lying Extensions	3	8–12
Rope Pushdowns	3	8–12
External Rotations/Internal Rotations	2 each	15–20

ROUTINE (5b)

Tuesday-Friday

EXERCISE	SETS	REPS
Bent-Over Rows	3	8–12
Lat Pulldowns	3	8–12
Dumbell Presses	3	8–12
Upright Rows	3	8–12
Barbell Shrugs	3	8–12
Preacher Curls	3	8–12
Alternating Dumbell Curls	3	8–12
Reverse Crunches	3	15–20
Swiss-Ball Crunches	3	15–20

ROUTINE (6a)

Monday-Thursday

EXERCISE	SETS	REPS
Leg Presses	3	8–12
Hack Squats	3	8–12
Stiff-Leg Deadlifts	3	8–12
Donkey Calf Raises	3	8–12
Dips	3	8–12
Incline Flyes	3	8–12
Narrow Presses	3	8–12
One-Arm Extensions	3	8–12
External Rotations/Internal Rotations	2 each	15–20

ROUTINE (6b)

Tuesday-Friday

EXERCISE	SETS	REPS
T-Bar Rows	3	8–12
One-Arm Rows	3	8–12
Dumbell Presses	3	8–12
Cable Laterals	3	8–12
Upright Rows	3	8–12
Dumbell Curls	3	8–12
Preacher Curls	3	8–12
Crunches	3	8–12
Rope Crunches	3	8–12

Some exercises are better for building mass, but even the so-called shaping exercises will stimulate muscle growth.

ROUTINE (7a)

EXERCISE	SETS	REPS
Decline Barbell Presses	3	8–12
Incline Dumbell Presses	3	8–12
Barbell Rows	3	8–12
Chin-Ups	3	8–12
Barbell Curls	3	8–12
Incline Dumbell Curls	3	8–12
External Rotations	2	15–20
Internal Rotations	2	15–20
Swiss-Ball Crunches	3	15–20
Hanging Leg Raises	3	15–20

ROUTINE (7b)

Tuesday-Friday

EXERCISE	SETS	REPS
Squats	3	8–12
Sissy Squats	3	8–12
Lying Leg Curls	3	8–12
Standing Calf Raises	3	8–12
Seated Calf Raises	3	8–12
Front Barbell Presses	3	8–12
Lateral Raises	3	8–12
Barbell Shrugs	3	8–12
Lying Triceps Extensions	3	8–12
Pushdowns	3	8–12

ROUTINE (8a)

Monday-Thursday

EXERCISE	SETS	REPS
Incline Barbell Presses	3	8–12
Flat Dumbell Flyes	3	8–12
Chin-Ups	3	8–12
T-Bar Rows	3	8–12
Preacher Curls	3	8–12
Concentration Curls	3	8–12
External Rotations/Internal Rotations	2 each	15–20
Crunches	3	15–20
Reverse Crunches	3	15–20

ROUTINE (8b)

Tuesday-Friday

EXERCISE	SETS	REPS
Leg Presses	3	8–12
Leg Extensions	3	8–12
Lying Leg Curls	3	8–12
Standing Calf Raises	3	15–20
Seated Calf Raises	3	15–20
Front Barbell Presses	3	8–12
Bent-Over Raises	3	8–12
Lying Dumbell Extensions	3	8–12
Triceps Pushdowns	3	8–12

ROUTINE (9a)

Monday-Thursday

EXERCISE	SETS	REPS
Dips	3	8–12
Incline Dumbell Presses	3	8–12
Lat Pulldowns	3	8–12
Barbell Rows	3	8–12
Lateral Raises	3	8–12
Upright Rows	3	8–12
External Rotations/Internal Rotations	2 each	15–20
Swiss-Ball Crunches	3	15–20
Hanging Leg Raises	3	15–20

ROUTINE (9b)

Tuesday-Friday

EXERCISE	SETS	REPS
Squats	3	8–12
Hack Squats	3	8–12
Stiff-Leg Deadlifts	3	8–12
Toe Presses	3	15–20
Seated Calf Raises	3	15–20
Barbell Curls	3	8–12
Incline Curls	3	8–12
Narrow Presses	3	8–12
Kickbacks	3	8–12

ROUTINE (10a)

Monday-Thursday

EXERCISE	SETS	REPS
Smith-Machine Incline Presses	3	8–12
Dips	3	8–12
Seated Cable Rows	3	8–12
Dumbell Pullovers	3	8–12
Cable Curls	3	8–12
Incline Curls	3	8–12
External Rotations/Internal Rotations	2 each	15–20
Crunches	3	15–20
Medicine-Ball Twists	3	15–20

ROUTINE (10b)

Tuesday-Friday

EXERCISE	SETS	REPS
Squats	3	8–12
Lunges	3	8–12
Standing Calf Raises	3	15–20
Seated Calf Raises	3	15–20
Front Barbell Presses	3	8–12
Cable Laterals	3	8–12
Dumbell Extensions	3	8–12
Bench Dips	3	8–12
Lying Extensions	3	8–12

ROUTINE (11a)

Monday-Thursday

EXERCISE (machine only – not counting abs)	SETS	REPS
Pec-Deck Flyes	3	8–12
Smith-Machine Incline Presses	3	8–12
Front Pulldowns	3	8–12
Seated Pulley Rows	3	8–12
Front Machine Presses	3	8–12
Lateral Raise Machine	3	8–12
Cable External/Internal Rotations	2 each	15–20
Swiss-Ball Crunches	3	15–20
Reverse Crunches	3	15–20

ROUTINE (11b)

Tuesday-Friday

EXERCISE (machine only – not counting abs)	SETS	REPS
Leg Presses	3	8–12
Leg Extensions	3	8–12
Lying Leg Curls	3	15–20
Standing Calf Raises	3	15–20
Seated Calf Raises	3	15–20
Cable Curls	3	8–12
Preacher-Machine Curls	3	8–12
Triceps Pushdowns	3	8–12
Behind-Head Rope Extensions	3	8–12

ROUTINE (12a)

Monday-Thursday

EXERCISE (machine only – not counting abs)	SETS	REPS
Squats/Lunges	3 each	8–12
Stiff-Leg Deadlifts	3	8–12
One-Leg Calf Raises	3	15–20
Lying EZ-Bar Extensions	3	8–12
Dumbell Extensions	3	8–12
Preacher Curls/Incline Curls	3 each	8–12
External Rotations/Internal Rotations	2 each	15–20
Swiss-Ball/Reverse Crunches	3 each	15–20

ROUTINE (12b)

Tuesday-Friday

EXERCISE (free weight only – not counting rotations)	SETS	REPS
Flat Barbell Presses	3	8–12
Incline Dumbell Presses	3	8–12
Chin-Ups	3	15–20
Barbell Rows	3	15–20
Dumbell Presses	3	15–20
Barbell Shrugs	3	8–12
Lateral Raises	3	8–12
Bent-Over Raises	3	8–12

CHAPTER 41

Dumbell-Only Training

"Using dumbells can help you break past a frustrating plateau. You can hit your muscles from a myriad of angles and do exercises in ways you never thought of. If you haven't been improving for awhile then try two weeks' of dumbell-only training. You might be surprised at the result."

– Gerard Thorne, regular contributor to *Reps!* magazine and author of numerous books on bodybuilding, on training with dumbells.

Dumbells are often referred to as the barbell's little brothers. And as is the case with many younger siblings, their big brothers' accomplishments often overshadow them. Most of the exercises we use for measuring strength – bench presses, deadlifts, clean and jerks, and squats – are performed using barbells. Rarely do we hear guys asking one another: "How much can you dumbell press?" or "What's your max on the lateral raise?" But these often-neglected little jewels of iron have an important role to play, and in fact may be the key to jazzing up your workouts and breaking through training plateaus.

THE DUMBELL ADVANTAGE

1 They stress both sides of the body evenly. Although barbells are far superior to machines in this regard, you're still holding one object with two hands. The stronger side will always dominate to a certain extent. But with two dumbells the weaker side will be subjected to the exact same weight as the stronger. Over time, dumbells do a better job of correcting muscle imbalances.

2 They offer a greater range of motion on some exercises. On an exercise such as the barbell bench press you can lower the bar only so far before it touches your chest. You can lower dumbells further and therefore get a greater stretch at the bottom.

3 They are versatile. Every major muscle in the human body can be exercised with dumbells – and usually with multiple exercises. Machines are usually muscle specific, and even the much-vaunted barbell generally gives you one or perhaps two exercises for each muscle. Dumbells allow you to do many different versions of the same exercise, from numerous angles.

4 An extension of #3: You can change the angles of an exercise to stress a muscle better or to work around an injury.

5 They are great for unilateral training. All barbell and most machine exercises force you to train both sides of the body at the same time, but dumbells allow you to train each side separately if you wish. This is great if you want to do a few extra sets for a lagging muscle group. Unilateral training also allows you to concentrate better on each muscle.

You may even realize a physiological benefit with unilateral training. Scientists have determined that when you train both sides at the same time, the brain has to split the nerve impulse. When you train each side separately (or in an alternating fashion) the entire nerve impulse is directed just one way. This may lead to a better overall muscle contraction.

A final advantage to using dumbells is safety. Unlike squats or bench presses where a spotter is an absolute must on heavy lifts, dumbells are much safer and if anything goes wrong, they can be dropped without trapping you underneath.

SO LET'S GET TWO IT!

Hopefully by now you are starting to see why dumbells should not be considered the junior members of the strength-training family. Here are a few sample full-body routines based solely on dumbells:

Photo of Vander Van Assche by Irvin Gelb

Dumbells offer a variety of benefits, but are superior for correcting muscle imbalances because they work each side of the body equally.

Alternating sides when training with dumbells affects the
nerve impulses such that a
better muscle contraction
may be achieved.

ROUTINE 1

EXERCISE	SETS	REPS
Bodypart – Legs		
Dumbell Squats	2–3	8–12
Stiff-Leg Deadlifts (with dumbells)	2–3	8–12
One-Leg Dumbell Calf Raises	2–3	15–20
Bodypart – Chest		
Flat Dumbell Presses	2–3	8–12
Incline Dumbell Flyes	2–3	8–12
Bodypart – Back		
Dumbell Pullovers	2–3	8–12
One-Arm Dumbell Rows	2–3	8–12
Bodypart – Shoulders		
Dumbell Shoulder Presses	2–3	8–12
Side Lateral Raises	2–3	8–12
Bent-Over Dumbell Raises	2–3	8–12
Bodypart – Biceps		
Standing Dumbell Curls	2–3	8–12
Incline Dumbell Curls	2–3	8–12
Bodypart – Triceps		
Lying Dumbell Extensions	2–3	8–12
Seated Dumbell Extensions (two hands, one dumbell)	2–3	8–12

ROUTINE 2

EXERCISE	SETS	REPS
Bodypart – Legs		
Dumbell or Walking Lunges	2–3	8–12
Lying Dumbell Hamstring Curls	2–3	8–12
Two-Leg Dumbell Calf Raises	2–3	15–20
Bodypart – Chest		
Flat Dumbell Flyes	2–3	8–12
Incline Dumbell Presses	2–3	8–12
Bodypart – Back		
Dumbell Upright Rows	2–3	8–12
Two-Arm Dumbell Rows	2–3	8–12
Bodypart – Shoulders		
Front Dumbell Raises	2–3	8–12
One-Arm Lateral Raises	2–3	8–12
Dumbell Shrugs	2–3	8–12
Bodypart – Biceps		
Dumbell Preacher Curls	2–3	8–12
Concentration Curls	2–3	8–12
Bodypart – Triceps		
Dumbell Kickbacks	2–3	8–12
Seated Dumbell Extensions (one hand, one dumbell)	2–3	8–12

CHAPTER 42

Training Injuries – When Things Go Wrong

"The truth is, most top bodybuilders squat, bench or deadlift truly heavy only once or twice a month. The top champs have long known that they cannot train all-out every workout. Their joints won't take the punishment and their bodies can't recover from constant high-intensity training."

– Greg Zulak, regular *MuscleMag Inernational* contributor, commenting on why most top bodybuilders cycle their training intensities.

"Many bodybuilders try and work through the pain, not understanding the tendon's function. They unwittingly worsen the situation."

– Dr. Marc Darrow

Before we look at some of the common training injuries and their prevention and treatment, a word of caution: Please don't read this chapter and consider yourself medically trained. Far from it. Hundreds if not thousands of different injuries can potentially occur to the body's muscles, tendons, ligaments, cartilage and bones. In fact every single structure in the human body is a site for a potential injury. This chapter merely gives you a general introduction to sports-related injuries. It is not meant to be a self-diagnostic manual. At the first sign of a serious injury, immediately put down the weights, leave the gym and seek medical advice. Don't let Danny Deltoid or Billy Biceps tell you "oh it's nothing" and force out two more reps. Doing so may turn a minor injury into a major one – possibly lifelong. Don't let your bodybuilding career come to halt simply because you listened to some gym rat.

SORENESS VS. INJURY

For virtually every bodybuilder the sign of a great workout is soreness. This is not surprising, as any time you subject the muscles to a greater than normal level of stress, one of the most recognizable post-workout symptoms is soreness – and added stress is necessary to elicit muscle growth. Bodybuilders welcome this "sweet pain." In fact, a workout followed by little or no soreness is deemed a waste by many bodybuilders.

While muscle soreness is indeed a form of injury, the injury has occurred at the microscopic level and is the precursor to muscular growth – remember the body heals injured muscle fibers by making them slightly bigger and stronger.

The key to injury prevention is to listen to your body and recognize when it's trying to tell you something. Once you've been training for a while you will recognize the difference between muscle soreness from training and pain from injury. And don't trivialize severe muscle soreness from training, either. It could be a sign that you're training too hard or not leaving adequate time between workouts for recovery.

A NEW LOOK AT MUSCLE SORENESS

No doubt by now you've experienced two types of muscle soreness – the intense burning that occurs during your workouts, and the deeper, more widespread soreness that occurs the next day. The soreness you experience during your workout is primarily caused by a buildup of metabolic byproducts of exercise, especially lactic acid. When these byproducts reach high enough levels they start impeding muscle contraction. As lactic acid is the most familiar byproduct I'll limit my discussion to it.

The body's chief short-term energy molecule is called ATP – adenosine triphosphate. The body can produce ATP through two primary pathways – aerobic, or "with oxygen" and anaerobic, or "without oxygen." The aerobic pathway is the source of energy for low-intensity, long-duration exercise such as marathon running. Short-term, high-intensity training such as bodybuilding relies primarily on the anaerobic pathway. One of the byproducts of anaerobic metabolism is lactic acid, which, despite being referred to as a waste product, can actually be used as an energy source itself. However, high concentrations can impede many metabolic reactions, including muscle concentration. For example, the high acidity of lactic acid can interfere with enzymes that help break down glycogen.

Post-workout soreness, or more accurately "delayed onset muscle soreness," or DOMS, usually appears about 12 hours after the workout and tends to become more pronounced as the day goes on. Generally you'll get over simple soreness within a couple of days. In more severe cases you may need to help the body along using one of these methods: stretching the area, massage, sauna or even very light, high-rep exercise to increase the blood flow to the area. If the soreness becomes more pronounced, doesn't go away, you can't train the muscle without intense pain or it begins to take on a different "feel," then you might have injured the area.

COMMON CAUSES OF INJURIES

"*Chronic stress causes connective tissue to shorten, rigidify, bunch up, adhere and lose mobility. This unwanted gluing and bonding is a major factor in the stiffness and reduction of elasticity associated with repeated strain and poorly healed injuries.*"
– Chris Rand, *MuscleMag International* contributor, offering an explanation for one of the common causes of injuries.

There are a whole host of reasons injuries occur. The most common include lack of concentration when working out, overtraining, poor exercise technique, too much weight, inadequate warmup, lack of stretching, exercise type, poor equipment, muscle imbalance, reaction to biochemicals and even poor nutrition. Any or all of these circumstances can cause a severe injury.

LACK OF CONCENTRATION

In simple terms, concentration means keeping your mind focused on the task at hand. In the case of bodybuilding it

TRAIN ENOUGH, BUT DON'T NEGLECT REST

Working out once or twice a week for less than 30 minutes per session won't be enough to make a dramatic change in body composition. To burn fat, it's best to train at least four times a week for one hour each session. But don't work out every day. The body needs time to recharge itself. Remember: Exercise is the stimulus, rest is for repair. Overtraining will lead to fatigue, which will slow down your metabolism. Be sure to get enough sleep to get the most from your workouts and still have enough gas left in the tank to get through the day with plenty of energy.

means keeping your undivided attention on every rep of a given exercise. It means concentrating on proper form and feeling the muscle work as opposed to haphazardly hoisting and dropping the weight with no thought to purpose and technique.

Whether you're an absolute beginner or 10-year veteran, the key to injury prevention is mental focus. Every time you enter the gym do your absolute best to leave the outside world behind you. The last thing you want to be doing on such exercises as squats, bench presses and deadlifts is worrying about your social life or sizing up the pretty redhead on the crosstrainer. Lose your focus on these exercises and sooner or later an injury will come knocking on your door.

Besides your social life, another potential cause of concentration loss is your training routine. Most bodybuilders get stuck in a comfort zone and perform the same exercises and exercise sequences over and over. Not only will this usually lead to stagnation, but it's difficult to stay focused when you're doing the same boring routine over and over. You end up simply going through the motions. When you find yourself in such a training rut, revamp your program. Not only will the new exercises jumpstart your muscles, performing different exercises will also force you to concentrate that much more.

OVERTRAINING

"Yes, my friend, you are overtraining. Does the word recuperation mean anything to you? In order to grow your muscles need time to rest. Your training method is totally counterproductive to what you are trying to achieve."
– Frank Sepe, bodybuilding model and writer, offering a beginning bodybuilder some sound training advice.

As this topic is of such importance, I'll be devoting an entire chapter to it later in the book. For now suffice it to say that a body in a continuous state of overtraining is far more susceptible to injuries than one in which full recovery is allowed to take place between workouts. As it applies to athletics, overtraining means overtaxing the body to the point that it never fully recovers. It can also mean not allowing enough time for growth and repair between workouts. These concepts are slightly different but related. Generally speaking, a stressed muscle requires a minimum of 48 to 72 hours for full repair to occur. There is just no way the average person can subject a given muscle group to 10 to 15 high-intensity sets of an exercise on Monday and expect it to be fully repaired by Wednesday. Many bodybuilders are so convinced that they have to follow their training plan or risk atrophy that they ignore the classic signs of overtraining (chronic fatigue, loss of size and strength,

Illustration by Mark Collins

decreased motivation levels) and continue to train regardless of what their bodies are telling them. As they continuously overtrain, their bodies become more and more susceptible to injury. The primary cure for overtraining is to listen to your body. It makes far more sense to take a week off than be laid up for six months with a torn ligament, tendon or muscle. Besides, after your week off you will likely find yourself stronger and more enthusiastic than ever before. The occasional week off does wonders for your progress.

POOR EXERCISE TECHNIQUE

"Tendon injury is a real concern for anyone who lifts weights on a regular basis. Lifting weights increases tendon strength, but the adaptive change in tendons occurs at a slower rate than the strength increases in the attached muscle."

– Dr. Nick Evans, regular *MuscleMag International* columnist

Contrary to most people's beliefs, neither the amount of weight being lifted nor the speed at which the exercise is performed causes most injuries. The most common reason for bodybuilding injuries is improper technique or form. Granted, an injury will likely be worse if it occurs with heavy weights as opposed to light, but as long as good technique is being used the individual using the heavier weight is at no greater risk of experiencing an injury than the person training with the lighter weight.

Bouncing and jerking the weight up with little or no attention to correct form is a typical example of bad form. At the very least such foolishness defeats the purpose of the exercise, which is to stimulate muscle fibers. In most cases other muscles take over and the individual gets little benefit from the movement except perhaps an inflated ego. In many cases, however, the sudden starts and stops brought on by poor exercise technique end up placing enormous stress on the person's muscle origins and insertions, as well as the surrounding soft tissues such as the ligaments and cartilage. This is why most chest injuries occur at the bottom of the barbell bench

press, when the bar is changing direction. In fact, bouncing the bar at the bottom puts far more stress on the joints and soft tissues than does loading up the bar with extra weight and doing the exercise in good form. But go into any gym and a quick glance in the direction of the free-weight section will see guys bouncing bars off their chest with hundreds of pounds. It's no wonder so many bodybuilders have shoulder injuries later in life. For the sake of a few extra pounds on the bar, these guys are greatly increasing the chances of developing a severe injury. The shoulder joint is extremely susceptible to injuries from poor form on chest exercises. An added risk is that of the pectoral tendons tearing away from where they attach to the upper arms. As gruesome as this sounds, it feels a whole lot worse, requires surgery to fix, and takes many months of rehab and physical therapy to recover from. Even then you may never achieve 100 percent of your pre-injury self.

Not to focus all the attention on the bench press; the squat rack can be the source of much injury as well. Like bench presses, most squat injuries occur at the bottom of the exercise when you change direction. Done properly, squats are probably the best exercise for building the thighs and glutes. They'll do wonders for stimulating overall muscle size as well. The problem, however, is that many bodybuilders use their knees as springs and bounce at the bottom of the exercise. The end result is torn knee or lower back ligaments. Then these same bodybuilders condemn squats as being dangerous! Again, is it worth tearing your knees or lower back for the sake of a few extra plates on the bar? I think not.

No discussion of injuries would be complete without mentioning that most glamorous of all muscles – the biceps. Unfortunately, in their quest for mountainous biceps many bodybuilders sit at the preacher bench and commence to bounce the bar at the bottom of the exercise. At the very least doing so might tear one of the biceps heads, but often the injury is oh so much worse. The biceps muscles are attached to the forearm bones by tendons. A number of bodybuilders – even the pros who should know better – have torn the biceps right away from the tendon or right off the forearm bones. The biceps then rolls up into a little ball at the shoulder. In both cases the only solution is surgery and months of rehab.

The best cure for all of these injuries is prevention. And by this I mean proper technique at all times. Rome wasn't built in a day and neither will your muscles be. Give it time and before long you'll be lifting heavy, muscle-building weight, but using good form.

TOO MUCH WEIGHT

Closely related to poor form is the issue of how much weight a trainer is attempting to lift. Poor form is often the result of the individual trying to lift more weight than he's capable of lifting. This will cause the trainer to speed up the exercise, twist his or her body, use other muscles or leverage, and jerk or bounce the weight. Remember this at all times while you train: if you can't lift the weight in good form, it's too heavy. This doesn't mean you can never do a cheat rep or two, but you should be controlling the weight at all times, never the other way around. Just because you read how the current national heavyweight champion can bench press 405 for reps or curl 225 pounds doesn't mean you should go for the same weights. Trust me, those individuals you read about didn't start out hoisting that kind of iron – and if they tried to do so, that was no doubt their first taste of injury. Then they went back to training the proper way: using enough weight to stimulate their muscles without sacrificing good form.

SKIPPING THE WARMUP

If you're living such a fast-paced life that you don't have time for a 10-minute warmup, then I strongly urge you to slow down and sort out your priorities. No doubt your workouts are among the favorite part of your day. If so, stop for a minute and visualize what life will be like if you couldn't work out for a few months. Not a pleasant picture, is it? But that's what the future may hold if you make skipping warmups a regular occurrence.

As we saw earlier there are three types of warmups: cardiovascular, general or whole body, and a warmup for the individual muscles being exercised that day. If time permits do all three, but at the very least do the third to prevent injuries. Under no circumstances do you ever begin your training using your maximum weight. Start with a light weight and do 15 to 20 reps. Next add a few more pounds and do a medium set of 12 to 15 reps. Do not attempt to lift your maximum weight until at least the third set. If you are going heavy, even this may be too soon. If for example you're going up to 300+ pounds on the bench press or 400+ pounds on the squat, play it safe and do at least three or four lead-in sets of gradually increasing weight. Below is an example for someone working up to 315 pounds on the bench press:

Photo of Pete Ciccone by Ralph DeHaan

Set 1	135 pounds	15–20 reps
Set 2	225 pounds	12–15 reps
Set 3	275 pounds	6 reps
Set 4	315 pounds	6 reps

Trying to lift too much weight often leads to poor form, making you more susceptible to injury.

Photo of Binais Begovic by Robert Reiff

UNCOOPERATIVE EXERCISES

"The behind-the-head barbell press is touted as one of the best exercises to add mass to your deltoids, but it carries a significant risk of shoulder injury. Believe me, as an orthopedic surgeon I know a thing or two about shoulder injuries and in my opinion the behind-the-head barbell press is a biomechanical time bomb."

– Dr. Nick Evans, *MuscleMag International* columnist, commenting on the dangers of behind-the-head barbell presses.

Unless you're that one in a million, odds are after a few weeks of training you'll discover a couple of exercises that "just don't feel right." Your technique may be fine and your weight selection appropriate, but for some reason these particular exercises don't suit your body's biomechanics.

EXERCISES TO AVOID!

Before leaving this section I should mention a few exercises that probably should be avoided by everyone:

SEATED TWISTS – They won't shrink your waist, but they will add undue stress to your lower back.

BENCH SQUATS – Slamming your butt down on a solid surface such as a bench is a great way to add compression force to your spine.

WEIGHTED SIDE BENDS – As with seated twists, they do nothing to shrink the waist, but do place stress on the spinal column.

These exercises offer few benefits from a bodybuilding point of view and place improper stress on the spinal column. My advice is to avoid them completely.

Some bodybuilders find that squats place too much stress on the knees and lower back, even when their form is spot on. If you fall into this category, stop doing the exercise. Just because squats are considered one of the best lower-body exercises doesn't mean you should force yourself to keep doing them if they are causing pain. Why risk damaging your knees or lower back when you can build a great set of legs using a combination of other exercises?

The barbell preacher curl is another exercise that often proves problematic. Even with proper form and technique you may find the movement too stressful on the biceps tendons. Again, either switch to dumbells or avoid the exercise all together.

A third exercise that can cause grief is the barbell upright row. While one of the best side shoulder and trapezius exercises, upright rows can cause severe shoulder impingement in many people. They can also be stressful on the wrists. Switching to a rope and doing the exercise on a low pulley may solve the wrist pain but the shoulder impingement may remain. If so, eliminate the exercise.

Just because a certain exercise is considered "the best" doesn't necessarily mean it's suited for you. Everyone's physiology is different. If any of the exercises outlined in this book cause pain or just don't feel comfortable, don't do them. If most of the exercises for a given muscle cause pain, then you should consult your physician, as this is indicative of something more severe than individual variation.

POORLY MADE EQUIPMENT

While most of the top equipment manufacturers these days offer excellent products, and most gyms are kept in good repair, there will always be some unscrupulous gym owners who try to save a buck by taking shortcuts. For example, they may hire a friend to weld together some equipment by trying to copy the big companies' designs. This is extremely dangerous. All the top manufacturers (Atlantis, Cybex, Nautilus, Polaris, Life Fitness) use kinesi-

ologists to help the engineers design and construct their equipment lines. You can't just slap a few iron bars together and call it a leg press or vertical bench press machine. The machine must respect the natural movement of the body's muscles. Many homemade machines don't take this into account.

A second problem with many homemade machines is construction. Unless the welder is a serious bodybuilder himself, he'll have no idea of just how much weight that machine may have to support. An intermediate-level bodybuilder could easily press 400 or 500 pounds with his legs. Some of the larger bodybuilders can use over 1,000 pounds. Odds are the guy who got paid in beer had no idea his machine would need to be able to support a half-ton of weight. If you're in doubt as to a machine's construction – avoid it.

Homemade equipment doesn't have a monopoly on poor design. Many of the older brand-name machines from the 1960s and 1970s didn't exactly mimic proper biomechanics. One of the most notorious was the older version of the Universal leg press. Most users found this particular machine stressful on the knees.

MAINTENANCE

Anything mechanical with moving parts will eventually wear out. If the owners of your gym are safety conscious (and get good legal advice) they'll do routine maintenance on their equipment (i.e. replace bushings, bearings, cables, etc). Frequent "out of order" signs on strength equipment means preventative maintenance is not a priority for your gym. If the equipment is being properly looked after it should rarely break down. Just imagine what will happen if the leg press or lat pulldown were to break in the middle of your rep.

MUSCLE IMBALANCES

"Most people in the gym train hard on chest and arms, but when it comes to core training, they do a half-assed, lazy job. If you want your lower-back pain to be a thing

of the past and want to build awesome abs in the process, take my advice and hit a solid core-training program."
– Rahim Kassam, *MuscleMag International* columnist, responding to a reader's inquiry about lower-back pain during his workouts.

The exercise programs in this book have been designed to work the body evenly – that is, to keep the muscles in balance and proportion. Unfortunately many bodybuilders skip the less visible or glamorous muscles and focus on the showy muscles (chest and biceps). Besides the obvious outcome of poor proportions, they create the more serious condition of muscle imbalance. Many lower-back and shoulder problems are not so much caused by damage to those areas as they are by over-development in surrounding areas. For example, most athletes have over-developed thighs and underdeveloped hamstrings. This is one reason pulled hamstrings are much more common than thigh injuries. Likewise many lower-back problems are caused by over-developed chest muscles and neglected upper-back muscles. The result is a drawing forward of the shoulder girdle, a change in the person's center of gravity and ultimately increased stress on the lower back.

Whether you follow the programs outlined in this book or design your own (as most readers will eventually do) remember that the body's muscles evolved to work in concert as a unit. Avoid doing the "Friday-night pump up" (chest and biceps) and train the body evenly. Not only will your physique look much better, you'll greatly reduce the risk of injuries.

POOR NUTRITION

Surprising as it may sound, your diet can contribute to injuries. As soon as you leave the gym your body starts rebuilding the muscle tissue that was broken down during your workout. If you fail to consume the right types and amounts of nutrients, your body won't be able to fully recover before your next workout. You need protein for building new muscle, carbohydrates to supply the energy, fats for hormone production, and vitamins and minerals to help power the untold number of chemical reactions that make up the recovery process. The only way you can get an adequate amount of all these nutrients is through your diet. It's because of the importance of nutrition to bodybuilding recovery and health that I devoted numerous chapters to it earlier in the book. If you're not sure about something, flip back the pages.

Training is only part of the bodybuilding equation – without proper nutrition your muscles lack the fuel for growth.

Photo of Robert Hatch by Ralph DeHaan

CATEGORIES OF INJURIES

"Now don't get me wrong. I'm not condemning the barbell squat. On the contrary I like squatting. But as I've become older the doctor in me always considers safety first, and I do not want to suffer from chronic knee pain in the years to come. So I pre-exhaust my quads with leg extensions first."

– Dr. Nick Evans, *MuscleMag International* columnist

Although every muscle, tendon, ligament or bone is a potential injury site, sports injuries can be placed into 10 broad categories:

Strains

Strains are one of the most common injuries and involve damage to the muscles or tendons.

Sprains

You can think of a sprain as a strain to a ligament or joint. While sprains and strains are really the same, doctors use the term sprain for ligament damage and strain for tendon or muscle damage.

Tears

Tears are among the most painful of injuries and can be partial or full, occurring in muscles, ligaments or tendons.

Dislocation

This occurs when the round "ball-shaped" end of one bone slips out of the socket of the adjacent bone. Dislocations are painful, as in the process of slipping out, there is usually muscle and ligament damage.

Tendonitis

This is the usually temporary inflammation of a tendon. It is caused when collagen-like proteins attach to the outer covering of the tendon, decreasing the lubrication of the tendon and irritating the surrounding nerves.

Bursitis

Bursae are sac-like structures that surround joints and hold in the lubricating synovial fluid. As with sprains and strains, bursitis tends to be amplified by heat and responds better to ice and elevation.

Spasms

Spasms are involuntary intermittent contractions of muscles. The mildest forms we call "twitches." Spasms generally last only a few minutes but in extreme cases can be very painful and last for hours. They are believed to be caused by nerve pressure or electrochemical imbalances.

Cramps

Cramps are more severe versions of spasms that may involve a continuous contraction of a muscle. Mild cramps are usually caused by dehydration while severe cramps may indicate electrochemical imbalances.

Hernia

Hernias are tears in the thin sheath that protects and encloses internal organs. In severe cases the internal organs may start protruding through the tear. The most common site for a hernia is the lower abdominal region.

Fractures

Fractures involve partial or full breaks in the body's bones. Fractures are rare in bodybuilding, as the associated muscles and tendons will usually tear before the bone breaks. Still, a few bodybuilders have broken bones by bouncing at the bottom of preacher curls or bouncing the bar off the chest on the bench press. As fractures are very serious (they can lead to internal bleeding and shock), seek immediate medical attention.

LISTEN TO YOUR BODY

Sprains, strains and tendonitis are probably the most common injuries experienced by bodybuilders. A typical injury will start with a mild case of tendonitis that is at first ignored and then treated with painkillers as it gets progressively worse. At the same time, the muscles surrounding the area begin to ache. Eventually the slight soreness becomes intense pain. Smart bodybuilders usually stop there and rest the area. But a few foolish individuals pop even more painkillers and try to work through the pain. Sometimes the tendonitis clears up on its own but often the mild case of tendonitis may become chronic. What could have been solved with a few days of rest in the beginning might now take weeks or months to heal, and in many cases it never heals.

I cannot repeat enough that you should listen to what your body is trying to say. A couple of days of rest will not only prevent a serious injury from occurring, but you'll also find that when you resume training your energy and motivation levels will be much higher and your workouts more valuable and rewarding.

With regards to strains and sprains, the usual culprits are poor technique and little or no warming up. As with most injuries the condition might be mild, moderate or severe. Often the bodybuilder's initial response

may determine in what direction the injury progresses. Although the two primary symptoms of strains and sprains are pain and swelling, these two symptoms are also common to more severe injuries (tears, dislocations, etc). Therefore you should seek medical attention if you ever experience severe pain or swelling.

INJURY SOLUTIONS
While no two injuries are the same, the following generalizations can be followed:

Stop training and apply ice immediately — one of the biggest reasons injuries take a long time to heal is because of swelling and not the injury itself. Remember RICE: Rest, Ice, Compression and Elevation. Spending the first 24 to 48 hours after an injury following this procedure can mean the difference between a week's recuperation and months of rehab.

Gradually try to rehabilitate the area with light exercise.

Be patient and don't rush back to heavy training.

Photo of Jerome Ferguson and Dr. Marc Darrow by Robert Reiff

CHAPTER 43

Overtraining – Pushing Yourself Over The Limit

"One of the biggest mistakes made by bodybuilders, especially naïve beginners, is believing that every workout should be an all-out effort and that muscle growth is constant. This just isn't so. Sometimes muscle growth has to be coaxed, not forced."

– Greg Zulak, regular *MuscleMag International* contributor, commenting on the perils of overtraining.

Believe it or not, the biggest mistake most bodybuilders make is training too much, not too little. In their quest to dethrone Jay Cutler, many follow the adage: "If some is good, more is better." There is a fine line between doing just enough exercise to stimulate muscle growth and doing so much that the body can't recover.

Overtraining occurs when exercise volume or intensity outstrips the individual's ability to recover. When this happens, little or no muscle growth will occur. In fact, muscle tissue may even be lost if the person doesn't break out of the overtraining state. While muscle loss is bad, getting an injury as a result of overtraining is worse. It's important to recognize the warning signs.

"Sometimes sleep of an hour or two under conditions of complete relaxation will accomplish more reconstruction than a whole night's restless, dream-racked sleep."

– Nelson Montana, regular *MuscleMag International* contributor

OVERTRAINING HAS FIVE POTENTIAL CAUSES:

1 Performing too many sets on too many days a week, even when the intensity levels are low – in other words, simply never giving your muscles enough rest time to recover.

2 Training with high-intensity sets too often each week. The end result is an overloaded central nervous system, adrenal glands taxed to the limit, and overall body fatigue.

3 Training with the right number of sets and reps, but for too many days per week. Again, the nervous system becomes fatigued and overloaded. This form of overtraining leads to fatigue, staleness and reduced motivation levels.

4 Training with adequate sets and reps but with too high an intensity. The body becomes overstressed and flooded with catabolic hormones that prevent muscle growth such as cortisol.

5 Training the same muscle groups too many times per week. Many bodybuilders overtrain the arms and chest. Most individuals need to hit the same muscles only twice per week.

Notice that all five states involve the failure to allow the recovery system adequate time to keep pace with the training volume. At the very least muscle growth stops, but in some cases existing muscle tissue might be broken down.

UNDERGAINING

For those readers who suggest that it's possible to make gains while overtraining, you're correct. But you will be expending far more time and effort than is needed. You work years to make gains that could come in as little as a few months. It is for this reason that many writers use the term undergaining rather than overtraining.

Undergaining means that your efforts are disproportionate to your results. If one bodybuilder spends twice as much time in the gym as another, you would think he would make twice the gains. But this is rarely the case. When overtrainers notice the discrepancy between gains and time invested, they often compound the problem by increasing training volume. This places even more demand on their recovery systems, and a vicious cycle begins!

OTHER CONSEQUENCES

Overtraining does more than just affect the body's physical structures (muscles, tendons and ligaments). There is a psychological component as well. Bodybuilders in a severe state of overtraining report a number of emotional problems, including anxiety, lack of motivation and even depression.

Finally, the relationship between overtraining and sickness must not be overlooked. Both scientific research and anecdotal reports suggest overtraining can weaken and depress the body's immune system, leaving it susceptible to bacteria, viruses and other pathogens.

BREAKING FREE

So what's the first step in combating overtraining? Recognition, of course! Here is a list of the 12 most common symptoms associated with overtraining:

- Reduced or insignificant strength and size gains
- Weight loss – particularly muscle mass
- Swollen lymph nodes
- Little or no training motivation
- Increased irritability
- Insomnia
- Frequent injuries
- Frequent colds and infections
- Elevated heart rate, especially upon waking up
- Persistent tendonitis
- Constant fatigue
- Tremors or twitches

While one or two of these symptoms might not indicate that you are overtraining, three or more probably does.

Once you've established that you're probably pushing things too hard and are overtraining, the next step is often the hardest: You do nothing! That's right, you take a couple of weeks off and avoid the gym completely. A couple of weeks off means your energy stores can replenish, nagging injuries can heal and your nervous system gets a chance to relax. Don't worry about losing muscle mass. In fact, most bodybuilders find they gain size and strength during this time. This is not surprising, because as we have learned, it is during recovery that you make the most gains.

After a couple of weeks off, your motivation level will also climb. But before you rush back into the gym and pick up where you left off, beware: if your previous workout routine put you in a state of overtraining, what makes you think that things will be any different this time around? Within a few weeks you'll be back to where you started. The smart thing to do is re-evaluate your entire training program. Understand that as you get stronger you'll be at a much greater risk for overtraining. Someone using 300+ pounds on a bench press will place a proportionally greater stress on his recovery system than a beginner using 100 pounds.

TIPS TO AVOID OVERTRAINING:

1 Add sets to only one or two bodyparts at a time. Any more than this and the body's recovery system will quickly become overloaded. For example, if you decide to specialize on your legs, fine. Just leave the number of sets for the other muscle groups where they are. In fact, if you are following a true specialization program you will want to reduce the number of sets for one of your stronger muscle groups.

2 Follow an appropriate training routine based on your experience level. Ronnie Coleman's biceps routine or Gustavo Badell's thigh routine are far too intense for beginner- or intermediate-level bodybuilders. Even most advanced trainers would soon be overtrained following the routines of the pros.

3 Pay close attention to any signals your body is giving you. If you feel tired and sluggish before you even enter the gym, a normal-intensity workout may be too much. You might be getting sick, and a hard workout will not only be difficult to accomplish, it will lower your immune system. Next thing you know you are sick from the illness you would have fought off had you not trained

too hard. Likewise, a stressful day at the office or school may mean taking it easier. Remember there is a fine line between adequate training and overtraining. Listen carefully when your body talks!

4 When you decide to start adding advanced training techniques to your program (rest-pause, pre-exhaustion, drop-sets, etc.) do so sparingly. Don't perform every set of every exercise in advanced fashion.

5 Cycle your workouts on a weekly basis. For example, perform a heavy week using heavy weights for 6 to 8 reps and a lighter week using light weights for 12 to 15 reps. This approach also helps your muscles develop more fully.

6 Play close attention to your diet. Make sure you are consuming all of the essential nutrients needed to maximize your recovery abilities.

7 Get adequate rest. Without proper rest your body is never given a chance to recover. If for some reason you miss a few hours sleep from the night before, try taking a nap during the day. It's amazing what a 15- to 20-minute nap can do for your energy level.

Photo of Alexander Fedorov by Irvin Gelb

CHAPTER 44

Instinctive Training and Returning After a Layoff

"To really make instinctive training work for you, you have to know your body inside and out, and you need a strong work ethic. Otherwise it's too easy to be lazy and call it 'instinctive training.'"

– Frank Sepe, top bodybuilding model and columnist for *MuscleMag International*, offering caveats on instinctive training.

When you first begin bodybuilding you can't go wrong by following an organized, preset program. Use the information you find in books such as this one and magazines such as *Reps!* and *MuscleMag International*. Make sure to also learn firsthand from knowledgeable trainers at your gym. Look for someone with a good attitude who has a body you want to emulate. If you read and learn, your workouts will be both productive and safe. Eventually, after all this reading, learning (and most important, doing!) you'll become more in tune with your body. You will know its strengths and weaknesses. You'll recognize what exercises give you great results and which ones seem almost useless for you. Perhaps most important, you'll be able to recognize when you are just being lazy and when you really do need a day off.

The instinctive principle is without doubt the most advanced and important of all training philosophies. But its success depends on you and you alone. No one else can tell you what works best for your physique. It takes years to master instinctive training, but once you do, you'll be master of your own destiny.

The instinctive principle can be applied both short term and long term. Short term refers to modifying your workouts on a daily basis to suit your individual body needs and rhythms. Let's face it, there will be days when you can't

max out on your exercises. There will even be days
when your body is warning you that the best thing to d
that day is avoid the gym entirely. Odds are this was
ceded by a stretch of great workouts using maximur
near-maximum workout poundage. The secret is k
ing when your body is telling you this and when
mind is telling you that it's a really nice day and
n't you rather sit on a patio somewhere drinkin

Instinctive training also means listening to the
ual bodyparts. Let's say one day you plan on w
chest but before your workout you realize yo
like they are lacking. You might decide to w
day and move your chest to the next day.

Long-term instinctive training mear
dropping exercises to suit you body's
tics. In short it means experimenting.
bodybuilding books (this one included
bell presses, squats and chin-ups to b
beginning and intermediate level ma
But for some bodybuilders barbel
ing more than tear up the shoul
Likewise, squats may do more
thighs. And chins, while being
back workout, might leave y
but do nothing for your lats.
months you discover that so
nothing in regards to your
What's the use of doing a
do?" Use your instinct a
for you.

However, it must
also be used as an ex
working back today,
feels the need, just b
back. Maybe you
ing for you becaus
You must always
changing your ro

Besides usir
training, you c
some time off

Photo of Brian Chamberlain by Ralph DeHaan

job, there's someone new in your life or you just needed time away from the gym. No matter what the reason, you haven't even seen a dumbell in two or three months and that latest issue of *MuscleMag International* with Jay Cutler on the cover has got you chomping at the bit. So what's the first thing you should do? How do you get back into the swing of things without tearing yourself up or pushing your body back into an overtrained state?

THE COMEBACK WORKOUT

Few workouts are as important as the one following a layoff. In fact it's probably more important than

the very first one you ever performed. You're now much stronger and capable of subjecting your body to far more stress than when you started training. Your technique may have been primitive the first time you strolled into the gym, but the lighter weight would probably allow you to escape serious injuries. It took many months, if not years, to condition your body to rep with hundreds of pounds of weight. You don't just take a couple of months off and then walk back in the gym and pick up where you left off. Unfortunately that's what many bodybuilders attempt to do. The end result is either extreme soreness or worse: some sort of injury.

Your first step on your return to working out is deciding what to wear. My suggestion is to dress "heavier" than normal. By this I mean a sweatshirt and track pants instead of a tank top or T-shirt and shorts. The extra clothes will keep you warm as well as preventing you from staring into the mirror to see if you shrunk while you were off. Trust me, you haven't, but you'd be surprised how many bodybuilders think they have.

The next step is to design a 12- to 14-day introductory training program. I suggest doing full-body training, one exercise per bodypart and keep it short and sweet; say 1 to 2 sets of 12 to 15 reps. Your workout should take no more than 45 minutes. If you think this is a simple workout, you're right. It is. But it's supposed to be. After a couple of months off, this is about all your body can handle. In fact, after being off for a few months this is all you'll need in the way of stimulation to get your muscles to grow again.

Besides the low number of sets, select a weight that is about half of what you'd normally use. Even if your strength levels are still high, resist the urge to put more weight on the bar or stack. Remember, the goal is to simply get the muscles used to contracting again. Subjecting them to hundreds of pounds after many weeks of doing nothing is neither necessary nor safe.

Stick with this routine for about two weeks. You can gradually ease back to regular training poundage, but always make sure you've warmed up properly. If you're like most bodybuilders you were probably becoming set in your ways before your layoff. In fact it could very well have been such monotonous training that led you to stop training in the first place. If so, don't make the mistake of falling back into the same rut. Your motivation level may be sky-high upon resuming training, but it won't take many weeks of such repetitiveness to push you back to square one. Try experimenting with a whole new program when you get back to the gym. Shift muscle groups around, try new exercises, incorporate some new training techniques. Odds are you'll end up with a routine far more productive than the one you were following before the layoff.

Here are a few tips to keep in mind when resuming training after a layoff:

- Always dress warmly to prevent injuries.
- Don't attempt to pick up where you left off. Ease back into training.
- Perform only one exercise per bodypart.
- Keep the number of sets to 1 or 2.
- Keep the rep range medium to high – 12 to 15.
- Use only 50 to 75 percent of the weight your strength levels will allow.
- Resist the urge to put more weight on the bar.
- Experiment with new exercises and techniques after a few weeks of training.

RETURNING TO ACTION

Here is a sample workout you can follow for a few weeks to get you back into the swing of things after a layoff. You may switch the exercises, but don't add extra sets.

EXERCISE	SETS	REPS
Bodypart – Legs		
Squats	2	12–15
Leg Curls	2	12–15
Standing Calf Raises	2	15–20
Bodypart – Chest		
Flat Barbell Presses	2	12–15
Bodypart – Back		
Chin-Ups	2	12–15
Bodypart – Shoulders		
Dumbell Front Presses	2	12–15
Bodypart – Biceps		
Barbell Curls	2	12–15
Bodypart – Triceps		
Triceps Pushdowns	2	12–15
Bodypart – Abdominals		
Swiss-Ball Crunches	2	12–15

There you have it – 18 sets in total. Allowing for about a minute to do a set and a minute between sets you should be able to complete this comeback workout in 35 to 40 minutes. After a couple of weeks you can revert back to a split routine if you wish.

ADVANCED-LEVEL TRAINING

CHAPTER 45

Advanced Bodybuilding

"As most bodybuilders know, if you want to continue building your physique, every now and then you have to shock your muscles by hitting them from odd angles or with equipment that has a different feel."

– Nelson Montana, regular *MuscleMag International* contributor

"Have you ever noticed how many guys train the same way every time they come to the gym? They always do the same exercises with the same weight in the same sequence, come hell or high water. The rest they take between sets is the same. So is the way they move the weight. Never do they incorporate new or different training principles. For some strange reason they usually look the same too — year after year after year."

– Greg Zulak, long-time *MuscleMag International* contributor, commenting on the reasons some bodybuilders never improve.

t's hard to say exactly when you leave the intermediate level and officially become an advanced trainer. Everyone is different and will progress at different rates. However, I can give you a reasonable time period.

TIME
If you're average, then after about a solid year of smart training you should have gained about 15 to 20 pounds of solid muscular bodyweight. Your arms should now be in the 17-inch range and you should have changed your waist-chest differential by at least six to eight inches. Those former slender thighs should now be filling out your pants and your overall shape should easily let others know you work out. Of course these are average gains. Some readers may reach this level after three months of training while others may need another year.

CONTINUED OR LACK OF PROGRESS?
Another guide is to evaluate the progress you're making on your current training program. The human body has incredible powers of adaptation. After your initial few months of training you probably experienced a slowing-down period. To keep the muscles growing you had to start employing such intermediate

techniques as split routines and multiple exercises for each muscle. Now after about a year of training you've entered that slow-down period again. It's time to address the situation and start applying advanced training techniques to kickstart your muscles into growing again.

INCREASED MUSCLE MASS

I suggest modifying your entire routine every five workouts. To keep the muscles growing you have to increase the work performed during your workouts. There are three ways to do this. First, you can simply add more weight or number of sets to your workout. Second, you can perform the same amount of work in a shorter time period. Or third, you can increase the intensity of work during the same amount of time.

Increasing workout duration by adding sets offers limited returns. Doing more sets at the same intensity level will work, but only up to a point. A beginner doubling his sets from 3 to 6 will in all likelihood make excellent progress. But going from 6 to 12 sets probably won't give the same degree of results. As I discussed in the last chapter, the gains will not match the work invested. A few bodybuilders realize these increased sets are not doing the job and make other changes, but most think the solution is even more sets. Before they know it they're doing 20 sets per muscle group, making no progress and feeling overtrained. With the exception of a few genetically gifted individuals (most notably Serge Nubret, with his 30 to 40 sets of bench presses, and Roy Callender's 60+ set back workouts), most bodybuilders won't achieve proportionate gains from more than 10 to 12 sets per muscle group.

So if increasing the length of your workouts by adding extra sets has limited benefits, what about increasing intensity levels by increasing the amount of weight lifted or decreasing the time between sets? Is this the key?

Let's start with lifting more weight. You can probably see the problem with this approach. You don't just decide to lift more weight – you have to be physically able to do so. And if you could lift heavier weight you'd probably already be doing it.

Part of advanced training is making sure to incorporate change and variety into your workouts.

As for decreasing the time between sets, there are two ways to do this and both have limitations. If you attempt to move the weight faster you'll probably end up getting sloppy and cheating. Not only is the effectiveness of the exercise decreased this way, you greatly increase the risk of an injury. On the other hand, most muscles need from 45 to 60 seconds of recovery time between sets. If you try shortening this to, say, 30 seconds, you won't be able to lift the same amount of weight. Then you break one of the fundamental principles of bodybuilding – decreasing the workload placed on the muscle and therefore not forcing it to adapt by growing and getting stronger.

So what's the solution? Increase set duration and intensity at the same time. This is not simply a case of doing more reps with lighter weight, because in that case the muscle does not get much out of the first 8 or 10 reps. The idea is to make the first 10 reps just as productive as the last. This leads us to the topic of advanced training techniques.

Photo of Serge Nubret

The cheat principle is an effective advanced technique that's fairly easily applied to most muscle groups.

The following are among the most effective techniques for increasing workout intensity without increasing the length of time you're in the gym. In fact, some of them will allow you to do shorter workouts. Virtually all of today's top bodybuilding stars, including Jay Cutler, Ronnie Coleman, Mustafa Mohammad, Victor Martinez, Dexter Jackson, Gustavo Badell and Toney Freeman, employ these techniques in their workouts on a regular basis.

ADVANCED TRAINING TECHNIQUES
Cheat Reps

"What's this, you ask? Cheat! Isn't cheating forbidden?" Cheating is indeed forbidden, but only when you cheat to make an exercise easier – as in less challenging. If you use cheating to make the set more challenging, then it's not only okay, it helps produce phenomenal growth. Cheating is probably the first advanced training technique most bodybuilders discover. Remember that last set of barbell curls when you failed at 10 reps? Instead of putting the bar on the rack you used a little bit of body swing to keep going. You may not have realized it

at the time, but that's when you discovered the cheating principle. Done properly it allows you to hit deeper muscle fibers. Done improperly and you waste your time and set yourself up for an injury.

By bodybuilding definitions, cheating is using additional muscles to help you complete a few extra reps after the targeted muscles are incapable of continuing on their own. In the biceps curl, for example, once you have completed as many reps as you can strictly, you can get a few more reps by swinging your body slightly, which uses your legs, your back, and momentum to help your biceps finish the last reps. You can see that you are not missing out on any stimulation by cheating. Not only are you getting the full set, you are getting a few bonus reps.

You should use the cheating principle only once you are failing with strict reps. If you need to cheat from the first rep or two, you're using way too much weight. Also understand that there are correct and incorrect ways to cheat. One of the worst things to do is bounce the weight up from the bottom. As I explained earlier in the book, bouncing places undue stress on the body's soft connective tissues. The key to effective cheating is knowing both how and when to cheat.

YOU CAN APPLY THE CHEAT PRINCIPLE TO MOST MUSCLE GROUPS

Biceps

For example, let's take the preacher curl. Instead of bouncing at the bottom of the exercise once you have a hard time completing more reps, lock your arms tight to your upper body, thrust your hips forward, and swing the weight up using your upper body and legs. This little movement will force the bar past the sticking point (usually close to the bottom of the exercise) and should allow you to complete a few extra reps. Try lowering the weight a bit more slowly than normal to emphasize the negative portion of the exercise. When you can no longer lower the weight in a slow and controlled manner, terminate the set. Under no circumstances do you keep lifting the bar solely with body momentum or bouncing.

Shoulders

On barbell shoulder presses you can stand up and use a slight leg dip and torso bounce to keep the bar moving after failing at the desired number of reps. Just be careful you don't excessively hyperextend your lower back as you force out the extra couple of reps. The best shoulder exercises to use constructive cheating on are front and side dumbell raises. You use the same leg kick and torso assistance as the shoulder press, but because the weight is much lighter you will not encounter the same degree of lower-back pressure.

Back

The best back exercises for cheating are the pull-down movements. As soon as you reach failure in strict style, start swinging slightly – just enough to keep the bar moving.

Legs

Given the amount of weight used, and the severity of any potential injury, I strongly advise you not to cheat on squats. Squats are one of those exercises where your technique must be perfect at all times. Any deviation could end your training permanently.

The leg press is another story. Even though you'll be handling huge poundage (if not now, you soon will be) you can easily cheat on this exercise by pushing on your knees with your hands to complete a few extra reps. Odds are it won't be the weight but pain that will cause you to stop. Leg presses burn like hell under normal circumstances and cheat reps are absolute murder – but they'll pack size on your thighs like few other exercises.

Chest

The flat barbell bench press is another exercise for which you should probably avoid cheating. Bouncing the bar off the chest is a good way to break a rib. Likewise, arching the lower back can lead to spine damage.

No doubt many readers are wondering how many cheat reps to perform. Arnold cheated on almost every rep. I suggest performing the first 8 to 10 reps in strict style and then adding two or three cheat reps at the end. Also, use effort to determine when you should stop. When you reach the point that you have to bounce and sway the whole body just to keep the weight moving, terminate the set right there.

Cheating is one of the simplest but most effective of the advanced training techniques. If properly employed it will break you out of a training rut and add new strength and size to your physique.

PARTIAL REPS, OR "BURNS"

Partial reps, or burns, were first made famous by training guru Vince Gironda. Burns are nothing more than partial reps performed at the end of a regular set of an exercise. Let's say you can manage only 10 reps of a barbell curl. Instead of stopping the set at the 10th rep, you bring the bar to the top and squeeze out a few more. You may be able to curl the weight only six to eight inches, but that's fine. You're still hitting muscle fibers you wouldn't have been hitting had you stopped the set after the last full rep.

You'll quickly discover where the name "burns" comes from, because the muscle will burn as though it's on fire.

ULTRASLOW REPS

Most bodybuilders take two to four seconds to complete a rep. But on occasion, to stress your muscles differently you might want to experiment with ultraslow reps. How slow? Try anywhere from 10 to 30 seconds to complete one rep!

Ultraslow training has a number of benefits to offer. It eliminates almost all body momentum – and thus cheating. Lifting and lowering a weight in ultraslow motion takes pure muscle power. Another advantage is safety. Most injuries are caused by lifting too much weight too fast. Such abrupt stopping and starting can damage the tendons, ligaments and muscles. Slow training eliminates virtually all these dangerous actions. Keep in mind that lifting a weight using 10- to 30-second reps will require the use of much lighter poundage. On the surface this sounds counterproductive, but don't forget you'll be lifting this lighter weight strictly with muscle power, not body momentum. By lifting the weight slowly you'll have to

fully focus on the task at hand. Most bodybuilders also find that they'll lift the weight through a greater range of motion when they perform ultraslow reps.

Why are slow reps so effective? Well, muscle fibers work on an all-or-none principle. There's no in between. Muscle power is based on the number of fibers contracting, not a graded response by individual fibers. During an ultraslow-rep set, the muscle fibers will tire very quickly, so the body will have to recruit more muscle fibers to complete the set.

A second reason for their effectiveness is that ultraslow reps raise the threshold of the muscles' Golgi tendon organs. As we saw in the chapter on stretching, Golgi tendon organs are stretch receptors in muscles that will shut down if they think that the muscle is undergoing excessive strain. In many cases you terminate a set not because of muscle fatigue, but because the Golgi tendon organs shut down. Ultraslow reps have been found to reset the Golgi tendon organs' firing threshold. This allows you to complete more reps before the muscle shuts down.

With the possible exceptions of squats and bench presses, you can perform ultraslow reps on just about every exercise you can think of. As with cheating, ultraslow reps on squats and bench presses are risky because of the weight used and the potential to become trapped under the weight if you collapse.

ULTRAFAST REPS

Having explained the merits of ultraslow training, it makes sense to discuss the opposite – using high-speed training during your workouts. As the name suggests, ultrafast reps involve lifting as much weight as you can handle with the fastest reps possible. This does not mean bouncing or jerking the weight up rapidly; you still use good technique and pay attention to form. Some bodybuilders call it "racing the clock" – you try to perform the greatest number of reps in the shortest time possible.

Ultrafast reps also have the benefit of allowing you to lift heavier weight. As we saw earlier, one of the primary stimulus for maximum muscle growth is using

Photo of Vince Gironda

progressively heavier weight. All other things being equal, the bodybuilders using the heaviest weights during their workouts are usually the largest. The key, however, is lifting the weight in good style no matter what your rep speed.

STRIP SETS, DROP SETS, DESCENDING SETS, OR DOWN-THE-RACK TRAINING

Strip sets are simple to do and produce outstanding results. As the name suggests, you "strip" some weight off the bar when you can no longer perform an additional rep. For example, say you are using 200 pounds on the bench press for 10 reps. Once you fail on the 10th rep, quickly rack the bar and remove 20 or 25 pounds (instead of taking your normal rest period). Your chest, triceps and shoulder muscles may not be able to handle 200 pounds but no doubt they're capable of continuing with 175 or 180 for a few more reps. Once you fail at that weight, you remove more plates and get back to it. You could go on like this and keep removing weight until you're left with just the bar, but most bodybuilders do only two or three drops. Reducing the weight three times is called triple dropping, or triple-drop sets.

The stripping technique is not limited to barbell exercises. You can use it on dumbell and machine exercises as well. If using dumbells, simply grab a lighter set of dumbells. Since most gyms have their dumbells arranged from smallest to largest, work your way "down the rack." The next time you're doing shoulders try a few down-the-rack sets of side raises or dumbell presses.

21s

Twenty-Ones are named as such because of the number of reps you do during the set. While they can be performed on most exercises, they are best suited to curling movements. Grab a barbell and curl the bar from the bottom to the halfway point (i.e. your forearm is parallel with the floor). Do this for 7 reps. Then curl the bar between the halfway point and the top for 7 reps. Then lower the bar back to your thighs and try to complete an additional 7 reps with a regular full curl.

It will take you only one set of 21s (now you see where the name comes from: 3 X 7 = 21) to discover that you won't be able to use your normal workout poundage. Don't worry about it. The partial movements will force the biceps to work just as hard, if not harder, than straight sets with heavier weight. Understand that while 21 is the traditional pattern of reps for this technique, you could just as easily do 3 X 6 (= 18) or 3 X 8 (= 24).

STAGGERED SETS

No, this is not some training technique performed after a late night on the town. Let's say that after a few months you begin to notice your forearms or calves are lagging behind the rest of your physique. Besides working them

Negative reps are an ideal advanced technique to do with your training partner.

during their normal time, you can add in a few extra sets while working other muscle groups. For example, while training your chest you can slip in a few sets of calf raises between your chest exercises. Although calf training hurts, they don't require much energy, so training them won't interfere with training your chest. Likewise, you can add in extra forearm work while training legs.

Notice that I suggested doing calves with chest or other upper-body exercises, and forearms with leg work. There's a good reason for this. You need your calves for stabilizing on most leg exercises, and your forearms play a big role in training the upper body. In fact, you'll need your forearms for gripping on every upper-body exercise. If you were to train forearms between chest or back exercises, you won't be able to use the same amount of weight or do the same number of sets.

NEGATIVE REPS

A great deal of research has demonstrated that the negative, or eccentric part of an exercise is just as productive as the positive, or concentric part. Most bodybuilders find negative training makes them more exhausted and sore than when they train with the concentration on positives. Negative-only training received a big endorsement from Dr. Arthur Jones, inventor of the Nautilus line of strength-training equipment.

There are three ways to perform negatives. The first is to simply lower the weight in the same slow and controlled manner as you lift it. In other words, you're not just hoisting the weight into position and then letting gravity take it downwards; you're using muscle power to keep the weight under control.

The other way is to load more weight on the bar than you can lift in the normal positive fashion and then lower it as slowly as possible, trying to stop the weight on the way down. For example, on the barbell bench press you'd have a training partner help you bring the bar back to the arms locked out position and then slowly lower it using the chest, shoulder and triceps muscles. The usual way to do this is after a regular set. When you can no longer lift the weight, you can still lower it. Do your full set by yourself, then have your partner help you do a few negative reps.

You can also do negatives on your own on a few exercises (though you'll have to really concentrate on safety). For example, on the barbell curl you'd lob the weight up using body momentum and then slowly lower it using just the biceps. You can do the same thing on various lateral raises for shoulders. For obvious reasons, you shouldn't try negatives on an exercise such as squats. The amount of weight being lifted could be more than you and your partner can safely control.

YOU GO, I GO

This is another simple but highly effective technique virtually guaranteed to shock you into new muscle growth. As the name suggests, it involves having one trainer perform a set of a given exercise to failure and then passes the dumbells or barbell to his partner, who also trains to failure. The two go back and forth training to failure with no break between sets. After a few of these sets you'll be wishing your partner were going at a slower pace. Because of the sheer intensity of the technique, it's best limited to smaller muscles such as arms and shoulders.

REST-PAUSE

Rest-pause is one of those advanced training techniques that will separate the true bodybuilders from the wussies! To perform rest-pause, load the bar (or machine) with enough weight to limit you to just one rep. Perform the rep and then place the bar back on the rack. Wait 10 to 15 seconds and then do another rep. Repeat this pattern for 8 to 10 reps. Rest-pause is based on the principle that a muscle will regain most of its strength in as little as 10 to 15 seconds. It's a great technique for blasting through sticking points, because you're using 100 percent of your one-rep maximum weight on every set. If you find that you can manage only 5 or 6 one-rep sets, reduce the weight by about 10 percent.

Some examples to illustrate the concept:

Many bodybuilders find barbell presses do more for their triceps and front shoulders than their chest. This is because the triceps and front delts, which support the pecs, tire first. The chest is never fully stimulated. To combat this problem, first perform an isolation exercise such as flat dumbell flyes or pec-deck flyes, and then do a set of barbell presses. The flyes tend to target just the chest muscles, leaving the triceps and shoulders relatively fresh. When you switch to the flat barbell presses, the chest muscles are now the "weak link" and will tire and fatigue before the still-energized triceps and front shoulders.

PRE-EXHAUST

I came up with the pre-exhaust training principle back in 1968. This technique is great for eliminating the "weak link in the chain" that often limits the effectiveness of many otherwise great exercises.

For example, during most back exercises the much smaller biceps give out before the targeted back muscles. Likewise, on chest training, the triceps or front delts may fatigue before your chest muscles are adequately stimulated. Pre-exhaustion means you fatigue or "pre-exhaust" the primary muscles first with an isolation exercise. You then perform a compound movement that allows the fresh secondary muscles to carry the targeted muscle to new depths of stimulation.

PRE-EXHAUST EXAMPLE

To pre-exhaust, simply perform an isolation exercise followed by a compound exercise. Here are some of the best:

ISOLATION EXERCISES	COMPOUND EXERCISES
Leg Extensions	Squats or Leg Presses
Shrugs	Barbell Rows
Preacher Curls	Narrow-Grip Chin-Ups
Dumbell Extensions	Narrow-Grip Bench Presses
Lateral Raises	Front Barbell or Dumbell Presses
Flat or Incline Flyes	Flat or Incline Presses
Leg Raises	Reverse Crunches

Photo of Joel Stubbs by Robert Reiff

SUPERSETS

They're quick, fun and efficient. Supersets involve performing two exercises in an alternating fashion, but rather than wait the usual 45 to 60 seconds between exercises, you rest only as long as it takes to switch from the first exercise to the second.

There are two primary versions of supersets. The first involves alternating two exercises for the same muscle group. For example, a set of flat barbell presses could be followed with a set of incline dumbell flyes. Or you could alternate incline barbell presses with dips. Most bodybuilders try to superset exercises that hit the muscle from different angles or different parts of the muscle. For example: lower and upper chest, inner and outer back, and front and rear shoulders.

The second variation of supersets involves alternating two exercises for different muscle groups. Most bodybuilders superset exercises for opposing muscle groups such as back and chest, thighs and hamstrings, and biceps and triceps. The reason for this is that working one muscle brings blood, and therefore nutrients, into the area. If you work the opposing muscle between sets you take advantage of the blood and nutrients while resting the first muscle.

SUPERSETS FOR THE SAME MUSCLE GROUPS:

Quads
Leg extensions + Squats
Hack squats + Leg presses

Hamstrings
Lying leg curls + Stiff-leg deadlifts
Stiff-leg deadlifts + Seated leg curls

Chest
Flat flyes + Barbell bench presses
Incline dumbell presses + Incline dumbell flyes
Flat dumbell presses + Dips

Back
Straight-arm pushdowns + Front pulldowns
Chin-ups + Barbell rows
Seated rows + T-bar rows

Shoulders
Side dumbell raises + Dumbell press
Front dumbell raises + Upright rows

Biceps
Incline curls + Standing barbell curls
Preacher curls + Narrow-grip reverse chin-ups

Triceps
Lying extensions + Narrow presses
Triceps pushdowns + Dips

Abs
Swiss-ball crunches + Reverse crunches
Hanging leg raises + Medicine-ball twists

Calves
Standing calf raises + Seated calf raises
Donkey calf raises + Seated calf raises
Seated calf raises + Toe presses

Supersetting your abs is a quick and effective method to achieve a chiseled midsection.

Photo of Kamal El Gargni by Robert Reiff

SUPERSETS FOR OPPOSING MUSCLE GROUPS

Quads and Hamstrings

Leg presses + Stiff-leg deadlifts

Squats + Lying leg curls

Leg extensions + Seated leg curls

Chest and Back

Flat barbell presses + Chin-ups

Incline dumbell presses + Seated rows

Flat dumbell flyes + Lat pulldowns

Biceps and Triceps

Barbell curls + Lying barbell extensions

Incline dumbell curls + Two-arm dumbell extensions

Cable curls + Triceps pushdowns

Abs and Lower Back

Swiss-ball crunches + Back extensions

Reverse crunches + Stiff-leg deadlifts

TRISETS

As soon as bodybuilders started putting two exercises together, back to back, it was only a matter of time before someone started alternating three different movements. Trisets are great for shocking the muscles out of the doldrums. You can hit them from every conceivable angle. Like supersets, they also save you time.

TRISET COMBINATIONS

Quads

Squats + Leg presses + Leg extensions (About as painful, but effective, a combination as there is.)

Hamstrings

Stiff-leg deadlifts + Lying leg curls + Seated leg curls

Chest

Flat barbell presses + Incline dumbell presses + Dips

Incline dumbell flyes + Dips + Cable crossovers

Back

Chin-ups + T-bar rows + Front pulldowns

Barbell rows + Narrow pulldowns + Seated cable rows

Use caution when doing giant sets. This technique is very intense, as you're combining four or more movements.

Shoulders

Side dumbell raises + Dumbell presses
+ Reverse pec-deck flyes
Front barbell presses + Side cable raises
+ Bent-over lateral raises

Biceps

Preacher curls + Hammer curls + Incline dumbell curls
Barbell curls + Narrow chin-ups + Standing dumbell curls

Triceps

Lying triceps extensions + Narrow press + Bench dips
Two-arm dumbell extensions + Triceps pushdowns
+ Behind-the-head cable extensions

Abs

Swiss-ball crunches + Reverse crunches
+ Medicine-ball twists
Hanging leg raises + Floor crunches + Ball passes

Calves

Standing calf raises + Seated calf raises + Toe presses

GIANT SETS

Instead of putting three exercises together, you combine four or more movements for the same muscle group. I caution you that giant sets are a very intense form of training and you won't want to do more than two or three giant sets for bigger muscles and one or two for smaller. In fact, since the arms will be getting a good deal of stimulation from training the chest, back and shoulders, you'll probably only need to do one giant set.

GIANT SET COMBINATIONS

Quads

Squats + Leg presses + Leg extensions + Hack squats
Lunges + Sissy squats + Leg extensions
+ Smith-machine squats

Hamstrings

Lying leg curls + Seated leg curls + Stiff-leg deadlifts
+ Back extensions

Calves

Toes presses + Standing calf raises + Seated calf raises
+ Donkey calf raises

Chest

Flat barbell presses + Incline dumbell presses
+ Flat dumbell flyes + Dips
Incline dumbell presses + Flat dumbell flyes
+ Dips + Cable crossovers

Back

Chin-ups + T-bar rows + Front pulldowns + Barbell rows
Seated rows + T-bar rows + Front pulldowns +
+ Reverse-grip chin-ups

Shoulders

Dumbell presses + Side dumbell raises
+ Reverse pec-deck flyes + Upright rows
Barbell presses + Side cable raises
+ Bent-over lateral raises + Barbell shrugs

Biceps

Preacher curls + Incline dumbell curls
+ Standing dumbell curls + Hammer curls
Barbell curls + Standing dumbell curls + Cable curls
+ Preacher curls

Triceps

Lying barbell extensions + Narrow presses + Bench dips
+ Two-arm dumbell extensions
Triceps pushdowns + Lying dumbell extensions
+ Behind-the-head cable extensions + Triceps pushdowns

Abdominals

Hanging leg raises + Swiss-ball crunches + Reverse
crunches + Medicine-ball twists
Ball passes + Planks + Swiss-ball crunches + Lying leg raises

Doing multiple exercises in one workout enables you to attack the muscle from a variety of angles.

LIMITATIONS OF TRISETS AND GIANT SETS

If there's a downside to trisets and giant sets it's that they're difficult to perform in a crowded gym. As soon as you leave one exercise to do another, someone's bound to move in and take your piece of equipment. If you decide to do them at a busy time, try to use equipment available in multiple copies. For example, most gyms have numerous barbells and at least two sets of each weight of dumbell. Another benefit of free weights is that you can do different exercises using the same barbell or dumbbell, so you can do a triset using the same piece of equipment for each set. Most machines are good for only one specific exercise and muscle group. If you do incorporate machines into your trisets or giant sets workout, try using them on weekends or during less busy times of the day.

EXTENDED SETS

Although not as popular as some other intensity techniques, extended sets are second to none when it comes to increasing training intensity, and thus muscle size. To perform extended sets, carry an exercise to positive failure and then immediately switch to an exercise that puts you in a better biomechanical position.

For Triceps: After you reach failure after a set of lying barbell extensions quickly bring the bar to your mid-chest and rep out with narrow presses.

For Chest: Dumbell flyes and dumbell presses. Start with the dumbell flye and when you can no longer continue, rotate your hands and continue on with dumbell presses. You are stronger in the press than the flye since the press brings in more of the triceps and front shoulders. In effect, you are using these still-fresh muscles to stimulate the chest muscles deeper than if you had terminated the set with the flyes. You can do the flye/press combination for both flat and incline versions.

For Lats: Wide and narrow pulldowns. After going to failure on the front pulldown, switch over to the narrow, reverse-grip pulldown. The underhand grip brings more of the biceps into play and allows you to push the lats past the normal failure point.

For Deltoids: Try doing lateral dumbell raises followed by dumbell presses. Although you'll likely have to use less weight than you normally would on the pressing movement, doing the side raises first will tire out the shoulders and you'll still be working them hard.

For Biceps: Nothing blasts the biceps like incline dumbell curls followed by standing barbell curls. Although both exercises work the biceps, the standing curl brings in more forearms and allows you to lift more weight. If you really want to maximize the biceps, add a few cheat curls at the end of your barbell curls. It won't take many sets of this dynamic combo to pack some muscle on your upper arms.

For Thighs: If you're looking to shock the thighs into new growth, try the front and back squat extended-set combination. Front squats reduce the amount of lower-back and glute involvement and are more isolating for the thighs. As soon as your thighs are fatigued from the front squats, rack the bar, step in under it and perform as many reps as possible of regular back squats (usually just called squats). The still-strong lower back and glutes will push the thighs to new depths of stimulation (and pain!).

For Abs: You can even do extended sets for the abs. Start with crunches on the Swiss ball or floor, and once the abs are sufficiently fatigued, switch over to reverse crunches. Reverse crunches allow you to use the hip flexors to continue working the abs.

Remember that with most advanced training techniques it's quite easy to go overboard with extended sets. For most intermediate bodybuilders, one to two extended-set combinations will be more than sufficient. Any more and you risk overtraining.

MULTIPLE EXERCISES

There are numerous advantages to training a muscle using multiple exercises during one workout. The most important is that you can attack the muscle from a variety of different angles. The more angles you hit the muscle from, the more muscle fibers are stimulated and the greater the overall degree of development. For example, on chest you can do declines for the lower and outer chest, flats for the lower and center chest, inclines for the upper chest, and pec-deck flyes and cable crossovers for the inner chest.

Another advantage of multiple exercises is variety. Even though most bodybuilders love training, doing the same workout over and over can get pretty boring. Changing the exercises keeps things fresh.

If there's one disadvantage to multiple exercises, however, it's that it's very easy to fall into the overtraining trap. Take shoulders for example: If you were to do one exercise for each of the three heads, plus another exercise for the trapezius, you'd end up doing 12 to 16 sets in total (assuming 3 to 4 sets per exercise). For the genetically blessed or pharmaceutically enhanced this is probably no concern. But the average natural bodybuilder will quickly find himself overtrained.

10 SETS OF 10, OR GERMAN VOLUME TRAINING

One solution to this is to adopt a one-exercise-per-bodypart-per-workout approach. The technique was first made popular as 10 sets of 10 by Vince Gironda in the 1950s and '60s. (In the 1970s it was renamed "German volume training.") Over the last 10 to 15 years, world-renowned strength-training coach Charles Poliquin has reintroduced the technique to a whole new generation of bodybuilders.

As the name suggests, you pick just one exercise for a muscle and perform 10 sets of 10 reps. Obviously you won't be able to do this with the amount of weight you'd use for 3 or 4 sets. You'll be lucky to use 50 percent of your usual weight. Don't let the first few sets

one exercise for the full 10 sets. Another benefit is that you won't have to worry about cooling down while changing exercises if the equipment you had planned on using is in use. A couple of minutes may not seem like a long time, but sometimes it's long enough for the muscles to cool down. By doing just one exercise you'll never be more than 45 to 60 seconds between sets.

A third advantage of doing just one exercise lies in thoroughness. It usually takes two or three sets before the muscles even feel like they're working. With multiple-exercise routines you may complete the first exercise and not even feel it. But if you're doing just one exercise, you know it won't be long before the muscles starting burning from that particular movement.

You may be concerned about the lack of variety if you only perform one exercise per workout. To prevent this, simply switch exercises every workout or so. For example, you could do flat barbell presses during one workout, incline dumbell presses the next, and dips on the third (tough to do as your bodyweight may eventually be too heavy to complete the last couple of sets). By alternating the exercises you're still hitting the muscle from different angles – just not during the same workout.

mislead you. They will feel easy, but trust me, by the time you're up to set 7 or 8 the muscle will be howling! You'll be lucky to complete 10 sets.

There are numerous advantages to performing just one exercise per bodypart. The most obvious is that once you start, your entire focus is kept on that

SAMPLE WORKOUTS

The following table consists of three sample workouts that you can perform for each bodypart. You can still follow your traditional muscle group splits (i.e. three, four, or six days per week) but you do only one exercise per bodypart. This means your total workout for any given day is only going to be two or three exercises.

MUSCLE GROUP	DAY ONE	DAY TWO	DAY THREE
Quads	Leg Presses	Squats	Hack Squats
Hamstrings	Seated Leg Curls	Standing Leg Curls	Stiff-Leg Deadlifts
Calves	Standing Calf Raises	Toe Presses	Seated Calf Raises
Chest	Flat Barbell Presses	Incline Dumbell Presses	Dips
Back	Chin-Ups	Barbell Rows	Seated Cable Rows
Shoulders	Dumbell Presses	Bent-Over Raises	Side Dumbell Raises
Biceps	Barbell Curls	Preacher Curls	Incline Dumbell Curls
Triceps	Lying Extensions	Bench Dips	Cable Pushdowns
Abdominals	Swiss-Ball Crunches	Reverse Crunches	Hanging Leg Raises

ADVANCED TRAINING ROUTINES

It's now time to start incorporating the advanced techniques into your training. The following routines are examples of four- and six-day-per-week splits. Wherever possible I have included some of the advanced training techniques, and with time you can begin designing your own routines. For example, the book's routine may stress the upper chest, but after some time in the gym, you realize that your center back needs extra work. No problem. Simply cut back on the sets and techniques for your upper chest and focus more on your center back. Remember, these programs are meant as a guide. In most cases, the rep range is between 8 and 12, but you can use lower reps (say 6 to 8) if you wish – or you may rotate between ranges. As discussed earlier, rep range is a personal thing and with time you'll discover which range works best for you.

SOME WORDS OF CAUTION

Before jumping into the routines, here are some important words of caution.

First, don't make the mistake of using these techniques on every set. If the routine calls for 4 sets of an exercise, perform the advanced technique on just the last set or two.

Second, perform advanced sets only once per week for each muscle group. Just do straight sets during the next workout. In other words alternate an intense workout with a less-intense workout. Doing so gives the body time to recover.

Third, limit these techniques to a maximum of four to six weeks. Few but the most genetically gifted bodybuilders can handle such intensity year round.

Finally, resist the urge to do more. Odds are within a few weeks of beginning these techniques you'll begin to see rapid changes in your muscle size and strength. This is great, but for many bodybuilders it can be a double-edged sword. They assume that if one or two drop sets or rest-pause sets are good, then three or four are better. For a week or two they may be right. However,

soon their gains will slow down or stop altogether. There's a very fine line between training enough and overtraining. You have to apply the maximum amount of intensity that stimulates muscle growth, but without overtaxing your recovery system.

On days when your energy and motivation level are high, great! Take advantage of it. Do that extra set or advanced technique. Virtually all the top bodybuilders in the world will tell you that the greatest advanced-training principle is the instinctive principle. When your body tells you that you're capable of pushing harder, go for it. Conversely, when your body hints that you've done enough, listen to it. It takes many years to get in touch with your body and learn when to push it and when to hold back. For now, use the following as a guide and make changes only when you want to prioritize one muscle over the other.

Advanced techniques offer numerous advantages, but there's a fine line between using and overusing them.

ROUTINE 1 (four-day-per-week)

Day One & Day Three

EXERCISE	SETS	REPS
Barbell Bench Presses	4	8–12
SUPERSET: Incline Dumbell Presses with Incline Dumbell Flyes	3	8–12
Barbell Rows	3	8–12
EXTENDED SET: Front Pulldowns with Narrow Reverse Pulldowns	3	8–12 (or to failure)
PRE-EXHAUST COMBINATION: Preacher Curls with Standing Barbell Curls	3	8–12
Crunches	3	15–20
Reverse Crunches	3	15–20

Day Two & Day Four

EXERCISE	SETS	REPS
Squats	3–4	8–12
DROP SET: Hack Squats*	3–4	8–12
Lying Leg Curls	3–4	8–12
Standing Calf Raises	3–4	15–20
DROP SET: Seated Leg Curls*	3–4	15–20
PRE-EXHAUST COMBINATION: Side Dumbell Raises with Front Barbell Presses	3–4	8–12
Reverse Pec-Deck Flyes	3–4	8–12
SUPERSET: Lying Barbell Extensions with Narrow Barbell Presses	3–4	8–12
Rope Pushdowns	3–4	8–12

* Perform drop sets on last set only.

ROUTINE 2 (four-day-per-week)

Day One & Day Three

EXERCISE	SETS	REPS
PRE-EXHAUST COMBINATION: Incline Dumbell Flyes with Incline Barbell Presses	3–4	8–12
Dips	3–4	8–12
T-Bar Rows	3–4	8–12
DROP SET: Seated Pulley Rows*	3–4	8–12
Preacher Curls	3–4	8–12
Incline Dumbell Curls^	3–4	8–12
Medicine-Ball Twists	3–4	15–20

Day Two & Day Four

EXERCISE	SETS	REPS
STRIP SET: Leg Presses#	3–4	8–12
Leg Extensions	3–4	8–12
Lying Leg Curls	3–4	8–12
Stiff-Leg Deadlifts	3–4	8–12
TRISET: Standing Calf Raises with Seated Calf Raises and Toe Presses	3–4	15–20
Dumbell Presses	3–4	8–12
Side Dumbell Raises^	3–4	8–12
Upright Rows	3–4	8–12
SUPERSET: Lying Dumbell Extensions with Bench Dips	3–4	8–12

* Perform drop sets on last set only.
^ Perform down the rack on last set only.
\# Perform strip set on last set only.

ROUTINE 3 (four-day-per-week)

Day One & Day Three (The following is an excellent split for specializing on your legs.)

EXERCISE	SETS	REPS
TRISET: Squats with Leg Presses and Leg Extensions	3–4	8–12
STRIP SET: Lying Leg Curls*	3–4	8–12
Stiff-Leg Deadlifts	3–4	15–20
10 X 10: Standing Calf Raises	10	10
GIANT SET^: Swiss-Ball Crunches, Reverse Crunches, Hanging Leg Raises and Medicine-Ball Twists	2	15–20

Day Two & Day Four

EXERCISE	SETS	REPS
10 X 10: Incline Dumbell Presses	10	10
Barbell Rows	3–4	8–12
Seated Pulley Rows	3–4	8–12
Front Pulldowns	3–4	8–12
GIANT SET^: Side Dumbell Raises, Front Dumbell Raises, Bent-Over Dumbell Raises and Rope Upright Rows	2	8–12
SUPERSET: Lying Barbell Extensions with Standing Barbell Curls	3	8–12

* Perform strip set on last set only.
^ Do two circuits of all four exercises.
Note: Because you are training the three large torso muscles on this day you'll only need to do 3 supersets (6 sets total) for arms.

ROUTINE 1 (six-day-per-week)

Day One & Day Four

EXERCISE	SETS	REPS
Flat Barbell Presses	3	8–12
REST-PAUSE: Incline Dumbell Presses*	3–4	8–12
Dips	3–4	8–12 (or to failure)
Chin-Ups	3–4	8–12
SUPERSET: T-Bar Rows with Front Pulldowns	3–4	8–12

Day Two & Day Five

EXERCISE	SETS	REPS
Front Barbell Presses	3–4	8–12
DROP SET: Cable Lateral Raises^	3–4	8–12
Reverse Pec-Deck Flyes	3–4	8–12
Dumbell Extensions	3–4	8–12
SUPERSET: Triceps Pushdowns with Bench Dips	3–4	8–12
21s: Barbell Curls	3	21
Concentration Curls	3	8–12

Day Three & Day Six

EXERCISE	SETS	REPS
Squats	3–4	8–12
Hack Squats	3–4	8–12
SUPERSET: Leg Extensions with Lying Leg Curls	3–4	8–12
Stiff-Leg Deadlifts	3–4	8–12
TRISET: Reverse Crunches with Hanging Leg Raises and Medicine-Ball Twists	3–4	15–20

* Perform rest-pause on last set only.
^ Perform drop set on last set only.

ROUTINE 2 (six-day-per-week)

Day One & Day Four

EXERCISE	SETS	REPS
Incline Barbell Presses	3–4	8–12
Flat Dumbell Flyes	3–4	8–12
Dips (Hold the dumbell between your feet and when you can't do another, drop the dumbell and do as many extra reps as possible.)	3–4	8–12
Front Barbell Presses	3–4	8–12
Side Dumbell Raises	3–4	8–12
DROP SET: Upright Rows*	3–4	8–12
Barbell Shrugs	3–4	8–12

Day Two & Day Five

EXERCISE	SETS	REPS
SUPERSET: Barbell Rows with Front Pulldowns	3–4	8–12
One-Arm Dumbell Rows	3–4	8–12
DROP SET: Standing Barbell Curls^	4	8–12
Dumbell Curls	3–4	8–12

Day Three & Day Six

EXERCISE	SETS	REPS
PRE-EXHAUST COMBINATION: Leg Extensions with Leg Presses	3–4	8–12
Hack Squats	3–4	8–12
Lying Leg Curls	3–4	8–12
Seated Leg Curls	3–4	8–12
10 X 10: Swiss-Ball Crunch	10	10

* Perform drop set on last set only.
^ Perform drop set on last two sets.

CHAPTER 46

Sticking Points – How to Become Unstuck

"In order to make progress in bodybuilding, all the basic components must fit perfectly together like the pieces in a jigsaw puzzle. If you're not witnessing positive changes in your physique, you'll need to carefully evaluate your workout regimen and dietary habits."

– Dr. Nick Evans, *MuscleMag International* columnist, commenting on the first step toward overcoming a training plateau.

Over its five million years or more of evolution, the human body has developed remarkable powers of adaptation. As soon as it encounters some form of stress, a series of biochemical changes take place to counter that stress and help the body to survive. As you read earlier, muscle growth (in response to the "stress" of increased physical demand) is one such adaptation.

Unless the genetic gods are on your side, you'll notice after a few months of consistent training that your muscle gains will start slowing down, if not stop altogether. Even if you train harder – or lay off a little if you realize you are overtraining – your muscles may still refuse to respond. Try not to panic. Most bodybuilders, from beginners to 20-year veterans, experience training plateaus, or sticking points. When you get stuck you have two choices: Keep training exactly the same way and hope the problem solves itself, or try to solve the problem. Since sticking points rarely sort themselves out, obviously I suggest the latter.

Bodybuilding legend Vince Gironda once suggested that bodybuilding is 85 percent nutrition.

Photo of Carlo Filippone by Jason Mathas

Once you have identified a sticking point you must stop and evaluate your entire workout philosophy. Remember that building muscle takes more than just hoisting weight. You need to STRESS the muscle with your training; you need REST time in order for your body to repair your damaged muscle cells, thereby building new muscle; and you need proper NUTRITION to provide your body with its rebuilding tools, not to mention what it needs for optimal daily functioning and to give it enough energy for effective training. Given the importance of all three, I'll address them separately.

NUTRITION

Like any machine the human body needs various compounds to run properly. If you're deficient in carbohydrates, then you won't have the necessary energy reserves to complete your workout – or you won't do as much as you might have been able to. And since carbohydrate plays a role in protein synthesis, a shortage of this valuable fuel source could interfere with your recovery abilities. Speaking of protein, failure to eat enough of this primary building material could easily set your muscle gains back for months, if not years. Then there are the various vitamins, minerals and even fats that power the biochemical reactions to build new muscle tissue. Bodybuilding legend Vince Gironda once suggested that bodybuilding is 85 percent nutrition. Although some may debate the exact percentage, everyone agrees that poor nutrition is one of the surest ways to bring training success to a halt. Make sure you eat a nutritious meal with complex carbs, protein and healthy fats every two to three hours.

TRAINING

Some experts have estimated that at least 90 percent of all bodybuilders are in a constant state of overtraining. Most of these individuals are beginners to moderately experienced bodybuilders who are following some pro bodybuilder's routine they found in a magazine. Few but the most genetically gifted or pharmacologically enhanced can endure a pro's routine. In fact, most of the routines you see quoted in the magazines are their pre-contest muscle-refining programs and not their muscle-building off-season routines. Few try to build strength and size on a 20- to 25-set-per-bodypart program. So if this sport's genetically gifted and often pharmacologically enhanced superstars follow such high-intensity training for only a few short months, what makes you think your body will be able to handle it, let alone grow on it? If your training program is composed of such mega-set routines and you're not making strength and size gains, there's a good chance this is where your problem lies. Cut your sets by at least half and then see what happens. Try doing 8 to 10 sets for the larger muscles and just 6 to 8 for the smaller.

Another suggestion is to alternate heavy with light days. Again, don't let magazine star Johnny Pro who uses 1,200 pounds for 6 to 8 reps on the leg press influence you. I assure you that Johnny Pro doesn't max out on every single workout! He can't – no one can. The human joints are just not designed to handle that kind of stress on a regular basis. For the most, pros train heavy just once a week. Many have backed it off even further and train super heavy only on every third or fourth workout.

If you're trying to both set record lifts and maximize muscle gains during every single workout, but end up doing neither, take a lesson from the pros and start cycling your workout poundage. Go heavy one workout and light to medium the next. Alternate a heavy, 6- to 8-rep workout with a lighter, 12- to 15-rep workout. The heavy weight will build size and strength while the higher reps will stimulate capillary formation and muscle endurance. Cycling in such a manner will also allow the body sufficient time to recover between workouts without overtaxing your recovery system.

REST

And here's something else most pros do: they take a week or two off every couple of months and do absolutely nothing. That's right, they don't go near the gym! This gives their bodies a chance to heal any nagging injuries and fully recover from the day-in, day-out training. After their time off they resume training, but only for two or three easy workouts – usually at about 50- to 75-percent intensity. A few more weeks will see them back to their four or five times per week training. It's only during the few months before a big show that they switch to a six-day per week routine. You can only increase training intensity up to a certain point before you will slip into a state of overtraining. But by cycling your training you can enjoy those heavy sessions without burning out or getting stuck.

You also have to make sure you're getting enough sleep on a daily basis. Most people need at least seven hours of sleep each night. You need more. When you stress your body as bodybuilders do, it is in constant need of repair – which is what bodybuilding is all about: building muscle by repairing it. But this repair takes place during sleep. If you are not getting enough sleep each day, your body's repair system simply does not have the time to get the job done. If you want to build muscle you have to train enough, eat enough and sleep enough. Simple as that.

CHAPTER 47

Shock it to Them

"Having competed 10 times as an amateur and four times as an IFBB pro, I have learned a lot. I have also trained plenty of other people for competition and one thing remains constant: different things work for different people."

– Brian Chamberlain, IFBB pro

The body's ability to adapt to new situations is beneficial from a bodybuilding perspective. As we increase the load (weight) on a muscle, our body responds by increasing the size of that muscle. But a point comes when increasing the weight no longer has the desired effect. Especially if you work out at the same time of the day, using the same exercises for the same number of sets and the same number of reps – even if the weight has increased. When movements become predictable for the body, it ceases growing. The dreaded training plateau or sticking point has arrived. Your next step should be obvious – you need to shock your body and wake it up!

When it comes to shocking your muscles, nothing beats variety. Predictability put you into this situation in the first place, and unpredictability will shock you out of it. One of the simplest (if your daily schedule permits) ways to shock your body is to change your workout time. If it's used to training at 5 p.m. every workout day, try training at 7 a.m. or 8 p.m. Another rela-

tively easy shocking technique is to vary your set-and-rep numbers. For example, if you normally do 3 sets of 12 reps, surprise your body by doing 5 sets of 15 reps. If you always start your chest workouts with flat barbell presses, try incline dumbell presses as your first exercise. Or how about ditching ALL your exercises for a few weeks and substituting them with a whole new set, complete with all new exercises and routines. By changing your exercises you keep your body guessing, and the outcome is bound to be new gains in strength and size.

You can also alternate the order of exercise execution. If you normally train chest first (and what bodybuilder doesn't like to do barbell bench presses first?) try beginning your workout with back. Of course you'd be wise not to work arms or shoulders before chest or back, as tiring these smaller muscles will only inhibit your workout's effectiveness and safety.

Don't forget what you learned earlier in the book. Incorporating some advanced training techniques into your training is a fantastic way to shock the body into new growth. Throw in a few strip sets, supersets, or forced reps to shock those slumbering muscles!

A few bodybuilders carry the shocking principle to the extreme and perform a different workout every day. I don't recommend this because, believe it or not, the body can actually adapt to variety (although this sounds like a contradiction, it does happen.) Furthermore, you need a certain amount of regularity in your workouts to gain muscular strength and size. By continuously changing the exercises you'll limit your progression. The shocking principle, like most techniques outlined in this book, is a valuable tool that should be used, not abused. The key to shocking lies in its novelty.

MUSCLE PRIORITY

As the years progress, you'll discover that some muscles grow faster than others. Your thighs might be columns of power, but your upper body might be mediocre. Your biceps may rival Ronnie Coleman's, but your triceps wouldn't even make the state-level championship. While genetics is sometimes to blame, your training order is the likelier culprit. It's safe to declare that most bodybuilders train their favorite muscles early in their workout and leave their least favorites until the end. It's also safe to say that the weak muscles tend to be trained last. The three best examples of this are thighs/hamstrings, chest/back and biceps/triceps.

Virtually everyone will start their leg workouts with quads and then proceed to hamstrings. This makes sense early in your training career because your quads are the bigger muscle and will require the most energy to train. But as soon as your quads start overshadowing your hamstrings, you should switch things around. Train your hamstrings first when you have the most energy. Don't worry if you can't go as heavy on your quad exercises after training your hams; maintaining existing muscle size is much easier than building it in the first place.

We see the same problem with chest and back training. Most bodybuilders who train these two muscles during the same workout always start with chest – and usually with the good ol' faithful flat barbell bench presses. Something about the bench press just appeals to most bodybuilders. Most of us are determined to join the 300-, 400-, even 500-pound bench-press "clubs." For this reason we'd never dare waste precious energy on back exercises.

The other reason is simple anatomy. Being located on the front of the body, the chest symbolizes power and masculinity. This is why you'll often see proud owners hitting a few chest poses in the mirror. The back, however, is extremely hard to see. Unless you set up two mirrors, it's not really visible in most poses, either. Although a well-developed back will earn you just as many points as a great chest on a bodybuilding stage, most bodybuilders do not give the same amount of training attention to back muscles.

The biceps is another "mirror" muscle. Even young children flex their biceps when they want to show how strong they are. When was the last time someone asked you to flex a triceps? The fact that the triceps is about two-thirds the mass of the upper arm and contributes more to upper-body strength than the biceps is usually forgotten. But most people become consumed with biceps – highly visible and symbolically powerful. Thus, the triceps tend to be neglected.

The problems develop when the muscles you train first in your workout begin to overshadow the rest. Odds are they eventually will. As soon as this begins to happen, you must start prioritizing the weaker muscles. The best way to do this is by shifting them to the beginning of your workout. Instead of starting with quads, do your leg curls and stiff-leg deadlifts first. Similarly, perform your rows and chins before your flat and incline presses. Finally, work the triceps before you train biceps. You don't need to worry that your favorite muscles will lose their mass. They will stay the same. You are simply giving your weaker muscles a chance to catch up.

SPECIALIZATION

You may also notice that parts of individual muscles may start lagging behind. For example, the lower chest may grow quite easily, but the upper chest may lack thickness. Your back might be wide, but have no depth. Your upper biceps might be full, but your lower biceps may not stretch all the way to the elbow joints. Squatting may have built you a great set of glutes and upper quads, but your outer and lower quads are not full.

Once again genetics might interfere here, but more often than not it's your training that needs revamping. Earlier in the book I suggested that the bulk of your beginner-level training should be composed of compound exercises. This is because compound exercises work more than one muscle and allow you to lift heavier weights. But one disadvantage to compound movements is that they place most of the tension on the central belly of the muscle. The upper and lower sections of the muscle often receive less stimulation. Over time the ends of the muscles start lagging behind the belly of the muscles in terms of fullness and development. The best way to address this problem is to start adding in isolation exercises – particularly movements that target the weak areas. Bodybuilders use the term specialization. This means giving extra attention to the areas of muscles that are lagging behind. As soon as a weakness is discovered it must be addressed right away because the longer you leave it, the harder it will be to fix later on. If this means eliminating a must-do exercise such as squats or bench presses, so be it. As you progress, your training will evolve from primarily compound exercises to a mixture of compound and isolation. Once you have the basic underlying mass (for most people this will be gained in the first four to five years) your best move is to devote most of your attention to refining your physique and bringing up weak areas.

Here are a few suggestions on how to incorporate specialization into your workouts:

1 Prioritize your weak points by training them first in your workouts. This way you'll be able to hit them while your energy reserves are highest.

2 If you have the time, split your workouts in two and train your weak muscles on their own. For example, train your upper chest or lower biceps earlier in the day and come back later for your regular workout.

3 To avoid overtraining, do not use a specialized program for more than six to eight weeks. If you start experiencing the symptoms of overtraining, cut back on the specialization.

4 If, after you give it time, a weak area doesn't respond to "normal" specialization training, try training it six days in a row for two weeks. While this is a radical approach that should not be your first choice, it usually works to shock a weak area.

Photo of Monty Rogers by Robert Reiff

Certain muscles grow faster than others – for this reason, it's important to pay attention to your training order.

CHAPTER 48

Asymmetric Training

"Dumbell training has helped me balance out my physique. Many of us have a muscular imbalance: perhaps one biceps is bigger than the other. My left biceps was half an inch smaller than my right, and I balanced them out with a unilateral routine."

– Frank Sepe, regular *MuscleMag International* columnist

Ever notice how sore you get after you do something different, such as moving a piece of furniture … or even after a day of gardening? All those tons of weight lifted every day in the gym, yet one moved couch or dug flowerbed puts you in agony for three days. No wonder your relatives say muscle is only good for show! You get sore after doing something unusual such as moving a piece of heavy furniture because the movement is different than what you're used to performing in the gym.

When was the last time you walked across the gym floor carrying a 50-pound weight? You may have shifted a 45-pound plate from the rack to a barbell or grabbed a dumbell off a rack and shifted to a bench, but you may never have actually carried a weight across the room. Likewise, how often do you climb up steps in the gym with a barbell on your shoulder?

These are not the type of movements you perform in your training, but they are the movements you often carry out in and around your house or apartment. Let's look at it another way: how often during the day are your arms and legs performing identical movements at the exact same time? Few forms of physical activity outside the gym place equal stress on both sides of the body. In fact, just about the only time you employ bilateral movements is in the gym. Most weight-training exercises involve training both legs, arms,

ble that using say, 150-pounds on the stack could place 90 pounds on one side and only 60 on the other.

2 The All-Important Mind-Muscle Connection. This may sound self evident, but it's much easier to concentrate on the working muscle when only one muscle is being worked. Here's a little experiment for you to try the next time you're in the gym. Do a set of barbell curls and try to concentrate on both biceps at the same time. Not easy, is it? Now grab a dumbell and do a set of concentration curls. Notice any difference? It's much easier to concentrate on contracting one biceps muscle than both at the same time, and the mind-muscle connection can mean a huge difference in muscle gains.

3 Your Neuropathways. A third advantage to asymmetric training lies with neurobiology. There is some evidence to suggest that the brain has to split nerve impulses to stimulate both sides of the body at the same time. Training only one side at a time allows for full nervous stimulation of the muscle.

4 Time For a Change. If your body is used to training both sides at the same time, a few weeks of asymmetric training will produce the ideal shock to get it back to growing again.

Here are some of the best exercises to add variety to your training and to help correct muscle imbalances. Most of them are also terrific for working the core stabilizer muscles (abs, spinal erectors, etc.). Besides the following list, just about every exercise you can think of can be done asymmetrically. Just switch to a dumbell. However, I don't recommend one-legged squats. As a word of caution, many of the following exercises will require you to twist your torso or lower body slightly to keep from falling over. Always pay attention to any warning signals that the body may give you. This is especially true in regard to the lower back. At the first instance of excessive spine pressure, reduce the weight, re-align your body or drop the exercise entirely. Remember to keep your core locked during all of these movements.

pecs, lats or other bilateral muscles at the same time, for example, barbell curls, squats, chin-ups, bench presses, lat pulldowns, etc.

Bodybuilders fear that asymmetrical training (training one side at a time) will produce an unbalanced-looking physique, with one side larger than the other. However, the opposite is more likely true. When you train both sides at the same time, your stronger side normally takes on more of the work to compensate for the weaker side. While machines are famous for allowing this to occur, it is also the case with barbells. The end result is a muscle on one side of the body that is slightly more developed than the matching muscle on the other side. Most bodybuilders have one leg or arm that's slightly fuller than the opposing limb and this is often because of unequal stress experienced when training both legs or arms simultaneously.

There are a number of advantages to training asymmetrically. Here are a few:

1 Keep Both Sides Equal. If you use a 50-pound dumbell for one-arm rows, you can be sure both sides are being subjected to the same 50 pounds. But the same can't be said for front pulldowns. It's possi-

Asymmetrical training helps to ensure that you keep both sides equal, preventing muscle imbalances.

Calves
One-leg toe presses
One-leg standing calf raises
One-leg seated calf raises
One-leg dumbell calf raises

Back
One-arm rows
One-arm lat pulldowns

Shoulders
One-arm front raises
One-arm lateral raises
One-arm reverse pec-deck

Triceps
One-arm dumbell kickbacks
One-arm cable kickbacks
One-arm dumbell extensions
One-arm triceps pushdowns

Quads
One-leg leg press
One-leg leg extensions
Lunges

Hamstrings
One-leg lying leg curls
One-leg seated leg curls
One-leg stiff-leg deadlifts

Chest
One-arm pec-deck flyes
One-arm flyes
One-arm dumbell presses
One-arm cable crossovers

Biceps
One-arm cable curls
One-arm dumbell curls
Concentration curls

CHAPTER 49

Working the Lowers

"There is a tendency for limbs to be built more in the upper extremities. The lower legs, lower quads, lower biceps, lower triceps, the forearms and even the lower abs frequently lack development. The 'lowers' need specialized attention."

– Editorial in *MuscleMag International*, on the need to build a complete muscle.

The business world calls it a return on your investment. If you invest more money you should see a proportionately larger amount of financial return. Bodybuilding works this way too – at least in the beginning. You should put most of your energy and time into training the larger muscle groups. Training the legs, chest and back with basic exercises lays down a good foundation and stimulates the smaller muscles too.

However, eventually you'll start noticing that your physique lacks a certain completeness. Your thighs are massive and trunk-like in size, but your calves, particularly your lower calves, appear almost puny. Your upper biceps start looking mountainous, but there is a noticeable gap between your lower biceps and forearms.

These areas (and a few others) are what bodybuilders call "the lowers," and when properly developed they help give your physique that classical Greek God look. I'll admit that training these sections doesn't carry the same degree of enjoyment or satisfaction as the training the larger, more showy parts. But trust me, the results will speak for themselves.

The following exercises are among the best for bringing up the "lowers" and adding that final degree of polish to your physique.

LOWER BICEPS

Granted, biceps length is genetic and there's nothing you can do to lengthen a short biceps, but by working the lower biceps – where the biceps muscle inserts near the elbow – you can create the illusion of length. The following are some of the best exercises to build up the lower biceps.

Barbell Preacher Curls: Set the chair so your upper arms rest comfortably on the pad. Slowly lower the barbell down to just short of a lockout. Again I remind you not to bounce at the bottom, as this can cause a biceps tear. Slowly curl the bar back up until your forearms are just short of vertical.

Dumbell Preacher Curls: Perform this exercise in the same manner as the barbell version. Dumbells give you the option of curling with one or two arms.

Reverse Curls: Besides working the lower biceps with preacher curls, you can help bring up the area with reverse curls. Reverse curls target both the lower biceps and upper forearms – particularly the brachialis muscle. Think of both exercises as the two doors that close the hole between your biceps and forearms. This exercise is identical to regular barbell curls with the exception that you grip the bar with your palms facing the floor rather than the ceiling.

LOWER CALVES

Because of their size and strength, most people spend far more time training the larger upper gastrocnemius part of the calves and very little time on the lower soleus muscles. It's much more fun to be lifting 500+ pounds on the standing calf raise than a mere hundred or two on the seated calf raise. But it's the seated calf that will bring out the full diamond-shape to your lower legs and help get rid of that dreaded high-calves look.

Seated Calf Raises: Load the machine. Sit down on the chair and lower the pads until they are resting snug on your thighs. Extend your ankles (go up on your toes) until the weight support falls away (on most machines this will happen as soon as the weight is lifted). Slowly

drop your heels as far as your flexibility allows. Now push up on to your tiptoes.

Bent-Leg Toe Presses: Sit down in the leg press and place your feet on the lower part of the pressing platform (only your toes and balls of your feet should be resting on the platform). Unlike the regular toe press, which is performed with the legs locked out straight, try to keep the knees bent slightly. Bending the knees activates the soleus more than the gastrocnemius. Slowly drop your heels away from you and then stand on your tiptoes.

Bent-Leg Standing Calf Raises: Perform this exercise exactly as you would the straight-leg version, but with your knees slightly bent. As with bent-leg toe presses, bent-leg standing raises do a great job of targeting the lower soleus muscle.

Photo of Alfonso Del Rio by Jason Breeze

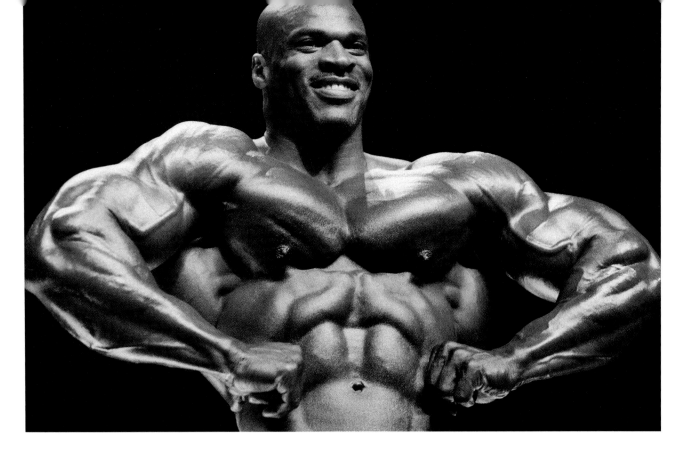

LOWER CHEST

There is nothing as impressive as a set of pecs that look like you could lose a quarter up under them. But while most bodybuilders seem to have no problem building the lower chest (years of heavy flat barbell presses are quite effective for this), a few individuals are not so lucky. Flat presses seem to do nothing but build their front shoulders and triceps. Their front-delt tie-ins are quite impressive, and their collarbones are hidden by copious amounts of beef, but their lower chest appears shallow. If you want that clean line that separates the lower chest from the upper abdominals, try the following exercises:

Dips: The late great Vince Gironda called this the best overall chest exercise there is. The key is to use the correct technique. Grab two parallel bars (or V-shaped bars, as Gironda preferred) and slowly lower down between them by bending at the elbows. Keep your chin on your chest, elbows flared out to the sides, and lean slightly forward. If you lean back with the elbows in close to your sides the exercise becomes more of a triceps builder.

Decline Barbell Presses: Either use a decline bench or prop up the lower end of the flat bench press rack with a few plates or block of wood. Do the bench press the way you normally would, but bring the bar down to the nipple region instead of lowering the bar to the mid chest.

Decline Flyes: Again, use a bench designed for declines or place a few plates or block of wood under one end of a regular flat bench. From here the exercise is the same as regular flat flyes. Try making a big hugging-type movement without bouncing at the bottom.

Decline Dumbell Presses: The two main differences between flyes and presses is that with presses you keep the hands pointing forward and push straight up and just slightly inwards, whereas with flyes you make a hugging motion and face the hands toward the body.

LOWER ABS

"What most people fail to realize is that right there, lurking under layers of adipose tissue and water, they already have abs. If you have been training for any length of time, your abs are most likely well developed. Tense them and you can feel them."

– Ron Harris, regular *MuscleMag International* contributor

Photo of Ronnie Coleman by Alex Ardenti

The lower abs are harder to bring out than the uppers for a number of reasons. The biggest problem is that the lower abdominal area tends to collect fat and does not like to give it up. So even if you have great lower abdominals you might not see them. In addition, most of the popular ab exercises, such as crunches, primarily target the upper abs. Then again, many of the exercises for the lower abs also bring the hip flexors into play – in fact the hip flexors may do most of the work.

While burning off excess fat is probably the most important plan, the following exercises will bring out the ridges of the lower washboard:

Reverse Crunches: Lie back on a bench, holding the bench above your head. With a very slight bend in your knees, slowly pull your legs back toward your chest, lifting your butt off the bench. Slowly extend your legs forward, gently kiss the floor with your feet, and lift again.

Lying Leg Raises: Lie back on the floor and, with a slight bend at the knees, slowly raise your legs up until they are forming about a 75-degree angle with the floor. Slowly lower back down to within an inch or two of the floor and lift again.

Hanging Leg Raises: Grab an overhead chinning bar and slowly draw your legs up in front of you. The idea is to bring your hips toward your sternum. At the beginning you might need to do this exercise with bent knees, but as your abdominal strength improves you can do them with straight legs.

LOWER LATS

High lats are similar to short biceps in that the condition is primarily genetic. You can't do anything to change where your lats attach. But by concentrating on building the lower sections of the lats, where they attach to the lower torso, you can give your back that sweeping, V-shaped look. The following examples are among the best lower-lat exercises:

Narrow Reverse-Grip Chins: Grab the chin-up bar with a shoulder-width grip, palms facing toward you. Pull yourself up until the bar is in line with your collarbone. Slowly lower back until your arms are just shy of lockout.

Narrow Reverse-Grip Pulldowns: Like narrow reverse-grip chins, this exercise is performed with a narrow grip, palms facing toward you. Sit down on the chair and slowly pull the bar down to your upper chest (as opposed to your chin or collarbone on wide pulldowns). Slowly stretch the arms overhead to just short of lockout.

Reverse-Grip Seated Rows: Attach a medium or long bar to the seated-row machine. Using a shoulder-width reverse grip (palms facing upward), slowly pull the bar to the lower ribcage. Slowly return to the starting position with your arms just short of lockout. Keep your knees bent to reduce the stress on your lower back.

Photo of Dennis Wolf by Josef Adlt

BODYBUILDING — THE GREATEST OF SPORTS

CHAPTER 50

Go For It!

"Sit down before your next competition and outline some of the objectives you want to achieve by competition day. If you've never before set a concrete goal and instead have gone blindly into contest prep, I guarantee you'll do even better the next show with a plan on paper."

– Charles Glass, pro bodybuilding coach and trainer, offering great advice on bodybuilding competition.

"For me the urge to compete never seems to go away. It's always there. Perhaps it's the thrill of being in front of a cheering crowd, the thrill of going through a posing routine, and the thrill of winning ... it's a part of the bodybuilding life that I couldn't do without."

– Rich Scimeca, amateur bodybuilder, as passionate about bodybuilding as he was back in the mid-1970s.

Congratulations and well done. You've arrived. After a year or two of training day in and day out, you've built a physique that has the size and shape to garner you compliments no matter where you go. It's now time to take the next step – strutting your stuff on a bodybuilding stage. The following chapters offer numerous tips and strategies to help you look your competitive best on contest day. You have no intentions of ever competing? In fact most people who regularly work out have no desire to step out onto a bodybuilding stage. However, much of what I discuss over the next few chapters can be applied to looking your best anywhere – whether on the beach or the posing platform. Besides, many of today's greatest bodybuilders had no intentions of ever competing. It was only after they started seeing their bodies developing and after attending a few shows they decided to give it a go. Who knows? You might be next!

THE TWO EXTREMES

Competitive bodybuilders generally fall into two categories. At one end we have the gung-ho types who feel ready to take the Mr.. Olympia title after only a couple of months of training. While the occasional genetic freak does come along who'll put 30 or 40 pounds on his frame in six months, for the

Stepping onto a bodybuilding stage is no easy task, as it requires detailed preparation and practice.

Photo of Silvio Samuel, Johnnie Jackson and Phil Heath by Irvin Gelb

most part the average person will need at least a solid year of training under his belt before being competitive at the local level. There's no way a person can have the knowledge necessary to compete after only a couple of months of training experience. It normally takes about 12 weeks of dieting and practicing posing to be ready, forget the muscle building. Those who compete too early on will usually be carrying too much body fat and won't look comfortable onstage. Even though they'll probably place where they deserve, they'll blame the judges and possibly give up the sport for good. This is too bad, as many potentially great bodybuilding careers ended this way before they even got started.

At the other end we have what can only be called the procrastinators, or the "just one more year's." These are the guys who train for 10 years or more, have more than enough size and knowledge to compete, but spend too much time comparing themselves to Ronnie Coleman or Jay Cutler. They're so hard on themselves that they keep putting things off for another year but unfortunately that one more year becomes 10 years, and before they know it their best competitive years are behind them. You can spot these guys in the audience at local body-

building contests. They're usually in their 30s or 40s and carry more muscle mass than the overall winner of the contest. It's sad when a contest with two or three contestants per weight class could have had 10 competitors per class if many of those in the audience would only decide to compete. But there they sit year after year.

THE BENEFITS OF COMPETETITION

"So let's say you've decided to accept the challenge. That's usually the reason people enter shows. It's a challenge getting in the best shape possible. But unless you have one-in-a-million genetics and are willing to take outrageous amounts of steroids and other performance-enhancing drugs, forget about making money by competing. Entering a show for most people is a personal struggle."
– Nelson Montana, regular *MuscleMag International* contributor, highlighting the reason most people decide to enter a bodybuilding contest.

Besides the end result of perhaps winning the contest, there are numerous reasons to give competitive bodybuilding a go. For starters it may be one of the greatest learning experiences of your life. Let's face it, competing in a bodybuilding contest will necessitate a whole new approach to your training. You'll need to adopt new strategies and exercises. You'll also need to learn the ins and outs of pre-contest dieting.

Another benefit of competing is that you'll probably make the best progress of your life. The primary reason is that you'll need to cycle your training in the months leading up to the contest. Even though your goal at this point is refinement more than growth, most bodybuilders discover that they actually add muscle size during their pre-contest training. The increased number of reps and sets seems to shock their bodies out of the state of staleness that many have fallen into.

Competition tends to bring out the best in people and do wonders for their training drive. A fifth-place finish will motivate most people to train even harder during the off-season. This constant drive to be the best has but one outcome – increased size and a much better physique.

Give it some serious thought. Unlike such sports as wrestling, judo or rugby, where getting in over your head can have serious consequences, bodybuilding is perfectly safe. Granted your ego may receive the occasional bruise, but my experience has been that most competitors use a poor placing to train harder and improve for their next outing.

THE TITLES — WHAT YOU'RE SHOOTING FOR

With the reorganization of bodybuilding back in the 1980s, the old familiar "Mr." titles became all but extinct. The Mr. and Ms. Olympias are still around. So is the NABBA Mr. Universe. But by and large the Mr. and Ms. titles are now called Championships. For example, the very prestigious Mr. America has become the U.S. National Championships. Instead of Mr. California, the winner is now called the California State Bodybuilding Champion. The Amateur Mr. Universe is now called the World Bodybuilding Championships, and the Professional Mr. Universe is now the Arnold Classic. Of course you don't just decide to enter the World Championships. The hierarchy is usually city to state (or provincial) to national to world. Some bodybuilders enter regional shows after winning the state or provincial championships.

Besides the name change, most contests now have separate weight divisions similar to those in boxing. The most common divisions are bantamweight, lightweight, middleweight, light heavyweight, heavyweight, and super heavyweight. Once the winners have been chosen for each weight division, an overall winner is picked. But it's not necessary to win the overall title to progress to the next level.

Most local contests are called "closed," meaning you must live in a certain geographic area to be eligible to compete. Other events, called "open," are accessible to anyone regardless of where the contestants live.

Most contests, even major ones, are amateur events. This means there are no cash prizes for the winners. But as with most sports, the line between amateur and professional is very murky these days. Most top amateur body-builders make thousands of dollars doing posing exhibitions and seminars. Others make millions endorsing supplements. If the bodybuilder had not won a major contest he would not earn this money, but because he doesn't earn it specifically for winning a contest, by definition he is considered amateur.

Once bodybuilders have won the World Championships, North American Championships or some other top qualifying event, they receive their professional card and are then eligible to compete in the sport's professional shows such as the Arnold Classic and the Olympia.

Like most pro athletes, pro bodybuilders compete for cash in the various pro contests. The top prizes are found at the Arnold Classic and Mr. Olympia and while $150,000 might not sound like much compared to the $1 million plus awarded to the winners of golf and tennis tournaments, it's still a long way from the tins of protein powder the winners received decades ago, and it's even a long way from what Olympic athletes receive.

Photo of Jay Cutler by Irvin Gelb

Competing is a learning experience. Each time you participate you'll be motivated to train harder and make improvements.

THE BIGGEST ONE

For those readers who plan on becoming part of bodybuilding immortality, the top contest is the Mr. Olympia, first awarded to Larry Scott in 1965. The Mr. Olympia was created by bodybuilding publisher Joe Weider to see who was the greatest bodybuilder alive. It was only open to former Mr. Universe winners. Since Scott's first win in 1965, this contest has been won by just 11 individuals. The winners since 1965 are:

Photo of Larry Scott by Robert Kennedy

MR. OLYMPIA RESULTS

YEAR	WINNER	CITY	YEAR	WINNER	CITY
1965	Larry Scott	New York	1987	Lee Haney	Gothenburg
1966	Larry Scott	New York	1988	Lee Haney	Los Angeles
1967	Sergio Oliva	New York	1989	Lee Haney	Rimini
1968	Sergio Oliva	New York	1990	Lee Haney	Chicago
1969	Sergio Oliva	New York	1991	Lee Haney	Orlando
1970	Arnold Schwarzenegger	New York	1992	Dorian Yates	Helsinki
1971	Arnold Schwarzenegger	Paris	1993	Dorian Yates	Atlanta
1972	Arnold Schwarzenegger	Essen	1994	Dorian Yates	Atlanta
1973	Arnold Schwarzenegger	New York	1995	Dorian Yates	Atlanta
1974	Arnold Schwarzenegger	New York	1996	Dorian Yates	Chicago
1975	Arnold Schwarzenegger	Pretoria	1997	Dorian Yates	Los Angeles
1976	Franco Columbu	Columbus	1998	Ronnie Coleman	New York
1977	Frank Zane	Columbus	1999	Ronnie Coleman	Las Vegas
1978	Frank Zane	Columbus	2000	Ronnie Coleman	Las Vegas
1979	Frank Zane	Columbus	2001	Ronnie Coleman	Las Vegas
1980	Arnold Schwarzenegger	Sydney	2002	Ronnie Coleman	Las Vegas
1981	Franco Columbu	Columbus	2003	Ronnie Coleman	Las Vegas
1982	Chris Dickerson	London	2004	Ronnie Coleman	Las Vegas
1983	Samir Bannout	Munich	2005	Ronnie Coleman	Las Vegas
1984	Lee Haney	New York	2006	Jay Cutler	Las Vegas
1985	Lee Haney	Brussels	2007	Jay Cutler	Las Vegas
1986	Lee Haney	Columbus		2008 results undecided as of publication	

THE MS. OLYMPIA

Although relatively new compared to its male equivalent, the Ms. Olympia has seen many battles over the years. As with the Mr. Olympia, the Ms. Olympia tends to be dominated for long stretches by the same winners. Lenda Murray is the most dominant, with eight Ms. Olympia titles to her credit. The winners since 1980 are:

MS. OLYMPIA RESULTS

YEAR	WINNER	CITY
1980	Rachel McLish	Philadelphia
1981	Kike Elomaa	Philadelphia
1982	Rachel McLish	Atlantic City
1983	Carla Dunlap	Warmister
1984	Cory Everson	Montreal
1985	Cory Everson	New York
1986	Cory Everson	New York
1987	Cory Everson	New York
1988	Cory Everson	New York
1989	Cory Everson	New York
1990	Lenda Murray	New York
1991	Lenda Murray	Los Angeles
1992	Lenda Murray	Chicago
1993	Lenda Murray	New York
1994	Lenda Murray	Atlanta
1995	Lenda Murray	Atlanta
1996	Kim Chizevsky	Chicago
1997	Kim Chizevsky	New York
1998	Kim Chizevsky	Prague
1999	Kim Chizevsky	Secaucus
2000	Valentina Chepiga (HW)	Las Vegas
2000	Andrulla Blanchette (LW)	Las Vegas
2001	Juliette Bergman	Las Vegas
2002	Lenda Murray	Las Vegas
2003	Lenda Murray	Las Vegas
2004	Iris Kyle	Las Vegas
2005	Yaxeni Oriquen	Las Vegas
2006	Iris Kyle	Las Vegas
2007	Iris Kyle	Las Vegas

2008 results undecided as of publication

Photo of Iris Kyle by Irvin Gelb

Holding poses is very tiring, and combined with the hot lights this makes for a group of very tired and very dehydrated bodybuilders.

THE EVENING SHOW

"Over weeks and months of dieting and preparation it seems the contest will never arrive. All of a sudden it's time to put on the contest color, don your trunks, and head off to the venue to compete. Then it's all over in the blink of an eye."

– Ron Harris, regular *MuscleMag International* contributor

The evening show usually starts around 7 or 8 p.m. It resembles the prejudging, but has a much larger audience, along with one or two entertainment acts (usually martial arts demonstrations), and a guest poser. The audience deserves a special comment. If this is your first bodybuilding contest you're in for a treat. This is definitely not a night at the opera! Within a minute of the first contestants strolling onstage you'll see what I mean. Bodybuilding audiences are among the loudest, noisiest and most vocal, around. And nowhere is this more evident than at a city or state contest.

A typical bodybuilding audience is made up of camps, or cliques (just think of the old high school cafeteria), each loyal to one or more contestants. The real wars start when you have groups of competitors from rival gyms. If you think polite applause and the occasional catcall is the extent of it, think again. As soon as the contestants start flexing their stuff the most vocal of the audience members will start yelling their support. From one corner it's: "squeeze it, squeeze it!" From another it's: "come on show those abs!" Add in an assortment of "hold its" and "oh yeahs" and you end up with nothing short of verbal mayhem. But this is what makes a bodybuilding contest so exciting and memorable. It seems no matter how hard the competitors try to outdo one another, the audience wants more.

Of course, between the bellowing and screaming there is an actual event. The first three rounds are identical to the prejudging, and then a fourth round is added. Affectionately called the posedown, it's reminiscent of the knights of old going head to head. The top four or five competitors from the class are asked to step forward and are given one minute to outflex their opponents. Each competitor does his best to match shots with his opponent. By this point most of the competitors know the one to beat, and they converge on him like drones around a queen bee. The objective in the posedown is to try and get the judges to reconsider their rankings – for the better, of course! While this rarely happens, it does make for perhaps the most exciting 60 seconds in bodybuilding.

After the posedown the head judges will ask the competitors to step back and relax. From then on it's a matter of announcing the winners. In most contests the top five are announced with fourth and fifth receiving medals and first, second and third receiving trophies. There may be the scattered boo during the announcements, but for the most part the judges place the contestants in the same order as the majority of the audience.

Once the winners of the individual classes are determined, they are asked to come back onstage and an overall winner is chosen. At the local levels the overall winner usually comes from the middleweight or light heavyweight divisions, as these are usually the most competitive classes. At the city level many of the heavyweights are either too smooth or just not carrying enough muscle for their height. Conversely, the majority of bantamweights and lightweights seem to get overshadowed by the middle- and light heavyweights. As you work your way up the levels you'll see the heavyweights starting to dominate the overall class, since by this time they have the muscle mass to fill in their taller frames and overpower the lighter divisions. All things being equal, a good tall bodybuilder will defeat a good shorter opponent.

So what do you think? Are you hooked yet? If so, great. The next time you go to a contest, many of those yells will be directed at you. Of course there are a few intermediate stops along the way, and that's where I come in.

CHAPTER 52

Step One – Which Contest to Choose?

"Not all of us can stand onstage at the Mr. Olympia and trade poses with Ronnie, Jay and Dexter, and that's okay. Even if you never win a first-place trophy – even if you never compete, period, you can be assured of victory if you set the goal of improving year after year and being the best that you can be. That's what real bodybuilding is all about."

– Ron Harris, regular *MuscleMag International* contributor

The first step in your assault on Ronnie Coleman's record is choosing an appropriate first contest. By this I mean picking the show most applicable to your physique development. Most local contests feature a teen division these days, so teens should have a great selection. If you're older than 19 but have never competed before, you have the option of competing in the novice division or in the open or regular classes. If you're older than 35 or 40 (the age limit varies depending on the contest and the federation) you may have the option of competing in a masters division. It's even possible to do all three.

In general, you start at the city level and work your way up. Occasionally a bodybuilder will emerge who is obviously destined for the pro ranks and will be given an exception and be allowed to go straight to a regional event, but for the most part you're expected to earn your dues. Besides, even if your physique is way ahead of the competition, what you'll learn about contest preparation at the local level will be invaluable when you reach the regional or national shows.

A WEIGHTY MATTER

Virtually all shows are broken down into weight classes. At one time contests had only two categories: either tall and short or above and below 200 pounds. But since a big push has been on to make bodybuilding accepted as a competitive sport, competitors are now separated by narrow weight classes, as they are in boxing and wrestling. The most common weight classes are bantamweight, lightweight, middleweight, light heavyweight, heavyweight, and occasionally super heavyweight.

Most bodybuilders try to compete at the top of a weight division. It may sound glamorous to compete as a heavyweight, but a big, ripped light heavyweight will

variables as skin color and thickness and stage presence are taken into account. So you can see that the judges have a lot on their minds when it comes to sorting and ranking the competitors.

In IFBB contests the judging panel is made up of anywhere from seven to nine judges. At local levels this number might be five. Judging panels are made up of odd numbers to help prevent ties. Most judges are former bodybuilders who work their way up the judging ranks in the same manner as the contestants. You don't just decide to judge the Arnold Classic or Mr. Olympia. You start at the local level and work your way up from city to state to national to pro. Most judges will have judged dozens, if not hundreds, of contests by the time

CHAPTER 53

Step Two – Round by Round

"Placing a competitor 13th instead of 11th is understandable, but no mistake should ever occur in the top six ... we must hold the judges accountable for their placings. Their signed scorecards should be published along with the contest report in bodybuilding publications."

– Paul G. Brier, bodybuilding fan, in a letter to *MuscleMag International*.

Now that you know how you'll be scored, it's time to look at the rounds in more detail. In today's highly competitive bodybuilding arena you must make a good impression all the rounds. Don't spend all your time preparing for the compulsories and string together a haphazard free-posing routine. Conversely, don't think the compulsories are simply a matter of holding the pose for a few seconds. Posing is an intense form of exercise (called isometric contraction) and will be just as physically demanding as the free-posing round.

THE COMPULSORY ROUND

Round 1 – Although the most basic of the four rounds, Round 1, or the "relaxed" round is where you make your first impression on the judges. You'll first be asked to stand facing the judges, hands at your sides. As simple as this sounds, there are definite do's and don'ts. For starters, don't let your gut hang out. Keep your abs either tensed or sucked back. Also, try to moderately tense every muscle in your body, especially the lats and quads. Years ago the relaxed round was just that – relaxed. But no more. Now relaxed means "tensed." Try not to tense too hard though. The strain will show on your face, and you'll be increasing the odds of a muscle cramping up. You may be standing there for 15 or 20 minutes, so practice standing this way for ever-increasing lengths of time. Also, keep in mind that for as long as you're onstage the odds are good to excellent that at least one judge is looking at you at any given moment – even if you're not in the group being judged. Assume that you're being judged from the minute you step onstage until you step off.

If you're in the group being judged, the head judge will next ask you to make a quarter turn to the right so your left side is facing the judges. As before, keep your abs tucked in. Make sure your hamstrings and calves are flexed. To fully flex the calf, pivot up on your toes and turn your lower leg just slightly towards the judging panel. Keep your left arm straight and slightly behind you, and your right arm slightly forward. This helps to show off the triceps and chest to your best advantage.

Another quarter turn brings your back in full view of the judges. Make sure your lats are fully flexed and outstretched to bring out your width and V-taper, and try flexing your calves by pushing down on the floor with the balls of your feet. After a close scrutiny you'll be asked to do another quarter turn so your right-hand side is now facing the judges. As before, keep the arms slightly forward and back to show your body off to its best advantage (but reversed, with your right arm slightly behind you and left arm slightly forward). Your final quarter turn brings you back to facing the front.

You may think it's redundant to present both sides to the judges separately, but few bodybuilders are perfectly symmetrical. Whether from genetics, poor training or an injury, most bodybuilders have a best side and the judges know this. In most cases the difference is insignificant, but occasionally a bodybuilder may step onstage with a glaring defect.

Although muscle size is important during Round 1, the judges are also looking at symmetry, proportion, and definition (body-fat percentage).

Judges often want to see both sides of a competitor's physique to assess symmetry and look for imbalances.

CHAPTER 54

Step Three – Round Two

"At the press conference Coleman was taken to task for his prediction that Victor Martinez was in line to win an Olympia. Ronnie's prediction became credible when Victor stepped onstage to perform his compulsory poses."

– Garry Bartlett, *MuscleMag International* correspondent, on the results of the 2006 Mr. Olympia.

This is the coldest and most clinical round in bodybuilding. When the average person on the street thinks of a bodybuilding contest, this is usually what they envision: a group of guys standing next to one another comparing muscles. Round 2 consists of seven poses called compulsory poses. These allow the judges to both scrutinize your physique and see how well it stacks up against your opponents'. These seven poses have set the standard over the years, and you must be able to do them in your sleep before you step onstage. While the judges normally allow you to pick your best side in such poses that can be performed to the right or left, you want to be well practiced at doing them from both sides.

THE SEVEN COMPULSORY POSES

- Front double biceps
- Front lat spread
- Rear double biceps
- Rear lat spread
- Side chest
- Side triceps
- Abdominal and thigh

Oliva, Coleman and Cutler, dwarfed the competition with this pose. It's not surprising that these bodybuilders also had some of the greatest arms in history.

The other variation to this pose is to twist the body slightly, bend and lean more on one leg, and hold one arm slightly higher than the other. By hitting the pose this way you can emphasize your overall proportions more than arm size and body mass. Such bodybuilders as Frank Zane, Lee Labrada and Dexter Jackson use or used this variation to compete with (and beat) larger opponents.

I should add that two of the sport's greats, Lee Haney (eight-time Mr. Olympia) and Dorian Yates (six-time Mr Olympia) often performed both versions in their careers. Despite their incredible muscle mass, neither was particularly famous for their biceps development (their triceps, on the other hand, were incredible). Both men would check out the competition and then choose to either hit the pose straight on (where their overall mass would make up for their moderate biceps development) or use the artistic version to show the judges that they where just as symmetrical and well proportioned as some of the smaller competitors. You'll know early on in your bodybuilding career whether your arms will be among the best onstage or merely average.

No matter which variation you use, don't forget your legs – they are equally on display. Start the pose by making a V with your feet (toes pointing outward) and flexing the quads. Then start pushing on the floor with the heels and balls of your feet. Pushing with the heels brings out the inner thighs while pushing with the balls of the feet helps flex the calves. Once the legs are set you can flex your arms. You can go straight into the pose or hold the arms out straight for a few seconds and then curl your forearms inwards and flex the biceps.

Rear Double Biceps

Most of what I just said about the front double biceps also applies to the rear version. However, one difference is that you'll probably be required to place one leg back and rise up on the toes to show the calf. You'll also be showing your back muscles, so make sure you know how to flex

and hold both the larger latissimus muscles (lats) and the smaller teres and rhomboids. This pose also gives the judges an excellent opportunity for checking out your deltoids, so learn how to control them too. In fact, despite the name this pose does a much better job showing the legs, shoulders and back muscles than the biceps – unless you're Ronnie Coleman, in which case there's just no way you can hide those mountainous biceps!

Side Chest

Despite the increased size of today's pro bodybuilders, no one can duplicate this pose the way Arnold Schwarzenegger did back in his prime in the early- to mid-1970s. Many writers said that Arnold's massive pecs resembled two sacks of flour laid on top of his ribcage. They were that large.

As with most poses, the side chest also displays other muscles. In fact, this pose is an excellent way to compare the relative sizes of the quads, hamstrings and calves. While most bodybuilders have decent size in their quads, any shallow hamstring development becomes apparent when they turn sideways. Likewise, superior hamstring development will be apparent. The side chest pose is also a great way to display the arms.

Start the pose by turning your best side to the judges (make sure to practice both sides, just in case). To flex the hamstring, bend the knee of the outer leg (closest to the judges) and rise up on the toes to flex the calf. Don't forget to turn the heel slightly forward to give the judges a clear view of your calf. With regards to the arms, you have a number of options. If you have long, full biceps you should keep the palm of your flexed arm pointing completely upwards. If you have a slight gap between your forearm and biceps, rotate your palm slightly inwards. This will help fill in the space. Finally, if you have great intercostals (the finger-like muscles located on the side of the lower ribs) – flex them! Years ago the great Robby Robinson displayed a set of intercostals that left most fellow competitors shaking their heads. These days Silvio Samuel and Dexter Jackson draw the same gasps of astonishment and appreciation.

Side Triceps

The side triceps is almost identical to the side chest pose; the only difference is the position of the arms. First, set your legs in exactly the same way as for your side chest. But instead of clasping your hands in front of your body, clasp them straight down and behind. You can clasp either the fingers or the wrist. As with the side chest you'll probably be able to pick your best side, but practice holding the pose from both sides.

Front Lat Spread

The front lat spread is one of the most impressive poses in bodybuilding, and one of the best to highlight a bodybuilder's classic V shape. Like the rear double biceps pose, it does a poor job of displaying the muscles for which it is named – the lats. It's very difficult to see the lats on anyone with large arms and pectoral muscles. You may catch a glimpse between the torso and arms but that's about it. For this reason many bodybuilders tilt backwards slightly when doing this pose.

Start the pose by setting the legs in the same way as for the front double biceps (slight V stance, quads flexed, pushing the floor with the heels and balls of the feet). Rest your knuckles or thumbs along the sides of your lower ribcage with the elbows slightly behind you. Slowly rotate your elbows forward until they are in line with your shoulders or just slightly in front.

Rear Lat Spread

Back in the 1970s, two-time Mr. Olympia Franco Columbu stopped audiences with this pose. His lats looked like a pair of bat wings. These days Jay Cutler, Toney Freeman and Ronnie Coleman tend to rule this pose.

Other than extending one leg back and pivoting up on the toes (and the fact that you're facing the back!), the rear lat spread is identical to the front version.

Abdominal and Thigh

It's said that if a bodybuilder comes in displaying a great set of abdominals then he'll be at or very near the top. Whether or not this is true, a great set of abdominals is indicative of how low a person's body-fat percentage is. The midsection is normally the first place body fat accumulates, and the lower abdominal region is usually the last place fat disappears from. Therefore the abs are a measuring stick to the leanness of the whole physique.

This pose also displays the thighs. The most common way to perform this pose is to place the hands behind the head, extend one leg forward and flex. To really draw in the waist and flex the abs, blow all the air out of your lungs just before hitting the pose. If you've got great thighs, one trick is to relax the forward leg and gently sway it back and forth and then forcefully flex it so that the striations, cross striations and separations suddenly leap out.

Most Muscular

Although not a formal compulsory pose, many contests add this one to the set. As the name suggests, the most muscular, or "crab," is designed to display just about every pose in the body at the same time. One of the best examples of this pose was Lou Ferrigno playing TV's Incredible Hulk. The instant Dave Banner turned into the Hulk, the creature would slam his hands together in front of his body and growl. In most cases that's all it took for villains to get the message and take flight.

To start the most muscular, set your legs first. You can keep them together as in the front lat spread or front double biceps, or you can take a small step forward with one leg. Next, bend the torso forward slightly and, with a slight bend at the elbow, make fists and bring the knuckles of both hands together. While you're doing this you should be squeezing the pecs and trying to hunch the shoulders so the traps bunch up around your ears. When you see guys like Gustavo Badell, Ronnie Coleman, Mustafa Mohammad, Jay Cutler and Markus Ruhl hitting this pose, you understand the name. From the eye-popping veins and striations to the inhuman muscularity and cuts, the most muscular is both frightening and a work of art at the same time.

ONE FINAL POINTER

Before moving on to Round 3 there is a final but important point to consider. As the judges will be sitting in a row, they'll each have a slightly different view of the competitors. The judges sitting in the middle will have the best view while those on the ends will be viewing at an angle (this will be compounded more if you happen to be unlucky enough to be standing at one end of the competitors' lineup). If you hit your poses straight on and square to the audience, only those judges in the middle will get the full effect. The way around this, of course, is to twist your torso slightly as you pose. A good practice is to look each judge in the eye as you hold the pose slightly toward him/her. By doing this you are ensuring that every judge sees your full physique – not just certain parts of it. It would be sad to have the best physique onstage but place low because of something as simple as a viewing angle. Judges are also aware of this problem and the smart ones will have the contestants rotate to make sure each judge gets an equal view.

Posing takes practice, practice and more practice. Each pose has to be mastered for bodybuilding success.

CHAPTER 55

Step Four – Round Three

"You have only two or three minutes to express yourself and show the audience what you've been training so hard for. You need to have music that suits your physique and personality."

– Ed Corney, master poser, offering his views on the free-posing round.

Round 3, or the free-posing round, can win or lose a close contest for you. The free-posing round is also the last chance the judges have to see you before the posedown. You may have been "just another competitor" during the earlier rounds, but now you have your chance to really stand out and make the judges take notice. Also, don't forget that the majority of the audience didn't attend the prejudging, so here's your chance to really win them over. There's nothing like a well-polished and dramatic posing routine to get an audience on your side screaming and clapping. Given that the judges are only human such a response could tilt a close contest in your favor.

If you've attended any bodybuilding contests, you've seen many different routines. Odds are that you remember the dismal and the spectacular. A few boring presentations would have been a great cure for insomnia, while others were nothing short of poetry in motion. There may have been one bodybuilder who captivated the judges and audience alike from the moment he strolled onstage to the moment he left. Time seemed to stand still. That's the impression you want to make, and the key to it is practice and preparation. So let's start.

Photo of Chris Cormier by Irvin Gelb

MUSIC SELECTION

Few things are as important to a great free-posing routine as your choice in music. Your music must excite the
audience as well as suit your physique. Larger physiques
can get away with hard rock or classical, but smaller
bodybuilders should probably stick to something more
upbeat. You need a tremendous physique to get away
with posing to slow classical music. Guys like Arnold
and Lee Haney could get away with it back it the '70s
and '80s because their bodies were huge and spectacular.
The audience was mesmerized. But a 5'6", 160-pounder
will only put the audience (and more importantly, the
judges) to sleep with Beethoven.

If there's any doubt, stick with pop or rock music.
The best choice is something that's currently on the
charts. Most of the audience is in their teens, 20s and
early 30s, so modern music helps get them on your side.
Besides, modern pop music has an upbeat tempo that's
ideally suited for hitting poses to, and has the added benefit of getting the audience clapping along. Unless your

physique is way off, such a favorable reaction from the
audience can't help but influence the judges.

Something else to keep in mind is that your music
selection should complement your posing routine, not
distract from it. While catchy to listen to, soundtracks
from movies – especially science fiction movies with laser
blasts – can overpower your posing routine. You also
want to think twice about using speaking voices within
your music selection. Some bodybuilders have managed
to mimic the voices on their music selections with great
results but it takes a great deal of practice to keep your
poses and voice in sync with an audio track. And then
there's rap. Pure rap music is virtually all talk, and while
perhaps a powerful way to make a social statement, is
an extremely awkward form of music to set a posing
routine to. If you have the time, physique and desire to
use rap music, give it a go. But I still think you should
play it safe for your first show and use a pop song.

DRIVE-BY POSING

If you still have trouble deciding what type of music to
pose to, try this little tip. As you're driving around, visualize posing to the various songs you hear on the radio.
As the music climaxes, visualize hitting a dynamic pose
such as a most muscular or double biceps. As the music
slows or drops in tempo, picture yourself hitting some
classic poses or kneeling shots. Over a period of a few
weeks you'll discover that some songs have the right
spacing between tempos to build a complete posing routine around. Or you may discover that parts of different
songs seem to work well together.

CREATING YOUR CD

Whether you decide to splice different songs or use just
90 seconds of one song, make sure you get someone
who knows what they're doing to do it for you. If you
have the money a professional sound engineer will do a
great job, but even a local disc jockey can make a CD
without it sounding amateurish.

Ed Corney flexes his biceps.

Make two or three copies of your CD. This may sound trivial, but you're tempting fate if you rely on just one copy of your music. Besides, you can't forget your fellow competitors, some of whom have been known to play such games as "hide and seek" with your stuff backstage – especially if they think you're their main competition. My suggestion is to carry two copies with you and have a trusted friend who will be present hold on to a third.

These days probably all contests use CDs, but make sure you ask. You'd hate to show up with CDs and find that they are demanding tapes. If you are using tapes make sure they are rewound to the beginning. It's also a good idea to leave some blank space (about 5 to 10 seconds) at the beginning so you have time to set yourself in position onstage. Of course some bodybuilders have the music start before they step onstage and simply build their posing routine around this.

At the amateur level you'll generally be limited to 90 seconds for your posing routine. But again you'll want to check with the promoter to make sure. You may have only 60 seconds, or for that matter, you might have two minutes. If you're talented enough to make it to the pro level, you normally won't have a time limit, but you should still stick to no more than two minutes. Any more and you'll overstay your welcome, any less and the judges won't get a good look. A good rule of thumb is to stay just long enough to highlight your strong points but short enough to leave the audience wanting just a little bit more.

As a final suggestion, it's probably a good idea to start collecting posing routines on DVD. There are numerous sources for this, including contests televised on ESPN and DVDs advertised in the various muscle magazines. Also, check out YouTube. Use the routines for both inspiration and instruction.

SWITCHING SONGS AND ROUTINES?

If you have a talent for posing (and don't be surprised if you do – some of the sport's greatest posers didn't realize they did until they started working on their first routine), it might be a good idea to prepare two routines with two different music selections. By following the advice to use current pop music, you certainly risk ending up with the same song as another competitor. Nothing is as frustrating as having to follow a competitor who used the same music selection as you. Even if your routine is better than his, much of the impact is lost. You can easily avoid this if you have a second posing routine set to a different song all set to go.

Besides the risk of duplication there's another reason why you might want to alternate songs – dramatic effect. Nothing impresses the judges as much originality, and a bodybuilder who has obviously done his homework. A few bodybuilders switch posing routines between the prejudging and evening show (some also change the color of their posing trunks).

Before leaving this topic I should leave you with a word of caution. If this is your first bodybuilding competition then no doubt you'll be nervous. Your first time onstage will be stressful to say the least and it's hard enough to remember the sequence of poses in one routine let alone two. If you do decide to use two different routines, make sure that you have the routines memorized and down pat. You should be able to flip through the poses in your sleep. If you have any doubt, stick with one routine. With time comes experience. In your subsequent contests you can start experimenting with multiple posing routines.

PUTTING IT ALL TOGETHER – THE POSES

"I always worked hard at it. Posing is so emotional for me. There are so many parts to it. You have your facial expressions, hand gestures, foot movements. I went to ballet classes in L.A. and learned more. I was never mechanical, never afraid to express myself."

– Ed Corney, Mr. Universe winner and master poser, giving his views on posing.

Once you have selected your music, the next order of business is building a posing routine around it. Pick your poses by answering the fundamental question: "What's the purpose of the posing routine?" The answer should be straightforward: you want to show your body to its best advantage by highlighting its strong points and minimizing its weak points. For those who say they have no weak points, my response is dream on! Every – and I mean every – bodybuilder has weak points. Just take a look at the lineup from last year's Mr. Olympia. You'll notice some bodybuilders with upper bodies too large for their legs, lower chests that overpower the uppers, backs that come nowhere near the quality of the fronts, and, as is becoming very common these days, large, bloated-looking midsections. You may think I'm being too critical and perhaps you're right. But the fact remains that every bodybuilder who ever lived had some flaws that needed to be made less apparent. Your goal is to do the same.

Your first step is to make a complete evaluation of your entire physique. Unlike music selection, for which your opinion probably counts the most, objectively analyzing your physique is best left to others. If you're like most bodybuilders you'll probably only see your good points and ignore or minimize your weak areas. Here's where an honest second or third party comes in. Get someone to scrutinize your physique from head to toe, and make sure this person is both knowledgeable and not afraid to hurt your feelings. The best person is a judge or another competitive bodybuilder (obviously not one entering the same contest as you!). Have this observer make notes as he takes you through the compulsory poses. In fact, hit as many different poses as you can think of so he or she can get a complete look at your physique. Then get him to rank the poses from best to worst.

The next step is to start picking the poses you'll use. There are two schools of thought on this. Some bodybuilders believe that since you'll be doing the compulsory poses in round 2, there's no need to include them all in your free-posing routine. The counter argument is that since the compulsory poses tend to be the best ones for highlighting your physique, you must work them into your routine. And the judges may feel that a bodybuilder who avoids hitting compulsory poses is trying to hide something. My advice is to try to use some if not all of the compulsory poses in your routine. If a couple of them really don't do your physique justice then perhaps omit them, but put the rest in there somewhere.

Keep in mind that you have only about 90 seconds to work with. Allowing for a couple of seconds to hold each pose and another second or two in between will give you room for 15 to 20 poses. So choose wisely.

Once you have the poses ranked, the next step is to arrange them in a logical order. By this I mean placing them so that you make the best impression on the judges. Generally speaking, you want to start and finish your routine with your best poses. If you have great arms you can't go wrong by doing a couple of arm shots, including the front double biceps. If you're ripped to shreds and have a set of abs that look like stacked bricks, use them. Hit a couple of ab shots to demonstrate to the judges that you mean business and took your pre-contest dieting seriously. In fact, with most of the other competitors probably starting out with the old standby poses, you'll stand out for your originality by opening with an ab shot. From here the choices are almost endless. Make your poses fluid, so they flow easily from one to the next. It doesn't make sense to try going from a front pose to a back pose all in one motion. Most people would have a hard time making it look graceful. It's much easier to stop halfway and hit a few side poses before continuing on to the full back shots. One of the things that separates the great posers from everyone else is the way they move almost effortlessly from one pose to another. Most bodybuilders try to stay flexed at all times but the great posers relax slightly between poses so when they stop and hit a pose, the muscles, veins and striations seem to pop out from nowhere. This makes a much more dramatic effect on the judges and audience than if the muscles were tensed at all times.

Most bodybuilders save the most-muscular pose for last, as it shows just about every muscle on the body and gives a great idea of your overall body-fat percentage. A totally ripped bodybuilder will display veins, striations and cross striations when hitting the most-muscular pose.

TRANSITION

Once bodybuilding became more popular and the quality of the physiques increased, competitors began to realize that it was going to take more than a collection of individual poses to win. For those who have seen the documentary *Pumping Iron*, one of the opening scenes shows Arnold Schwarzenegger and his good buddy Franco Columbu posing under the direction of a dance instructor. Arnold was probably the first big bodybuilder to put as much effort into moving between poses as he put into the poses themselves. The great Cuban-born Sergio Oliva

carried as much muscle as Arnold (perhaps more given his shorter stature), but looked awkward and unsure of himself when posing onstage. Arnold moved gracefully from one pose to the next. It was this attention to detail that helped make Arnold the superstar he became.

The art of moving between poses is called transition and it takes as much practice to master as holding individual poses. It's for this reason that many pro bodybuilders hire professional dance choreographers to help them with their posing routines. And if you think that dance and ballet are for sissies, think again. I assure you that after a couple of minutes of posing, whether holding individual poses or moving from one pose to another, you'll be huffing and puffing like you were on your last set of squats … and squats are not for sissies, right? So if you can afford it, take advantage of it. Instead of giving the audience and judges just another mediocre posing routine, start establishing your reputation as a dynamic poser.

FINAL TOUCHES

It's easy to spot the bodybuilders who started practicing months in advance and those who have left it 'til the last week. The last-minute guys usually look awkward and seem to be searching for the next pose. They rarely interact with the audience and can't seem to get it over with fast enough. Those who practice, however, appear confident and move gracefully from one pose to the next. They seem to be enjoying every minute and love interacting with the audience. They also do something very simple but important – they smile! Arnold may not smile much in his movies, but he always had a confident grin on his face during his Mr. Olympia days. Today such competitors as Dexter Jackson, Jay Cutler, Gustavo Badell, Ronnie Coleman, Mustafa Mohammad, Victor Martinez, Markus Ruhl and Toney Freeman flash the pearly whites every chance they get. They also make eye contact with the judges throughout their posing routines.

As you practice your posing routine, leave nothing to chance. This includes walking to and from the stage.

A well-polished, dramatic posing routine with great music will get the audience on your side.

Every now and then a competitor will trip on the stairs leading to the posing stage or platform. If possible, practice walking from one room to another and up a flight of stars and then doing your posing routine. If you can, try sneaking into the actual contest venue and practicing. A great posing routine can take months to perfect but the results are worth the time and effort.

TIPS FOR MASTERING THE FREE-POSING ROUND: RECAP

Tip #1: Don't make the first one your first one.

Don't make the mistake of making your very first body-building contest the one you compete in. Attend at least one and preferably two or three contests as a spectator. Pay particular attention to the following: the length of time each pose is held for, how the competitors move from pose to pose, which competitor looks most relaxed (and who looks like they'd prefer to be somewhere else!), which competitor is too light or too dark. Also, study the audience. Figure out which routine(s) seems to go over better. Finally, determine which competitors are prepared and the ones who appear to be making it up "on the spot."

Tip #2: Start posing months in advance

Unless you want to be one of those competitors we criticized earlier, start your pre-contest posing preparations at least two and preferably three months in advance. Holding poses is isometric exercise. You may be able to bang out 8 reps with 300 pounds on the bench press, but trust me, flexing every muscle in your body and holding it for 10 to 20 seconds is nothing short of brutal! Besides practice for the contest, posing helps harden your physique. Try to practice posing 30 minutes a day to give your physique a ripped, muscular look.

Tip #3: Shoot yourself! (No, we don't mean develop suicide tendencies!)

Have a friend take a dozen photos from different angles. Group the photos into good, fair and bad. Unless they're compulsories, toss the bad ones. You want to start and finish your routine with your best poses. You can also use these photos to try and improve.

Tip #4: Master the compulsories

The free-posing round will allow you to be creative and camouflage weaknesses. But you won't be able to do this as well in the compulsory round. The compulsory poses are there specifically to give the judges a close look at your entire physique. In fact, most placements are decided in the compulsory round. For this reason, you must have all seven or eight poses mastered.

Tip #5: Watch some TV

Hundreds of contests are out on DVD these days. In fact, many of the top bodybuilders have their own DVDs that instruct you how to pose. This is a great resource to help you learn and practice posing in the privacy of your own home.

Tip #6: Make your own videos. (No, not like Paris Hilton or Pamela Anderson!)

Have a friend or relative shoot a video of your posing routine. Sit back and watch. Different, isn't it? This is how the judges and audience will view you on contest day. Use the video to evaluate everything about your routines, from your static poses and transition moves to your facial expressions and confidence.

Tip #7: Variety is the bodybuilding spice of life

Do not rely on the same couple of poses over and over. Yes, you may have the best arms in the show, but what about the rest of you? The judges award points for creativity; they also penalize competitors who are repetitive. The key to impressing the judges is to display a well-balanced routine that incorporates the compulsory poses in combination with original poses.

Tip #8: Dance – no, wait – pose to the music!

Although music selection is a personal thing, there are a few points to consider. Only the largest competitors can get away with slow classical music. The rest of us will put both the judges and audience to sleep with such music. Play it safe and pick something modern and upbeat. Or blend a couple of songs with different tempos together.

Tip #9: Bring two copies of your music

Bodybuilding competitors are known to play head games backstage, and accidentally "misplacing" someone else's music tape is one such game. Or maybe the copy you brought just doesn't work right. Play it safe and bring at least two copies of your music. It probably wouldn't hurt to have a third in the safe hands of a friend. Don't forget to check with the promoter to see if they'd prefer tapes or CDs.

Tip #10: Posing transition – like poetry in motion

Take a look at great posers like Ed Corney, Frank Zane, Chris Dickerson, Lee Labrada, Vince Taylor and Melvin Anthony. All these great bodybuilders had or have one thing in common: they make posing look effortless and fun. When putting your own posing routine together, try to infuse a sense of style and personality. Also, while you don't have to be a ballet star, try to ensure your poses flow seamlessly from one to the next.

Tip #11: Mix it up in the posedown

Don't be afraid to mix it up; this is no time to be meek and mild. By this round, you'll know who your closest competitor is. You'll also know how you stack up on a bodypart-by-bodypart basis. As soon as he hits one of his best shots, counter it with one of your own. Try to outdo him at every opportunity. Don't hold back. In a close contest, a show of aggressiveness may be enough to push the judges in your favor.

Tip #12: Relax and smile!

Even though it's tough work, try to make your posing appear effortless and relaxed. Try to smile at all times – even during the most difficult of poses. This is another reason you should begin practicing a couple of months in advance. One or two weeks of preparation is simply not

enough time to train the muscles for holding forceful, static contractions, all while appearing relaxed.

Tip #13: Display confidence at all times

You must constantly believe in yourself and feel that you are the best. Try to straddle the fence between cockiness and confidence. If you're still not sure, watch *Pumping Iron* and pay close attention to Arnold's attitude. At no time did Arnold appear as though he felt second best. In his mind he was the best, period. Believing in yourself will come through onstage – you'll hold your head higher, hit your poses more forcefully, and appear relaxed and confident. And besides, if you appear to think you're not up to par, then the judges and the audience will think you must know best.

Tip #14: Practice, practice, practice

Posing will fatigue you just as much as any chest or leg workout, because you'll be flexing and contracting every muscle in your body. The best posers practice for 30 to 60 minutes every single day. They treat posing the same as a workout and perform "sets and reps." Put the time in and you will be rewarded on contest day.

Photo of Dexter Jackson by Irvin Gelb

CHAPTER 56

Step Five – The Posedown

"Gunter has been a huge crowd favorite, as his Herculean development and movie-star charisma always raised the level of excitement in the final posedowns."

– Muscleaneous, a feature in *Reps!* magazine

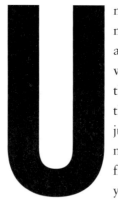

Unlike the first three rounds, which are more formal in nature and can be rehearsed, Round 4 is improvising at its best. You literally make it up on the spot and go with the flow. A typical posedown consists of the top three to five competitors. You'll be asked to line up at the front of the stage and, after a signal from the head judge, given one minute to show your stuff. For the next minute you and your competitors will be trying to out-flex one another and convince the judges that you and you alone deserve the winner's trophy. The posedown is in many respects a chess match, and the strategy is to highlight your strong points while minimizing your weak points. At the same time you'll be trying to use your strong points to bring your opponents' weak points to light.

Although it's difficult to prepare for the posedown, you can give yourself an edge. If at all possible, try to have some idea of who'll you'll be posing against (another reason to view your first contest from the audience rather than the stage). Most competitors tend to hit the same poses in the same order. If you find yourself competing against any competitors that you've seen in action before, you can be ready for them. Let's say they have a great set of arms and usually go for a front double biceps first. You, on the other hand, have the better legs and abs. As soon as they hit their biceps shots, you wait a second,

The posedown gives competitors a chance to try and outflex one another and highlight their strong points.

Photo of Vince Taylor and Flavio Baccianini by Robert Kennedy

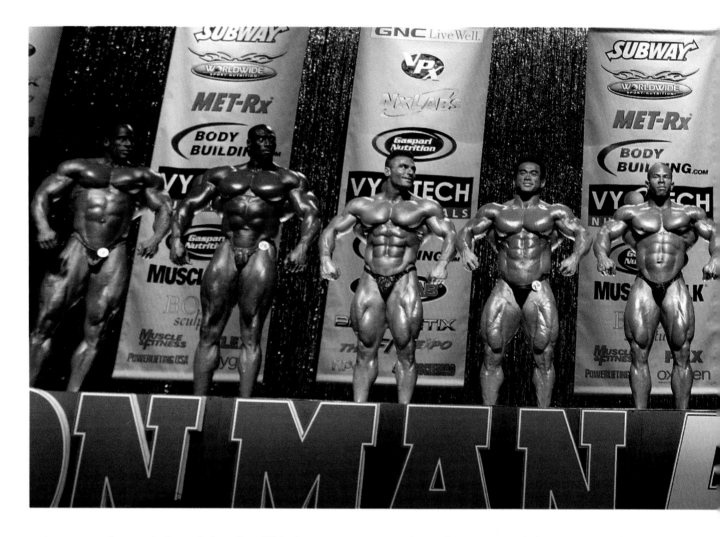

point to your legs and abs and then flex. This draws the judges' attention away from their strong points and over to yours. If they hit a front lat shot that looks pretty decent, you can flip around and do a back lat spread or double biceps – assuming of course that you look good in these poses. The idea is to offset their strong points with your own. Don't be afraid to match poses either, especially when you know you look better. If your great-arm competitor hits his double-biceps pose and you just happen to have a great set of arms of your own, fine! Accept the challenge and join the fray.

Another point to keep in mind is that the posedown takes place at the end of your class. After a day of strenuous posing under the hot lights, having been living on a low-carb and calorie diet for weeks and then reduced water for the last couple of days, you're going to be tired

– extremely tired. So it's a good idea to practice the posedown in the weeks before the contest. To make it a bit more fun, invite a few of your friends from the gym to tag along. The three of you can pretend that you're at the Olympia: with Coleman, Cutler and Badell disposed of, it's down to the three or four of you.

As a typical posedown at the local and state level usually lasts about a minute, try practicing for a minimum of two minutes – three to four if you have the energy.

POSING – NOT JUST FOR SHOW!

Before leaving this chapter a few words are needed on a vital but sometimes forgotten aspect to posing. In one of the early chapters I told you about how the great Charles Atlas made millions on his comic ad

Photo by Jason Breeze

telling teens how to build their bodies to fight off bullies. The heart of Atlas' training courses was Dynamic Tension. The exercises that made up Dynamic Tension primarily involved contracting the muscles against immovable objects such as walls and floors. Other exercises involved flexing the muscles against themselves. While static-contraction exercises (now more commonly called isometric exercises – exercises for which the muscle doesn't change length) are not as effective as isotonic movements (the familiar exercises where the muscle contracts and shortens), they do offer some ability to increase size and strength. So what has all this got to do with posing? Well it just so happens that posing – especially holding poses – is a form of isometric exercise. You'll discover this the first day you start practicing your posing. You'll find a cou-

ple of minutes of all-out posing to be just as tiring as a heavy set of squats or bench presses. And the odds are good to excellent that you'll be just as sore the next day as from any weight-training workout.

Besides the fact that practicing helps you do your best on contest day, posing practice is a great way to harden and refine your physique – especially the smaller muscles that often get short-changed with traditional weight-training exercises. Many bodybuilders actually look their best two or three days after the contest because of all the posing they did on contest day. In fact, the greatest bodybuilders in the world spend one to two hours each day practicing their posing. They practice compulsories, holding shots and transition moves, and even the posedown. Nothing is left to chance and everything is rehearsed, practiced and repeated.

CHAPTER 57

Pre-contest Eating

"I'm amazed that almost everyone thinks there is some kind of trick to getting ripped and dry. Diet is the most important aspect of contest training, even up to the day of the show. All this carb-up, sodium-loading, diuretic, insulin-taking crap is a sure way to screw up four to five months of contest prep."

– King Kamali, *MuscleMag International* columnist, offering his opinion on the most important factor for success in contest preparation.

"I love and hate bodybuilding at the same time. While I love lifting heavy weight and eating huge quantities of foods, I dread dieting like the plague. Anything that helps me survive the torture of dieting is always welcome."

– Gustavo Badell, top IFBB pro

If they're honest, most bodybuilders will probably tell you that pre-contest dieting is just about the hardest part of preparing for a bodybuilding contest. And this goes double for drug-free bodybuilders. A bodybuilder who is huge in the off-season might turn up onstage looking like a scrawnier version of his former self. Not exactly what you want on contest day. Those 30 or 40 pounds of muscle that took years to obtain were gone within a matter of a few months.

The problem is not so much their muscles as their brains – and I'm not talking about intelligence here. The trouble is, your brain uses only carbohydrate as a source of energy, and your body will do just about everything in its power to protect the brain. When blood sugar levels fall very low, the body thinks it's entering a period of starvation. As a form of defense, it begins releasing stress hormones, including cortisol. Cortisol is a catabolic hormone that breaks muscle protein down into carbohydrate to give the brain its energy source. The end result is muscle wasting. Don't despair, however, as a combination of smart dieting and daily data collecting will have you looking both big and ripped on contest day.

YOUR PRE-CONTEST PREPARATION KIT

To really get organized and serious about pre-contest dieting you should put together a little kit. Take an hour or
two and pick up the following:

- Weight scales
- Notebook
- Measuring tape
- Food scale
- Food nutrition guide (you can also use some of the
  online sites such as www.nutritiondata.com)
- Mirror
- Skinfold calipers

Start your pre-contest dieting at least three to four months
before the contest. Yes, you read correctly – three to four
months. Most bodybuilders underestimate how much fat
they need to lose to end up in decent contest shape.
They also fail to realize that you can't do it in one or
two months by following a crash diet. A crash diet is the
surest way to cause that muscle loss I was just discussing.

One of the first things you should do is get an accurate assessment of your body composition – particularly
body-fat percentage. Get it measured at the gym, a local
university (medical school or exercise physiology department), or at a hospital. An even easier method would be
to use one of those body-fat measuring machines that
you simply stand on or hold on to with your hands – if
you can find an accurate one. They operate by sending a
very small electrical current through your body. The
speed it takes the current to travel through your body
determines how much body fat you have. There was a
time when you'd need to spend thousands of dollars for
an accurate body-fat machine but no longer. Those cheap
Wal-Mart versions are nearly as accurate as the more
expensive units. In fact many of the newer digital scales
have a body-fat percentage analyzer built in. Do keep in
mind though that these are still not totally accurate, and
that many do not work for athletes. Do your homework.

You should aim to carry about five percent body fat
by contest time. Once you know your body fat percentage, you can calculate how much fat you have to lose.

Pre-contest dieting is a highly calculated and planned program that should start at least three months before a contest.

Let's say you weigh 200 pounds, carrying 20 percent
body fat. If we multiply your weight by the percentage,
or 200 X 0.20, we see that you have 40 pounds of fat
spread over your body. If you want to get down to 5
percent body fat, you would need to lose 15 percent, or
30 pounds of fat.

LOSING FAT WITHOUT LOSING MUSCLE

*"It is a well-known fact that the body tends to hoard fat
during periods of starvation, and extended pre-contest
dieting is viewed by the body as starvation. As a result
the body will naturally prefer to cannibalize muscle tissue while sparing survival fat stores."*
– Ron Clark, president of the National Federation of Professional
Trainers, offering his views on extended pre-contest dieting.

For many years weight-loss experts have used the
"bucket" theory: Calories in, calories out. Bodybuilders
have never followed this method of fat loss. As always
seems to happen, competitive bodybuilders learn what

The first step to pre-contest clean eating is to cut out all junk food and avoid processed foods.

Photo of Binais Begovic by Robert Reiff

works and what doesn't in regards to building muscle and losing fat light years before everyone else. The scientists are now agreeing with what bodybuilders have said for years: one calorie is not the same as the next.

Your first step in getting ripped is figuring out how long you need to diet for. Two to three pounds a week is about the fastest rate that will allow you to both lose fat and keep your muscle. That got you thinking, didn't it? If you have 30 pounds to lose that means you are dieting for anywhere from 10 to 15 weeks. Given the fact that you will likely see a plateau during that time you should probably give yourself a little more time rather than less.

WHAT TO EAT

Now you have to take a good look at what you've been eating. Have you been eating clean? Do you know what clean eating is? Well, you've got to figure it out, start doing it, and as the next 12 or so weeks go by you're going to have to get stricter and stricter with it.

Start by cutting out all junk. No more chocolates, candies, cakes, creams, sauces, fried food, cookies, soda, pizza, burgers or beer ... in fact, no alcohol at all. Really! You also have to avoid white flour, cheese, sugar and any processed foods. Since you should be eating to feed your muscles in the off-season, you this should not be a big stretch for you.

That's the first step. Plus, you have to make sure you eat every two to three hours. But you should be pretty used to that already.

As the each week passes you will have to cut down more and more on such foods as starchy carbs, fruits, nuts and milk products. By the last week or two you will be eating almost nothing but lean meat, protein powder and green leafy vegetables. This is not easy, and it's where your resolve will be tested more than at any other time.

HOW MUCH TO EAT

"I guess I've become known for showing up at every contest as one of the most, if not the most shredded bodybuilder onstage. It's one thing to be huge, but if you're not ripped you might as well take a lawn chair with you to the contest."
– Art Dilkes, IFBB pro, affectionately known as "Mr. Ripped" in bodybuilding circles

CARBOHYDRATE LOADING

When you start attending bodybuilding contests on a regular basis you'll notice that some competitors look small and flat at the prejudging, but full and vascular at the evening show. Others look pathetic for the full contest day but would easily win the overall on Sunday or Monday. This even happens at the pro level, and you'll hear such explanations as: "I missed my peak" or "I left it too late" at the Sunday or Monday photo shoot when they're displaying the physique they should have brought to the show on Saturday.

So what is it that explains the dramatic change in a bodybuilder's physique in as little as 12 or 24 hours? The biological explanation lies with a unique interplay between water and glycogen (stored carbohydrate). By first depleting and then ingesting (called "loading") carbohydrates, bodybuilders can show up on contest day as big as a house and ripped to shreds. But if they miss the timing just slightly and they'll appear small, flat and smooth. It's that simple and here's how it works:

The stored form of sugar is called glycogen – each gram of which holds three to four grams of water. Competitive bodybuilders make use of this fact by depleting their carbohydrate levels starting about a week before the contest. They also restrict their water intake. After a couple of days of depleting (usually Sunday to Tuesday), they then switch to a carb-loading phase (usually Wednesday to Friday evening) to greatly increase glycogen levels. In fact, muscles will store more glycogen after a period of depletion than under normal circumstances. In addition, because each gram of glycogen is capable of holding three to four grams of water, the muscles start drawing water from under the skin. The end result is muscles filled with glycogen and therefore much larger and fuller. And because that glycogen draws water from under the skin, the individual's vascularity will be that more visible and pronounced. The whole process can take as little as 8 hours or as long as 72. This is why bodybuilders who look flat and smooth at the prejudging can look so much fuller and harder at the evening show. And the reason so many bodybuilders look so good the day after the contest is that traditionally there is a post-show pig-out. Most promoters rent a nightclub or restaurant, and after a couple of months of strict pre-contest eating most bodybuilders let loose in an orgy of nutritional debauchery. The next morning they wake up fully glycogen loaded and hard as nails. Of course, by then it's too late. But this gets back to what I said earlier about keeping notes. If you keep detailed notes about what you eat and how you look you'll know how far in advance to start your preparations for the next contest. If you looked your best at the evening show, then start your loading a half-day earlier next time. If you're in top form on Sunday, then shift everything forward a full day for future contests. A Friday peak means you'll need to start things a day later next year.

Of course there is a limit to how much glycogen the muscles can hold, and once they are saturated excess glycogen may be stored in the body's tissues. This can lead to a buildup of water under the skin, which leads to that dreaded "smooth" or "holding water" look. The worst scenario is appearing smooth at the prejudging and then arriving rock hard for the evening show. All the posing during the prejudging under the hot lights sweats out the excess water, allowing the person's true muscularity to show through. The problem is that the effect won't be seen until the evening show. And since most of the placings are decided at the prejudging, the competitor won't place as high as he could have. This puzzles the audience, as they can't understand how the best-looking physique didn't win. Those who had attended the prejudging would realize what had happened.

You can read every bodybuilder's advice about timing and dieting, but the truth is there's only one person who can determine how your body will respond to a given set of circumstances and that's you. But you will have to experiment to find out. You may need as little as 12 hours to fully carb-load or it may take three or four days. The odds are good to excellent that you won't nail it the first time. But when you do the results are worth it and undeniable.

WATER RETENTION

It only makes sense to follow the topic of carb-loading with that of water retention, as they are related. You probably understand that, all other things being equal, the bodybuilder who is the hardest and with the most defined muscles will more than likely win. Two variables control how hard a physique will look: fat and water. Keeping body-fat levels low takes a year-round approach in combination with some strict precontest dieting, and come contest week there's not much you can do to alter your fat level. It's work with what you got.

When it comes to water retention, however, you can make drastic changes in the days leading up to the contest. As discussed, you can use carb loading to fill up your muscles and make your skin look paper thin. Another strategy employed by competitive bodybuilders is to reduce salt intake. Salt causes the body to retain

water. That's one of the reasons salt tablets are included in survival kits. Water conservation may be vital in the desert or the frozen tundra, but not when standing on a bodybuilding stage. Unfortunately, salt (sodium) is added to most foods. This is especially true of tinned food. As soon as you start your pre-contest diet, start eliminating most if not all tinned food.

Another strategy is to slowly start restricting your fluid intake in the weeks before the contest. For obvious reasons you shouldn't cut out water entirely, but don't make a practice of consuming great quantities. If possible, try to drink distilled water (normally available in grocery stores), as it has all the sodium removed.

Given the amount of salt and water lost in sweat, it wouldn't hurt to add in a few extra sessions of light cardio in the weeks leading up to a contest. You'll probably be doing the cardio as part of your fat-loss strategy anyway, but now's the time to be extra diligent.

CHEMICAL HINDRANCE

As some drugs are notorious for causing water retention, check with your doctor or pharmacist if you are using any medication. Obviously if it's a drug for a serious medical problem then you're going to need to keep taking it, but if it's something that you can discontinue for a few weeks or even months, then give it some serious consideration. Some drugs such as anabolic steroids (discussed in much more detail later in the book) and cortisone cause the body to conserve large amounts of water. Even many over-the-counter painkillers can cause water retention. If you have any doubt as to a particular drug's water retaining effects consult someone.

CHEMICAL ASSISTANCE?

I'd be negligent if I left the topic of water retention without discussing the pharmaceutical approach to shedding water. Just as some athletes turn to chemicals to build muscle and lose fat, many do the same to get rid of water. There are two approaches to shedding water by chemical means – natural and drug. Natural means using a mild herbal product such as dandelion root to help the body increase water excretion or decrease water conservation. While most of these natural means are safe, they are generally not very effective either. This tends to be a hit-or-miss approach.

The drug route is the most effective way to shed water – it also the most dangerous and could kill you. In fact, diuretics are thought to have been at least part of the reason for one pro bodybuilder's death. Most diuretics are water-shedding drugs that work by interfering with aldersterone – the body's primary water-conserving hormone. The bodybuilders who use diuretics usually take them in the days before a show to drop the extra water.

The problem is not so much the water loss as the electrolytes that go with it. Electrolytes are electrically charged substances called ions, that control the body's various electrochemical systems including muscle contraction, nerve signal conduction, and heartbeat. It's quite common for diuretic-using bodybuilders to experience muscle cramping during a contest – particularly as they're posing. This is not fatal, but it's very painful. It also won't win you any extra votes from the judges. The real problem is the risk of heart arrhythmia (irregular heart beat) or even heart attack. Your heart is under the control of such electrolytes as sodium, calcium and potassium, and interfering with their levels could easily put you in the emergency room or morgue. In 1992 one of the top pro bodybuilders in the world – Mohammad Benaziza, died of a massive heart attack just after winning the Belgian Grand Prix. His death was believed to be directly related to the diuretics he used before the contest to shed water. It was ironic having a bodybuilder who supposedly epitomized health and fitness dropping dead of a heart attack just hours after being proclaimed a champion.

While Benaziza is the most famous bodybuilder to have died from using diuretics, others have come close, and muscle cramping is common at pro events. My advice is to stay away from diuretic drugs and rely on natural means to shed water.

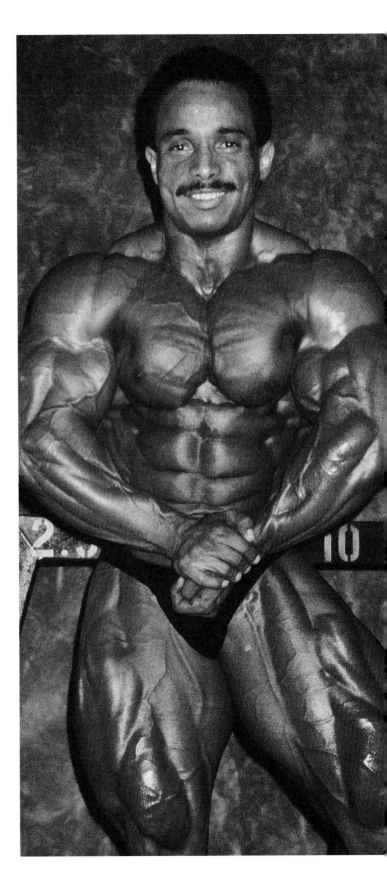

Photo of Mohammad Benaziza by Garry Bartlett

CHAPTER 58

Looking Your Best Onstage

"People see pictures of competitive bodybuilders shaved down, oiled up, wearing tiny posing suits, and form their own opinion. They don't understand how the sport works or how it's judged."

– Ron Harris, regular *MuscleMag International* contributor, on why you should follow your dreams and not worry about other people.

No doubt many readers wear eyeglasses. If you are one, then you've probably discovered how annoying it is to keep having to adjust them during your workouts. No matter how well they fit, glasses will invariably start sliding down your face as the sweat begins to flow. The bodybuilding stage offers no reprieve. The combination of posing and hot lights will have your glasses resting on the tip of your nose like a crusty old librarian in no time. Since you really don't want to have to adjust your glasses while you're standing in the lineup, and since it's virtually impossible to do so during your free-posing routine, you're going to have to do something about them.

The simplest option is to ditch the glasses and go onstage half blind. While feasible for some people whose eyesight isn't too terrible, this solution does have its drawbacks. You run the risk of tripping on the stairs, or banging into stage equipment or other competitors. But even if you can manage to get around all that, not being able to see properly will affect your performance. With the exception of the free-posing round, the bulk of a bodybuilding contest is interactive with the judges and the other competitors. You'll need to be able to see both if you hope to look your best and offer some real personality to the performance. How do you make eye contact with the judges and match the other competitors pose for pose if you can't see them? Ditch the glasses and opt for contact lenses. Yes they'll set you back a few dollars (On average $50 to $100 for a three-month supply), but the results will be worth it. You'll have perfect vision with no blurred edges, and you won't have any of the annoyances associated with glasses including slipping off during workouts, drying off during rain showers, fogging up in the cold and having to keep cleaning off smudges and dirt.

If money is no object you have the option of going all the way and getting laser surgery. Laser surgery is one of the great advances in corrective eye care and you'll have your vision restored to its pre-glasses state. Without going into the technical details suffice it to say that laser surgery involves using a laser to reshape the lenses in your eye so they produce a sharp image. If laser surgery has a downside, it's cost. The ads might say "from $499!" but the average procedure costs $2,000 to $3,000. Still, once it's over you'll have great vision without the need for glasses or contact lenses.

A HAIRY SITUATION

Up until Arnold came on the scene, most Hollywood hunks had copious amounts of hair on their chests. It seems men were supposed to sport the shaggy look to emphasize their masculinity. This is one of the reasons bodybuilding took so long to become accepted. Any sport that involved men with smooth skin must be for sissies, right? Yeah, just try telling that to Toney Freeman as he's pressing 150-pound dumbells, or Ronnie Coleman as he squats 800 pounds.

Despite being associated with masculinity for all those years, hair is a big disadvantage for competitive bodybuilders. You've spent months, if not years, building a great body and don't want it obscured by a layer of coarse hair. And I don't think I need to tell you just what a sight you'll make with inch-long body hair soaked with posing oil!

So the hair has to go. The first time you remove it you'll see your body in a whole new light and odds are you'll want to keep it that way.

HAIR TODAY GONE TODAY!

There are numerous options for removing hair, and each has pros and cons. My advice is to experiment and find the method that works best for you.

Photo of Brad Baker by Irvin Gelb

SHAVING

By far the most popular method for removing body hair is simply shaving with razor blades or an electric shaver – usually a combination of both. Now a few words of caution are in order. Your facial skin may be used to shaving but if this is your first time shaving your body hair you'll need to go easy. The skin on your body is likely not used to having a sharp piece of metal dragged across it. You may also want to avoid using shaving cream. While you're used to the unique curves of your face, you'll be less familiar with the curves and bumps that characterize your muscles, and the shaving cream will serve to obscure these areas. Also, extremely long body hair plus shaving cream makes for a cloggy situation. Glycerine soap is a good choice. You'll get the best, and safest, results in a warm shower or bath. If you try to shave your body without enough soapy water you'll scrape your skin, and if you get too cold you will get

Hair removal is an important factor in competitive bodybuilding – you don't want your hard-earned body masked by a thick layer of hair.

goosebumps. This will cause a bad shave at best, and scraped up skin is again likely.

The other popular form of shaving is to use an electric shaver. Most electric shavers have a side attachment used for trimming beards and moustaches. This also does a great job of removing body hair. Don't use the regular shaving attachment (usually three circular heads). These small blades are not designed for cutting thick body hair. You also run the risk of getting the long hair caught in the revolving heads and may end up yanking more hair out than cutting it. Besides, you may burn out the motor.

Electric shavers offer numerous advantages over blades. For one thing they're much faster. It may take you an hour or more to shave down with a blade but 10 or 15 minutes should do it with the electric shaver. Shavers are also safer. It's virtually impossible to cut yourself with an electric shaver but you're bound to get a cut or two shaving with a razor – especially in bony locations such as your shins.

Most bodybuilders use a combination. They start about a month before the contest, to have their skin smooth and prepared by contest time. Starting in advance gives any nicks and cuts and rashes a chance to heal.

Finally and I know this seems common sense, but under no circumstance do you use an electric shaver in the shower or bath! Water and electricity don't mix – actually they mix far too well – and every now and then you'll read in the newspaper how someone was electrocuted by a electric shaver or hair dryer falling into the tub. Use the shaver away from water, and make sure to unplug it when you're done.

HAIR REMOVAL CREAMS

Although they may seem to be the exclusive domain of women, hair removal creams will work just as well on men's hair. In some respects you can consider this form of hair removal to be external digestion, as the cream contains ingredients that literally break down the protein structure of the hair. Just smear the cream on the area, leave it for five to ten minutes and wipe it off with a cloth or in the shower. Hair removal creams do an excellent job of leaving the skin hairless and smooth. The other option is to use a hair removal cream that's designed for men. One of the best is called the Lex Hair Removal System. Consisting of three products that remove hair, soften the skin and keep the hair from regrowing, this system is produced by Lex Advanced Skin Technologies of Georgetown, Ontario,Canada.

No matter which product you use, do a little test first before smearing the whole body. Some individuals may be allergic to the cream so place a small amount on the back of your hand or forearm and leave it for five or ten minutes. Wait for 24 hours. If no rash or redness appears it's probably safe to use it on the rest of your body. If you do have an allergic reaction, you can try another brand. If you still develop a rash it probably means that you are allergic to the active ingredients in the cream and you'll probably need to use a razor.

WAXING

Waxing is a hair-removal technique that is getting more and more acceptable with guys. In fact, back waxing is getting very common and many estheticians say men are beginning to come in as often as women. Waxing is a very effective and long-lasting method for shedding the fur coat, but it can be rather painful.

The technique is fairly straightforward. You simply melt the wax, smear it over the area, let it cool, and then rip it off. Now, a word of caution about the last step. If you have long, coarse hair, there is a right way and wrong way to do this. Waxing is not much different than grabbing a handful of grass and pulling it up by its roots. If you try ripping slowly, every single hair is going to add its voice to the collective experience known as intense pain. Ripping fast still hurts, but not as much as ripping slowly. And keep in mind that ripping hair out by its roots may leave a rash and even leave small drops of blood. There is a classic scene in the movie *The 40-Year-Old Virgin* that may serve to enlighten (or frighten!) you on the joys and tribulations of waxing.

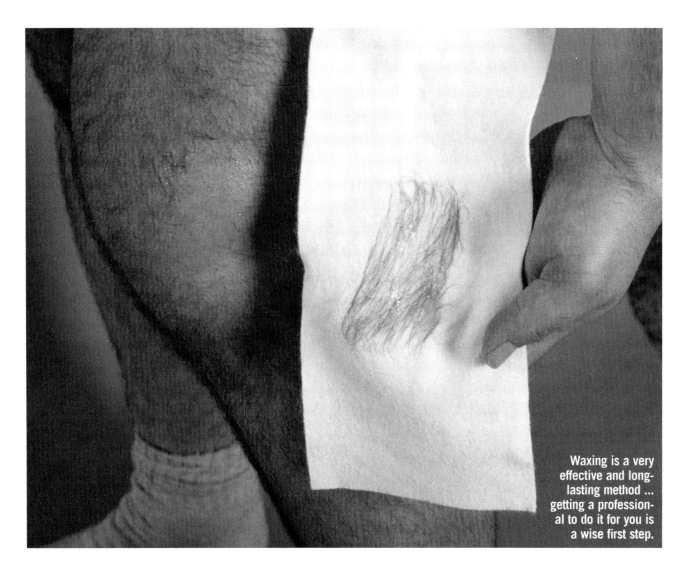

Photo by Robert Kennedy

Waxing is a very effective and long-lasting method ... getting a professional to do it for you is a wise first step.

The truth is, getting a professional to do it for you is a wise first step. After you've had it done a few times you may want to do it yourself – or you could do the parts of your body that are easy and hire someone to do the parts you can't reach yourself.

ELECTROLYSIS

As with laser eye surgery, modern science has offered an expensive alternative for hair removal. As the name suggests, electrolysis involves zapping the hair follicle with a blast of electricity. While great in theory, it's honestly not all it's cracked up to be. For one thing each hair has to be targeted separately. Take a look at those hairy thighs of

yours and do the math. You're in for a long day. Also, you have to consider the cost – hundreds of dollars for a small area and many thousands for the full body. Finally, despite what advertisers claim, electrolysis is not permanent. There will be some hair re-growth. Given the effectiveness and speed of the cheaper hair removal methods (shaving, creams, etc.) I suggest leaving electrolysis to those with deep pockets trying to shed hair from smaller areas.

SKIN CARE

It only makes sense to follow the topic of hair removal with that of skin care, as there is some overlap. All those days baking in the sun, sweating in the gym, and ravishing it with sharp steel or creams can leave the skin looking years, if not decades, older than it really is. Given that the skin is the body's first line of defense against invading germs, you have to treat it with care and kindness. Also, keep in mind that you're involved in a sport that is concerned primarily with looks – especially healthy, youthful looks.

Even if the damage you inflict now is not visible for 10 or 20 years, you're still accelerating the aging process. The primary culprits that cause wrinkly skin are prolonged exposure to sunlight, facial expressions, and unhealthy habits such as drinking, smoking and eating nutritionally bereft foods.

Weight-training athletes often scrunch their faces up into strange expressions when working on heavy weights, and they also subject their skin to the harsh conditions brought on by excessive sweating. Sweat contains more than just water. It's loaded with salt and the waste byproducts of exercise – all of which tend to dry out and wrinkle the skin. When you add in the various rashes and acne that often accompanies regular exercise, I think you'll see why skin care should be a high priority.

The following skin-care techniques will take just four or five minutes to perform in the morning and before bed, but the results will keep your skin looking healthy and youthful. Now, before you skip ahead to the next section, don't think skin care is a "women-only" issue. If you've ever seen the aged and weathered skin of a 50-year-old alcoholic, you'll understand how unattractive it is to have prematurely aged skin.

Cleansing

The first step in skin care is to clean it with a mild non-detergent lotion. If possible use an unscented brand, as the scented versions often leave an oily clogging residue behind. Also avoid rubbing with a harsh cloth, as this may irritate the skin and spread or cause acne. Most skin-care experts recommend cleansing the skin first thing in the morning and again before bed in the evening.

Toning

The next step to healthy skin care is toning. Toners remove the residue left behind by washing. No matter what type of soap or cleansing solution you use, there'll always be some residue left behind. The best applicator to use is a small cotton ball or quilted pad, but a light cloth will do just as well. Use circular motions as you apply the toner and avoid getting close to the eyes. You may also want to apply some toner just after your workout to help remove some of the dirt left by sweating. And if your gym buddies razz you when they see the cotton balls, just remember that in 20 or 30 years, while your skin still looks youthful, theirs will begin to look like an old pineapple!

Moisturizing

One of the primary reasons skin begins to look terrible is dehydration. Just imagine two pieces of leather left out in the sun. One is left untreated and the other regularly covered with a thin layer of oil. Which one do you think will dry out and crack the fastest? Well your skin behaves in much the same way.

Although the body continuously tries to keep the skin hydrated with water, much of it evaporates. Sealing the water in with a moisturizer will keep your skin soft and pliable (stretchable). The type of moisturizer you select depends on the type of skin you have. If you have dry skin you can go for a heavier moisturizing cream. Those with normal to slightly oily skin may want to use a light moisturizing lotion.

Exfoliating

Besides the three previous skin-care techniques, which should be performed on a daily basis, it's also a good idea to exfoliate about once a week. Exfoliation is the process by which old, dead cells are removed. Although your skin does this naturally, and regular shaving also helps remove dead skin cells, a good exfoliant will speed up the process.

There are numerous exfoliant products on the market but some can be very harsh on the skin and actually cause burning, a rash and even skin damage. In some respects exfoliation is like scrapping off old paint before you apply a new coat. You don't want to scrub so hard that you damage the wood underneath – just remove the old peeled paint. The same applies to skin exfoliation. The goal is to use a product that removes the old dead cells yet not harm the underlying new cells. Unfortunately some commercial products will do just that. If in doubt check with a licensed cosmetician or dermatologist before hand.

No matter which exfoliant product you use, don't scrub too hard and never rub in the same place for more than a few seconds. Keep moving your hand over your entire face and avoid getting the product into your eyes or mouth. After you've finished rinse with cold water or as some experts recommend, run an ice cube over the face.

STRETCH MARKS

The next time you're in the gym take a close (but discrete!) look at some of the larger bodybuilders. Many will have long purplish streaks along their bodies, particularly around the pec-delt tie-in region (where the chest muscles join the front shoulders). These streaks are called stretch marks and are in fact tears in the skin. They are caused by a number of factors, including rapid weight gain and poor nutrition.

Basically what happens is that the underlying muscles grow faster than the overlying skin. The end result is stretching and eventually tearing of the skin, which leads to that purplish streaking look. The reason the pec-delt tie-in is prone to stretch marks is because it's the sight of the most rapid muscle growth in the body.

Virtually every bodybuilder will develop stretch marks. In fact many bodybuilders welcome them and consider them a rite of passage. If you'd rather not have so many purple streaks in your skin, make sure you are following a diet that is well balanced and fortified with all the essential vitamins and minerals. A diet deficient in nutrients causes the skin to become less elastic and stretchable, so instead of expanding to accommodate the growing muscle, the skin tears.

Illustration by Mark Collins

Another suggestion is to avoid following the old concept of "bulking up" in the off-season. While bulking up will help you gain muscle size, the extra calories will also pack excess fat on your body. The result: stretch marks.

If you've already developed stretch marks, a number of over-the-counter products may help. A good place to start is with vitamin E capsules. Break them open and spread the oil on the affected area. Coca butter is also supposed to help. Many skin-care companies produce stretch-mark creams that are supposed to help. Also, dark tanning products are not only necessary for competition, but they also help camouflage stretch marks.

STRETCH MARKS

When the natural collagen and elastin fibers within the body are strained due to rapid changes in weight and muscle, the underlying tissue tears and the body responds by forming unsightly scar tissue. Skin structure is genetically determined; we are predisposed to developing stretch marks. The skin has lost much of its original elasticity and will never look quite the same. Stretch marks do not go away entirely; however, you can massage your skin with a massage brush or glove to increase circulation; apply moisturizing cream on a daily basis to keep the skin supple; and eat foods that contribute to the overall health of the skin, such as those high in vitamins C and E, zinc and silica (which helps to form collagen). Treat stretch marks as early as possible to minimize their appearance.

CHAPTER 59

Tanning and Oiling

"They often look more stupid than muscular. Not applying under the chin gives them the 'white strap around the neck' look. Not rubbing color into the hairline or eye sockets, behind the ears, or under the arms can also distract from the physique big time."

– Nelson Montana, regular *MuscleMag International* contributor, commenting on the tanning mistakes some novice bodybuilders make.

> **"** He starts tanning in a tanning bed four times a week for 20 minutes, 10 weeks before a contest. He stops tanning one week before the show. On the Thursday night before prejudging, he applies three coats of Pro Tan. On Friday, with one last application of Pro Tan to his face, he is ready to go."
>
> – Larry Pepe, *MuscleMag International* contributor, commenting on the skin darkening preparations of IFBB pro, Will Harris.

Everyone these days seems to be after the California Golden look, whether a competitive bodybuilder or a sedentary accountant. Those living in northern climates spend thousands of dollars on trips down south, tanning beds and creams. Kind of ironic, given that just over a 100 years ago a tanned skin was the sign of the lower classes and anyone with money was expected to remain lily white.

For bodybuilders tanning has two purposes. Regular suntanning helps tighten the skin, making it hug the muscles. The end result is a more striated and ripped appearance. This is why most African American bodybuilders spend as much time tanning as their Caucasian counterparts.

The second and most important reason is that all things being equal the darker bodybuilder will invariably place higher than a lighter opponent. The bright stage lights that flood down on the competitors tend to wash out and blur muscle definition and separation, and a light skin emphasizes this. Under any circumstances a bodybuilder with fairer skin will look smoother than one with darker skin. During bodybuilding's early days of the 1940s and early 1950s it was discovered that those bodybuilders from California (and to a lesser extent Florida), with their dark tans, looked better onstage than their northern rivals. It wasn't long before tanning – either natural or through artificial means – became as much a part of the bodybuilder's pre-contest preparations as dieting, posing and increased cardio.

Things were going along quite nicely until scientists spoiled the party by announcing that sunbathing leads to skin cancer.

Besides the risk of skin cancer, excessive exposure to sunlight destroys the skin's elasticity, leaving it wrinkled and old looking (again I remind readers of the dried out leather analogy). You can see this with laborers who spend most of their day outside in the sun. Their skin has a dark leathery look often covered with moles.

THANK YOUR ANCESTORS

When humans first evolved in the equatorial regions of Africa, the intense sunlight necessitated protection in the form of dark skin pigmentation. As humans migrated northward the reduced sunlight caused the evolution of lighter, thinner skin to aid in the development of vitamin D in sun-scarce winters. Increased sunlight causes fairer skin to darken as a form of protection. We call this temporary darkening tanning, and while most people view it in social terms (i.e. it looks healthier and more attractive) it's really a defensive measure against solar radiation.

For most people, true tanning takes a week to 10 days. For light-skinned individuals (i.e. Nordic ancestry) it could take two weeks or more to develop what could be considered a dark tan. For extremely fair red and light blond hair it can take months to get even a moderate tan. Given this, it doesn't make sense to spend three or four hours in the sun a couple of days before a contest. All you'll end up with is a severe sunburn and look like an overripe, probably peeling, tomato. You also run the risk of developing 1st, 2nd, or even 3rd degree burns, which will leave you puffy, swollen, and in all probability bandaged.

The best procedure for developing a natural-looking tan is to start weeks in advance. How early depends on your skin type. If you tan easily then you might start only two or three weeks out. Light to fair-skinned individuals may need a month or more. Also keep in mind that you want to tan the whole body. I have often seen competitors standing onstage sporting a great tan only to ruin the effect when they raise their arms for their first pose, revealing two brilliant white armpits. Every inch of your body except for what lies behind a skimpy suit will be displayed during the contest, so you must tan every part of your body. This won't happen if you lie on your back all the time. You'll need to lie at awkward angles to let the sun's rays reach every part of your skin.

SUNSCREEN

"Scientists have determined that exposure to ultraviolet (UV) is the major cause of melanoma. This is an invading type of cancer that develops deep in the skin, arising from cells that produce the skin-coloring pigment called melanin."

– Jean-Claude Favreaux, *MuscleMag International* contributor

No matter what your ancestry – from almost black African American to lily-white Nordic – I strongly urge you to wear a sunscreen or sun block. A good sunscreen will help filter out some of he sun's harmful rays and will allow you to stay out in the sun longer. Suncreen is rated by a system developed by the Food and Drug Administration (FDA) back in the 1970s, called SPF or sun protection factor. The scale ranks lotions based on their effectiveness in blocking UV rays. Initially the scale ranked from 2 to 22, but every year a manufacturer releases a higher number. As of this publication the FDA is re-evaluating the entire SPF scale.

Don't let the numbers confuse you. They do not correspond to minutes or hours. An SPF of 10 does not mean you can stay out in the sun for 10 hours. It simply means that you can stay out in the sun 10 times longer without burning than if you didn't wear a lotion. For example if you normally start to burn after 10 minutes, then using a sunscreen with an SPF of 10 will allow you to stay out in the sun for about 100 minutes. However, for these num-

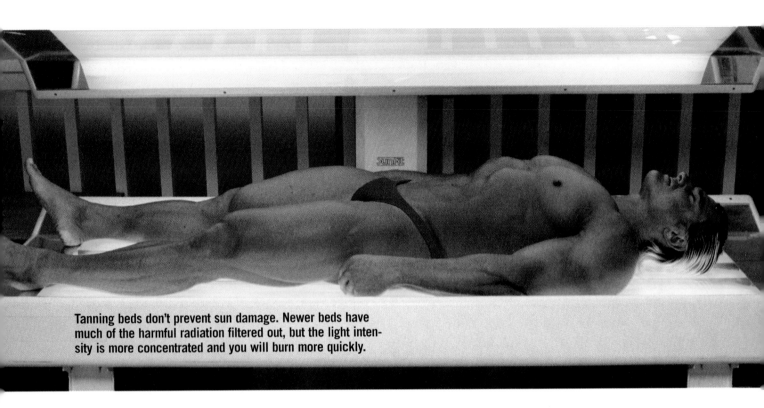

Tanning beds don't prevent sun damage. Newer beds have much of the harmful radiation filtered out, but the light intensity is more concentrated and you will burn more quickly.

bers to be accurate you must make sure to slather on enough of the stuff, make sure to cover the tiniest spot of skin, and you can't swim or sweat it off.

And keep in mind that by the time you start noticing your skin turning red, it's too late. You've already become sunburned and you won't know the full extent until later in the evening.

The following guidelines can be used for suntanning. Just remember that everyone responds differently so know your limits.

Apply the first layer of sunscreen at least a half-hour before going out in the sun. This gives the lotion time to be absorbed by the skin.

To help reduce the risk of skin cancer, use a suncreen a minimum SPF of 6. Some doctors recommend no less than 15.

No matter how dark your skin, never stay in direct sunlight for more than an hour.

Put multiple coats of suncreen on throughout the day, as much of it will be washed away by sweat.

It takes at least two weeks to develop a good tan, so slowly build your exposure time.

Contrary to what most people believe, water-based sunscreens are better if you're exercising, as oil-based products interfere with sweating.

For those who are extremely sensitive to the sun, apply a zinc-oxide product to such areas as the nose, ears, lips, and – dare I say – bald spots!

If you live in an area that receives ozone warnings, pay attention. On days that the levels are high, either avoid the sun or use a 15+ suncreen.

To prevent accidentally looking into the sun and damaging your eyes, wear sunglasses when you lie on your back.

ARTIFICAL TANNING

"Tanning alone won't cut it. You'll definitely need to use some type of tanning or skin-coloring product."
– Scott Abey, master trainer and *MuscleMag International* contributor, commenting on artificial tanning products.

For those of you who live in areas that don't receive much sun, there are alternatives. Tanning beds are everywhere these days. There are two basic types – the

Photo of Tom Platz by Art Zeller

lie down waffle-iron version and the stand-up tanning booth. Both will give you much the same tan as sunlight but have the added benefit of being quicker and available when ever it's convenient for you. Of course with speed and convenience comes a cost (usually 50 cents to $1 per minute), but most tanning salons will let you buy in bulk for a cheaper fee.

One of the myths about tanning beds is that they won't cause cancer. While the newer beds do have much of the harmful radiation filtered out, they still carry a risk. Light is a form of radiation and over time will cause skin damage. (Why do you think your body is releasing pigment to protect you from it?!) You should also remember that the intensity of artificial tanning lights is more concentrated than sunlight and will burn you more quickly. Start out with just a couple of minutes and slowly work up to 15 or 20 minutes.

For those who want to avoid any exposure to light sources, there is another option you can use. For the past couple of decades skin-care companies have made available a number of products that will, for want of a better phrase, paint you to perfection. They're called artificial tanning lotions or dyes, and if used properly will have you looking as dark as if you'd spent three weeks in the Caribbean.

There are two types of artificial tanning products. Some of the products work by interacting with enzymes in the skin. Just spread them on and wait a few hours and before you know it you're chocolate brown – at least that's the theory. How dark you become depends heavily on your individual genetics. Some individuals go orange or yellow instead of brown, and every now and then you'll see some bodybuilder step out onstage looking as if he's in the final stages of liver disease.

The other type of artificial tanning products can be considered body painting. They're nothing more than brown dyes that you apply with a brush (or spray bottle). While they'll probably give you a darker color than the enzyme-reactors, you'll still need to put on three or four coats. Most bodybuilders put on one coat before the Friday night weigh-in, another after the weigh-in,

and then a third early Saturday morning before the pre-judging. Depending on how they look onstage Saturday morning, many will add a fourth coat Saturday afternoon. There's an old saying among competitive bodybuilders that you can never be too dark.

Like hair removers, artificial tanners can cause allergic reactions in some individuals, so you should probably test a small amount of the product on your skin before applying to the whole body. As many of the enzyme-reactors are accelerated by sunlight you should alternate a few days of tanning lotion application with using natural or artificial light. Most artificial tanning lotions don't contain a sunscreen, so even if you look tanned you'll still need to use your normal sunscreen product.

Whatever you use, you should apply all over your body – including your face! Many bodybuilders totally forget to apply the spray or lotion to their face. Also, don't neglect the hard-to-see areas such as under the armpits and inner thighs.

A word of caution about applying lotion to your face. The area around the eyebrows and hairline tends to stain slightly darker than the surrounding skin, so try to minimize your use of the product on these areas. Don't make the mistake of applying the lotion with your bare hands, either. Your hands are covered with skin after all and they'll darken just as much as the rest of your body. In fact your palms will go darker, given that thicker skin seems to soak up the lotion more than thinner skin. Either use a pair of disposable latex gloves or have someone else apply it for you.

The most popular brands these days are Pro Tan, Dream Tan, Quick Tan, and Jan Tana. If your local drug store or health food store doesn't carry them, check out the ads in *MuscleMag International.*

TAN IN A PILL?

Before leaving this topic I need to say a word on tanning pills. Like most things these days, if you look hard enough you'll find manufacturers that offer pills that supposedly

speed up the tanning process. As of this publication none of these products are FDA approved. At the very least you'll be wasting your money, but more important they may be downright dangerous.

While on the topic of tanning pills you should check with your doctor to see if any medication you might be on makes your skin more sensitive to sunlight. For example, many antibiotics will increase the sensitivity of your skin to sunlight, so check with your doctor or pharmacist before hopping in the tanning booth.

OIL RIGHT THEN!

The bright stage lights used at bodybuilding lighten the body and make it less muscular looking. They also tend to "wash out" the physique, making it look flat. The reason for this is that the skin – whether light or dark – is flat and absorbs most of the light. The old-time strongmen found that by putting a light coat of oil on the skin they could offset the detrimental effects of lights and make their bodies look that more impressive. Modern bodybuilders have adopted this technique and use oil to emphasize their bodies' shape and musculature.

TYPES

Like most things associated with competitive bodybuilding there is a right and wrong approach to oiling. For

one thing there are two primary types of oil – vegetable and mineral – and they have major differences when it comes to bodybuilding applications. Mineral oils are poorly absorbed by the skin and tend to sit on top of it rather than sink into it. So while you may be tempted to go out and buy baby oil, the end result is a high-gloss finish that makes it look like your body is wrapped in cellophane. Vegetable oils, on the other hand, absorb quite nicely and then are slowly released as you sweat. Instead of the high luster produced by the mineral oil you're left with a muscle-highlighting sheen. Olive and almond oils seem to be the most popular, but tons of bodybuilders use Pam cooking spray.

YOUR OILER

One of the most important ships in any navy is the fleet oiler, and backstage at a bodybuilding contest is no different. Most federations allow the competitors to bring an assistant backstage, and on contest day this trusty individual will be worth his or her weight in gold (or protein powder). Some contests have general assistants backstage to help, but do they know how to apply oil correctly? More important, are they friends other competitors in your weight class? The last thing you want is someone doing a half-assed job of your oiling. The same caution should be considered before you ask another competitor – especially someone in your weight-class. Bodybuilders are very close knit as a group, but competition is competition, and you really don't want to put too much faith in your opponents on contest day.

Have your assistant practice your oiling one to two weeks before the show. This way you can get the bugs out early. The big thing to watch out for is applying too much oil. Walking onstage looking like an advertisement for Exon or Mobil will not get you any extra points.

Finally, common courtesy dictates that you should try to clean up after yourself. A pool of oil on the floor is an accident waiting to happen. At the very least, wipe up after you apply the oil. Even better, stand on a towel as you're being oiled.

Photo of Frank McGrath by Irvin Gelb

CHAPTER 60

Hair Style

"Receding hairline? Don't despair. Bodybuilders these days are taking a cue from athletes in many other sports. The bald look is in. Even athletes with naturally full heads of hair are taking a razor and buzzing it all off."

– Gerard Thorne, regular contributor to *Reps!* magazine and author of numerous books on bodybuilding, on losing hair.

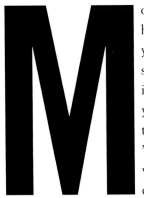

Most bodybuilders take great pride in how their hair looks. Besides the extra touch it will add to your physical appearance, there are practical reasons for keeping your hair neat and tidy. For instance, a large mass of hair will actually make your shoulders look smaller. Just look at many of the great African American bodybuilders from the '70s with their afro hairstyles and compare them with photos from the early '80s. See the difference? While the afro may have been all the rage, it certainly didn't do the bodybuilders of that era any favors. Of course, if you have long flowing locks, much of your musculature won't just look smaller by comparison, it will actually be hidden. If your hair tends to be fuzzy, curly, or you just have too much of it, seriously consider getting it trimmed way back. Your traps and shoulders (and the bodybuilding judges!) will thank you for it.

Another reason to avoid long hair will quickly become apparent at the contest. Given the heat of the lights plus the sweat you'll work up from posing, it won't be long before that long hair of yours will become soaked and strung out. This is fine if you're going for the drowned-rat look, but odds are it won't garner you any extra points from the judges. If you must wear your hair long, tie it up and out of the way.

The other extreme of hairstyles is to get rid of it all completely. Many bodybuilders start balding prematurely because of steroid use, and decide to shave it all off instead of having hair in patches. There are numerous advantages to the cue-ball look. For starters it's one less issue to worry about on contest day (or any other day, for that matter). And as we already saw, short

or no hair creates the illusion of wider shoulders. Finally, a bald head is considered downright sexy by many women. You'll have more women trying to touch you than you ever dreamed possible. Give it a thought.

THE LOOK

If you have any doubt as to whether your hairstyle suits your body, get a second or third opinion. While your buddies can offer suggestions I'll have to admit that the best people to talk to are women. Women tend to be best at judging men's hairstyles (and clothes). Head to a men's hair salon and drop a few dollars. Ask the hairstylist to recommend something that will suit your face and lifestyle. Even better, experiment a few months in advance and see which hairstyle most people think suits you best.

Some hairstyles will detract from your physique. Take the time to figure out which style will best suit your features.

Photo (Left) of Lee Priest by Raymond Cassar
Photo (Right) of Dave Draper

CHAPTER 61

The Brief on Briefs

"My manhood hid, only just, beneath briefs bought at Kmart not two hours before. The Sandman had put me through hell preparing for a contest, but had neglected to tell me not to wear underwear onstage."

– Paul Dillett, IFBB champion, writing about his first contest.

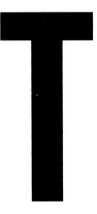

Thirty or 40 years ago all a competitive bodybuilder had to do was haul on a pair of swim trunks and hit the posing dias. But times have changed. Posing trunks can make or break your appearance. There are numerous factors to consider when choosing your posing trunks. Everything from style and color to cost and availability will need to be evaluated before you stroll out onstage. It takes time to make a proper assessment, so don't leave it until the last minute. For example, you may need to order your trunks online and you could wait weeks to receive them.

WITH STYLE

Probably the most important characteristic to consider when buying your posing trunks is their style or "cut." You want to choose a style that complements your physique. The most important point in this regard is the length of your legs and torso. A bodybuilder with a long torso and legs can get away with low-cut trunks. A short bodybuilder will want to create the illusion of leg length and will need to wear high-cut trunks. The higher cut (i.e. the less material) will reveal more of the leg and will help a shorter bodybuilder look more balanced.

Besides leg and torso length, body type will also need to be considered. Those with slender builds can get away with smaller trunks while thicker bodybuilders will probably look better wearing fuller styles.

Another factor is the condition of your legs. If you're in great shape and the separation in your thighs goes right up to your lower abs, you want to emphasize this to the judges. In this case a high cut pair of trunks will show

more of your legs. You might also want to consider your glutes. If you're ripped and have great glutes, you don't want to hide them behind too full a cut. Show them off!

Although the trend nowadays is to go for smaller trunks, most bodybuilding federations won't allow trunks with less than one inch of material between the upper leg and lower waist. Anything less is considered G-string territory and while this may win you points with the ladies, it's frowned upon by the judges. If there's any doubt in your mind, contact your local bodybuilding federation.

COLOR

Besides style, the color of your posing trunks must be carefully considered. Most federations, including the IFBB, state that the trunks must be solid – no patterns, lines, or dots. They also must not be "too shiny." While this one is a bit harder to define, stay away from metallic colors such as silver and gold. The color of your trunks should absorb most of the light and not reflect it back to the audience.

Try to stay with basic colors such as purple, red and blue. Black will work for Caucasian bodybuilders but African American bodybuilders will need to avoid black as it will blend in with their skin and give the illusion that they're wearing nothing at all. Likewise, most bodybuilders of all racial backgrounds should avoid brown, as this is the color their skin will be. You should also avoid light colors including white, as lighter colors tend to make the waist look bigger than it actually is.

WHERE TO BUY

Those who live in larger centers may be able to buy posing trunks in a store that sells regular beach wear. If they don't have actual bodybuilding trunks some of the smaller briefs may work. If you know someone who is handy with a needle and thread, maybe you can get a pair made by hand. Many gyms and health food stores sell bodybuilding clothes or have a member who sells them, so there's another option. Finally, there are a number of reputable companies that sell posing trunks through ads in

MuscleMag International. Perhaps the best known is former Mr. International Andreas Cahling's line at www.andreascahling.com. The average pair of men's posing trunks will set you back $40 to $50.

BRIEF POINTS

If you can afford it, buy two pairs of posing trunks and bring both with you to the show. Posing oils and quick tanning lotions can stain trunks and if you really make a mess of one pair, you have the other pair as a back up. You may even want to change colors between the prejudging and evening show. Finally, competitors have been known to play numerous tricks backstage (with Ken Waller stealing Mike Katz's shirt in *Pumping Iron* being the most famous). There you are backstage getting ready for your weight class when you discover that some trickster has stolen your only pair of posing trunks. Do yourself a favor and keep an extra pair on hand.

Finally, you must consider the issue of size. You may fit comfortably into a size large two or three months out, but odds are you'll drop to a medium or even small by contest time. If possible, check around with other competitive bodybuilders of your frame size to see what size briefs they wore on contest day. If you're in doubt either order two different sizes or order the smaller size. It's better to put up with the discomfort of a pair of briefs that are too small than having to keep pulling up a pair that are too large.

Ultimately the style and color of your trunks is your decision. As with hairstyle, why not try a number of different styles and colors and take a few pictures. If you can't obtain the genuine article, modern computer photo software will easily allow you to change the color of your trunks. Simple wear a pair, take a digital picture and open it up in Photoshop or some other photo editing program. With one or two clicks of the mouse you can change the color of the trunks. The bottom line is that your posing trunks should highlight your physique to its fullest. As the crusader knight said to Indiana Jones in *The Search for the Holy Grail*: "Choose wisely."

CHAPTER 62

Showtime!

"King uses Pam spray as his posing oil of choice. He also has a backstage routine he follows before going onstage."

– MuscleMag International Precontest Report

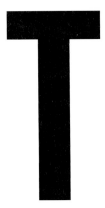

The big moment has arrived. In less than 24 hours you're going to compete in your first bodybuilding contest. The years of training and months of dieting have left you in the best shape of your life. All three heads of your deltoids are clearly visible and you can separate your quads into four slabs of meat at a second's notice. Your pecs have striations and cross striations and your abs remind your grandmother of an old-time washboard. Your posing routine is poetry in motion and you just can't wait to do battle. Well done. You're already a winner in my book.

YOUR CONTEST KIT

Before taking you through the contest from weigh-in to post-contest pig-out, I need you to take a few minutes and put together a gym bag containing some items that will be invaluable on contest day. We'll call it your contest kit. While some of the items may seem common sense, you'd be surprised what gets omitted in the excitement and confusion the day or two before the show.

Two Pairs of Posing Trunks: The first item to pack is really two items. While I discussed this before it deserves a second mention. Your most important piece of clothing on contest day is your posing trunks. Given their importance it only makes sense to have two pairs. Wear one pair to the venue and have another pair in your gym bag.

> It was the greatest feeling in my life and I hope it was not the last win of my career. To work so hard and finally get that reward is beyond words. Now I know why Ronnie Coleman cries every time he wins the Olympia."
>
> – Markus Ruhl, IFBB pro, on his Toronto Pro International win.

Photo by Jason Breeze

Posing Oil: Include at least one bottle of oil. If you're the generous type and want to make friends, bring an extra bottle. Who knows maybe some fitness or figure contestant will have forgot hers!

Tanning Lotion: Even though you'll have on at least three coats of tanning lotion, the sweat and clothes will rub some of it off. Bring along a bottle of the instant tan to touch up any light areas that appear on your body.

Towels: The odds of towels being supplied backstage are slim, so bring along a few. It makes sense to use cheap towels, as quick-tan stains are extremely difficult to remove. Bring at least one large towel to stand on and one or two smaller towels for wiping off sweat.

Warmup Clothes: You may be under the hot lights onstage, but you'll be standing around throughout the women's fitness and figure and throughout all the other weight classes. Most backstage areas are cold, so make sure to bring along some warmup clothes. A tracksuit is best. Besides keeping you warm, the extra clothes give the added psychological benefit of keeping your physique hidden from the other competitors until the last minute (more on psychological warfare later).

Portable Exercise Equipment: Some contest venues may have a few light dumbells backstage, but most won't. Therefore it's up to the contestants themselves to bring something along. Probably the most convenient is a chest-expander spring set (a misleading name, since the springs can be used to train just about every muscle but the chest!). These sets are small, light, and easy to stuff into a gym bag.

A Small Toiletry Kit Containing:

- Soap
- Shampoo
- Deodorant
- Brush or comb
- Small mirror
- Small hair dryer
- Toothbrush and toothpaste

Other items to consider are rubbing alcohol to remove oil, bottled water, slippers or sandals, and a lock, in case lockers are provided.

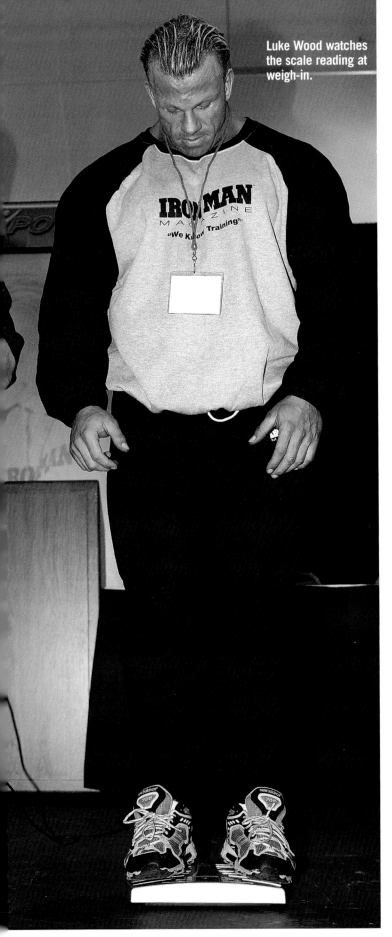

Luke Wood watches the scale reading at weigh-in.

WEIGH-IN

The weigh-in for most bodybuilding federations is Friday night. If you're not familiar with the area, you may want to get directions beforehand and give yourself extra time to find your way there. It's far better to be too early than too late. At the weigh-in a representative from the federation will go through the rules and procedures for the show and then give competitors an opportunity to ask questions. Don't be shy. If there's something you're not sure of, ask. Once it seems everyone understands how the contest will proceed, you'll be weighed. If you're over your weight class limit by a couple of pounds most federations will give you an hour to lose it. Some bodybuilders hit the sauna. Others who had an idea that they'd be over will rely on diuretics to shed the weight in the form of water. If you're still over at the second weigh-in you'll just have to be content to go in at the bottom of the next weight class. If you're ripped then you still have a fighting chance, but odds are you'll be giving up 10 to 15 pounds against guys just as hard as you are. Such are the perils of mistiming your dieting or water loss.

After the weigh-in I strongly suggest that you head back to wherever you're staying and turn in for the night. You have a big day ahead of you tomorrow and you'll need all the rest you can get. Save the late night partying for Saturday night after the show. Oh, and don't forget to set the alarm clock.

THE PREJUDGING

As most federations start the prejudging around 10, you'll be required to be there by 9. This means that you should get up around 7 to give yourself time to prepare. As you'll probably be wearing instant tan, I suggest giving the shower a pass. In fact you probably won't shower from when you put on your first coat on Thursday or Friday night, to after the evening show Saturday night. By all means eat some breakfast, but keep it light. You'll want full control over your abs in a couple of hours and a stomach full of food is not that easy to flex. A piece of fruit and a glass of juice or coffee will probably suffice.

Photo of Luke Wood by Irvin Gelb

Before you leave go through your checklist to see that you have everything you need. At times like this it wouldn't hurt to have a second person double check for you.

If you happen to be in one of the heavier weight classes you can watch some of the women's events and lighter men's classes from the audience. This probably won't be an option at the evening show as they tend to be sold out. Likewise, if you're in an earlier show you can probably watch the heavier divisions from the audience as well.

The prejudging will be conducted by weight class, with the men's and women's light or bantamweights coming on first and then progressing upwards. A women's figure contest will usually be divided into tall and short classes and fit in somewhere between the light and middleweight bodybuilding classes. Procedures vary from federation to federation, so don't be surprised if the order of judging is different. To help the competitors out, most promoters will have someone organizing the classes and making sure everyone receives enough warning to go backstage and get ready.

Also popular nowadays are guest posers. At the very least you will have a top national competitor as guest poser, but there's a good chance it will be a top pro such as Jay Cutler, Ronnie Coleman or Gustavo Badell. As these guys will easily be the largest bodybuilders in the venue, most promoters put them on toward the end of the show. It's bad enough that the light heavyweights or heavyweights have to follow one of these behemoths but it would look ridiculous to have 290 pounds of Jay Cutler come and then have the bantamweights stroll on stage!

PUMPING UP

Once you head backstage, immediately strip down to your posing trunks and start getting ready. The first order of business is to pump up. For those new to the sport, pumping up is the practice of performing a few high-rep sets of different exercises to force blood into the muscles. While a few bodybuilders find that flexing alone is sufficient, most bodybuilders like to use some light weights to get a good pump going before hitting the stage.

Victor Martinez pumps up his biceps before hitting the stage.

Photo of Victor Martinez by Irvin Gelb

The primary advantage to pumping up is that it enlarges the muscles to a certain degree. Now I'm not talking inches here, but it's no problem increasing your arm from 17 ½ to 18 inches. Likewise a good lat pump will make you feel ready to take on Ronnie Coleman.

As you might expect, pumping up has a few disadvantages as well. A muscle fully engorged with blood is sometimes harder to control than an unpumped muscle. Also, fully pumped muscles may lose some sharpness and definition because of the extra blood. You also have to consider the process of pumping up and its impact on your energy level. You'll need all the energy you can manage when posing onstage. It would be pretty big mistake to perform a full workout backstage before you go on.

With regards to which muscles to pump up, the consensus is to pump up your weakest muscles. Years ago the biceps and chest received the most pumping but in most bodybuilders these muscles are overdeveloped to begin with. It makes more sense to try and enlarge your weaker areas to help balance out your physique.

gym using a cable machine. To hit the rear shoulders, grab a handle in each hand, bend over slightly at the waist and pull outwards until your arms are locked out straight. Great rear deltoids are rarely seen at beginner or intermediate-level contests. If you've got them, you want to get a good pump in there to show the judges.

The Lats: The V-taper is perhaps the bodybuilder's trademark. Even in clothes the classic inverted triangle should be evident. To really give the lats a good pump you can do one-arm dumbell rows or barbell rows if a light barbell is available. While there probably won't be a chin-up bar, an exposed overhead pipe may work. Just make sure it will support your weight before grabbing hold. The last thing you want is to flood out the backstage area! The most common lat-pumping exercise is the towel pull. As the name suggests, you have your partner hold one end of a towel while you pull it toward you.

Chest and Triceps: Dumbell presses are great for these muscles if they're available. If not, hit the floor and bang out 15 or 20 push-ups. To add variety to the exercise try doing push-ups with your feet or hands elevated. If there are a couple of chairs available (or two benches) you can do dips.

Thighs: As most thigh exercises require a considerable amount of weight, there's not much you can do backstage. One option is sissy squats. Simply grab a stationary upright, lean slightly backwards, and squat down. You can also do dumbell squats. Don't go overboard training the legs. As I said earlier, you'll need most of your energy for the contest.

Biceps: Your biceps will probably get a good pump from working your lat muscles. They'll also be heavily stimulated from all the arm shots you're no doubt hitting every couple of minutes. If you want to get extra blood in there you can use your spring set again. Stand on one handle with your foot, as before, and perform one-arm cable curls.

Three muscles you don't want to pump up are the calves, forearms and abdominals. The calves and forearms won't pump up that much, and the calves are notorious for cramping, especially onstage when posing. Given your dehydrated state the last thing you want to do is give the calves another reason to cramp up. As for the abdominals, this is not a muscle group you want enlarged. Besides, pumping up the abs makes it much more difficult to flex and control them.

The following muscles are my recommendations for pumping up before hitting the stage. Try to hit as many poses as possible between sets. This helps speed the influx of blood to the muscles as well as loosen you up for the show.

The Shoulders: One of the statements you'll never hear at a bodybuilding contest is: "His shoulders are too wide." If light dumbells are supplied backstage, do a few sets of front, side and bent-over raises. Getting a good pump in the shoulders will not only make your shoulders appear larger, it will also bring out the separation between the three deltoid heads. If there are no dumbells around, break out your chest expander set and anchor one handle to the floor by standing on it. From here you can do one-arm front and side raises just the same as if in the

Photo of Mustafa Mohammad by Irvin Gelb

POST PUMP-UP

Once you're fully pumped up, have your assistant apply your oil. Make sure it's applied evenly over your entire body. Don't put it on too thick, as you'll be making a mess backstage as well as looking too shiny and reflective. You'll probably be given a five-minute warning, so use it wisely. Make a few quick checks in the mirror. Is your entire body oiled? Are there any glaring light patches on your body? Is your hair neat and tidy? Is your competitor number pinned to your trunks? This is a must, as the judges won't call you by name. From now on you're competitor number such and such and you must have your number memorized. You'll look stupid just standing there as the head judge calls out your number three or four times.

One of the first things you'll notice when you walk out onstage is how bright the lights are. It will take a few minutes before your eyes become fully accustomed to the brightness. Try to avoid staring at the lights. This is not only dangerous for your eyes, but could make you dizzy. If there's one advantage to such brilliance it's that you'll only be able to see the first few rows. It will be far less stressful to see only a couple of dozen people in the audience as opposed to many hundreds or thousands.

Once you're standing in line onstage it's only a matter of following the instructions of the head judge. You'll first go through the mandatory poses and then the various comparisons will be made. If you find yourself involved in a number of comparisons you can be reasonably confident that you're in the top three to five. Who knows, you might even be battling for the top spot!

POST-PREJUDGING

Once the prejudging has ended you'll want to spend the rest of the day in an appropriate fashion. The first order of priority is replacing your lost fluids. That bottle of water I told you to pack earlier will now be worth its weight in gold. Don't make the mistake of gulping down the whole bottle all at once. This could give you cramps.

Sip it slowly over the next hour or so. The only exception is if you are severely dehydrated from trying to make a weight class using the sauna or other water-loss techniques. In this case try consuming the bottle in about 15 to 20 minutes.

Before putting on your clothes either take a quick shower if facilities are available or wipe the excess sweat and oil off your body with an old towel. You'll want to use an old towel because oil and instant tan stains are virtually impossible to remove. The same goes for your clothes. It makes sense to wear the oldest in your closet. If you don't have anything that you consider disposable, head to a thrift store and you can no doubt pick up an old pair of sweats for a few bucks.

After you get dressed check with someone to confirm when you have to return for the evening show. As with the prejudging it will probably be an hour before curtain time but check to make sure. Also keep in mind that there will be a much bigger crowd at the evening show and you might have difficulty finding a parking spot.

The next four to six hours are yours to do with as you please. Most competitive bodybuilders go for a quick meal to recharge their energy levels. Nothing major, just a light snack containing a few carbs, maybe a baked potato or some steamed rice. The goal is to alleviate your hunger pangs without giving you a bloated-looking stomach. If there is a guest poser he may give a seminar during the afternoon. By all means attend if you feel up to it. For the sake of $10 to $20 you can listen as one of the sport's top superstars reveals his training, nutritional and competitive strategies.

If you're really dragged out I suggest going back to your home or hotel room and taking a nap. As you'll be dragged out from both the prejudging and lack of sleep the night before, I strongly urge you to set the alarm clock or have a trusted friend call you after an hour or two. Don't sleep any longer than this or your body could slip into deep sleep and when you wake up you'll need a couple of hours to fully wake up. The goal is to sleep long enough to recharge your batteries without shutting your body down for the day.

As soon as you wake up, lie back for a few minutes and visualize the morning's proceedings. How did your posing routine go? Was the audience's reaction favorable or subdued? Who do you think are your closest competitors? From watching them backstage and onstage you probably know where you stack up bodypart by bodypart. Keep this in mind if you make it to the posedown.

Give yourself at least two hours to prepare for the evening show. Before you leave you can use the same checklist you used in the morning. Once you and your assistant have determined that you're ready, leave for the contest venue.

THE EVENING SHOW

"This is your night. Look at those abs! Enjoy the attention. Share the camaraderie of your fellow competitors. You all have a common bond. Revel in fact that this is not something that just anyone can do."
– Nelson Montana, regular *MuscleMag International* contributor

There's no need to go into detail on the evening show. With the exception of a few minor additions such as one or two appearances by the guest poser and perhaps some sort of demonstration by a local martial arts or gymnastics club, it's identical to the prejudging. The first three rounds will be the same, and even though most of the placings will have been determined in the morning, you may have to go through comparison call outs again. Once the top three to five competitors in each class have been determined, they'll be given a minute to "flex off" against one another in the posedown.

Perhaps the most important aspect to the whole evening show is your reaction to your placing. Obviously if you win all I have to say is congratulations and well done. Hold up your winner's trophy with style and grace, pose for a few photos for the local press and then exit the stage. If you place second or third or don't even make the top three, accept the results wholeheartedly. Even if you and a majority of the audience felt that you were robbed, don't make a scene. Don't stand there with a peculiar look on your face, give the judges the finger, or throw your trophy backstage. Everyone loves a great sportsman and hates a sore loser. The best example I can use to illustrate this was Tom Platz's reaction to placing third at the 1981 Mr. Olympia. By all accounts Tom was at his all-time best that day. Conversely the winner, Franco Columbu, was woefully deficient in the leg department. Lesser bodybuilders would have stormed off the stage cursing and swearing. But not Tom. True to the gentleman he was, Tom accepted the results with professionalism and congratulated the winner. It was this stellar display of sportsmanship that garnered Tom thousands of new fans and no doubt contributed greatly to his future success in business.

The lesson to be learned here is that the judges are only human and occasionally they make mistakes. One of the best guides for this is the audience's response to the placings. The occasional boo is to be expected, but if the whole audience erupts in one negative chorus, then chances are the judges missed one. I'll be the first to admit that in a few cases politics may determine the placings – but very rarely and certainly not as often as is rumored. If you are the victim of such blatant injustice then you have my sympathy. It's not fair to you (or any other wrongly placed competitor) to go through the rigors of pre-contest training and dieting only to lose because someone else is a friend of the head judge. As I said, the odds of this happening are very slim but if it happens it happens. Jumping up and down and cursing a blue streak at the judges won't change things. In fact it may ruin your chances the next time you compete, since at the local and state levels the judging panels usually consist of the same individuals. They have long memories for competitors who insult their ancestry or give them the finger. My advice is to take a page from Tom Platz's book and accept the results with class. Afterward in private you can vent to your friends and channel that excess negative energy towards your training. Make it so next year you're in such outstanding shape that the judges have no choice but to award you first place.

Photos of Ronnie Coleman and Jay Cutler by Ralph DeHaan

CHAPTER 63

Psychological Warfare

"Winning comes from the mind far more than it comes from the body, and if you find you are not reaching your goals, then look to your mind for the answer."

– Aidan Turrell, sports psychologist

One of the highlights of the sporting world during the 1970s was listening to the great Muhammad Ali before an upcoming fight. With a mastery of the English language that was a combination of Shakespeare and rap, Ali would verbally spar with opponents and convince them of his superiority before he even stepped into the ring. Whether it had any influence on guys like Joe Frazier or Ken Norton, who knows? But no doubt many a lesser opponent had their confidence shaken by Ali's colorful rhetoric.

While psychological warfare has probably existed as long as competition itself, Ali was probably the first superstar athlete to refine it to an art form. Also during the 1970s, bodybuilding had its own Ali – the one and only Arnold Schwarzenegger. Arnold is the first to admit that a couple of his contests were won as much with his brain as with his body. The most frequent victim of these psychological tactics was the Cuban-born Sergio Oliva.

Even by today's Synthol-steroid-growth hormone-induced standards, Sergio Oliva was an awesome sight. From that 28-inch waist to those cannonball-sized deltoids to those larger-than-his-head arms, Oliva took a backseat to no one when it came to pure muscle mass. After his second-place finish to Sergio at the 1969 Mr. Olympia, Arnold realized that he would need more than a great physique to beat Oliva. As the story goes, Arnold suggested to Oliva at the 1970 Mr. World contest that he would need a few extra pounds at the upcoming Mr. Olympia contest. Oliva, who was always a bit insecure in his younger days, took the advice to heart. He came in heavier but softer at the Olympia and lost to a rather confident Arnold.

Arnold was a master of psychological tactics during his bodybuilding career.

Two years later Oliva was yet again the victim of Arnold's "advice." From both the photos and witness reports, Oliva was in the best shape of his life. Realizing that he was "up against it" Arnold suggested to the judges that they hold the prejudging in another room. What he failed to point out was that the room had brown walls. While his lighter skin stood out, the Cuban-born Oliva blended right in. Whether a different prejudging setting would have made any difference is debated to this day. The bottom line is that Arnold wasn't prepared to let his physique alone do battle. When the need arose he would use every psychological trick in the book.

Another victim of Arnold's was Lou Ferrigno in 1975. With the groundbreaking film *Pumping Iron* being shot that year, Arnold invited the entire Ferrigno family to breakfast on the morning of the contest. As the 19-year-old Ferrigno hung on every word, Arnold casually mentioned how it was a pity that Ferrigno didn't have another two weeks of preparation to perhaps win the title. But then Arnold added that if Ferrigno had another two weeks so would he, and the outcome would be just the same – another win for Arnold! Poor Lou took the comments seriously and he was never sure of himself afterward.

Of course Arnold may have won all those contests regardless of his psychological games. With the possible exception of Oliva in 1972, no one had a physique to rival Arnold during the '70s.

With the amount of prize money being offered at today's contests, pro competitors rarely play tricks on one another backstage like Ken Waller did stealing Mike Katz's shirt in *Pumping Iron*. As for verbal sparring, most of it takes place in the magazines with such stars as Shawn Ray, Paul Dillet and King Kamali. All of these pros developed reputations for saying what's on their minds – particularly as it relates to other bodybuilders.

If you decide to engage in a little psychological warfare, keep it light-hearted and simple. Such comments as: "Maybe you should have started dieting two weeks earlier," or "I thought your arms were bigger than that," probably won't get you into trouble. Just don't make the

mistake of making your comments seem serious and personal. With the carb-depleted states some bodybuilders are in these days, there could be fireworks!

If you happen to be on the receiving end of another competitor's barbs or negative comments, simply let it go in one ear and out the other. You know the old saying about sticks and stones? Well it's not just for schoolyards. If you've dieted properly and prepared a great posing routine, you have nothing to worry about. Bodybuilders who make a habit of insulting and putting down other competitors are usually covering up their own insecurities.

One trick you can try is to keep your opponents guessing as to the shape you're in. About a month out from the show start wearing a full-length tracksuit when you work out. This will hide your physique from your opponents. The only time they'll get to take a peak is when you're oiling up just before you go onstage. The advantage of doing this is that it never allows your them time to plan a strategy to challenge you, whereas you'll have been watching them all along.

Photo of Arnold Schwarzenegger

BOOK VIII

EARNING A LIVING THROUGH BODYBUILDING

CHAPTER 64

Making a Living Through Bodybuilding

"A good trainer is worth his weight in gold. Don't hire some skinny kid still wet behind the ears, but rather someone who looks the part because he or she actually lives the lifestyle."

– Editors of *MuscleMag International*, answering a reader's inquiry about how to start working out.

Chapter sixty-four will deal with making a living as a professional bodybuilder. But even if your genetics aren't up to par, or if you simply don't want to become the next Mr. Olympia, you can still make a living through your love of training. Here are some ideas.

PERSONAL TRAINING

Five to 10 years ago the personal-training industry held great promise for bodybuilders, but things have changed, and not for the better I'm afraid. Most gyms 10 years ago allowed independent personal trainers to access their facilities, provided that both trainer and client had memberships or paid a day fee. But a combination of legal liability and greed has changed all that. Because of a few lawsuits, gyms started banning independent trainers from their premises. Even with proper certification and with both parties having insurance, a number of legal cases ended up costing gyms and fitness centers big bucks.

Then the gyms started thinking profit. With the average personal trainer making $50 to $100 per hour, it's not surprising that gym owners wanted in on the action. So many gyms (not all, but most) banned independent trainers and hired their own. The problem with this is that gyms keep most of the money and pay their trainers only $20 to $30 per hour. Not a bad hourly wage, but a far cry from what they were making before. Besides, as a personal trainer you might work one hour and then wait an hour for your next appointment. It's not like you are working an eight-hour shift each day. So it's not surprising that many of the best trainers got out of the personal-training business. Trainers employed by gyms these days tend to be young and inexperienced. Of course the clients can be sure the trainer is certified, and some of these young trainers know their stuff and have the youthful enthusiasm to go along with it. But you just can't beat experience when it comes to designing a safe and effective exercise program and helping clients reach their goals.

If you're still interested in becoming a personal trainer I strongly recommend you get certified. It's true that you don't have to, as long as someone is willing to pay you money for your services. But be aware that virtually no gym will look at you if you're not certified – if they hired an uncertified trainer and a client got injured, their insurance would not cover damages. Likewise, if you're going to be training clients on your own you'll need to obtain insurance, and guess what? No insurance company will even consider you if you're not certified.

At last count there were nearly 500 certifying agencies in the United States and Canada. As expected, some are considered more worthwhile than others. Their reputation is usually based on the thoroughness of the course itself. Some courses invlove nothing more than sending in $50 and answering a short quiz. Others are almost as in depth as a college course. While on the pricier side, these will establish you as an expert in the personal-training field.

Some of the more credible agencies that grant personal-training certification are:

American Council on Exercise - ACE

American College of Sports Medicine - ACSM

Cooper Institute - CI

National Academy of Sports Medicine - NASM

National Strength & Conditioning Association - NSCA

National Council on Strength and Fitness - NCSF

National Federation of Professional Trainers

Can-Fit-Pro

YOUR WAY OR THEIR WAY?

"When you work for someone else, obviously they are going to take a percentage. This cut is usually 40 percent or more. It's not that they're greedy, but that's the only way the company could be profitable. Their expenses of running a business are higher than yours and the money has to come from somewhere."
– John Platero, *MuscleMag International* contributor, commenting on one of the primary disadvantages of working as a personal trainer for someone else.

> Working out with a trainer makes bodybuilding easier. On my own I would simply wander around aimlessly, lifting each piece of equipment only once or twice. Then comes the masochistic part. The trainer fulfills the role of timer, cheerleader and slave driver. Reminding me of some of my old college professors, he is not happy until he sees me cry out in pain and fail."
>
> – Dr. Glen Joshpe, *MuscleMag International* contributor, after a session with his personal trainer; a Christmas gift from his family.

Once you become certified your next step is deciding whether you want to go it alone or work for a gym. Going it alone gives you freedom, a much higher salary if you can get the clients and the ability to set your own hours of work. The downside is that your income will never be guaranteed and will change from week to week. You may also have a hard time finding clients, as most people look for a trainer at their gym. You'll also need to find a training facility that will allow access to you and your clients. In a large city this may be possible, but in small cities and towns you're out of luck if the local gym has their own staff and bans independent trainers, as is usually the case. And don't forget that if you're working for yourself you'll need to cover all your expenses including traveling, training, re-certification, supplies and insurance.

If you're the type of person who prefers stability, working for a gym is probably your best option. Not only will your income be more consistent and regular, you'll have sales personnel working with you to book clients. The gym will cover all expenses, and, while you won't get rich making $20 to $30 per hour, it's a respectable living that allows you to do what you love.

Before moving on I should mention that personal training is one of the most rewarding careers you'll ever become involved in. You'll be helping people improve both their physical and mental health, and this will have a profound change in their overall self-confidence. In short, you'll literally be saving lives. Not many people can honestly say the same about their jobs.

MAIL-ORDER AND INTERNET TRAINING COURSES

When Arnold Schwarzenegger first came to America, one of the first business ventures he got involved in was mail-order training courses. There was nothing fancy about the courses, just good basic training and nutrition information, laid out in small training booklets. With overhead cost kept to a minimum, the courses made Arnold a tidy sum of money. In fact, *MuscleMag International* was started from money made from mail-order bodybuilding courses that *MMI*'s editor-in-chief and I put out together. That was how we made our living back then, and the magazine was a natural transition.

Most of the top bodybuilders these days offer individualized training programs online, but mail-order courses have pretty much gone the way of the do-do.

BODYBUILDING CAMPS AND CONFERENCES

For some bodybuilders and fitness enthusiasts, reading books and magazine articles is not enough. They want a more personalized, hands-on approach. To meet this demand a number of ingenious promoters have established training centers where individuals can go and do nothing but think, talk and practice bodybuilding and fitness. The fees can range from a few hundred to a few thousand dollars, depending on the length of stay and list of presenters.

Perhaps the greatest benefit of training camps is the degree of individual attention. At some point every bodybuilder tries to follow other people's training programs and then wonders why he isn't seeing results. An expert can observe your training and make adjustments depending on your individual body mechanics. He can look at your workouts and your body and see where you might want to make some changes. This kind of thoroughness is not possible through the mail or Internet, or even private phone consultations.

These days the trend is for a promoter to organize the camp and book various experts to hold workshops and perform one-on-one training. In this regard bodybuilding camps have evolved into something more like conferences.

Bodybuilding camps are not for everyone. You have to pay travel costs and registration fees, and you may have to take time off school or work. Still, if you have the time and money, spending some time in Florida or California working out with some of your bodybuilding heroes is an experience of a lifetime. So why is this section in the "making money" chapter instead of the "spending money" chapter? Because you, my friend, could present one of these camps. If you do it right, you will not only make money, but you'll get to attend the camp and hang out with your favorite bodybuilders. There is risk with this type of venture, because you'll have to pay your experts no matter how many attend. Your best bet is to go to some of these yourself, see how they do it, see how they market it, and then go for it.

BEING AN EXPERT

You can also make money being one of the hired experts. If you decide you want to be a presenter you'll need to send a press package to the promoter. Besides a list of your accomplishments – both academic and previous presentations – you should send along a DVD showing you presenting a seminar. This doesn't have to be a two-hour documentary. Something as simple as 10 minutes from a previous presentation is more than adequate to give the promoter an idea of your presenting style and appearance.

The key to being a popular presenter is a combination of knowledge and delivery. Obviously being a top bodybuilding competitor is an asset, but many of the top presenters in the world have never even won an amateur event much less a pro contest. Once you establish a reputation as someone who knows his stuff and has an engaging delivery style, your problem won't be trying to land conference dates, but rather trying to fit in all the requests.

WRITING

> "When Arnold works with you on a project he is very hands-on. He isn't one to hire a ghost-writer and let it go at that. He gets involved and is very demanding, so it was a lot of work."
>
> – Bill Dobbins, one of bodybuilding's most famous writers, promoters and photographers.

Bodybuilding magazines have always featured training tips from the stars, but the truth is that most articles were written by the magazines' staff. Even articles attributed to certain pros were in all likelihood ghost written. That all changed in the late '70s and early '80s as many pro bodybuilders put down the barbell in favor of the pen. In fact, Arnold himself wrote for *MuscleMag International* for a couple of years in the '70s. A couple of former Mr. Universe winners, Rick Wayne and Mike Mentzer, became as famous for their articles and books as for their competitive accomplishments. Mike influenced millions with his articles on overtraining and high-intensity training, and Rick's articles, particularly those on bodybuilding history and behind-the-scenes politics, are considered classics.

Many of the top bodybuilding stars over the past 50 years have released training and autobiography books (again either penned by themselves or ghost written). Arnold's *Education of a Bodybuilder* and *Encyclopedia of Modern Bodybuilding* have sold millions. Likewise Franco Columbu's *Coming on Strong* is a best seller. Bill Pearl's *Keys to the Inner Universe* is one of the all-time classics.

Besides bodybuilders, such notables as the late Bill Reynolds, Joe Weider, Ellington Darden, George Snyder and Bill Dobbins have authored or co-authored hundreds of books between them. I have also written over 50 books on bodybuilding, some of them New York Times bestsellers.

SO YOU WANT TO BE A WRITER

Unless you happen to be Mr. Olympia or an established nonfiction writer, you don't just write a book on bodybuilding (or any other topic for that matter) and get it

Arnold stands beside me showing the camera an early issue of *MuscleMag International*.

published. Just like a struggling actor or musician, you have to break into the business.

Most aspiring writers start by writing training and nutrition articles and submitting them to bodybuilding and fitness magazines. As hundreds of other writers will be doing the same, you have to make your article jump out at the editor. They get hundreds of articles called: "How to Build Bigger Arms," but what about "Biceps Building After an Injury" or "The Top-Five Biceps Exercises of All Time?" Submit a few articles to local publications and Web sites, too. All magazines are more likely to publish your work if you've been published elsewhere, and the more times the better. Most newspapers have a health and fitness column these days, and they often accept articles from free-lance writers. You may have to deviate from your first love of hardcore bodybuilding and make it more about fitness. Don't go looking for money at this stage, either. Your number-one goal is to get published and build a resumé for yourself. Once you have a number of articles to your name, the magazine publishers may even come looking for you. You can also approach bodybuilders and other fitness professionals about ghost writing for them.

MAGAZINE PUBLISHING

It's been well over 30 years since I took a little bit of money made from a mail-order business and sat with my good friend Johnny Fitness at the kitchen table creating the first issue of *MuscleMag International*. Since those first few lean years *MuscleMag* has jumped to and remained at or near the top of the bodybuilding magazines.

Bodybuilding magazines, or muscle mags as they are affectionately called, are the unofficial journals of the bodybuilding world. Most are published on a monthly basis and feature a mix of training, nutrition, supplement and competition articles.

Besides educating millions of aspiring Mr. Olympia wannabes, the monthly magazines play a huge role in promoting the top bodybuilding stars. Pro and top amateur bodybuilders know that one training article in *MuscleMag International* or *Flex* can catapult them to the very top of the bodybuilding world and help their careers enormously.

Besides the star profiles and training articles, bodybuilding magazines also contain advertisements for bodybuilding merchandise. While clothing and equipment accounts for some of the advertising, it's the full-page glossy ads for food supplements that dominate the pages. As annoying as these ads may be to readers, they are vital to publishers as most of the magazine's operating revenue is derived from the supplement manufacturers.

ACTING

Although Arnold Schwarzenegger has unquestionably done the most to sell bodybuilding to the masses, it was Steve Reeves who first demonstrated the drawing potential of the bodybuilding physique to Hollywood. In fact, for a couple of years during the 1950s, Steve Reeves was the number-one box-office draw in the world. Until Reeves emerged on the scene, the Olympic pool was where Hollywood producers turned for great-looking physiques (with Johnny Weissmuller and Buster Crabbe being two of the most famous). But with his manly good

> " Consider that bodybuilders in Venice are a dime a dozen. If you have dreams of the silver screen and modeling, get a reality check. Don't get me wrong. You can do it. Dreams do come true. However you need to be strong-willed and dedicated. A little dash of genetics helps."
>
> – Anita Ramsey, *MuscleMag International* contributor, giving her views on leaping from competitive bodybuilding to stardom.

looks and Greek God-like physique, Reeves was the perfect choice to play Hercules during the 1950s.

During the 1960s such bodybuilders as Reg Park, Dave Draper and Larry Scott appeared in a number of movies – Park in a series of Hercules movies and Draper and Scott in a number of beach movies with Frankie Avalon and Annette Funicello.

Although *Pumping Iron* is considered Arnold's first starring role, he actually appeared as Hercules in the rather forgettable 1970 movie *Hercules in New York*. Because of his thick accent his voice was dubbed, and his last name changed to Strong. Not exactly the most promising start for the future governor of California.

Starting with *Conan the Barbarian* in 1982 and *Terminator* in 1984, Arnold quickly vaulted to the head of Hollywood's A-list of action heroes, and by the early 1990s had established himself as the biggest box-office draw in the world. Not bad for the 19-year-old who stepped off the plane in 1968 with little formal education and who spoke no English.

Besides Arnold, *Pumping Iron* helped launch the career of another bodybuilder turned actor – Lou Ferrigno. As Lou was getting ready for the 1977 Mr. Olympia, TV producers were casting for a big bodybuilder to play the title role in "The Incredible Hulk.". At 6'5" and 275 pounds, Lou was the biggest bodybuilder around, and during the late 1970s and early 1980s, he played the avenging green character on TV and in a couple of TV movies. He later appeared in a number of movies, including *Hercules* and *Cage*. Lou never enjoyed the phenomenal success of Arnold, but he nevertheless helped lay the groundwork for other bodybuilders to become successful actors.

In 1982 Arnold played the action hero in *Conan the Barbarian*.

YOUR FIRST BIG BREAK

"I was in the 'Beverly Hillbillies' for an episode where Granny was trying to cure my illness. I was sick with barbell disease or something."
– Dave "The Blond Bomber" Draper, bodybuilding legend, reminiscing about his acting days in the 1960s.

As most action movies require a heavy or two, there are a number of small acting parts for bodybuilders available in the movies. Unfortunately, you'll almost certainly need to be based in Los Angeles to get a chance to audition for the roles. Before you head to the airport with visions of stardom in your eyes, please heed these words of advice: Every week sees hundreds of acting hopefuls depart planes at LAX hoping to be the next Arnold. It's safe to say that during a typical year tens of thousands of aspiring actors

and actresses head to Hollywood to break into show business. Most end up with nothing more than a very expensive trip, and return home broke. In your hometown you may be the big fish, but in L.A. you're just another minnow in a sea of hungry sharks. And what a feeding frenzy it is. For every small movie role there are hundreds if not thousands of actors seeking the role. And you can be sure that most of them have a physique at least as good as yours.

Virtually every bodybuilder who made it in the movies had achieved a high level of bodybuilding success. From Steve Reeves and Reg Park to Arnold and Lou Ferrigno, all had won the Mr. America or Mr. Universe. In fact it was their bodybuilding accomplishments that first brought them to the attention of TV and movie producers. I don't mean to discourage you, but it's virtually impossible for an unknown to walk off a plane and right onto a movie or TV set.

If you still have your sights set on the silver screen my

Photo of Arnold Schwarzenegger

first suggestion is to stay where you are and try to break into the business in your own region. Unless you live in a small town, most cities have drama clubs and theater groups. Not only will there be far less competition, but you'll get a taste for the acting profession. It may seem glamorous to walk the red carpet at the Academy Awards, but what you don't see under all the flashbulbs and glitz are the 18-hour days in all forms of weather most foul, staying in character for hour upon hour as you shoot the same scene again and again, only to find out that you have to come back and try again tomorrow. If you can't handle a few days of rehearsal for a local play, how do you think you'll manage on a movie set for six months? Many people start out fantasizing about being a TV or movie star, but when they actually get involved in the industry they realize it's not at all what they really had in mind. Besides, even experience on a local level will be worth something when you're looking for your first acting gigs.

OWNING A GYM

Many of the most popular body-building gyms were started by former bodybuilders. Two of the most famous, Gold's and World Gym, were founded by Joe Gold. While he never won the Mr. Universe, Joe was one of the original Muscle Beach gang in the 1940s and 1950s, and at one time was part of Mae West's entourage.

If you're like most serious body-builders, the idea of owning and operating your own gym will probably cross your mind. It could be that the one or two gyms in your town are crowded and you see potential for another. Or maybe you feel there is a whole untapped market of bodybuilders that are not being catered to by existing gyms. Whatever the reason, the business bug has bitten you and you want to own your own establishment. In the following section I'll

> **"Bodybuilders could never repay what they owe Joe Gold. Without his ingenuity, weight training would remain a little-known pastime instead of the widespread passion it is today. Joe's gyms have helped lift bodybuilding from obscurity to worldwide acceptance."**
>
> – Loren Franck, *MuscleMag International* contributor

look at the two primary types of gyms and what's involved in owning and operating one.

Franchise and Private Gyms

The largest and most familiar gyms in bodybuilding are franchise gyms. Franchise gyms are part of a chain, just like McDonald's, 7-Eleven, or any other franchise. When you go into one of these establishments you know exactly what you're getting, since all of them must meet the same standards set by the head office. Such names as Gold's, World, and Powerhouse have become cemented in the minds of bodybuilders the world over. Franchise gyms are large and outfitted with multiple lines of weight training and cardio equipment.

Like all gyms, franchise gyms owe much of their existence to Joe Gold, who started the original Gold's Gym in 1965 in Venice Beach, California. With Joe's gift for manufacturing training equipment, it wasn't long before Gold's Gym was the place to train. During the late '60s and '70s the top bodybuilding stars trained there as they prepared for the top titles. If you strolled into Gold's during the early 1970s you'd see Arnold and Franco Columbu in one corner pumping away on their chests, while in another corner, Robby Robinson would be inflating his enormous biceps like two balloons. A quick glance around would see such other '70s superstars as Mike Katz, Ken Waller, Bill Grant, Frank Zane and Ed Corney.

After selling the gym in the early '70s and taking a break from bodybuilding, Joe decided to get back into the business. However, since his name was now a trademark, he opened up his new gym with the name World Gym. With the fitness boom of the 1980s both Gold's and World decided to license out their names across North America. Soon other gyms did the same, and the era of franchise gyms had arrived.

Private gyms are just that – privately owned by one or two individuals. There is no head office and all expenses are incurred by the owners. Private gyms tend to be smaller than franchise gyms and more specialized with regards to their clientele (i.e. hardcore bodybuilding, women only, health spa). While they might not have the same amount of equipment as the larger franchise gyms, they do offer personal service that the larger facilities can't match. You can be just a number at the big gyms, and many of the bigger gyms seem to care more about signing members than servicing the members they already have.

GETTING STARTED

If you're looking for a challenge in your life, starting a gym will definitely fit the bill. With a combination of hard work, long hours and luck you can make a comfortable living. On the other hand, if you don't manage your money well, try to take too much time off, trust your business to other people or simply don't manage it well, you may end up spending many years paying off your debts after your business shuts its doors.

The first decision you'll have to make is whether to go the franchise or private route. The advantage of the franchise gym is that from day one you'll have instant name recognition. As soon as you open a World, Gold's, Powerhouse or other franchise you'll immediately attract a large clientele strictly on the name alone. In addition, most people will know exactly what they're going to get before they even enter your gym. You'll get new members and take members from competing gyms. You'll also get a lot of support and advice from the franchise head office. This only makes sense, as they have a vested interest in your business as well.

Of course this close contact with head office can work both ways. You will need to have all your i's dotted and t's crossed before you approach a franchise head office. Before they grant you a license to use their name they'll want to see a business plan. And do you blame

> "Shortly after I sold my Pacific Avenue gym, Arnold and Franco begged me to open another gym. 'I'll support you,' they said. And they did. Arnold put World Gym on the map. I give a lot of credit to Arnold and Franco.
>
> – Joe Gold, founder of both the Gold's and World Gym franchises

them? Who wants to lend their name to a business venture that may be bankrupt in six months? In your business plan you'll need to outline such things as location, start-up costs, whether you'll rent a building or build from the ground up, the number of potential members you hope to attract and how you plan to do it, maintenance costs, staff training, salary costs, as well as growth potential. Only after assessing the feasibility of your business proposal will a major gym chain grant you the rights to use their name on your gym.

If you decide to go it alone, the previous considerations still apply, but even then not all of the decision-making will be yours. Instead of bringing your business plan to a franchise head office you go to a bank or other financial institution. Chances are you'll have to go to at least a few before hearing a yes. If the bank does decide to grant you a loan, you've cleared your first hurdle. You now have to implement your business plan. The facility will need to be renovated or built and the equipment bought or leased and delivered. If you can, arrange for a grand opening featuring a top bodybuilder – even if just for an hour or two. Nothing will attract potential new members like a pro bodybuilder.

The first few months will be hectic. Keep the operation simple and hire minimal staff. But make sure your training staff are all certified. You don't want a lawsuit because some idiot put a 70-year-old newbie under the squat rack.

I'll be honest. You'll need to put in long hours at the beginning to get your gym up and running, and that beginning may last two or three years. But with a little luck and perseverance, you'll slowly build up a client base and start turning a profit. And who knows? Maybe down the road someone will approach you and want to use your name on his gym. Congratulations! You've just started a franchise!

Photos of Joe Gold

Joe Gold laid the groundwork for two of the most famous franchise gyms: Gold's and World Gym.

CHAPTER 65

Turn that Winning Body into Cash

"In addition to having his image portrayed on the covers of over 50 romance novels, Frank has appeared five times in skits on 'Late Night With Conan O'Brien,' as well as being a regular on the 'Howard Stern' radio and television shows."

– Ron Harris, regular *MuscleMag International* contributor, commenting on the success of top bodybuilding model, Frank Sepe.

When the first bodybuilding contests were held back in the 1940s the top prizes consisted of a trophy, a medal and perhaps a few tins of protein powder. But as the saying goes: Times, they are a-changin'. Today's bodybuilders can look forward to making a decent living from the sport, provided they see themselves as a product to be marketed and sold. It's no use to win a big title and sit back waiting for Robert Kennedy to come knocking on your door. Every year sees a whole new crop of title winners and it's a very competitive world out there. Time after time the sport has witnessed the "next Arnold" go crashing down in flames because the individual failed to seize the moment and capitalize on the opportunity. Ask yourself: Wouldn't you rather be making a living from the sport you love than from doing whatever it is you're doing right now? Thought so!

The key to complete bodybuilding success (as opposed to simply winning a few titles) is to get out of the gym and expend just as much energy marketing yourself as you would doing that all-out set of squats or deadlifts. Earlier in the

book I talked about setting long-term and short-term goals for building your physique. Now you must do the same with any business venture you would like to pursue.

As soon as Arnold established himself as the sport's top bodybuilder he began working on the business side of things. First he set up a mail-order business to sell his training programs. Next he started taking business courses. He also began taking acting classes. He began writing for *MuscleMag International*. Finally he learned as much as he could about real estate and began investing. In short, Arnold didn't sit on his squat-built ass and wait for things to magically happen. He took the bull by the horns and went after it.

Now, I'm by no means suggesting that you'll end up winning seven Mr. Olympia titles, be Hollywood's top box-office draw and get elected governor. But there's no reason why you can't convert that great physique of yours into hard cash with a little bit of ingenuity and drive. Virtually all the top pro and amateur body-

builders have business sidelines these days. In fact most make far more money from these other businesses than from prize money.

The following are some of the primary areas in which a resourceful bodybuilder can make money. Some will yield direct income while others can be used to increase your marketing potential. If you plan on making a living from the sport someday, this section is a must read.

> **"** Unless you're winning the Mr. Olympia you probably can't afford the lifestyle of a pro bodybuilder. That's the reality."
>
> – 1980s pro, Mike Christian, commenting on the realities of being a pro bodybuilder.

PRIZE MONEY

"Turning pro is such a long shot. It all boils down to why you work out in the first place. If you're in bodybuilding only for fame and money, you're grasping for the wrong stars. If you're more interested in living a good, healthy lifestyle with balance among family, career and training, your odds of success are infinitely better."

– Anita Ramsey, *MuscleMag International* contributor, commenting on what it sometimes takes to make it to the pro level in bodybuilding.

Photo Dexter Jackson by Irvin Gelb

Despite the name, prize money is one of the least lucrative sources of income in bodybuilding. While the winner of the Mr. Olympia or Arnold Classic may receive upwards of $150,000, the money for the remaining placings diminishes rapidly. With only six to eight pro contests each year, a bodybuilder would have to win a couple or place high in many to bring in what could be called real money. The future might see the prize money for bodybuilding contests increasing, but the truth is that prize money comes from sponsorship. Until Nike, Adidas or some other multinational conglomerate takes on bodybuilding, making a living as a pro will be a challenge. As it stands now there are easier ways to make money from bodybuilding. Read on.

GUEST POSING

Back in the old days the top bodybuilders were lucky to get a trophy and some protein powder for their wins. Then pro bodybuilding began. But while being professional means you make money, many pros don't even make enough from competition to pay for their supplements each year.

Modern bodybuilders can thank Arnold Schwarzenegger and Franco Columbu for the income they can make from guest posing. Up until Arnold and Franco came on the scene, guest posing was more of a sideline. But Arnold and Franco saw the potential income guest posing could generate and turned it into the lucrative endeavor it is today. Most pro bodybuilders now make far more money from guest posing than from competing.

Guest posing has changed the fitness strategy of bodybuilders. Instead of the old practice of bulking up by 30 or 40 pounds in the off-season, most bodybuilders now try to stay within 15 or 20 pounds of their competitive weight. If a promoter pays a pro a couple of thousand to guest pose at his contest, the last thing he wants is for the Pillsbury Doughboy to show up – the audience wants to see their favorite stars bearing some resemblance to their magazine photos. If their favorite pro weighs 250 pounds for a contest, they won't be too happy when a 300-pound blimp lumbers onto the stage. Having said this, a few pro

bodybuilders who guest pose looking more like sumo wrestlers than competitive bodybuilders. However, these guys are at the top of their game and get away with it.

For those future guest posers reading, I have a few suggestions to offer:

First of all, don't allow your weight to drift more than 15 to 20 pounds above your contest weight. If you're on the tall side you may be able to stretch this to 30 pounds, but there is no reason to look like the "before" picture in a weight-loss contest. Keep in mind that the bodybuilding fraternity is a close-knit one. All it takes is one or two fat appearances and your guest-posing career will dry up faster than spit in the desert.

Second, always be on time. Bodybuilding contests, especially evening shows, run on tight schedules. The whole evening can be thrown off if you stroll in late. Besides, showing up early gives you a chance to interact with fans and perhaps sell some merchandise. And let's not forget the extra points you're adding to your reputation. News travels fast and promoters quickly hear whether certain guest posers are professional or cause headaches.

SEMINARS

As the two often go hand in hand, it only makes sense to follow the section on guest posing with the topic of seminars. Most bodybuilders who guest pose at a contest also do a seminar. The usual time is Saturday between the prejudging and evening show, but some bodybuilders hold two or three sessions on Friday night, Saturday afternoon and even Sunday. The typical seminar is broken down into three sections: training, nutrition and supplementation, and competition. If you get a chance to attend one of these sessions, go! As great as books and magazines are, they're nothing like having a top pro (or top amateur, for that matter) talking to you in person. Virtually all are walking libraries of knowledge, and instead of spending weeks or months looking for the answer to a particular problem, you may get the answer with just one welldirected question. Don't be afraid to take notes, either. Topics that seem irrelevant now may become crucial in a year or two. For example, if you're a beginner your primary focus should be building muscle mass, not pre-contest dieting. But this time next year you may decide to enter your first contest, and in that case the pro's pre-contest advice will be invaluable.

For those readers who do decide to conduct seminars there are two primary areas that you'll need to become adept in. The first is knowledge. The second is delivering the knowledge. Just the fact that you've reached this level in bodybuilding and have been asked to conduct a seminar indicates that you know your stuff, but knowing something and being able to pass that knowledge on to other people are two different skills. Some of the most highly educated people in the world haven't got a clue about teaching. I need only point you in the direction of the nearest university or college to confirm this. Conversely, there are those who have a true gift for passing along what information they do possess.

So what does all this have to do with conducting a bodybuilding seminar? This: You'll be getting in front of dozens, if

> "I'm gone at least 20 weekends out of the year. The busiest time is the main contest season from March to July, when I'm booked every weekend."
>
> – Jay Cutler, Mr. Olympia winner, commenting on his hectic seminar and posing schedule.

not hundreds, of enthusiastic bodybuilders who will be hanging on your every word. Do you have any experience in public speaking? If not you're going to have a tough couple of hours. Not only will you stress yourself out, but you'll also sadly disappoint a lot of potential fans.

Unless you're one of those naturally gifted individuals who thrives on public attention, you're probably going to be nervous speaking in front of a large group of people. If so, my first suggestion is to enroll in a public-speaking course. These range from the Toastmaster program to once-a-week community college courses to full-fledged business courses offered by such prestigious organizations as Dale Carnegie. At the very least, pick up a good book on public speaking. If you're in high school or college or university, jump at every opportunity to get up in front of an audience. Yes the first couple of sessions will probably be nerve racking. But like most things you'll get better and become more relaxed with time.

Perhaps the most important aspect of good public speaking is learning to relax. Remaining calm often takes

Many bodybuilders, like Jay Cutler, will guest pose and do a seminar at a contest.

Photo Jay Cutler by Garry Bartlett

care of many of the other facets of public communication. If you get nervous and uptight at the mere sight of a microphone it's going to have a profound effect on what you say and how you say it.

Good public speaking also depends on the speed at which you talk. Don't race along trying to fit as many words as possible into one sentence. Try to speak slowly and deliberately.

If your day-to-day speaking involves frequent use of words of the four-letter variety, I suggest you start cleaning it up right now. Coarse and vulgar language may be fine with your friends but it's a no-no in public. Besides, you want to appear professional and intelligent, not like some piece of gutter trash.

Another suggestion is to tape record yourself at some point just to see how you sound. Don't be shocked the first time you play it back. Most people don't realize how they sound to others. Once you get over the initial "do I really sound like that?" shock, replay the tape a couple of times and analyze it. Pay particular attention to how fast you're speaking and how you pronounce each letter. If you have a sharp dialect you may want to consider modifying it. It's not that accents and dialects are wrong, but what you're saying should be clear and understandable. Arnold Schwarzenegger and Lou Ferrigno spent years working on speech – Arnold because of his thick Austrian accent and Lou because of a hearing loss suffered in childhood. Both ended up among the sport's best public speakers.

You must also be conscious of how many "uhs" and "ahs" you work into your speech. Try not to string sentences along with such idiosyncratic grunts. Finish one sentence and then start the next. Don't pause in between with an "uh" or "ah."

A final mistake many people make when first learning to speak in public is trying to use as many big, unfamiliar words as possible. Trust me. Trying to imitate a thesaurus will not make you look more intelligent – just foolish.

PHOTOS

Virtually all the new bodybuilding stars have photos for sale including Ronnie Coleman, Jay Cutler, Gustavo Badell, Mustafa Mohammad, Markus Ruhl and Toney

Signed photographs are a great way to promote yourself.

Freeman. But it's not just the new generation's photos that sell. Classic shots of Schwarzenegger, Zane, Oliva, Ferrigno, Columbu, Park and Reeves also do brisk business. Besides showing the various poses, these photos serve as inspiration. In fact, you might have some inspirational bodybuilding photos on your wall right now! These photos may be color or black and white and usually sell for $10 to $20. In many cases you'll get a discount if your order them in sets.

When your physique starts winning top amateur contests, get a series of photos done while you're in contest shape. Take them with you to seminars and posing exhibitions to sell (autographed, of course). They'll not only please your fans but they'll also improve your marketability. There's no such thing as overexposure in bodybuilding.

DVDs

"You have to know your competition, so do some research. Setting a price is always a balancing act of maximizing your profits while not overwhelming the consumer. This is a good time to step back and objectively evaluate the chances of success for your new product."
– Don Mochrie, *MuscleMag International* contributor

Older bodybuilders remember the filmstrips of the top bodybuilding stars of the '50s and '60s that were available through ads in the various muscle magazines. With the intro-

Photo Lee Priest by Rich Baker

duction of VHS and DVD video technology there has been an explosion in the number of such products.

There are generally three categories of bodybuilding videos available. The first consists of posing videos, featuring bodybuilding stars both past and present posing at exotic locations around the world. Besides serving as a source of inspiration, such videos are great educational tools when it comes time to putting together your posing routine.

The second is DVDs of the major contests. Every year the Arnold Classic, Mr. Olympia, Iron Man, and the various Grand Prix events are recorded by professional filmographers and made available on VHS tapes and DVDs to the general public. A double DVD normally costs around $39.99.

The third category is training videos released by the individual bodybuilding superstars. Most are shot in commercial gyms and follow the stars as they go through a workout for each bodypart. Although such videos were available in the 1980s, it was six-time Mr. Olympia Dorian Yates who really established such products with his *Blood and Guts* video released in the 1990s. While previous videos had been more fluff than anything, Yates got down and dirty and showed viewers just how hard pro bodybuilders really train. He used real workout poundage, and that was real sweat dripping off his forehead. *Blood and Guts* set the standard for training videos, and virtually every top bodybuilding star now has a series of similarly styled videos. You can see Ronnie Coleman blasting those enormous arms of his and Jay Cutler hammering his tree-trunk-sized thighs.

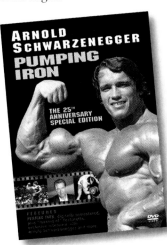

If you start winning top amateur titles, you should seriously consider making your own training DVDs. Start with a shorter full-body training DVD and if the sales are decent, you can expand to include DVDs for individual bodyparts. Don't cut corners on the production costs, either. Having a buddy chase you around with a $300 video camcorder won't come close to the quality of a professional filmographer with thousands of dollars in lighting and video equipment. You want to establish a reputation for professionalism, and if someone pays once for an unprofessional product, you can bet he won't be paying twice.

SUPPLEMENT ENDORSING

By far the most lucrative form of financial reward for bodybuilders is endorsing food supplements. Every year the top supplement lines such as MuscleTech, Twin Lab EAS, Pro Lab and Weider battle it out for a piece of the billion-dollar supplement pie. A flip through a recent copy of any one of the major bodybuilding magazines and you'll see just how competitive this industry is. Those full-color, multi-page ads that you see cost thousands of dollars per page. While perhaps interruptive to readers, the ads are vital to the survival of the magazines.

Given the competition in this industry it's not surprising that virtually all the supplement companies hire top bodybuilders to promote and endorse their products. Super bodybuilding promoter and publisher Joe Weider was the first to recognize the potential of this arrangement back in the 1950s and 1960s. Weider protein powder ads with such top stars as Larry Scott, Dave Draper, or Arnold surrounded by a bevy of beach babes have become classics. They also helped Weider become by far the biggest name in the supplement industry, a position that went unchallenged until the mid 1990s, when such newcomers as EAS, Twin Lab and MuscleTech came on the scene.

Weider responded to the new competition by putting many of the top pro bodybuilders under contract. This meant they could endorse only his products, no matter how much money the other companies offered. Initially this worked well, as Weider had the deepest products and the top stars naturally went to him. But once the other companies started building their bank accounts they immediately started offering the next generation of body-

Advertisements from supplement companies are crucial to the financial survival of bodybuilding magazines.

Photo by Rich Baker

builders similar-sized deals. It wasn't long before some of the established pros switched camps when their contracts with Weider expired. It's reached the point now that the Weider line of supplements is just another player on the scene. Most bodybuilders under the age of 30 or 40 have no idea of the monopoly that Weider had before the arrival of the new guns.

While many readers no doubt hope to be in the enviable position of signing a supplement contract with one of the major supplement companies, I'll be the first to admit that it's a tough road to travel. Supplement companies won't even look at you until you reach the upper echelons of the pro bodybuilding ranks. You might not need to win the Mr. Olympia or Arnold Classic, but you must consistently place in the top 10, and you must be very popular with the fans.

You also need to have "the right look." This is hard to define, but essentially means that you have good facial features to match your phenomenal physique. The only goal of putting you on supplement labels or featuring you in the ads is to increase sales. Every year supplement companies spend millions of dollars on marketing research, trying to determine what approach has the greatest impact on sales. If they don't feel that you have the "look," then there's not much you can do to change their opinions.

The classic example occurred with Joe Weider back in the late 1960s. At the time Sergio Oliva was the number-one bodybuilder in the world, but despite his success on the posing platform he just didn't sell products. Whether it was his Cuban birth, his shy presence around fans, or his African ancestry (remember this was the 1960s, when African Americans still fought to go to school with whites). Who knows? But the bottom line for Weider was that having Sergio endorse supplements wasn't paying off. Then along came the Austrian-born Schwarzenegger. He possessed an equal body, was white and had a charisma that to this day has been unmatched. It's easy to see why Weider immediately started promoting Arnold. He brought Arnold to America, helped him set up his mail-order business, and began featuring him in his magazines. The rest, as they say, is history. Arnold's close association with Weider greatly benefited both: Arnold got paid to support a lifestyle which allowed him to win a then-record six straight Mr. Olympia titles, and sales of Weider's supplements went through the roof.

CLOTHING

It was only a matter of time before bodybuilders joined the fashion set. Tattered worn-out T-shirts have been replaced by the latest in workout fashions. Besides, bodybuilders need their own clothing lines. Most clothes are built for either big fat people or small lean people. It's hard to get clothes that will fit big broad shoulders and lats and a lean waist. Many bodybuilders have turned their talents to endorsing workout clothing lines and a few, such as Gary Strydom and Mike Christian, have created their own clothing lines.

Normally you would get into the clothing business as a product endorser. This is similar to being taken on by a supplement company. First you need to establish yourself as a top-ranked competitor and win or place high in a few contests. Since you'll be endorsing clothes you'll need that certain "look." How can you expect customers to buy the clothes if you don't look good in them?

The other option for getting involved with the clothing business is to create your own. This is not as simple as it seems. You can't just slap a few pieces of material together and call it a workout suit (although with some of the items that pass for fashion these days I sometimes wonder). The clothes must be both stylish and functional. The material should keep you cool and be able to endure repeated stretching and chaffing. It should also be capable of surviving heavy doses of human sweat. Once you have the material picked out you'll need to design the clothes (or have someone else design them), manufacture them and find a distributor to market them to various retail stores. Oh, and one other thing, the price must be competitive with the workout clothes offered by department and sports specialty stores. Getting into the clothing industry is not a piece of cake. But if you make a success of it, the financial rewards can be huge.

CHAPTER 66

Contest Promotion

"The fact is, the purpose of promoting a competition is to make money. The risks are huge with questionable rewards."

– Garry Bartlett, *MuscleMag International* correspondent, on Joe Spinello and the return of the Montreal Pro Classic.

Like any business venture, contest promotion is tough and there are financial risks involved. The following is by no means an all-encompassing guide to contest promoting. Instead I'll touch on the main points that will need to be addressed if you want to ensure that your show is both financially successful and enjoyable for both the audience and competitors.

AFFILIATION

Before you decide to get into the contest-promoting business you'll need to first become affiliated with one of the bodybuilding federations. Although the IFBB (International Federation of Bodybuilders) is the largest, there are others, so check out what's available in your region.

Once you have your affiliation with a certain federation, the next step is to see if there's an opportunity available to run a contest in your area. If the given federation is already running a contest in your area, the odds are good to excellent that the parent federation will let that promoter keep managing it. You don't fix a wheel that's not broke.

However, if the previous promoter decides to retire or is asked to step aside, then the door is now open for you to become involved. But there's a good chance

Gustavo Badell shows his muscles before the 2007 Mr. Olympia contest.

Photo Gustavo Badell by Irvin Gelb

that you won't be the only interested party; other budding entrepreneurs might also jump at the chance. This means that you'll have to bid on the rights to hold the show. And just like most business tenders, the lowest bidder normally wins (although higher bidders with better overall presentation packages occasionally get the nod, and you will certainly be given the upper hand if you have previous experience hosting events of this nature).

GET SOME BACKGROUND

If you are lucky enough to be successful in your bid to hold the contest, the fun begins. You now have a year or two to prepare. The job can be done is less time, but if you want your first contest to be successful you'll want to give yourself plenty of time to work out the bugs – and I assure you there'll be plenty.

One of the first things you should do is contact previous promoters or promoters from other (similar) regions. If contest promotion has not left a sour taste in their mouths, and assuming they're the friendly types, they should be happy to help you out. Of course if you find out that they lost money three years in a row you may want to rethink the whole venture. In fact it wouldn't hurt to scope this out before you even start bidding on contest rights.

Besides the financial dirt, previous promoters can also give you a list of people you'll need to help run the contest. For the sake of an hour or two on the phone, you can make contact with a few people who will make your life a whole lot easier. Also, people who have been involved

before can let you in on all the little issues that usually crop up that you couldn't possibly know about yet. They can also get you some names of reliable people to work with. Once you're armed with a decent plan of attack it's simply a case of executing it.

GETTING THE VENUE READY

One of the first and most important tasks is arranging the contest venue. For a smaller local contest you can probably get by with a high school gym, but as you rise up the competitive ladder, the audience and competitors expect better facilities. Most cities and large towns have arts cen-

ters and theatres that make ideal contest venues, but you don't just phone up a week before. Most will be booked months if not years in advance – especially on Friday and Saturday nights. And as expected the more posh and ritzier the facility the higher the cost. You'll need to factor this into your operating expenses.

Once you have the venue booked your next step is hiring a lighting contractor. It's true that most high schools and arts theaters have their own lighting, but odds are it won't be suitable for a bodybuilding contest. A good lighting contractor will have his own lights and the expertise to go along with them. Lighting contractors can cost from a few hundred to many thousands of dollars, and as with ven-

Photo by Irvin Gelb

The contest venue is critical for the success of the contest itself – think size, lighting and sound.

the night before so any potential issues and acoustics can be ironed out the night before.

MARKETING

With the venue, lighting and sound taken care of, the next step is promotion. The greatest show in the world is useless if people don't attend because they didn't know about it. For a bodybuilding contest it's not just the audience that you're trying to entice either. What's a bodybuilding contest without bodybuilders? In fact, the more bodybuilders you attract to compete in your show the larger the audience turnout, since each competitor is bound to bring a dozen or more friends and relatives.

If you leave the advertising until too late you'll doom your show to mediocrity at best, but more likely total failure right from the start. The average competitive bodybuilder needs at least three months to diet and prepare for a contest. If you don't give potential competitors enough time to both decide to compete and then prepare for competition, most will simply skip your show. Let all the gyms in the contest area know about your show at least four to six months in advance. Besides the gyms it wouldn't hurt to send advertising flyers to high schools and food supplement stores either. Teenage bodybuilding is growing by leaps and bounds and virtually every bodybuilder goes into a supplement store at some point. You should also send a brief description of your contest to the major bodybuilding magazines so they can post it in their "Upcoming Events" section. And remember that magazines plan these sections three to four months before the magazine comes out, so this should be done first and often.

One great source of advertising is the local media such as newspapers and TV. Newspapers are always looking for something different, and bodybuilding can fit that bill. If you have a contact at the local paper, try to convince him or her to write a story on bodybuilding featuring a couple of the contestants. You'll get free advertising and they'll get a catchy story about local personalities. If you can't get a story, at least buy some advertising space – preferably in the sports section – and run an ad. Besides,

ues, should be booked months or even years in advance. You should also arrange to have the contractor set up the night before if possible and test out the lights using real people. I've attended contests where the promoters and lighting contractors didn't test the lights until an hour before prejudging. In many cases they had to stop the contest because some spots on the stage were better lit than others.

Besides lighting you'll need a sound person to look after the music for the competitors' posing routines plus the posedown. Once again the venue may have it's own stereo system, but if there's any doubt as to the quality of the in-house sound system, hire a contractor. As with lighting, see if the person can set up and check things out

the way most papers work (especially smaller papers) is that they'll do a story if you run an ad.

If you have the cash, a brief mention on the radio wouldn't hurt either. Radio ads are much cheaper than TV and you'll be sure that you're reaching a wide audience. If money is tight, limit the ad to whatever radio station in your area caters to the 15- to 30-year-old age bracket. The bulk of your competitors will be coming from this age group and it won't make sense to advertise on an oldies radio station.

If you really have deep pockets then you can do up a catchy TV ad. Of course this will set you back thousands of dollars. If a full-blown TV ad is out of your reach, most local cable companies have community channels offering scroll news that features upcoming events. Given the prevalence of remote-controlitis in our society, odds are good to excellent that potential competitors and audience members will see your ad.

OTHER PEOPLE YOU'LL NEED

Another important task is to book an emcee. Radio or TV personalities make great emcees, as they're usually personable and know how to keep an audience entertained. Besides, most in the audience will know them and treat them like a local celebrity (which in a way they are). One piece of advice is to avoid hiring some wisecracking comedian. Chances are good that he will use the stage as a platform to try out his latest repertoire of anti-bodybuilding jokes. The last thing you want is someone belittling the sport. It's taken bodybuilding decades to achieve a decent level of credibility and such idiots don't further our cause. No matter how popular a radio or TV personality might be, ditch them if you think they'll treat our sport with disrespect. In fact, you should build right into their contract a clause that they may not demean the sport or competitors in any way.

Another individual you'll need to consider is a guest poser. An average contest can be quickly turned into a once-in-a-lifetime event if you have a top Mr. Olympia-level pro turn up. Once local bodybuilders know that

someone of the caliber of Jay Cutler, Ronnie Coleman or Dexter Jackson will be in attendance, your problem won't be unsold seats, but scalpers!

Most pros charge between $3,000 and $5,000 for an appearance, but someone like Ronnie Coleman or Jay Cutler could set you back $10,000 or more. Besides the appearance fees, virtually every pro will want traveling, food and accommodation expenses included as well. On the surface this may sound like a lot of money, but you'll easily recoup this expense from the number of extra seats you'll sell if you do book them. If you set up a seminar or two with him, you'll stand to make even more money.

With all the commotion going on there is one group of individuals that you may forget to line up – the judges! Not much use parading a group of bodybuilders onstage if there's no one to judge them. Rounding up the judges is usually fairly easy. Odds are the previous promoter will have a list. Judges may approach you to offer their services. Unless the decisions made at the last few contests were way off, you're safe to use the same judges. It never hurts to train in new judges in case you need to change the judging panel in future years (you'll also lose a few by normal attrition). Most federations require prospective new judges to serve as test judges for a few contests before becoming qualified. Test judges sit at the judging table and go through exactly the same procedures as the regular judges, but their decisions don't count. At the end of the contest the head judge will compare the test judge scores to the actual scores. As long as the test judges placed the contestants in the same range as the regular judges, then after a few years they can serve as full judges in future shows. Different federations have different rules on qualifying test judges, so check things out.

You'll need a number of volunteers to carry out an assortment of tasks including collecting and selling tickets, helping out backstage, ushering audience members, and looking after the guest poser. There shouldn't be a need to pay any of these people. Many will gladly do it just for the thrill of being associated with the contest in some way. The free pass plus maybe some free food afterward is all it should cost. Make sure to have a volunteer coordinator,

Running a contest is no small feat, but starting local may just be the first step to becoming a top promoter.

Photo by Irvin Gelb

too. The advantage of delegating many of these tasks to other people is that it frees up your time to coordinate the whole show.

OTHER STUFF

You will need to pick up a few items. Have a local printer run off the exact number of prejudging and evening show tickets that you'll need. Under no circumstances do you take a page out of the airlines' handbook and oversell the show. Bodybuilding fans are a loyal bunch and you can be sure that 99 percent of them will show up. You don't want a dozen VERY LARGE individuals being turned away at the door. If your theater seats 2,000 people you print 2,000 tickets. Period.

I can't guarantee that your first show will be successful or problem free, but it certainly will be rewarding and challenging. But if you take the time and plan it out well in advance, and you have some good people helping you, there's no reason that the contestants and fans won't be pleased with your efforts. If you do manage to put together a number of great shows and develop a reputation for promotion, don't be surprised if you're asked to run a state or regional contest. And who knows, maybe one day you'll be in charge of the Nationals or a Grand Prix event. Just like bodybuilders, most of the top promoters got their first big break at the local level. There's no reason why you can't do the same.

Photo of Ronny Rockel by Alex Ardenti

THE BIG SEVEN

CHAPTER 67

The Barbell Row

"While wide-grip chins and lat pulldowns widen the lat muscles.
They do not add a great deal to the actual mass of the lats,
especially the lower areas. The bent-over row is the answer."

– Editorial in *MuscleMag International*, on giving your lats more mass in the lower regions.

Be honest and admit it. Your back training hasn't been nearly as intense as it could be. How do I know? Take a look around any gym and you'll see for yourself. With all the super-smooth machines and cable devices designed to train this bodypart almost an entire generation of bodybuilders has all but forgotten one of the most effective back developers around: the bent-over barbell row.

The main reason for the abandonment of the barbell row is that it's uncomfortable. Unlike cable pulldowns, low-cable rows or even machines designed to simulate the action of a barbell row, a free-weight row requires the back to stabilize on its own accord. You have nothing to sit or lie on – no back supports, no knee braces and no platforms – just the natural support of your spine and the erector muscles in your lower back.

Not only does the bent-over position place stress on your spinal erectors, it places additional stress on your ability to breathe. To top it all off, the hamstrings are placed under tension (to stabilize the upper body) and too many factors appear to be working against you for you to efficiently work the latissimus dorsi muscles you're looking to target. But hold on just a second. All is not as it seems.

When the body is fully braced, as it is in a machine, the lats may be more specifically isolated, but the end results are subpar because the back is a muscle group that works as a unit. The lats, rhomboids and erectors are all components integrated to work in tandem. Even the traps get involved, yet most bodybuilders treat this muscle group as a separate entity.

Many bodybuilders think traps are primarily shoulder muscles. They don't realize this bodypart extends down along the spine to the bottom of the ribcage. When these muscles contract they affect muscles throughout the entire back. For instance, when the traps are activated the scapula moves down and in, resulting in deeply etched grooves throughout the back.

When performing isolated exercises such as lat pulldowns, other back muscles barely come into play. That's the reason trainers who rely on machines have shallow backs. They may have decent lat development when viewed from the front, but when they turn around to the side or back … well, there's just nothing there.

TEAMWORK

If you want thick, dense muscle throughout your back you must work the area the way nature intended: as a unit. The back muscles must all be forced to stabilize. All the muscles must come into play. This bodypart must also be worked heavy, with no support and no assistance. That means awkward, painful and uncomfortable barbell rows, which may cause difficulties with your breathing. There's just no way around it.

PROPER FORM

Proper technique when performing barbell rows is important. Loose lifting and heaving of the weight won't work the muscles sufficiently and can lead to potential damage. You need to remain strict and contract completely. Again, a very uncomfortable action, but one that's vital for complete development. Remember, the function of the back is not only to pull, but to arch. If you do not complete the final phase of the exercise (the contraction), you simply will not achieve full development.

INJURY PREVENTION

Your back must also remain in a contracted, or arched, position to prevent injury. As long as the lower back is flat

Photo of Jae Jung by Paul Buceta

and slightly arched (as opposed to rounded), you shouldn't have a problem. Be careful, though. Back injuries are the most common of all training injuries. This is almost always the result of rounding the back, which compromises the integrity of the small muscles in the lower region. Every day people hurt their backs merely by picking up something light if they are rounding their backs, so you can imagine what happens when you add a couple of hundred pounds. As soon as the lower-back muscles are stabilized they can lift tremendous poundage.

BARBELL ROWS – PROPER TECHNIQUE

- Bend down over the barbell while consciously keeping your lower back horizontally straight and tight. Stick your butt out to help with the correct positioning.
- Lower your arms to grab the barbell while keeping your back straight. Trainers normally use an overhand grip, but an underhand grip is an excellent variation to place more emphasis on the lower lats. The underhand barbell row was a favorite of six-time Mr. Olympia Dorian Yates.
- Maintain a straight, slightly arched back and keep your arms extended (shoulders a tad higher than your hips). Find a spot on the wall directly in front of you and keep your eyes focused on that spot throughout. Doing so helps you keep your back arched. You can also look into your own eyes in the mirror for the same effect.
- Row the bar up and just under your chest while keeping your torso parallel to the floor and your legs

slightly bent. Once the bar is in the fully contracted position, hold it and squeeze the back muscles and shoulder blades together for one or two seconds.
- Slowly lower the bar. Once again, keep your back arched. Think of your arms as handles, serving as hooks for the back muscles. Make your back do the work.
- Repeat for 8 to 10 reps.

That's all there is to it. Easier said than done, right? Heavy barbell rows are brutal. They not only demand a lot physically, but to derive the ultimate benefit and prevent injury they also require extreme concentration. They aren't a knock-out-a-few-sets and get-it-over-with exercise by any means. They're the real deal. But I guarantee that when you set your mind and motivation toward making this exercise the main movement in your back training, you're going to see some drastic changes. Thick, defined back mass from all angles will be yours. All you need to do is supply the effort. In the end, you're going to look big and broad – coming and going.

Photo of Con Demetriou by Alex Ardenti

A bodybuilder's diet needs all the macronutrients – not just protein. Experiment with herbs and spices to keep it interesting.

Photo of Dan Decker by Robert Reiff

CHAPTER 68

The Squat

"If you spend enough time working in a gym you'll hear plenty of reasons for not squatting. Usually they're not good reasons. We had a category for those who left the squat out of their training. We called them 'lightbulb lifters' because we could envision the developed upper body tapering down to thin, underdeveloped underpinnings."

– Bob Shaefer, *MuscleMag International* contributor, giving his views on bodybuilders who avoid doing squats.

The regular back squat is undeniably the best-known builder of quad mass. When you squat you simultaneously involve all the biggest muscle groups: the back, glutes and quads. This increases your lung efficiency, revs the metabolism and causes release of growth hormone, stimulating all-over muscular body growth. But unfortunately squats are also one of the most neglected and abused of bodybuilding exercises. Go into any gym and you may have to wait 20 minutes to use a leg-extension machine, but odds are you'll be able to walk right up to the squat or power rack. Why? Because squats separate the men from the wusses, that's why! Besides working the legs and lower back, squats stress just about the whole body. When you have that amount of muscle mass being stimulated all at once the end result is pain and fatigue. Many would-be bodybuilders are unwilling to endure either and instead opt for the leg extensions.

Then are those who claim that squats are bad for the knees. While it is true that this area is subjected to some stress during squats, and some people truly cannot do them – or at least not heavy squats – the same holds true for leg extensions. In fact from a kinesiological point of view leg extensions are actually harder on the knees than squats. Extensions are an example of an "open-chain movement." This means that while the quads are contracting and pulling on the knee ligaments and attachments, there is little or no counter action by the hamstrings. During squats, the contracting hamstrings help to stabilize the knee region (which is why the squat is considered a closed-chain exercise). Done properly squats are no more dangerous than leg extensions. In fact many kinesiologists and physical therapists recommend doing squats as opposed to extensions because squats mimic a natural movement while leg extensions don't resemble any movement you'd make during the day.

Some people avoid squats because they think they'll build huge glutes. Again some myths never seem to disappear. While squats do stimulate the glutes more than leg extensions, they won't build you a wide ass! Large asses are usually the result of overeating. Besides, you need a decent set of glutes to both balance out the physique and reduce the pressure on the lower back. A bodybuilder with an ironing board for a butt won't win any contests.

No, it's safe to say that the main reason why many people avoid squats is because of sheer laziness. They just don't want to work hard at the squat rack. Well I'm here to tell you that if you have any hopes of building a great set of legs, you will have a very difficult go of it unless you squat on a regular basis. Not only will squats give you pillars of power, they'll add slabs of muscle to your upper body as well. As Peary Radar, the original publisher of *Iron Man* magazine said first (though others followed), "If you want big arms, squat!" This may surprise you. But as

I said earlier, the more muscle mass being stimulated the more of an indirect growth-promoting effect is placed on the rest of the muscles.

TYPES OF SQUATS

There are three main squatting routines, and each serves its own purpose. Bodybuilders intent of building muscle mass and shape can benefit from all three to give variety to their training sessions. Keep surprising the muscles and they will keep growing.

Straight Sets with Increasing Weight

This is the most common squatting routine. Do 4 to 6 sets of squats with a three-minute rest between sets. Repetitions should be between 8 and 12 per set. Add weight disks each set, building up to your maximum weight on the final set.

Powerlifting Routine

This is the quickest way to build true quad power. Put your feet a little more than shoulder-width apart. Add weight plates on each set for 8 sets. Keep repetitions between 2 and 6 per set. Because of the extra-heavy resistance, make sure the descent into the squat position is careful, slow and controlled, or you may blow out a knee.

The Breathing Squat

The breathing squat made its first appearance over 60 years ago. The science behind it is to increase the size of

WATCH THOSE KNEES

Older bodybuilders find that those 500-pound squats they used to crank out begin to take their toll. To keep your knees healthy always use correct form when squatting, lunging and leg pressing. If you feel aches and pains in or around your knees, rest and consult your physician.

Proper technique is essential in the squat if you want a functional spine.

Photo of Geovanny Gouea by Paul Buceta

the ribcage (in addition to the quads) and to rev up the metabolism so the whole body benefits with added muscle growth. Do the first 10 reps of the 20-rep set without pausing between reps. For the last 10 reps, pause between each repetition. During the pause, take three deep breaths before squatting down for the next rep.

At the conclusion of each 20-rep set, go straight to the flat bench for 15 to 20 reps of light straight-arm pullovers, breathing deeply between each repetition.

FREQUENCY

Once-a-week leg training is adequate to build both power and mass. The most important factors in making training progress are hard work and recuperation. If you are missing either of these aspects you won't grow.

If you train all bodyparts once a week, full recuperation is not too difficult with correct rest, nutrition and supplementation. Training a bodypart twice a week can improve progress, but it also makes complete recuperation more difficult. Should you want to specialize on squatting for an 8- to 12-week period, you can do your leg (squat) workouts twice a week while holding your other bodypart training frequency to once each week.

SQUATTING TIPS

- A squat rack is essential. The bar should be a 7-foot Olympic bar, placed on the squat rack just a few inches below shoulder height.
- Clothing should be comfortable so as to not restrict breathing. Track pants should be reasonably tight so they are snug against the upper legs, giving a sense of security. Footwear should be solidly constructed.
- The warmup should be for 2 or 3 sets of 12 to 15 reps using light to medium weight.
- Tighten the belt to maximum just before the working set. This gives a stronger sense of security and ultimate confidence.
- Do not bounce out of the squat. Do not lower all the way to the ground.

- Approach the racked bar, addressing it with studied concentration and seriousness of purpose. Grab the bar with a hand width comfortably wider than your shoulders. Duck under the bar, feet side by side and shoulder-width apart, butt out, back arched – not rounded. Lift the bar from the racks and back up in small steps until you are clear of the racks and catchers.
- Keep your head up and back flat, feet shoulder-width apart, toes pointing slightly out. Lower under control until your thighs are parallel to the floor or just below. Push up through the hips and heels without excessive forward lean.

Photo of Tarek Elsetuhi by Robert Reiff

CHAPTER 69

The Bench Press

"A good bencher will plant his feet tightly on the floor, and he will maintain his tight grip throughout the movement. Think of gripping the floor with your toes and keep them that way. Don't let your feet move, slip or rise."

– Bill Starr, regular *MuscleMag International* contributor

The bench press has always been a mainstay in bodybuilding routines because it is such a great exercise for building an impressive upper body. Strength athletes such as shot putters and football players benefit from handling heavy weights in this exercise.

Two events occurred to increase the popularity of bench pressing. The first was the emergence of the sport of powerlifting, in which the bench press was and still is a part of the competition. The other was the acceptance and inclusion of strength training for athletes. In high schools and colleges the flat bench was shown to be an ideal exercise to improve upper-body strength and could be done with a minimum of equipment. Some schools even kept the benches in the locker room. Not ideal, but it worked. Another bonus was that the exercise was easy to teach.

In a short period of time the bench press replaced the military press as the standard of strength. When someone asks, "How much can you bench?" he's really asking: "How strong are you?" Personally I'm more impressed with a big squat, deadlift or even incline press, but there's no disputing that the flat bench press is king in the eyes of many people.

Photo of Brian Wiefering by Robert Reiff

THE IMPORTANCE OF CORRECT TECHNIQUE

The-end-justifies-the-means attitude has caused many of the injuries associated with bench pressing. When sloppy form is practiced consistently, the areas of the body usually injured are the elbows, crowns of the shoulders and the rotator cuffs. If the lifter bangs the bar off his chest continuously over an extended period of time he can expect some damage to his pecs.

The rapid rise in rotator-cuff injuries can be traced directly to the burgeoning popularity of the bench press in the early 1970s. Up to that point the military, or overhead, press was the gauge of strength. Rotator-cuff problems were very rare. However, once the flat bench replaced the military press as the king of upper-body exercises, trainers and doctors began seeing a succession of injuries to the rotator cuff.

Keep in mind the exercise is not the villain. Done correctly the bench press is a safe and beneficial exercise. Sloppy form and overuse are the causes of injury, not the bench press itself. The shoulders, elbows and rotator cuffs are delicate, and if they are abused repeatedly with improper technique – often with heavy weights – they will become traumatized. If the individual ignores the warning signs and continues to pound away, he may hurt himself so severely he will be forced to stop benching. In some cases he has to stop training altogether.

Maintaining proper form also makes the exercise more effective because you hit the target muscles more thoroughly. Done correctly, the bench press works the pecs, deltoids and triceps completely. However, when technique is abused, these muscle groups do not receive as much work. For example, bouncing the bar off the chest bypasses the particular pec muscles that are responsible for driving the bar from the chest. Similarly, bridging denies the triceps the opportunity to finish the lift. (Bridging is when a lifter arches his back off the bench to give himself more power. This movement is illegal in powerlifting.)

Bouncing the bar off your chest may cause a broken rib or sternum.

I believe one reason so many people do the exercise incorrectly is because the lift is thought of as being very simple to do. Compared to such exercises as the power clean, the flat bench is relatively easy to learn – which often prompts coaches and personal trainers to spend much time teaching the finer points of squatting or cleaning while allowing the lifter to do his benches without any guidance. After all, the flat bench is just a matter of taking a bar from the rack, lowering the bar to the chest, and then pressing it back, right? Those instructions are fine when using light weights, but when the bar gets loaded up you need to know a great deal more about bench pressing. Younger lifters need to learn how to press correctly. Doing so is extremely important. The flat bench is generally their favorite exercise and also the most dangerous. Since the bar is suspended over the lifter's face and neck, a slip or mistake can be disastrous. Every year a number of young men die while doing unsupervised bench presses. I am not trying to be an alarmist. Rather I am pointing out the necessity of learning how to do the lift correctly, part of which means having a spotter present.

BENCH PRESSING 101

These tips are geared toward beginners and those who are just starting back to training after a layoff:

The Grip

Hold the bar so your wrists are directly above your elbows. This means your forearms will always be vertical. If your grip is too close or too wide you are giving up some power because you are putting a portion of your energy into moving the bar laterally rather than vertically. If you're doing a high-rep light-weight set then a slight variation in your grip will not matter much. However, if the poundage is heavy an ideal grip is critical. Many coaches urge benchers to use a very wide grip in order to involve the pecs more. I prefer a narrower grip so the deltoids and triceps are forced to contribute more to the exercise. A narrower grip also helps build up the inner chest where the muscles attach to the sternum. This helps pro-

duce the line that gives the chest that two-slabs-of-armor look. As well, an exaggerated, wide grip can be most stressful to the shoulders of any beginner. The strength base has to be firm before the grip can be moved out wider. All this being said, different grips will work better for different people, and you may find a wider grip is best for you.

After finding a grip that suits you, learn to lock your wrists and keep them locked throughout the entire exercise. Many lifters pick up the habit of cocking or turning their wrists while the bar is in motion, trying to coax it through the sticking point of the exercise. The trouble is, all the twisting and turning of the wrists isn't helping. In fact, the twists and turns work against you. The unnecessary movement of the wrists diminishes the power generated by your chest, shoulders and arms. When you keep your wrists locked, that power goes upward into the bar. Bear in mind the wrists are small joints that are very susceptible to injury. The constant twisting of the wrists while benching can irritate them. Once you hurt your wrists, they are extremely difficult to rehabilitate and you may in fact have problems with them for the rest of your life. Avoiding the trouble is far easier.

If you have developed the habit of cocking or twisting your wrists during the bench press, or any other pressing movement for that matter, start taping your wrists. Taping the wrists will help keep them locked and straight, and will also protect them from being dinged.

Another point concerning the grip is that you must hold the bar securely. Grip the bar firmly, making sure your thumbs are secured around the bar. I realize many trainers prefer the false grip, in which the thumbs are not around the bar. But using this grip is far too risky, especially for beginners. The slightest slip will send you to the dentist, doctor or possibly the morgue. I am aware of the argument that a false grip allows the lifter to apply more upward thrust, but such an advantage is not worth your health and safety, I assure you. Besides, I'm not convinced the false grip even increases the amount one can lift.

I've noticed those who employ the false grip have a habit of bridging once the bar hits the sticking point because they are not able to keep the bar from running forward. Without their thumbs around the bar they have no way to guide it backward into the proper groove. Having the thumbs around the bar is much safer, and safety should always be your prime consideration.

On the subject of safety, always, always, always use a spotter when doing benches. The spotter's job is to assist the lifter in taking the bar on and off the rack, and helping if the lifter gets stuck.

Once the Grip is Set

Let's move from the hands down to the feet. This part of benching – what the feet should be doing – is often over-looked. But bench pressing starts with the feet. All too often the lifter will merely lie down on a bench and allow his legs to dangle freely while he does the exercise. When the going gets tough his feet will move around, sometimes even leaving the floor.

Bracing your feet on the floor before lying back on the bench assures you a solid base throughout the exercise. Then, when the bar hits the sticking point – it always does, sooner or later – you can bring power up to the pressing muscles from that firm foundation. However, without that base, no source of power is available. The only way, then, to nudge the bar upward is by twisting or bridging – two major no-nos.

Instead of just lying back on the bench as you would

on a couch, push down into the bench until you become almost a part of it. Lock your buttocks and shoulder blades tightly to it. Following these steps, along with planting your feet firmly on the floor, will ensure you maintain a solid foundation throughout the lift.

Lifting and Lowering

Once your hands and feet are set, have the spotter hand you the bar. Some trainers prefer to take the weight off the rack themselves because this helps them feel more in control. Either way is fine. With locked wrists, lower the bar in a controlled manner to the lower end of your sternum (breastbone). Naturally, some variations exist in which the bar touches the chest, but don't let it touch down too low or high on the chest, as this will adversely affect the lift. Remember, you always want your wrists to stay directly above your elbows.

When the bar touches your chest, pause briefly. A half-second is enough and will keep you from the ugly habit of rebounding the bar off your chest. Rebounding may seem like a good idea early on because you will be able to use a bit more weight than when you include a pause before you lift. However, in the long run this bad habit will work against you. First of all, rebounding the bar causes you to neglect those muscles that initiate the start of the press from your chest. In other words, by pausing you will ultimately get stronger than you would if

Photo of Tito Raymond by Alex Ardenti

VARY YOUR BENCH GRIP

If you want to clearly outline your pecs, vary your routine by simply changing the grip you use on your bench press. Try two easy variations: wide grip and close grip. Wide-grip bench press means you hold the bar with as wide a grip as possible. You will notice you do not have the same range of motion as with your usual grip, and you cannot lift as much weight. The wide grip gives you a great stretch in your pectorals as you lift and lower the bar. This method hits the outer pecs, bringing high definition to the area. To do the narrow-grip bench press, lie on a bench with your elbows out to your sides. Grip the bar with hands about one to two hand widths apart. The movement will feel awkward at first, and you may have difficulty balancing the weight. Using a narrow grip will add mass to those inner pecs.

you bounce the weight off your chest, even though at the time this may not seem to be the case. Besides, excessive banging of the bar will eventually damage the pecs. I have found that if someone is disciplined enough to pause on his bench presses from the very beginning he will always pause, even when he starts handling big weights.

Once the barbell is in position on your chest, drive it upward in a forceful manner. Until you learn the proper groove, this upward thrust will be more deliberate than forceful. With practice and concentration you will be able to drive the bar off your chest in a perfectly straight line. Then the bar will glide slightly backward at the conclusion of the lift so it ends up above your chin or neck. However, the bar should not move any further back. It will travel in an arc, but only a slight one.

Throughout the exercise your elbows have to remain below your wrists. This, too, takes practice, but affords

you a great deal of control of the bar as well as ensuring the power source is always under the bar where it needs to be. Remember, if your elbows move ahead or behind the bar, you are diluting the upward thrust. Try to make every rep exactly as the one before. Over time you will establish a tight, hairline groove.

When to breathe while benching is an important consideration, and many trainers breathe improperly – primarily because they have been taught to breathe in and out during the execution of the exercise. If you're doing 12 or 15 reps with a light weight, how you breathe really doesn't matter. However, if you are doing heavy fives, threes or singles, your breathing matters very much. Inhaling or exhaling while the bar is in motion forces your ribcage to relax, thereby preventing you from maintaining a solid foundation. Here's the correct breathing procedure. Take the bar from the rack, lock your arms, set yourself and take a deep breath. Lower the bar to your chest, pause, drive the bar to lockout and exhale. Pause, take another breath and do the next rep. If you exhale too soon on a rep, it is going to be much more difficult to complete.

Only a few seconds at the most is required to do a rep in the bench press, so holding your breath isn't a big deal. And this may seem unimportant, but it's critical for handling heavy weights because holding your breathe ensures your diaphragm stays locked, creating positive intrathoracic pressure.

The bar should be lowered to your chest in a controlled manner, slower rather than faster. This control keeps the bar from crashing onto your chest and also helps you to place the bar in the exact same spot on every rep. Take a brief pause, then explode into the bar and follow through that strong drive to the lockout position. Go down slow, up fast. Think of the start as a boxing punch – short and powerful.

Concentrate on using perfect form, all the way from the light warmup sets to the heavy working sets. Once you have mastered the technique on the bench press the numbers will take care of themselves. Most importantly, your gains will be made safely.

Illustration by Mark Collins

CHAPTER 70

Barbell Curls

"No biceps exercise has such an extensive track record for bulking up even the scrawniest biceps as the good old barbell curl."

– Ron Harris, regular *MuscleMag International* contributor, on surefire ways to blast your biceps.

onsidered the bench press of curling, barbell curls allow you to curl the greatest amount of weight. Sadly, they are also the most abused biceps exercise in terms of form. Go into any gym and you'll see bodybuilders loading up bars and lobbing them to the midpoint by hip thrusting and then simply leaning back so the bar essentially falls toward their shoulders. Sure they're moving a lot of weight, but they're not building great biceps.

PROPER TECHNIQUE

To execute a strict barbell curl, stand up straight with your feet no further than shoulder-width apart. Begin with the bar a couple of inches from the bottom position. This will discourage any heaving or swinging to initiate the movement. Also, keep your elbows pressed firmly at your sides for the entire set. If your elbows move even remotely forward during a curl, your biceps will lose the tension and the stress will shift to the front shoulders. From here slowly curl the bar up until your biceps are fully contracted. Don't let the bar touch your chest at any time. Depending on your arm length, your biceps should reach full

contraction at about the point where the bar clears your nipples. Another suggestion is to pay attention to the feeling in your biceps. The cramping sensation you feel when you've completely contracted the muscle is what you should aim for with every rep. After contracting your biceps hard against the resistance for a full count, slowly lower the bar back down to the start position.

Don't worry if you can only lift half the weight you were normally swinging and cheating up. You could choose to spend the next 10 years lifting too much weight with poor form and getting nowhere with your biceps or be can be sensible and select a weight that exhausts your biceps within 8 to 12 strict reps. When you can no longer move the bar with proper form, the set is over.

Many bodybuilders prefer to use an EZ-curl bar for this exercise to protect their wrists. Either a straight bar or an EZ-curl bar is fine. Keep in mind, however, that the EZ-curl bar's shape impacts which head of the biceps is hit hardest. A close grip will target the outer head, while gripping the bars at the wider bend will work the inner head. Utilize both grips equally to ensure full development of the muscle.

TO CHEAT OR NOT

There's nothing wrong with adding a few cheat reps, but you must do so at the end of the set. And the key word there is "adding." If you start swinging right from the beginning of the set, you're only defeating the purpose of the exercise. To build great biceps you want them to do virtually all of the lifting until they start fatiguing toward the end of the set. It's then – and only then – that you add a little bit of body momentum to help the biceps complete a few additional reps. Now you are getting the full strict set, then are giving your biceps the stimulation of a few more reps even if they do not offer full stimulation.

Mark Dugdale performs strict reps.

Photo of Mark Dugdale by Robert Reiff

CHAPTER 71

The Deadlift

"Remember, deadlifts take a lot more out of you than leg extensions. Make sure you get lots of rest and make sure you eat for mass."

– Rahim Kassam, strength-training columnist for *MuscleMag International*

Ever wandered over to a fully loaded bar, checked to make sure no one was watching, and then tried to lift it? Sure you have. Most bodybuilders just can't resist having a go. Have you ever tried to lift a bar and find yourself unable to make it clear the ground even a quarter-inch?

Few gym scenes are more impressive than a 250-pounder grabbing a barbell loaded with a quarter-ton or more of weight and lift it from the floor in one continuous motion. Serious deadlifting ranks right up there with squatting for separating the men from the boys. Traps strain; delts swell to bursting; bis, tris and forearms struggle; quads scream out in pain; and knuckles turn white in the attempt to defy gravity.

Deadlifts are one of those exercises that stimulate just about every muscle in the human body. They'll pack meat on your upper back as well as any rowing exercise, and build you a set of python-like spinal erectors. And they are about the only exercise other than squats that will build you a thunder-

> **I'LL BE BAAACK!**

MCC

ARNOLD'S FAVE: THE DEADLIFT

You're always wise to wear a weight belt when doing any heavy barbell work. While the exercise might be referred to in full as the stiff-leg deadlift, do not straighten your legs completely. Straight-leg exercises will destroy your lower back in a heartbeat.

Stand on a bench or a chair with a loaded barbell within reach. Slowly bend forward and feel the stretch deep in your hamstrings. Keep your back straight and resist the temptation to round your spine. Lift the bar, exploding from the hams. Don't bob or jerk. If you can't get your rep out cleanly, use less weight. For a serious increase in muscular strength keep the reps in the 5-to-7 range for 3 sets.

Photo of Michael Ferrer by Mark Collins / Illustration by Paul Buceta

ous set of thighs. In fact it's likely the aspects of deadlifts that are similar to squats that keep many bodybuilders from adding them to their arsenal of exercises – this exercise is tough. And like squats, deadlifts must be performed with flawless technique.

WANT TO TEST YOUR DEADLIFTING POWER?

Before trying to hoist some serious iron off the floor there are a few pointers you need to follow. First, always warm up thoroughly. Safe deadlifting requires a strong back, and warm back muscles are stronger and more capable of effort than cold ones. Begin with a few minutes of cardio followed by lots of stretching, back bending and toe touching. Once the lower back is warm and loose, move on to 3 sets of light back extensions, free squats and dumbell shrugs. These exercises are great for warming up the three primary muscles stressed by deadlifts – the lower back, quads and traps. Finally, do at least 3 sets of strict, non-bouncing barbell deadlifts working your way up to a weight that enables you to do 3 comfortable reps. I should add that you shouldn't attempt heavy deadlifts if you have a history of back injuries or have not lifted before.

HOW TO DO DEADLIFTS

Although a few prefer to deadlift with both hands in either an overhand or underhand position, by far the best way to lift really heavy is with the one-over/one-under (knuckles up and knuckles down) grip. The bar is more secure with this grip.

Once you've warmed up thoroughly, add two 20-pound disks to the weight you could manage to lift for 3 reps, squat down, take your grip (without straps), take three deep breaths, flatten your back and slowly lift the

bar off the floor by straightening your legs. In a manner of speaking a deadlift is just a squat with the bar held by the hands and not across the shoulders. Make sure you don't ever lower the bar too quickly and bounce the weight. If you do you will jar your lower back. Settle the bar and release both your grip and your back muscles slowly. If you experience any pain whatsoever, discontinue.

Deadlifts work the entire body – from traps and spinal erectors to forearms and hamstrings.

Photo of David Hoffman (left) and Brian Yersky (right) by Robert Reiff

CHAPTER 72

Dips

"Struggling to pack size onto your arms? Simply start dipping – with weights. Once you can dip with 50 to 100 pounds, you should have created a couple of bazookas."

– Terrance Abbott, *MuscleMag International* contributor

There was a time in the not-so-distant past when just about everyone who trained with weights – bodybuilders, competitive weightlifters and strength athletes – did some form of dips. Some did them with bodyweight only, while others made them a strength event and piled on lots of weight. For recreational bodybuilders and those interested in general fitness, freehand dips are sufficient. But if you want to add size and strength to your upper body, you have to add weight.

Although you can fix a dumbell between your legs to do weighted dips, at some point this method becomes awkward and troublesome. At this point a dip belt comes in handy. This is a simple apparatus – little more than a leather lifting belt with a chain and hook. You loop the chain through the hole in the center of a plate and secure it to the belt with a hook. Dip belts are readily available, not expensive and an absolute necessity if you are serious about doing dips with big weights.

Before you start adding weight, do freehand dips. This is advisable for anyone, regardless of his strength level. The weighted dip is a core exercise that you need to approach like any other primary movement. You have to build a solid base before climbing to a higher level. The rule is to hold off on adding resistance until you are able to do 4 sets of at least 20 reps with bodyweight only.

HOW TO DO DIPS

Most people find the dip to be a natural movement and do the exercise correctly from the very beginning. Start the exercise by grabbing the two bars (either parallel or V-shaped) with your palms facing inward and arms locked out straight. Slowly lower your torso between the bars by bending the elbows. Lower to a comfortable stretch (for most the nipple region of the chest will be in line with the bars), and then return to the starting position by locking the arms out straight.

Like most weight-training exercises, the fuller the range of motion the better, so the lower you stretch, the more muscle groups become involved. But bodybuilders who experience shoulder and elbow pain when they dip should try experimenting with different dipping depths and stopping just short of the range that gives you pain.

Dips done vertically, with elbows in, work triceps. Dips done leaning forward, with elbows out, work chest.

Photo of Peter Putnam by Robert Reiff

Bench dips are another common variation to hit the triceps and pack on mass.

Illustration by Mark Collins
Photo (Top) of Craig Richardson by Jason Breeze

If there's pain before or just as you bend at the elbows then you should avoid the exercise.

DIP VARIATIONS

There are a number of different variations of the dip. The late Vince Gironda, the Iron Guru, was the champion of wide-grip dips for enhancing pec development. I have always believed they help enhance the lower pec line.

Wide-grip dips do work, but be careful when you do them for the first time. Move your grip out cautiously. Let your elbows flare out wide and lean your torso forward slightly. Wide-grip dips place much more stress on the lower and outer chest.

TRICEPS

Many bodybuilders like to do dips for the triceps. so they use a narrower grip and keep the torso vertical. They also keep their elbows close to their sides. This position takes much of your chest out of play, so you will use less weight. You'll probably discover that your bodyweight is sufficient, unlike with wide grips, where the involvement of the chest will probably necessitate adding weight to the exercise.

Whether you have limited facilities and can do only bodyweight dips or are able to take advantage of a nicely equipped gym, add dips to your routine. They've long been standard procedure for building Herculean shoulders, horseshoe triceps and well-defined pecs.

WIDE-GRIP DIPS

Vince Gironda had a unique way of executing parallel bar dips that built his side pecs, enhancing his V-shape. To do this version, your hands should be at least 31 inches apart. Throughout the dipping motion it is important to keep your feet forward, chin on chest, and elbows out to the sides of the body. (This is a completely different movement than regular triceps dips that are done with elbows close to the body, feet tucked under the torso, and head up.) Stretch down as far as you can, and rise. The effect will be felt in the pectorals after a few sets.

CHAPTER 73

Chin-Ups

"This one is simplicity itself. Find a bar and chin is what you do, and thicker, wider lats are what you get."

– Greg Zulak, *MuscleMag International* contributor, discussing the most effective exercises.

Remember those physical fitness tests you performed in junior high and high school? Each student performed as many chin-ups as possible and was then ranked according to national scores. Arguments have raged over whether these tests were a good idea, but regardless, why did we stop doing chin-ups? Whether or not machines are the reason, the decline of chin-ups seemed to coincide directly with the increasing popularity of pulldown machines. Some people call the lat pulldown the lazy man's chin-up.

Chin-ups are the best back-widening exercise. In fact the top bodybuilders of all levels make them the mainstay of their back routines. They are an important part of building that great V-shape. When doing the movement, concentrate on pulling with the large back muscles (latissimus dorsi) and not the biceps and forearms. And don't drop back to the starting position in such a manner that you practically yank your arms out of the shoulder sockets. Do the exercise nice and slow.

Chinning is tough – but the effort is worth it.

Chins primarily work the large latissimus dorsi muscles (lats). They also stress the smaller back muscles such as the teres major. Finally, the rear delts and biceps are brought into play. You will find that by pulling to the front, the lower parts of the lats are worked the most. Conversely, pulling behind the head stresses the upper section. Keep in mind that these divisions are not carved in stone, and at the beginning level, it is adequate to do either one. If you have the strength, you might alternate the two on the same day or alternate days. Also keep in mind that behind the head chin-ups can put extra stress on the rotator cuff complex.

HOW TO DO CHIN-UPS

You will need access to an overhead bar to perform this exercise. Most Universal multi-stations have one attached, but a wall-mounted version is just as good. Jump up and grab the bar with a grip about twice your shoulder width. Now pull yourself up and try to touch the bar with your chest. Lower back to the starting position in a controlled manner. If you find the wide-grip version too difficult, try taking a shoulder-width reverse grip (i.e. your palms are facing you). If even this version is too difficult, most gyms have an assisted chin-up machine that will help you. You simply stand or kneel on a pad and add weight to the assisting stack. Unlike other machines, with this one your goal is to use less and less weight until you can lift your bodyweight.

Besides wide- and reverse-grip chins you can hook numerous attachments onto the bar for variety. The double-D, often used for seated rows, is a popular attachment.

While you don't have to do chins in your back workout, personally I think you'll be missing out if you don't. The chin is a core exercise that just can't be duplicated by machines. Together with rows they'll build you a back that will impress judges and fellow competitors alike.

Photo of Joel Stubbs by Robert Reiff

Photo of Mike Ergas by Robert Reiff

THE M.A.S.S. SYSTEM OF TRAINING

CHAPTER 74

The M.A.S.S. System of Training – Phase I

"Basic, compound free-weight exercises are the toughest to perform, but they are by far the most effective at stimulating muscle growth."

– Ron Harris, regular *MuscleMag International* contributor

Y ou can consider Phase I of the *MuscleMag* Anabolic Size & Strength (M.A.S.S.) system your ticket to putting on a solid 15 to 20 pounds of muscle over a period of three months. The program consists of three phases, each based on basic free-weight and machine exercises, which are combined in the most effective manner to maximize your size and strength gains. You'll be training with heavy weights and making changes to your reps and exercises over the course of the three-month period to add variety and continue muscle growth. If you follow the workouts closely you'll make strength and size gains that you previously thought impossible. Make sure to put aside a little extra money, because you'll need to invest in a new wardrobe as your body expands and fills out over the next few months.

Phase-One Highlights
For the first five weeks of the M.A.S.S. program the focus is primarily on building muscle size (hypertrophy) using basic compound exercises, performed in the optimal sets-and-reps ranges to stimulate solid muscle growth.

TRAINING SPLITS
You'll start by doing three different workouts that cover all the major muscle groups, training on a three-days-on/two-days-off schedule, repeating that cycle

Photo of Will Harris by Robert Reiff

MuscleMag's Anabolic Size & Strength program consists of three phases that will help you put on 15 to 20 pounds of muscle over a three-month period.

for the entire phase. This means every sixth day you'll be repeating a workout, which provides enough muscle recovery time without too much off time between sessions. If your schedule prevents you from working out on consecutive days, you'll have the option of moving workouts and rest days around, as long as you train three out of every five days and then repeat the cycle.

The three workouts are Push (pushing muscles include the chest, delts and triceps), Pull (back, biceps and abs) and Legs (glutes, quads, hamstrings and calves). You can do the three workouts in any order (I describe Pull followed by Push and then Legs), but some individuals like to precede their leg training with a rest day, so feel free to make whatever adjustments you like. Just be sure to meet the three-days-out-of-five requirement.

To generate the maximal amount of hormonal response and to overload the working muscles in the most effective manner, you'll be doing 3 working sets of each movement over the course of this five-week program. Note that this doesn't include warmup sets. You may include as many warmup sets as you need, especially toward the beginning of your workout when your muscles, ligaments and tendons are less pliable. The appropriate number of warmup sets typically depends on your age, experience and working weight, but always make sure to use a controlled speed and perfect technique. The total number of working sets amounts to about 9 for larger muscle groups (remember, you're training up to three muscle groups in a single workout during Phase I, so increasing the volume will adversely affect your strength toward the end of your workout) and 6 for smaller ones. Calves and abs are worked with just one exercise each at the end of your workout.

EXERCISE SELECTION

I've selected the M.A.S.S. exercises with one purpose in mind: to stimulate as much muscle gain as possible. To do this, M.A.S.S. recommends that a majority of the movements consist of compound, or multijoint, exercises. These include the squat, leg press, row and pressing movements for both chest and shoulders. These exercises engage the greatest number of muscle fibers because more than one joint is being activated. For example, the bench press involves movement at both the elbow and shoulder joint. It therefore recruits the triceps and shoulders into the action as well as the chest.

Compound movements call on several muscles at once, so you'll be able to lift significantly more weight. Because of this, compound exercises stimulate better overall mass development than isolation (also called single-joint) exercises. Another benefit follows from including movements that tax the body more heavily: they promote a higher anabolic hormonal response, flooding your system in a natural way with the very hormones most responsible for muscle building. While I included some single-joint movements in this program, their role is limited to working smaller muscle groups (such as the arms) or to help work the target muscle from a slightly different angle than the main compound move.

Exercise order is crucial: You want to use compound exercises earlier in your workout when your strength levels are highest. Unless your goal is to pre-exhaust a particular muscle group that has plateaued, starting a workout with an isolation movement (such as leg extensions) will limit your ability to lift heavier weights with compound movements (such as squats).

Perform all moves with textbook form through a full range of motion, from a completely stretched position to a peak-contracted position, using a smooth and controlled rep speed.

REPS & WEIGHT

When considering how much weight to use for a given exercise, look first at your target rep number. During the first week, that target is 8 reps. This means (after your warmup sets) you choose a weight with which you can complete just 8 reps with good form – that is, you can't do a 9th rep. So the muscle will reach positive failure by the 8th rep. It might also mean that you have to experiment with the poundage until you find the right resistance. Unless you've got a memory like one of the kids at the

M.A.S.S. SYSTEM : PHASE 1 FIVE-WEEK TRAINING CYCLE

	MONDAY	TUESDAY	WEDNESDAY	THURSDAY	FRIDAY	SATURDAY	SUNDAY
WEEK 1	Pull #1	Push #1	Legs #1	Rest	Rest	Pull #2	Push #2
WEEK 2	Legs #2	Rest	Rest	Pull #3	Push #3	Legs #3	Rest
WEEK 3	Rest	Pull #4	Push #4	Legs #4	Rest	Rest	Pull #5
WEEK 4	Push #5	Legs #5	Rest	Rest	Pull #6	Push #6	Legs #6
WEEK 5	Rest	Rest	Pull #7	Push #7	Legs #7	Rest	Rest

This three-days-on/two-days-off configuration starts with pulling movements (back, biceps, abs), followed by pushing exercises (chest, shoulders, triceps) and finishes with legs (quads, glutes, hamstrings, calves). Though I chose to start with Pull, you can rearrange your workout schedule depending on your own timetable and needs, as long as you continue to train each group every sixth day and take two days off for optimal recovery.

Phase I of the M.A.S.S. program consists of three workouts: Push, Pull and Legs, which are done in a three-days-out-of-five format.

Photo of Will Harris by Robert Reiff

PULL WORKOUT

EXERCISE	WORKOUT 1 SETS	WORKOUT 1 REPS	WORKOUT 2–3 SETS	WORKOUT 2–3 REPS	WORKOUT 4 SETS	WORKOUT 4 REPS	WORKOUT 5–6 SETS	WORKOUT 5–6 REPS	WORKOUT 7 SETS	WORKOUT 7 REPS
Bent-over barbell rows	3	8	3	9	3	10	3	11	3	12
One-arm dumbell rows	3	8	3	9	3	10	3	11	3	12
Front lat pulldowns	3	8	3	9	3	10	3	11	3	12
Standing barbell curls	3	8	3	9	3	10	3	11	3	12
Alternating dumbell curls	3	8	3	9	3	10	3	11	3	12
Machine crunches	4	8	4	9	4	10	4	11	4	12

The Pull workout involves dumbell, barbell and machine moves.

PUSH WORKOUT

EXERCISE	WORKOUT 1 SETS	WORKOUT 1 REPS	WORKOUT 2–3 SETS	WORKOUT 2–3 REPS	WORKOUT 4 SETS	WORKOUT 4 REPS	WORKOUT 5–6 SETS	WORKOUT 5–6 REPS	WORKOUT 7 SETS	WORKOUT 7 REPS
Bench presses	3	8	3	9	3	10	3	11	3	12
Incline dumbell presses	3	8	3	9	3	10	3	11	3	12
Dips	3	8	3	9	3	10	3	11	3	12
Barbell overhead presses	3	8	3	9	3	10	3	11	3	12
EZ-bar upright rows	3	8	3	9	3	10	3	11	3	12
Dumbell lateral raises	3	8	3	9	3	10	3	11	3	12
Skullcrushers	3	8	3	9	3	10	3	11	3	12
Dumbell extensions	3	8	3	9	3	10	3	11	3	12

The Push workout focuses on your chest, delts and triceps.

Photos of Will Harris by Robert Reiff

LEG WORKOUT

EXERCISE	WORKOUT 1		WORKOUT 2–3		WORKOUT 4		WORKOUT 5–6		WORKOUT 7	
	SETS	REPS	SETS	REPS	SETS	REPS	SETS	REPS	SETS	REPS
Squats	3	8	3	9	3	10	3	11	3	12
Leg presses	3	8	3	9	3	10	3	11	3	12
Leg extensions	3	8	3	9	3	10	3	11	3	12
Stiff-leg deadlifts	3	8	3	9	3	10	3	11	3	12
Lying leg curls	3	8	3	9	3	10	3	11	3	12
Standing calf raises	3	8	3	9	3	10	3	11	3	12

Some people prefer to train their legs after a rest day – you can adjust the order of the cycle to whatever works best for you.

national spelling bee, jot down those weights, because you're going to be using the exact same poundage on each set for every workout during Phase I.

Rest just long enough for your working muscles to recover, and strive to hit the same target rep for each of the additional sets. Don't employ high-intensity techniques (such as forced reps or drop sets), which can adversely affect your strength on succeeding sets; just do straight sets, using the same weight for the same target rep.

The goal here is to be able to complete an additional rep for the same exercise in all 3 sets the next time you do this workout. That is, if you did 8 reps today, in six days you'll be reaching for 9. Progressive overload occurs when you increase either your working weight or the number of reps you perform. During the first phase, we're trying to add a single rep on all three sets with each successive workout for that bodypart. But don't increase the weight as you get stronger. Because you may not always be able to achieve this goal with every workout, we're giving you seven workouts to increase your reps by 4. So by the end of the five weeks (seven workouts for each bodypart), you'll be doing 12 reps with the same weight, not 8. And at the end of the five weeks, you'll also have a new, higher working weight with which you can do just 8 reps when you start the next M.A.S.S. phase.

The repetition range you're working through (starting at 8, finishing at 12) is generally considered the best for achieving maximum muscular development and the consequent hormonal response. On the other hand, completing a relatively low number of reps (fewer than 6) generates greater strength (but not muscle growth).

GETTING WARMED UP

Precede each workout with a 5- to 10-minute cardio warmup, which can be done on a stationary bicycle or similar piece of cardio equipment at low-to-medium intensity. This will help to get your muscles and connective tissues warm and to elevate your core temperature, preparing you for vigorous weight training.

Unless you have particularly tight muscles, do stretching moves after your workout, not before. If you do need to stretch before training, do it after your warmup. Stretching a cold, inelastic muscle is far less effective and more dangerous. Finally, don't forget to start your workout with warmup sets of the actual exercise you'll be performing. This will help with both mental and physical rehearsal of the move before you tackle the heavy weights. While warming up may seem to be a waste, you'll actually be able to lift heavier poundage – meaning your muscles will be working harder and therefore growing more afterward – if you have properly warmed up. Besides, part of successful weight training is having the proper neuropathways, and a warmup set helps to set those pathways.

OVERTRAINING & REST

To reduce the possibility of overtraining – a state in which muscle growth can actually reverse itself – don't do more work than is prescribed here, and don't attempt to train more frequently. Each muscle group needs time to recover and will grow stronger over time, assuming you are following proper nutrition and getting enough sleep. Muscle growth, as you may recall, occurs not in the gym but rather when the muscles are rebuilding themselves after a hard workout. If you like to party all night or do too many other physical activities, you won't be making the gains you might otherwise be. Train hard, eat well and get plenty of rest. Intense weight training with an emphasis on basic movements is one of the most incredible stresses you can inflict on your body. Depriving it of adequate rest, sleep and nutrition will not only diminish your potential gains but also predispose you to injury and illness (by weakening your immune system). In that sense, too much enthusiasm and energy can have a reverse effect on your body.

Ultimately, combining the right mass-building workouts with a weight-gain nutrition program and getting plenty of rest will help your physique explode with new growth. Here's all the info you need to get started. You've got to supply the sweat.

Photos of Will Harris by Robert Reiff

CHAPTER 75

The M.A.S.S. System of Training — Phase II

"If you think cycle training is a principle used only by weightlifters obsessed with complicated formulas like percentage of maximums for various lifts and exercises, think again. Cycling is a very important principle for bodybuilders too."

– Greg Zulak, *MuscleMag International* contributor

Welcome to the second phase of the M.A.S.S. system. Here you'll build on the progressive workouts from the previous chapter. Phase II of the *MuscleMag* Anabolic Size & Strength system is not for beginners; it's a challenging multi-day training system that works every bodypart with greater volume and intensity and then gives you time off for your muscles to recover. Whereas Phase I focused on increasing the number of reps you could complete over the five-week course with a given weight, this four-week companion makes a number of significant changes to promote further gains in strength and size:

• You'll go from a three-day to a four-day split, meaning you'll work each muscle group with more exercises and volume.
• You'll do completely different moves in a different order to work each bodypart from a variety of angles, promoting optimal muscular development.
• You'll stack on the plates and train in fairly low rep ranges (early in your workout when your energy levels are highest), a method proven to build strength, and eventually size. You'll also extend your rest periods between sets for better recovery.

• On the last exercise for each bodypart, you'll up the intensity by adding an advanced technique such as drop sets or partial reps, pushing your body to its limit and delivering a monster muscle pump.

TRAINING SPLITS

You'll follow a four-day split, doing back, hamstrings and calves on day 1; shoulders, triceps and abs on day 2; quads, glutes and calves on day 3; and chest, biceps and abs on day 4. Depending on your personal recovery needs, you can follow each workout with one to two rest days. Be careful about moving your training days around; the split presented here ensures you won't overtrain a particular muscle group. The hams, which get worked to some

4-DAY SPLIT

DAY	MUSCLE GROUPS WORKED
1	Back, Hamstrings, Calves
2	Shoulders, Triceps, Abs
3	Quads/Glutes, Calves
4	Chest, Biceps, Abs
5	Rest Day
6	REPEAT CYCLE

degree on quad/glutes day, will get at least 48 hours' rest after you train them with shoulders, and the same goes for triceps, chest and shoulders. Your back and biceps will get plenty of rest between their workouts as well.

EXERCISE SELECTION

Once again you'll start with compound exercises, but you'll use different exercises from new angles to ensure you work each muscle a bit differently than you did in Phase I. For example, you started with flat bench presses for chest last month. Now you'll do your inclines first to hit your upper-pec fibers when your energy levels are highest.

REPS & WEIGHT

With Phase I you started the program with a weight that allowed you to do only 8 reps with good form, and your goal was to increase your number of reps (rather than weight) over the five-week period. This time, after your warmup sets, you'll be going heavier, challenging the target muscles with weights that allow you to complete only 6 reps. The focus here will be to increase overall strength. This applies to the first two working sets of your first two compound exercises for each major muscle group. You'll slightly decrease the weight for higher reps on compound

M.A.S.S. Phase II involves moving to a four-day split where you'll work each muscle group with more exercises and volume.

Photos of Mike Ergas by Robert Reiff

DAY 1

TARGET MUSCLES: Back, Hamstrings, Calves

EXERCISE	SETS	REPS
Wide-grip chin-ups		40
T-bar rows	4	10, 6, 6, 6, 10
Seated cable rows	3	6, 6, 10
Neutral-grip pulldowns	3	8, 8, 8
Romanian deadlifts	4	10, 6, 6, 10
Single-leg curls	4	10, 6, 6, 10
Donkey calf raises	4	15, 15, 15, 15

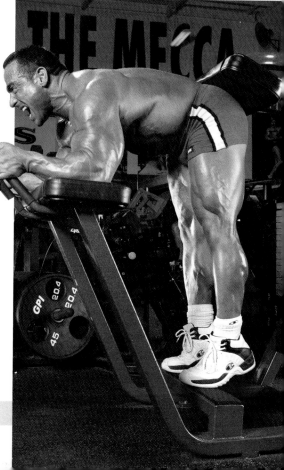

DAY 2

TARGET MUSCLES: Shoulders, Triceps, Abs

EXERCISE	SETS	REPS
Dumbell overhead presses	5	12, 10, 6, 6, 10
Bent-over lateral raises	3	10, 10, 10
Front cable raises with rope	3	10, 10, 10
Leaning dumbell lateral raises	3	10, 10, 10
Dumbell shrugs	4	12, 6, 6, 10
Close-grip bench presses	4	12, 6, 6, 10
Triceps dip machine	3	6, 6, 10
Cable kickbacks	3	10, 10, 10
Weighted incline crunches	4	15, 15, 15, 15
Crunches		

Photos of Mike Egan by Robert Reiff

During Phase II you'll be going heavier in order to challenge the target muscles with a focus to increase overall strength.

DAY 3

TARGET MUSCLES: Quads/Glutes, Calves		
EXERCISE	SETS	REPS
Hack squats	5	12, 10, 6, 6, 10
Smith-machine squats	3	10, 10, 10
Walking lunges	3	10, 10, 10
Single-leg extensions	3	10, 10, 10
Donkey calf raises	4	12, 6, 6, 10

You're aiming to reach muscle failure on each set by the target rep, so using the correct weight is critical.

DAY 4

TARGET MUSCLES: Chest, Biceps, Abs

EXERCISE	SETS	REPS
Incline dumbell presses	5	12, 10, 6, 6, 10
Smith-machine decline presses	4	10, 6, 6, 10
Machine bench presses	3	8, 8, 8
Pec-deck flyes	3	10, 10, 10
EZ-bar preacher curls	4	10, 6, 6, 10
Two-arm upper cable curls	3	10, 10, 10
Standing one-arm cable curls	3	6, 6, 10
Weighted incline crunches	4	15, 15, 15, 15
Crunches		

Photos of Mike Ergas by Robert Reiff

exercises that come later in your workout and for isolation (single-joint exercises) such as leg extensions, pec-deck flyes and straight-arm raises.

Choosing the correct weight is critical, and your goal is to reach muscle failure on each set by the target rep. Keep a log so you can remember your weights and reps next time around. That way you won't waste valuable energy on sets that are either too heavy or too light to produce the effect you desire. Also, if you can complete more than the listed number of reps (say, you've become stronger between workouts, which happens), don't do extra reps. Instead, add more weight so you'll still be training within the target rep range.

THE LAST SET

Finally, on the last set for each bodypart, I want you to employ one of the advanced training techniques I discussed earlier in the book. The idea is to work the muscle well past the point of failure by doing drop sets, partial reps, cheat reps or any other advanced training principle that super-fatigues the muscle group. If you still have energy after you've completed these workouts, you simply didn't train at a high enough intensity level.

POINTS TO CONSIDER:

- Your first set of many exercises (listed by higher reps) is a warmup set, but do as many warmup sets as you need before tackling the heavy weights.
- After your warmup sets, choose a weight that allows you to reach muscle failure by the listed rep number.
- On the wide-grip chin-ups, do as many sets as it takes for you to complete 40 total reps with good form.
- On your heavy sets (all sets for which you're doing just 6 reps), take an extra 45-second rest between sets to ensure full recovery.
- After your heavy sets do a back-off set in which you choose a slightly lighter weight to further pump the muscle for a few extra reps (where indicated).
- On your last set(s) of certain exercises for each major muscle group, you'll use an advanced tech-

nique to increase the intensity of your workout.
- For the Smith-machine squat, do 2 sets with your feet underneath your torso and 2 sets with your feet about 18 inches in front of you (after your warmup set).

- Unlike the stiff-leg deadlift, where your knees are slightly bent, during the Romanian deadlift your knees are straight. You slide the bar down your legs, pushing your hips back farther than in the stiff-leg version. Use this when you want to target the glutes and hamstrings without placing added stress on your lower back. Given that you'll be sliding the bar along your lower legs, you might want to wear some sort of protection such as wraps or track pants. **Execution:** Stand upright with your feet about shoulder-width apart and grab the barbell with an overhand grip. Slowly lower the bar by pushing your hips back and centering your weight over your heels, always keeping the bar in contact with your legs. Lower the bar until it touches just below your knees and you feel a good stretch in your hamstrings. Return to the starting position by contracting your hamstrings and glutes, forcing the weight of your body down through your heels as you push your hips forward. Always keep your legs completely locked and maintain the natural curve in your lower back throughout the movement.

Photo of Mike Ergas by Robert Reiff

During Phase II moving your training days around isn't as simple because the split is designed to ensure you won't overtrain a specific muscle group.

CHAPTER 76

The M.A.S.S. System of Training — Phase III

"Rest-pause training was popularized through the writings of the late Mike Mentzer in the 1980s, and more recently has gained converts through the followers of DC (DoggCrapp) Training."

– Ron Harris, regular *MuscleMag International* contributor

If you've been diligently following the M.A.S.S. program, you've no doubt added pounds of new muscle tissue to your physique and have seen your motivation level go through the roof. Great! You're right on track. But you're not done yet.

TRAINING SPLITS

During the five weeks of Phase III you'll follow a five-day split. You'll never do more than one major bodypart in a given workout (though you will train both biceps and triceps together, and you'll add either calves or abs after each larger muscle group). This split will allow for maximal recuperation because the intensity and volume are so demanding.

You'll use some new exercises in this workout, but you'll always start with the best mass-builders (called compound movements), and you'll hit each muscle group from a number of angles.

Because you'll be pushing yourself beyond levels that you're probably accustomed to, barbells and machines are better for you to use than dumbells, which can become harder to control toward the end of a workout.

Earlier in your workout, while you're still fresh, you'll start with moves for which you'll use relatively heavier weights, progressing to lighter-weight exercises as you fatigue.

REST INTERVALS

You'll take slightly longer rest periods after you complete each five-segment set. Rest two minutes for smaller muscle groups and up to three with larger ones.

DECREASED EXERCISES – INCREASED INTENSITY

You'll finish off many workouts for larger muscle groups with a single-joint exercise for straight sets. The overall workload might look meager – the leg day includes only five exercises, for example. But the total volume is high because each set consists of 15 to 25 total reps done at a very high intensity. You'll do abs and calves in regular sets after you train the larger bodyparts. Most of the exercises will not require a spotter, but it may be a good idea to have one for certain moves such as the Smith-machine squat and bench press.

TO THE NEXT LEVEL WITH REST-PAUSE

At the heart of Phase III of the M.A.S.S. system is an advanced training principle that's both highly intense and highly regarded for its mass-building qualities. The principle is called rest-pause, and just about every top bodybuilder today uses it to some degree in his training.

Rest-pause is a method of training in which you do one rep of a heavy weight – think around 80 percent of your one-rep max, place the weight down, wait for 10 to 20 seconds and then do it again. One set of rest-pause might be 6 or 8 reps, but remember this is a weight you normally might only get 2 or 3 reps with, so you've vastly increased the work you would normally do.

Do 2 or 3 such sets for each exercise, hitting the working muscles from a couple of different angles, and you're system will be flooded with powerful muscle-building anabolic hormones. This method is simple, but it's downright brutal and hugely growth inspiring.

Some trainers use different variations of the rest-pause method, including relative weight used, the number of reps you do, the amount of time you spend resting

Photo of Quincy Taylor by Robert Reiff

M.A.S.S. PHASE III SPLIT	
DAY	MUSCLE GROUPS WORKED
1*	Chest, Abs
2	Back, Calves
3	Shoulders, Upper Traps, Abs
4	Quads/Glutes, Hamstrings
5	Rest Day
6	Rest Day
7	REPEAT CYCLE

*Try swapping the order of these muscle groups on a regular basis.

By Phase III you should be seeing noticeable changes to your physique in the form of added pounds of new muscle tissue.

DAY 1

TARGET MUSCLES: Chest, Abs

EXERCISE	SETS	REPS
Bench presses	2	1+1+1+1+1
Smith-machine incline presses	2	4+4+4+4+4
Decline machine presses	2	5+5+5+5+5
Pec-deck flyes	3	15, 15, 15
Cable crunches	4	15, 15, 15, 15
Floor crunches	3	20, 20, 20

DAY 2

TARGET MUSCLES: Back, Calves

EXERCISE	SETS	REPS
Bent-over barbell rows	2	1+1+1+1+1
Wide-grip front pulldowns	2	4+4+4+4+4
Seated cable rows	2	5+5+5+5+5
Straight-arm pulldowns	3	12, 12, 12
Donkey calf raises	4	15, 15, 15, 15
Seated calf raises	3	15, 15, 15

Rest intervals are slightly longer in Phase III – two minutes for smaller muscle groups and up to three for larger groups.

Photos of Quincy Taylor by Robert Reiff

DAY 3

TARGET MUSCLES: Shoulders, Upper Traps, Abs

EXERCISE	SETS	REPS
Seated barbell overhead presses	2	1+1+1+1+1
Barbell upright rows	2	4+4+4+4+4
Machine lateral raises	2	5+5+5+5+5
Reverse pec-deck flyes	3	12, 12, 12
Dumbell shrugs	2	4+4+4+4+4
Cable crunches	4	15, 15, 15
Floor crunches	3	20, 20, 20

Phase III involves working one major bodypart in each workout and includes either abs or calves after each larger muscle group.

Photo of Quincy Taylor by Robert Reiff

DAY 4

TARGET MUSCLES: Quads/Glutes, Hamstrings

EXERCISE	SETS	REPS
Smith-machine squats	2	1+1+1+1+1
Leg presses	2	4+4+4+4+4
Leg extensions	2	5+5+5+5+5
Smith-machine romanian deadlifts	2	1+1+1+1+1
Lying leg curls	3	5+5+5+5+5

DAY 5

TARGET MUSCLES: Biceps, Triceps, Calves

EXERCISE	SETS	REPS
Standing barbell curls	2	1+1+1+1+1
Incline dumbell curls	2	4+4+4+4+4
Machine preacher curls	2	5+5+5+5+5
Close-grip bench presses	2	3+3+3+3+3
Triceps dip machine	2	4+4+4+4+4
Pressdowns	2	5+5+5+5+5
Donkey calf raises	4	15, 15, 15, 15
Seated calf raises	3	15, 15, 15

between segments, the number of segments that constitute a single set, the number of sets you complete for a single move, and the number of exercises you do for a given bodypart. But most bodybuilders do one rep then rest, and the rest period is under 20 seconds. Too much rest and you are no longer doing rest-pauses, but rather one-rep sets.

Given that bodybuilding is not an exact science and your personal characteristics (such as training level, age, recuperative abilities, etc.) must be taken into account, your routine will likely need some adjusting. Still, start with the program as presented here, follow a solid mass-gaining nutrition plan, get plenty of rest when you're not in the gym, and give the program five good weeks before passing judgment. The science may be inexact, but the results are anything but.

M.A.S.S. PHASE III WORKOUT

After your warmup sets for each muscle group, choose a fairly heavy weight for your first exercise. The weight you select should barely allow you to complete 3 reps, but do only 1. Rack the weight and rest for 10 to 20 seconds. Repeat this process a total of five times to make 1 extended set. Rest for two to three minutes before repeating the entire cycle. (Rest periods should be closer to two minutes for smaller muscle groups such as arms, and three minutes for larger muscle groups such as legs, chest and back.)

On your second exercise for the same bodypart, choose a lighter weight – one with which you can complete just 7 reps with good form, but do only 4. Rack the weight and rest for 20 seconds. Then immediately continue the set, repeating this process a total of five times. After a two-to-three-minute break, do a second set in similar fashion, again resting for two to three minutes afterward.

On your third exercise for each bodypart, choose a weight with which you can complete only 9 reps with good form, but do only 5. Rack it and rest 20 seconds, continuing this process a total of five times. After a two-to-three-minute rest, repeat for another set.

Keep your rest periods for all sets in which you're not using rest-pause to between 60 and 90 seconds.

Photo of Quincy Taylor by Robert Reiff

A solid nutrition program and ample rest are just as important as the actual workouts in the M.A.S.S. program.

Photo of the Priest and Rusty Jeffers by Robert Kennedy

TRAINING WITH THE SUPERSTARS

CHAPTER 77

Back Training

"A man's back is a statement of sorts. A narrow back suggests frailty. A wide one exudes power. Even the term 'a strong backbone' stems from the fact that the back is the source of all upper-body power. Bulging biceps and a big chest are less impressive without it."

– Nelson Montana, longtime bodybuilding writer, commenting on how a large, powerful back symbolizes porwerful masculinity.

W hen properly developed, the muscles of the upper and outer back give bodybuilders their classic V-shape. Great back shape and size creates the illusion of a small waist and enhances the overall look of the upper body. Current bodybuilders famous for their backs include Ronnie Coleman, Dexter Jackson, Gustavo Badell and Jay Cutler. Previous-generation bodybuilders who dominated back poses include Arnold Schwarzenegger, Sergio Oliva, Franco Columbu, Roy Callander, Lee Haney and Dorian Yates.

"The truth is, as the upper back accumulates more muscle mass it becomes wider simply because it is expanding away from the spine. Both vertical and horizontal pulling movements contribute to this phenomenon, so no one should rely on either at the expense of the other."

– Ron Harris, regular *MuscleMag International* contributor, explaining why you should do both types of back exercises in your back training.

ANATOMY

When we say back we are really talking about a group of muscles. The largest are the latissimus dorsi (lats), which are shaped like two large wings. When properly developed they give the bodybuilder a manta-ray look. The primary function of the lats is to draw the arms downwards and back. They also play a major role in scapular retraction (pulling the shoulder blades together).

Other large muscles of the back include the teres major and minor, and the rhomboids, which attach to and are primarily used to stabilize and move the shoulder blades. They also assist the lats in moving the arms.

The trapezius muscles (traps) are also technically part of the back region, but most bodybuilders prefer to train them with shoulders. The trapezius muscles attach to the base of the skull and extend down the center of the back. Their primary function is to lift and rotate the shoulder girdle complex. They also help protect the neck. Well-built traps help football players and wrestlers to get that "no neck" look.

Finally, the back contains two long, thin but powerful snake-like muscles called the spinal erectors that attach to the pelvic girdle and run up the center of the back. Although the larger upper back muscles tend to look more impressive and receive the most attention by bodybuilders, the spinal erectors are the real power behind many of the primary mass-building exercises such as squats, deadlifts and bent-over rows.

TRAINING THE BACK

Bodybuilders tend to divide back-training exercises into three categories: those for width, those for thickness and those for the lower back.

- Width exercises place most of their stimulation on the outer edges of the upper and lower lats, helping to emphasize the V-shape. The best width exercises are variations of chin-ups and pulldowns.
- Thickness exercises tend to place most of their stress on the center of the back, giving it a meaty look. Many bodybuilders have good back width but their central back area looks shallow. The best exercises for adding mass to the center of the back are rowing movements.
- Finally, the spinal erectors are directly trained using back-extension exercises and indirectly with rowing and deadlift movements.

The following exercises are among the most popular used by pro bodybuilders for adding width, thickness and strength to the upper, lower and central back areas. I left out trap exercises because most bodybuilders train traps with shoulders.

Photo of Ronnie Coleman by Jason Mathas

WIDTH EXERCISES

- Wide-grip chin-ups
- Narrow-grip chin-ups
- Chin-ups using V-grip attachment
- Reverse-grip chin-ups
- Front pulldowns
- Narrow-grip pulldowns
- Pulldowns using V-grip attachment
- Reverse pulldowns
- One-arm pulldowns
- Behind-the-head pulldowns (This exercise is not recommended because it puts your shoulders in a vulnerable position, but it is still performed by a few bodybuilders).

THICKNESS EXERCISES

- Wide-grip barbell rows
- Reverse-grip barbell rows
- T-bar rows
- One-arm dumbell rows
- Seated cable rows

Ronnie Coleman displays his well-developed back, highlighting his classic V-shape.

THE CHAMPS' ROUTINES

Dexter Jackson

"I tend to get bigger as I diet. My calories don't increase when I diet but I eat better foods more frequently and that seems to make me bigger."
– Dexter Jackson, multi-time Arnold Classic winner, commenting on his body's unique response to dieting.

Despite routinely being outweighed by 50 pounds or more, top IFBB pro Dexter Jackson has more than held his own on today's highly competitive bodybuilding stage, having won numerous pro contests around the world, including the Arnold Classic on three occasions as of this printing.

Dexter has a unique philosophy on training. He works his entire body over three workouts, hitting each bodypart just once per week. He also keeps the total number of sets below 10 for every muscle group. With one of the widest and most detailed backs in bodybuilding today, it's hard to believe he maintains it with just two exercises per workout!

Dexter starts his back workout with one of the two staple width exercises – front chins or front pulldowns. If he does chins he'll use just his body weight and aim for 3 or 4 sets of 10 to 15 reps. If he opts for pulldowns he'll use enough weight to keep the reps in the 6-to-8 range.

To add thickness to his central back, Dexter will do 3 or 4 sets of 6 to 8 reps of either barbell rows or one-arm dumbell rows.

JACKSON'S BACK WORKOUT

EXERCISE	SETS	REPS
Chins	3–4	10–15
Front Pulldowns	3–4	6–8
Barbell or Dumbell Rows	3–4	6–8
Dexter does either chins or front pulldowns.		

Dexter Jackson maintains one of the widest backs in bodybuilding today with just two exercises per workout.

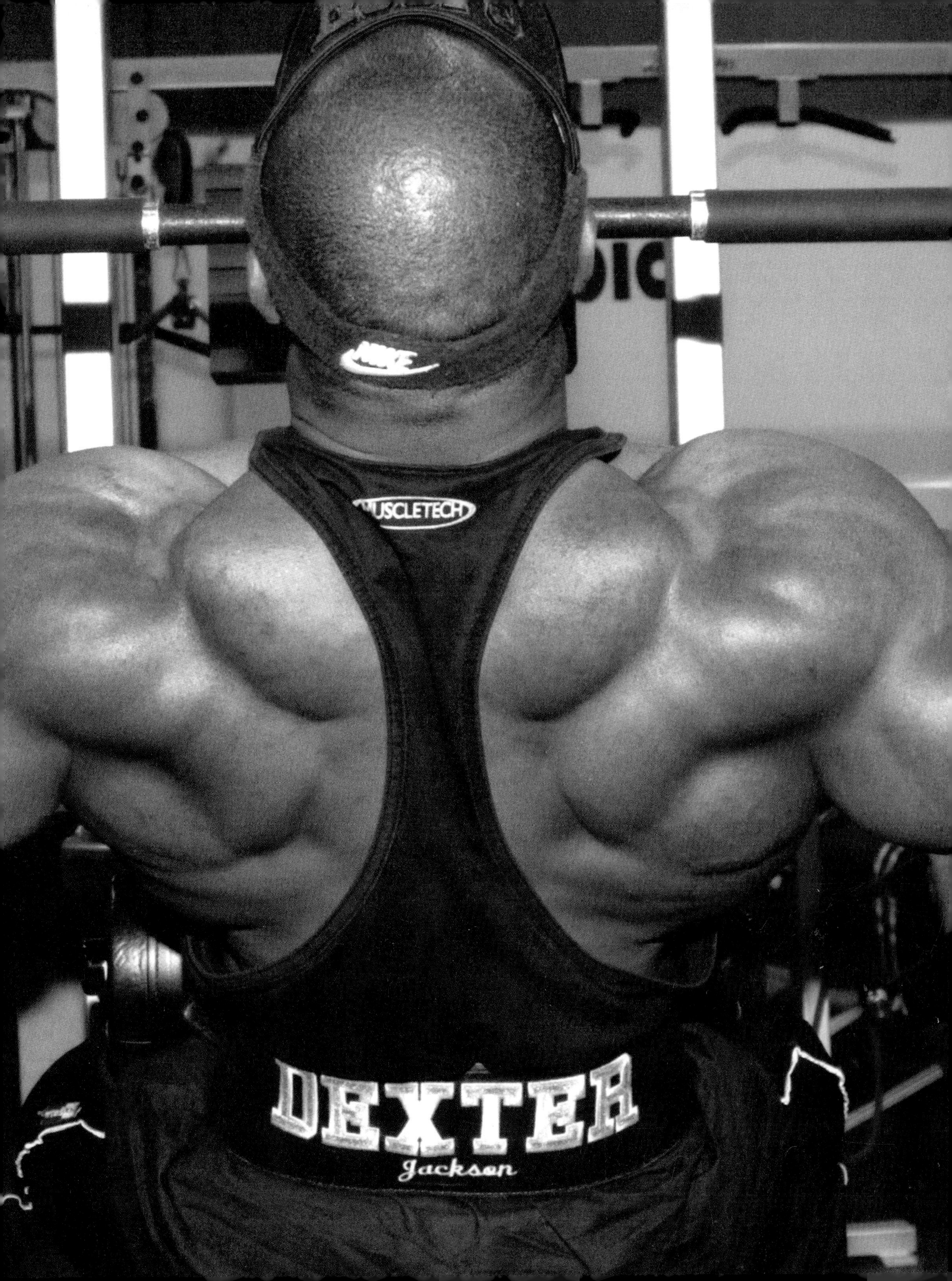
DEXTER
Jackson

King credits most of
his back development
to rowing movements
– he does three in his
back workout.

20
30
40
50
60
70
80
90
100
110
120
130
140
150
160
170
180
190

THE CHAMPS' ROUTINES

King Kamali

"You want to feel your back muscles doing most of the work. As you pull the weight back toward you, lift and expand your chest and your shoulder blades will almost touch together."

– King Kamali, top bodybuilding pro and regular *MuscleMag International* columnist

With his 1999 NPC heavyweight class win and fourth place at the 2001 Arnold Classic – his first pro contest – King Kamali (real name Shahriar Kamali), was quick to cement himself as one of the new forces in bodybuilding. Never afraid to speak his mind, Kamali quickly gained a reputation as one of bodybuilding's bad boys. This strategy paid off, as he's one of the most sought-after guest posers and speakers in the sport. He also writes an outspoken column in *MuscleMag International* magazine.

Packing 240 to 250 pounds in contest shape on his 5'10" frame, Kamali is no slouch in the mass department and easily holds his own with most of the mass monsters on the pro circuit.

One of Kamail's best bodyparts is his back. He attributes most of his back development to rowing exercises, and a typical back workout will see him doing three rowing exercises and only one pulldown or chin-up exercise.

Kamali usually starts his back workout with quarter deadlifts. Over the years he has found this exercise great for building up his lower back. He also discovered that it's a great way to add thickness to his traps and central upper back. During a typical workout King will do 4 sets of 12 to 15 reps.

King's next exercise is a seldom-seen back movement – one arm barbell rows. He starts by putting one end of an Olympic bar in a corner or against the base of a machine and has a training partner stand on it with one foot. He then bends forward and grabs the bar just below the sleeve. With the elbow of his free arm braced across his knee, he slowly pulls the bar up as if doing a T-bar row. Again he does 4 sets of 12 to 15 reps.

For his third exercise King moves on to seated cable rows. He begins by sitting on the machine's pad and, with his feet on the foot rests and knees slightly bent, he slowly pulls the handle in to his lower ribcage. He then returns to the starting position by slowly stretching his torso forward. King says the key to this exercise is to pull with the lat muscles and not jerk the weight up with the lower back. Not only does the jerking movement defeat the purpose of the exercise, it's a great way to injury your lower back ligaments. As you might have guessed by now, he does 4 sets of 12 to 15 reps.

After two rowing movements and the deadlifts you'd think King might be finished, but there's still more to be done. Next up is wide front pulldowns. With a grip just slightly wider than shoulder width. He pulls the bar down to his collarbone and then slowly stretches it back over his head to just short of lockout. For variety King likes to use different grips on the bar (i.e. wide, narrow, reverse). As usual, he does 4 sets of 12 to 15 reps.

To finish off his back, King does one final rowing movement – one-arm cable rows. Unlike most people, who brace themselves on a bench, King does cable rows while standing, bent slightly forward. He also rotates his hand as he pulls the cable to his hips. He starts with his palms facing inward and then rotates his arm so at the top of the exercise his palms face rearward. Again it's 4 sets of 12 to 15 reps.

KAMALI'S BACK WORKOUT

EXERCISE	SETS	REPS
Quarter Deadlifts	4	12–15
One-Arm Barbell Rows	4	12–15
Seated Rows	4	12–15
Wide-Grip Front Pulldowns	4	12–15
One-Arm Cable Rows	4	12–15

Mark focuses on form and feeling when training his back.

THE CHAMPS' ROUTINES
Mark Dugdale

"Don't get me wrong, I still train as heavy as I can, but my focus is on feeling the back muscles through the entire range of motion. So I guess you could say I made one major change: I switched my focus from poundage to feel."

– Mark Dugdale, IFBB pro, dicussing how he modified his back-training philosophy.

Like many inexperienced bodybuilders, Mark Dugdale had trouble developing his back. Even after winning the 2004 USA Championships, Mark felt that his back was way behind the rest of his physique. It may have been sufficient to win the USAs, but it was nowhere good enough to stand an assault from the likes of Jay Cutler, Victor Martinez and Ronnie Coleman on the Olympia stage.

As Mark discovered, it wasn't a lack of busting ass that kept his back development lagging. No, it was that common trap of using too much weight and letting his form get sloppy. This way of training may work with some other muscle groups, but not the back.

Nowadays when he hits his back, Mark keeps his mind focused on every single rep. He still trains heavy, but his form is immaculate and the priority is on how much stimulation his back muscles receive and not how much weight is on the stack or bar.

Mark typically starts his back workouts with seated pulley rows. If you want to see what Mark means by proper form, you need look no further than this exercise. With a slight bend at his knees to reduce lower back stress, Mark pulls the V-shaped attachment into his lower ribcage, fully contracting his shoulder blades as he pulls. He then stretches his arms out to just short of a locked-out position, being careful to stretch his torso forward only a few degrees. Many bodybuilders stretch all the way forward and set up a rocking motion. In Mark's mind this is defeating the purpose of the exercise, not to mention placing unwanted stress on the lower back. After 2 warmup sets Mark does 2 working sets of 6 to 12 reps.

For his second back exercise Mark pulls out one of six-time Mr. Olympia Dorian Yates's favorites – reverse-grip pulldowns. With a shoulder-width reverse grip, Mark slowly pulls the bar down to his mid chest, being careful to fully contract his shoulder blades and arch his chest at the bottom. He then stretches his arms above his head to just short of a locked-out position. Again he does 2 working sets of 6 to 12 reps.

Exercise number three is bent-over rows on the Smith machine. He prefers the straight-line motion of the Smith machine to the barbell, as it allows him to focus on working his back muscles rather than concentrating on balancing the bar. With his torso just short of parallel with the floor, Mark pulls the bar to his lower waist. There is absolutely no rocking or jerking the weight on this exercise. As you might guess, it's 2 sets of 6 to 12 reps.

To finish off his back, Mark supersets 2 sets of 6 to 12 reps of wide-grip front pulldowns with straight-arm rope pushdowns. While wide pulldowns are familiar to most readers, rope pushdowns may need a brief description. Mark attaches a rope attachment to a high pulley and, with just a slight bend at his (locked) elbows, pushes it down to his thighs. He finds this exercise great for the lower lats and serratus.

DUGDALE'S BACK WORKOUT

EXERCISE	SETS	REPS
Seated Cable Rows	2	6–12
Reverse-Grip Pulldowns	2	6–12
Smith-Machine Rows	2	6–12
Rope Pushdowns (superset with) Wide Pulldowns	2	6–12

Photo of Mark Dugdale by Jason Mathas

Dennis Wolf is quickly becoming a force to be reckoned with in the bodybuilding world.

THE CHAMPS' ROUTINES

Dennis Wolf

Following in the footsteps of Markus Ruhl, Gunter Schlierkamp and of course Arnold Schwarzenegger, 260-pound Dennis Wolf is yet another Germanic bodybuilder who seems to have come from nowhere to frighten the current crop of IFBB pros. After winning overall titles at the 2005 German and World Championships, Dennis quickly placed in the top 10 in a number of pro shows before winning the 2007 Keystone Pro Classic. His 5th place finish at the 2007 Mr. Olympia – many had him as high as third – only furthered his reputation as one of the new faces (and chests, and backs, and arms …) to be feared.

Dennis typically starts his back workout with front pulldowns to his chest. Unlike many bodybuilders, who use body momentum to train their egos and simply lift more weight, Dennis keeps his torso stationary and concentrates on pulling only with his lats.

Next up: He does 3 sets of seated pulley rows. He uses a wide underhand grip on this one to bring in more of his lowers lats.

Dennis' third exercise is one of his favorites – one-armed seated pulley rows. He finds this movement one of the most effective for working the lower, outer edges of his lats.

To finish his back workout Dennis does straight-arm pushdowns. Like many other champs, Dennis looks to Dorian Yates for inspiration, as this exercise was one Dorian's favorites. Dennis adds that the key to this exercise is to use just enough weight to work the lats and serratus without having to swing the body or bend the elbows, which would bring the triceps into play.

WOLF'S BACK WORKOUT

EXERCISE	SETS	REPS
Front Pulldowns	3	10–12
Seated Pulley Rows	3	10–12
One-Arm Pulley Rows	3	10–12
Straight-Arm Pushdowns	3	10–12

THE CHAMPS' ROUTINES
Jay Cutler

"Deadlifts and barbell rows were two exercises I got really strong on, but I was just lifting the weight. I wasn't feeling my back work at all, and so it wasn't improving in spite of my ability to use huge weight."

– Jay Cutler, multi-Mr. Olympia, commenting on how his back didn't respond the way he wanted although he was very strong.

Lesser individuals would have given up the second time. The more determined among them might have given it just one more shot. But Jay Cutler is made of sterner stuff than most. Despite placing second to Ronnie Coleman at the Mr. Olympia on four occasions he vowed that come hell or high water he would win bodybuilding's ultimate prize.

Since his first runner-up placing in 2001, Jay knew that although he could hold his own or surpass Coleman on many poses, the contest was all but over when they turned around. Coleman's back had set new standards in size, thickness and detail. Jay knew that if he hoped to snatch the Sandow trophy from big Ronnie some day, he would need to bring his back up to Coleman's level. The rest, as they say, is history. Jay did just that and relegated Coleman to second place in 2006. He then proved it was no fluke by defending his title in 2007, pushing Ronnie down to fourth place.

One of the first things Jay did to improve his back was to split his training into two parts. He did mostly upper back in the morning and lower back and traps in the evening. Jay is quick to point out that the average bodybuilder would quickly overtrain by following such a heavy workload.

Jay usually starts his back attack with front pulldowns. Even though he admits chins are probably a better exercise, there's just no way a guy like him weighing over 300 pounds in the off-season could chin effectively with that kind of weight. He usually does 6 sets of 8 to 12 reps, using two different grip styles.

His first is the shoulder-width reverse-grip pulldown made popular by six-time Mr Olympia, Dorian Yates. He follows this up by using a standard grip with a slightly wider than shoulder-width grip.

Jay's second exercise is the T-bar row. He attributes this movement more than any other for adding the extra thickness he needed in his center back. He'll typically do one set with two 45-pound plates and then work up to four or five plates for 3 sets of 6 to 8 reps.

After T-bar rows it's on to one-arm dumbell rows. Initially he did the standard hands-on-the-bench version, but found that his lower back got involved, so now he does them in a more vertical manner, with his free hand holding a dumbell rack. He starts with a 120-pound dumbell and then does 2 sets with a 140-pounder for 7 to 9 reps.

For his fourth back exercise Jay does another basic mass-builder: the barbell row. As with one-arm rows he discovered that when he stands at 70 degrees as opposed to the traditional 45 degrees, his back receives more stimulation. He found he had a tendency to swing more when in the lower position. Jay normally does 3 sets of 6 to 8 reps, using about 315 pounds.

Exercise number five is the seated cable row. Jay does the basic exercise, doing 2 to 3 working sets of 6 to 8 reps.

CUTLER'S UPPER BACK WORKOUT

EXERCISE	SETS	REPS
Pulldowns (two grips)	6	8–12
T-Bar Rows	3	6–8
One-Arm Dumbell Rows	2	7–9
Barbell Rows	3	6–8
Seated Cable Rows	2–3	6–8

Jay's approach to improve his back involved splitting his training into two parts – upper back and lower back with traps.

As opposed to his arms, which respond quickly to training, Lee had to work very hard to bring up his back.

THE CHAMPS' ROUTINES
Lee Priest

"But the real proof came during the quarter turns in round one. Lee looked great from the front with his tremendous delts and eight-pack abs. From the side his amazing arms were evident. Now for the back. Long considered a bit of an Achilles' heel, Lee's back looked better than it has in a long time ... maybe ever."

– Larry Pepe, regular *MuscleMag International* contributor, commenting on Lee Priest's condition at the 2004 Iron Man.

It's not so much the 220 pounds of striated beef that he carries into combat. Nor is it those 22-inch guns that swell from his shoulders. What really causes fans and fellow competitors to stand back in awe is the fact that all of this weaponry is displayed on a 5'4" frame. Most bodybuilders with these dimensions are strutting around with frames pushing six feet or more.

While his arms have always responded quickly to training, Lee's back took a concentrated effort of determination and persistence on his part to bring it up to the same level as the rest of his physique. When he started evaluating his back, Lee immediately noted that it definitely needed more width. This is why he usually starts his back training with front pulldowns. Unlike many bodybuilders who load up the machine and then throw their whole body into it, Lee's reps are rock solid. No body sway or jerking for the Australian pocket Hercules. A typical day will see him doing 5 sets of 8 to 12 reps.

Lee's second exercise is another width movement: front chins. Like most bodybuilders Lee doesn't do this exercise year-round, as he is usually too heavy (Lee sometimes gets up to 270 pounds in the off-season), but as soon as his weight starts dropping he does 4 to 5 sets to failure, averaging 10 to 15 reps per set.

With two width exercises completed, Lee moves on to rowing exercises to add thickness and density. One of his favorites is seated cable rows. Again, Lee does not cheat by rocking his body back and forth. With the exception of a slight stretch forward at the end, Lee keeps his torso relatively straight throughout. Again it's 4 to 5 sets of 8 to 12 reps.

Exercises four and five are a unique Priest combination. Lee will load up an EZ-bar with three or four 45-pound plates per side and bang out 8 to 12 reps of bent-over rows. He prefers the EZ-bar over the straight bar as it's both easier on his back and seems to provide a stronger back contraction. As soon as he completes the last rep he stands up straight and squeezes out 8 to 12 reps of shrugs. Lee typically does 5 supersets of both exercises.

Most bodybuilders would be done by now but not Lee. For his sixth exercise, Lee does 5 sets of V-bar pulldowns. He finds this exercise excellent for filling in the area of his back between his lower traps and lower lats. He's always careful to keep his torso arched throughout the full range of motion on this exercise.

To finish off his back workout Lee does 3 or 4 sets of 12 to 15 reps of back extensions. Lee does this all-important exercise both to balance out his lower back with his upper back, and to provide his lower back with the strength necessary to endure such heavy movements as squats, deadlifts and rows.

PRIEST'S BACK WORKOUT

EXERCISE	SETS	REPS
Chins	5	8–12
Front Pulldowns	5	8–12
Seated Cable Rows	5	8–12
EZ-Bar Rows	5	8–12
EZ-Bar Shrugs	5	8–12
V-Bar Pulldowns	5	8–12
Back Extensions	3–4	12–15

CHAPTER 78

Chest Training

"Striated mountains of pectoral mass – a sight to behold, on or off the stage."

– Casey Gately, *MuscleMag International* contributor

With the possible exception of the biceps, no other muscle group receives the same degree of attention as the chest. It's one of the primary symbols of toughness and masculinity.

There are several reasons chest training is so popular. For one thing the chest is the center of the upper body's power. You rarely hear bodybuilders asking one another how much they can row or pressdown, but it seems all bodybuilders are preoccupied with their bench press. The location of the chest also makes it easy to see as you train it, and whenever you look in the mirror. Unlike the back or shoulders, you can see every muscle fiber contract as you perform chest exercises. Training chest is also fun compared to such other muscles as calves, back or thighs, which often end up shortchanged because of visibility or difficulty. Not so with the chest. It's a low-pain, highly visible muscle, and once pumped up it feels like two plates of armor.

Bodybuilders famous for their chests include Ronnie Coleman, Lee Haney, Arnold Schwarzenegger, Serge Nubret, Franco Columbu, Branch Warren, Jay Cutler and Markus Ruhl.

ANATOMY

When we talk about the chest we are primarily refer-ring to two regions, the larger outer chest muscles called the pectoralis major, and the smaller pectoralis minor that are located underneath the pectorals major. Although they play a role in adding strength and size to your chest, bodybuilders don't really focus on the pectorals minor when training. For the purposes of this book when I talk about chest exercises I'm refer-ring to the pectorals major.

The primary function of the chest muscles is to draw the arms and shoulders toward the center of the body. To put it simply, the chest muscles allow you to make a bear-hug type motion with your arms. These muscles can be considered in opposition to the back muscles.

TRAINING

Bodybuilders generally divide chest training into two parts: upper and lower. As time goes on you may have to specialize on such areas as the inner, outer and pec-delt tie-in regions. At the intermediate level of training you should include at least one lower-chest and one upper-chest exercise in your workouts.

CHEST EXERCISES

- Flat barbell bench presses
- Incline barbell bench presses
- Decline barbell bench presses
- Flat dumbell presses
- Incline dumbell presses
- Decline dumbell presses
- Flat dumbell flyes
- Incline dumbell flyes
- Decline dumbell flyes
- Dips
- Pullovers
- Cable crossovers
- Vertical press machine
- Pec-deck machine

Photo of Branch Warren by Ralph DeHaan

Branch Warren sports one of the most famous chests in body-building.

Jay credits his chest development to changing his exercises to those that allowed him to feel his chest muscles working.

Photo of Jay Cutler by Irvin Gelb

THE CHAMPS' ROUTINES

Jay Cutler

"When people try to criticize me for not using as much weight as they think I should be using, I always remember how crappy my chest was when I was caught up in using the heaviest weights possible."

– Jay Cutler, multi-Mr. Olympia winner, responding to a reporter's question on why he doesn't train heavier.

When Jay Cutler snatched the Mr. Olympia crown from eight-time winner Ronnie Coleman in 2006, he did it by playing Ronnie's game: carrying the maximum amount of striated beef on his frame. From thighs to back to arms, Jay's physique was complete, and he was rewarded for his efforts with the coveted Sandow statue.

Despite the two armor plates that he sports across his ribcage nowadays, his chest wasn't always one of his best bodyparts. As he's quick to point out, the problem was self-inflicted. Like many bodybuilders he got too hung up on seeing how much weight he could handle on the flat barbell bench press. The end result was a massive set of shoulders that made his chest look shallow.

Once he realized the error of his ways he ditched the barbell presses in favor of exercises that allowed him to squeeze and feel his chest muscles working. Another change he made was to alternate compound exercises with isolation movements. He finds this puts less stress on his joints and greatly reduces the risk of injuries.

Jay usually starts his chest training with flat dumbell presses. He finds that not only do the dumbells allow him to work his chest through a greater range of motion, they allow him to move his hands closer together at the top of the exercise. He starts off with a couple of warmup sets of 10 to 12 reps using from 75 to 100 pounds, and then does 2 to 3 sets of 8 reps using 125- to 130-pound dumbells.

Jay's second exercise is high cable crossovers. While most bodybuilders consider cable crossovers more of a shaping exercise, Jay is convinced that this exercise has added extra size to his inner chest. Since his chest is fully warmed up from the flat dumbell presses, Jay dives straight into his 3 working sets for 10 to 12 reps.

Next up is incline dumbell presses. Jay offers this advice to beginner and intermediate bodybuilders: "If the development of your upper chest does not match your middle and lower chest, you should do this exercise first in your routine." On most days Jay will do one lighter set of 10 reps and then 2 to 3 sets of 6 to 8 reps using much the same weight as with the flat dumbell presses.

For his fourth exercise Jay does 2 sets of 10 to 12 reps of dumbell pullovers using a 100-pound dumbell. While most bodybuilders do this exercise early in their careers to try and expand their ribcages, Jay uses them to add size to his chest.

To finish off his chest, Jay does 3 sets of low cable crossovers. For those not familiar with the exercise, you start by putting the cable pulley at the floor. With a slight bend at the elbow, slowly sweep the arms upwards and together to just below the chest.

CUTLER'S CHEST WORKOUT

EXERCISE	SETS	REPS
Flat Dumbell Presses	2–3	8
High Cable Crossovers	3	10–12
Incline Dumbell Presses	2–3	6–8
Dumbell Pullovers	2	10–12
Low Cable Crossovers	3	9–12

Photo of Jay Cutler by Irvin Gelb

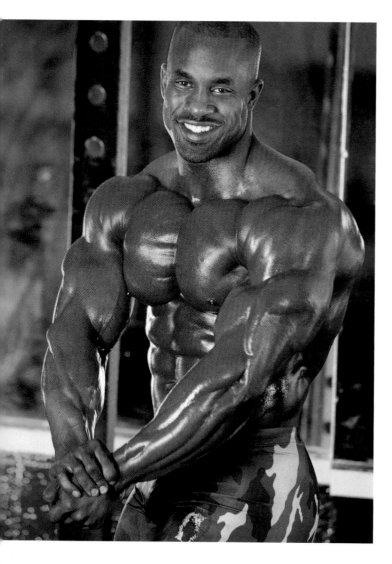

To shock his muscles and keep them guessing, Victor rotates his starting chest exercise every three workouts.

THE CHAMPS' ROUTINES

Victor Martinez

"As a kid I overtrained the hell out of my chest. I would do two kinds of flat press every workout, plus two kinds of incline presses, along with pullovers and pec-deck. I was doing drop sets on every set – and this was twice a week! I honestly wasn't feeling my chest work at all and it didn't grow very much during that time."

– Victor Martinez, top IFBB pro, commenting on the training mistakes he made when younger.

With his win at the 2007 Arnold Classic and second place to Jay Cutler at the 2007 Mr. Olympia, Victor Martinez has locked himself into place as one of the top pro bodybuilders in the world. Many in the know believe it's only a matter of time before he wins bodybuilding's most coveted crown.

As expected of a second-place Olympia competitor, Victor's physique is densely packed from head to toe. Victor attributes much of this mass to his career as a powerlifter before switching to bodybuilding. At a weight of 198 pounds, Victor has done an official 475-pound bench press and lifted over 500 pounds in the gym.

During the off-season, when adding new mass is Victor's goal, he relies primarily on pressing movements and weighted dips. As contest time approaches he'll add in cable crossovers and machines. He also rotates the starting exercise every three chest workouts, to keep his muscles shocked and off guard.

Photo of Victor Martinez by Irvin Gelb

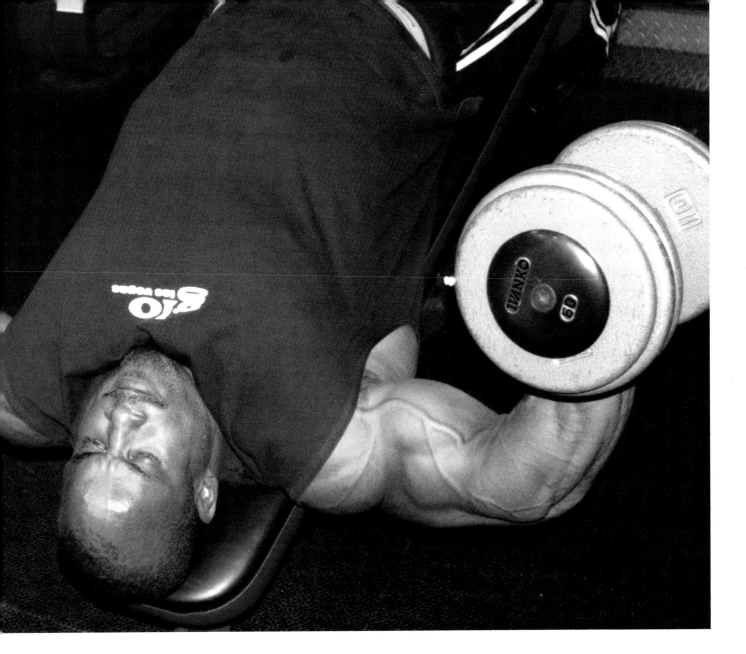

Photo of Victor Martinez by Raymond Cassar

A typical Martinez chest workout will start with flat barbell bench presses. His warmup is impressive to say the least: he does 225 pounds for 20 fast-tempo reps. He'll then go 315 for 10 reps, 405 for 10 reps, and then 455 for 10 reps. Victor will penalize himself at this point if he can't do 10 reps with 455. He'll drop the weight to 315 and again to 225 and force out as many reps as possible.

Victor's second exercise is often incline dumbell presses. He'll start with 80-pound dumbells for two quick warmup sets of 20 reps each, and then do 4 sets of 10 reps using the 100s, 120s, 125s, and 150s. During the off-season he'll occasionally go up to the 170s or 180s if he feels strong.

To finish off his chest, Victor does 3 sets of incline dumbell flyes using 75- to 95-pound dumbells for 10 to 12 reps. This is the only isolation exercise he does in the off-season.

MARTINEZ'S CHEST WORKOUT

EXERCISE	SETS	REPS
Flat Barbell Presses	5*	10
Incline Dumbell Presses	6**	10
Incline Dumbell Flyes	3	10–12
* 3 working sets ** 4 working sets		

Photo of Dexter Jackson by Raymond Cassar

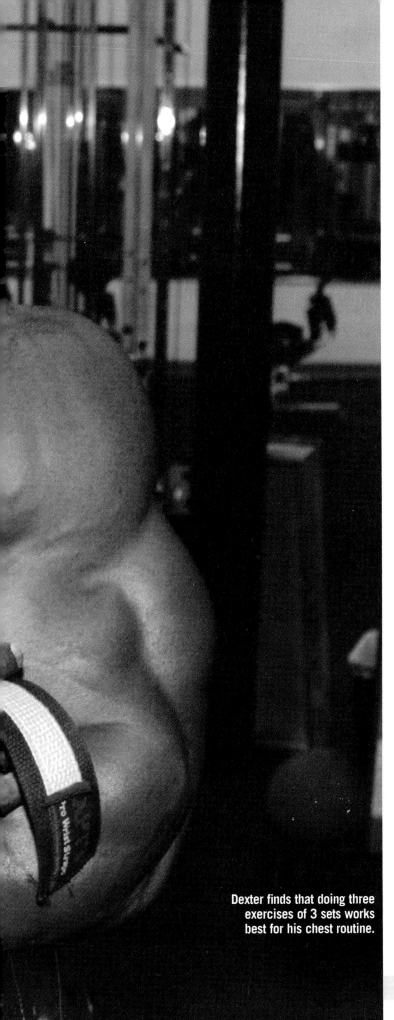

Dexter finds that doing three exercises of 3 sets works best for his chest routine.

THE CHAMPS' ROUTINES

Dexter Jackson

"I think I'm very balanced, and that has been the key to my success."

- Dexter Jackson, top IFBB pro, with an understatement about how well balanced his physique is.

In a sport dominated by 270- to 280-pound freaks, 220-pound Dexter Jackson has managed to do quite well for himself, thank you very much. Since winning the 1998 North American Championships, Dexter has vaulted to the upper echelon of pro bodybuilding. With the exception of the Mr. Olympia, Dexter has won just about every pro bodybuilding contest, including the Iron Man and two Arnold Classic titles.

You'll likely be surprised to discover how simple his chest routine actually is. Never one for high-volume training, Dexter does just three exercises of 3 sets each. He has found over the years that any more than 9 or 10 sets per muscle group is just too taxing on his recovery system.

His first exercise is usually a pressing movement – either barbell or dumbell. As this is his first chest exercise he'll do 2 to 3 light warmup sets and then 3 working sets of 4 to 8 reps.

To hit his upper chest Dexter relies on an incline movement – usually incline Smith presses. As his chest is fully warmed up from the 5 to 6 sets of flat presses, he'll go straight into his 3 working sets of 4 to 8 reps.

Dexter usually concludes his chest training with a flye exercise – either flat dumbell or pec-deck. Again it's 3 sets but he'll go slightly higher on the rep range – usually 6 to 8.

JACKSON'S CHEST WORKOUT

EXERCISE	SETS	REPS
Flat Barbell Presses	3	4–8
Incline Smith Presses	3	4–8
Flat Dumbell or Pec-Deck Flyes	3	6–8

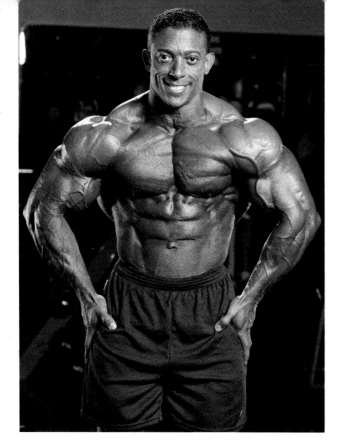

THE CHAMPS' ROUTINES
Troy Alves

"I couldn't even get the ball from center field to the pitcher. You can imagine how depressing that was for me."
– Troy Alves, 2002 NPC Nationals champion, commenting on how an injury forced him to abandon his major league baseball ambitions and focus on bodybuilding instead.

Troy Alves is a perfect example of how an accident can be a blessing in disguise. As the future 2002 NPC Nationals champion was growing up, his idols weren't Arnold or Lee Haney, but baseball legends Hank Aaron and Reggie Jackson. Troy eventually became good enough at baseball to be scouted by the California Angels and earn a scholarship to Arizona Community College. Unfortunately, an injury that occurred while attempting a heavy bench press ended his baseball future and his educational scholarship. But Troy's gray cloud had a silver lining. He soon discovered that he had the type of body that responded quickly to any type of resistance training. Even the push-ups he did in his preteen years for karate changed his chest dramatically.

Troy has one of the most proportionate chests on the pro tour, but it wasn't always that way. Like many bodybuilders Troy spent too many years starting his chest workouts with flat barbell presses. The end result was great lower and outer pec development but a shallow upper chest.

Once Troy realized that to make a name for himself as a pro bodybuilder he would have to bring his chest up to standard, he redesigned his workouts. He now begins virtually every workout with an incline pressing movement – either barbell or dumbell. If using barbells he'll do warmup sets with 135 and 225 pounds and then work up to 405 for 3 to 4 sets of 6 to 10 reps. These are not half reps, either. Troy makes sure to lower the bar all the way to his collarbone. If using dumbells Troy will work up to 150 to 160 pounders for 3 to 4 sets of 6 to 10 reps.

Troy's second exercise is a flat press – usually dumbells. Whether barbell or dumbell, Troy doesn't begin the exercise until he has a slight arch in his lower back and his shoulder blades are pulled together. These two little movements shift most of the stress from the front shoulders to the pecs. When using the dumbells Troy will work up to the 150s for 3 to 4 sets of 6 to 10 reps. If doing flat barbell presses he'll use about 405 pounds for the same number of sets and reps.

For his third exercise Troy moves back to the incline bench and does what he calls an incline press/flye. With his hands in the traditional palms-facing-inwards flye position, Troy pushes the dumbells straight up like a press. He doesn't "hug" them together as in a flye movement. He knows this isn't a typical way to do these exercises but he finds it the best variation for stressing his upper chest. He usually does 3 sets of 6 to 10 reps using 75 to 85 pounds.

Troy finishes his chest by alternating the incline press/flye exercise with the flat version. On most days he'll use 85 to 100 pounds for 3 to 4 sets of 6 to 10 reps.

ALVES' CHEST WORKOUT

EXERCISE	SETS	REPS
Incline Barbell or Dumbell Presses	3–4	6–10
Flat Dumbell or Barbell Presses	3–4	6–10
Incline or Flat Presses/Flyes	3–4	6–10

To maintain one of the most proportionate chests on the pro tour, Troy starts every workout with an incline pressing move.

Chris "The Real Deal" Cormier now limits his barbell work since overcoming a lower-back infection in 2006.

THE CHAMPS' ROUTINES
Chris Cormier

"I don't expect people to kiss my ass or bow down to me but I wish my fellow pros would recognize the longevity I have had in this sport, and my accomplishments."
– Chris Cormier, top IFBB pro, responding to a reporter's question on how he deals with the negative comments of some of the newer members of the sport.

When it comes to longevity, Chris Cormier is at the top of the list. Nicknamed "The Real Deal" because of his facial resemblance to former Heavyweight boxing champion, Evander "The Real Deal" Holyfield, Chris is one of the true superstars in the sport of bodybuilding. With over a 100 contests to his credit and dozens of wins and second-place finishes, Chris is always a force to be reckoned with. A serious lower-back infection in 2006 temporarily paralyzed him, but even that couldn't send him into retirement, and he came back with a very respectable 4th place finish at the 2007 Montreal Grand Prix.

An ironic aspect to Chris's longevity is that he's also one of the sport's stronger individuals. Most guys who throw around huge poundage have short careers. However, save for the lower-back injury in 2006, Chris seems to have escaped serious injury. How strong is Chris? Well at one time he was doing 12 reps with 405 pounds on the incline barbell press. Most bodybuilders would be lucky to do one rep with this weight on the flat barbell press. Chris could also use 200-pound dumbells for flat and incline dumbell presses. You just have to see it to believe it.

Nowadays Chris limits his barbell work. Since he has both great chest mass and a more cautious view to training, he now uses more flyes and machines in his training. Chris usually starts his chest training with incline Hammer Strength presses. He'll typically do a couple of warmup sets and then work up to four or five 45-pound plates a side for 4 sets of 12 to 15 reps.

For his second exercise, Chris switches over to the flat version of the Hammer Strength press. Again he finds that he can go as heavy as he wants without the same joint pain experienced while using barbells. A nor-

mal day will see Chris throwing six 45-pound plates on each side and doing 4 sets of 12 to 15 reps.

Chris' third exercise is incline dumbell presses. Instead of the 180 to 200 pounders that he used years ago, he now keeps the weight "down" in the 120- or 130-pound zone. To keep up the intensity, he does higher reps – 12 to 15 versus 6 to 8. This not only puts less stress on his joints but gives his upper chest a much better pump. Again he does 4 sets of this exercise.

To finish off his chest, Chris adds in 4 sets of 12 to 15 reps of incline dumbell flyes. By this point his chest is tired, so there's no need to go super heavy. Chris will typically use 75 to 90 pounds for ultra slow and strict reps. As he says: "Most guys don't do these right. They use too much weight and treat it as some half-assed press."

CORMIER'S CHEST WORKOUT

EXERCISE	SETS	REPS
Incline Hammer Strength Presses	4	12–15
Flat Hammer Strength Presses	4	12–15
Incline Dumbell Presses	4	12–15
Incline Dumbell Flyes	4	12–15

Photos of Chris Cormier by Robert Reiff

To maintain his exceptional proportions, Craig keeps his workouts short but intense.

THE CHAMPS' ROUTINES

Craig Richardson

"As I developed, I noticed two things were happening to my physique. First: my front delts were getting huge, but were really overshadowing my chest development. Second: my upper-pec area was lacking."

– Craig Richardson, IFBB pro, on the common peril of young body-builders relying too much on the flat barbell press for chest development.

Although he's competed in only a dozen or so pro con-tests since 2003, Craig Richardson has made a mark on the bodybuilding scene. With the exception of his first Night of Champions and the 2005 Mr. Olympia, he has consistently placed in the top 10. Like Dexter Jackson and Shawn Ray before him, Craig holds his own against guys who outweigh him by 50 pounds by displaying near flawless proportions.

Like many bodybuilders who came of age during the 1990s, Craig was heavily influenced by the training philosophy of Dorian Yates, and keeps his workouts short but intense.

Craig realized early on that he was relying on the flat barbell press too much for his chest development. Like many bodybuilders his lower chest and front shoulders were far outpacing his upper chest. As tough as it was, Craig decided to drop the flat barbell press altogether and concentrate on incline movements to

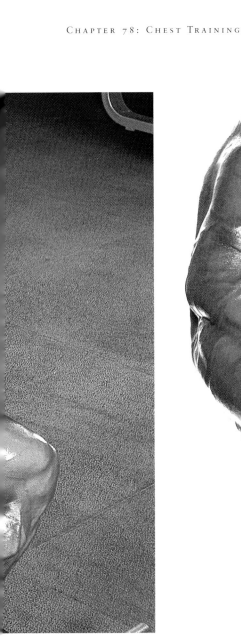

Photos of Craig Richardson by Jason Breeze

balance out his upper chest. He was rewarded for his efforts by winning the Light Heavyweight class at the 2000 NPC Nationals.

Nowadays Craig starts his chest training with either incline Smith-machine presses or incline dumbell presses. Unlike most bodybuilders he finds angles of 30 degrees or less still place most of the stress on his lower chest. For this reason he sets the bench angle at 45 degrees. Craig typically does a few light warmup sets and then does 3 sets of 6 to 8 reps.

With his upper chest training out of the way, Craig's next exercise is the decline Hammer Strength press. He prefers pressing on Hammer Strength machines to dumb-

ells or barbells because he can concentrate on squeezing and contracting his pecs. There's no having to worry about getting the dumbells into position or controlling them. Again he does 3 heavy working sets of 6 to 8 reps.

To finish off his chest Craig does 3 sets of 12 to 15 reps of either cable crossovers or pec-deck flyes.

RICHARDSON'S CHEST WORKOUT

EXERCISE	SETS	REPS
Incline Smith or Dumbell Presses	3	6–8
Decline Hammer Strength Presses	3	6–8
Cable Crossover or Pec-Deck Flyes	3	12–15

Lee Priest and Paul Dillett go head-to-head showing off their chests.

Photo of Lee Priest and Paul Dillett by Josef Adlt

THE CHAMPS' ROUTINES

Lee Priest

When you're one of the sport's most popular and controversial bodybuilders you'd better have the physique to back up your words. In this regard, Australia's Lee Priest easily surpasses all expectations. Carrying 220 pounds on his 5'4" frame (275 to 280 in the off-season!), Lee is one of the most massive bodybuilders of all time. He's also one of the strongest, with 800-pound squats and 500-pound bench presses a common occurrence in the off-season.

Lee comes from the old school of training styles and a chest workout will see him easily do 4 or 5 exercises for at least 20 sets in total. He rotates his exercises on a regular basis, gravitating more toward machines during the pre-contest season. The following is a typical Lee Priest pre-contest chest workout.

His first exercise, which he doesn't even consider part of his chest routine, is the standing cable crossover. He finds this exercise great for warming up his chest and he'll use a moderate amount of weight for 4 sets of 12 to 15 reps. Lee is especially proud of the fact that in all the years he has been training he has never had a chest or shoulder injury.

Lee's second exercise is usually a seated machine press. During the off-season he'll do flat dumbell presses with 180-pound dumbells, but he finds the machine better for stability and injury prevention during the pre-contest season. He starts with 3 lighter sets and then works up to as much weight as he can handle for 5 sets of 6 to 8 reps.

Lee's one free-weight exercise during the pre-contest season is the incline dumbell flye. He'll typically use 100-pound dumbells for 5 sets of 6 to 8 reps, going for a full stretch at the bottom of the exercise and bringing his arms to a lockout position at the top.

To finish off his pro-sized pecs, Lee bangs out 4 sets of bodyweight dips to failure. He doesn't need to strap weight around his waist, as his chest is already well fatigued by this point.

PRIEST'S CHEST WORKOUT

EXERCISE	SETS	REPS
Cable Crossovers	4	12–15
Seated Machine Presses	5	6–8
Incline Dumbell Flyes	5	6–8
Dips	4	failure

Photos of Lee Priest by Jason Mathas

THE CHAMPS' ROUTINES
Quincy Taylor

"I've never trained heavier or harder, and that has made all the difference in bringing my chest and back up to pro standards. When we get to the gym we're like two warriors going into battle."

– Quincy Taylor, IFBB pro, commenting on working with his training partner, former powerlifting champion Jesse Esparza.

Although he now displays a chest that rivals anything on the Olympia stage, it wasn't always that way for Quincy Taylor. Even once he reached the national level, his gargantuan arms and shoulders were overpowering his chest and back.

Not willing to be just another big-armed bodybuilder on the pro circuit, Quincy set about modifying his workout schedule so his chest and back could catch up to his arms and shoulders. One of his first changes was to train chest as his first muscle group following a complete day off. This allowed him to attack his chest workouts in a fresh state. He also found he made better gains by hitting his chest hard only once every seven or eight days.

Quincy usually starts his chest training with incline dumbell presses. After a couple of warmup sets in the 70- to 120-pound range he does 4 all-out sets, working up to 150- or 160-pound dumbells for 10 to 12 reps. These are not sloppy; nor are they half-reps. He starts at the top with his arms locked completely out and lowers the dumbells down until his elbows are below his back.

Next up are flat dumbell presses. As his chest is now fully warmed up from the inclines, Quincy goes right into his working sets. He typically does 4 sets of 10 to 12 reps, working up to 180-pound dumbells.

With his two basic dumbell exercises out of the way, Quincy next moves on to vertical machine presses. He'll do 4 sets of 8 to 10 full reps and then have his training partner help him do another 8 half-reps. By this point his pecs are all but destroyed.

As if they needed it, Quincy finishes off his chest training with 4 sets of pec-deck flyes. Quincy has his own unique style on this exercise. Instead of placing his elbows and forearms on the vertical pads, he places his palms right in the middle of the pads and squeezes his arms together. As with the vertical machine press, Quincy does 8 to 10 full reps followed by 8 half-reps.

TAYLOR'S CHEST WORKOUT

EXERCISE	SETS	REPS
Incline Dumbell Presses	4	10–12
Flat Dumbell Presses	4	10–12
Vertical Machine Presses	4	8–10*
Pec-Deck Flyes	4	8–10*
* Plus 8 half-reps.		

Photo of Quincy Taylor by David Paul

Quincy Taylor proves that he's not just another big-armed bodybuilder – his chest rivals anything on the Olympia stage.

THE CHAMPS' ROUTINES

Will Harris

"It was frustrating as hell. I would pound it [his chest] and pound it year after year, and it improved but never got close to the rest of my upper body. I needed a chest bad! Then in 2001 I made some changes and it exploded."
– Will Harris, 2004 NPC USA heavyweight champion, commenting on how his chest wasn't always one of his best bodyparts.

Like many bodybuilders trying to bring up a lagging bodypart, Will Harris made the classic mistake of doing more sets rather than fewer. The end result was a chronic state of overtraining. Luckily he wasn't willing to settle for mediocrity and took a page out of Dorian Yates' book. He made two changes to his chest training. He cut the total number of sets in half – from 25 down to about 12. He also increased his rep range from 8 to 12 to 12 to 20. The end result was that his chest vaulted from being one of his worst bodyparts to one of his best.

Will's a big fan of Hammer Strength and usually starts his chest training with their vertical press machine. Although many bodybuilders prefer the balance factor required by dumbells and barbells, Will finds that not having to balance the weight leads to a better chest workout. He'll typically do 4 or 5 sets of 12 to 15 reps.

To hit his upper chest, Will moves on to Hammer Strength's incline press machine. As his chest is fully warmed up from the vertical press, he'll go slightly heavier on this exercise and do lower reps – in the neighborhood of 8 to 12.

With the two Hammer Strength machines out of the way, Will moves on to good old-fashioned dips. He performs these in the same manner recommended by the late Iron Guru, Vince Gironda: elbows out, chin on chest, torso leaning forward. Will tries to bang out 3 sets of 15 reps using his bodyweight.

To finish off his chest Will does 3 sets of either cable crossovers or pec-deck flyes. He's not really fussy which one he uses and goes by instinct. Rather than get too worried about weight on these exercises, Will goes relatively light and keeps the reps in the 15-to-20 range.

HARRIS' CHEST WORKOUT

EXERCISE	SETS	REPS
Vertical Hammer Strength Presses	4–5	12–20
Incline Hammer Strength Presses	4	8–12
Dips	3	15
Cable Crossovers or Pec-Deck Flyes	3	15–20

Will often finishes his chest routine with pec-deck flyes.

Photo of Will Harris by Jason Mathas

THE CHAMPS' ROUTINES

Dennis James

When he won the super heavyweight class and overall title at the 1998 USA Championships, many in the audience had a feeling that the 5'8" Dennis James would be making his mark on the pro scene. These predictions were to quickly come true, as within a few years Dennis had won the Hungary Grand Prix and achieved a hoist of top-five finishes.

Dennis was among a new generation of pros who emerged on the scene in the late 1990s. He carried as much mass on his 5'8" frame as do most guys over 6 feet tall. Although solid from head to toe, Dennis' chest is noteworthy.

He's a traditionalist when it comes to training: 3 or 4 exercises for 3 or 4 sets each. A typical day will see Dennis start with incline Smith presses. There was a time when machine exercises were frowned upon by most bodybuilders, but nowadays you're just as likely to see a Mr. Olympia competitor repping out on a machine as using barbells or dumbells. Dennis is one such convert. He starts by setting the bench at about 30 degrees. Then, using a slightly wider than shoulder-width grip, he lowers the bar to his collarbone. One thing Dennis likes to do on this exercise is pause at the top of the exercise, when his arms are fully locked out, and contract his pecs forcefully. He does 3 or 4 sets of 8 to 12 reps.

For his second exercise Dennis moves on to flat Hammer Strength presses. Once again he finds the machine gives his chest a better workout than the barbell. Dennis typically does 3 or 4 sets of 8 to 12 reps. Again the reps are performed in a slow, fluid, piston-like motion.

With his two primary pressing exercises out of the way, Dennis moves on to flat or incline dumbell flyes. He performs these in the traditional "hugging the tree" motion and makes sure never to bounce at the bottom of the exercise. He does 3 or 4 sets of 8 to 12 reps.

Dennis' fourth exercise is either cable crossovers or pec-deck flyes. He does either of these exercises to emphasize the inner section of his chest and help bring

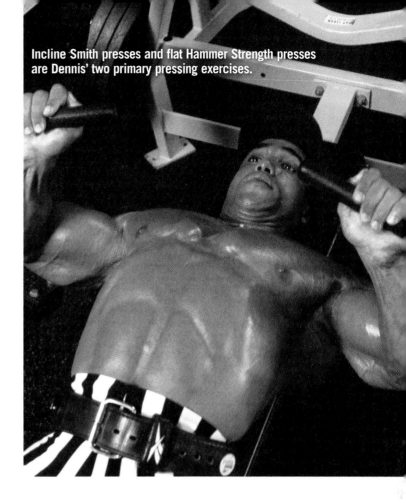

Incline Smith presses and flat Hammer Strength presses are Dennis' two primary pressing exercises.

out that clean line that divides his chest into two equal but massive slabs. Dennis prefers the version of the pec-deck with the 90-degree pads to the vertical-handled version that also doubles as a reverse flye. While he's the first to admit that this machine can be harder on the rotator cuff, he has never had any problems in this area. As expected, he does 3 or 4 sets of 8 to 12 reps.

To finish off his Grand Prix-winning chest, Dennis does 3 or 4 sets of machine dips. The machine Dennis uses is similar in function to a decline press and helps put that clean line under his lower pecs. While he usually sticks to his standard 8 to 12 range, he'll occasionally go as high as 15.

JAMES' CHEST WORKOUT		
EXERCISE	SETS	REPS
Incline Smith Presses	3–4	8–12
Flat Hammer Strength Presses	3–4	8–12
Incline or Flat Dumbell Flyes	3–4	8–12
Pec-Deck or Cable Crossovers	3–4	8–12
Machine Dips	3–4	8–12

Markus Ruhl is one of bodybuilding's true titans, and his chest is one of the best in the sport.

THE CHAMPS' ROUTINES

Markus Ruhl

"He had built every muscle group to the maximum and the end result is a physique many feel is the most representative of the word 'bodybuilding.' As he was inspired over a decade ago in his native Germany by Arnold Schwarzenegger, images of him in magazines all around the world are now motivation for the next generation of young iron pumpers to follow in his footsteps."
– Ron Harris, regular *MuscleMag International* contributor, commenting on 2000 Toronto Pro Invitational winner, Markus Ruhl.

Back in the 1980s Wendy's had one of the most memorable ads in history. It featured three elderly ladies, one of whom asked: "Where's the beef?" Well, one look at Germany's Markus Ruhl and that question is easily answered. At a little under six feet tall and weighing an incredible 285 pounds in contest shape, Markus Ruhl is one of the true behemoths in the sport.

Markus' first love was soccer, but at age 17 (and 140 pounds!) he took up weight training. It wasn't long before his outstanding genetics for building muscle emerged, and within a few years he was bench pressing 500 pounds on both flat and incline exercises. In recent years Markus has given up most flat pressing movements in favor of more incline work. As thick and as powerful as his upper chest is, he feels that a bodybuilder can never overdevelop this area.

For his first exercise, Markus usually does incline dumbell presses. Given the poundage he will be working up to, Markus does four warmup sets of 8 to 12

reps to really prepare his muscles and joints for the assault that is about to come. He then does anywhere from 6 to 10 working sets using as much weight as he can handle for 5 to 6 reps. As an example of how strong he is, Markus regularly uses anywhere from 170- to 200-pound dumbells in the off-season.

With a flip of his wrist Markus moves on to his second exercise – incline dumbell flyes. Again the strength displayed by the big German is unbelievable and he'll do 4 to 5 sets of 8 to 12 reps using 130- to 150-pound dumbells. Most bodybuilders can't even flat press dumbells this heavy, let alone incline flye them.

For his third chest exercise Markus likes to dip back to the glory years of bodybuilding – Arnold's Gold's Gym days in California in the 1970s. One of the most popular exercises for Arnold and the other regulars at the time was dumbell pullovers. Besides working the chest and back muscles, the exercise was great for stretching the ribcage ligaments. This could easily add a couple of inches to a bodybuilder's chest measurement. Markus is convinced that much of his ribcage size and overall chest shape is from doing heavy dumbell pullovers since day one. He prefers the cross bench version as it allows him to arch and get a better stretch. Again he does 4 to 5 sets of 8 to 12 reps.

To finish off those two slabs of meat that he calls his chest, Markus hits the cable crossover machine. During the off-season he'll just do the movement with the pulleys in the high position, but close to a contest he adds in mid and low versions of the exercise. Unlike most bodybuilders, who prefer to do higher reps on this exercise, Markus stays true to his 8-to-12 range with heavy weights.

RUHL'S CHEST WORKOUT

EXERCISE	SETS	REPS
Incline Dumbell Presses	6–10	5–6
Incline Dumbell Flyes	4–5	8–12
Dumbell Pullovers	4–5	8–12
Cable Crossovers	4–5	8–12

CHAPTER 79

Shoulder Training

"We all want them, don't we? Wide shoulders that scream to the world we are muscular stallions, powerful and virile enough to take on any challenge. Every male heroic figure through the ages, from Samson to Superman, has been depicted as owning a set of imposing, broad deltoids."

– Ron Harris, regular *MuscleMag International* contributor

> "The truth is, as the upper back accumulates more muscle mass it becomes wider simply because it is expanding away from the spine. Both vertical and horizontal pulling movements contribute to this phenomenon, so no one should rely on either at the expense of the other."
>
> – Ron Harris, regular *MuscleMag International* contributor, explaining why you should do both types of back exercises in your back training.

O f all the major muscles on display at a bodybuilding competition, few are as hard to hide as the shoulders. Creative posing can hide most of the other muscles but the shoulders are visible in every single pose you do. The shoulders are also one of the few muscles that will stand out even when you are dressed. It's possible to hide a set of 22-inch arms under a jacket, and the largest of chests can be kept from view with loose clothing, but no matter what you wear there'll be no hiding a wide set of shoulders. Virtually all the top pro bodybuilders have great shoulder development these days. In the past such bodybuilders as Sergio Oliva, Lee Haney, Paul Dillett, Mike Matarazzo and Larry Scott were famous for their cannonball-like deltoids.

ANATOMY

Like the back, the shoulders, or deltoids, are really a series of muscles. The deltoids are composed of three sub-muscles called heads – the front (anterior), side (lateral or medial) and rear (posterior). Each head raises the arm in

the direction for which it is named. In other words, the front deltoid lifts the arms to the front, the side deltoid raises the arms to the side, and you guessed it, the rear deltoid draws the arms back and raises them rearward.

Besides the deltoids the shoulder muscles also include the trapezius (the traps). Earlier I mentioned that, while they are technically part of the back musculature, most bodybuilders train traps with their shoulders.

SHOULDER TRAINING

For maximum shoulder impressiveness you must ensure equal development of all four distinct but important areas. Having said this, you rarely see it at bodybuilding contests. Most bodybuilders have great front shoulder development from all the years of pressing movements for their chest, but rare is the great set of rear shoulders. Chest training may bring up the front shoulders, but back training rarely leads to great rear deltoids. This is why you must include rear deltoid exercises to balance out your shoulder development. With regards to the side shoulders, let me say here and now that there has never been a bodybuilder penalized for having shoulders too wide!

Before performing any heavy shoulder training you really should warm up the shoulder region. Along with the knees and lower back, the shoulders are among the most injured areas. The unfortunate part of shoulder injuries is that they don't happen all at once but gradually from many years of heavy pressing exercises. By the time you realize you have a problem with this joint, the damage becomes cumulative and it's far more difficult to treat. Always take a couple of minutes to warm up the shoulders with some light exercises before moving on to heavier pressing and lateral movements. And always be sure to do rotator-cuff exercises two or three times a week. Guys hate to do these because the weights are so low. Besides, they feel as if they are wasting their time because they get no muscular development from the movement. But look at it this way: if you do rotator-cuff exercises, a few years down the road you will still

Photo of Paul Dillett

be able to do heavy chest, back, shoulder and arm work, whereas those who did not strengthen their inner shoulders will be using pansy-ass weights trying in vain to save whatever muscle they already built.

Shoulder exercises can be divided into pressing movements, raises and shrugs. You can also throw upright rows in there. Pressing exercises tend to work the front and side shoulders, while raises isolate the three heads separately. Shrugs are the main exercise aimed at developing the traps, but bodybuilders also use narrow-grip upright rows to hit this muscle. Wide-grip upright rows target the delts with some trap involvement. Most bodybuilders use medium-grip upright rows to target both areas equally and to avoid too much wrist strain from close-grip uprights.

BEST SHOULDER EXERCISES
- Front barbell presses
- Dumbell presses
- Front raises
- Side laterals
- Bent-over laterals
- Upright rows
- Shrugs
- Cable raises

THE CHAMPS' ROUTINES

Phil Heath

It didn't take Phil Heath long to cement his reputation on the IFBB pro circuit. He had barely walked away with the overall 2005 NPC championships when he won the first two pro tournaments he entered – the 2006 New York Pro and Colorado Pro championships. With a second-place finish to Dexter Jackson at the 2008 Arnold Classic and a win at the 2008 Iron Man, Phil is a force to be reckoned with.

He is packed head to toe with 240 pounds of striated muscle on his 5'9" frame, but Phil's shoulders are among his most impressive bodyparts. Unlike many of the current pros, Phil loves to incorporate lots of sets in his shoulder training. A typical shoulder workout will see Phil bang out 15 to 20 sets for those cannonball-sized delts. He usually starts with 3 solid sets of front military presses for overall size and then incorporates numerous dumbell lateral exercises to bring out the separation between the three shoulder heads. He then achieves a slightly different angle from the barbell military press by doing dumbell military presses. He both finishes off his delts and ties in his traps with 3 sets of upright rows.

Here's a typical shoulder workout from one of bodybuilding's most exciting pros.

HEATH'S SHOULDER WORKOUT

EXERCISE	SETS	REPS
Barbell Military Presses	3	8–10
Side Laterals	3	8–10
Front Dumbell Raises	3	8–10
Rear Laterals	3	10
Dumbell Military Presses	3	12
Upright Rows	3	12

Phil Heath exhibits one of his best bodyparts – his shoulders.

Using dumbbells for shoulder training is a technique that Armin feels gives him a better contraction.

THE CHAMPS' ROUTINES
Armin Scholz

"Personally I don't think they're so overpowering or incredible. Maybe it's because I have always thought of the shoulders as the one part of the body that can never be too big."

– Armin Scholz, German pro bodybuilder, expressing modesty on two of the largest sets of deltoids in bodybuilding.

There must be something in the blood of the ancient Teutonic Knights, as some of the largest pro bodybuilders have originated in Germanic countries. First there was Arnold Schwarzenegger, from Austria. Two of the largest pros on the circuit are Germans Markus Ruhl and Gunter Schlierkamp. Now a fourth name can be added to the list of German giants – Armin Scholtz.

At 6'2" and 270 pounds, Armin easily stands out in a pro lineup. It was this size that helped him to easily win three Mr. Germany titles. In the fall of 2005 he used his 23-inch arms and outstanding muscle mass to place a respectable 10th at his first pro contest – the Europa Super Show.

Armin starts his shoulder training with that most basic and productive of all shoulder exercises – presses. Armin prefers to use dumbells, as he feels they give him a better contraction. He finds pressing to the front with a barbell too much front shoulder, and pressing behind the head too stressful on his shoulder joints. He usually pyramids up in weight from 60 to 90 pounds, averaging 3 or 4 sets of 10 to 12 reps per set.

To hit his side shoulders, Armin bangs out 3 drop sets of dumbell lateral raises. He starts with a pair of 90s and just manages to get 8 reps. He'll then have a training partner help him get 4 more reps. Finally he'll drop the 90s and grab the 45s, grinding out another 8 reps on his own and 4 reps assisted. For variety Armin substitutes one-arm lateral raises for 3 or 4 sets of 8 to 12 reps. Again he does 8 strict reps and then uses slight body momentum to complete an additional 4 reps.

For his third exercise Armin includes 4 sets of one-arm cable raises. Armin adds in the second side raise exercise as he feels that the side shoulders can never be too big. He uses about 35 pounds for 4 sets of 15 reps per arm.

For his fourth and final exercise, Armin finishes off with 3 or 4 sets of bent-over dumbell raises. To really isolate the rear delts and reduce the stress on his lower back, Armin performs the movement lying facedown on a 30-degree incline bench. Over the years Armin has discovered that his rear delts respond better to higher rep ranges so he keeps the reps in the 18-to-20 range using 25- to 30-pound dumbells.

SCHOLZ'S SHOULDER WORKOUT

EXERCISE	SETS	REPS
Dumbell Presses	3–4	10–12
Side Dumbell Laterals	3*	12
One-Arm Cable Raises	3–4	15
Bent-Over Laterals	3–4	18–20

* Drop sets

Photos of Armin Scholz by Robert Reiff

THE CHAMPS' ROUTINES
Jay Cutler

"Being a successful bodybuilder is all about being smart, not feeding your ego with such heavy weight that you can't feel the muscle you're supposed to be working."
– Jay Cutler, Mr. Olympia, commenting on what separates great bodybuilders from average bodybuilders: intelligence.

In 2006 Jay Cutler did what many deemed impossible – he prevented Ronnie Coleman from winning an unprecedented ninth consecutive Mr. Olympia title. With his four second-place finishes to Coleman and a physique that improved with each passing year, many in the bodybuilding world expected that the title would one day be his, but the win over Coleman was still a shock when it came.

Given his chest and arm thickness it's not surprising that Jay has had to work hard to keep his shoulders in proportion. He has tried many training styles over the years but the one that seems to yield the best results is pre-exhaustion. Pre-exhaustion involves doing an isolation exercise for a particular muscle group and then following up with a compound exercise that brings other fresh muscles into play.

Jay starts with that old-school side-delt builder: standing dumbell laterals. Jay does the movement using both arms simultaneously rather than one arm at a time. Starting with the dumbells by his sides he raises them outwards and upwards until his arms are parallel with the floor. Any higher, he says, and you'll be bringing in more of the traps. At all times he tries to keep his elbows slightly bent. He starts with his palms facing his body and ends with them facing the floor. He'll first do 2 warm-up sets of 15-to-20 reps and then 4 or 5 working sets of 6 to 12 reps.

With his shoulders now fully warmed up and pre-exhausted Jay moves on to his second exercise – seated dumbell raises. He keeps his hands facing to the front at all times and is careful never to bounce at the bottom of the exercise. He'll do 1 set with an 80-pound dumbell and then 2 or 3 work sets, going up to 100- to 130-pound dumbells.

For his third exercise Jay bangs out 2 or 3 sets of alternate front raises. He doesn't bother to do warmup sets on this exercise, as his shoulders are fully warmed up from the previous movements. He's tried different hand positions over the years, but the one that feels the most effective and comfortable is having his hands facing the floor at all times. A typical rep range is 8 to 10.

To give his shoulders the complete look, Jay finishes off with bent-over dumbell raises. Again he goes straight into the working sets without a warmup. Unlike some bodybuilders who prefer to lie down on an incline bench, Jay does them standing but bent over at the midsection, making sure his back is arched. He'll typically perform 2 or 3 sets of 8 to 10 reps.

CUTLER'S SHOULDER WORKOUT

EXERCISE	SETS	REPS
Side Dumbell Raises	4–5	6–12
Seated Dumbell Presses	2–3	5–8
Alternating Front Raises	2–3	8–10
Bent-Over Dumbell Raises	2–3	8–10

Photo of Jay Cutler by Alex Ardenti

Jay works hard to keep his
shoulders in proportion to his
arms and chest.

THE CHAMPS' ROUTINES

Dennis James

"In his first weeks of serious lifting he gained an average of two pounds of muscle every day. This makes him one of the easiest gainers ever reported in the history of bodybuilding."

– Ron Harris, *MuscleMag International* contributor, commenting on the awesome genetic potential of IFBB pro Dennis James.

When he burst on the pro bodybuilding scene in 2000/2001, few had ever heard of the 5'8" 260-pound Dennis James. It didn't take Dennis long, however, to make his mark. After several top-five finishes, he won the 2001 Hungary Grand Prix, then followed that up with a second at the Australian Grand Prix and a third at the Arnold Classic. With training and nutrition advice from Milos Sarcev, Dennis has now had numerous top-10 finishes in over 75 pro contests.

While densely packed with meaty muscle, Dennis's shoulders are particularly impressive. He usually begins his shoulder workouts with one-arm cable laterals. Dennis got the idea for this exercise from watching six-time Mr. Olympia Dorian Yates train. Like Yates, Dennis likes to do the exercise behind his back rather than to the front. He finds that the standard front version brings too much of his front shoulders into play. He wants to isolate his side shoulders as much as possible. During a typical workout he'll do 4 sets of 8 to 12 reps.

Next up is seated dumbell presses. Unlike many bodybuilders, who try to hoist up as much weight as possible without any thought to proper form, Dennis maintains immaculate form on this exercise. He does this to effectively stimulate his front and side shoulders as well as reduce the risk of developing a shoulder injury. As with cable raises, Dennis will do 4 sets of 8 to 12 reps. I should add that during the pre-contest season, when he's lower in bodyweight and more susceptible to injury, Dennis substitutes machine presses for dumbell presses.

To bring in his traps, Dennis does 3 or 4 sets of upright rows using a narrow grip on an EZ-curl bar. Unlike many bodybuilders, who stop the movement at mid-chest level, Dennis pulls the bar all the way up to his chin.

For the fourth and final exercise, Dennis does 4 sets of bent-over cable laterals. As with side cable laterals, Dennis prefers the feel of the cables to that of dumbells. He'll stand between the two pulley machines and grab the lower left handle with his right hand and the lower right handle with his left hand. From here he'll bend forward and pull the handles outwards and upwards until his arms are parallel to the floor.

JAMES' BACK WORKOUT		
EXERCISE	SETS	REPS
Side Cable Laterals	4	8–12
Dumbell or Machine Presses	4	8–12
Upright Rows	3–4	8–12
Bent-Over Cable Laterals	4	8–12

Photo of Dennis James by Robert Kennedy

THE CHAMPS' ROUTINES
Markus Ruhl

"When I first saw pictures of Dorian in the magazines, he had a look of ruggedness and power that I had never seen in a bodybuilder before. You just knew that he was incredibly strong. As soon as I started to find out how he trained my respect grew for him more. The way he pushed himself beyond normal limits of pain and effort was even more impressive to me than his physique. I resolved to model myself after him."

– Markus Ruhl, mass monster and 2002 New York Night of Champions winner, commenting on England's Dorian Yates – the main inspiration for his training style.

It's not surprising that a guy who modeled his training after Dorian Yates would sport the degree of rugged muscle mass that highlights Markus Ruhl's physique. While he'll never win any awards for aesthetics, few bodybuilders thrill audiences as this German behemoth does.

Markus usually starts his shoulder training with a basic pressing movement, either dumbell or front barbell. At one time in his career he did both during the same workout but now that he has most of the mass he needs, he alternates between the two. A typical workout will see him doing 10 to 12 working sets on the pressing exercise. Although he favors a higher volume of work than his idol Dorian did, the last 4 to 6 sets might be done for just 4 or 5 reps, so it's not as extreme as it first sounds.

To add extra width to his already yard-wide shoulders, Markus moves on to one-arm side laterals. Like most bodybuilders he spent years doing the two-arm version but on a whim one day he tried the one-arm version and became hooked on the extra degree of concentration it gave him in the side head of his shoulders. With his free arm braced on a power rack or Smith machine, Markus performs 8 to 10 sets of 8 to 10 reps.

For his third exercise Markus likes to do front dumbell raises – again working one arm at a time. Markus believes he neglected his front delts for many years, feeling that they received adequate stimulation from all his chest exercises. But once his side shoulders began to overpower his front shoulders he knew he'd need to

modify his training. A typical day will see Markus perform 6 to 8 sets for 8 to 10 reps.

Another favorite exercise on shoulder day is upright rows. Markus feels that this is one of the most underrated of all shoulder exercises and is a great way to work both the side shoulders and traps. Markus usually uses an EZ-curl bar as it places less stress on his wrist than a straight bar. As his shoulders are starting to fatigue by this point, Markus usually limits the sets to 4 or 5, with reps in the 8-to-10 range.

To finish off his shoulder workout, Markus performs 6 to 8 sets of rear lateral raises. He prefers the lying version to the standing version, as lying on the bench places less stress on his lower back. Most days will see him work up to 45- to 60-pound dumbells for 8 to ten reps.

RUHL'S SHOULDER WORKOUT		
EXERCISE	**SETS**	**REPS**
Dumbell or Barbell Front Presses	10–15	4–10
One-Arm Side Laterals	8–10	8–10
Upright Rows	4–5	8–10
Rear Laterals	6–8	8–10

Photo of Markus Ruhl by Irvin Gelb

Rusty spots while Lee
hammers out some extra reps.

THE CHAMPS' ROUTINES

Lee Priest

"Anyone who has weak shoulders would probably be better off training them first on a separate day, maybe pairing them with biceps or triceps."

– Lee Priest, top IFBB pro, offering advice to bodybuilders who find their shoulder development lagging behind.

When you're just 5'4" and 220 pounds and competing against guys in the 280- to 300-pound range, you need every single muscle developed to the max. Australia's Lee Priest has accomplished this and then some. His arms and legs are as large as those on guys a foot taller, and his back and chest can hold their own with just about anyone. Then you have his shoulders. Has there ever been a bodybuilder at such a diminutive height who sported such deltoid mass? Lee's shoulders had never been his best bodypart, but after nearly 25 years of training they now give our pocket Hercules that yard-wide look.

Given the size of his arms, Lee realized his side deltoids needed the most size for purposes of visual proportion. It's for this reason that he usually begins his shoulder workout with side dumbell raises. He starts with the dumbells in front of his thighs and lifts them to just above shoulder level. To reduce the stress on his shoulder joint Lee keeps a slight bend at his elbows at all times. Typically he does 5 sets of 8 to 12 reps.

Most bodybuilders at this point would move on to presses, but Lee realizes his rear delts will garner him more points at contests than his front delts, so for his second exercise he moves on to bent-over lateral raises. To begin, Lee grabs a set of dumbells and bends forward so his torso is nearly parallel with the floor. From here he raises the dumbells outwards and upwards. To keep the traps and rhomboids from taking over, Lee never allows his shoulder blades to touch.

Lee's third shoulder exercise is a pressing movement. He's not that fussy which one he does, and therefore rotates barbell, dumbell, machine and Smith-machine presses on a regular basis. A typical day will see Lee banging out 5 or 6 sets of 8 to 15 reps.

To finish off his shoulders, Lee will do 5 or 6 sets of dumbell shrugs. He prefers the increased range of motion that dumbells provide. At one point Lee would go up to 200-pound dumbells in this exercise, but now keeps the weight in the 120- to 150-pound range.

PRIEST'S SHOULDER WORKOUT

EXERCISE	SETS	REPS
Side Laterals	5	8–12
Bent-Over Laterals	5	8–12
Front Presses	5–6	8–15
Dumbell Shrugs	5	8–12

Photo of Lee Priest by Raymond Cassar

circuit who can stand next to such guys as Jay Cutler, Ronnie Coleman and Victor Martinez, and not look out of place. In fact big Quincy outweighs all three and towers over them at 6'4". While picking a "best body-part" on the Taylor physique is difficult, his shoulders ooze special quality.

A typical Taylor shoulder workout will start with side lateral raises. Although he'll occasionally do cable laterals during the pre-contest season, most of his off-season training is done with dumbells. Quincy is quick to point out that he alternates both the exercises and their order – the following is but one shoulder routine in his arsenal. Quincy will alternate one- and two-arm laterals depending on how he's feeling that day. He typically does 3 sets of 8 to 10 reps using 50 to 60 pounds.

Quincy's second exercise is often a pressing movement – usually the Smith machine. Quincy adds that no matter which pressing exercise he does, he'll press to the front. Behind-the-head presses are murder on the rotator cuff, he adds. Quincy is especially strong on this exercise, going up to 315 pounds for 3 sets of 8 to 12 reps.

To finish off his side shoulders and bring in his traps, Quincy does 3 sets of barbell upright rows. Like most bodybuilders Quincy takes a medium-width grip and pulls the bar up to his clavicles. Again the reps are in the 8 to 12 range.

For his fourth and final exercise, Quincy does bent-over laterals using dumbells or cables, or uses a rear-delt machine. He uses such variety because, unlike his side shoulders, which always responded to dumbells, he's had more difficulty bringing his rear shoulders up. He usually does 3 sets of 10 to 12 reps.

THE CHAMPS' ROUTINES
Quincy Taylor

"I like cables for isolation and getting a very deep pump in the muscle, but my own experience has shown that dumbells are better for me in the off-season."
– Quincy Taylor, IFBB pro, comparing the effectiveness of cable laterals to dumbells for adding mass to his shoulders.

At nearly 300 pounds in contest shape, Quincy Taylor is an imposing sight. He's one of the few men on the pro

TAYLOR'S SHOULDER WORKOUT

EXERCISE	SETS	REPS
Side Dumbell Raises	3	8–10
Smith-Machine Presses	3	8–12
Barbell Upright Rows	3	8–12
Bent-Over Laterals or Rear Delt Machine	3	10–12

Photo of Quincy Taylor by Ralph DeHaan

THE CHAMPS' ROUTINES
Mark Dugdale

"When I did an honest assessment of my genetics I realized that I am not structurally broad. Therefore I felt I had to prioritize my shoulders to create as much muscular width as possible."

– Mark Dugdale, new IFBB pro, commenting on how being honest with one's self can lead to positive results.

As if guys like Jay Cutler and Ronnie Coleman didn't have enough to worry about, along comes Mark Dugdale. Packing an incredible 220 pounds on a 5'6" frame, Mark is proportionally one of the thickest competitors on the pro circuit. He's also one of the most symmetrical and balanced.

One of Mark's most impressive bodyparts is his shoulders. Round, full and striated, each coconut is the envy of his opponents everywhere.

Mark's approach to shoulder training is a little different than most, in that he tends to superset a lot of his deltoid exercises with trap exercises. His first superset combo is likely to be standing Hammer Strength shrugs and seated side laterals. He'll do one warmup set of each and then two supersets of 6 to 12 reps.

His next superset consists of seated barbell raises and seated dumbell shrugs. The seated shrugs are probably self-explanatory, but the front barbell raises may be new to many readers. He starts by placing a barbell on his thighs and grabbing it with a palms-up, shoulder-width grip (as if doing a barbell curl). From here he lifts the bar in an arc until it's above his forehead. He then lowers it slowly to just short of touching his thighs. Again he keeps the reps in the 6-to-12 range.

Mark's next two exercises are done as straight sets. For front presses he prefers a machine to free weights. The machine at his gym goes straight up as opposed to having a backward arc. The machines with a backward movement, says Mark, threaten to damage your rotator cuff. He'll do 2 sets of 6 to 12 reps.

For his fourth and final exercise, Mark bangs out 2 sets of 6 to 12 reps of reverse pec-deck flyes. Mark adds that you have to really concentrate on pulling with the rear delts and not the lats on this exercise. The body tends to get lazy and tries to use the larger back muscles to pull the handles.

DUGDALE'S SHOULDER WORKOUT

EXERCISE	SETS	REPS
Hammer Strength Shrugs (superset with) Side Laterals	2	6–12
Front Barbell Raises (superset with) Seated Dumbell Shrugs	2	6–12
Seated Machine Presses	2	6–12
Reverse Pec-Deck Flyes	2	6–12

THE CHAMPS' ROUTINES

Will Harris

"I've always been a big fan of the seated dumbell press and I always keep things simple. I don't move or twist my hands during the movement. I've seen too many guys blow out their shoulders, so I'm not taking any unnecessary risks."

– Will Harris, IFBB pro, talking about how strict form is essential during pressing exercises.

Despite the hundreds of pounds of beef that make up Will Harris' physique, three bodyparts immediately jump out at you: First he has a tight, rock-hard midsection that most lightweights would kill for. Then there's his back, which can easily hold its own with such top guns as Jay Cutler and Ronnie Coleman. Finally, his shoulders give his physique that coveted yard-wide look.

It's not surprising that Will likes to train his shoulders using basic movements. You won't find a lot of cable or fluffy exercises in the Harris shoulder workout. His first exercise is invariably seated dumbell or Hammer Strength presses. Regardless of which exercise he does, Will uses relatively high reps. He finds that higher reps not only give his shoulders a better workout, but the lighter weight he's forced to use greatly reduces the stress on his shoulder joints. Will typically does 3 or 4 sets of 12 to 20 reps.

For his second exercise Will does standing dumbell laterals for his side shoulders. Although there are different versions of this exercise, Will finds dumbells give him the desired feeling in his side delts. To keep the stress on his side shoulders and not his front shoulders or traps, Will lifts the dumbells just to shoulder height and tries to keep his elbows as the highest point at all times. He does 3 to 5 sets of 12 to 20 reps.

To finish off those contest-winning monsters of his, Will does 3 or 4 sets of 12 to 20 reps of either reverse pec-deck flyes or bent-over dumbell raises. If using the pec-deck he pulls his arms back until they are in line with his body. Any further, he says, and the traps and lats take over.

Will prefers bent-over laterals to lying rear laterals. He is careful not to swing his body or pull with his lower back.

HARRIS' SHOULDER WORKOUT

EXERCISE	SETS	REPS
Dumbell or Hammer Strength Presses	3–4	12–20
Side Laterals	3–5	12–20
Reverse Pec-Deck or Bent-Over Laterals	3–4	12–20

THE CHAMPS' ROUTINES

Victor Martinez

History records that Jay Cutler successfully defended his Mr. Olympia title in 2007, but it wasn't a free ride. Hot on his heels was Victor Martinez. With his convincing win at the 2007 Arnold Classic, Victor was one of the favorites going into Las Vegas, and he didn't disappoint. Carrying 250 pounds of striated beef on a 5'9" frame, Victor was one of the thickest yet best-proportioned bodybuilders onstage at the Olympia, and he pushed Cutler to the limit. Most bodybuilding experts feel the sport's grandest prize will be his some day.

Photo of Victor Martinez

As expected of an Arnold Classic winner, Victor's shoulders are a sight to behold. All three heads are fully developed and help give his upper body a supreme V-taper. Besides his shoulder mass, Victor is proud of the fact that his deltoids have the same separation and quality of a light or middleweight. He achieved this result by training intelligently. Unlike most bodybuilders, who have oversized front shoulders from beginning their shoulder training with front presses, Victor always starts his shoulder workout with rear delts. He'll typically do 4 or 5 sets of either bent-over cable or dumbell raises. If using dumbells he'll start with the 40s for 1 set of 10 to 12 and then do 3 or 4 sets of 10 to 12 reps using the 60s.

Next up is side dumbell laterals. Victor finds that by bringing the dumbells up from beside his body, rather than in front, he can keep stricter exercise form. He typically does 3 or 4 sets of 10 to 12 reps using 50- to 70-pound dumbells.

Exercise number three is either dumbell or barbell presses. At one point he did behind-the-head presses, but he gave up the exercise when he started feeling twinges in his rotator cuffs. If he uses dumbells he'll work up to a pair of 140s. Barbell presses usually see Victor maxing out at anywhere from 275 to 315 pounds. In either case it's 3 or 4 sets of 10 to 12 reps.

To finish off his Olympia-level shoulders, Victor does either front raises or upright rows. He primarily does the uprights for his side shoulders, so he uses a shoulder-width grip. If it's a relatively light day he'll use a straight bar on the uprights, but on heavy days he'll use an EZ-curl bar as it's easier on his wrists. Again he does 3 or 4 sets of 10 to 12 reps.

MARTINEZ'S SHOULDER WORKOUT

EXERCISE	SETS	REPS
Bent-Over Laterals	4–5	10–12
Side Laterals	3–4	10–12
Dumbell or Barbell Presses	3–4	10–12
Shoulder-Width Grip Upright Rows	3–4	10–12

CHAPTER 80

Quad and Hamstring Training

"Hamstring strength and flexibility are not only crucial in the size and shape of the rear portion of your upper leg, they also assist in the development of your quadriceps and lower back, and contribute to any type of movement that is performed while you are on your feet."

– John S. Comereski, *MuscleMag International* contributor

"As almost any bodybuilder will admit, even those who loathe and fear the exercise, squatting is the best way to develop large muscular thighs. Squats, squats and more squats have been the main mass-building leg exercise for bodybuilding champions for the past 75 years."

– Greg Zulak, regular *MuscleMag International* contributor, commenting on the importance of squatting for leg building.

Those who follow boxing have no doubt heard announcers saying how a certain boxer lost because "his legs gave out." And just where would soccer or hockey players be without great leg development?

Most sports require great leg strength and power, and bodybuilding is no different. In fact, not only must your legs be strong but they must also be well developed and proportionate to the rest of your body. Nothing in bodybuilding looks as dumb as a 50-inch chest and set of 20-inch arms teetering about on a set of 23-inch quads.

When I released my bestselling book *Hardcore Bodybuilding* back in the early 1980s, I could have selected any photo from my archive of hundreds of thousands. Instead of using a great chest shot or double biceps pose, I chose a mind-blowing photo of Tom Platz doing a leg pose. Even by today's standards Tom is considered to have the greatest set of legs in bodybuilding history. From his massive quads to steel-chord hamstrings, to balloon-sized calves, Tom's legs were the envy of millions. Today such bodybuilders as Ronnie Coleman, Jay Cutler, Mustafa Mohammad, Paco Bautista and Branch Warren set the standard for leg development.

ANATOMY

"You must first separate your quad training from your hamstring training. When training the quads and hamstrings together, most lifters put most of their energy into their quad training. They are just going through the motions by the time they get to their hamstrings."
– Rahim Kassam, *MuscleMag International* columnist, answering a reader's question on how to bring up his lagging hamstrings.

The legs consist of three primary muscle groups. The largest are the four-headed quadriceps that runs from the pelvis to the knee. The quads are the "triceps" of the lower body and as such are extensors. Their primary function is to extend the lower leg at the knee joint, but they also play a role in hip flexion. The hamstrings can be considered the leg version of the biceps and in fact are often referred to as the leg biceps. Their function is to flex, or bend, the leg at the knee joint, drawing the lower leg toward the upper leg. The alternation of quad and hamstring relaxing and contracting allows for such movements as walking, running and climbing stairs.

The calf is made up of two muscles: the gastrocnemius is the diamond-shaped muscle located at the back of the lower leg. The soleus is located underneath the gastrocnemius. Both these muscles are used to extend the foot at the ankle joint. Ballet dancers and gymnasts usually have great calves because of the amount of time they spend on their toes. Since most bodybuilders treat their calves as a separate entity all their own, I'm going to devote an entire chapter to them later in the book.

LEG TRAINING

Unlike the upper body, for which most bodybuilders train the larger muscles separately, the vast majority of pro bodybuilders train the quads and hamstrings during the same workout. As time goes on you may want to split them up, especially if you notice your quads starting to overshadow your hamstrings.

Most bodybuilders begin leg training with the quads, as they require the most energy. You may want to train hamstrings first if you notice them lagging behind.

Photo of Paul DeMayo by Jason Mathas

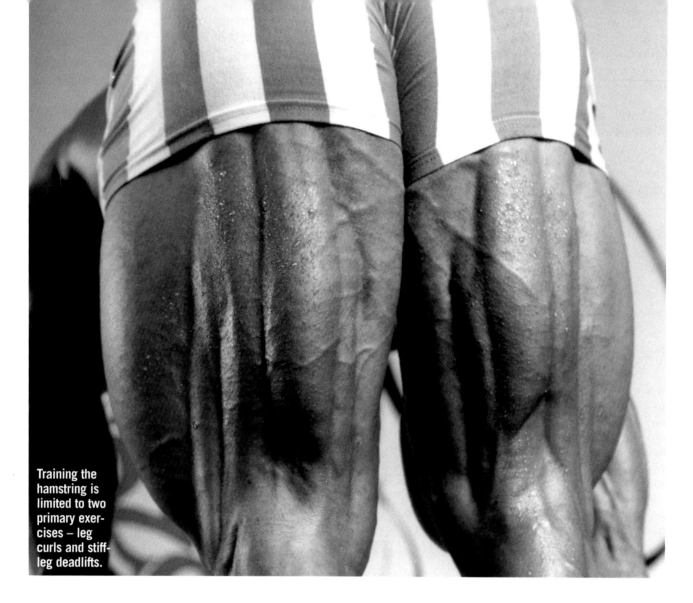

Training the hamstring is limited to two primary exercises – leg curls and stiff-leg deadlifts.

By far the best all-round leg exercise is the barbell squat. Although leg presses are a good substitute in some cases (more on this later), squats have built more championship legs than any other exercise. It's safe to say that every top bodybuilder over the past 50 years has spend thousands of hours at the squat rack.

Having said all that, there may be cases where you should limit or avoid squats altogether. For starters, squats tend to place tremendous stress on the lower back. Now, lower-back strength should keep pace with your quad development, provided you gradually increase the weight. But if you have lower-back problems or make a sudden jump in weight, your legs may be capable of handling it but your back probably won't. Likewise if you injure your lower back by some other means, squats may only prolong the healing process or aggravate it further.

Then there are the knees to consider. Again, knee problems shouldn't come from squatting if you gradually increase the weight over the years. But knee injuries take place for many reasons, and if you have bad knees you should probably not do squats – at least not heavy squats.

Another reason to cut back on squats is proportion. Squats are a terrific quad builder, but they'll also build a powerful set of glutes. You do need some glute size to balance out your lower body, but if you start getting a butt that would do J-Lo proud, either narrow your stance when doing squats (so most of the stress shifts to the center/outer quads) or avoid them altogether, at least for awhile. You will also find if squats are your main leg builder that your quads will eventually outpace your hamstrings, so sometimes you may want to take a break from squats to bring your legs into balance.

Unless you have one of these issues, I can't emphasize enough the value of squats to your bodybuilding workouts. They'll not only build you a powerful set of legs, but they'll even help you gain muscle on your upper body. There are two reasons for this. For one, you'll need to contract every muscle in your upper body just to support the barbell on your shoulders. And it won't be long before you'll be easily squatting with 300+ pounds on your shoulders. The second reason is not fully understood, but because squatting is such a challenging exercise for so many large muscle groups it makes the body release extra growth hormone, which helps increase the size of all your muscles. So get thee to thy squat rack!

The other primary quad exercise is the leg press, which, while not quite as effective as the squat, is a close second. The advantages of leg press over squat are that you can alter your foot position on the platform and thus have more control over the angle of stimulation, you can protect your knees, and you can avoid glute involvement. For these reasons leg presses make a good substitute for those who have pre-existing lower-back or knee problems or wish to reduce the amount of glute development.

Without repeating the exercise description found later in the book, I must stress an important point about leg presses. Within a few months you'll be using a few hundred pounds on the leg press, and after a year or so you'll likely be capable of moving 500+ pounds. The last thing you want to do with this amount of weight is slam the legs into a locked-out position. There is a great risk of hyperextending the legs at the knee joint if you do this. I suggest doing the exercise in a three-quarters style, where you lower the weight until you have an 80- to 90-degree angle between the upper and lower legs, and then extend upward to just short of a lockout.

Besides squats and leg presses, two other quad exercises performed by most bodybuilders are leg extensions and hack squats. Leg extensions are great for total isolation, while hack squats put a nice sweep to the outer quads. Both exercises play a major role in separating the four heads in the months leading up to a contest.

Unlike most muscle groups, for which you literally have dozens of exercises to choose from, training the hamstrings is limited to two primary exercises: leg curls and stiff-leg deadlifts. For this reason you must make frequent use of the advanced training techniques discussed earlier in the book.

FINAL CONSIDERATIONS

While warming up is recommended for all muscle groups, it's an absolute must before leg training. You don't just walk in off the street and start doing 300-pound squats or 500-pound leg presses. If you're working up to, say, 315 pounds on the squat, perform 15 to 20 reps with just the bar, and then go 135, 225, 275 and then 315. These are suggested weights and you will need to modify the weight to suit your own strength levels. The bottom line is that one set of 135 pounds before your work sets is not a warmup, it's an accident waiting to happen. Not only the leg muscles are at risk. The knees and lower back play a huge role in stabilizing and moving that weight. Both must be warmed up as well. All it takes is a few minutes of your time to enjoy a lifetime of injury-free leg training.

BEST QUADRICEPS EXERCISES
- Squats
- Leg presses
- Hack squats
- Leg extensions
- Lunges

BEST HAMSTRING EXERCISES
- Stiff-leg deadlifts
- Lying leg curls
- Seated leg curls
- Standing leg curls
- Back extensions

before we see the first 300-pounder hoisting the coveted Sandow statue.

Ronnie's success was built on his overall size and balance. At his best the man had no weakness. Although Ronnie's back and arms tend to receive the most attention, his legs are also among the best in bodybuilding history. They are huge and crisscrossed with splits and cuts. As you might expect, Ronnie has performed just about every leg exercise and training combination over the years, and the following routine is but one of the many he used during his Mr. Olympia run.

A typical leg workout would see Ronnie start with the king of leg exercises – squats. Ronnie would usually pyramid up in weight from 135 to over 500 and even up to 800 pounds. It's difficult to nail Ronnie down on rep ranges, but he probably did sets of 12 most often.

With his basic power movement out of the way, Ronnie would move on to hack squats. Again he would pyramid up in weight from four to five to six plates or more per side. Again he favored sets of 12 reps.

Until Ronnie, many bodybuilders considered lunges a sissy exercise. One look at Ronnie's legs convinced them otherwise. Ronnie typically did 3 to 5 sets of walking lunges using from 135 to 185 pounds and lunging a distance of about 100 yards per leg.

After murdering his quads, Ronnie moves on to hamstrings. One of his favorite routines was to superset lying with seated leg curls. A typical day would see him do 4 or 5 such supersets.

THE CHAMPS' ROUTINES
Ronnie Coleman

With his record-tying run of eight Mr. Olympia wins, Ronnie Coleman has secured his place in bodybuilding history. When you talk about the greatest bodybuilders ever, Ronnie's name has to be in the top few.

Ronnie continued the trend of ever-heavier Mr. Olympia winners. It started with Sergio Oliva at 230, Arnold at 240, Lee Haney at 250, Dorian Yates at 260, and finally Coleman's 280 to 290. With Jay Cutler also weighing in the 280+ range it's only a matter of time

COLEMAN'S QUAD WORKOUT

EXERCISE	SETS	REPS
Squats	4–5	12
Hack Squats	4–5	12
Walking Lunges	3–5	100 yds

COLEMAN'S HAMSTRING WORKOUT

EXERCISE	SETS	REPS
Lying Leg Curls (superset with) Seated Leg Curls	4–5	12

Photo of Ronnie Coleman by Irvin Gelb

Ronnie's superior quads and hamstrings helped him achieve his eight Mr. Olympia titles.

Quincy always fully warms up his thighs because of the heavy weight he uses on basic mass exercises.

THE CHAMPS' ROUTINES

Quincy Taylor

One of the problems faced by tall bodybuilders is managing to keep their legs in proportion to their upper bodies. Ironically for 6'4" Quincy Taylor, his legs have always been one of his best bodyparts despite having 300 pounds of beef spread over his frame.

Given the weight he uses on basic mass exercises such as squats and leg presses, Quincy likes to fully warm up his quads with leg extensions before beginning. During a typical workout he'll do four good warmup sets of leg extensions. Although the reps may vary, he generally does 10 to 12 reps per set.

With his quads now warmed up it's on to his first compound exercise: leg presses. There's no need to list the weight he uses here. Suffice it to say that he might as well be pressing a small car. During a typical workout he'll blast out 4 excruciating sets of 8 to 10 reps.

Next up is 4 sets of Smith-machine squats. While he'll occasionally perform barbell squats, Quincy finds the Smith machine better for isolating his quads and reducing the stress on his lower back. It also allows him to position his feet in such a way that his glutes are not as heavily involved.

During the pre-contest season Quincy will go back to the leg extension and do another 8 sets of 10 to 12 reps. Yes, you read that correctly – 8 sets! Is it any wonder that his wheels are among the most striated and separated on the pro circuit?

With his quads annihilated Quincy moves on to inflict the same degree of punishment on his hamstrings. He usually starts with stiff-leg deadlifts. When doing this exercise Quincy pays strict attention to technique. It's very easy to get carried away and pull with the lower back rather than forcing the hamstrings to do most of the lifting. He typically does 4 sets of 15 to 20 reps.

Next up: 4 sets of lying leg curls. Again strict style is important and Quincy makes sure not to throw his butt into the air or pull with his arms. As he considers this is basic power movement for hamstrings he'll go as heavy as possible for 10 to 12 reps.

Photos of Quincy Taylor by Jason Mathas

To finish off his hamstrings Quincy will do 4 sets of either seated or standing leg curls. On some days he'll superset the two together for 4 sets of 10 to 12 reps

TAYLOR'S QUAD WORKOUT

EXERCISE	SETS	REPS
Leg Extensions	4	10–12
Leg Presses	4	8–10
Smith-Machine Squats	4	8–10
Leg Extensions (pre-contest)	8	10–12

TAYLOR'S HAMSTRING WORKOUT

EXERCISE	SETS	REPS
Stiff-Leg Deadlifts	4	15–20
Lying Leg Curls	4	10–12
Seated or Standing Leg Curls	4	10–12

THE CHAMPS' ROUTINES
Lee Priest

"Leg days were the worst you could imagine. He would have us do supersets, giant sets, high reps, forced reps, anything to inflict more pain. After this hellish workout he would expect me to be lying on the floor moaning for an hour. Instead I would act exhausted for a minute and then start doing a little dance. That used to drive him nuts."

– Lee Priest, top pro bodybuilder, describing what a leg day was like when training with Tom Platz.

Despite his 5'4" height, Australia's Blond Myth, Lee Priest, is not afraid to mix it up onstage with the "big boys." Why would he be intimidated? At 220 pounds he packs more muscle mass on his frame than just about any bodybuilder in history. While famous for his over-22-inch arms, Lee's legs are among the best on bodybuilding stages these days as well.

Of course Lee's workouts change often, so the following is just a sample of the exercises he has used over the years to pack mass on his quads.

Lee often starts his quad training with leg extensions. They serve to warm up and pre-exhaust his quads, so he doesn't need to go as heavy on leg presses and squats. A typical day will see Lee perform 4 or 5 sets of 15 to 20 reps of Leg extensions

With his legs now fully warmed up Lee moves on to his second exercise – often squats. Over the years Lee has discovered that his legs respond both to heavy weight for low reps and lighter weight for high reps. At one time he squatted 800 pounds for 3 reps and has banged out an incredible 30 reps with 405 pounds. Unlike many bodybuilders Lee will occasionally substitute Smith-machine squats for barbell squats. One thing is for sure though, whether barbell or Smith machine, Lee comes from the old school regarding depth and tries to squat down until his butt is just short of the floor.

Another favorite mass-builder for Lee is leg presses on the vertical press machine. Lee got inspired to do vertical leg presses from looking at old photos of Arnold, Dave Draper and Franco Columbu doing the exercise at the old Gold's Gym in Venice Beach, California.

Photo of Lee Priest

After squats or leg presses, Lee likes to finish off his quads with hack squats. Lee credits this exercise with putting the most sweep on his outer quads over the years. Although at one time he could work up to 1,000 pounds on hack squats, these days he usually does 4 or 5 sets of 10 to 12 reps using between 315 and 495 pounds.

PRIEST'S QUAD WORKOUT

EXERCISE	SETS	REPS
Leg Extensions	4–5	15–20
Squats or Leg Presses	4–5	3–30
Hack Squats	4–5	10–12

To develop and maintain his famous legs, Lee changes his quad exercises fairly often.

Photos of Lee Priest by Paul Buceta

THE CHAMPS' ROUTINES

Jay Cutler

"I remember trying to squat 135 and not being able to budge it, though I already weighed about 180."
– Jay Cutler, multi-Mr. Olympia winner, telling an interviewer about his early days at he gym.

When he dethroned Ronnie Coleman from the Mr. Olympia perch in 2006, many in the audience said that sure he was the best that day, but look out next year. Ronnie will be back. Well Ronnie did come back, but so did Jay – bigger and harder than ever. The end result was a second Mr. Olympia title for Jay and fourth place for Ronnie. With his second Mr. Olympia title, Jay proved it was no fluke and he cemented himself as the number one bodybuilder in the world.

What gives Jay the nod over his closest rivals is his completeness. From head to toe you'll see nothing but Grade A beef. And speaking of beef, you need look no higher than Jay's quads to see what I'm talking about. Not since Tom Platz has the Mr. Olympia stage witnessed such a pair of striated quads.

Jay attributes much of his quad development to his early years watching a local bodybuilder named Rich Warfield training legs. Rich had huge legs and spent a considerable amount of time at the squat rack. Although he had done various machine exercises, it wasn't until he began squatting that Jay's legs began to grow. It wasn't long before the days of struggling with one 45-pound plate per side disappeared and he started loading up the bar with six or seven plates instead.

Jay's legs responded so well that he actually had to back off the heavy squats. He now limits the weight to 400 pounds or less and does the exercise on an infrequent basis.

A typical Cutler quad workout nowadays starts with leg extensions. He doesn't really consider this exercise part of his workout and only does a couple of light sets to warm up his joints and leg muscles. He usually keeps the weight at about 60 pounds and does two easy sets of 15 to 20 reps.

With his quads and knees warmed up Jay moves on to his first power movement: leg presses. He does 2 medium-weight sets for 12 to 15 reps and then moves on to two heavy sets for 7 to 10 reps. To maintain stress on his quads and not his knees, Jay never locks out at the top of the exercise. Nor does he bounce at the bottom and use his knees as springs.

Jay's second quad exercise is the hack squat. Jay finds this exercise is great for putting that superior sweep on his outer quads. Unlike many bodybuilders who go only partway down because they use too much weight, Jay has opted for quality over quantity. All his reps are rock bottom. He does 3 sets of 6 to 8 reps.

To finish off his over-30-inch quads, Jay goes back to the leg extension machine. This time the exercise is not a warmup, however, and these last 3 sets are done to absolute failure. He also limits his rest period to 30 seconds or less to emphasize the burn and pumped feeling.

Photos of Jay Cutler by Irvin Gelb

CUTLER'S QUAD WORKOUT

EXERCISE	SETS	REPS
Leg Extensions	2	15–20
Leg Presses	4	12–15
Hack Squats	3	6–8
Leg Extensions	3	10

280-pounders in the sport, Dexter's physique looks both functional and athletic. He doesn't have a bunched-up blocky look, and his waist resembles those of the bodybuilders of old – small, tight, wasp-like ... and ripped.

While picking a "best" bodypart on the Jackson physique is difficult, his legs deserve special mention. When you have one of the best upper bodies in the business it only makes sense to keep the wheels in proportion, and his is the perfect X-frame.

When it comes to training his quads, Dexter's a traditionalist. You won't find many exotic machine exercises in his quad routine. He usually starts his quad workouts with barbell squats. While he can handle some tremendous weight in this movement, he doesn't jump right into his top weight. He'll do two warmup sets with 185 pounds and then 5 sets of 8 to 10 reps, working up from 225 to 545 pounds.

For his second exercise, Dexter moves on to hack squats. Like most bodybuilders he finds this exercise great for putting that wide sweep on his outer quads. He'll typically do a warmup set using 135 pounds and then pyramid up in weight from 225 to 405 pounds for sets of 10 reps.

Exercise number three is the seated leg extension. As his quads are warmed up by now, he goes straight into his working sets, doing 4 sets of 10 reps using half, two-thirds, three-quarters and the full stack.

To finish off his quads, Dexter adds in 3 sets of 15 to 20 reps (steps) of walking dumbell lunges. The way Dexter looks at it, it doesn't make sense to build muscle if it's not functional.

THE CHAMPS' ROUTINES
Dexter Jackson

"You have to get in the gym, hit your legs hard, and then get out and let them rest. If you don't you won't have the energy to train as hard as you should."
– Dexter Jackson, top IFBB pro, commenting on his approach to training legs.

When you ask the question who the top bodybuilders are in the world today, you are likely to hear the names Ronnie Coleman and Jay Cutler. But if you modify the question and ask which bodybuilder would you most like to look like, then more often than not the name mentioned is Dexter "The Blade" Jackson.

Standing just 5'6", Dexter carries 230 pounds of prime beef into battle. And unlike some of the

JACKSON'S QUAD WORKOUT		
EXERCISE	**SETS**	**REPS**
Barbell Squats	7	10
Hack Squats	4	10
Leg Extensions	4	10
Walking Dumbell Lunges	3	20*
		* Number of steps per leg

Photo of Dexter Jackson by Irvin Gelb

THE CHAMPS' ROUTINES
Will Harris

When Will Harris decided he wanted to get serious about bodybuilding he realized that he'd need to bring his legs up to the level of his upper body. Will was blessed with a unique ability to add mass to his back, arms and delts almost by looking at weights. His legs, on the other hand, continued to display a degree of stubbornness. Realizing that normal training techniques just weren't cutting it, Will adopted a high-rep training style for his leg workouts. Instead of the usual 8 to 12 reps he was using with success for his other muscle groups, Will started doing 30 reps per set on all his leg exercises. His second place finish at the 2007 Europa Super Show demonstrates that Will's philosophy has paid off.

Will typically begins his leg workouts with leg extensions. He likes the intense burn that leg extensions give his quads. He also believes that leg extensions are probably the best warmup exercise for the quads and one of the primary reasons he has never had a serious leg injury over the years. Will normally does 4 sets of 30 reps of leg extensions. As you can imagine his quads are literally exploding with pain by the time he reaches those last couple of reps.

Exercise number two for big Will is the 45-degree leg press. Again it's 4 sets of 30 reps, but don't be misled into thinking that these are light sets or half-rep sets. He brings his knees down until they touch his chest. He also uses considerable weight, starting with six 45-pound plates per side and working up to 10 to 14 plates per side.

To really kill his quads, Will finishes of with three sets of bodyweight squats. As his quads are pretty well spent from the two previous exercises, Will finds that he doesn't need to use a barbell. He'll typically go to failure, which on many days is upwards of 100 reps per set. For those who consider this a wussy exercise, Will challenges you to give them a try and just see how your quads will howl with pain!

Will's hamstring workouts are very similar to his quad training – high-rep sets in the 20 to 30 range. He starts with lying leg curls. The key to this, says Will, is to not throw your butt up into the air. This not only cheats the hamstrings out of getting the maximum stimulation, but also puts stress on the lower back. He'll typically do 3 or 4 sets of 20 to 30 reps.

Hamstring exercise number two is the Hammer Strength seated leg curl – 3 or 4 sets of 20 to 30 reps.

Will finishes his hamstrings in the same manner as his quads, with a bodyweight-only exercise. In this case it's lunges (which actually works all the muscles of the leg, plus the glutes). Will prefers to step back as opposed to forward, but the finished position is the same. He'll go to failure on one leg and then switch legs. Once again it could be 50 reps or a hundred. It all depends on the day.

HARRIS' QUAD WORKOUT

EXERCISE	SETS	REPS
Leg Extensions	4–5	30
45-Degree Leg Presses	4	30
Bodyweight Squats	3	failure

HARRIS' HAMSTRING WORKOUT

EXERCISE	SETS	REPS
Lying Leg Curls	3–4	20–30
Seated Leg Curls	3–4	20–30
Bodyweight Lunges	3	failure

Photo of Will Harris by Jason Mathas

CHAPTER 81

Calf Training

"My dad was wearing shorts and I noticed that he had the exact same calves as mine, and you think my dad ever trained them? Not a single day in his life!"

– Stan McQuay, 2006 NPC light heavyweight champion, commenting on the secret to his great calves – outstanding genetics.

"The fact is, calves are difficult and stubborn and don't often respond to the type of training and basic exercises that other bodyparts do. That's because calf development depends largely on genetics. The good news is, genetics can mostly be bypassed – even overridden – with the correct type of training."

– Lori Grannis, regular *MuscleMag International* contributor

f one word can be used to describe the calves, it's stubborn. We often hear bodybuilders complaining that despite the "blasting" they give their calves, they just refuse to grow. While in some cases genetics are in fact the primary culprit, in most cases it's the bodybuilders' generous use of the word "blasting" that lies at the heart of the problem. Blasting does not mean performing a few half-hearted sets at the end of the workout. Blasting means training your calves like every other muscle group and then some. You're doing 8, 10, 12 or more sets each for your biceps and chest. Shouldn't you treat the calves with the same diligence? Unfortunately most bodybuilders don't. After a few months of half-assed training they give up, citing "poor genetics" as the reason for the poor calf development.

Sure there are exceptions. I'm sure you've seen guys with monster calves who never did a calf raise in their lives. These genetically gifted wonders then have the audacity to say how their mother or great aunt has even bigger lower legs! The winner of the 1982 Mr. Olympia, Chris Dickerson, owner of two of the greatest calves in bodybuilding history, was fond of saying that his two brothers (Chris was one of a set of triplets) had calves nearly the same size as he did, and yet neither worked out.

At the other extreme we find the genetically disadvantaged who do in fact spend years blasting their calves with just about every exercise known, and still can't get the little buggers to stretch the tape to more than 15 or 16 inches.

So why is it that so many bodybuilders have poor to mediocre calves? Well for starters you don't know what pain is until you start training your calves properly. Like the thighs and abdominals, calf training is downright agonizing. Training the calves might not fatigue you like thigh training, but the little devils take a backseat to no one when it comes to misery. Many bodybuilders are simply unwilling to put up with such pain – especially for what will probably be a long period of training.

Another reason lies with their location. Unlike the biceps and pectorals, which are displayed prominently

The calf muscles don't always respond to basic training – monster calves require the correct exercises and focused effort.

for all to see, the calves are "way down there" and usually covered by a pair of pants. Many bodybuilders just don't want to devote that much time and effort in developing a muscle that rarely gets seen.

A third reason can be blamed on ego. When people know that you work out they'll often ask you to "show me your muscles." Now, you don't pull up your pants leg and flex a calf; you hit a double biceps. No matter how big and impressive your calves, they'll never be considered "muscles" by the general population. Though a great set of calves will make bodybuilders the envy of their gym buddies and hold them in great esteem by the judges, the fact remains that bodybuilders would sooner spend most of their time working the big showy muscles like the chest and arms.

A final reason relates to what I mentioned earlier. Unless you're that naturally blessed one in a million, odds are you're going to have to work hard – very hard – to get your calves to respond. The calves are among the most stubborn muscles when it comes to growth. You may spend months if not years doing standing and seated calf raises with little observable growth. Conversely some of the other muscle groups such as your chest, back or thighs may start shaping up in weeks. The bottom line is that you must – absolutely must – work your calves if you hope to do well in any contest these days.

ANATOMY

The calf is made up of two muscles: the gastrocnemius and the soleus. The bulk of the calf is made up of the gastrocnemius, the large heart-(or diamond) shaped muscle at the rear of the lower leg. The primary function of the gastrocnemius is to flex the foot at the ankle and raise you onto your toes when your legs are straight.

The other main part of the calf is the soleus, a broad but flat muscle that connects to the Achilles tendon. This muscle is located partially underneath and partially below the gastrocnemius. The soleus also flexes the foot at the ankle joint, but plays a bigger role when the knees are bent.

When working his calves with donkey calf raises, Arnold routinely had more than one person sit across his back.

Photo of Arnold Schwarzenegger, Bill Grant and Franco Columbu by Art Zeller

TRAINING

Yes, training the calves is both painful and tedious. But it's also necessary and highly rewarding – especially when other bodybuilders start admiring those diamond-shaped lower legs of yours. If you need a lesson in determination look no further than Arnold Schwarzenegger. When Arnold first started winning contests in Europe he usually had the biggest upper body onstage. But then he began losing contests to smaller bodybuilders with better proportions, including better calves. After watching his idol Reg Park training his calves with 1,000+ pounds on the calf machine, Arnold changed his mindset and made calf training a priority.

Calf training exercises generally fall into two types – standing and seated. Standing calf exercises such as the standing calf raise machine primarily work the larger gastrocnemius muscle and allow you to use hundreds of pounds of weight. Seated calf raises primarily work the smaller soleus section of the calves, and will not take as much weight.

Besides machine raises, one of the best calf exercises is the donkey calf raise. Flip through an old issue of *MuscleMag International* or *Muscle Builder/Power* and you might see Arnold bent over, working calves with one or two people sitting across his back. While seldom seen in gyms anymore because of the "look" of the exercise, you can't dispute its effectiveness.

Besides using different exercises, you can also target different parts of the calf by turning the toes in or out. You can also train calves in your socks or bare feet. The theory behind this is that having the feet free of the constraints of a sneaker, allows for a greater range of motion. While this is true, keep in mind that you'll will need some ankle support when doing calf raises with a couple of hundred pounds of weight. Also keep in mind that many gyms have policies against going bare foot in their gyms (both for safety and hygiene reasons).

There's no magic time to train your calves. Most bodybuilders work them after they train thighs. You can do the same as long as your calves don't start lagging behind your other muscles. As soon as you notice your upper legs overshadowing your lower legs, revise your training and either do calves first or switch them to a separate day. You may even want to perform staggered sets – train between other muscle groups.

No matter which calf routine you follow you must train at least as hard as you do the other muscle groups. You'll also notice that traditional reps and sets (i.e. 3 to 4 sets of 8 to 12 reps) don't often yield results. Most bodybuilders find alternating high-rep (15 to 20) days and low-rep (6 to 8) days to be the best approach.

THE BEST CALF EXERCISES

- Standing calf raises and seated calf raises
- Toe presses on leg-press machine
- Donkey calf raises
- Calf raises on hack machine

THE CHAMPS' ROUTINES

Given the limited number of exercises for calf training, it's not surprising that most of the top pros follow similar routines. The following are a few sample calf workouts:

MARTINEZ'S CALF WORKOUT

EXERCISE	SETS	REPS
Standing Calf Raises	3	15–20
Seated Calf Raises	3	15–20
Toe Presses on Leg-Press Machine	3	15–20

JACKSON'S CALF WORKOUT

EXERCISE	SETS	REPS
Standing Calf Raises	3	15–20
Seated Calf Raises	3	15–20

CUTLER'S CALF WORKOUT

EXERCISE	SETS	REPS
Standing Calf Raises	3	10–12
Seated Calf Raises	3	10–12
Donkey Calf Raises	3	8–12

CHAPTER 82

Biceps and Triceps Training

"I knew after the 2003 USA that if I was going to come back and fulfill my goal of winning in 2004 I was going to need to bring up my arms a bit more and continue to improve my back."

– Mark Dugdale, IFBB pro, as told to Larry Pepe

t's safe to say the photo on the cover of Arnold Schwarzenegger's book *Education of a Bodybuilder* did more to inspire the 1980s generation of bodybuilders than any other. Even by today's standards, no one has been able to duplicate that single biceps pose performed by Arnold on a California hilltop.

Building a bigger set of arms is probably the No. 1 goal of just about every bodybuilder. Even if the arms are among the body's smaller major muscles, there's something highly desirable about having a set of "hams" hanging from your shoulders.

While it's true that two of the sport's greatest Mr. Olympias, Dorian Yates and Lee Haney, had average-sized arms (compared to their other muscle groups), most of the top bodybuilders of the past 40 years have had outstanding arms. From Sergio Oliva and Arnold to Ronnie Coleman and Jay Cutler, it seems bodybuilding's greatest are synonymous with arm development.

ANATOMY

Perhaps the most ironic thing about the arms is that while the biceps get the most attention, it's the triceps that make up most of the upper arms' mass. Furthermore, it's the triceps that play the biggest role in most sports. In a manner of speaking you can think of the arms as upper-body legs. In fact human arms were at one point a second pair of legs, but became adapted for other functions when our ancestors stood up on two legs years ago.

But the largest muscle in your leg – the quadriceps – just happens to correspond to the largest muscle in your arms – the triceps. Both work to

straighten, or extend, their respective limbs. Likewise, both the legs and arms have biceps muscles (in the legs we call them the hamstrings) for flexing the limbs.

While the arms and legs are virtually identical from an anatomical point of view, most bodybuilders start their leg training with the quads but start their arm training with the biceps. This doesn't make a lot of sense, given the larger size of the triceps. If your goal is building the largest pair of arms possible, you should train the triceps as hard as, if not harder than, the biceps.

TRAINING

With the possible exception of the barbell bench press, by far the most popular exercise seen in free-weight gyms is the standing barbell curl. There are numerous reasons for the popularity of barbell curls. For starters it's probably the best exercise for building the biceps. And any exercise that builds the biceps is going to place very high on the popularity scale. Another reason for the popularity of barbell curls is their simplicity. All you need is a barbell and a few plates. No cables, pulleys or racks are needed. Finally, you can perform barbell curls just about anywhere – in gyms, basements, even hotel rooms.

Besides barbells, bodybuilders use dumbells, cables and machines to work the biceps. Dumbell curls are virtually as effective as barbell curls and have the advantage of placing less stress on the wrists. Cables are great for pre-contest and keep the tension on the biceps for the full range of motion (as opposed to barbells, where there is less tension on the biceps as the forearm approaches the vertical). Machine curls are loved and hated. Take your pick. I usually suggest giving them all a try and seeing how they feel. If you seem to be getting something out of them, include them in your training.

As I stressed earlier, the real key to building large arms is triceps development. Unlike biceps training, where the barbell curl is by far the most popular exercise, there doesn't seem to be one favorite movement for working the triceps. The most popular and effective are variations of lying extensions, pushdowns and dips.

Photo of Ronnie Coleman by Alex Ardenti

I should stress that because the biceps and triceps receive a great deal of stimulation when training the large torso muscles, you don't need to kill them when you work out. Chest and shoulder training is heavily dependent on the triceps, and the biceps are given a great workout on most back exercises. For most bodybuilders 6 to 8 sets in total is probably sufficient. Even the top pro bodybuilders rarely go over 10 to 12 sets when they train their biceps and triceps.

BEST BICEPS EXERCISES

- Barbell curls
- Dumbell curls
- Preacher curls
- Cable curls
- Incline curls
- Concentration curls
- Machine curls

BEST TRICEPS EXERCISES

- Lying barbell extensions
- Lying dumbell extensions
- Behind-head dumbell extensions
- Kickbacks
- Pushdowns
- Narrow presses
- Dips
- Bench dips

THE CHAMPS' ROUTINES

Jay Cutler

"They always had good shape, but I knew they need-ed a lot more size to match."

– Jay Cutler, commenting on probably the most sought-after goal in bodybuilding: larger arms!

When you're trying to dethrone an eight-time Mr. Olympia who has two of the largest arms in history, you need a decent pair of your own. Jay always had a great set of guns, but just didn't have the necessary mass to trade arm shots with Ronnie Coleman. One of the first things he did was get his ego under control and not worry about how much he could curl. Now he goes for quality and slightly higher reps.

Jay has a group of favorite biceps and triceps exercises that he picks from, but the following usually make up the core of his arm workouts.

His first biceps exercise is usually preacher curls with a dumbell. He finds one-arm preacher curls a great way to pre-exhaust his biceps and keeps him from get-ting too carried away with heavier weight on the barbell curls. He'll start with a couple of light warmup sets, then a 35-pound dumbell for 15 reps and then two addi-tional sets of 8 to 15 reps using a 45-pound dumbell.

With his biceps now fully warmed up, Jay moves on to standing barbell curls. At one point in his career he was using over 225 pounds on this exercise, but no longer. Now he'll do one set with just 75 pounds and then bring the weight up to 135 pounds and bang out 3 sets of 12 to 15 reps.

Next up our multi-Mr. Olympia winner moves on to standing alternating dumbell curls. He certainly needs no warmup sets at this point and he launches right into 3 sets of 8 to 12 reps using between 50- and

Photo of Jay Cutler by Irvin Gelb

60-pound dumbells. Like most bodybuilders, Jay supinates his hands as he curls the dumbells.

For his fourth exercise Jay does 3 sets of cable curls. Besides keeping the tension on his biceps throughout the full range of motion, Jay finds cable curls an excellent exercise for drop sets or rest-pause. If doing rest-pause he'll pick as heavy a weight as he can handle for 5 reps, put it down and count to 5, and then pick it back up and try to squeeze out another 5 reps.

Jay ends his biceps onslaught with one-arm cable curls. With his free hand placed on his hip for balance Jay squeezes every rep as hard as he can. Again it's 3 sets of anywhere from 8 to 15 reps, depending on the mood he's in.

TRICEPS

For his first triceps exercise Jay likes to do one-arm cable pushdowns. This exercise serves the same purpose as one-arm preacher curls for his biceps – it both warms up his triceps and pre-exhausts them before the heavier compound exercises come later. Jay typically does 3 sets of 10 to 12 reps.

For his second exercise, Jay does 3 sets of 10 to 12 reps of straight-bar pushdowns. Unlike most bodybuilders, who use a narrow, 6- to 8-inch grip on this exercise, Jay says his triceps seem to get the most out of a shoulder-width grip.

Next up is two-arm behind-the-head dumbell extensions. Although many bodybuilders consider dumbell triceps exercises more shaping than mass-building exercises, Jay disagrees. This is not surprising given the 200+ pound dumbells he uses. Again it's 3 sets of 10 to 12 reps.

Exercise number four is bodyweight dips. For those who question a Mr. Olympia using just his bodyweight, remember that Jay weighs over 300 pounds in the off-season. As you can imagine that's plenty to stimulate his triceps after his previous sets. Jay typically does 3 sets of 10 to 12 reps.

Jay adds a fifth exercise to blast his triceps – close-grip barbell presses. It's amazing to think that

after four exercises he's still strong enough to use 250 pounds on this exercise, but such is the power of those Cutler horseshoes!

CUTLER'S BICEPS WORKOUT

EXERCISE	SETS	REPS
One-Arm Preacher Curls	5	8–15
Barbell Curls	3	8–15
Alternating Dumbell Curls	3	8–15
Cable Curls	3	8–15
One-Arm Cable Curls	3	8–12

CUTLER'S TRICEPS WORKOUT

EXERCISE	SETS	REPS
One-Arm Cable Pushdowns	3	10–12
Wide-Grip Pushdowns	3	10–12
Two-Arm Dumbell Extensions	3	10–12
Bodyweight Dips	3	10–12
Close-Grip Bench Presses	3	10–12

Photo of Jay Cutler by Alex Ardenti

Melvin has amazing 21-inch guns, which he achieves with high-volume training.

Photo (Top) of Melvin Anthony by Jim Amentler
Photo (Bottom) of Melvin Anthony by Robert Reiff

THE CHAMPS' ROUTINES
Melvin Anthony

Since the 2000 New York Night of Champions, "Marvelous" Melvin Anthony has placed out of the top 10 only twice in the dozens of IFBB pro contests he has entered. Along the way he won the 2004 New York Night of Champions and came 2nd at both the 2008 Australian and New Zealand Grand Prix. Over the years Melvin has developed a reputation for being one of the sport's greatest posers.

BICEPS

Melvin is one of the thickest competitors on the pro scene, carrying 240 to 245 pounds on his 5'8" physique. Among his greatest attributes are his 21-inch arms.

In this age of heavy-duty or high-intensity training, Melvin is not one to shy away from high volume. He typically does 25 to 30 sets for his biceps. Most would consider this overtraining, but it works for him and in his mind, that's all that counts. Melvin's also a big fan of supersets and he often performs six biceps exercises in three groups of two exercises each.

ANTHONY'S BICEPS WORKOUT

EXERCISE	SETS	REPS
Standing Barbell Curls (superset with) Dumbell Concentration Curls	5	10
Standing Alternating Dumbell Curls Standing Straight-Bar Cable Curls	5	10
One-Arm Preacher Curls (superset with) Incline Dumbell Curls	5	10

THE CHAMPS' ROUTINES
Quincy Taylor

"Bodybuilding is purely a visual sport anyway, so why would you even bother to exaggerate any of that stuff?"
– Quincy Taylor, 2001 NPC champion and bodybuilding pro, responding to a reporter's question about other competitors exaggerating the size of their arms.

At 6'4" and 330 pounds in contest shape, Quincy is another of those supersized pros favored to win the coveted Mr. Olympia title some day. With arms that measure a genuine 22 inches, Quincy is not afraid to trade front double biceps shots with guys like Ronnie Coleman and Jay Cutler.

Quincy always tries to train his biceps and triceps at least two days before or after his chest and back training, since the arm muscles are heavily stimulated by training chest and back.

Quincy's first biceps exercise is preacher curls using a straight bar. He typically starts with a couple of warm-up sets using 60 and 80 pounds for 12 reps, and then pyramids up in weight for four sets, going from 100 to 150 pounds. Quincy is quick to add that while he could go heavier, he's not one of these bodybuilders who rocks the weight up with body momentum. Nothing but raw biceps power is where Quincy's at.

His next exercise is alternating dumbell curls. Quincy prefers to do this exercise seated to prevent body momentum. He also supinates his palms as he raises the dumbells. Quincy starts with 2 sets of 12 reps using 50- and 60-pound dumbbells and works up to 2 sets using 70s.

For his third exercise Quincy does a very seldom seen biceps exercise – biceps curls on a lat pulldown machine. He learned this exercise from eight-time Mr. Olympia Lee Haney. Quincy starts by leaning back on a preacher bench and grabbing the straight lat bar attachment with a reverse (palms up) shoulder-width grip. He usually does 4 sets of 8 to 12 reps using a moderate amount of weight.

Next up is overhead cable curls using the cable crossover machine. Quincy figured if Mr. Biceps himself, Ronnie Coleman, does them, they must be good.

The exercise looks similar to the front double biceps pose except you hold on to a set of handles attached to the upper pulleys on the crossover machine. Again it's 4 sets of 8 to 12 reps.

To finish off his enormous biceps and to help fill in the gap between his biceps and forearms, Quincy does 4 sets of dumbell hammer curls using 50- or 55-pound dumbells. This exercise is one of the best for developing the brachialis muscle, and one look at Quincy's and you'll see the proof.

TRICEPS

With biceps out of the way it's on to triceps. Quincy's first exercise is invariably skullcrushers. While he rotates most of the other exercises on a regular basis, skullcrushers have always been part of his triceps workouts. He prefers to do the movement on a flat bench. He starts with a 25-pound plate on each side of the EZ-curl bar and does 15 slow, easy reps. He then puts a 45 on each side and does a few more warmup sets. From here he does 4 work sets, going from 150 to more than 200 pounds for 10 to 12 reps.

Next up it's 3 sets of close-grip cable pushdowns. It's not surprising that someone as strong as Quincy needs to pin an extra 45-pound plate or two to the whole weight stack to keep his reps in the 10-to-12 range. These are strict reps, too, with his elbows pinned close to his sides.

Exercise number three takes just a flip of the wrist and a slighty wider grip as he bangs out 3 sets of reverse-grip pushdowns. Although the bar is harder to hold on to, Quincy still manages to use some tremendous poundages on this exercise. Reps are still kept in the 10-to-12 range.

With three heavy movements out of the way, Quincy moves on to single-arm reverse pushdowns. As he's using his exercise to isolate his triceps, he doesn't use near the same amount of weight as for the previous cable exercises. He's also careful to squeeze into a fully locked-out position at the bottom of the exercise. Each arm gets 3 sets of 10 to 12 reps.

As if the four previous execises were not enough, Quincy adds in a fifth exercise – rope pushdowns – to finish off his triceps. This is the one exercise where he often deviates from his normal 10-to-12 rep range and often goes as high as 20 reps to really finish off his triceps with a good pump.

TAYLOR'S BICEPS WORKOUT

EXERCISE	SETS	REPS
Preacher Curls	4	12
Alternating Dumbell Curls	4	12
Lat-Machine Curls	4	8–12
Standing Cable Crossover Curls	4	8–12
Hammer Curls	4	12

TAYLOR'S TRICEPS WORKOUT

EXERCISE	SETS	REPS
Skullcrushers	6–7	10–12
Close-Grip Pushdowns	3	10–12
Reverse Pushdowns	3	10–12
One-Arm Reverse Pushdowns	3	10–12
Rope Pushdowns	3	15–20

Photo of Ronnie Coleman by Jason Mathas

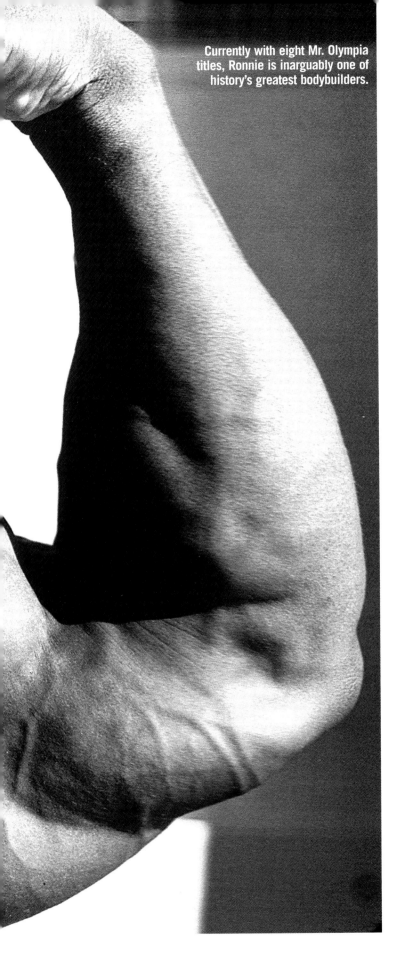

THE CHAMPS' ROUTINES

Ronnie Coleman

"I've always had big arms. I hate to say it but they've been the easiest thing in the world for me to build."
- Ronnie Coleman, eight-time Mr. Olympia, telling *MuscleMag International* contributor Lori Grannis how lucky he was in the arm-building department.

Although he didn't win that coveted ninth-straight Mr. Olympia title, Ronnie Coleman is undoubtedly one of the greatest bodybuilders in history. During his record-tying stretch of eight Mr. Olympia titles, Ronnie had no equals. It's also safe to say that Ronnie's arms – particularly his biceps – are among the greatest of all time. They rank right up there with Arnold Schwarzenegger, Robby Robinson and Lee Priest.

Typical of most of the bodybuilders who refined their art during the 1990s, Ronnie favors shorter, more intense workouts to the high-volume training style that was popular in the '70s and '80s. His biceps workout is a perfect example. Ronnie has two workouts for his biceps, each consisting of 3 exercises performed for 3 sets of 10 to 12 reps. Ronnie has experimented with numerous rep ranges over the years but keeps coming back to the 10-to-12 range. He just doesn't find that lower rep ranges keep his biceps contracted long enough for adequate stimulation.

COLEMAN'S BICEPS WORKOUT (A)

EXERCISE	SETS	REPS
One-Arm Preacher Curls	3	10–12
Standing Cable Curls	3	10–12
Barbell Preacher Curls	3	10–12

COLEMAN'S BICEPS WORKOUT (B)

EXERCISE	SETS	REPS
Standing Barbell Curls or Barbell 21s	3	10–12
One-Arm Cable Curls	3	10–12
Low Narrow-Grip Cable Curls	3	10–12

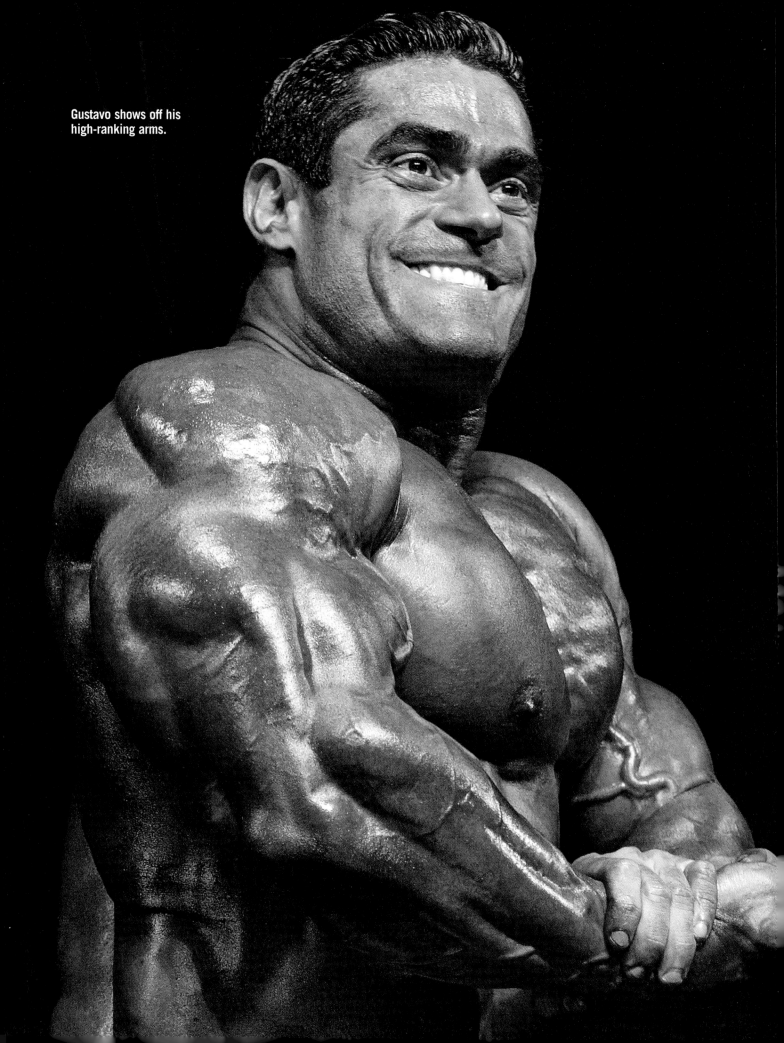

Gustavo shows off his high-ranking arms.

THE CHAMPS' ROUTINES

Gustavo Badell

In a sport where huge arms are almost a must for popularity, (two notable exceptions being Dorian Yates and Lee Haney), Puerto Rico's Gustavo Badell ranks right up there with such big-gunned greats as Ronnie Coleman, Jay Cutler and Arnold.

Gustavo is definitely from the old school of high-volume training, as he averages four to six exercises for his biceps and triceps, doing 4 sets per exercise.

As expected of someone who sports 21- to 22-inch arms, Gustavo begins most biceps workouts with standing barbell curls. He usually uses a straight bar and holds it with a slightly wider than shoulder-width grip. He normally does 4 sets of 8 to 10 reps working up to about 200 pounds.

To target his brachialis Gustavo usually makes standing alternating hammer curls his second exercise. For variety he likes to change his foot stance. Although most bodybuilders don't find foot stance makes much difference on biceps exercises, Gustavo has discovered that by changing his foot position he gets a different feel as he works his biceps. Again he does 4 sets of 8 to 10 reps.

For his third exercise Gustavo does 4 sets of seated alternating dumbell curls. Depending on the day he may supinate his hands or keep them facing straight up at all times. One thing he's careful to do is not swing. He sees so many young bodybuilders cheating just to lift heavier dumbells. It's no wonder, he says, they're not getting the results they want.

Next up is concentration curls. Gustavo prefers to do this in a standing bent-over position, the version made famous by Arnold. Unlike most bodybuilders who alternate from side to side, Gustavo does 4 complete sets with one arm before switching to the other arm.

By now most bodybuilders are in the shower or have moved on to another muscle group – but not Mr. Badell. For his fifth exercise he does 4 sets of seated preacher curls using an EZ-curl bar. For variety he alternates between a wide and narrow grip: "My training is never boring and never dull," he says.

To finish off his biceps, Gustavo does 4 sets of one-arm concentration curls. As this is his final exercise, he tends to go lighter and perform higher reps – say 12 to 15.

TRICEPS

Gustavo almost always starts his triceps training with skullcrushers. Although other bodybuilders like to do a lighter pumping exercise first, Gustavo prefers to go straight into his primary mass-builder. He usually starts with two light sets of 20 to 30 reps and then adds a set of 45-pound plates to the bar for another set of 15 to 20 reps. He then keeps adding weight and decreasing the reps until he has two 45-pound plates on each side of the bar, at which time he does 10 to 12 reps.

Gustavo is such a fan of skullcrushers that he makes his second exercise another version of the same exercise – this time on an incline bench. As his triceps are fully warmed up by now, he launches straight into 3 sets of 10 to 12 reps.

With his two basic mass-building exercises complete, Gustavo moves on to overhead rope extensions as his third exercise. With the pulley wheel set in the top position, Gustavo leans forward and extends the rope to an arms-locked-out position. While many bodybuilders flare the rope ends apart at the end, Gustavo prefers to keep them together at all times. Over the years he found that separating the rope ends limited the amount of weight he could use and didn't really add anything extra to the exercise. Typically he'll do 3 sets of 10 to 12 reps.

For his fourth and final exercise, Gustavo bangs out 3 sets of 10 to 12 reps of rope pushdowns. Again he does not flare the rope at the end.

BADELL'S TRICEPS WORKOUT		
EXERCISE	**SETS**	**REPS**
Skullcrushers	5	10–20
Incline Skullcrushers	3	10–12
Overhead Rope Extensions	3	10–12
Rope Pushdowns	3	10–12

Photo of Gustavo Badell by Irvin Gelb

THE CHAMPS' ROUTINES
Lee Priest

"Much of Lee Priest's mystique stems from his spectacular arms. He stands just 5'4" but by the time he won three Mr. Australia titles, those gifted guns were already taping out at the magic number that separates the genetic have's from the have-not's in our sport: 20 inches."
– Ron Harris, *MuscleMag International* contributor, commenting on the arms of top IFBB Pro, Lee Priest.

He's called the Blond Myth and for good reason. Australia's Lee Priest is one of the most densely packed bodybuilders of all time. When he goes into battle he carries 220 heavily striated pounds, topped off by a set of guns that measure upwards of 22 inches.

Given his superior genetics and love of training, it's not surprising that Lee prefers the high-volume approach to working out. You won't catch him doing one of the late Mike Mentzer's one-set-to-failure workouts.

The first exercise in Lee's biceps attack is that old standby: barbell curls. As Lee is fond of saying, if it worked for Arnold, Oliva and most of the other greats in the past, why not him? On most days he'll do 5 sets of 6 to 8 reps, but if the energy and strength is there he'll bang out 7 or 8 sets. Lee is exceptionally strong on this exercise and at one time could cheat curl 310 pounds. These days he keeps the weight in the 185- to 225-pound range. Although he tries to maintain strict style, he's not immune to adding a few cheat reps towards the end of his sets.

Next up for the Blond Myth is standing alternating dumbell curls. At his heaviest bodyweight Lee can use 100-pound dumbells on this exercise, but most times he keeps the weight in the 65- to 80-pound range and does 4 or 5 sets of 6 to 8 reps. Like most bodybuilders Lee supinates his hands as he curls the dumbells upwards.

When you have upper arms as large as Lee's it only makes sense to keep the forearms in proportion. For this reason Lee usually makes reverse barbell curls his third exercise. He prefers to use a straight bar on this exercise and uses a shoulder-width grip. He typically works up to 120 to 150 pounds for 4 or 5 sets of 6 to 8 reps.

Exercise number four is likely to be standing cable curls. Lee calls them "crucifix curls," as that's the position he's in during the exercise – like Christ on the cross. Lee sets the pulley wheels just slightly above his head and performs the movement as if doing a front double biceps pose. He usually does 4 or 5 sets of 6 to 8 reps.

Lee's fifth and final exercise (although he admits that sometimes he makes this his first exercise) is standing cable curls. Whether warming up or finishing off his biceps, this is the one exercise where Lee deviates from his normal 6 to 8 reps, preferring instead to go up to 15 reps per set.

TRICEPS

Given the stress that his triceps and elbows will be under with some of the other exercises, Lee usually does rope pushdowns as his first triceps exercise. He finds this exercise great for warming up his triceps and joints. Unlike with the other exercises, Lee's not too concerned with weight and he usually pumps out 3 sets of 15 to 30 reps.

With his triceps now fully warmed up, Lee moves on to his first mass-building exercise: close-grip bench presses. When I tell you that Lee works up to 385 pounds on this exercise you'll begin to understand why he started out with the high-rep sets of rope pushdowns. He doesn't start with this weight, however. He'll first put 75 pounds on the bar and then work up to 375 over the course of 4 or 5 sets. He keeps the reps in the 6 to 8 range. One thing Lee has learned over the years is that a lot of the elbow pain experienced by many bodybuilders while doing this exercise is from doing it with the elbows flared outwards. The key to reducing joint pain and stimulating the triceps to the maximum is to keep the elbows pointing at the feet.

Lee next moves on to skullcrushers. Again he goes super heavy and will work up to 4 or 5 sets using anywhere from 200 to 250 pounds. If it's one of those days that his elbows are sore, he'll limit the weight to 120 to 180 pounds. Lee likes to lower the bar to within a few

Photo of Lee Priest by Irvin Gelb

inches of his forehead rather than behind his head. Lee finds that the latter version turns the exercise into more of a pullover and brings his lats and chest into play.

Lee's third exercise is either one- or two-arm dumbell extensions. Although he prefers to sit down for this exercise, he doesn't use any back support. No matter which version he does, Lee tries to keep his elbows pointed at the ceiling and his upper arms locked perpendicular to the floor (vertical). He usually does 4 or 5 sets of 6 to 8 reps working up to 60 to 70 pounds for the two-handed version.

Exercise number four is seated cable extensions. He does this exercise by using an EZ-bar attachment on a low pulley. As with the dumbell extensions he keeps his elbows pointed at the ceiling throughout the full range of the exercise. He does 4 or 5 sets of 6 to 8 reps.

For his fifth and final exercise Lee likes to do one-arm reverse cable pushdowns. This exercise is great for bringing out the long rear head of the triceps. As this is more of an isolation exercise, Lee doesn't get too carried away with the weight. He goes more for the muscle pump and will do slightly higher reps – in the 12-to-15 range.

PRIEST'S BICEPS WORKOUT

EXERCISE	SETS	REPS
Barbell Curls	4–5	6–8
Alternating Dumbell Curls	4–5	6–8
Reverse Barbell Curls	4	6–8
"Crucifix" Curls	4	6–8
Cable Curls	4	12–15

PRIEST'S TRICEPS WORKOUT

EXERCISE	SETS	REPS
Close-Grip Bench Presses	4–5	6–8
Skullcrushers	4–5	6–8
One- or Two-Arm Dumbell Extensions	4–5	6–8
Seated Cable Extensions	4–5	6–8
One-Arm Reverse Pushdowns	4–5	12–15

CHAPTER 83

Forearm Training

"Virtually every exercise we do works the forearms to some degree, but only a few bodybuilders actually concentrate on the forearms with specialized lower-arm exercises such as wrist curls using both underhand and overhand grips. If you have weak forearms you should make a habit of doing specialized forearm work."

– Editors of *MuscleMag International,* explaining the importance of forearm work.

One of the most popular cartoons of the 1950s and '60s was "Popeye the Sailorman." Unlike most superheros, who were built from head to toe, Popeye had but one notable feature – his gargantuan forearms. All it took was one can of spinach and heaven help anyone who got between him and his girl, Olive Oyl!

There was a time when large muscular forearms were a necessity for survival. Most occupations required gripping tools and equipment. Sailors needed to be able to grab and haul thick ropes in the worst kind of weather. Fishermen relied on their gripping power to haul nets and fish lines. Carpenters and lumberjacks needed great forearm strength to cut wood.

With the advent of the industrial revolution many positions that stressed physical strength were eliminated. With the exception of plumbers and a few other occupations requiring some degree of physical labor, great forearm development has gone the way of the dinosaur.

ANATOMY

Contrary to popular belief it's the muscles of the forearm, and not the hand, that give you a powerful grip. It's true that there are small muscles located in the fingers that help in holding on to objects, but they have nowhere near the strength and power of the larger forearm muscles.

"Bill Pearl had forearms to die for, no doubt built in part from his habit of tearing car license plates in half, three at a time, which he did at his frequent strongman demonstrations some years ago."

– Gerard Thorne,

Reps! magazine contributor

The forearms are made up of a number of muscles, including the flexor digitorum, flexor carpi ulnaris, and extensor carpi radialis longus and brevis. The forearm muscles interact to contract and relax the fingers, allowing you to grip and twist such objects as barbells, bottle caps and ropes. From a bodybuilding perspective the forearm muscles are involved in just about every upper-body exercise and most of the lower-body exercises. In fact, the forearms often give out before the primary muscles being worked.

TRAINING

In many respects the forearms are the calves of the arms. And as such, they are composed of the same dense muscle tissue that hurts like hell when you train them. The reason the forearms are composed of such dense muscle fibers is that they are in continuous use just about every minute you are awake. Nature compensated for this by packing in a high percentage of muscle fibers that can endure long periods of exercise. From a biological point of view this makes sense, but from a training point of view it can be pure murder.

There are two trains of thought with regards to forearm training. Many bodybuilders find that they get all the forearm stimulation they need from training their other muscle groups. Let's face it, just about every exercise you perform requires you to grip a barbell, dumbell or handle. This is often enough to keep the forearms in proportion to the upper arms. The less fortunate bodybuilders who find that indirect training is not adequate will need to incorporate some forearm training into their workouts. Even here there will be differences, with some bodybuilders responding better to high rep ranges (15 to 20) and others finding that heavy weight and low reps (6 to 8) work best. My advice is to experiment with both ranges and see which works for you. You may even need to perform both rep ranges to shock the forearms into growth.

Forearm exercises generally fall into two categories: flexor and extensor movements. Variations of the wrist curl (where you curl the hands toward the insides of your forearms) primarily work the flexors, while reverse wrist curls (curling the backs of the hands toward the top of the forearms) primarily work the extensors. Besides the flexors and extensors, bodybuilders like to train the brachialis muscles with their forearms. The brachialis is a medium-sized muscle that connects the forearms to the upper arms and when developed helps fill in the gap between the upper and lower arms. The best exercise for training the brachialis is called the reverse curl. It's performed like a regular barbell curl, but the bar is gripped with the hands facing downwards and not palms up.

You should train your forearms after your other muscles – especially the upper body torso muscles, and even lower body, if you use free weights. As I said earlier, the forearms will be needed for gripping when you train the chest, back and shoulders. But you also grip a barbell when squatting, don't you? If you fatigue your forearms first, you'll have trouble gripping when you train the other muscles, and for some exercises tired forearms are downright dangerous.

Another option is to train your forearms entirely on their own. This is definitely an option for those who need to do extra work on their forearms. Even though training the forearms is painful, it doesn't require much energy or time. So you don't have to worry about depleting your recovery system by adding in an extra couple of 10- or 15-minute workouts. A couple of months of such specialization will not only give you bigger and stronger forearms, but will also enable you to lift more weight on the exercises for your larger torso muscles.

BEST FOREARM EXERCISES
- Barbell wrist curls
- Dumbell wrist curls
- Reverse barbell wrist curls
- Dumbell reverse wrist curls
- Reverse barbell curls
- Hammer curls

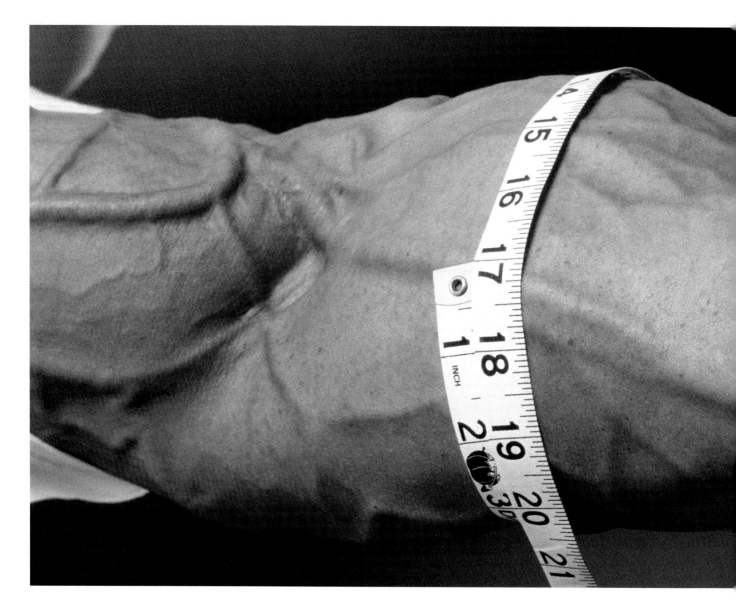

THE CHAMPS' ROUTINES

Frank McGrath

As with calves, many of the best forearms around are owned by the genetically blessed. Still no matter how favorable a person's DNA, he'll need to spend countless hours to bring out that great genetic potential.

When 250-pound Frank McGrath stepped onstage at the 2003 Canadian Nationals he gave the audience members a view of two of the greatest arms to ever grace the national stage. In fact, Frank's arms surpass most pro bodybuilders. From forearms to biceps to triceps, Frank's arms are complete in every way. It's safe to say that no

one on the pro scene – save perhaps Lee Priest – has forearms that compare to Frank's.

While Frank's forearms have never been a weak point, he still had to work hard to turn them into the steelchords of power that burst forth from his shirtsleeves.

Like many bodybuilders Frank doesn't have a rigid schedule when it comes to training. He has a core group of exercises that he rotates on a regular basis. Forearms are no different.

One of his favorites is the standing barbell reverse curl. This exercise is almost identical to the barbell curl, except you grab the bar with a palms-down rather than

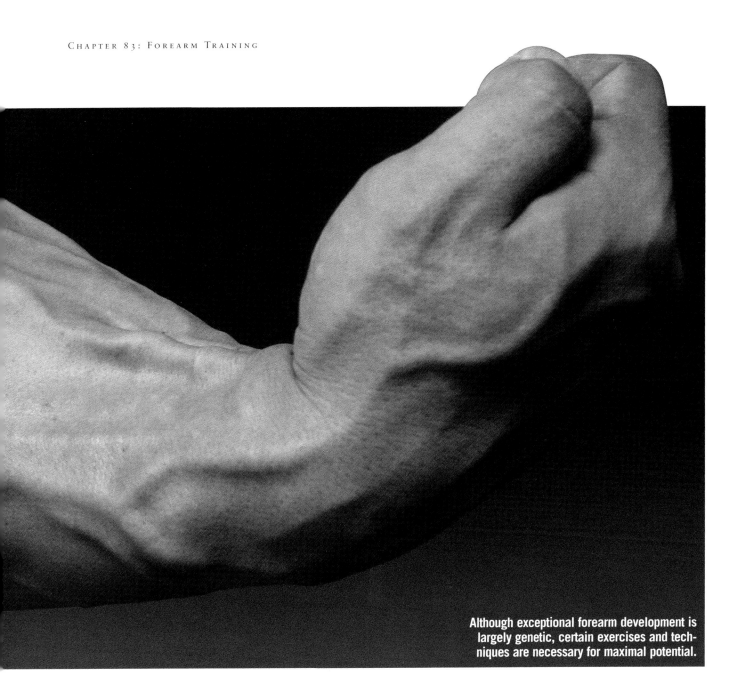

Although exceptional forearm development is largely genetic, certain exercises and techniques are necessary for maximal potential.

Photo of Frank McGrath by Robert Kennedy

palms-up grip. This shifts most of the stress from the biceps to the forearm extensors. On most days Frank will bang out 3 or 4 sets of 12 to 20 reps.

Another McGrath favorite is hammer curls. This exercise is similar to regular dumbell curls except you keep the palms facing inward at all times. This movement is great for working the brachialis – the muscle that joins the biceps to the forearms. There are two versions of this exercise. You can curl the dumbell straight up and down or across the front of the chest, as Frank prefers. Again it's 3 or 4 sets of 12 to 20 reps.

To work the extensor muscles of his forearms,

Frank will do the old tried-and-true barbell wrist curls. No less an authority than Dorian Yates has said that barbell wrist curls across a bench are probably the best overall forearm exercise there is. Typically sets and reps for Frank are 3 or 4 sets of 15 to 20 reps.

McGRATH'S FOREARM WORKOUT

EXERCISE	SETS	REPS
Reverse Barbell Curls	3–4	12–20
Across-Body Hammer Curls	3–4	12–20
Barbell Wrist Curls	3–4	15–20

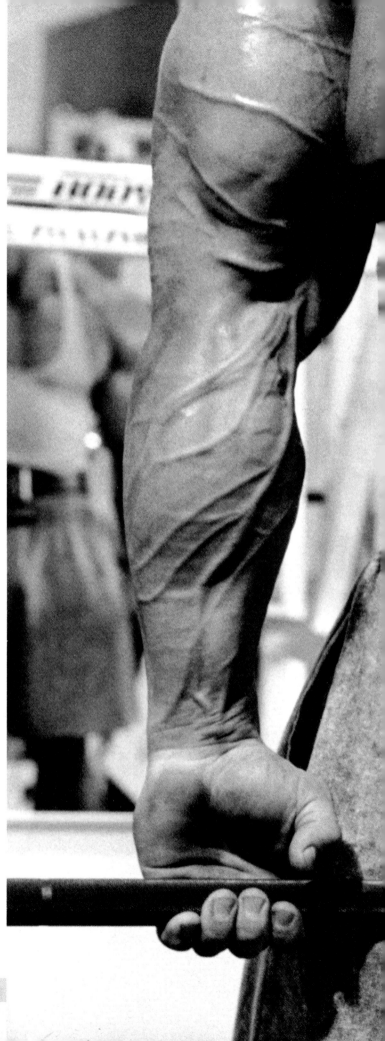

THE CHAMPS' ROUTINES
Jay Cutler

In some respects placing second to Ronnie Coleman at the Mr. Olympia on four different occasions was a blessing in disguise. It forced Jay to keep re-evaluating and trying to improve his physique rather than resting on his laurels. For the first few years of his bodybuilding life his forearms kept pace because of all the indirect stimulation they received from his other training. But once his upper arms passed the 20-inch mark Jay realized that he'd need to work hard to keep his forearms in proportion. Although he's tried numerous exercises in the past, the two he keeps coming back to are reverse curls and wrist curls. He's also experimented with different rep ranges, and despite the popularity of high-rep sets for the forearms, Jay discovered that his responded better to lower reps using heavy weight.

CUTLER'S FOREARM WORKOUT

EXERCISE	SETS	REPS
Wrist Curls	3	8–10
Reverse Curls	3	8–10

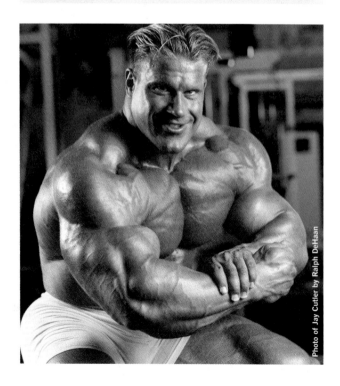

Photo of Jay Cutler by Ralph DeHaan

If he hadn't concentrated on building up his forearms, Lee's superior biceps and triceps might have easily overshadowed his lower arms.

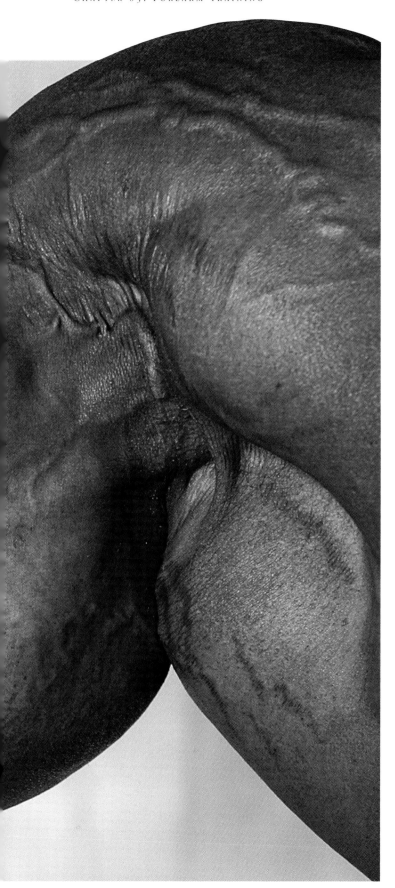

THE CHAMPS' ROUTINES
Lee Priest

While packed with muscle from head to toe, Lee's arms are easily one of his best muscle groups. Most bodybuilding experts place them in the top five in bodybuilding history. Given the great guns that have appeared on the scene over the past 50 years or so, that's quite the accomplishment on Lee's part. What makes the Aussie's arms stand out is their completeness. His baseball-sized biceps are balanced out by a tremendous set of horseshoe-shaped triceps. And as for those forearms … the creators of "Popeye the Sailorman" must have had Lee in mind when they created the character all those years ago.

Like Jay Cutler, Lee realized that carrying such a huge set of upper arms had one disadvantage – their ability to make his forearms look small. With his eyes set firmly on the bodybuilding pro circuit, Lee had no intentions of being held back by mediocrity in his lower arms. He set out to give them the same harsh treatment as his gargantuan upper arms. Given the mass of muscle that protrudes from his shirtsleeves, I think it's safe to say that he succeeded.

PRIEST'S FOREARM WORKOUT

EXERCISE	SETS	REPS
Cambered-Bar Reverse Curls	3	12–18
Alternating Dumbell Hammer Curls	3	12–18
Barbell Wrist Curls	3	12–18

CHAPTER 84

Abdominal Training

"By far the biggest misconception surrounding abdominal training is that exercising the abs will burn the fat that covers them. What you eat, when you eat and in what portions, the amount of cardio you do and when you do it – these things will determine how much body fat you carry and whether you can see your abs."

– Ron Harris, regular *MuscleMag International* contributor, explaining the real secret to great-looking abs.

No one with a full deck wants a big waist. It's safe to say that just about everyone who joins a gym has as one of their primary goals the shrinking of their waistline. That's why the manufacturers of those abdominal contraptions you see advertised on TV make hundreds of millions of dollars.

For the average person, keeping the pants size stationary is probably adequate. But for competitive bodybuilders, a small waist is not good enough. It also must be rock hard, with all abdominal ridges clearly separated and visible. Anything less than a fat-free six-pack just won't cut it.

Besides impressing the judges, a small tight waist will go a long way in improving your success with the ladies. Interviews with women show that next to a small tight butt, a slim waist is considered very sexy by women. So guys, the beer-belly look is definitely out.

Hopefully by now most readers are aware of the keys to developing a small midsection. The average Joe or Jill off the street still thinks that performing endless sets and reps of crunches and leg raises will somehow magically shrink their waists. Abdominal exercises only target the muscle, not the overlying fat. Fat is stored energy and must be burnt off with cardio and by boosting the body's metabolism with an overall weight-training program. While abdominal exercises do burn calories, cardio exercises such as cycling, swimming and running burn far more calories per unit of time. An extra five minutes on the treadmill or cycle will do more for your abs than 15 or 20 minutes of crunches or leg raises. Also, keep in mind that you can't spot reduce. The advertisers of those top-selling gizmos make it seem that if you perform crunches for the waist you'll somehow be telling the body where to take the fat from. Unfortunately it doesn't work that way. The body will take stored fat from all over, and as the waist is usually the first place fat is stored, it's usually the last place that fat will remain.

Super abdominals are built with exercise and honed with diet. In other words, you use various abdominal exercises to strengthen and tone the muscles, and then keep your fat levels low with diet. It's a two-front war, and performing thousands of crunches is not the answer.

A final point to be made concerns stomach distension. Think of your stomach as a series of springs. If you repeatedly stretch a spring it eventually won't go all the way back to it's original length. The smooth muscle lining your stomach walls is similar. If you keep overstretching it by stuffing your stomach with huge volumes of food and drink, you'll end up with that paunch, or beer-belly look. This is another reason you should eat four to six small meals per day rather than two or three large ones. It's also a great reason why you should limit your alcohol intake (not to mention the calories you'll save by not overindulging on a regular basis).

ANATOMY

When we think of abs, we normally picture the rectus abdominis. This muscle starts at the ribcage and attaches to the pelvic region. A properly developed and fat-free midsection is arranged in four to eight "blocks" (normally six) and resembles an old-time washboard (hence the terms "six-pack" and "washboard abs").

There is considerable variation among individuals with regards to abdominal development. Some bodybuilders show eight distinct blocks of abdominal muscles (four complete rows) while others are lucky to get four blocks to peak out (two rows). This may be in spite of the fact that these bodybuilders may have similar body-fat percentages. If you don't have a full six- or eight-pack, don't worry. As long as your midsection is fat free you'll be just as competitive as someone with four distinct rows.

The primary function of the abdominals is to contract and shorten the distance between the upper and lower body. If you're lying on your back, a full ab contraction will move your shoulders only about eight to ten inches off the floor. Those old sit-ups you may have done in gym class (where you go all the way up to your knees) are rarely done anymore, as most of the movement is being carried out by your hip flexors.

Other muscles that make up the abdominal region are the obliques, serratus and intercostals. They all contribute to core stability and movement by helping to twist and stabilize the torso. They also play a role in helping you breathe.

TRAINING

Abdominal training generally falls into two categories – upper and lower. In a way this is misleading. From an anatomical point of view there are no upper and lower abs. This misconception arises because the abdominal ridges (those blocks I talked about earlier) are arranged left to right, not up and down. But the abdominal fibers run from ribcage to pelvis. Still, from an exercise point of view it is possible to target the upper and lower regions with different exercises.

Generally speaking, to hit the upper abdominals you perform movements where the legs are stationary and your sternum moves toward the legs (e.g. crunches). Conversely, to bring in more of the lower abdominals you keep the upper body stationary and move the legs toward the sternum (e.g. reverse crunches, leg raises).

One of the big changes in abdominal-training strategy in recent years concerns the number of sets and reps performed. Back in the '60s and '70s bodybuilders routinely banged out sets of 50 to 100 reps or more for their abs. They also trained their abs four to six times per week. But it eventually became apparent that those bodybuilders who treated their abs like any other muscle had abs as good as the 100-reppers. Most pros now pick two or three exercises and perform three or four sets of 20 to 25 reps for their abs and that's it. Occasionally they may use a 10-pound plate or dumbell to add a little bit of extra resistance to the exercise, but for the most part the exercises are done with just bodyweight.

As a final comment I should address the issue of overtraining the abdominals. Unlike most muscles, where training every day or even three or four days per week would quickly lead to burnout and overtraining, the abs seem to recover much more quickly. Theoretically you could train the abs every day and not have to worry about overtraining. The question is why would you want to? The goal, remember, is to strengthen and tone the muscles. This can easily be accomplished by training them a couple of times per week. The real key to great-looking abdominals is a low body fat percentage, and all the crunches and leg raises in the world won't make a difference. Only by following a clean diet and burning excess calories with cardio will you develop eye-catching, contest-winning abdominals

THE BEST ABDOMINAL EXERCISES

- Crunches
- Reverse crunches
- Swiss-ball crunches
- Leg raises
- Hanging leg raises
- Roman-chair sit-ups
- Rope crunches
- Medicine-ball twists
- Ball passes

Photo (Top) of Frank Zane by George Greenwood
Photo (Bottom) of Thierry Pastel

A majority of today's pro bodybuilders pick two or three ab exercises and do them with just bodyweight.

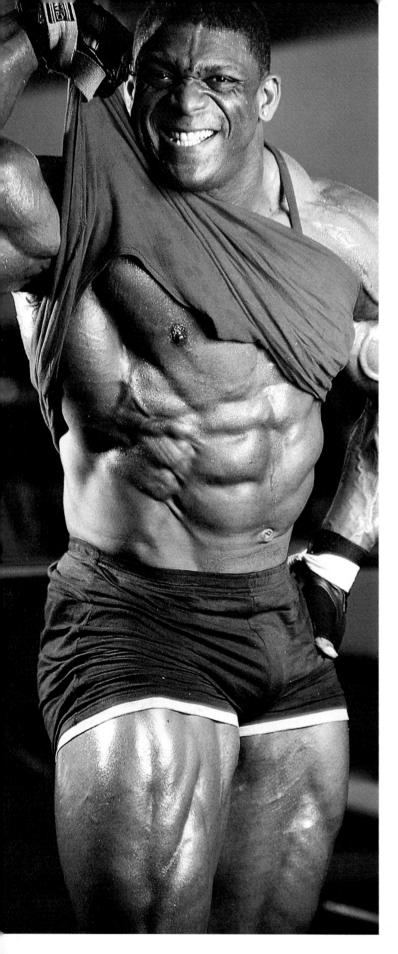

THE CHAMPS' ROUTINES
Quincy Taylor

"The abs are critical, especially if you're a big guy. So many of the other monsters in the sport don't have great abs that mine really give me an advantage when I battle them come showtime."

– Quincy Taylor, top pro, commenting on the importance of great abdominals to his success.

Quincy Taylor has established himself as one of the true mass monsters in the sport. But unlike many of the other 280- to 300-pounders, Quincy sports a set of abdominals that rival the best lightweights.

Quincy prefers to train abdominals at the beginning of his workout – not at the end. He finds that training the abs first not only warms up the entire body, but it gives him time to concentrate and plan out what he'll be doing for the rest of his workout. He also differs from most other bodybuilders in that he does only crunches – no leg raises or direct serratus work. The way he looks at it: "I've been training abs that way for years and I see no reason to change what's working."

Quincy's first exercise is usually lying crunches. He lies on his back and with his hands crossed across his chest he raises his shoulder girdle about 8 to 10 inches off the floor. Once at the top he holds the contracted position for about two seconds and then slowly lowers back down to the starting position. He usually does 4 sets of 20 reps.

For his second and last (yes, last!) exercise, Quincy does 4 sets of 20 reps on the machine crunch. He uses the version that you sit in and grab the handles by the sides of the head. He performs machine crunches in the same manner as floor crunches. At one time he did this exercise using extra weight, but once his abs developed the thickness he desired, he dropped the weight and now just uses his bodyweight.

TAYLOR'S AB WORKOUT		
EXERCISE	SETS	REPS
Lying Floor Crunches	4	20
Machine Crunches	4	20

Photo of Quincy Taylor by Jason Mathas

THE CHAMPS' ROUTINES

Jeramy Freeman

"Unlike many bodybuilders terrified that weights will thicken the abs and waistline, Jeramy trains abs heavy, just as he would any other muscle group."

– Jon Simmons, *MuscleMag International* contributor, commenting on the ab-training approach of 270-pound 2001 North American super heavyweight champion Jeramy Freeman.

When he won the 2001 North American Championships at 270 pounds, super heavyweight Jeramy Freeman displayed a set of abdominals and intercostals that were the envy of most lightweights and middleweights.

A typical day will see Jeramy start with hanging leg raises from a chin-up bar. Instead of doing high reps he'll hold a dumbell between his feet and do three sets of 15 reps. Jeramy says the key to this exercise is to rock the pelvis forward and upward as you do the movement. Failure to add this little movement in will result in the hip flexors doing most of the exercise.

For his second exercise Jeramy will bang out 3 sets of reverse crunches lying on a flat bench. As with hanging leg raises, he prefers to hold a dumbell between his feet and do lower reps.

For his third and final exercise, Jeramy does 3 sets of 15 reps of decline sit-ups. As he crunches forward he blows all the air from his lungs so he can get the maximum ab contraction. He also forgoes going all the way up or down on the movement, to minimize the stress on his lower back or bring his hip flexors into play.

FREEMAN'S AB WORKOUT		
EXERCISE	SETS	REPS
Hanging Leg Raises	3	15
Reverse Crunches on Flat Bench	3	15
Incline Sit-Ups	3	15

Photo of Jeramy Freeman by Alex Ardenti

Ahmad's abs are so great that he's been nicknamed "Abzilla" in their honor.

THE CHAMPS' ROUTINES

Ahmad Haidar

"Many bodybuilders don't work their abs in the off-season. They train them for only a few months before the show. That's why they don't have really good abs."
– Ahmad Haidar, IFBB pro, commenting on the mistake many bodybuilders make in their abdominal training.

You know you have a great bodypart when people start nicknaming you in honor of it. Take Lebanon-born Ahmad Haidar. Despite weighing 230 pounds at a height of 5'7", Ahmad sports a set of abdominals that rival the lightweights at a national championship. So good were his abs that it wasn't long before people were calling him "Abzilla" (in the same manner that the late Paul DeMayo was nicknamed "Quadzilla" because of his huge quads).

When it comes to developing his washboard abs, Ahmad is a firm believer in both high reps and frequency. He typically does sets of 50 to 150 reps on every workout day.

Typically he'll start with 4 sets of crunches, doing an astounding 150 reps per set. Like most bodybuilders Ahmad finds that crunches are probably the best exercise for bring out the upper abs.

Next up it's 4 sets of leg raises, averaging 40 to 50 reps per set. Whereas the crunches are the best upper ab exercise, Ahmad finds that leg raises really rip up his lower abs.

To balance out his abs, Ahmad finishes off with 4 sets of side crunches. He does 100 reps per set on each side to develop his obliques and intercostals.

HAIDAR'S AB WORKOUT

EXERCISE	SETS	REPS
Crunches	4	150
Leg Raises	4	40–50
Side Crunches	4*	100

* Number of sets per side.

THE CHAMPS' ROUTINES

Troy Alves

"When they relax, their guts often stick out farther than their chests. I don't think that's how a bodybuilder should look."

– Troy Alves, commenting on some of the bigger bodybuilders on the pro circuit.

While Troy Alves is not the biggest man on the pro circuit, he doesn't need to be. Some guys keep trying to pack more mass on their frames, but Troy has kept his competitive weight in the 215-to-220 range at 5'8" and symbolizes what the Greeks had in mind when they began to sculpt statues out of marble. Like Lee Labrada, Frank Zane and Shawn Ray before him, Troy prefers to focus on symmetry, size and proportion.

Unlike those "large gut" bodybuilders he was alluding to in the opening quote, Troy's midsection is nothing but small, tight and rock hard. No 40-inch bellies for him – just 29 inches of chiseled granite.

Troy usually trains his abs twice per week using three exercises for 3 sets of 15 to 20 reps. His first exercise is often leg raises on a flat bench. With his legs straight and feet just inches from the floor, Troy lifts his legs until they are at about a 45-degree angle to the floor. To keep momentum out of the picture and really feel the burn, Troy takes about 4 to 6 seconds to perform each rep.

Next up are 3 sets of crunches. Troy frequently sees bodybuilders performing this exercise incorrectly and says the key to isolating the abs and reducing the stress on the lower back is to keep your lower to mid back on the floor at all times. As soon as your lower back leaves the floor your hip flexors start taking over.

To give his midsection that finished look, Troy switches from straight crunches to twisting crunches. Curling up to one side forces the obliques and intercostals to do much of the work.

ALVES' AB WORKOUT

EXERCISE	SETS	REPS
Leg Raises	3	15–20
Crunches	3	15–20
Twisting Crunches	3	15–20

THE CHAMPS' ROUTINES
Rodney Davis

"I must lose about eight inches when I get ready for a contest. In fact during the first four weeks of my diet, the only thing that changes on my body is that my waist just keeps getting smaller and smaller."

– Rodney Davis, 2006 NPC Masters super heavyweight champion, commenting on his midsection during the weeks leading up to a contest.

Rodney Davis is another bodybuilder who proves that just because you're a super heavyweight doesn't mean you can't display a tight, trim midsection. In this age of 40-inch waists on 280-pound bodybuilders, Rodney sports a waist that is the envy of lighweights and super heavyweights alike.

Rodney has a "one from column A and one from column B" approach to ab training. He has two exercises for his upper abs and two for his lower abs. During a typical workout he'll pick one from each column. Close to a contest he'll add in an intercostal/serratus exercise. He also trains fast, resting only 45 seconds between sets, and usually completes his ab workout in 10 to 12 minutes.

Rodney's two upper-ab exercises are lying crunches or incline board sit-ups. If doing the crunches he'll squeeze out 30 to 35 reps for 4 sets. To reduce the stress on his lower back he keeps his thighs perpendicular to the floor. When he does incline sit-ups he'll set the incline board at about 20 degrees and anchor his feet in under the roller pads. He does 4 sets of 20 to 25 reps, stopping each rep when he feels the tension coming off his abs.

For lower abs Rodney does either hanging leg raises or knee-ins at the end of a bench. At his gym the chinning bar has a set of straps that allow him to hang from the bar without having to grip with his forearms. This allows him to bring his lower abs to failure rather than having to stop because his forearms give out. To reduce the stress on his lower back, Rodney keeps his knees bent as he lifts his thighs up to his midsection. He does 4 sets of 15 to 20 reps.

For knee-ins on the end of a flat bench he leans back at about 45 degrees and grabs the bench behind his butt

with his hands. From here he lifts his knees to his chest and then back down to the starting position. Again it's 4 sets of 15 to 20 reps.

About 4 to 6 weeks out from a contest, Rodney adds in one-arm cable side crunches for his intercostals and serratus. He starts by standing with his side toward a high pulley and grabs the handle with one hand. From here he crunches his torso down toward his hip. He'll typically do 2 sets per side.

DAVIS' AB WORKOUT		
EXERCISE	**SETS**	**REPS**
Lying Crunches or Incline Sit-Ups	4	20–35
Hanging Leg Raises or Knee-Ins	4	15–20
One-Arm Side Cable Crunches (pre-contest)	2	30–35

Photo of Rodney Davis by Jason Mathas

CHAPTER 85

Serratus, Lower Back and Neck

"There is no reason for a bodybuilder to get so out of shape that he looks fat. Arnold said years ago that once you can no longer see at least the outlines of your serratus, you are no longer a bodybuilder."

– Stan McQuay, top model and IFBB pro

" In a survey of those who did not engage in any strenuous physical activity, eight out of 10 adults indicated they experienced back pain that was severe enough to require medical attention and often surgery as well."

– Bill Starr, regular *MuscleMag International* contributor

While many bodybuilders develop these three regions indirectly from training the other muscles, you may notice sooner or later that one or more of these areas starts lagging behind. If this happens you'll want to start specializing.

THE SERRATUS
Contest-Winning Fingers

Take a look at some photos of Robby Robinson from the 1970s and 1980s. Despite being famous for his arms and back, Robby also displayed a set of serratus that literally looked like two open hands laid against the sides of his ribcage. When properly developed they help frame the midsection and give your physique a polished look. They also tell the judges about your overall conditioning, especially your body-fat percentage, as you have to be extremely ripped to bring out the serratus.

ANATOMY

The serratus are those long, thin, almost rib-like muscles located between the lats and obliques. Although relatively small compared to most other muscles in the torso, they play an important role in assisting the lats and chest to move the arms. They are also involved in helping with the breathing process.

TRAINING THE SERRATUS

As with the abdominals, you have to approach serratus development from two fronts – training and diet. The diet aspect was discussed earlier in the book. Suffice it to say that the greatest serratus in the world are wasted if they're covered by a layer of fat. If you want to see them you have to get rid of the covering. Simple as that.

Training the serratus is relatively straightforward. Most bodybuilders consider pullovers – both barbell and dumbell – to be the most effective movement for the job. The main difference between the two is that for the barbell version you lie lengthwise on the bench, while for dumbell pullovers you lie across the bench. The dumbell version tends to get the nod by more bodybuilders, as lying across the bench allows you to arch the spine and stretch the ribcage more. There's no need to get carried away with the amount of weight, either. As with abs, you're not trying to build huge serratus muscles, but

rather strengthen and tone them. Pick a weight that allows you to perform 15 to 20 reps.

For variety you can substitute a pullover machine in place of the barbell or dumbell. Machine pullovers are a great way to finish off chest and back training and begin serratus and abdominal training.

Besides pullovers, other great serratus builders are close-grip versions of chins and pulldowns. These movements are great for emphasizing the connection between the lower lats and serratus. Many bodybuilders find that wide-grip dips also bring the serratus into play.

Finally, a seldom seen but highly effective serratus exercise is the kneeling rope pulldown. Attach the rope attachment to a high-cable machine and kneel down on the floor. With a firm grip on the ends of the rope bend forward until you're in the fetal position. Slowly return to the starting position.

Posing can also help bring out these muscles. One of the best is what's called the vacuum pose – made famous by three-time Mr. Olympia Frank Zane. Place both hands behind your head and point your elbows at the ceiling. Now gently push forward with your hands and at the same time take in a huge volume of air. Hold the pose for 15 to 20 seconds and then relax. Do three to four sets of this pose after your abdominal workout. Not only will it help bring out your serratus, it's great practice for competition.

Photos of Robby Robinson, Mohammed Makkawy and Shawn Ray

THE LOWER BACK
Developing Your Back Pythons

It's ironic that most bodybuilders spend countless hours working the large showy muscles such as the chest, back and shoulders, and often totally neglect the one muscle group that could potentially save their bodybuilding careers.

Besides the large upper-back muscles we think of as "the back," there are two long snake-like muscles that attach to the lower back and run up the center of the upper back. These muscles, called the spinal erectors, serve to protect the spinal column as well as allowing the body to remain upright and move. The spinal erectors play a huge role in allowing you to pick heavy objects off the floor, and they stabilize you on such exercises as squats and deadlifts.

Given their importance you'd think that the spinal erectors would be given equal opportunity in the gym, but unfortunately this is not the case. Unless they're indirectly worked on such exercises as seated and barbell rows, most bodybuilders ignore them and hope for the best.

The problem with this attitude is that the lower back ranks right up there with the knees and shoulders when it comes to becoming injured. Lower-back injuries have ended the careers of thousands of athletes and curtailed the Mr. Olympia ambitions of numerous amateur bodybuilders. This is crazy, considering that training the

lower back is neither painful nor difficult. All you have to do is put lower-back training into your schedule. Not only will you prevent injuries, but well-developed spinal erector muscles make the judges sit up and take notice.

ANATOMY

The two long spinal erector muscles start at the base of the spine and extend up the center of the back to the base of the neck. For bodybuilding purposes it's the lower regions that concern us. The spinal erectors are relatively relaxed when sitting down and mainly come into play when the torso bends backwards. In this regard the spinal erectors act to oppose the abdominals, which contract to bring the torso forward.

TRAINING THE LOWER BACK

The first piece of advice I can give you with regards to training the lower back is to avoid any exercise that causes pain in the area. Now I'm not talking muscle soreness, but rather pain that feels deep within the base of the spinal chord and perhaps radiates down one or both legs, especially if that pain is sharp. You're trying to strengthen the lower-back muscles, not end up in traction for six months! If you find that virtually all the exercises involving lower-back movement cause such pain, go see a physician, chiropractor or physiotherapist. You've obviously got something going on there that needs to be looked at.

The next suggestion is to not get carried away with the amount of weight you're using. In the beginning you may not want to use any weight at all. Sure some powerlifters can lift impressive weight with their lower back. But first of all you're likely not a powerlifter, and more important, these guys didn't start out lifting that kind of weight. They worked up to it over a period of a few years. You'll get great results using moderate weight for 15 to 20 reps per set. Above all, perform every set with impeccable style and technique. Lower-back exercises are not movements to cheat on.

Photo of Dorian Yates by Jon Davey

Always start your lower-back training with a light warmup. Two of the best are back extensions and good mornings. For back extensions you can lie facedown on the floor, a Swiss ball, or a specially designed machine. Good mornings are performed in a standing position. Don't hold any weight at this point. Your torso weight is more than sufficient for a warmup. Perform 15 to 20 slow easy reps for one or two sets of both exercises. Once your back is fully warmed up, do the following triset. If you are a real beginner then do only one. As you get stronger you can move up to two, then three trisets.

Good Mornings: Stand straight up and with your legs locked straight. Slowly bend forward trying to reach a point where your torso is parallel with the floor. Slowly return to the starting position.

Back Extensions (formerly known as hyperextensions): Lying facedown on a Swiss ball with your hands behind your head, gently lower your torso down in front of the ball. Slowly lift your torso back up until it's just slightly past being in line with your legs. Don't arch excessively, as the human spine was not designed to hyperextend to any great degree. You can also do this exercise on the hyperextension machine, but again do not lift your shoulders far above the line with your legs.

Stiff-Leg Deadlifts: You should do this exercise as part of your hamstring training, but it also makes a great lower-back exercise. If you have the flexibility, stand on a bench or low platform so you can lower the bar past your feet level. Keep in mind that your legs do not have to be completely straight, but they should not have more than a slight bend. As with the two previous exercises, always perform stiff-leg deadlifts in a slow and controlled manner with no bouncing or jerking movements.

Once you reach a point that 15 to 20 reps is excessively easy, start adding light weight to the exercises. Just pay close attention to any warning signals your back may give you. Remember your goal is to prevent future injuries, not cause one.

Photos of Monty Rogers by Robert Reiff

THE NECK
Hold Your Head Up

Sooner or later after the start of football season you'll hear some reporter referring to a player as having "no neck." Despite the 300 pounds of musculature the person may be carrying, it's the bull-like neck that seems to grab the reporter's attention.

While a few bodybuilders over the years have made neck training a priority, by far most avoid it altogether. They think only wrestlers and football players have thick necks. This may have been true years ago, but no longer. In today's highly competitive bodybuilding arena, a well-developed neck is a big advantage. And if you play such sports as wrestling, rugby, football and judo, a powerful neck is an absolute necessity.

ANATOMY OF THE NECK

The neck is one of the body's most complex regions and includes various "hyoid" muscles (i.e. thyrohyoid, sternocleidomastoid, mylohyoid) that interact to move the head forward, backward, and sideways. They also allow you to twist the head upward of 200 degrees. Besides moving the skull, the neck muscles form a strong support network for protecting the head. This is why wrestlers and football players usually have such great neck development.

PREVENTATIVE MAINTENANCE

In many respects the neck is like the lower back – you're not even aware of it until you injury it. Everything's going along great until you wake up one morning with a stiff neck. Next thing you know you can barely even drive. Many of the best bodybuilding exercises can be dangerous on the neck if performed incorrectly. For example, many bodybuilders balance most of their bodyweight on their glutes and head when performing flat barbell presses. Then the next morning they wake up with a stiff or sore neck and wonder where it came from. Another exercise that may cause neck problems is the squat. Many

bodybuilders force their heads back against the bar as they perform the exercise.

Other exercises that can lead to neck problems are shoulder presses, shrugs, deadlifts and lying barbell extensions. When performing these exercises (and all others for that matter), try to keep your head in neutral alignment (i.e. in line with your spine).

TRAINING THE NECK

You can train the neck either directly or indirectly. You may need to be creative, as most gyms don't have neck-training equipment. With the exception of a few old Nautilus and Universal machines, manufacturers have neglected to design devices for this important muscle group.

One of the simplest exercises to perform is to lie on a flat bench and rest a weight plate on your forehead (you may want to wrap it in a towel). With your head positioned over the end of the bench, tilt it backwards to a comfortable stretch, and then raise it so your chin nearly touches your chest. You'll need to hold the plate in position with your hand. Start out using lighter weight for 15 to 20 reps, and work up to heavier weight for 8 to 12 reps. It's probably not a good idea to ever use extremely heavy weight for low reps (i.e. 4 to 6), as the risks outweigh the benefits.

Another exercise that doesn't require fancy equipment is the wrestler's bridge. Lie on your back on the floor and arch upward so you are supporting your body with just your head and feet. Slowly rock back and forth as many times as possible.

Wrestler's bridges are similar to chin-ups and dips in that it's all or none from day one. By this I mean you'll need to be strong enough to support your entire body-weight from the beginning. If you can't, or can only do one or two reps, I suggest you wait until your neck muscles have strengthened from the other exercises before attempting to do it again.

At the other end are those who may be able to perform 20 or 30 reps with ease. In this case you'll need to add extra weight to the exercise. Wrestlers often get a partner to sit on their chest, but since it's unlikely you are that strong, it probably makes more sense to have your partner lay a weight plate across your chest. Start out with a 10- or 25-pound plate and work up to a 35- or 45-pounder. Be careful not to let the plate slip and hit your throat.

If your gym has them you can use one of the commercial neck machines that are available. The version by Nautilus has a pad that you rest your head on and then tilt in various directions. The muscles on the side of the neck (sternocleidomastoids) give the neck a wide, bull-like appearance. The muscles along the back that tie into the trapezius help give the upper back a full look. The nice thing about the neck machine is that you can alternate directions just by changing the position of your head. There are no cables, straps or partners involved. This makes it ideal for supersetting and trisetting.

If your gym doesn't have a proper neck machine you can use a strap or neck harness. These can be bought or easily made. Simply slip the harness on over your head and attach a weight plate to the other end. From here it's just a matter of rotating your head in different directions to target the different neck muscles. By leaning forward and nodding your head you are working the neck muscles at the base of your skull. Lie faceup with your head hanging off a bench and you target the neck muscles along the front. Lie to one side and you work the muscles on the other side and vice versa.

There are also numerous ways to train the neck indirectly. Most versions of the shrug bring the neck muscles into play. One of the best is the calf-machine shrug. You stand under the machine as if you were going to do calf raises, but instead of flexing at the ankles, you simply shrug your shoulders up. You probably won't get the same degree of motion as with a regular barbell or dumbell shrug, but the exercise is still great for working the neck and traps.

Unless you are blessed with great genetics you'll probably need to do some direct neck training. Take a couple of the previous exercises and do two to three sets – either in a straight set fashion or as supersets or trisets. Before long people will be referring to you as the one with no neck.

"The neck is one of the body's most complex regions ... the muscles form a strong support network for protecting the head."

Photo by David Paul

CHAPTER 86

Classic Routines of the Superstars

"It's interesting to note that in spite of all the new selectorized weight-stack machines, the pulleys, cams and air-pressure apparatus, virtually every successful bodybuilder agrees: nothing builds huge muscles faster than rugged workouts with free weights. And it was in the golden era of bodybulding, from the '50s to the '70s, that all the principles of training were invented."

– Editorial in *MuscleMag International*

Having looked at the training routines for many of the current champs, I thought it might be interesting to show you how some of the champs from the past trained. As there are virtually thousands of workouts to choose from I've selected what I call a "best body-parts" routine from some of the greatest bodybuilding superstars in the history of the sport. Enjoy.

ARNOLD SCHWARZENEGGER
Chest

When it comes to the most famous bodybuilders of all time, Arnold Schwarzenegger definitely ranks number one. In fact Arnold's name seems to get mentioned more often than all the rest combined. What separates Arnold from the rest is that he became just as successful in movies and politics as he did on the Olympia stage. It's safe to say that the sport of bodybuilding wouldn't be where it is now without Arnold's popularity. Not bad for 19-year-old who got off a plane in Los Angeles in 1968 with nothing but a great body – and ambition to spare.

Even by today's standards Arnold's chest was one of the greatest of all time. From sternum to ribcage to pec-delt tie-in, Arnold's chest was and still is the envy of millions. Given that he trained during the 1960s and 1970s, it's not surprising that he relied heavily on barbells and dumbells to build those two slabs of beef. At that time, few machines were available with the exceptions of the Universal multi-station and the cable crossover. By today's standards Arnold's chest routine may seem outdated, but look at the results. How many current Mr. Olympia competitors could have compared side chest shots with Arnold at his best? Not many, I assure you.

A typical chest day would see Arnold and his good friend Franco Columbu starting out with 4 or 5 sets of flat barbell presses for 8 to 10 reps. Most of his sets were carried to positive failure, but occasionally he'd have Franco give him one or two forced reps.

After flat presses Arnold moved on to incline barbell presses for 5 quality sets to failure of 8 to 10 reps per set.

With his two primary mass-builders complete, Arnold's third exercise was flat dumbell flyes. For those who question the training intensity of the "old guys" of the sport, rent *Pumping Iron* and take a look at Arnold doing flat flyes. If that doesn't inspire you, please change sports!

To finish off his 58-inch chest, Arnold did 5 sets of standing cable crossovers. Again the reps were carried to positive failure and performed in a slow and controlled manner.

SCHWARZENEGGER'S CHEST WORKOUT

EXERCISE	SETS	REPS
Flat Barbell Presses	5	8–10
Incline Barbell Presses	5	8–10
Flat Dumbell Flyes	5	8–10
Cable Crossovers	5	8–10

Photo of Arnold Schwarzenegger

Arnold displays his still-envied chest in this side-chest shot

Few people would disagree that the best legs of all time belonged to Tom Platz.

TOM PLATZ

Legs

Given the thousands of bodybuilders who have made it to the national or pro level of the sport it's bold to claim that one bodybuilder or another had the best-ever version of any particular bodypart. I say Arnold had the best chest, others counter with Serge Nubret or Lou Ferrigno. Yates' back gets top marks from many, but guys like Haney, Coleman and Cutler are right there as well. For shoulders Oliva was considered king, but how about Christian and Dillett? For every best there is a counter best.

When it comes to legs, however, few will argue that the best belonged to Tom Platz. Even among today's top pros, no one has the same degree of leg size, completion and separation, as Tom's legs from the early 1980s. In many respects Tom's legs actually held him back as he could never bring his upper body up to the level of those 30+ inch monsters.

One writer from the 1980s said watching Tom Platz train legs was like watching a freight train careening out of control. How does 600-pound squats for 20 reps grab you?

During his heyday Tom had three different leg workouts that he rotated. On the first leg workout he'd do squats and hack squats. The second he'd do all hack squats. Finally for his third leg workout he'd do high-rep squats. Then close to a competition he'd add in leg extensions on day two.

Although Tom's hamstrings were also among the best of all time, his hamstring workout usually consisted of just one exercise: lying leg curls (remember there weren't many seated or standing leg curls available in the '70s and early '80s).

PLATZ'S LEG WORKOUT

EXERCISE	SETS	REPS
Squats	8–10	5–35
Hack Squats	5–8	10–15
Lying Leg Curls	6–8	10–15

Photo of Tom Platz

Sergio believed in training opposing muscles together – his superior chest and back were proof that this practice worked.

SERGIO OLIVA

Chest and Back

He was nicknamed "The Myth," and for good reason. Most competitors didn't believe that he was for real. Pound for pound the Cuban-born Oliva carried as much muscle as any bodybuilder in history – past or present. But what made Oliva's physique so devastating was that in this age of 35- and even 40-inch midsections, Oliva's waist was down in the 28-inch range. When you combined this with his over-55-inch chest and two of the largest sets of delts and arms in history, the end result was nothing short of frightening. Even Arnold Schwarzenegger was taken aback the first time he saw Oliva in person.

Oliva was a firm believer that since the body's opposing muscles evolved to function together they should be trained together. For this reason he often trained chest and back together in a superset fashion. A typical Oliva chest-and-back day would look something like this:

OLIVA'S CHEST-AND-BACK WORKOUT

EXERCISE	SETS	REPS
Wide-Grip Chins (superset with) Flat Bench Presses	4–5	8–10
Narrow-Grip Chins (superset with) Incline Barbell Presses	3–4	6–8
Wide-Grip Rows (superset with) Narrow-Grip Rows	3–4	6–8
Deadlifts (superset with) Good Mornings	3–4	6–8
T-Bar Rows (superset with) Machine Pullovers	3–4	6–8

MIKE CHRISTIAN

Shoulders

Although Lee Haney dominated bodybuilding for most of the 1980s, it wasn't a complete walk in the park for the big Georgian. One of his fiercest competitors was Mike Christian. While Haney had the edge in most muscle groups, as far as shoulders went, mighty Mike held his own and then some.

Mike is the first to admit that his shoulders always responded quickly to training. In fact he often went long stretches without even training them as they received adequate stimulation from just doing his chest and back workouts.

When he did train them, Mike liked to alternate a heavy day with a light day. He was also more partial to free weights, primarily using barbells and dumbells for most of his shoulder exercises. The only exception was the reverse pec-deck for his rear deltoids.

CHRISTIAN'S SHOULDER WORKOUT

EXERCISE	SETS	REPS
Behind-the-Neck Barbell Presses	4	10–12
Side Dumbell Raises	4	10–12
Front Dumbell Raises	4	10–12
Reverse Pec-Deck	4	10–12

Mike's shoulders responded well to training and he used this genetically gifted bodypart to his advantage.

Photo of Mike Christian

Flex flexes one of his greatest assets – his back.

FLEX WHEELER

Back

According to many bodybuilding fans, bodybuilding reached its zenith in the early to mid 1990s with Flex Wheeler. At his best (around 1993) Flex carried about 230 pounds on his near-flawless physique. Many believed he combined the best of both worlds: massive size along with shape and proportions. No part of the Wheeler physique was underdeveloped or overpowering. It was perfect balance all around.

It's not surprising that a physique this proportioned was built with great variety. Flex was a firm believer in rotating his exercises on a regular basis and his back training was no different. Flex was one of the few guys in the 1990s who could hold his own in back shots with six-time Mr Olympia Dorian Yates. Here's a typical back workout for Flex:

WHEELER'S BACK WORKOUT		
EXERCISE	**SETS**	**REPS**
Wide-Grip Front Pulldowns	5–6	10
One-Arm Dumbell Rows	5–6	10
Close-Grip Pulldowns	5–6	10

ARNOLD SCHWARZENEGGER

Calves

It's hard to believe that a guy who became famous for his calves had at one time totally neglected them. But repeated goading from Reg Park and Joe Weider (and a desire to be the absolute best in the sport) convinced Arnold to get serious about his calf training. Once Arnold decided to start blasting his calves it was all-out war. Typically he'd pick four exercises and do 5 or 6 sets of higher reps of each exercise. Within five years Arnold's calves had become full-blown cows, and to this day few bodybuilders sport the same calf development as did the Austrian Oak.

SCHWARZENEGGER'S CALF WORKOUT

EXERCISE	SETS	REPS
Donkey Calf Raises	5–6	15–20
Standing Calf Raises	5–6	12–15
Seated Calf Raises	5–6	12–15
Toe Presses on Leg Press Machine	5–6	12–15

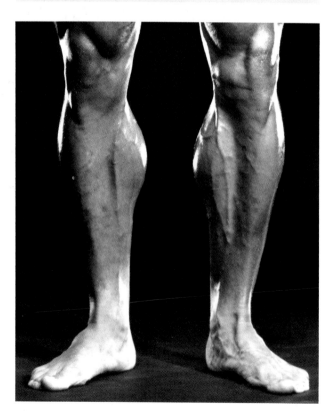

The Oak had a set of calves still largely unrivaled in the sport.

Photo of Arnold Schwarzenegger

SERGE NUBRET
Chest

Serge Nubret, born in Guadeloupe in the French West Indies, won just about every top bodybuilding contest. If not for a combination of Arnold Schwarzenegger and politics, Serge Nubret may well have been the dominant bodybuilder of the 1970s. Odds are he would have won the Mr. Olympia if not for Arnold's presence.

Realizing that he probably could never beat Arnold, and having had a falling out with the IFBB, Serge started competing in rival organizations during the late '70s and early '80s. While his lower body was never his strong point, his upper body is considered one of the greatest of all time. With one of the greatest waist/chest differentials in history, it's safe to say that few bodybuilders looked as good as Serge did just standing there.

Serge's training style was as unique as it was effective. In a time of high-volume training Serge took things to the extreme. He routinely did 20 to 30 sets for his muscle groups and used weights that most modern bodybuilders would consider warmup weights. But the results speak for themselves.

Other than perhaps his abdominals, Serge's chest was his greatest asset. From collarbone to lower ribcage, Serge's chest resembled two oversized balloons. Perhaps the most amazing thing about Serge's chest was how he built it. Believe it or not, he used just one exercise throughout his long training career – the flat barbell press. During a typical workout Serge would use from 185 to 225 pounds and do 20 sets of 15 to 20 reps. That was it. If you've been doing multiple-exercise chest workouts using heavy weight without seeing results, why not give Serge's workout a try?

Photo of Serge Nubret by Chris Lund

NUBRET'S CHEST WORKOUT		
EXERCISE	SETS	REPS
Flat Barbell Presses	20	15–20

Serge followed a unique training style and possessed one of the greatest upper bodies of all time.

MOHAMMED MAKKAWY
Abdominals

When you weigh 170 to 175 pounds at your best and you're competing against guys weighing 240 and 250 pounds, you quickly realize that you need to present the judges with a complete package if you hope to have any chance of winning. Such a complete package was Egypt's Mohammed Makkawy. During the early 1980s, this near-perfect example of humanity won numerous Grand Prix events including victories over future eight-time Mr. Olympia winner, Lee Haney.

Mohammed won these contests by playing his own game, not by trying to match mass with the 240-pounders. Once he figured out that nothing less than perfect proportions would beat Haney and company, he modified his training to accomplish this goal. At the center of his great physique was a small, tight, rock-hard set of abdominals. Mohammed never believed that diet alone would bring out the abs, so he treated them like any other muscle.

During a typical ab workout he would do various combinations of crunches, leg raises and twists, to bring out his upper and lower abs and obliques.

Because he weighed less than most of his opponents, Mohammed focused on perfecting his proportions.

Photo of Mohammed Makkawy by Roger Shelley

MAKKAWY'S AB WORKOUT		
EXERCISE	SETS	REPS
Hanging Leg Raises	4–5	15–20
Bench Leg Raises	4–5	15–20
Crunches	4–5	15–20
Stick Twists	4–5	40–50

ROBBY ROBINSON
Biceps

Robby Robinson is one of the true legends of the sport, having won pro contests in three decades. Robby first got inspired to compete after seeing pictures of Sergio Oliva competing at the 1967 Mr. Olympia. From his first major win at the 1975 Mr. America to his win at the 50-and-over Masters Mr. Olympia in 1997, Robby Robinson has served as a role model for millions of bodybuilders the world over.

While Robby could be criticized for having calves a tad too small to be proportionate with the rest of his physique, they never held him back in competition. As for his upper body, Robby's was one of the greatest ever. The centerpiece of Robby's awe-inspiring physique was his pair of arms. In short, they were perfect. His biceps resembled two baseballs and his triceps had that beefy horseshoe look. Unlike some bodybuilders with one arm slighter bigger or higher peaked than the other (Arnold being the best example) Robby's arms were like mirror images of one another.

Robby usually began his biceps workout with standing barbell curls. After a couple of light warmup sets Robby would blast out 4 sets of 6 to 8 reps.

Another favorite Robinson exercise was preacher curls. While on occassion he'd substitute dumbells, more often than not he'd use the barbell. As with standing curls he typically did 4 sets of 6 to 8 reps.

To finish off those great guns of his, Robby did 4 sets of one-arm dumbell concentration curls. Every rep was performed in a slow and deliberate manner with no bouncing or jerking. As this was his last exercise, he did slightly higher reps – usually in the 8-to-12 range.

A true body-building legend, Robby Robinson had an impressive upper body.

ROBINSON'S BICEPS WORKOUT

EXERCISE	SETS	REPS
Standing Barbell Curls	4	6–8
Preacher Curls	4	6–8
Concentration Curls	4	8–12

DORIAN YATES

Back

If Arnold owned the 1970s and Lee Haney dominated the 1980s, then the 1990s were surely the era of "The Shadow" – England's Dorian Yates. Dorian didn't fit the mold of the typical champion bodybuilder. Not only did he live far away from the sandy beaches of California, his training style was also unique for the time. Borrowing heavily on the writings of Dr. Arthur Jones and Mike Mentzer, Dorian averaged about 6 to 8 sets per muscle group. At the time, the vast majority of bodybuilders followed the high-volume approach to training and it wasn't uncommon to see bodybuilders slaving away in the gym for two, three or more hours every day. While Mentzer had some success on the competitive stage, it was Yates with his six straight Mr. Olympia wins that influenced a whole generation of bodybuilders.

Of all the parts that made up his solid 260-pound body his back stood out the most. He was probably the first bodybuilder to demonstrate that white athletes could develop a back just as thick and detailed as black athletes. In fact for most of his Mr. Olympia years, Dorian's back was the standard by which all others were measured.

Many consider the 1990s to have been dominated by Dorian Yates, "The Shadow," from England.

Photo of Dorian Yates

YATES' BACK WORKOUT

EXERCISE	SETS	REPS
Reverse-Grip Pulldowns	3	8–15
Reverse-Grip Barbell Rows	2	8–12
Seated Cable Rows	2	8–12
Back Extensions or Deadlifts	2	8–12

LOU FERRIGNO
Chest

Not counting Arnold Schwarzenegger, the most famous bodybuilder of the 1970s was Lou Ferrigno. Standing 6'5" and weighing around 270 in contest condition, Lou was by far the largest bodybuilder competing at the time. With wins at the Mr. America and Mr. Universe and a starring role in the 1975 ground-breaking documentary *Pumping Iron*, big Lou was set to inherit Arnold's Mr. Olympia title. But then Hollywood came calling. Lou was cast as the Marvel comics super-hero The Incredible Hulk, and every week millions tuned in to see mild mannered David Banner turn into the hulking green socially conscious monster. When Lou (playing the Hulk) hit those famous most-muscular growls, his upper body would explode into a series of bulges, bumps and striations. At the center of this eruption was Lou's 60-inch chest.

As expected of someone who idolized Sergio and Arnold, Lou's chest routines were primarily done with barbells and dumbells. He didn't add in cables until close to contest time. A typical chest workout from Lou's Incredible Hulk days would look like this:

Lou idolized Arnold and Sergio and performed his chest training mostly with barbell and dumbell moves.

Photo of Lou Ferrigno

FERRIGNO'S SHOULDER WORKOUT

EXERCISE	SETS	REPS
Flat Barbell or Dumbell Presses	4	8–10
Flat or Incline Flyes	4	8–10
Flat or Incline Presses	4	8–10
Cable Crossovers	4	8–10

The most famous set of biceps in the history of bodybuilding.

ARNOLD SCHWARZENEGGER
Biceps

It only makes sense to end this chapter with perhaps the most famous set of biceps in bodybuilding history. Today's champions may be popular and their routines may be followed, but Arnold's biceps routines are probably still the most popular in the world. The photo on the cover of his autobiography *Education of a Bodybuilder* has yet to be duplicated.

Although he varied his exercises on a regular basis, Arnold always included a couple of barbell and dumbell exercises in his biceps workouts. He also tended to divide his training into nine months of mass building and three months of pre-contest refining. A typical Schwarzenegger off-season workout would look like this:

SCHWARZENEGGER'S BICEPS WORKOUT

EXERCISE	SETS	REPS
Standing Barbell Curls	4–5	8–10
Preacher Curls	4–5	8–10
Standing Alternate Dumbell Curls	4–5	8–10
Standing Bent-Over Concentration Curl	4–5	8–10

THE COMPLETE BODYBUILDER

CHAPTER 87

Tips for the Traveling Bodybuilder

"I suggest you watch your eating habits closely when traveling. The less you do, the fewer calories you need."

– Bill Pearl, one of the top bodybuilders of all time, offering suggestions on traveling as a bodybuilder.

An unexpected business trip or even a planned vacation can seriously interfere with a bodybuilder's training and goals. But your workouts don't need to go down the tiolet just because you're in another city, or even another country. You can find ways to keep up your training while on the road.

The first thing to understand is that you have to make training a priority, regardless of where you are or why you are there. Your success will depend upon your being both dedicated and organized. One of the best ways to do this is to have a detailed itinerary prepared before your departure. If you leave it until the last minute, both your workout and your nutrition will falter. You will make dismal food choices and your workouts will be forgotten at worst or mediocre at best.

Tip #1: Know your hotel

Most hotels feature a Web site that lists their services. Before booking into the cheapest accommodations, compare the different hotels in the area where you'll be staying. For a few extra dollars you may get access to a pool and fitness center. Many hotels also put their menus on their site. If possible, select a hotel that offers healthy nutritional choices. This way you will have no excuse for not eating healthy the majority of the time. You can also phone them ahead to ask if they will cook special items for you such as egg-white omelets. Sometimes you may have to go somewhere with limited choices, so you are allowed an occasional cheat meal. Just make sure the majority of your meals are sound.

Tip #2: A man and his kitchenette

Although you'll have to pay more for a room equipped with a kitchenette, it's well worth the money. Instead of relying on someone else to prepare your meals (with goodness only knows what kind of high-fat, high-sodium ingredients) you can prepare your own. At the first opportunity, drop by a supermarket to stock up on fresh meat, fruits and vegetables. Then you can whip up tasty, home-made, low-fat, high-protein bodybuilding meals in no time. Besides, you'll likely save more in the long run by not having to purchase every meal at a restaurant.

Tip #3: Check the gyms

If your hotel does not have a gym, or you would rather have access to more equipment, buying a short-term pass at a local gym is a great way to go. The easiest way to see if there is an adequate gym in the area is to go online and type in the name of the town or city you are going to. The business bureaus of most towns and cities will list what's available. They'll also give you a little map to show you where each gym is located. You can then check the gyms out online or give them a call. You can also simply call your hotel and ask them about the gyms nearby.

Tip #4: Scope out the restaurants

While you are checking out the gyms online, check out your restaurant selection as well. Like hotels, most of the

better eating establishments have Web sites that post their menus. You can save time – and your waistline – by browsing the menu before you even go through the doors. By pre-planning your selection, there is less chance you'll order an inappropriate meal in the spur of the moment.

Tip #5: Pack you workout clothes first

You'd be surprised what gets left behind in the hassle of packing a suitcase prior to an important business trip or vacation. Before any shirts, dress pants or swim trunks get folded into your suitcase, toss in at least one workout outfit. You don't need anything fancy – a T-shirt or two, a pair of shorts and sneakers are sufficient.

Tip #6: Bring equipment

If your trip is to be taken by car, you have another way to get your workout in: bring your own equipment. You don't have to lug around squat and bench-press racks, but there's no reason you can't pop a few adjustable dumbells – and maybe even a barbell – into the trunk. If you have the room, toss in a small adjustable bench (you know, the $50 one that most guys get for Christmas at least once in their lives!). You don't need a truckload of fancy equipment to get a good workout. When he was young and living in Germany, Arnold Schwarzenegger would take one day each week, go into the woods with a few buddies and do nothing but barbell exercises. Need I say more?

Tip #7: Experiment with weight-training routines

Sometimes not being able to use the same familiar equipment is a blessing in disguise. Most people are creatures of habit and bodybuilders are no different. There's nothing like changing up your training routine to shock the muscles into new growth. Even if the gym has most of what you're used to, give it a pass and experiment with new exercises and new equipment. You'll probably experience a degree of soreness the next day that you haven't felt in a while.

Tip #8: Experiment with different forms of cardio

Even though your primary goal as a bodybuilder is to build muscle mass, you don't want it covered by a layer of

EATING ON THE GO

Traveling can put a wrench in your diet plans, but if you think ahead you can come out on top. First of all, avoid airport food whenever possible. When flying, drink lots of water to keep hydrated. Choose snacks that have a high water content such as apples and pears. If you have a small cooler with you, yogurt and cheese will provide you with amino acids to help increase blood flow and tryptophan, which helps with relaxation (especially helpful if you're scared of flying). Almonds make good snacks while low-sodium beef jerky will keep you feeling full and provide you with lots of protein.

fat. You should be doing at least three sessions of 20 to 30 minutes of cardio each week. Sorry to break it to you, but being on the road is no excuse for missing your cardio workouts. As with weight training, try a new cardio machine if the opportunity presents itself. Better still; check out the gym's cardio classes. If regular aerobics doesn't grab your fancy, try a spinning class or one of the martial arts-based classes.

Tip #9: Go for a walk

If you are tied up in meetings until late every night, you can always rely on that reliable old standby of physical activity: walking. Walking is the most natural form of exercise there is, and can be tailored to just about any intensity level. If this is too low impact for you, how about changing it to a jog? Both walking and jogging provide you with an opportunity to explore the area you are staying in.

Tip #10: Stay bodybuilding and fitness minded

Perhaps the best tip is to stay focused. Sometimes all it takes is a loss of focus to derail your eating and training habits. If you're on the road for only a day or two, then taking time off training and loosening your diet won't set you back. But if you're traveling for four days or more, you'll want to get organized and stay committed. Buy some bodybuilding magazines for inspiration.

THE EXERCISES

Although the following exercises are great for those on the road, they can be followed by just about anyone. All you need are a few inexpensive pieces of equipment and some

items that can be found around your house or hotel room. Not only will they help you maintain your present condition, they may help you improve on it, since the exercises will be a shock to the body.

For simplicity I have divided the body into muscle groups. The exercises are arranged to target the largest muscle groups first. In most cases I have included three or four exercises for each muscle group. You can pick a couple of them and perform three or four straight sets, or do them all in one or two giant sets.

EQUIPMENT NEEDED:

Two chairs

Two books

Set of chest-expander springs

Hand grips

Bed

Legs

You probably won't find a squat rack in your hotel room, but that's not a reason to neglect training your legs. Here are a few exercises that will keep your legs in shape while on the road.

Sissy squats: Sissy squats are definitely not for sissies, and should not be limited to hotel rooms. You should also incorporate them into your regular workouts at the gym. Position yourself in a doorway and grab one side with your hand. Lean back slightly on your heels and squat down so your legs are parallel with the floor. Return to the starting position. Try to keep your thighs and glutes tensed throughout the entire range of motion. If you have something heavy on hand (dumbell, heavy book, brief-

Illustration by Mark Collins

case, etc.), hold it to your upper chest. You'll be surprised at the difference five or ten pounds will make.

Chair lunges: Most hotel rooms contain at least one chair, but the bed can also be used. Place one foot on the chair and step far forward, lowering yourself until your hamstring is just short of touching your calf. Pause at the bottom and then return to the standing position. Perform 15 to 20 reps per leg.

Limbo squats, or between-door squats: Open the bathroom door (you could use the main door but the other guests may get the wrong idea!) and grab both sides with your hands. Lean back as far as possible and squat down into a full squat position. Pause for a second and then return to the starting position. Limbo squats are similar to sissy squats, but by holding on with both hands you can lean back further and place more stress on the quads.

One-leg squats: Those with knee or back problems may want to avoid this exercise. Even with good technique there is some slight lateral stress on the knees and lower back. As the name suggests, you perform this exercise as you would regular squats, but you stand on just one leg. Hold a doorframe or the back of a chair for balance. One-leg squats are very challenging and don't be surprised if you can only manage 8 to 10 reps. A slightly different version involves bending the opposite leg to the one being worked, and using just your toes for balance. This can allow for better positioning, but you will likely need a weight.

One-leg calf raises: All you need for this exercise is a three- or four-inch block or thick book to stand on. Position the block or book in a doorway and stand on the edge with the ball of one foot. With the other foot bent behind you, lower your heel as far as possible. To make up for the lack

Photo of Diego Azizi by Paul Buceta

of weight you'll need to do ultraslow reps for high reps – at least 20 to 30.

Squat-down calf raises: This exercise is almost identical to one-leg calf raises, except you perform the movement in a squat position. This shifts most of the stress from the gastrocnemius (upper calf) to the soleus (lower calf). Since your lower calves are not as strong as your upper, you may need to do the exercise using both legs. Again do high reps, however.

Chest

Despite the popularity of barbell and dumbell presses for working the chest, you can give the area a great workout with just your bodyweight and two chairs. Dips and pushups were building pectoral muscles long before barbells and dumbells arrived on the scene.

Push-ups: Push-ups are one of the most basic and effective bodyweight exercises. Besides working the chest, they give the front shoulders and triceps a great workout. This exercise is basically a reverse bench press. Instead of lying faceup and pushing the weight away from you, you lie facedown and push yourself away from the floor. If you're not used to doing push-ups you may want to start with half push-ups, whereby you keep your knees on the floor. You can also do sets of both full and half push-ups to ensure a good chest workout.

Push-ups with feet elevated: To shift most of the stress from the lower to the upper chest, position your feet on a chair or bed. From here the exercise is performed like standard push-ups.

Dips between chairs: Place two chairs just slightly wider than shoulder width apart and, with your hands resting on the seat of the chair and feet on the ground, slowly lower your torso between them. As with dips on V-shaped or parallel bars, don't bounce at the bottom of the exercise, as you could tear the pec-delt tie-in region. Although this exercise works your whole chest, this angle places most of the stress on the lower and outer chest regions.

Dips between chairs with feet elevated: Perform this exercise in the same manner, but with your feet placed on a third chair or side of the bed. Because of the change in angle, your upper chest is brought more into play. Being elevated on the chairs also allows for a greater range of motion, for both push-ups and dips.

Back

Although the back is one of the harder areas to train without specialized equipment, it can be done. You just need a chest-expander set and a long piece of strong, solid rounded wood such as a broom handle or a solid piece of pipe instead.

Chins between chairs: Place two chairs about three to four feet apart and place your bar or stick across them. Make sure it's secure. Lie on your back between the chairs and grab the bar with a slightly wider than shoulder-width grip. Slowly pull your body up to the bar as if doing a chin-up. If the bar is of sufficient strength (eg. a piece of iron pipe) you can perform the exercise with a narrow reverse grip. Chins between chairs are sort of a cross between a chin-up and a row. You're pulling yourself upward like a standard chin-up, but the angle is closer to that of a rowing motion. Perform as many reps as you can.

Spring rows: Spring sets, more commonly called chest-expander sets, are a godsend for those on the road. They consist of a series of springs attached by two handles. The more springs attached at any given time, the more tension. Anchor one handle on a leg of the bed and grab the other handle with both hands. With your knees and torso slightly bent, slowly pull the handle toward the lower ribcage. Stretch your arms back out. Try to stand (or sit) far enough from the anchored handle that the tension remains on your lats even when your arms are fully extended. You can also use the spring set in this manner to do one-arm rows.

Shoulders

Although your shoulders have received some work from the chest and back exercises, it's still a good idea to perform some direct work for them. Two heavy books and the chest-expander set will do the trick.

Front, side and rear raises: As these three exercises are similar I'll describe them all here. To work the front shoulders grab a pair of heavy books and lift them to the front as you would a pair of dumbells. Likewise, for the side shoulders lift them to the sides as if doing dumbell side laterals. To hit the rear delts lean forward and perform bent-over raises, again holding the books.

Spring raises: Anchor one handle of the chest-expander set under your foot and slowly lift the other handle to the front or side. To hit the rear shoulders, bend over, grab a handle in each hand and slowly pull outwards to an arms-locked position.

Upright rows: Again lock one handle of the chest-expander set under your foot. Grab the other handle with both hands and slowly pull straight up the center of the body.

Biceps and Triceps

You can perform dozens of arm exercises on the road. Give the following a try.

Triceps chair dips: This exercise is performed exactly the same as the gym version of bench dips, except you use two chairs instead of two benches. Set the two chairs about four feet apart and, with your heels resting on one chair and your hands on the other, slowly bend at the elbows and lower yourself to a comfortable stretch. Pause at the bottom and then push back up to an arms-locked position. If you find one chair is not wide enough for both hands, you can set two side by side. Make sure they won't tip!

Close-grip push-ups: Just like the standard push-up, but place your hands about 8 to 10 inches apart. This shifts most of the stress from the front shoulders and chest to the triceps.

Spring curls: With one end of the chest-expander set anchored beneath your feet, grasp the other end and curl upward. For variety you can lift with the opposite arm and curl across the front of the body.

Book curls: While the handles on the chest-expander set are more convenient to hold on to, you can also use a book. It will take some practice to find out the most

give the biceps a good workout. With the heaviest books only weighing five pounds or so, you'll need to use an ultraslow motion to make up for the lack of weight. You can also use a towel for this exercise. Stand on the end of a towel and curl the other end up.

Abdominals

As most abdominal exercises don't require specialized equipment, you can perform just about any ab exercise while on the road. Simply lie back on the floor and alternate various versions of leg raises, crunches and reverse crunches. To make things more challenging, try holding a weight or other heavy object.

Now you have some great tips and exercises for staying in shape while on the road. Just remember that a change of environment and in your normal routine doesn't have to signal an end to your workouts. Remember muscles grow in response to new stimuli, and while increasing the weight is one way, changing the exercises also shocks them into new growth. So don't be surprised if you actually make gains while traveling.

Photo of Billy Begovic by Alex Ardenti

CHAPTER 88

The Corporate Quickie

"You can always find an excuse not to succeed. Instead you have to find a way to make sure you do succeed."

– Editorial in *MuscleMag International*

f you're like many people, time seems to be in short supply. There may be 24 hours in the day but there are weeks when 30-hour days wouldn't cut it. Whether from school, work or family responsibilities, there will be times when your training will need to be put on hold. But does it really need to be put on hold? What if you could train the entire body in 20 minutes with just seven basic compound exercises?

The beauty of compound exercises is that they work more than one muscle group. This is why beginning trainers are told to put most of their emphasis on compound movements rather than isolation exercises. By utilizing multiple muscles compound exercises allow you to lift more weight and hence stimulate more muscle mass.

Compound exercises also save you time. For example, barbell bench presses – either flat or incline – will work the chest, front shoulders and triceps. Chin-ups or pulldowns – particularly the reverse narrow versions – will target the back, rear shoulders and biceps. These two exercises alone will work virtually all of the upper body. Add in a couple of sets of side raises and you're done.

The same approach can be used with the lower body. Squats, lunges and leg

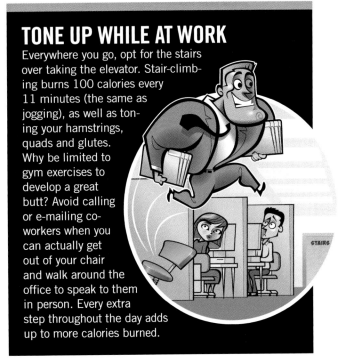

TONE UP WHILE AT WORK

Everywhere you go, opt for the stairs over taking the elevator. Stair-climbing burns 100 calories every 11 minutes (the same as jogging), as well as toning your hamstrings, quads and glutes. Why be limited to gym exercises to develop a great butt? Avoid calling or e-mailing co-workers when you can actually get out of your chair and walk around the office to speak to them in person. Every extra step throughout the day adds up to more calories burned.

presses work the thighs, hamstrings and glutes, all in one motion. Add in toe presses or calf raises and you've worked your entire lower body. To complete your workout, perform a little circuit of crunches and back extensions for the abdominals and lower-back muscles.

The same workout using isolation movements would take you over an hour – perhaps two if you did three or four sets per exercise. But these seven movements can be performed in as little as 10 to 15 minutes if you do only one set of each, or 25 to 30 minutes if you have enough time to do three sets.

THE CORPORATE QUICKIE

EXERCISE	MUSCLES	SETS	REPS
Leg presses, lunges or squats	Quads/Hamstrings/Calves	2	10–12
Flat or incline barbell bench presses	Chest/Shoulders/Triceps	2	10–12
Narrow reverse-grip pulldowns or chin-ups	Back/Shoulders/Biceps	2	10–12
Dumbell or machine lateral raises	Shoulders	2	10–12
Crunches	Abdominals	2	15–20
Back extensions	Lower Back	2	15–20
Toe presses or calf raises	Calves	2	15–20

Pick compound exercises (to work more than one muscle group).
You can add a cardio component to the workout by reducing the weight and keeping between-set rest intervals to less than 20 seconds.

Illustration by Mark Collins

CHAPTER 89

PHA Training

"The good news is that there is a way for you to get your cardio exercise and lose the love handles that suits your personality more than a 10 k jog does. It's called circuit training."

– Wendy Morley, contributing editor of *Reps!* magazine

Okay so you've been squatting with enough weight to make a rhino cower in fear and you routinely bench a small car off your chest. Your leg presses require every 45-pound plate in the gym and most members view your workouts with the same air of bewilderment as a space shuttle launch. You've yelled and screamed your way to the top of the gym hierarchy and have the slabs of muscle all over your body to show for it. Unfortunately you're also carrying a spare tire around your waist, and climbing a set of stairs nearly puts you in labor. You've known for months that you have to address this situation, but you're not exactly sure how to go about doing it. Just the thought of running on a treadmill or hopping on a crosstrainer causes you to barf up your last two protein shakes. So how do you do it? How do you burn off that extra layer of blubber without sacrificing your hard-earned muscle mass?

If you hate to run, refuse to join an aerobics class and the idea of spending even one minute in a spinning class makes you question your sanity, then why not give PHA training a try. PHA stands for Peripheral Heart Action. It was first developed and popularized by former Mr. America Bob Gajda back in the 1960s. Over the years it has evolved (and in many cases been watered down) into what we now commonly call circuit training. Numerous athletes, bodybuilders and famous actors, including the late Bruce Lee, have used it

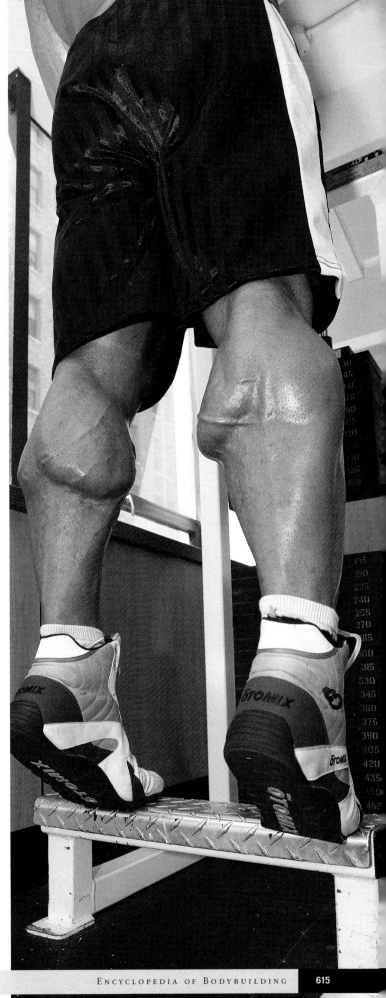

over the years to shred their physiques while maintaining muscle mass.

The primary benefit of PHA training over traditional cardio is that you'll be using standard weight-training exercises. This will enable you to maintain most if not all of your hard-earned muscle mass as you ditch the fat.

PHA training differs from normal weight training in that you do one set of an exercise and then quickly move on to another exercise that works a completely different muscle group, rather than doing multiple sets for one particular bodypart before moving on to the next. You also try to switch exercises as quickly as possible to keep your heart rate elevated and in the cardio zone. PHA is also different than the more familiar circuit training because you alternate upper and lower body movements instead of performing random exercises. The idea is to provide continuous blood flow throughout the entire body while taking little to no rest between sets.

I'll warn you from the start that PHA training is not some sissy little circuit routine that you'll see at the local health and beauty spa. The constant motion will tax your cardiovascular system to the max. But here lies the beauty of PHA training. You'll be building endurance and burning fat while lifting weights that are also stressing the muscles. Such an expenditure of energy quickly translates into fat loss. When you add in a revamping of your diet, you'll be amazed at how quickly you'll harden up and lean out.

Photo (Top) by Irvin Gelb
Photo (Right) of Alfonso Del Rio by Jason Breeze

You can't show your muscles off to their full dimensions until you lose the excess bodyfat that lies on top.

One of the more common PHA routines is to perform three rounds, or circuits, of one group of exercises and then perform three rounds of a second group of exercises. Try to pick compound exercises as opposed to isolation movements, since compound exercises target more muscle mass and require more energy.

Here is an example of a four-week PHA program:

GROUP 1:

Squats –15 reps

Bench presses –15 reps

Lying leg curls – 15 reps

Military presses –15 reps

Reverse crunches – 20 reps

Barbell rows – 15 reps

Complete three rounds without stopping, take a bit of a rest, and then quickly move to the next group of exercises. If this is too much for your cardiovascular system, do just two rounds. You may also want to rest a bit between exercises in the beginning and then gradually reduce the rest interval until you can perform the full group with no rest. For all exercises in each group, pick a weight that is relatively light for the first round, a bit heavier for the second, and the heaviest for the third.

GROUP 2:

Incline dumbbell press – 15 reps

Leg presses – 15 reps

Chin-ups (or front pulldowns) – 10 to 15 reps

Calf raises – 15 reps

Lying triceps extensions (or skullcrushers) – 15 reps

Stiff-leg deadlifts – 20 reps

Perform your PHA workouts on alternate days (i.e. Monday, Wednesday and Friday, or Tuesday, Thursday and Saturday. An alternative approach is to perform two days per week of PHA and two days of traditional weight training. This "50-50" approach will work on strength and endurance with equal emphasis. You won't shed fat as quickly as you would by performing just

PHA training alone, but it's a great way to transition from regular strength training into PHA. Here are a few tips to keep in mind:

- Before each workout, do a couple of minutes of light cardio to get your heart rate slightly elevated and your body warmed up.
- Perform compound rather than isolation exercises to stimulate the most muscle mass.
- Use medium weight for 15 to 20 reps.
- Keep your rest interval to a minimum (only as long as it takes to move from one exercise to the next).
- At no point should you train to total muscle failure.
- After you finish the workout, cool down by walking around for a few minutes to bring your heart rate back to normal.
- Have a low-calorie protein shake after each workout to enhance recovery.

Photo of Antoine Vaillant by Irvin Gelb

CHAPTER 90

To the Heart of the Matter with Cardio Training

"My emphasis is not on building muscle anymore, but on holding muscle and getting as lean as I can. I eat less and do more cardio, so I have to balance my energy expenditure. This new focus also cuts down on any risk of injury."

– Will Harris, IFBB pro

Although once shunned by most weight trainers it's now accepted that bodybuilders should do some sort of aerobic exercise, especially during the pre-contest phase of their training. Not only does it help get rid of body fat, it improves the health of the cardiovascular system, and everyone can use help with that.

Also keep in mind that a muscle completely fatigued in the absence of oxygen will build up lactic acid at a rate 25 times the normal level. And a fatigued muscle can only generate one-tenth the energy of a muscle that is rich in oxygen. Since there is only one way for oxygen to reach your muscles – by your cardiovascular system – it stands to reason that you must do everything possible to keep yours in top shape.

AEROBIC EXERCISE – WITH OXYGEN

Although you may be primarily concerned with the development of your skeletal muscles, don't forget that the heart is also a muscle. And while a well-developed heart won't win you extra points onstage, it is your most important muscle when it comes to overall long-term health.

In simple terms aerobic exercise is any extended activity that makes you breathe hard while using the large muscle groups at a regular, even pace. Aerobic activities help make your heart stronger and more efficient. They also use more calories than other activities. Some examples of aerobic activities include:

- Jogging
- Bicycling
- Swimming
- Aerobics class
- Boxing class
- Spinning
- Racquet sports
- Rowing
- Ice or roller skating
- Cross-country or downhill skiing
- Using cardio equipment (i.e. treadmill, stationary bike)
- Brisk walking
- Hiking

BENEFITS OF AEROBIC EXERCISE

When oxygen enters your lungs it's grabbed by red blood cells and transported back to the heart and then pumped throughout the body to the various tissues and cells. At the cellular level the oxygen is released and various waste products including carbon dioxide are carried back to the lungs and exhaled. One of the benefits of aerobic exercise is that after a period of time blood volume will increase. An average male can increase his circulating blood volume by up to a liter with regular aerobic exercise. More blood means more red blood cells. More red blood cells means more oxygen and waste-carrying capacity. I think you can see how this would be beneficial to hard-training bodybuilders. Not only will your muscles be receiving more oxygen, waste products will be removed that much faster.

>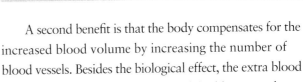
> The large majority of heavier strength athletes have a body-fat percentage that's too high. That puts them at risk for heart conditions and cardiovascular disease down the road. Powerlifters and other strength athletes suffer from heart attacks more frequently than do athletes in any other sport."
>
> – Rahim Kassam, regular *MuscleMag International* columnist

A second benefit is that the body compensates for the increased blood volume by increasing the number of blood vessels. Besides the biological effect, the extra blood vessels give bodybuilders a much more vascular look.

A final benefit to regular cardio exercise is that it increases the body's digestive abilities and mental alertness, and plays an important role in combating stress and ill temper.

STARTING AN AEROBIC PROGRAM

Like most forms of physical exercise you don't just dive right in at the highest intensity level. Just because you can squat 315 pounds for 12 reps doesn't mean your legs are capable of enduring an hour of cycling or running. Start out by doing two to three 15- to 20-

Photo of Pasi Schalin by Ricky Marconi

Photo of Armon Adibi by Alex Ardenti

For bodybuilding success you must learn to use cardio to lose fat while retaining muscle.

minute sessions at a light to moderate pace and gradually increase the duration to 30 to 45 minutes, four to five times per week.

UNDERSTANDING THE TARGET HEART-RATE ZONE

To get the most health benefits from aerobic activity, you should exercise at a level strenuous enough to raise your heart rate to what's called your target heart rate zone. Your target heart rate zone is 65 to 80 percent of your maximum heart rate (the fastest your heart can beat). To find your theoretical maximum heart rate subtract your age from 220. For a 30-year-old that equals 190 (220 - 30 = 190). Now take this number and multiply it by .65 and .80 to give you your target heart rate zone. For our 30-year-old that would be 124 to 152.

Check to see if you're in your ZONE

To see if you are exercising within your target heart rate zone, count the number of pulse beats at your wrist or neck for 10 seconds, then multiply by six to get the beats per minute. If your heart is beating faster than your target heart rate, you are exercising too hard and should slow down. If your heart is beating slower than your target heart rate, you should exercise a little harder.

Go easy!

When you begin your exercise program, aim for the lower end of your target zone (65 percent). As you get into better shape, slowly build up to the higher end of your target zone (80 percent).

FAT-LOSS ZONE AND CARDIO ZONE

You will no doubt hear about training in a lower-intensity fat-burning zone (60 to 70 percent of maximal heart rate) as opposed to a cardio zone (80 to 90 percent of maximal heart rate). The debate rages as to which is the best zone. While it's true that exercising at the lower zone will burn more calories in the form of fat by percentage, exercising in the higher zone will burn more calories overall for the same amount of time. And since total calorie expenditure is the key to losing fat, theoretically the higher zone should be the best zone. The key word there is "should," as everyone's body responds differently. The lower zone may work best for you. Working out in the lower zone may also help you to keep all your muscle while leaning out.

My advice is to start out at the lower zone and gradually work into the upper zone and see what happens. If there is a noticeable difference then select the one that works best. If on the other hand both seem to be yielding equal results, then alternate them. You can alternate them on a daily basis (i.e. high, low, high, low, etc.), or you can do one month high and the next low.

Another great alternative is to do HIIT training. This is great for both fitness and fat loss. In HIIT training you exercise at a lower intensity for a while and then at a very high intensity to get your heart rate right up into the high cardio zone for a brief period, then back to low intensity until you can catch your breath enough to go back into the high cardio zone. You keep going back and forth this way until your whole workout is done.

> "Man I do a lot of cardio. From the first week of my prep I do two 45-minute sessions a day, six days a week and one 45-minute session on the other day, which is my leg day."
>
> – Craig Richardson, IFBB pro, commenting on how much cardio he does during the pre-contest phase of training.

WHEN TO PERFORM YOUR CARDIO WORKOUTS

"If you live in the real world and your time is limited, you may want to do your weights and cardio in one long session at the gym. Think about investing in a piece of cardio equipment for your home so you have more options and don't always have to do your cardio at the gym. But plenty of bodybuilders do it all in one shot, both weights and cardio, and still manage to get decent results."
– Ron Harris, regular *MuscleMag International* contributor

While generally speaking there is no best time to perform your cardio workouts, there are a few guidelines that you might want to follow. It probably doesn't make much sense to do your cardio workout before a hard leg workout. Few bodybuilders can go for a 30- to 45-minute bike ride or jog and then bang out multiple sets with many hundreds of pounds on the squat or leg press. (And if you are used to squatting 315 then your legs won't be growing much when you reach failure at 6 reps with 135.) The opposite is also true – just how effective will your run or cycle be after a grueling leg workout? Besides, a 45- to 60-minute leg workout is highly aerobic anyway so why waste time doing both back to back?

There are numerous cardio/weight training combinations that you can follow. You could do all your cardio on your days off. The advantage to this is that you're only doing one form of exercise on each day. The disadvantage is that you're working out seven days a week. Give it a try and see how you feel. If none of the symptoms of overtraining start appearing, by all means keep going. Another option is to do your cardio on your upper-body weight-training days and then one or two of your days off. The benefit of this approach is that you give your body at least two days off from exercise each week.

If you have the time you can do your cardio and weight training at different times on the same day. Many bodybuilders like to do their cardio early in the morning before work or school and then go back later in the day for their weight training.

There is no right combination for your cardio and weight training. My advice is to try different combinations and see which one works best for you. And keep in mind that the best program is the one that fits into your schedule. You can map out the perfect training and cardio program, but if you find you skip workouts because the times don't work for you, then your physique will never benefit from your "perfect" program.

EARLY MORNING CARDIO?

Every now and then some bodybuilding writer will suggest that doing cardio first thing in the morning before breakfast is by far the best time to do cardio exercise. The theory is that since the brain primarily burns carbohydrates while you're asleep, when you wake up in the morning the only thing left to burn is fat. While there may be some truth to this, keep in mind that you don't deplete all your carbohydrate supplies while asleep. The difference in fat-burning early in the morning versus later in the day is so small that it's not really necessary that you haul yourself out of bed at 5 or 6 in the morning – unless you're an early riser to begin with. Besides, the few extra calories you burn might be made up for by the fact that your metabolism doesn't kick in until you eat.

The key to success is consistency far more than time of the day. As long as you're doing those three to five, 30- to 45-minute sessions per week you're doing fine. Don't let anyone tell you that you must exercise at any particular time.

OPTIMAL TIME FOR TRAINING

You can boost the success of your aerobic workout by training at specific times. Early morning is one of the best possible times to get in an aerobic workout, but it's not the only time that offers extra fat-burning benefits. Right after a weight-training session your body is in fat-burning mode. Your metabolism is high from the weight training and you have used most of your glycogen stores during the strength-training session. Your body burns off more fat for fuel sooner. Post-weightlifting is an excellent time to squeeze in an aerobic workout and take advantage of the fat-burning processes already at work.

PRECAUTIONS

Before looking at some of the more popular cardio machines a few precautionary points are in order. For starters, if you're overweight and/or new to exercise I strongly encourage you to check with your doctor before hopping on that cardio cycle or treadmill. That old ticker of yours is probably not used to exercise and a doctor's office is a much better place to find out its weakness than trotting along on the gym floor.

A second point concerns feedback signals from your body. Different machines put different stresses on the joints – particularly the knees and ankles. If you start experiencing pain in any of the joints (or lower back), stop the exercise and switch machines. For some people running on a treadmill is the most effective and enjoyable form of cardio. For others it's a fast route to destroyed knees. Switching from a flat run to an inclined power walk may prevent your having to use a cane in a few years. If the pain persists regardless of the machines, go see your doctor.

Finally, (though this doesn't happen to most bodybuilders) you may become addicted to cardio exercise. Cardio releases endorphins that give you a natural high. Yes there are worse addictions, but cardio is meant to complement your bodybuilding, not interfere with it. Spend too much time running, cycling or crosstraining, and you could lose much of your hard-earned muscle mass. This is especially true once your body fat percentage starts dipping into single digits. You only have so many calories to work with, and once your fat and carbohydrate levels are low, the body will switch to protein (in the form of muscle tissue) as a fuel source.

Ectomorphs may want to heed this advice for the same reasons. By definition ectomorphs have low body fat levels and high metabolisms to begin with. They should probably limit their cardio training to two or three 20-minute sessions per week.

Illustration by Mark Collins

CHOOSING A CARDIO MACHINE

Years ago the only choices bodybuilders had for indoor cardio were cycling and swimming, but today the choices are almost endless. You have treadmills for walking, jogging and running on; cycles for biking; rowers for rowing and a whole assortment of ellipticals, steppers and crosstrainers. The beauty is that one form of cardio is no better than the next. They all burn about the same number of calories per unit time (assuming equal exercise intensities). There might be a huge difference in comfort (i.e. how it feels on the joints), but as long as your heart rate is the same, most forms of cardio will give you the same results.

WHAT TYPE IS BEST?

My first piece of advice is to test each type of cardio machine and choose the one that feels best. Virtually all will work the legs and a few will bring in the arms, but there may be a huge difference in how they feel. If you don't notice any difference in the machines with regards to comfort, then alternate them on a daily or weekly basis. This keeps things entertaining and more challenging.

> Is it just me or is training on cardio machinery about as much fun as watching paint dry? I won't lie. There are days when I simply don't feel like hopping on that motionless bike or treadmill for yet another session of what seems to be an eternity in aerobic hell. On those days I have to dig deep down to muster the fortitude I need to get my cardio done."
>
> – Casey Gately, *MuscleMag International* contributor

Here's the scoop on each piece of cardio equipment:

Treadmill

The great thing about treadmills is that you can walk, jog or run on them. Walking stresses the joints the least, but jogging and running will burn more calories per minute. Most modern treadmills have a solid wooden deck that is cushioned by shock absorbers. It's for this reason that many joggers and runners prefer treadmills to running outside on the concrete sidewalk or pavement. Most treadmills also have handrails to hold on to, but you'll need to let your hands and arms swing by your sides as you jog or run. For those who find jogging and running difficult (or who don't have the cardiovascular conditioning just yet) you can get a great workout by walking uphill at a good speed. Most treadmills allow you to increase the angle from flat to 15 degrees. While 15 degrees doesn't sound like much, trust me you'll easily reach your target heart rate zone after five to ten minutes of power walking up this angle.

Stationary Bike

Stationary bikes or cardio cycles provide fairly intense workouts with little stress on the knees. Cardio cycles come in two styles: upright and recumbent. Upright cycles usually have two sets of handlebars – those that allow you to sit straight up, and those that let you lean forward like a Tour De France racer. They are equally effective, but the racing version may be slightly more stressful on the lower back for some.

Recumbent Cycle

As the name suggests, recumbent cycles allow you to sit down with your legs in front of the body. Recumbent cycles are not more or less effective than uprights, but they are less stressful on the lower back. For both upright and recumbent cycles you adjust the chair height until your outstretched leg is never able to completely lock out. There are two ways to increase the intensity of cycling: you can peddle faster and you can increase the tension on the peddles. Many cardio cycles have heart rate sensors built into the handles that will compare your actual heart rate to where it should be based on your age (you simply program in your age and duration at the beginning). From then on the bike will increase or decrease the tension to increase or decrease your heart rate in much the same way that a furnace and thermostat will work together to keep the temperature constant.

Rowing Machine

Although on the surface rowing appears to work mostly the upper body, a proper rowing stroke derives about 75 percent of its force from the legs. Despite its effectiveness, rowing is often perceived as being the most boring of indoor cardio exercises. Whether because it requires an unfamiliar movement, or because it's difficult to row and watch TV or read at the same time, who knows? However, rowing is just as effective for stimulating fat loss and increasing cardiovascular fitness as any of the other cardio machines, and you'll rarely have to wait for one.

Make sure when rowing that you sit up straight and don't overarch your back as you complete each stroke. Keep your elbows close to your body when pulling. You should be pulling with your arms and pushing with your legs. There should be little to no lower back involvement.

Stepper or StairMaster®

Other than the manually operated cardio cycle, and perhaps the treadmill, steppers were probably the first mass-produced indoor cardio machine. The version by StairMaster became so popular that most steppers became known as StairMasters.

Steppers consist of two steps connected to a motor. As you increase the speed the steps move faster, forcing you to increase your pace to keep up. Although the exercise is very easy to do, the constant up-and-down motion can play havoc on the ankles and knees. When ellipticals and crosstrainers came on the scene in the early 1990s, most step users switched because ellipticals and crosstrainers place far less stress on the ankles and knees. Most gyms these days have far fewer stepper machines than in their glory days of the 1980s.

Elliptical and Crosstrainer

Equipment manufacturers addressed the issue of joint injury from stepping by designing machines that forced the legs to make a circular or ellipse-type motion rather than a straight up-and-down motion. Although the names are often used interchangeably, crosstrainers have both moving peddles and arms, whereas ellipticals have stationary handles to hold on to. At no time does the path your foot takes become a straight up-and-down motion.

There is a misconception that because the crosstrainer has moving arms it is somehow more effective than the elliptical, but this is not the case. Both machines heavily stress the legs and the legs are such a large muscle group that once they start exercising they quickly bring your heart rate up to the target heart rate zone. The addition of the relatively small arm muscles is not really contributing that much extra. My suggestion is to try both and see which machine feels the most comfortable.

Step Mill

Although this machine is not often seen in gyms anymore, if your gym has one then be sure to give it a try. You can think of the step mill as a small escalator – except it never brings you anywhere (except to a superior level of fitness)! The step mill consists of a moving set of stairs that you can vary the speed on. Unlike some of the other cardio machines there is no coasting on this machine. If you coast you fall off. Simple as that.

Photo of Reggie McKee by Paul Buceta

Given their high cost, size (often between 7 and 8 feet high) and the fact that like steppers, step mills can be hard on the knees and ankles for some, they've fallen out of favor over the last 10 years. Actually, they've probably also fallen out of favor because they work you hard! Still, if you have access to one, give it a try. Your target heart rate zone will be mere seconds away!

CHAPTER 91

Spin Classes

"Spinning classes offer upbeat music and an instructor that pushes you to your max. You will sweat like crazy and you'll get an amazing cardio workout. Perfect for the bodybuilder who hates cardio machines and can't stand complicated moves."

– Carol Lepine, fitness coordinator, City of Richmond

f you just can't seem to talk yourself into traditional forms of cardio exercise, give spinning a try. Spinning® is a perfect example of an aerobic activity that seems to have staying power. The term "Spinning®" is actually a registered trademark of the Schwinn Corporation. However, most people use the word to describe any group cycling class on stationary cycles.

Spin classes are popular because they offer numerous fitness-related benefits while remaining gender neutral. Despite all the advances made in the last couple of decades, weight training is still seen as masculine, and cardio as feminine. But spin classes are for everyone, and most classes have an even mixture of men and women. It's a great way to stimulate the cardiovascular system as well as strengthen the muscles, particularly the leg muscles.

A lesser-known reason for the popularity of spin classes over other forms of cardio fitness is that it is very motivational. A combination of small class size, a dynamic instructor and tailored music all contribute to keeping participants interested and determined to finish the class. In a large aerobics class it's easy to slack off and simply go through the motions, but a spin class leaves no room for stragglers. Everyone is motivated to keep up, and it's far more fun than spending 30 minutes doing the exact same movement on a piece of stationary cardio equipment.

A typical class consists of one instructor and 10 participants. Instructors have different cycle arrangements, but most use a semi-circle pattern. Other than the cycle, the only equipment you need is a water bottle and a towel. The cycle itself bears little resemblance to those $5,000 cardio cycles that inhabit gyms these days. You won't find any bells or whistles – in fact you won't find electronics of any kind. This is cycling at its purist. The cycle will have a lever located just beneath the handlebars that allows you to increase the tension on the pedals. Push the lever all the way down and it acts as a brake. Keep this in mind – the large front flywheel weighs 40 or 50 pounds, and once it gets going you can't automatically stop it by just locking your legs. You must either gradually slow down and stop or push the brake lever down.

If spin cycles have one big disadvantage over regular cardio cycles it's comfort, or lack thereof. The seat on a typical cardio cycle is rather small and not blessed with the greatest amount of padding. After 10 or 15 minutes sitting on it, your squat-built hindquarters are going to start talking to you in unpleasant terms. However, during a spin class you'll be alternating sitting with standing and sprinting, so you won't be sitting on the seat for long stretches.

The class itself is like most forms of physical activity and can be divided into three phases: warmup, middle, and cool-down. The warmup consists of various stretches that start while standing on the floor and then progress to the cycle. Most instructors start with slow- to moderate-paced peddling, and then progress to the faster-paced peddling and sprinting, either seated or standing. During a typical class you'll alternate various speeds with different tensions on the wheels.

Spin classes are conducted in the presence of music. Most gyms have the stereo system controls located next to the instructor's cycle so he or she can alternate various music tempos throughout the class. Slow music is typically used for the warmup and cool-down, and faster paced music for the heart of the class. Some instructors use rock music, while others go for upbeat dance music.

The average spin class lasts 45 to 60 minutes, and is as good as it gets when it comes to cardiovascular conditioning. Spinning has an advantage over most other forms of aerobic exercise because of its strengthening effects on the muscles. Most forms of cardio only use the weight of

the body as resistance. For the first couple of weeks this may provide some strengthening benefits, but the leg muscles quickly adapt. With spinning the tension lever allows you to increase the resistance on demand. Many weight trainers report that their legs get as pumped from a spinning class as from a regular squat workout.

Some gyms charge extra for spin classes. Others include these classes in their fee structure. One suggestion is to check out different instructors. They should all have the same qualifications, but personality can play a big role. One instructor may motivate you to the point you could go for two hours, while another may make you decide to give up after 15 minutes. Or you may hate the music one instructor chooses while another plays your favorite motivational tunes. The bottom line is to choose the class and instructor that motivates you to keep coming back.

CHAPTER 92

Shaping Up at School

"I believe education is important. I played college sports and modeled, but neither was as important as my education."

– Bart Blackwell, *American Health and Fitness* contributor, commenting on the importance of education.

You thought the day would never come but here it is. You're on your own at college or university. The U-haul has been unloaded, the parents are gone and you're ready to meet new people, experience new things and prepare for your future. It's a great time of challenges, and hopefully some enjoyment along the way. Whether you're just starting out or are in the middle of your college experience, you'll want to know how to keep training while balancing academics and your social life.

THE RIGHT ATTITUDE

Perhaps the best piece of advice I can give you is to bring a fit attitude to campus. When you were growing up you probably kept yourself reasonably active, even if you never thought of your activities as exercise. You may not have played organized sports or attended a gym on a regular basis, but all through school you kept your circulatory system pumping with walking to friends' houses, using a bicycle as transportation before you had a car and just playing around.

Your life now will likely be different. If you are taking a full course load, partying on the weekends and holding down a part-time job to help offset the

Photo of James Davila by Alex Ardenti
Illustration by Mark Collins

high tuition and living expenses, time is something you don't have in abundance. You will need to make a special effort to remain active. The first step is to cultivate the attitude and the determination that you are going to stay fit.

The most straightforward way to gain, or re-gain, that attitude is to train consistently. If you've been going to the library to study every night, working at your part-time job or partying (after all it is college!), you'll likely notice that your energy level has decreased significantly. Don't worry, you'll quickly begin to feel better once you become active.

GET IN THE FITNESS HABIT

Getting into the habit of fitness does not have to take a lot of effort. Simply take an extra walk across campus. Ride your bike around town once or twice a week after class. Walk to class instead of taking the bus. If it's winter and outdoor activities are limited, do some ab work – crunches and leg raises – when you get up in the morning. Twice a week throw in some bodyweight exercises such as push-ups, chin-ups, and sissy squats. The bottom line is to be smart, be consistent and most of all, be active.

GET WALKING

Even if you're not in pre-contest mode, if you're logging fewer than 5,000 steps daily on your pedometer you need to step up your efforts. Walking 5,000 or fewer steps throughout the course of the day (about 2 1/2 miles) is deemed sedentary behavior, according to new activity guidelines. Most people log between 2,000 and 5,000 steps daily by doing everyday activities. To land in the "active" category you need to step it up to 10,000 steps daily. You'll look and feel better for it.

KEEP OFF THE GRASS

FITNESS UNITS

If you have trouble fitting in your activities, try to rearrange your schedule. If Monday consists of eight hours of class followed by two or three hours of study, take a 10- or 15-minute break during the day to stretch or go for a walk. Or take a half-hour to do something physical between your classes and your study time. If this is not feasible, do something the day before and day after. One of the disadvantages of college life is that the days lack repeated structure, so you can't always have a workout at 4 p.m., for example. No worries, though. Make the commitment to slot it in where you can at least four days a week and the rest of the time simply pick up your activity level.

Now that you have made the mental commitment, you can make accommodations that fit your schedule. You may no longer get the two-hour training sessions you had been used to. But that doesn't mean you have to give up. Think in terms of small segments of time. Find 15 minutes here, a half-hour there. Contact your campus athletic department to find out what recreational sports are offered. Check out the gym, pool and classes. Make note of the hours. Make the campus rec center your second home, and get in the habit of going there every time you have a break rather than sitting in a coffee shop.

FACILITIES AND EQUIPMENT

Every campus is different in regard to its fitness facilities. You may or may not have reasonable access to an indoor court if you want to play some basketball, volleyball or other activity that requires a relatively large area. You might have better access to handball or squash courts. Weight room availability and equipment also vary greatly. Some campuses have facilities where students can lift heavy iron, some restrict use of the best equipment to var-

> "Most fad diets work to help you shed those extra pounds – in the short term. But by the time you actually get to wear your new swim trunks, you're back to being harpooned while sunbathing on the beach! Fad diets are just that – fads. If you want to lose weight and keep it off you have to make lasting lifestyle changes. Learn to cook, shop and dine in a healthy way, and those pounds will stay off."
>
> – Melissa Swain O'Neill, *American Health and Fitness* contributor, commenting on the inefficacy of fad diets.

sity teams. Some have an abundance of machines and free weights, others have just the basics. You may even have to join a gym off campus to get access to some decent workout facilities. Off-campus gyms often offer great deals for students, so you might want to look into this option.

As for outdoor sports and recreation, geography will play a role. Campuses located in Florida or California offer endless outdoor fitness opportunities. If you are in an area of less than ideal weather conditions you may need to be a bit more creative. On sunny days do your workouts outdoors and save the indoor stuff for those rainy days. Likewise the seasons will dictate your activities. If you're in a northern climate try skiing, snowboarding or hiking to jazz up your recreation. There's nothing as refreshing as a hike through the woods on a cold, clear, crisp winter's day.

ON-CAMPUS NUTRITION

In the dark days of college life, just ten or twenty years ago, most campuses offered only "dorm food," which consisted of endless mounds of macaroni and unidentifiable meat. It was all about calories. Thankfully most colleges now offer healthier alternatives. Granted there are still guys who live on pizza and beer, but you can eat clean if you want to. Good selections include turkey or chicken breast, whole grain cereals, fruit and vegetables, and eggs.

When time is of the essence, try a meal replacement bar or shake. Make sure to read the ingredients! If you live off campus in your own apartment, you're better off as you'll have more control over what you eat.

Whatever your fitness goals or aspirations, college life can be a great time for setting you on a lifetime path of fitness success and enjoyment. Don't be afraid to be creative and experiment. Be determined. Get out there and do something!

Bodybuilding is important and takes thought and effort, but make sure to get enjoyment from other areas of life, too.

CHAPTER 93

Don't Drag from Jet Lag

"Travel complicates things more than any other variable when it comes to consistency. Again planning ahead helps. If you are vacationing in a certain area, check to see if there is a hotel with a gym. It may not have the equipment you need, but it will allow you to be consistent. Any workout is better than none."

– Bill Starr, *MuscleMag International* contributor, commenting on training while on the road.

Ever since the late 1950s when jet aircraft made traveling the globe a matter of hours and not days, people have been grappling with the effects of the biological upheaval of jet lag.

Jet lag is a temporary condition that some people experience following air travel across several time zones in a short period of time. This causes the traveler's internal clock to be out of sync with his/her external environment. People experiencing jet lag have a difficult time maintaining their internal sleep-wake pattern in their new location because external stimuli, like sunshine and local timetables, dictate a different pattern. For this reason, one can feel lethargic one moment and excited the next. Jet lag creates a double bind for vacationers and business people who must cross several time zones to reach their destination, but who are also intent on maximizing sightseeing or productivity. As travelers attempt to adjust their internal clocks to a new external environment, symptoms result with varying intensity.

TIPS ON REDUCING JET LAG

Eat Properly

One of the first steps in reducing the effects of jet lag is to try and maintain your daily routine. You don't want to deviate from your diet when you travel. Bad nutrition only makes a case of jet lag worse. This is ironic given that the first food you'll probably eat on your trip is airline food! If you plan on taking a trip that involves more than two time zones, avoid airline food and bring your own. This is actually a good idea no matter where you are flying to.

Meal replacement bars can help in this regard, as long as the ingredients are clean. Carrying some raw almonds along with some fruit is also a great idea. These items don't take up a lot of room in your carry-on luggage. You can also eat them anytime you want. No more waiting for the food-cart to reach your aisle.

Supplement

You should also pack some vitamins and minerals. Vitamins and minerals help reduce cramps, which become all too common on today's overcrowded aircraft. They also boost your immune system, which will be under attack from all the germs being circulated by the aircraft's air-conditioning system. Think of it this way: you are going to be stuffed into a narrow tube with 200 other people for many hours. Visualize the number of bacteria and viruses harbored by such a population. You want all the help you can get in warding off such assault.

Illustration by Mark Collins

Drink Your Fill

I can't stress enough the importance of drinking water. The constantly changing air pressure inside the cabin

TRAVELING TOO OFTEN

Do you travel a lot for business? Attend every bodybuilding competition you can? During these trips, do you suffer from jet lag? The most important thing you should do to help prevent jet lag is to maintain your routine as much as possible. Stick to your diet whenever you can. Avoid airline meals. Pack a bag with meal replacement bars, healthy snacks and plenty of water to get through the trip. Relax during the flight and get in a nap.

will quickly dehydrate you. Besides keeping you hydrated, drinking lots of water will force you to get out of your seat and visit the washroom. This may not seem important, (it may even seem a pain) but visiting the washroom means you get to stretch and flex your leg muscles. This helps prevent cramps and keeps the body from getting lethargic.

Keep Your Body Aligned

Another suggestion is to pack a good neck pillow. Sure the airlines sometimes provide them but the quality is pathetic. And do you really believe they clean all pillows between each flight? For the sake of $20 or so, pick up a good pillow to enable you to rest in comfort. Proper neck and body alignment will go a long way in reducing post-flight aches and pains. These pains alone have been known to cause jet lag.

Stay Informed and Inspired

Unless you're lucky enough to be treated to a just-released movie, odds are you've seen the onboard entertainment before (multiple times if you are a regular airline traveler). A useful way to pass the many hours is to read some fitness magazines. Most airports have a bookstore or magazine stand that offers the latest issues of *MuscleMag International*, *Maximum Fitness*, and *Reps!*. Or maybe you have a stack of them at home waiting to be read. Bring a couple along and brush up on your bodybuilding knowledge and inspiration.

Stay in Tune

Bring along an MP3 player. Sure the airlines offer onboard music, but chances are you won't like their selections. Bringing your own allows you to listen to what you want when you want. Besides the music, a portable music player insulates you from the many noises around you, like the annoying guy next to you, or the crying baby in the seat behind you.

Sleep Tight

Another must is to get a good night's sleep after you travel. Try to grab at least eight good hours of sleep the first night you arrive, and try to make sure to wake up close to the actual morning time.

Healthy Breakfast

As soon as you wake up, head to the nearest restaurant and have a nutritious meal. If you're thinking that means sausages and bacon, think again. Try hot cooked whole grain cereal, scrambled egg whites and a piece of fresh fruit. Then go back to your hotel room and take your supplements.

Work Out

A final suggestion is to hit a gym for a workout. Unless you are going to be in the area for a long period of time – say three weeks or more – your goal is maintenance, not setting any new records. Do at least 10 to 15 minutes of cardio to warm up and get the blood flowing, and then do some light stretching. Let's face it; your muscles were cramped up for many hours. They want to be eased back into operation. Perform a light to medium weight-training routine – nothing too intense. Performing one exercise and one set per bodypart is great. Keep the rep range between 12 and 15.

If your hotel gym leaves much to be desired, pick up a day or week pass from a local full-service gym. Doing so is well worth the few bucks.

CHAPTER 94

Bodybuilding in the Golden Years

"I didn't start training until I was in my 30s and was 34 at my first show. People told me I was too old to get into bodybuilding, that I couldn't build size and strength past my 20s. I never believed any of that and proved them all wrong. I won the California on my fourth try and I won most of my big titles in my 40s, so you're never too old."

– Ed Corney, bodybuilding legend and one of the stars of *Pumping Iron*, letting "older" readers know that it's never to late to compete.

There's an old saying that the only things you can be sure of in life are death and taxes. However, you can also be sure that your body will slow down, you'll take longer to heal and muscle will come less easily. No matter how much you may try to stop the biological clock, it's inevitable that as you get older things will begin to slow down. Digestion and circulation suffer at the hands of father time. Our reflexes slow down and our strength levels begin to decline.

Drs. William J. Evans and Irwin H. Rosenberg have broken aging down into 10 categories that can be used as markers for measuring how fast an individual is aging:

Albert Beckles won the 1991 Niagara Falls Pro Invitational at the age of 61!

Photos of Albert Beckles

TEN CATAGORIES OF AGING:

Muscle mass

Strength

Basal (resting) metabolism

Body fat percentage

Aerobic capacity

Blood-sugar tolerance

LDL and HDL cholesterol ratios

Blood pressure

Bone density

Temperature regulation

Besides biological changes we also experience psychological changes as we age. Most people find that as they get older their priorities change and they no longer have the same training drive or enthusiasm that they had when they were younger. The law of diminishing returns doesn't help – no matter how hard you try you just can't seem to hold on to the form that you had earlier in your life. There are exceptions of course, but as the years go by most bodybuilders change their values and attitudes towards training. The question is, should they?

THE "OLDER" BODYBUILDER

Young and old are relative terms. There are 20-year-olds whose health profiles might be similar to those of 50-year-old heart attack victims. Conversely we have 60-year-olds running marathons. While the 60-year-old is chronologically older than the 20-year-old, the 20-year-old might be older with regards to physical shape.

The late Vince Gironda was still going through body-

> My role model was Albert Beckles. The guy was awesome. When he was over 40 he beat much younger men. Too much!"
>
> – Quincy Taylor, IFBB pro, talking about his idol.

building workouts in his 80s and Albert Beckles was winning pro bodybuilding contests in his 50s. Bodybuilding legend Bill Pearl looks better in his 70s than most body-

IT'S NEVER TOO LATE

Exercise not only improves your health, but it can also reverse the aging process to an extent. Researchers have found strength training can reverse age-related effects on muscle. A study from the May online journal PLoS One suggests resistance training actually rejuvenates muscle tissue in healthy senior citizens.

Researchers took tissue samples from 25 healthy, nontraining older men and women (average age 70) and analyzed before and after gene-expression profiles. The participants did strength training twice a week for six months. The researchers compared their results with those from a similar analysis of younger healthy men and women (average age 26). They found the strength training resulted in a reversal of the genetic finger-print, reaching levels similar to those of the younger adults tested. Muscle strength increased for all participants, improving by 50 percent on average. Bodybuilding really could be the fountain of youth!
Source: IDEA *Fitness Journal*, Sept. '07

builders do in their 20s and 30s. After a five-year layoff, 51-year-old Vince Taylor placed third at the 2006 Australian Grand Prix. Even eight-time Mr. Olympia Ronnie Coleman was winning bodybuilding's top contest at 41 years of age. For these guys (and many others) age is just a number and

they have no intentions of slowing down.

Believe it or not I remember almost every day of my youthful training. Now after 50 years of working out with weights, I still love to train. True enough my former three-and-a-half-hour workouts are now only 45 minutes, but I train faster, follow a split routine and train an average of four days a week rather than six.

THE KEYS TO LONGEVITY

If I still haven't convinced you there's bodybuilding life after 40, let's look at it another way. If muscle size diminishes with age and gaining body fat becomes easier, doesn't it make sense to be doing something that can slow down these changes? Arnold Schwarzenegger once said: "It's not that you're too old to bodybuild, you're too old not to!" Sure you're probably not going to be a threat to Jay Cutler or Ronnie Coleman, but just look at all the positive effects bodybuilding will have on your body.

There's a famous study involving Boston nursing home patients, most of whom were in wheelchairs. After just two months of regular weight training many of the subjects were walking again, two without the use of canes. The only negative aspect to the whole story is that after the researchers left no one kept the exercise program going and all the patients ended up back in wheelchairs.

For those "older" people either new to bodybuilding or getting back to the weights after a 20- or 30-year layoff, the key is to make adjustments where necessary. You first must realize that your recovery system can't handle the same workouts it did 20 or 30 years ago. You'll get far better results following a 30- to 45-minute workout than you will trying to do those two-hour marathons you performed in the past.

Another consideration is your type of workout. At 20 you may have been able to skip cardio exercise and still say lean, but no longer. One of the virtual guarantees of aging is a slowdown in your basal metabolism. Your body will store more calories as fat than when you were younger. You can still train for strength and size, but you must include some sort of cardio exercise to burn off those extra calories as well as maintain your overall cardiovascular health.

THE KEY IS CONSISTENCY

No matter what your age you won't make the progress you desire if you skip workouts. If your goal is to look lousy and sport a potbelly, then by all means replace the gym with booze. But don't blame me if you start feeling your age.

Consistency may be king, but intensity is also important. Just because your birth certificate is slightly wrinkled doesn't mean you need to hold back. As long as you have no injuries, your energy level is high and your recovery abilities are up to scratch, give it your all (that is, once your body is used to working out again). One of the best ways to keep motivation levels high is to work out with a younger person. His (or her!) youth will keep you inspired

Your first gray hairs should inspire you to train more – not less.

Photo of Robby Robinson by Alex Ardenti

and force you to keep up. And let's face it, your age will have the same effect on your partner. No 30-year-old wants a 50- or 60-year-old to outlift him!

You may also want to start considering vitamins and minerals if you haven't already done so. As we age our digestive systems become less efficient at breaking down and absorbing food. In many cases the minor health problems experienced by older people are simply a matter of nutrient deficiency. While you don't need to load up on hundreds of dollars worth of supplements, I strongly urge you take a multivitamin and a good protein supplement. Such other proven supplements as creatine and glutamine probably wouldn't hurt either.

FINAL CONSIDERATIONS

If you follow the advice in this book, there is no reason not to make progress in your 50s, 60s, 70s and beyond. Always keep in mind that much of what we associate with aging is psychological, and as long as you keep a positive attitude, you'll be ahead of the game with regards to slowing the clock down. Instead of dwelling on what you used to bench press or squat, focus on what you can lift now. So what if you aren't as strong and fit as you were at 20? Not only will you be stronger, healthier, in better shape and more independent than practically everyone in your age group, you'll no doubt be in better physical condition than 90 percent of the general population.

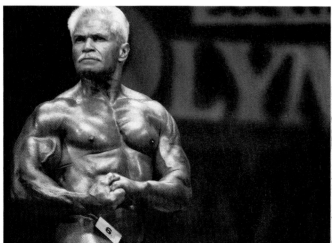

Photo (Top) of Clancy Ross
Photo (Left) of Ed Corney by Robert Kennedy
Photo (Bottom) of Larry Scott

BOOK XIII

BODYBUILDING SOCIOLOGY

CHAPTER 95

How You Fit In

"A guy left a huge puddle of sweat on a flat bench. As he started to walk off, a lady nearby said, "That's an awful nice puddle of sweat you've got there." "Thank you," he replied sarcastically and walked away."

– Casey Gately, *MuscleMag International* contributor

Y ou may find once you start looking like a bodybuilder that having a great physique doesn't necessarily attract the type of attention you desire. Much of the general public thinks bodybuilders are knuckleheads. Sometimes bodybuilders bring this on themselves. Let's face it, bodybuilding is no different than most sports in that it attracts a few idiots. Unfortunately, when these idiots happen to be loud and obnoxious 250-pound idiots, the effect is magnified.

The following chapter is a guide to the various social and behavioral manners by which bodybuilders should conduct themselves when working out. This chapter also takes a look at the unsavory side of the bodybuilding subculture.

WIPE IT DOWN

Yes, we all know you sweat. We don't have to either sit in the puddle you left behind on the bench or clean it up to know how hard you work. Most gyms provide paper towels and antibacterial cleansers. Use them. And while you're at it, bring a towel around from bench to bench and from machine to machine to sit or lie on. That way you'll have a lot less mess to clean up, too.

THAT'S GROSS!

Visualize this for a minute: You're having a great workout and lifting more iron than Pittsburgh. Those lost abs of yours are starting to reappear, and you've finally broken through the defenses of that cute redhead you see on the treadmill every day. Yes it's great to be a bodybuilder.

The one blemish is that you've forgotten your water bottle. No big deal. You head to the water fountain. And then the person in front of you spits a wad of gum into the water basin and follows it up with a large yellow ball of spit. I've even seen bodybuilders spit on the benches.

Besides being a great way to spread such diseases as hepatitis and mononucleosis, it's this type of gross behavior that gives bodybuilders such a bad reputation. Lots of people already think we're big and dumb, and such disgusting behaviors only reinforce these stereotypes. Maybe some bodybuilders will ignore or tolerate such behavior, but you shouldn't. If your gym doesn't have such rules posted, go see the owner and request them. If some people want to act like animals, then fine, they can go to the nearest barnyard. I'm sure the farmers could use the extra muscle.

Photo of Larry Vinette by Paul Buceta

WEIGHTS BACK

There are few things as irritating during a workout as spending half your time looking for the weights you want to use. Unless it's tripping over the weights that someone left lying on the floor. Or maybe having to remove the 800 pounds of plates left on the leg press before you work on rehabbing your left knee. Get the picture? As the old saying goes: if you're strong enough to use it, you're strong enough to put it back.

ON THE OFFENCE AGAINST BEING OFFENSIVE

One of the signs of a great workout is working up a good sweat. Unfortunately, in the process of releasing water to cool down, the body also takes the opportunity to flush out the waste products of exercise, including the bacteria that live in our skin pores. All it takes is a couple of days of sitting in your workout clothes and you're left with a stench that makes a zoo smell like a flower shop.

No doubt you've heard the expression: "This place smells like a gym." Well it shouldn't – at least not if you wash your clothes regularly. And I don't mean one day a month, or even once a week. If possible wash your clothes either daily or every second day. Why not have two or three sets of workout clothes. This way you'll need to wash only once or twice per week.

Besides your clothes, there's something else that needs to be washed regularly – you! You may think this point is self evident, but you should shower immediately after your workout. If the gym shower room turns you off, head straight home and do it. Don't leave the gym and go to a social gathering with an offensive layer of sweat adhering to your body. Maybe you can't smell it, but trust me others can. Grab a bar of soap and lather up.

Here's another tip you may not think of. It wouldn't hurt to brush your teeth before working out. You're going to be doing some heavy breathing, and a mouth smelling like a freshly opened coffin won't make it easy to get a spot – especially the second time. And what if by chance that sexy redhead on the treadmill starts chatting you up? How sexy do you think you'll come across with a disgusting case of bad breath? At the very least use some mouthwash.

With regards to sharing personal items in the locker room, my advice is don't – not under any circumstances. Let's start with razors. Razors and straight edges are designed to cut hair, but they also nick skin and draw blood. Do you really want to mix someone else's blood with your own? Not only is this a great way to spread skin diseases, but you could contract AIDS or hepatitis this way. Even something as simple as sharing your comb could get you a case of head lice. The same goes for water bottles. You'd be surprised the soup of nastiness that brews in people's mouths, and people are often contagious before they even know they have a flu or cold.

EWWWW...
Continuous use of the same towel after workouts without washing it can be hazardous to your health. It just takes a couple of days for infectious bacteria and fungi to breed on your towel and enter your nose or mouth when you use it. Can you say, "disgusting?" We recommend that you wash your gym towel every day – hanging it out to dry isn't enough.

EW!

Illustration by Mark Coll[

You know the old saying: "If you're strong enough to use the weight, you're strong enough to put it back."

CHAPTER 96

Can't We All Just Get Along?

"You may know the best way to do skullcrushers. But that doesn't mean the guy doing them wants to hear about it."

– Editors of *MuscleMag International*, stating some things they've learned over the years.

ost bodybuilding gyms have a social hierarchy, and the sooner you recognize it the sooner you'll adapt and fit in. At the bottom of the list we have the newbies – that is, people working out for the first time. Next up could be called the new regulars – people who have been working out for a couple of months to a year. At the top of the heap are the veteran bodybuilders who have been training for a year or more. Even within this dominant group there may be subgroups consisting of competitive and non-competitive bodybuilders.

As with any social hierarchy there are unwritten rules. In bodybuilding gyms those bodybuilders getting ready for contests get the right of way. This doesn't mean that they can (or will) kick you off a piece of equipment. But if the state champion is doing flat barbell bench presses on Monday at 5 p.m. there should be at least one rack free at this time. It doesn't matter that you might have waited half an hour for the rack. Move aside and wish the guy luck. It's not just the size or experience of competitive bodybuilders that gives them priority. Remember the last time some friend or relative tried to give up smoking or was on a diet? They were a barrel of chuckles and laughs, right? Well you have no idea how mean-spirited someone can get when they're on a pre-contest carb-depleted diet. And you don't want to find out! All it takes is a bit of watchfulness and you'll be accepted. Once you are one of the boys, these same individuals will go out of their way to help you prepare for your first contest. It's called the brotherhood of iron. While it takes a bit of patience to work your way in, once you are in, you have friends for life.

You should also avoid staring. Humans are primates after all, and in primates staring is a sign of aggression and challenge. There are times that bodybuilders want to be looked at and admired (i.e. onstage or when practicing posing), but not as they're working out. Sure, keep an eye on someone if you are spotting them or they asked you to check out their form on a particular exercise. But don't let your staring be misinterpreted as a sign of aggression, or even sexual interest. Given the emphasis on the male body's masculine beauty in bodybuilding it's not surprising that homosexuality is often associated with the sport. The last thing you want is some super-aggressive, straight 250-pound bodybuilder to start thinking you're "checking him out." And guys, contrary to popular belief, women go to the gym to work out – not to be ogled or drooled over. Many could probably kick your ass at the squat rack, so show some respect and discretion.

Photo of Larry Vinette by Paul Buceta

ASKING FOR AND GIVING ADVICE

Offering and asking for advice can be a double-edged sword. Some over-enthusiastic young bodybuilders memorize what they read in the magazines and then strut around the gym acting as if they're Charles Poliquin or Scott Able. Those who have this trait often have a lack of self-confidence. They are insecure and over-eager to become accepted. If a person risks serious injury by what he is doing, then go ahead and say something, but don't become the gym know-it-all, or the other trainers will start running in the opposite direction every time you come around.

You must also be wary about asking for advice. Most veteran bodybuilders are flattered and happy to help when some new trainer asks them for advice. Everyone likes to be recognized for having expertise, and bodybuilders are no different. But don't become a patronizing nuisance. Ask for advice on training or nutrition maybe once every week or two, not every five minutes. There is a fine line between flattering someone's ego and getting on their nerves.

THE SEEDIER SIDE

The local gym is normally a very safe and friendly place to hang out. You are all pursuing a healthy interest. You and your gym buddies have work issues, family issues and other things going on in your lives, and your workouts are often a source of stress relief. There's nothing like a great workout after a hard day at school or the office. Genuine friendships are forged at the gym and bodybuilders will go to great lengths to help and support one another. Because there is no money or top title to fight over, the local gym normally has a very relaxed and encouraging atmosphere.

The L.A. scene is entirely different. Southern California – particularly Santa Monica – is a "mecca" for the sport of bodybuilding. Every year thousands of eager young iron pumpers from around the world make the pilgrimage to Gold's or World Gyms in Santa Monica hoping to be discovered as the next Arnold or Jay Cutler. Hundreds of bodybuilding hopefuls, all trying to earn their pro card and then win the top titles. After the titles hopefully come the endorsement deals, movie roles and ulti-

Photo of Chris Jalali and Samir Bannout by Alex Ardenti

mately fame and fortune. When the stakes are that high some people will have no reservations of walking over whoever gets in their way. It's a dog-eat-dog atmosphere and greenhorns (i.e. – you!) are nothing more than something to be taken of advantage of, exploited and used.

Of the millions of amateur bodybuilders only a few hundred ever make it to the pro ranks. And of these probably fewer than a dozen earn six-figure salaries. It makes far more sense to invest your few dollars in furthering your education than to buy a plane ticket to L.A. A bodybuilder needs something to fall back on in the most likely event that he never reaches the pro ranks. Besides, most pros do not make a great income. In fact, the income many pros make does nothing more than pay their supplement bill. Those without a decent education can look forward to traditional bodybuilding jobs such as bouncing, security and construction. Bouncing and security will hardly support you, and though construction pays well when the economy is good, when the real estate market dries up you may be out of a job. Besides, construction work often means long tiring hours that might derail your bodybuilding efforts.

No doubt you've heard tales of young girls falling into the trap of prostitution after failing to make it as a star in Hollywood. Well I hate to break it to you but the same thing happens to guys – especially well-built guys trying to make it to the bodybuilding pro ranks. When the money runs low, many turn to hustling to pay the rent and put protein on the table. Their clients are often older men who prefer young male bodybuilders to women. As you might expect, the young male becomes confused, degraded and loses all self-respect, whether he is gay or straight.

THE DRUG SCENE

Later in the book I'll be looking at the issue of performance-enhancing drugs in more detail. For now I'll limit the discussion to the social side of things. If you haven't already, it won't be long before you encounter the bodybuilding drug scene. It's a fact that a number of amateur and virtually all pro bodybuilders use anabolic steroids and other performance-enhancing drugs. A few have done jail time for traf-

ficking in such drugs. While most keep their drug use to themselves, a few will be quite open about it. Often the guys who are most open about it are the ones selling the stuff.

If you become curious about steroids then I suggest doing your research on the Internet and from magazines or books – not the gym. With anabolic steroids classified as illegal drugs, law enforcement types routinely mount undercover operations in gyms. How do you know that the person you are asking the question about Winstrol prices is not an ambitious cop who's part of a sting operation? You could easily get dragged into something much bigger. You could lose your job, relationship and reputation, all because you wanted to know how much a bottle of Dianabol would cost.

You also have to be careful about the steroid dealers themselves. Dealers get very nervous when strangers start

> " These drugs are illegal in North America. Any time you buy them either through the mail or via a local dealer, you never know when a DEA agent might be around the corner ready to slap the cuffs on you."
>
> – Ron Harris, regular *MuscleMag International* contributor, offering some words of wisdom to those who contemplate using anabolic steroids.

asking them about their "products." Their first reaction is that you're an undercover narc who's trying to take them down. Why risk the black glove treatment in the parking lot when a few minutes on the Internet could get you the same information?

Besides cops and dealers, you have the owner to worry about. Even owners of the most hardcore gyms don't like open talk about steroids in their gyms. It's bad for business and they'll probably revoke your membership.

If by chance you do get approached by a dealer, just politely say you're not interested and walk away. I doubt that they'll persist as the last thing they want is to draw attention to themselves. If steroids are legal in your country you can probably get a prescription from a doctor and buy them much cheaper at a pharmacy (more on this later). If they're illegal, as they are in the U.S., then obey the law and avoid them like the plague.

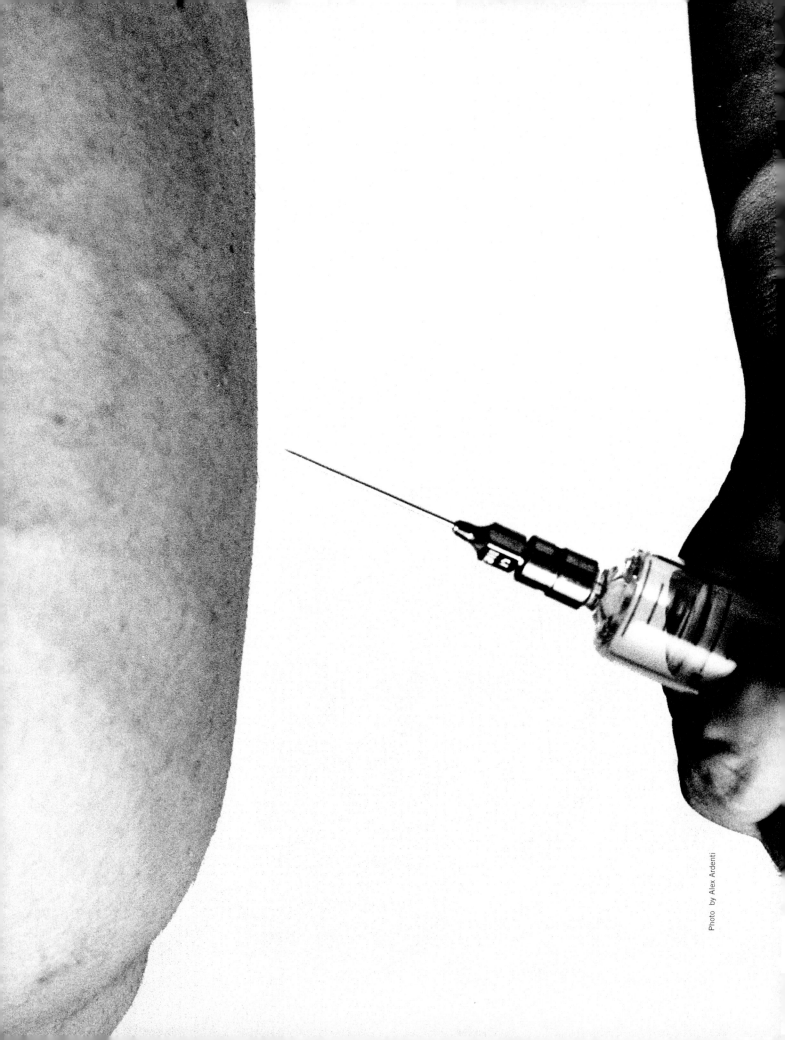

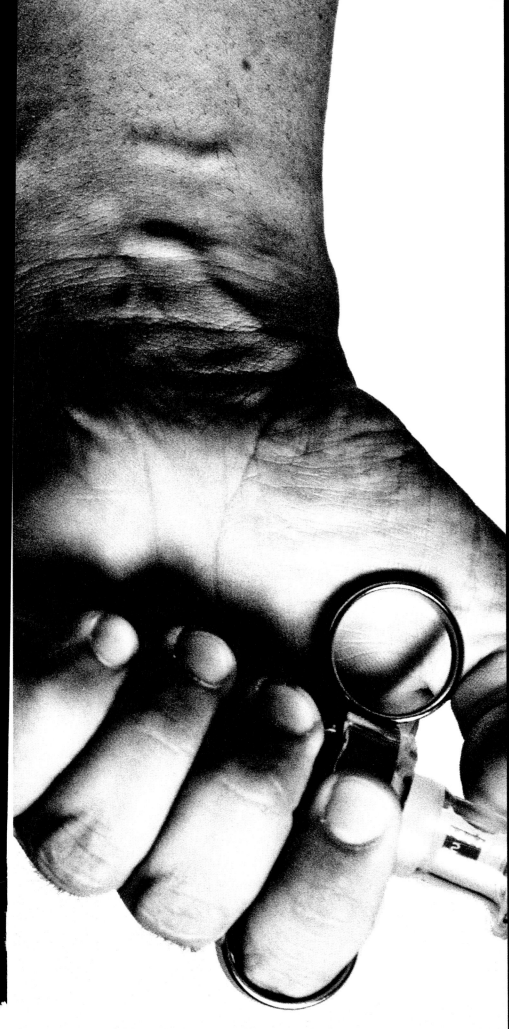

CHAPTER 97

The Key to Anabolic Growth

"By cycling your training you alter the stress loads on your body, preventing the exhaustion of the body's stress-activated chemicals."

– Greg Zulak, regular *MuscleMag International* contributor, offering advice on how to minimize catabolic reactions in the human body.

Many novice bodybuilders view building muscle as some mysterous adventure that can be achieved only by following the advice of pro bodybuilders. They think there is a dirty little secret that, once discovered, will lead them to the Holy Grail of freaky muscularity and maximum muscle size; that there is one best training routine or diet that will stimulate their anabolic growth potential and turn their average-looking bodies into pillars of muscle and power. I hate to break it to you if you fall victim to such beliefs, but there is no magic pill to pack pounds of striated muscle mass on your frame, and no secret potion to push you into the heavyweight class. Trust me, if there was, everybody would already be using it and gyms would be filled with 250-pounders repping with 500 pounds on the bench press.

The real key to gaining maximum muscle size is to create what's called an anabolic environment in your body. Without the internal environment necessary to stimulate growth, it doesn't matter what crazy training routine you follow, the music you listen to or the time of day your train.

ANABOLIC VS. CATABOLIC

Biochemists can be a funny lot. They love inventing new vocabulary – especially words that have little use in other areas. Let's take the word metabolism for example. Instead of just saying all the chemical reactions that take place in your body, they had to coin the word "metabolic." And guess what – it doesn't end there. Nope, metabolic itself can be subdivided into two more words – anabolic and catabolic. Now you've probably heard of anabolic before, since it applies to "anabolic steroids." The word itself means chemical reactions where small molecules are combined to create larger molecules. The best example of this occurs when amino acids are combined to form polypeptite chains which in turn are combined to form protein strands and ultimately muscle tissue. The name anabolic steroid means exactly that – a steroid molecule that stimulates anabolic reactions in the body.

Some compounds do just the opposite. They break down large molecules into smaller molecules. Such compounds are called catabolic steroids, and the best example is the hormone cortisol. During times of stress, the body releases large amounts of cortisol. On one hand cortisol will help you survive the stressful event, but on the other hand it causes the body to break muscle tissue down as an energy source. Not exactly what a hard-training bodybuilder wants.

ANABOLIC REACTIONS – A BODYBUILDER'S BEST FRIEND

It doesn't take a genius to figure out that bodybuilders should be striving to create anabolic reactions in their bodies. The last thing you want is to be in a catabolic state. Unless your body is continuously in a state of anabolism, you're virtually wasting your time in the gym.

> " Cortisol's major catabolic effect involves facilitating the conversion of protein in muscles and connective tissue into glucose and glycogen. Known as gluconeogenesis, this process involves both catabolizing protein already formed and discouraging the synthesis of new protein. Bottom line: Your growth potential is somewhere bound and gagged in the twilight zone."
>
> – Dr. George Redmon, *MuscleMag International* contributor

Muscle growth won't be taking place. In fact you could be experiencing just the opposite – suffering catabolism and losing muscle tissue. What's the use of busting your ass in the gym for hours every day only to be losing muscle and not gaining it?

PREVENTION IS THE KEY

Hopefully you're just a little bit concerned about whether your environment is catabolic. There's an old saying in the medical field that it's easier to prevent diseases than treat them. The same applies to reducing catabolic situations. Prevention is by far the best cure, and as a bodybuilder you can't leave anything to chance that might stop you from making gains, or even take away the gains you've already made.

The human body is either in an anabolic state, a catabolic state or a neutral state somewhere between the two extremes. As we saw earlier, an anabolic state is the ideal condition for your body, because this is where you'll make your best gains in muscle size and strength. The end result of anabolism is the synthesis of new cellular material, especially muscle proteins, cells, membranes and tissues. In short, we're talking about maximum muscle size.

Catabolism, meanwhile, is the process whereby large, complex molecules are broken down into simpler ones, especially for energy production. It's very easy for a bodybuilder to slip into a catabolic state. Ironically, the all-out high-intensity training we often subject ourselves to is treated as a form of stress by the body, and one its responses is to release the hormone cortisol. Cortisol is often called a stress hormone because the body manufactures and releases it in high concentrations during such stressful situations as disease, injury, and yes, even intense exercise. The reason cortisol is so detrimental to bodybuilding is that it increases the mobilization of amino acids from muscles and increases protein breakdown. As more and more protein is broken down, you start losing valuable muscle tissue.

If you're wondering how such things evolved, just blame your ancestors. Unlike most of us, who live relatively safe lives, our ancestors never had it easy. Whether going weeks without solid food or being chased by a sabre-tooth cat or cave bear, things were often stressful for our cave-dwelling ancestors. To increase their chances of survival, their bodies evolved and passed to us a number of preventative mechanisms – one of which is stress hormones. And while we rarely have to worry about being some animal's lunch these days, we still have these survival mechanisms that will fight us as we try to put on muscle mass.

So what can you do to maximize anabolic reactions and minimize catabolic reactions? How can you make sure that your body is always primed and ready to build new muscle tissue? What can you do to keep those dreaded catabolic reactions at bay? The fact is, you can do quite a lot. Let's take a look.

TRAINING

Even though I just said that intense training would cause the body to release cortisol and other stress hormones, weight training also stimulates the body to release such anabolic hormones as testosterone and human growth hormone (HGH). Testosterone, as most readers are aware, is the primary male sex hormone. Human growth hormone is also highly anabolic and can make huge differences in strength and size. These hormones are so effective at building muscle that during puberty a four-foot boy can add two feet to his height and gain 50 pounds or more. Now I'm not going to proclaim that every time you train you'll gain the equivalent of going through puberty. But intense training does cause the body to increase the production and release of these two hormones. The key is the type of training. It seems that short (45- to 60-minute) sessions of high-intensity training will cause the maximum amount of testosterone and HGH release, while at the same time produce the least amount of cortisol production. In other words, short to medium-length training ses-

Train intensely for short periods of time to optimize your balance of natural testosterone and growth hormone.

Photo of Joel Stubbs by Robert Reiff

ENERGY, FATIGUE AND SLEEP

Most people require an average of eight to nine hours of sleep a night, but it varies from person to person. If you're only getting four you are denying your body the sleep it needs to function properly. As a result, your natural immune system may become weaker, making you more susceptible to disease or infection, or you may not be able to concentrate as well. Muscle building is a growth process and most growth occurs during sleep. Many trainers take a nap during the day and find that to be a great way to restore energy.

sions keep the anabolic/catabolic ratio heavily weighted toward the anabolic side of the equation. Conversely, training sessions of two hours or more seem to have little impact on testosterone and HGH production but maximize cortisol production. This is the worst situation for developing freaky muscularity and maximum muscle size.

REST

With all the information floating around, it's amazing that some bodybuilders still think muscle growth takes place while training. Afraid not. You stimulate the muscle in the gym but actual recovery and growth takes place while you rest. So if you want to maximize your muscle and strength gains you must get adequate rest. If you're the late-night party type, routinely strolling in at 4 or 5 a.m., then you're not going to achieve the success you want. Sleep is the most anabolic time for the human body. In fact, both testosterone and GH levels reach their peak during sleep. Almost all growth and repair takes place during sleep. By interfering with sleep you're decreasing the body's ability to maximize its anabolic state. The end result is less muscle growth.

NUTRITION

The greatest bodybuilding routine in the world is virtually useless if you don't consume the right nutrients in the right amounts.

Intensive exercise is clearly a vital part of the whole muscle-building process, but achieving optimum muscle mass depends on consuming the raw building materials

the body converts into muscle. Proper nutrition depends on numerous factors and while there are others, the following are the most important:

Protein

When it comes to priming the anabolic environment and building freaky muscularity and maximum muscle size, nothing plays as important a role as protein. You can think of protein creating muscle as bricks create a wall. Protein supplies all the amino acids the body uses to repair and build muscle tissue following an intensive training session.

If you fail to consume enough protein you risk letting the body slip into a state of negative nitrogen balance. Biochemists predict protein synthesis and muscle growth by measuring the amount of nitrogen present. Nitrogen is one of the key ingredients in amino acid synthesis, and the more of it present the greater the rate of synthesis. When levels are high it's called positive nitrogen balance and when levels are low the term is negative nitrogen balance. Positive nitrogen balance, anabolism and muscle growth are all interlinked. If developing maximum muscle size is your goal then you should try to eat 1 to 1.5 grams of protein per pound of body weight each day from such high-protein food sources as beef, fish, poultry, eggs and low-fat dairy products. Try to spread the protein over at least five or six meals to derive the optimum benefits.

Carbohydrates

Think of your body as a high-performance racing car. It needs energy to operate. In the case of your body the energy comes in the form of carbohydrates (carbs). Carbohydrates

Illustration by Mark Collins

come in two forms – simple and complex. Simple carbs (sugar, white bread, fruit juice, some fruits, etc.) should be limited, as they tend to get stored as fat if not burned right away. Complex carbs (whole wheat pastas, many fruits, whole wheat breads, rice) are released much more slowly over time and less likely to be stored as fat. In order to maintain peak energy levels during your workouts carbohydrates should make up at least 50 percent of your total calories throughout most of the year. In the pre-contest diet you'll have to cut that proportion down.

Besides energy, carbs are also vital to the muscle-building process. Carbohydrates stimulate the release of insulin, which forces more amino acids into muscle cells to begin the process of growth and repair. However, if your carb levels are so low that your body does not have enough to fuel its daily activities, then your body will start cannibalizing its own muscle to convert into glycogen in order to meet its energy requirements. In simple terms, failure to eat enough quality carbs can put the body into a catabolic state.

INCREASE YOUR CALORIES

Unless you're carrying excess weight or gain fat very easily you need a positive caloric balance if you want to build new muscle tissue. Try to ensure that your daily caloric intake is about 10 percent higher than your daily energy expenditure for maintenance.

Eat Fat

One of the biggest changes in nutrition circles over the past 10 to 20 years is the viewpoint regarding fats. There was a time that all fats were lumped together and considered evil, but no longer. It's now known that fats are definitely either good or bad for you. Fats can be subdivided into two types: saturated and unsaturated. Saturated fats, including the evil trans fats, are killers. They tend to be solid at room temperature. These fats deserve their bad reputation. Over time they build up on arterial walls, causing heart disease and stroke. For optimum health

Photo of Lind Walter by Irvin Gelb

your goal is to try and eliminate all saturated and trans fat from your diet. Unsaturated fat, including EFAs, monounsaturated and polyunsaturated, are considered "good" fats and are vital to life. They tend to be liquid at room temperature. These fats do everything from lubricating the joints to protecting cellular walls to promoting protein synthesis by increasing the production of hormones, including testosterone. It's this last point that has led some nutritionists and bodybuilding experts to label unsaturated fats "anabolic" compounds. The best sources of unsaturated fats are fish and vegetable oils.

WATER WORKS

The human body is approximately 70 percent water by volume. While our ancestors left the seas hundreds of millions of years ago, we are still dependent on this simple but vital life-giving liquid. Failure to drink adequate quantities of water will lead to dehydration and will adversely affect your muscle mass. Even though there are many myths about water and nutrition floating around, one common saying that you've no doubt heard is true – you should drink at least eight glasses of water per day. And this is not counting the extra water you should be drinking on workout days. Water is cheap or free, depending on the source, and vital for life. Since all the chemical reactions in the human body are directly or indirectly dependent on water you should make consumption a priority.

SUPPLEMENTATION

Like fats, the role of supplementation in maximizing bodybuilding success has evolved over the decades. From simple protein powders and multivitamins to creatine, CLA and glutamine, the area of supplementation has been radically transformed. While some mainstream nutritionists may question the value of supplementation, it's pretty much accepted by most bodybuilding experts (and bodybuilders themselves) that supplementing makes a huge difference when it comes to building maximum-sized muscles.

Supplements can be divided into two categories – nutrients and performance enhancers. As the name suggests nutrient supplements are just extra amounts of the common nutrients such as protein, vitamins and minerals, and EFAs. While it is possible to receive adequate amounts through the diet, they will make a big difference if levels are low to begin with, and taking a little extra ensures you will always have enough. It only makes sense to supplement with protein or EFAs to ensure the raw materials are available for synthesizing new muscle tissue.

Although the quality of nutrient supplements has improved over the years, it's within the area of performance enhancement that the biggest advances have been made. Such state-of-the-art supplements as creatine, glutamine and nitric oxide are being used by millions of bodybuilders to bring their muscularity to new levels.

What separates these supplements from the nutrients is their ability to boost strength and size gains beyond what normal nutrition can provide. Creatine has a proven track record in helping bodybuilders build bigger muscles. Likewise, glutamine can help combat the stress of high-intensity workouts and keep the body in that all-important anabolic state of positive nitrogen balance. Nitric oxide has the ability to increase the transport of other nutrients into and from cells, as well as reduce joint and soft-tissue inflammation.

ZINC AND TESTOSTERONE PRODUCTION

Among its many functions, the evidence suggests that zinc plays a major role in testosterone production. Despite the fact that it's a trace element, zinc is involved in virtually hundreds of metabolic actions.

Approximately two to three grams of zinc in the body is found within the bones. The rest of the mineral is found mostly in the skin, nails and hair. To give you an idea of zinc's importance, most of the body's hormones, such as insulin, estrogen, testosterone and growth hormone are dependent on zinc. This has been confirmed in studies, which suggest that hard-training athletes are often deficient in zinc.

Zinc will not boost testosterone levels above normal. But if your zinc levels are low from training hard, then supplementing helps to ensure optimum hormone production. Unless you consume megadoses (500 to 1,000 milligrams per day), adverse reactions to zinc are rare. Excessive zinc can interact with other minerals like copper and iron, but this occurs only in extreme cases. Taking 15 to 30 milligrams per day as a supplement is perfectly safe for healthy individuals. For hard-training athletes the optimal dosage is 30 milligrams per day.

CHAPTER 98

The Medicated Edge

"I am no longer amazed at the size of the athletes of today. I am no longer stunned by their contest weight of 290 pounds at 1.5 percent body fat. I am amazed, rather, by the amount of chemicals they are putting into their bodies."

– Sean McDaniel, *MuscleMag International* guest writer, commenting on the state of modern athletics.

f there is one topic *MuscleMag International* has never shied away from over the years it's the issue of drug use in sports – particularly bodybuilding. While most rival magazines either ignore the issue or worse, distort the facts, *MuscleMag* does its utmost to present readers with a balanced approach to this very complex issue. Until Canadian sprinter Ben Johnson tested positive for anabolic steroids at the 1988 Summer Olympics, the vast majority of the general public had never heard of anabolic steroids much less growth hormone, beta agonists or Synthol. Despite steroids becoming front page news all over the world, it came as a shock to many that steroids had been used in sports since the 1950s, and that drug use in sports can be traced all the way back to the ancient Greeks.

While it is true that, as with all drugs, there are risks associated with using steroids, and some of those risks might be severe, it's also true that the majority of athletes who use steroids do not experience the horrendous side effects often reported in the media. Be that as it may, the following chapters are not meant to be "how to" guides on drug use. Since its founding in 1974, *MuscleMag International* has emphasized that bodybuilding is about improving one's overall health, not just about building bigger muscles.

Performance-enhancing drugs do carry side effects, and in some individuals the consequences can be deadly. You pays yer money you takes yer chances. So let me stress that I'm in no way condoning drug use for body-building purposes. Having said that I also realize some of you will use drugs anyhow. For this reason I think it makes more sense to give you the honest facts rather than preach horror stories. And who knows, if after reading these chapters you decide not to use steroids or other per-formance-enhancing drugs, then all the better for you.

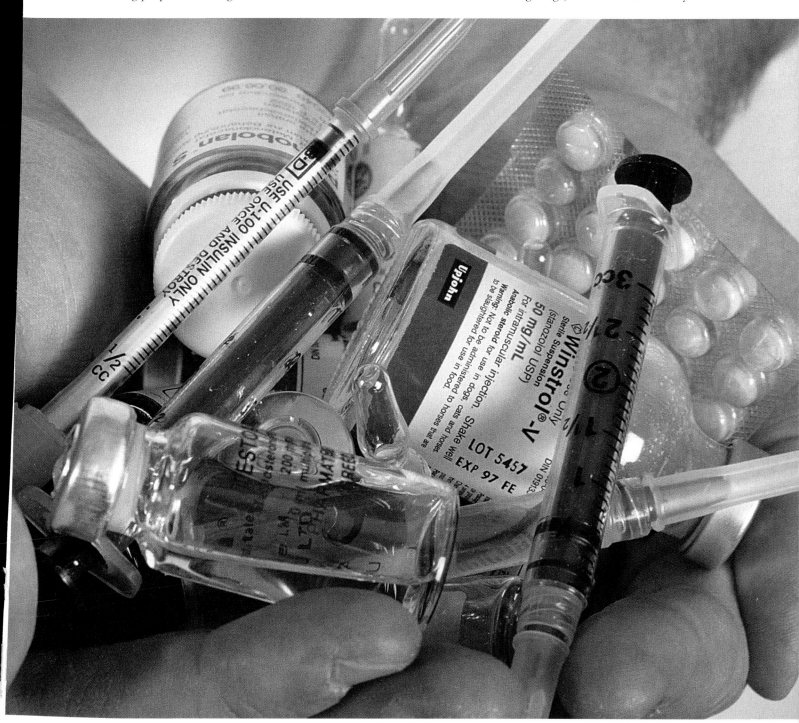

CHAPTER 99

Anabolic Steroids

"Many of the old-time bodybuilders look remarkably good for their ages. I don't think we'll be saying the same about some of the walking science projects competing today when they get to be around 50 years old."

– Nelson Montana, regular *MuscleMag International* contributor, comparing the bodybuilding superstars of decades ago with many of today's bodybuilders who are heavy users of performance-enhancing drugs.

Despite the increased popularity of some of the newer drugs, steroids are still by far the most popular performance-enhancing drugs in bodybuilding. They go by many different names including anabolic steroids, steroids, anabolics, juice, gear and roids. But no matter what you call them, these powerful muscle-building drugs are now ingrained in the consciousness of bodybuilders and athletes everywhere. It's safe to say that these drugs are rampant at all levels of sport, from low-level amateur to upper-echelon professional.

Anabolic-androgenic steroids are a class of testosterone-mimicking drugs that were first developed in the 1950s to stimulate muscle growth and treat males with endocrine problems. As news of the drug's muscle-promoting properties became known, it wasn't long before weightlifters, bodybuilders and athletes in other sports requiring strength and power started taking them.

Medically, these anabolic drugs are used for treating such conditions as delayed puberty, some forms of impotence, combating such wasting diseases as

Distended bellies are now a common sight on bodybuilding stages.

" Unless you either make your living from competitive bodybuilding or have serious potential to do so, I think you would be a fool to go on the gear. Steroids are illegal and they can cause many different health problems."

– Lee Priest, popular bodybuilding pro, responding to a beginner's question about using anabolic steroids.

AIDS and cancer, anemia and osteoporosis. Despite their legitimate medical uses, the biggest market for most of these drugs is in sports; and the sport most closely associated with these drugs is bodybuilding. Virtually all professional and top amateur competitive bodybuilders use steroids. And for every pro or national competitor who uses them, there are probably a thousand recreational bodybuilders using them, who will never even compete. But it's not just bodybuilders who use these muscle-building agents. Many of the world's top track and field athletes also use them. And such sports as football, rugby and powerlifting see rampant usage. Steroids have even made their way to Hollywood, and many of today's biggest stars have used steroids to quickly get in shape for movies that required the removal their shirts.

HOW THEY ARE USED

Anabolic steroids can be taken in a number of different ways. The two most common are orally (swallowing a pill) and injection (using a hypodermic needle to inject the steroid into the muscle). Orals are easiest to use, but because of their chemical modifications they produce more side effects. Injectables require the use of a needle and all the risks that accompany breaking the body's outer protective barrier. But this version is easier on the system, with fewer side effects. A third method of delivery

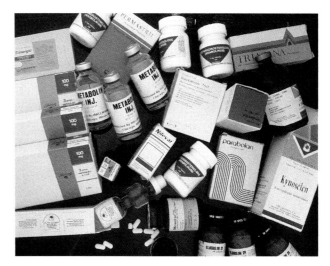

Photo (Top) by Irvin Gelb

involves a patch containing creams or gels that get absorbed through the skin directly into the body.

Cycles and Stacks

Most bodybuilders don't just randomly pop pills and stick needles into their asses (at least the smarter ones); they combine the drugs into stacks and cycles. A cycle is a period of drug use followed by a period of nonuse. The most popular

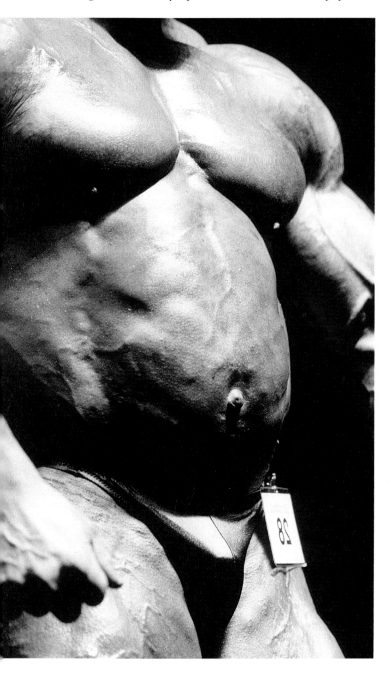

cycle would be 8 to 12 weeks on and 2 to 3 weeks off.

Probably the most popular variation of this cycle is called the pyramid cycle. In this case the dosages start out low, gradually increase in potency, peak for a few weeks, and then start to gradually decrease. A drug-free period follows after this cycle before the user may start again. It's thought that by arranging the dosages in this way, the body has time to adjust and avoid the side effects that sometimes occur. This type of cycle also gives bodybuilders and other athletes a better chance of passing drug tests.

Although the risks are greater the more they take, bodybuilders rarely take just one steroid in a cycle. Instead they take two or more drugs at the same time in what's called a stack. Bodybuilders stack steroids because they find that drugs sometimes magnify each other's effects by a process known as synergism.

SIDE EFFECTS

While the side effects attributed to steroids may have been exaggerated by the media, these drugs do present a risk. Most of the negative effects such as acne, oily skin and increased blood pressure are transitory and will disappear after the drugs are stopped. In women the effects of a deepened voice and masculinized genitalia may be permanent.

In males many steroids cause a suppression of the body's natural testosterone levels. The reason is associated with a mechanism called biofeedback. Essentially, the body continuously monitors its own hormone levels. When levels reach a certain peak, the body shuts down production. Conversely, when levels drop too low, the body increases production. Since the body treats anabolic steroids as natural testosterone (this is after all what steroids are – synthetic derivatives of the male hormone) it shuts down its own natural production. The problem for users is that it may take the body weeks if not months to get testosterone levels back to normal after steroid use is stopped. In some cases it could be a year or more. During this time some, if not all, of the strength and size gains made while on the cycle may be lost. This is why most bodybuilders take another drug called hCG (human

Chorionic Gonadotropin) after their steroid cycles. This drug stimulates the testes to begin testosterone production again, allowing levels to quickly get back to normal.

Roid Rage

So far the jury is out on whether or not roid rage exists. There is no conclusive proof to support its existence, but many in the medical community insist it is indeed real. Roid rage is probably not, however, responsible for every incident it's blamed for. It seems every act of violence perpetrated by someone suspected of using steroids gets blamed on the steroids. For example, in June of 2007 wrestling super-star Chris Benoit was found dead of an apparent suicide after murdering his wife and young son. Despite the lack of evidence, the media is calling it a case of roid rage. Did steroids have something to do with this tragedy? We'll likely never know. However, doctors do believe that if a person already has a psychological disorder then steroids can inten-sify the problem.

Some steroid users do become more aggressive while on the juice, and those who are already idiots may become more idiotic than usual. Luckily most users channel their aggression toward the weights or out on the football field and not at their neighbors, friends or family members.

I should point out that the risk of side effects, includ-ing aggression, is related to the nature of drug usage. Users who take multiple drugs in high dosages for extended periods of time are at greater risk of developing health problems than someone who does a one-drug, six-week cycle. It's also known that users of oral steroids are at much greater risk for developing side effects than those who use injectable steroids. The problem with many oral steroids is that they have been chemically modified to sur-vive the harsh environment of the digestive system. This chemical modification (called 17-alklylization, because the changes are made at the 17th carbon position on the steroid molecule) places much more stress on the liver – the body's primary detoxifying organ.

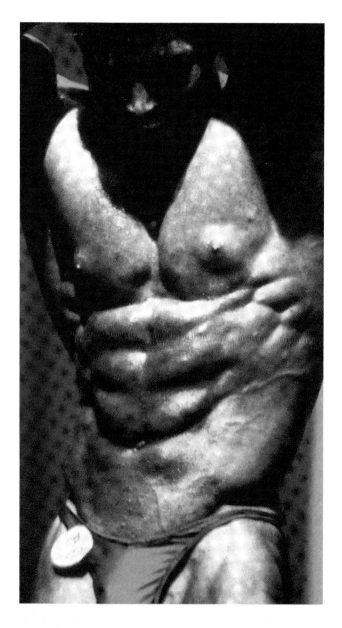

One of the most unsightly scenes in bodybuilding is called gynecomastia, also known as gyno or "bitch tits." As unflattering as the term is, this is essentially what the condition looks like – the teats on a female dog!

Gyno occurs when an enzyme in the male body, called aromatase, breaks testosterone down into the female hormone estrogen. The estrogen then stimulates estrogen receptors throughout the male's body, including in the nipple region. Since this same enzyme can also break many anabolic steroids down into the female hormone, the risk of developing gyno is always present with heavy steroid stacks.

This condition is usually first spotted by the appearance of a slight swelling or a small lump under the nipples. If not treated it can grow into a very unsightly mass of tissue, often irreversible without surgery. If you take a close look at many of today's top pro bodybuilders you'll see numerous cases of gynecomastia – or the scars from the removal of breast tissue.

It's for this reason that, besides the assortment of drugs that many pro bodybuilders use (i.e. anabolic steroids, insulin, growth hormone and thyroid drugs), many add the drug Nolvadex to their steroid stacks. Nolvadex is an estrogen blocker and helps reduce the risk of developing gyno during a cycle.

For those bodybuilders who develop the condition, things can get complicated. In some cases the condition will disappear after the steroids are stopped. Others find that post-steroid therapy with Nolvadex and other estrogen blockers will reverse the problem. In some cases, however, the only option is surgery. Besides the obvious cosmetic rea-

Gynecomastia

"Gynecomastia (or gyno) is a common problem in the bodybuilding world among both pros and amateurs. If you are using any compounds that elevate your testosterone, you are not only a candidate for gyno, you are also a potential candidate for breast cancer. Yes, breast cancer! Breast cancer is no different for men than women when the environment is the same. Men have the same breast tissue and potential for breast growth as women."

– Mark Foster, *MuscleMag International* contributor, adding yet another reason individuals should think twice about using anabolic steroids.

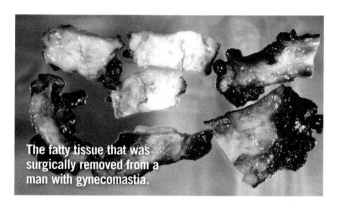

The fatty tissue that was surgically removed from a man with gynecomastia.

sons for the surgery (most males like to fondle breasts, but not their own!) untreated gyno can turn cancerous.

THE LONG ARM OF THE LAW

Ask the average citizen what anabolic steroids are and they'll say they are vile and deadly drugs used only by the depraved of society. The use of these drugs by adults for muscle building and fat loss is routinely labeled "drug abuse" and, not surprisingly thanks to the influence of the mainstream media, the average American puts steroid users into the same degenerate group as heroin or cocaine users.

> "Buying drugs on the black market is a sketchy venture. You never know for certain if what you're getting is real. Even if it does have active ingredients, you can't be sure the compound is indeed sterile."
>
> – Ron Harris, regular *MuscleMag International* contributor

Until the late 1980s, obtaining these drugs for muscle building and fat loss was relatively cheap, easy and safe. Doctors regularly prescribed them to athletes. If you didn't want to go to your doctor, you could easily find some at the local gym and purchase a six- to eight-week supply for less than $100. But with Ben Johnson's much-publicized positive drug test at the 1988 Olympics combined with the reclassifying of anabolic steroids as controlled substances in 1990, it's not surprising that they became part of the drug war in 1990.

Anabolic Steroid Control Act of 1990

The Anabolic Steroid Control Act of 1990 added anabolic steroids to the federal list of controlled substances, thereby making the possession of steroids for non-medical purposes a criminal offence. The Act essentially put steroids in the same legal class as such drugs as heroin, cocaine and barbiturates. Individuals caught illegally possessing anabolic drugs – even purely for personal use – face immediate arrest and prosecution. Also, under this Act it is unlawful for any person knowingly or intentionally to possess these drugs for fat loss or muscle building unless they were obtained directly by a prescription from a medical doctor. Other subsections of the act include:

Photo by Jim Amentler

- A first-offense simple possession conviction is punishable by a term of imprisonment of up to one year and/or a minimum fine of $1,000.
- Simple possession by a person with a previous conviction for certain offenses, including any drug or narcotic crimes, must get imprisonment of at least 15 days and up to two years, and a minimum fine of $2,500.
- Individuals with two or more such previous convictions face imprisonment of no less than 90 days but no more than three years, and a minimum fine of $5,000.
- Distributing, or possession with intent to distribute, is a federal felony.
- An individual who distributes or dispenses anabolic steroids or possesses with intent to distribute or dispense, is punishable by up to five years in prison (with at least two additional years of supervised release) and/or a $250,000 fine ($1,000,000 if the defendant is other than an individual). Penalties are higher for repeat offenders.

CHAPTER 100

Insulin

"Yes they are bigger, but at what cost? They have lost their aesthetics along the way. I think the early '90s was when the guys looked their best. Not long after that they started using insulin and the guts came along. Not everyone has suffered from this condition, but most have to some degree."

– King Kamali, regular *MuscleMag International* columnist, voicing his concerns over the state of modern bodybuilding.

nsulin is a perfect example of just how extreme some bodybuilders are willing to go to gain a competitive edge. Not happy with "just" using steroids, some careless bodybuilders have begun risking their lives with this potentially dangerous drug.

In the minds of many bodybuilders, insulin is almost the perfect drug. It's cheap, difficult to detect and actually enhances performance. Notice I said "almost," as this "perfect drug" has another side to it – it can be lethal.

Insulin is a natural peptide (protein) hormone secreted by the pancreas. Its primary role is in controlling the levels of glucose in the blood. Diabetics need to inject it to prevent a rise in blood glucose, as their pancreas' produce either insufficient or no insulin. The dangerous fact about the hormone is that if too much is injected it can drive blood sugar levels too low, putting the individual into a diabetic coma or even leading to death. In fact, insulin injection has been the suspected method of death in many murders.

So you may be wondering just why anyone in his right mind would use insulin for athletic purposes. Insulin use is thought to have first started with endurance athletes, who used the drug to force more glucose into muscle cells for storage as glycogen. Later, bodybuilders discovered that the hormone could also be used for muscle building by speeding up protein synthesis and increasing the delivery of amino acids to muscles.

A MEMBER OF THE BIG THREE!

Insulin probably became part of bodybuilding subculture around the same time as growth hormone – the early 1990s. Up until the late 1980s drug stacks and cycles primarily consisted of steroids and maybe an anti-estrogen. But as soon as word started circulating that a few pro bodybuilders were experimenting with insulin, gym rats everywhere jumped on the bandwagon and started using the drug for muscle building.

Together with anabolic steroids and growth hormone, insulin is one of the big three drugs in bodybuilding. These three drugs together are believed to produce a synergistic effect. This means each drug magnifies the others' effects. Whereas 240 solid pounds was considered huge back in the 1970s and 1980s, the new stacks pushed the average weight of the pros to 260 pounds, and it's not unusual now to see bodybuilders weighing 280, 290 or even more in contest shape.

For those readers contemplating using insulin, I strongly urge you to reconsider. Unlike steroids and growth hormone, which may cause side effects down the road, this is one drug that could literally kill you within minutes. The problem is that while you may be taking it to speed up amino acid transport and muscle-tissue syn-

thesis, the hormone will also start lowering blood sugar levels. You could very quickly end up in a coma. A number of bodybuilders have died from insulin-induced comas. You have to ask yourself if a few extra inches on your arms or chest worth dying for. I seriously doubt it.

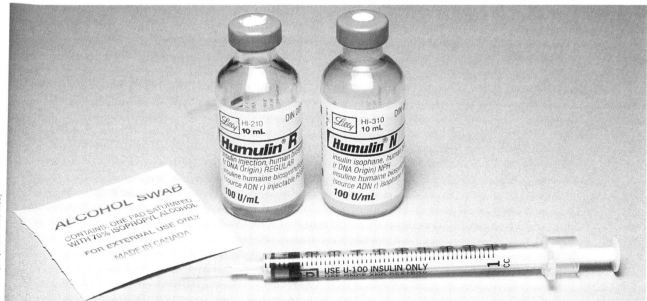

CHAPTER 101

Human Growth Hormone (HGH)

"Healthy aging is accompanied by a progressive reduction in production of anabolic hormones like testosterone and growth hormone."

– Dr. Nick Evans, bodybuilding expert and medical advice columnist for *MuscleMag International*

Like insulin, human growth hormone (HGH) is a polypeptide hormone that has made inroads from the legitimate medical field into bodybuilding and other sports. It is secreted by the anterior pituitary gland and has numerous functions, including regulating tissue growth, controlling energy levels, speeding fat loss, and increasing muscle growth. Growth hormone is often called the "master hormone," because it is released by the anterior pituitary gland (often called the "master gland"). While HGH is not necessary or critical to one's survival, it plays a vital role in human development.

During childhood a shortage of HGH leads to the condition of dwarfism, in which individuals grow to only about three feet in height. Conversely, an overabundance of HGH can lead to gigantism and heights of over eight feet are possible (the tallest being Robert Wadlow, who stood 8'11").

Bodybuilders have long dabbled in human growth hormone use, but until the mid 1990s it was limited to the very wealthy because of its cost. It was also one of the riskier drugs to use because it was all derived from cadavers (that's dead people), and sometimes contained a nasty little virus that causes an extremely rare but invariably fatal infection called Creutzfeldt-Jakob disease

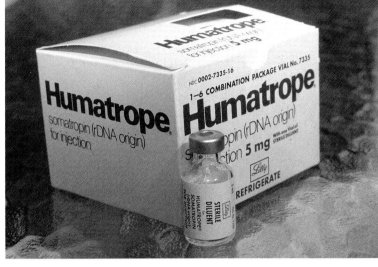

Sure HGH helps your muscles grow larger than they would otherwise be. But it helps internal organs grow larger than they would otherwise be, too.

(aka Mad Cow disease). It was when synthetic versions came onstream and the price dropped that HGH use became rampant at the pro level for maximizing muscle size.

By itself HGH doesn't seem to accomplish much, but when stacked with steroids and insulin the results are nothing short of spectacular. You can almost pinpoint the exact week a bodybuilder started taking HGH, as he'll gain 20, 30 or more pounds in a few months and show up onstage weighing 260 to 270, compared to his normal 220 to 230 from just six months before. And keep in mind this is in individuals who hadn't gained an ounce of new muscle tissue in years. Because of this effect many experts refer to HGH as a plateau buster.

Despite the new manufacturing techniques, human growth hormone is still probably the most expensive of bodybuilding drugs, and many pros are rumored to spend $5,000 to $10,000 per contest on growth hormone for maximizing muscle size.

CHAPTER 102

Synthol

"Synthol has no place in the sport at all. It's not real muscle. It's more like an implant. Synthol and the GH bellies are two ugly trends that do nothing but detract from physiques."

– Lee Labrada, popular former IFBB pro and owner of Labrada nutrition, as told to Ron Harris.

The genesis of Synthol was an Italian steroid called Esiclene that was quite popular in the 1980s. For those unfamiliar with Esiclene, it was not used for lasting mass gains, but instead immediately before a contest as a quick fix for visually weak bodyparts.

Acting primarily as a muscle inflammatory agent, this steroid was injected directly into the calves, arms or shoulders for a bit of extra size and fullness in whichever of these smaller muscle groups were lagging. The effect was fleeting, but the drug served its purpose. In the early '90s, a German named Chris Clark began to toy with the idea of an injectable substance that would yield more permanent gains in size. He came up with a formulation initially named Synthol, which he later learned was already a registered and trademarked pharmaceutical name. Clark quickly renamed his product Pump 'N Pose, but the first name stuck. Now, the word Synthol is as much a part of the hardcore bodybuilding vocabulary as Dianabol or Deca. Clark hit upon a gold mine, as there were thousands of steroid-using bodybuilders who were dissatisfied with the size of their arms, delts and calves. Let's face it, few have the genetics to build

an upper arm of 20 inches or more in lean condition, even with a boatload of anabolics and the most brutal training regimens imaginable.

One of Synthol's first users was a German strongman who billed himself as having "the world's largest arms" at 27 inches. The effect is quite obviously not natural, as the Synthol-enhanced muscles take on shapes never found growing naturally on any actual human being. You can go to any contest or large fitness expo and see several men who have injected enough oil into their bis and tris to satisfy their most extreme desires. Gains of two inches or more in the arms alone are quite commonplace. Synthol is also commonly used in the side delts and calves, as was Esiclene. Ironically, it is available legally, since the $400 bottles are labeled as

posing oil. Despite the high price tag, its makers have found it difficult at times to keep up the worldwide demand from bodybuilders.

WHAT IS SYNTHOL?

Synthol is composed of 85 percent medium-chain triglyceride oils (a fatty acid), 7.5 percent lidocaine (painkiller), and 7.5 percent benzyl alcohol. The preparation is injected deep into the muscle where it is encapsulated between the fascicles (bundles of muscle fibers). With repeated injections, a larger volume of oil builds up inside the muscle, expanding its size like a balloon filling up with air. About 30 percent of what is injected is metabolized by the body. The

other 70 percent remains lodged in the muscle, where it breaks down very slowly over three to five years. There seems to be some issue of debate among bodybuilders as to whether or not Synthol actually lasts this long, and some believe it is even longer. Chris Clark is convinced that it somehow leads to permanent muscle growth in the effected areas, though even he is unsure of the mechanisms that would make this possible. Synthol users report amazing pumps while training, though this could be a result of the extra pressure of the accumulated oil.

RISKS OF SYNTHOL USE

Although Mr. Clark claims Synthol is completely safe to use, he also said a few years ago that he is not legally responsible for bodybuilders using it for any reason other than as a posing oil. Of course, injecting any amount of fatty-acid material

> **All it takes is one little glob of this crap to plug one of your ventricles or the blood supply to your brain and that's it – you're dead."**
> – Ron Harris, *MuscleMag International* contributor, pulling no punches when it comes to Synthol usage.

intramuscularly can be perilous. This is complicated by the fact that few bodybuilders have any medical training. Without knowing the location of major nerves, it's easy to hit one by accident and cause permanent paralysis of muscle fibers in the area. With an injection of any type, abscess infections at the injection site are always a possibility. Often abscesses (extremely painful, large areas of infected tissue) require surgery to remove, not unlike a tumor.

You haven't heard the worst yet. Should you inject into a vein or artery by mistake (avoided by drawing back on the syringe to make sure there is no blood, a simple precaution many folks are too squeamish to take) the fatty acids could be transported to the lungs, causing a pulmonary embolism, to the heart, causing a heart attack, or perhaps even into the brain, leading to a cardioembolic stroke. All these cases are potentially fatal. Allegedly, IFBB

Photo by Bert Perry

pro Milos Sarcev had a scare when some of the Synthol in his arms traveled to his heart.

This sounds like an enormous amount of risk simply for the benefit of inflated arms and calves, but body-builders are not normal people. To some, it's worth the risk of death to finally have 21-inch arms just like the big genetic freaks they idolize. To date, there have been no publicized deaths related to Synthol or any of its several knock-offs currently available. However, this is a fairly new product that has only skyrocketed in use over the past five to ten years. Ultimately, Synthol users are adults who are responsible for their own health and safety and are free to make the choice themselves.

Photo (Top Right) by Robert Kennedy

CHAPTER 103

Thyroid Drugs

"An underactive thyroid will leave you so tired that you have to drag your butt around all day and you'll keep gaining weight. An overactive thyroid will make you sweat, feel anxious, suffer heart palpitations, have diarrhea, and lose lots of weight like crazy."

– Chris Rand, *MuscleMag International* contributor, in paraphrase.

There are literally dozens of products on the market that promote themselves as being the be-all and end-all to fat-burning. In fact there is such a huge demand for drugs and natural products to burn body fat that it has created an industry worth billions of dollars. In their quest for ripped muscle mass and shredded muscularity many bodybuilders bypass the over-the-counter choices and go straight to the prescription drugs. The most popular are thyroid derivatives, but as I'll show you later, messing around with the thyroid gland is not to be taken lightly.

THE THYROID GLAND – YOUR BODY'S METABOLIC MASTER

The thyroid is a small gland located just above the Adams apple in the neck. It produces several hormones vital for regulating metabolism. The two primary hormones are T3 and T4, and for many bodybuilders they play just as important a role in competition success as do steroids or growth hormone.

So what's the big deal about thyroid hormones and bodybuilding? Thyroid hormones play a huge role in directing basal metabolism. The more T3 and T4 you produce, the more calories the body burns, especially in the form of heat. One simple measure of thyroid functioning is to take your temperature first thing in the morning. Lowered body temperature is one of the classic signs of hypothyroidism.

The thyroid hormones are both anabolic and catabolic. A low to moderate level of T3 is primarily anabolic. But the higher this level gets, the more the catabolic action will start to predominate, while the anabolic activity comes to a halt. For optimum amounts of ripped muscle mass and shredded muscularity, individuals need to keep their T3 levels from skyrocketing out of control.

The thyroid hormones also have indirect actions. For example, thyroid hormones help you reduce fat (and gain muscle) by increasing the number of beta-receptors in the fat and muscle cells. You may have heard of these receptors because the popular fat-loss compound ephedrine works by stimulating beta-receptors.

DIET AND THYROID IMPLICATIONS

As you are aware, carbohydrates are one of the key macronutrients. They have direct actions on insulin and indirect actions on IGF-1. They also stimulate the production of thyroid hormones. Therefore, the more you decrease your carbohydrate intake during a diet and the longer your diet lasts, the more you will reduce the secretion of thyroid hormones. This is one of the big problems of carbohydrate-reduced diets. They drastically reduce the individual's basal metabolism, eventually producing the opposite of the desired effect – weight gain as opposed to weight loss. Therefore, replacing carbohydrates with protein may make some sense in the short term, but you don't want to stay on such a diet for too long. At the very least you should periodically increase your carbohydrate intake to restart the thyroid.

Long-term diets can impact on the muscles in a big way. If insulin is present in sufficient quantities, it can prevent the catabolism induced by the thyroid hormones. But when the level of insulin is low because of caloric restriction, the catabolism increases and muscle tissue will be lost. In fact the instant you go on a strict diet, your body starts decreasing the levels of thyroid hormones to try and preserve muscle tissue. This, of course, means your metabolism is lowered.

THYROID DRUGS

It's not surprising that bodybuilders would turn to thyroid drugs once word got out about how efficient they are for

burning body fat. For the modern bodybuilder trying to develop ripped muscle mass and shredded muscularity, thyroid medication seems like a logical step. The most popular thyroid drug is Cytomel.

Cytomel contains a synthetically manufactured compound called liothyronine sodium, which resembles the natural thyroid hormone T3. Bodybuilders seem to love Cytomel, as it causes a faster burning of carbohydrates, proteins and fats. The last point is especially important. Increased lipolysis (fat-burning) will leave them hard as a rock on contest day. Cytomel helps a competitor maintain an extremely low fat content without necessitating a loss in muscle tissue, which is a difficult accomplishment. Bodybuilders also report that low dosages of Cytomel combined with steroids make the steroids more effective. No one is sure of the reason for this, but one theory is that Cytomel's increased breakdown of protein leaves more available to be converted into new muscle tissue.

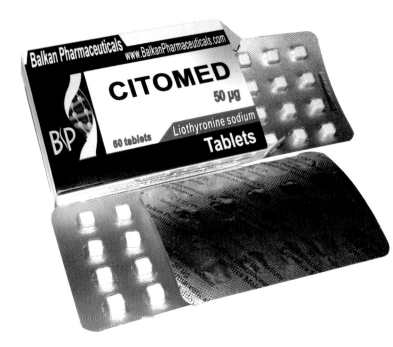

I'd be remiss if I forgot to mention that it's not just the men who are using Cytomel. The drug is also very popular among female bodybuilders and fitness contestants. Since women on average have slower metabolisms than men, in addition to having a naturally higher body fat levels, it is extremely difficult for them to develop the ripped muscle mass and shredded muscularity that judges expect these days. Instead of a drastic reduction of food and calories, the women simply add in Cytomel a few weeks before the show. While women are probably more susceptible to side effects than men, they can usually get good results from 50 mcg/day.

RISKS

As with insulin, all is not rosy with thyroid usage. Most bodybuilders use only small dosages two or three times per day rather than one large dosage all at once. They also stay on for no more than six weeks in a row. There must be at least two months of total abstinence from the drug following this usage. Those who fail to heed this advice and take high dosages of thyroid drugs over a long period of time are at risk of developing a chronic thyroid insufficiency. There are numerous stories circulating about bodybuilders and fitness stars having to take thyroid medication for the rest of their lives from earlier thyroid drug abuse. It is also important that the dosage be reduced gradually, rather than stopped cold turkey. Stopping abruptly places a tremendous shock on the system.

My advice is to stay clear of thyroid drugs and stick with such safe alternatives as increased cardio exercise and a reduced caloric intake. Avoid simple sugars. Why risk damaging your thyroid gland for a slightly lower body fat percentage?

Photo by John Butler

CHAPTER 104

Ephedrine

"In one study they took many samples of the top-10 weight-loss products (ephedrine/caffeine), measured each product batch-to-batch six months later, and guess what, huge differences between batches!"

– Dr. Serranno, bodybuilding nutrition expert, as told to John Paul Catanzaro

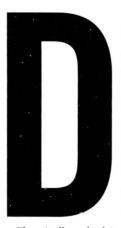

Despite the negative press and increased restrictions on its use, ephedrine is still one of the most popular bodybuilding supplements ever. Until it was banned a number of years back, it was the primary ingredient in most over-the-counter weight-loss products. Ephedrine, however, is not an invention of 20th century pharmacology. It was used in China for thousands of years. The most familiar form of ephedrine is derived from the Chinese herb ma huang (with ephedrine being the active ingredient).

Chemically, ephedrine is an alkaloid, and it acts both as a sympathetic amine (stimulant) and as a thermogenic aid (fat loss through heat generation). Medically, ephedrine is commonly used as a smooth-muscle dilator in the treatment of asthma, bronchitis and nasal congestion. Its close cousin pseudoephedrine is still one of the most common ingredients in cold and flu medications.

As a sympathetic amine, ephedrine acts to stimulate the sympathetic nervous system (this is the "flight or fight" system that kicks in when you're faced with a dangerous or frightening situation). It does this by causing nerve terminals to release norepinephrine – more commonly called noradrenaline (NA), into the synaptic space (space between two adjacent nerve fibers). Ephedrine also has the ability to increase circulating levels of adrenaline, the body's primary beta-2 agonist. Once released, noradrenaline stimulates adrenergic

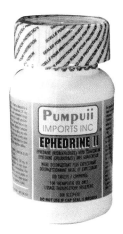

receptors on the surface of fat cells (called adipocytes). This in turn starts a chain of chemical events that ultimately leads to fat-burning, called lipolysis.

Bodybuilders use ephedrine products for its stimulant effects in addition to its fat-burning properties. Ephedrine ranks somewhere between caffeine and amphetamine on the stimulant scale and provides a definite "kick" to one's workout.

ized, you still can't be sure exactly just how much you are taking with each serving. There could be a huge discrepancy between equal dosages of two different products. You should also be aware that virtually all sports organizations have added ephedrine to their list of banned drugs.

One of the biggest detriments to taking drugs such as ephedrine is human nature. We always seem to think that if some is good, more is better. Almost all the cases of deaths associated with ephedrine use came about because the drug was abused. Excessive ephedrine use will likely make you very thin indeed – skeletal, in fact.

THE ECA (EPHEDRINE CAFFEINE ASPIRIN) STACK

Given their love for stacking multiple drugs together to produce a synergistic effect, it's not surprising that bodybuilders commonly combine ephedrine with two other compounds to increase its effectiveness. It didn't take long for bodybuilders to discover that stacking the compound with caffeine and Aspirin® magnified its fat-burning properties. In fact these three compounds when combined together produce what is arguably the most potent fat-burning product available.

The standard dosage is one 24/25 mg of ephedrine, 200 mg of caffeine (about one large cup of coffee) and one Aspirin®. However, ephedrine is now a restricted drug and cannot be purchased in dosages of over 8 mg.

NO FREE RIDE

Anyone considering taking ephedrine, caffeine and Aspirin® should be aware of potential side effects. Certainly individuals with pre-existing high blood pressure or other heart problems should not use stimulants such as ephedrine. If you are considering taking this product, please have a complete physical first, including a stress test. Also, when taking herbal forms of ephedrine, be sure you understand just how much is in each serving. Although herbal preparations are standard-

Photo by Jason Mathas

CHAPTER 105

Diuretics (Lasix)

"I was still so new I didn't know what Lasix was. I definitely didn't know what 40 mg of Lasix would do. The painful answer came soon enough."

– Paul Dillett, IFBB champion, telling about the famous time he froze onstage and had to be carried off.

Lasix is the trade name for the drug furosemide, a very powerful drug that belongs to a class of drugs known as loop diuretics, which cause the body to excrete water as well as potassium, sodium and chloride. Loop diuretics, and Lasix in particular, tend to be the drugs of choice for promoting water loss, as they're among the strongest such drugs available.

Bodybuilders and other athletes use diuretics for a number of different reasons. Many individual sports (including bodybuilding) are divided into weight classes. The drugs are used to drop water weight in an effort to make a lighter weight class. For most sports the goal is to come in at the top of the weight class and not the bottom. Since the weigh-in is usually the day before the competition, competitors can drop their bodyweight considerably and be back to normal within hours of rehydration with water. Bodybuilders rely heavily on diuretics when preparing for a contest, but they may or may not hydrate after the weigh-in. Unlike most sports, for which appearance is not an issue, bodybuilding contests are heavily dependent on having a ripped, defined look. And lower subcutaneous water concentrations play a huge role in developing that rock-hard appearance. Virtually all pro bodybuilders use prescription diuretics before a big contest.

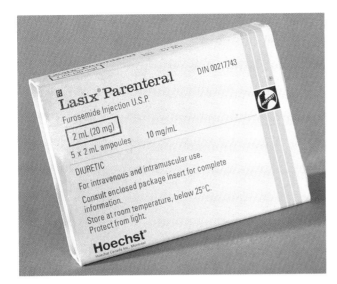

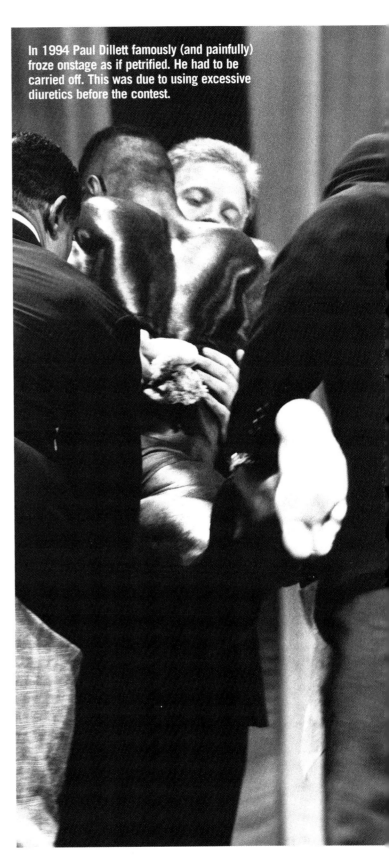

In 1994 Paul Dillett famously (and painfully) froze onstage as if petrified. He had to be carried off. This was due to using excessive diuretics before the contest.

SIDE EFFECTS

Diuretics can remain active for many hours. If you take Lasix or other diuretics you may find that you continue to dehydrate after you achieve the look you want. Since diuretics also cause a loss of potassium and other electrolytes, serious effects on the body's systems may occur, including the nervous, muscular and cardiovascular systems. Everything from your cells to your heart muscle depend on proper electrolyte balance to function properly.

Severe dehydration and electrolyte imbalance has taken the life of overambitious athletes. The most famous case in bodybuilding was Mohammad Benaziza, who died of a massive heart attack just after winning the Belgian Grand Prix in 1992. His death was believed to be directly related to the diuretics he used before the contest to shed water. Another famous dehydration incident involved Paul Dillett, whose body cramped up so badly onstage that he literally could not move and had to be carried off as if he were a statue.

The warning signs that Lasix may be causing severe dehydration include dizziness, cramping, vomiting, diarrhea, fainting and heart problems. I urge you to use extreme caution when considering using Lasix or other diuretics. If you do decide to use them, stay clear of the 500 mg tablets. These are meant to be used only in severe medical conditions and contain a dosage that could prove to be lethal for a healthy person.

Photo (Top) by Robert Kennedy

CHAPTER 106

Acne

"Four out of every five steroid users experience at least one of the more common side effects such as acne, gynecomastia, hair loss, stretch marks, testicle shrinkage, and mood swings. Users tend to accept these complications as a necessary consequence."

– Dr. Nick Evans, bodybuilding expert, author and *MuscleMag International* columnist

Few four letters have caused as much grief to teens, athletes and bodybuilders alike as acne. For teens the arrival of the first facial blemish conjures up fears of rejection and the end to their social lives. For bodybuilders the dreaded pineapple look only adds to the stress of pre-contest dieting and training. And as for the rest of us, skin that bears a striking resemblance to the lunar surface makes going shirtless at the beach all the more difficult.

One of the intriguing things about acne is that it's not picky; just about everyone will experience it to a greater or lesser degree at some point in their lives. It is the extent, however, that shows marked variation. Some experience only one rash of pimples that quickly disappears. Others have acne so bad they don't want to leave the house.

Generally speaking there are three categories of individuals who experience acne – teens, athletes and steroid users. Lets look at all three.

TEENS

As if the dramatic physical and emotional changes that take place during puberty where not enough, most teens can also look forward to developing acne. For some the first pimple is welcome as it signifies the beginning of the

"Bacne" – a common side effect of steroid use.

changes that will lead them into adulthood. For others, however, the slightest skin blemish is seen as an insult to their social standings.

The development of acne can be very traumatic for many teens. At this stage in their lives much of their self-worth is based on physical appearance. For a shy, 14-year-old male, those extra facial pimples may be the difference between asking that cute girl to the junior prom or not.

You'd think that something so common among the general population would be fully understood, but such is not the case. The most commonly accepted theory is that the hormonal changes that signal the beginning of puberty increase the skin's oil production, which serves as a perfect medium for bacteria-causing acne.

ATHLETES

The second group of individuals who may experience acne are athletes. Just about everyone who exercises on a regular basis can be included. Once again the exact cause is unknown, but a number of theories have been put forward. The first is that the increased amount of sweating causes an increase in waste production. Some byproducts of cellular respiration then act as a breeding ground for bacteria.

Another theory is that most sports cause an increase in testosterone production, and this hormone has been linked to an overproduction of skin oil (from sebaceous glands). As a result, a perfect growing medium for acne-causing bacteria has been produced.

The final theory is what could be called the chafing effect. Most sports require the athlete to make repetitious movements of the arms and legs while wearing some sort of uniform. Often the rubbing of the uniform material over the skin produces a rash, which in turn may become inflamed, leading to acne.

STEROID USERS

Most steroid users will experience acne. While this acne could take the form of facial pimples, it often reveals itself as large, blood-filled cysts along the shoulders and back. Minor skin blemishes tend to clear up after steroid use is discontinued, but the large black cysts often produce life-long scars.

The prevailing theory for steroid-induced acne is related to oil production and an increase in skin bacteria.

Photo by Steve Neece

TREATMENTS

Whether building a physique for the beach or stage, the last thing you want is a skin surface full of indentations and protrusions. There are numerous ways to treat acne – some based on folklore (don't eat chocolate, etc.) and others based on medical science. As with cold remedies, it seems everyone has a solution for clear skin.

Since oil is one of the prime conditions that leads to acne, it's not surprising that various acne cures are based on drying out the skin. The simplest is sunlight, which has the advantage of being free and easily obtainable. The downside, of course, is that exposure to the sun has been linked to skin damage. You may end up trading in acne for a dose of skin cancer. Despite its sometimes gruesome look, acne is not life threatening, but assure you skin cancer is.

The alternative to sunlight is a tanning bed. Most of the newer tanning beds have the harmful rays filtered out, but there is a risk just the same. And unlike Mother Nature, which gives you sunlight for free, tanning salons will charge you a pretty penny. For someone with severe acne this may mean year-round visits – a considerable financial investment.

Besides light, various drying creams, oils and lotions have come on the market. They work by reducing the build-up of oil, dead skin and other waste that serves as a breeding ground for those dastardly little acne-causing bacteria. For some acne sufferers the results are nothing short of miraculous, but for others the condition may in fact get worse, especially when using some of the creams and lotions.

In extreme cases of acne, the weapons of choice are antibiotics and Acutane®. As the name suggests, antibiotics work by killing the bacteria that cause acne. Again, the results vary from individual to individual. One of the drawbacks to long-term antibiotic treatment is the development of antibiotic-resistant strains of bacteria, such as MRSA. Since few antibiotics are specific for one specific type of bacteria, the risk of developing drug-resistant disease-causing bacteria is ever present.

Acutane® is a powerful drug that is perhaps the most effective method for treating acne. Virtually everyone who uses it shows a marked improvement in their skin, but unfortunately there are drawbacks. For starters Acutane® is

Illustration by Mark Collins

very expensive and only available by prescription. Not everyone has insurance that covers it. Perhaps the main reason physicians are reluctant to prescribe Acutane is its side effects: fatigue, nausea, dry skin and eyes, headaches, depression and fetal abnormalities.

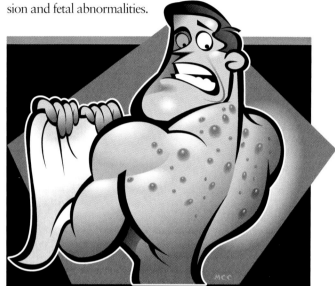

BACNE

Bacne, or back acne, causes red and purple pimples and bumps that line the upper back and neck of many bodybuilders. Apart from being embarrassing at the beach and gym, this skin condition can be painful and may cause more serious skin infections if it's not treated. If you suffer from bacne, here's some advice to help clear things up and prevent future breakouts.
• Do avoid tight-fitting clothing that can trap sweat and prevent airflow.
• Do avoid wearing backpacks for long periods of time.
• Do wear clothes made of cotton that will absorb sweat better, decreasing the chances of clogging pores.
• Do remove sweaty clothes as soon as possible.
• Do wash regularly with antibacterial soap. Scrub your back to remove dead cells and impurities. This will unclog your pores.
• Do avoid sun damage. Too much sun exposure can scar sensitive acne-covered skin.
• Don't use steroids or supplements that contain hormones. These products can increase your hormone levels, leading to severe body acne.
• Don't use moisturizing lotions or oils that clog pores and irritate your skin. They may enhance the appearance of your muscles, but those zits will be emphasized as well. Nobody wants to see that.
• Don't squeeze acne – it will spread bacteria and lead to scarring.
Seek treatment if you have severe acne.

Photo of Paul Dillett by Paul Buceta

APPENDIX I & II

APPENDIX I

Questions and Answers

S ince the first issue of *MuscleMag International* was published in 1974, I have received thousands of letters at *MuscleMag* headquarters every year. While a few offer comments and suggestions (some of which cannot be reprinted here!), the vast majority are inquiries from bodybuilders, all looking for that one piece of advice that will catapult them to bodybuilding stardom. I do my best to answer them all, either in the magazine or as a personal reply. The following is a selection of questions and answers drawn from over 30 years of *MuscleMag International*. Perhaps you'll see one of yours printed here. In any case, enjoy!

SQUATS – HOW HIGH AND HOW FAR?

Q. Should I perform my squats with my heels on a block of wood? Also, who was the first bodybuilder to employ this method? Last question: How far from the squat stands should I place the block if I use one?

A. Bodybuilders almost always use a block of wood to lift their heels during squatting. This throws most of the action on to the thighs and minimizes the work done by the hips and buttocks (provided you do not bend too far forward). Steve Reeves was the first bodybuilder to raise his heels on a block when squatting. As for your last question, the answer should be obvious. One step back from the squat stands to the block is the correct distance. With a heavy weight on your shoulders there's no reason to take a walk around town!

LOWER LEGS

Q. How do you develop the front of the lower leg, over the shin area?

A. The best exercise to develop the tibialis, the muscle covering the shin bone, is to do toe raises with a high block under the heels. Rise as high as you can and try to consciously flex and stretch the tibialis. Do 10 to 15 reps, until the area burns. Regular calf work, running, cycling and stretching the legs also works the area to some degree. To show a well-developed tibialis you should keep a low bodyfat level. It's hard to show any muscle if it's covered in fat.

PEAKING THE BICEPS

Q. Is there anything I can do to build a better peak on my biceps?

A. The best exercises to improve biceps peaks are concentration curls, pulley curls, supination curls, and lat-machine pulldown curls. Use a full range of motion on these exercises and consciously tense the biceps hard in the fully contracted position. Also, flex your biceps hard without using weights. Lift your elbow as high as you can, flex, and tense the biceps until it cramps. Some exceptionally peaked biceps are the result of a tear, though I don't recommend tearing your biceps for this purpose!

MACHINES VS. FREE WEIGHTS

Q. My friends tell me the only way to build power and thickness is to use free weights, meaning barbells and dumbells, and to stay away from machines. Is there any truth to this?

A. The old free-weight vs. machines question rears its ugly head again! Well, your friends are both right and wrong. It is definitely true that you need to train hard and heavy with free weights to add overall thickness to your body, but some machines are also beneficial. There is not a pro bodybuilder out there – or powerlifter, for that matter – who does not incorporate some sort of machine into his daily training routine. Machines these days are superior to the old-time machines because they mimic the actual free-lift movements.

The key to adding size and thickness is to train heavy, with or without the use of machines. Just as we do in our everyday life, your muscles need some variety to stay stimulated. You have to keep your body guessing into new-found growth. Mixing it up with free weights and machines is the best approach.

MORE VEINS

Q. I am 18 and a big fan of yours. I've been training for about a year now. My focus is on creating a more proportionate, muscular, defined body. I know all gains come in time with patience and correct training. My question is: How do you get vascular, or ripped? This might sound weird, but I would really love to have my veins show, especially on my biceps. My bodyfat is about 20 percent. Does vascularity come with time, or does it depend completely on bodyfat?

A. Vascularity is partly genetic. Some people's veins are naturally closer to the skin's surface, so they are more visible. But veins also show because of a low level of bodyfat. As you said yourself, patience and hard, correct training are the answers. As time goes by your body will become stronger, leaner, and yes, more vascular. I suggest you perform at least one set of 30 reps each biceps workout. High reps increase vascularity.

ARE SUPPLEMENTS NECESSARY?

Q. I weigh only 140 pounds at six feet. I'm 18 and have always been naturally thin. I see so many ads in the magazines that practically guarantee major gains in muscle size and mass. Do I need to take these supplements? Money is a problem as I'm going to school and working part time. Which supplements do you recommend I take?

A. The key to gaining size and mass is good eating and hard training. Supplements are just that: a supplement to your meals. To get big, you need to take in far more protein and calories than you currently manage (along with hard training, of course). Aim for one gram of protein per pound of bodyweight and about 30 calories per pound of bodyweight per day. These are minimums and you may need more.

As for supplements, I suggest you stick to the basics. Take a multivitamin/mineral and a good-quality whey protein powder. Protein shakes can be really useful for getting extra protein and calories, because drinking is easier than eating. Try to eat four or five meals a day, each of which contain some kind of protein (meat, egg whites, fish, poultry, cottage cheese), some kind of complex carbs (rice, potato, yams, steamed vegetables, salads), and some healthy simple carbs (fruit). Have two or three protein shakes between meals.

PECTORAL IMBALANCE

Q. I am having trouble with my pec development. Lately I've noticed my left pec has developed better than my right pec. Is this common? It's very annoying. I bench press with elbows aligned with my shoulders, but when I use heavy weights my right elbow tends to drift downward, bringing my right lat into play. What can I do to bring my right pec up to the development of my left pec?

A. It is fairly common for one lat, pec, arm or leg to be slightly more developed than the other. The best way to bring up such asymmetrical development is through the use of dumbells or one-arm exercises. When you use dumbells you force both sides to work equally hard. When you use a barbell there is a natural tendency to let the stronger side do more work than the weaker side. I suggest you try an all-dumbell chest routine for a while. Try flat dumbell bench presses for 4 sets of 8 to 10 reps, followed by a superset of incline dumbell presses and flat or incline flyes for another 4 sets of 8 to 12 reps. If the muscle imbalance is severe, try some one-arm pec-deck flyes or one-arm cable crossovers for 3 sets of 10 to 15 reps. This should help.

FOOTWEAR

Q. I have been bodybuilding for a couple of years, but I am still confused about the best footwear to use during workouts. Or is it best to train barefoot, like Arnold did?

A. Experts disagree about what is best. The late Vince Gironda said to do all calf work barefoot to get a complete, full stretch. Most bodybuilders train in running shoes of one kind or another. A few train in street shoes. You'll even see the occasional pair of workboots strolling around the gym. I do not recommend training barefoot.

TO TRAIN OR NOT TO TRAIN

Q. Sometimes before my workouts I feel too tired to train. Should I not exercise and just rest, or what?

A. In my experience a good workout is just what the doctor ordered in terms of renewed energy. Think about the analogy of a car sitting in traffic and getting loaded up with carbon and sludge. Once out of the city and away from traffic, the freely running car essentially cleans itself as it runs at top speed. I think the same holds true for humans. Work, deadlines, family responsibilities and stress all drain our energy. A workout will restore your energy levels, unless you are truly sleep deprived or genuinely exhausted from physical activity.

BICEPS GAP

Q. I have a wide gap between my elbow and biceps. Is there anything I can do to fill it in?

A. You cannot lengthen your biceps, but you can reshape it to provide an illusion. Do strict preacher curls on a 45-degree bench to build the lower biceps. Make sure you go all the way to a complete stretch at the bottom or you will take the stress away from the lower biceps area (but don't bounce). However, you can expect only moderate success filling in your gap.

HITTING THE LOWER ABS

Q. What are the best exercises for my lower abs? My upper abs are pretty good, but my lower abs lack development.

A. Try lying leg raises on an incline board set at any angle greater than 20 degrees. Take your legs back until your butt lifts off the board.

LOWER QUADS

Q. How can I get more development in my lower quads? All my development seems to be at the top of the thigh. I do squats and leg presses and leg curls for the thighs. What are the exercises that best hit the lower thigh?

A. While squats and leg presses are excellent quad exercises, they stress mostly the upper area, especially if you do your squats flatfooted. To hit the lower thigh area try doing your squats with your heels elevated on a two- or three-inch block. Hack squats and leg extensions (concentrating on fully locking out) also hit the area near the knee.

The size of the gap between your biceps muscle and the crook of your elbow is genetically determined.

Photo of Craig Richardson by Jason Breeze

Great lats are visible from the front or the back.

THE INNER PECS

Q. What's the best exercise for the inner part of the pecs?

A. Try close-grip bench presses, keeping your elbows to the side. The pec-deck is also great for the inner pecs, as are cable crossovers. Also, try squeezing the pecs together at the top of your dumbell flyes and presses.

LIMITED TIME

Q. My time for training is extremely limited. Can I build a decent physique on three or four workouts a week of 30 to 40 minutes? What exercises do you recommend I do and how many sets of each?

A. Some genetic superiors could build a fair body in 30 minutes a week, but most people could not. You will have to make every minute count. Never rest more than 60 seconds between exercises. Use a high degree of intensity. I suggest you superset your exercises (opposing muscle groups) to allow maximum work in the shortest period of time.

HIGH AND SHORT LATS

Q. My lats are high and short. How can I make my lats longer and lower?

A. Unfortunately, the muscle insertions that give you your high, short lat structure cannot be radically altered by exercise. What you should do is pick exercises that stress the lower lat area. This will give you the illusion of larger lats. Narrow-grip exercises are better than wide-grip exercises for hitting the lower lats. Try close-grip pulldowns or chins (normal or reverse grip) narrow-grip bent-over rows, one-arm dumbell rows, and perhaps one of the best for lower lats, reverse-grip bent-over rows. Use good style and concentrate on isolating the lower-lat area.

REAR DELTS

Q. When I do bent-over laterals I can't seem to feel it in the rear delts. What's a good exercise?

A. If you're not feeling it in the delts then you are probably using too much weight. Drop the weight and use better form. But to answer your question, laterals with cables is an excellent exercise. Try pulling the cables from different heights. You can also do this as a bent-over exercise.

LOCK OUT OR NOT?

Q. Is it best to lock out during exercises, or should I maintain constant tension by stopping the movement short of a full lockout?

A. This varies with each exercise. Personally I don't lock out on the triceps dumbell extension, but on triceps kickbacks I lock out and squeeze. On leg extensions I lock out, but on squats I don't. It's often a matter of personal preference and sometimes a matter of joint safety. You don't want to lock out on leg presses, for example. You will have to experiment a little to find out which exercises are made more effective by locking out.

THE OUTER PEC

Q. I want to develop the outer part of my pecs. I seem to have plenty of muscle near the center of my chest, but things get pretty thin in the outer region. What do you recommend?

A. I was always impressed by the outer pectorals of Arnold Schwarzenegger, yet he never handled more than 60-pound dumbells when he did flyes. And this was the exercise that gave him the wide outer pecs. I know for a fact that Arnold could have used more weight, but he used lighter dumbells to concentrate on stretching all the way down.

Other great outer-pec exercises are: wide-grip bench presses, dumbell presses with a slow, full stretch, and dips performed with the chin on the chest, leaning forward.

TRAINING VERSUS DIET

Q. What's more important to a bodybuilder's success, training or diet?

A. Diet, definitely! You have to liken your body to a sports car. It won't perform optimally if it doesn't receive the right kind of fuel. Super nutrition sets you up for maximum benefit in the gym, and without the right fuel your efforts in the gym will probably be wasted. Remember, lifting weights only stimulates growth. Proper recuperation requires plenty of rest and good food. You can't have one without the other. Ideally you should pay total attention to both diet and exercise.

IS FIVE YEARS ENOUGH?

Q. Do you think it's possible to reach one's ultimate potential in five years? I've been training for longer than that and can't seem to make any more gains.

A. Even though we are all definitely limited by our genetics, I don't feel anyone ever fully realizes his or her potential. There are always ways to push yourself further physically. Don't give up your fight in the gym. To break out of you training rut you probaby need a radical change in either diet or routine. One of my favorite plateau-busting methods is "boatloading." Eat everything you can get your hands on for a few weeks. Of course, try to keep the nutrition content high. Potato chips and chocolate bars won't help! Sit down and eat something every couple of hours. While I wouldn't suggest following this regimen indefinitely, it can certainly help kick-start your body into further muscle growth.

THE GREAT PUMP UP

Q. Is a pump necessary for muscle growth? I get a good pump most workouts, but my bodybuilding progress is slow and I wonder whether that might be because I don't always get a good pump.

A. A pump is not necessary for muscle growth. Many bodybuilders train regularly and seldom get a significant pump. Perhaps they either don't change their exercises often enough, work with low reps, or refrain from intense training. These same men do build muscle size, and this proves that a big pump each workout is not necessary.

Also, as you appear to have found out, an almighty pump every workout does not by any means indicate your muscles are on a positive growth pattern. Some bodybuilders train very effectively and pump up to an impressive appearance by the end of each workout, only to deflate by the time they walk out of the gym. Many do this month in, month out, and still do not gain size. However, as a bodybuilder moves into the advanced stages, say 18-inch arms, he has to get a pump to take his growth to the 19- or 20-inch-arm mark.

IF IT WORKS DON'T CHANGE IT

Q. I have been training somewhat hard six days a week, occasionally five, and for the last four months I have been making unbelievable gains everywhere. Will I build more muscle mass training heavy every other day or the way I am training now?

A. Do not change a thing. I like the every-other-day split principle of training (train half the body one day, rest next day, then train the other half the day after, indefinitely). But if you are making great gains as you say, then keep training as you are until progress slows down or comes to a halt.

UPRIGHT ROWS – HOW WIDE?

Q. Must the upright-row exercise be done with a narrow grip to make the shoulder area really grow?

A. The deltoids are worked with this exercise, but so are the trapezius, forearms and biceps. A wider grip will give more deltoid development, and a narrower grip will develop the trapezius to a greater degree.

TRAINING TO FAILURE

Q. Do you believe in training to failure?

A. Yes, I believe in training to failure, but perhaps not in the sense you mean. I believe in training to failure with good form. It is useless to continue an exercise if you have to use every muscle in the body to hoist it up in bad form.

CHINS OR PULLDOWNS?

Q. I don't have time (or energy) to use both the chinning bar and lat-pulldown machine. Which is the best apparatus to use for wide lat development?

A. Each exercise has a unique use. There is more tensile strength and nervous energy involved in chinning, but make sure to keep the elbows back throughout the entire movement. Most top bodybuilders regularly perform wide-grip chins, and there is a definite "look" about the back of a regular wide-grip chinner.

On the other hand, the lat pulldown is not quite so severe a movement. Less weight can be used, and the bar can be pulled right to the sternum or below for complete movement. Few bodybuilders can get this complete movement on the chinning bar, because they lack the strength. Of the two movements, and because most top bodybuilders find them extremely beneficial, I advise you to go with the chins, but don't discount the lat machine. When you have more time you should add a few sets of pulldowns to supplement your back training.

HALTING GAINS

Q. Is there any truth to the theory that regular swimming and other mild sports such as tennis or horseback riding will interfere with my bodybuilding gains?

A. You will lose muscle size if you swim and participate in other sports regularly. You have to fight hard to keep your capillaries and muscle cells at their fullest, and extra nonprogressive sports activity will hold back your gains.

However, if you are blessed with a huge number of muscle cells and gains come easily, then a moderate amount of extra sports activity will not hold back your progress.

CALLUSES

Q. Is there any way I can prevent getting calluses on my hands from regular weight training? I'm a massage therapist and cannot have callused hands.

A. Some bodybuilders train with light leather gloves, which can be purchased at sporting goods stores. If you can't find weightlifting gloves, thin gloves used for other sports will do.

LEG MASS

Q. I have been a serious bodybuilder for about a year now and cannot gain mass in my legs. I am doing all the normal exercises – leg curls, extensions, squats, etc. Could it be my diet? I eat as much salad as I can, along with tuna and steaks. Please help!

A. If you want size in your legs, lift heavy with compound exercises! Do fewer repetitions and use the heaviest poundages you can handle. Do supersets and giant sets. You should feel almost sick after leg training.

As far as your diet goes, you seem to be missing an important food type – carbohydrates! Salad is a great diet food, but to put on size you need protein combined with good complex carbs. Try adding carbs to your diet at least three times daily. Here are some good examples: potatoes, yams, oatmeal, rice, pasta, and beans. Make sure to eat at least five meals a day.

DO I NEED LIFTING STRAPS?

Q. Just how important are lifting straps in bodybuilding? I have friends who swear by them and friends who insist they're useless. Those who use them do not appear stronger or better built. I want to do every single thing I can to help my muscles grow, but I'm a bit lost. I see some guys with gloves and some without. Some who strap elbows and knees, and some who never do. I do wear a belt when training, but I'm not sure if I really should. Please help.

A. Bodybuilding, like any sport, will always attract people who buy all the latest clothing, trappings and accessories, whether useful or not. Remember, however, that if you are serious about getting those muscles to grow then you must never discount any innovation.

Common sense and intelligent trial and error must be your guide. Straps are definitely useful to the bodybuilder. They can help you maintain your grip when nursing an injury or when using heavy weight. They can also help you forget the grip and concentrate on form.

Try them out for yourself and see. Strapping an injured joint or using straps as a safety measure when going into heavy poundage is common sense.

Belts are a little different. While I advocate their use for the same two reasons – injury and heavy training – they can be overused and result in a weakening of the back. This can come about if you strap the belt on too tight and leave it on for the entire workout. To avoid a weaker lower back down the road, tighten your belt only for heavy work and loosen it or take it off for all other training.

THREE OR FOUR ROWS

Q. My workout buddy and I have good abs. John has four distinct rows of abdominal muscles above his navel, whereas I have only three. We have been arguing on and off as to whether my three sets are the more normal shape, or if his four are. I told him that his abs are deformed because his top row is divided. I bet him ten bucks that his four-ab set-up is so freakish that it is unique. What do you say?

A. Whereas your three sets of abs are the most common formation, there are lots of fours out there. They look especially good when ripped, so many bodybuilders who have the three or even two set-up wish they had the four. To be honest, while your abs are more common, his are far from freakish. You're going to have to hand over that ten!

CHEATING FOR SUCCESS

Q. I have been a reader of *MuscleMag International* for several years and have enjoyed all the articles, especially those by Greg Zulak, Dennis Weis, and yourself, Mr. Kennedy. My question involves the value of cheating when performing the various bodybuilding movements. After many years of bodybuilding I am still confused. Is it better to use loose form (cheating) when exercising, or will more muscle growth result from using a very strict exercise form?

A. I am glad you enjoy *MuscleMag*. As for your question, you should not think in terms of performing either a cheating workout or a strict workout. Rather you should adapt your chosen style to each selected exercise, bearing in mind of course that one can get results from a variety of training styles. Tailor your style to exhaust the area you are working in the most effective manner. You should also take into consideration your allotted workout time, your efficiency, energy levels and stage of development. Tune into your feelings, listen to your body's feedback and actively think out the effect you want to get from the exercise in question.

Age and condition have a lot to do with your decision. It would be madness to throw yourself into cheating lateral raises, for example, if you haven't worked your deltoids in months.

Champion bodybuilders use instinctive "creative cheating." Paying attention to their body's feedback is important. Before they start a set they know how they are going to approach it – heavy or light, strict or loose, fast or slow, to failure or not … it's all in the mind. Another option is to do a full set then use cheating to crank out a few more reps.

TO SIT UP OR NOT?

Q. Should I do sit-ups every day to keep my stomach flat? How many sets and reps would be enough?

A. I feel four times per week is plenty for training abs. With a proper (low-fat) diet and a good overall workout program this will be enough to keep your stomach area nice and tight. I recommend also including some type of leg raises in your abdominal training because they stress the lower abs a bit more. True sit-ups are not useful – you are probably referring to crunches.

WIDENING THE SHOULDERS

Q. I have narrow shoulders. I realize that I cannot widen my scapulae, but what in your opinion is the best exercise to make my delts look wider?

A. To look wider you must work on the side deltoid head. Lateral raises strongly work the side head if you keep your little finger higher than your thumb as you raise the dumbell. But I think the best shoulder broadener is the barbell upright row. To place emphasis on the side head, you must use a wide grip. Grasp the barbell with your hands 15 inches apart. Stand upright with your shoulders rounded, knees bent and the bar resting on the thighs. From this position, pull the bar up to your neck. Be sure not to hunch your shoulders. Keep them down or you will work the traps. You must keep the shoulders rounded and the elbows forward. Go for 4 sets of the following reps: 10, 8, 6, 15.

HIP REDUCTION

Q. I have been bodybuilding about 10 months and I have a problem. I can't reduce the size of my hips. My training partner tells me I shouldn't do heavy squats, but I love to squat. It's one of my favorite exercises.

A. No exercise acts as a fat emulsifier. Exercise builds muscle. It does not reduce it. Lack of exercise will cause muscle-tissue loss. To reduce hips that are too muscular-ly large you must cut out exercises that throw stress on the area, such as squats, half-squats, and leg presses. Instead, do exercises that throw stress on the legs and glutes: lunges, hack slides, sissy squats, Roman-chair squats and leg extensions. Your hip area might be too large because you are simply carrying too much fat. To solve this you must eat clean – plenty of lean meats and vegetables and whole grains. Let no junk food pass your lips.

ALL BODYPARTS HARD?

Q. Do professionals and top amateurs train all muscle groups equally hard all the time? When I try to follow the types of training routines so often seen in the magazines, I burn out after a few weeks.

A. The pros and world-class amateurs do not train all muscle groups equally hard all the time. The goal of bodybuilders should be perfect symmetry and proportions, and this takes some juggling when it comes to training the individual muscle groups. All top bodybuilders concentrate more energy on their bodyparts that do not grow as easily. Sometimes you might hear a pro say something like: "I'm training arms these days." This does not mean the pro is training only arms. It means he is specializing on his arms for six to eight weeks to bring them up relative to the other bodyparts. During this time he does maintenance training for the other muscle groups – just enough to maintain their size. I suggest you have something for every body part in your training but specialize on one area at a time. Focus most of your energy on the slower-growing muscle groups that give you trouble, and less on the muscle groups that grow easily.

GYNO

Q. I've got gyno, which I assume is because I have been using steroids for a couple of years. Is there any way to get rid of it without surgery?

A. Gynecomastia – feminization of the male breast – is a bitch isn't it? Excuse the pun unless you actually like having a pair of oh-so sensitive nipples protruding through your tank top.

This condition often disappears once you stop taking steroids. You may, however, have to wait about six months for the extra fatty tissue under your nipples to clear. The standard treatment for gyno is the anti-estrogen drug Nolvadex (Tamoxifen), 20 mg daily. Reducing your bodyfat level can help you clear up the condition. Surgical removal is the last resort but may be needed in cases where the patient is unresponsive to drug treatment.

MUSCLE SORENESS

Q. The day after a really good workout, my muscles are quite sore. Is this soreness good or bad? If it is bad, how can I prevent it and what should I do when it occurs?

A. If the soreness is so severe that you can hardly move, obviously this is not good. Besides being painful, it can inhibit your upcoming workouts. But a mild soreness is not bad, and champs claim that if you do not feel some soreness after a workout then you haven't worked the muscle hard enough to stimulate growth. Whether this is true or not is debatable.

The best way to rid muscles of the lactic-acid buildup that causes soreness is by doing light-weight, high-rep exercises to flood the muscles with blood and flush out the lactic acid. Massage is also useful in eliminating muscle soreness. If you are getting sore after every workout you might be overtraining, training too hard or getting insufficient nutrition.

TRAINING PARTNERS

Q. I have often read about the importance of training partners in bodybuilding, and also about the importance of increasing training intensity by reducing rest time between sets. How can you train with a partner and still reduce time between sets? Obviously you have to wait for your partner to finish his set before you can start yours, and that's about as fast as you can go, isn't it?

A. It isn't necessary to reduce time between sets to increase intensity. That's only one way to do it. You can superset, do pre-exhaust sets of super-high intensity, and you can have your training partner help you with forced reps and perhaps a few negatives. While you rest, he can do his pre-exhaust or superset. When doing this type of training, the length of time your partner takes to do his sets is hardly long enough to allow you to rest and recuperate for your sets. You wouldn't want to take less than 60-to-90 seconds' rest between his set and yours.

The whole idea of having a training partner is to train with greater intensity while using heavier weights. If you train too fast you must use much lighter weights and the cardiovascular system is brought into greater play. Decide what your priorities are: more size, via heavier weights and high intensity, or greater cardio fitness and reduced bodyfat, via light weights and fast sets.

HEAVY OR LIGHT?

Q. I'm pretty much a beginner, with three months of training. Should I be training heavy (reps in the 6-to-8 range) or lighter (reps in the 10-to-15 range) if my goal is to gain size and mass?

A. After a three-month break-in period you can start training heavy. The beginner must build a good foundation through heavy weights and strict form. Except for calves, forearms, and abs, I believe you should keep your reps in the 6-to-10 range. As you advance you can make good gains with lighter training, but build your base first.

TENDONITIS

Q. I am 17 years old and I have been lifting weights for almost two years. I have loved every minute of it except for a painful knee. My doctor said I have tendonitis. She gave me some advice on how to treat it, such as icing it

A good trainer is worth his weight in gold – as a spotter and as a coach.

and taking aspirin. I read that the best way to treat tendonitis is rest, so I haven't worked my legs lately. I am trying to search for the right exercise that will build the surrounding muscles in order to protect the infected joint. Is this the right thing to do?

My problem is that I can't find a leg exercise that doesn't put pressure on my knee. Can you help me? I don't want to give up bodybuilding – I've just started.

A. First of all, don't worry. With the right amount of exercise and rest you'll get rid of the tendonitis. Leg extensions are the best and safest exercise for you to start with. You must do this exercise and any other exercises with perfect technique. Bring your legs to the upper position, hold for a second, then slowly lower.

Control the movement. Never do fast, bouncing movements, and avoid overstretching.

Try other leg exercises, but if your tendonitis flares up, use only partial movements. For instance, try hack squats or leg presses using only half the range. This should strengthen the muscles gradually until you are able to do a more complete movement. Also, don't use too much resistance too soon.

STRENGTHENING THE LOWER BACK

Q. I have been lifting weights for a number of years and have strained my lower back several times. Could you please let me know which exercises will strengthen my lower back and prevent further injury to that area?

A. No problem! The lower back is susceptible to injury, especially when training heavy on basic exercises for the legs and back. Squats, deadlifts, bent-over rows, T-bar rows, and cable rowing are often the culprits, usually because of poor form or too much weight. If you squat or deadlift heavy, limit such workouts to no more than once a week. Do really heavy deadlifting no more than twice a month. To strengthen your lower back I recommend hyperextensions, 4 sets of 15 reps, or good mornings, 3 or 4 sets of 12 to 20 reps. On lower-back work never go to absolute failure, and never use really heavy weights. Try to get a nice pump, but never strain.

SQUATS ARE KING

Q. I have skinny legs and a small flat butt. What would be the best exercise to build up my legs and to fill out my glutes? Please advise me on sets and reps too.

A. That's an easy question to answer. Squats are the absolute best builder of legs and glutes for men and women. Try doing 4 sets of 10 to 15 reps, two or three times a week. Make your training progressive by regularly adding weight to the bar, working up to as heavy a weight as you can. I suggest bodyweight for 15 reps as a minimum goal. Leg presses and leg curls will also fill out the legs and glutes.

GETTING RID OF BODY HAIR

Q. How do bodybuilders get rid of body hair?

A. Most bodybuilders just shave their hair off. Get a pack of those disposable razor blades. Get in the shower and shave under the hot spray. As soon as one razor starts to pull and drag a bit, use a new one. Be careful though! Don't rush it. Don't try and shave your whole body in five minutes. Take your time or you'll nick yourself.

You can also use commercial hair removers such as Veet. Test a small area to see if you get an allergic reaction. If not, spread it over your arms, legs, chest and back if necessary; wait the amount of time it states on the bottle, get in the shower and rinse it off. This is a fast and convenient way to remove hair.

If you have the money, you can go to a salon and have your hair removed by waxing. But this is more costly (and painful) than shaving or using hair removers. One final tip: if you shave, do so three or four days before the contest. This gives small nicks, cuts and scratches a chance to heal.

OBLIQUES?

Q. It's always been my understanding that most bodybuilders want to have little if any obliques. But some do exercises that promote their growth. Where do you stand on this?

A. Obliques are only desirable if you have a small waist like Frank Zane. If you do not, you will ruin your taper by increasing their size.

CONFUSED – HEAVY WEIGHTS OR LIGHT?

Q. Should one use heavy, medium or light weights for a great body?

A. Opinions will always very. One thing's for sure; you can waste years of bodybuilding if you don't increase your weights. You have to push the poundage up, at least to a certain stage. Nubret and Arnold both reached 500-pound bench presses. I can also recall seeing Arnold deadlift 600 and cheat curl near 300. Every top bodybuilder alive can manage a 350-pound bench and squat considerably more. You simply must push for more weight during your earlier years in the sport to improve. Later you can moderate the weight used and learn to make the body "feel" it, even if it isn't heavy.

The best advice I can think of is try and make your workouts progressive from week to week, year to year. This does not always mean increasing poundage. You can do it by increasing sets, decreasing rest periods, improving style, concentrating on the action, using intensity techniques, adding reps, tensing and squeezing the muscles at the conclusion of each rep, and by adding resistance to the bar.

FOREARMS

Q. My forearms are so bad I am ashamed to wear a short-sleeve shirt. I have developed a pretty good chest and my upper arms are fair (16-1/4), but my forearms are long and skinny with virtually no development.

A. Many people have difficulty building forearms (and calves) because of insufficient cell allocation to that particular area. On the other hand, some thick-wristed naturals never need to do specific forearm work. Their forearms grow from regular exercises such as chins, rowing, curls, and pulley machines, all of which stimulate and work the forearms strongly.

People like you, with a long-wrist appearance and only a small amount of development near the crook of the elbow, should work their forearms regularly using the pre-exhaust system.

Try alternating wrist curls with overgrip chins, 4 sets each, your hands six inches apart, no rest between sets. Rest briefly and then alternate palms-up wrist curls with undergrip chins, 4 sets of each and no rest between sets.

CANCER

Q. I have heard that exercise can cure cancer. Is it true?

A. No! Exercise cannot cure cancer, but new findings indicate that regular vigorous exercise can drastically reduce your risk of getting cancer. Many studies show that people who do not exercise are 10 times more likely to get cancer than those who exercise vigorously.

According to noted cancer researcher, Dr. Ernst Van Asken, people who do not exercise run the risk of having their healthy cells turn into cancerous tissue. The regular eating of junk food and smoking of cigarettes and cigars intensifies this effect.

TRIPLE-DROP AND PYRAMIDING

Q. Please explain the triple-drop and pyramid training methods.

A. The triple-drop method is a system whereby weight is systematically decreased during a set to enable further repetitions to be achieved. Pyramid training involves increasing the weight each successive set and then decreasing the poundage each subsequent set. Both methods are used extensively by today's champs and many other bodybuilders worldwide.

HITTING THE TRAPS

Q. I have a long scraggly neck, no traps, and my clavicles angle up at about 30 degrees even when I try and force my shoulders down. I want to win all the top bodybuilding titles, so could you please give me the two best trap-building exercises in the book.

A. The two best trap exercises are high pulls from the floor and heavy shrugs. Your clavicle structure indicates that you are predominately ectomorphic. Bodybuilding will help you gain attractive muscular weight, but you will probably never win Mr. Olympia.

PRE-EXHAUST DETAILS

Q. I am currently using your pre-exhaust system and would like to know one thing. After you've done your isolation exercise could you use two combination movements in superset fashion, so as to hit the muscle at different angles?

A. No! Just use isolation sets to really tire the smaller muscle, and then follow immediately with only one set of a compound movement.

DOORWAY CHIN BARS

Q. Can you give me your thoughts on doorway chin bars? Are they safe?

A. Doorway chin bars unscrew to fit solidly between the uprights of any doorway. Pressure on the hard rubberized ends keeps the bar in place, not suction. If a bar is fitted properly it will hold a 300-pound man easily. The disadvantage is that the doorway chin bar is not suited for wide-grip chinning.

TRICEPS OUTER HEAD

Q. Please list some exercises for building the outer head of the triceps. The only equipment I have is a set of barbells and dumbells, an EZ-curl bar and an adjustable bench. Thanks for any help you can give me.

A. The best exercise for the outer head of the triceps is the supine triceps extension done with a light dumbell. Lie on your back on a bench and hold a single dumbell at arm's length with your right hand. Now lower the weight slowly with your thumb facing downward until the top of the dumbell touches the left pectoral. Return to the straight-arm position without any bounce from the weight, as this can defeat the purpose of the exercise. This was a great favorite of the late Steve Reeves, who used the exercise extensively.

LOSE GUT WITH LEG RAISES?

Q. I need to lose my gut. How many leg raises should I do each day?

A. Leg raises are a great exercise for the abdominal muscle, and the hard-to-reach lower abs in particular. However, they will not help you get rid of your gut. To lose excess fat around your middle – or anywhere else, for that matter, you have to eat clean and do some cardio. Avoid junk food and eat six nutritious meals each day.

TOO MUCH SUGAR

Q. I like to take sugar with my cereal at breakfast and also have it in my beverages. Is sugar so bad? I do not want to get fat.

A. The big problem with sugar is that we simply eat too much of it. Often we are unaware of just how much we eat. You may not realize it, but you're eating almost 50 percent sugar when sucrose is a number three ingredient in a box of cereal, corn syrup is a number five, or when honey is a number seven. It is beyond argument that sugar is a prime factor in tooth decay, and it is also the villain in hypoglycemia. Sugar is also accepted as contributing directly or indirectly to diabetes and heart disease. As a bodybuilder, sugar is your enemy. It has no nutritional value, yet it can cause obesity.

Read labels carefully. Look for sucrose substitutes such as corn syrup or corn sugar, and watch out for words that end in "ose" which indicates the presence of sugar. Keep clear of: soft drinks, cakes, cookies, candies, canned fruits, ice cream, jams, desserts, and syrups.

STUBBORN CALVES

Q. I have probably the worst set of calves in the world. I wouldn't dare wear shorts in public. Can you give me some tips or a routine that will help me build a decent set of calves?

A. Calves are the most difficult muscle to build, as far as I am concerned. Most people with outstanding calf development were blessed with great genes. That doesn't mean you can't make improvements to your skinny calves. It just means it will take a lot of time and hard work to bring them up to speed. The one tip that will help you most is this: Stretch.

Stretching is very important for complete calf development. Stretching will help facilitate muscle growth and increase circulation in the calves. Stretch both before and after a workout. Every set you do for calves should be followed by plenty of free-stretching movements using only your bodyweight. Here is a calf-specialization routine. Try this for four weeks. Then go back to a standard mass-building routine for your calves.

CALF-SPECIALIZATION ROUTINE

Calf stretching	(10 minutes)
Standing calf raises:	6 x 50/40/30/20/10/50
Seated calf raises:	3 x 6
Leg-press toe raises:	3 x 50/40/30
Donkey calf raises:	3 x 6
Stretching	(10 minutes)

OLD-SCHOOL CARDIO

Q. I have been training for three years now and I have made some great strides. I decided I'm ready to enter a bodybuilding competition. My friend has been in a couple of contests so I asked him to help put together a pre-contest training regimen for me. I can't understand why he put so much cardio in there! I told my friend this is a bodybuilding competition, not the Tour de France. I'm trying to look like Ronnie Coleman, not Lance Armstrong.

Now I find that most of today's top bodybuilders do two hours of cardio a day. I consider myself an old-school bodybuilder and I can't honestly see myself doing any cardio. I hate cardio. Can I get in good enough condition to win a bodybuilding contest without doing cardiovascular exercise?

A. So you consider yourself an old-school bodybuilder. That's cool. You might want to go out and rent *Pumping Iron*. I am sure if you are an old-school bodybuilder you have heard about *Pumping Iron*. Ask the guy at the Blockbuster counter for the bodybuilding movie set in the 1970s starring the Governator; Arnold Schwarzenegger. Anyway, in this movie Lou Ferrigno, at that time considered the largest of all bodybuilders, is getting ready for the Mr. Olympia. Lou does an extremely intense, heavy weight-training workout that I am sure an old-school bodybuilder like you would love. But if you listen carefully, you can hear Lou telling his trainer he is going to run a couple of miles. So the largest bodybuilder of the 1970s was doing cardio.

I don't know where you got the idea that old-school bodybuilders didn't do cardio. There is more to bodybuilding than training with heavy weights. So the answer to your question, "Can I get in good enough condition to win a show without doing cardio?" is a definite no. You have to drop the idea that bodybuilders who do cardio aren't hardcore. You know where you can see bodybuilders who don't do cardio? You can see them walking off the stage and going home after the top five in their class have been called out.

I don't know if you have noticed this, but the standards for bodybuilders have changed dramatically over the past 30 years. Having the biggest biceps won't guarantee victory. You have to come into a contest big, symmetrical and shredded, with nearly transparent skin, or you can forget about winning anything. If you want to be competitive you have to come in with ultra-low bodyfat. Cardio burns bodyfat. It's not rocket science.

I'm sure if you search long enough you can find a bodybuilder who says he doesn't have to do cardio, but such bodybuilders are as rare as two-dollar bills. Besides, many of these people who say they are genetically gifted are taking dangerous medications for thyroid or prescription fat-loss pills. I strongly suggest that you stay away from these medications and do it the old-school way: Do your cardio. If you're going to put all this time into your body then why not create the healthiest body you can? Doing these drugs would wreak havoc on your heart and central nervous system, so be smart.

SUPERSETS – TOO SEVERE?

Q. I have heard many bodybuilders state that they only use supersets prior to an important contest. They say supersets are too severe for the off-season and they would soon burn out. My question is, wouldn't supersets performed with less intensity during the off-season lead to shorter workouts while keeping the muscles growing?

A. You are assuming that the superset principle can be used moderately. But supersetting is by definition an intensity technique. The superset principle is not clearly defined. Some people superset chest and back, while others might superset two biceps exercises. The benefit of

supersetting is that it saves time. And obviously, when more work is done in a shorter period of time, the benefit is increased greatly, and so is the intensity.

If you always keep in mind that muscle-building gains come about from increased intensity (resulting in an increased blood flow – to pump up capillary size), as long as you provide the system with adequate nourishment and rest (to allow compensational growth to take place), you will not go wrong. No known exercise is "too severe," but you should use discretion on the number of sets performed. Too many sets can lead to overtraining and the resultant loss of muscle size.

VITAMIN C – HOW IMPORTANT?

Q. How important is vitamin C in the bodybuilder's diet?

A. I don't know if you could possibly single out any particular vitamin and stress its importance over another, because they are all important. But here are a few facts about vitamin C that might help you. Vitamin C is an antioxidant. One of its specific roles is promoting the formation of collagen, the single most important connective tissue protein in the body. Contrary to what I'm sure you have heard in the gym, the body also stores large amounts of vitamin C in the adrenal glands, where it is needed to aid in the production of the hormones epinephrine and norepinephrine.

MEDIUM-CHAIN TRIGLYCERIDES – MCTS

Q. What are medium-chain triglycerides?

A. Medium-chain triglycerides (MCTs) are special dietary nutrients derived from coconut oil. MCTs have been used for over 30 years in hospital nutrition. They contain over twice the energy of carbohydrates, but are absorbed and metabolized as easily as carbohydrates. Your red muscle fibers (back and legs) prefer MCTs as an energy source during exercise.

MCTs have been shown to reduce bodyfat, improve

the metabolism of carbohydrates and proteins, and enhance the absorption of essential elements like calcium and potassium. MCTs will give you extra energy during hard workouts and help you recover more quickly.

TOO SMALL A WAIST!

Q. My question may seem unusual. My waist area is definitely too small. I do not want to enter contests – I just want to look good on the beach. I have tried performing side bends with a dumbell in both hands, but my oblique muscles are not thickening up. Please do not doubt that my waist is too small; several friends have pointed it out to me. My waist measures 22 inches and my chest is 43.

A. I guess there's not much hope for Melvin Anthony or Dexter Jackson then, is there? At any rate, the obliques are not really worked when you use two dumbells. You may as well use none at all because you are balancing the weight when you use two. Try sidebends with one dumbell (3 sets of 30 reps). You will also find that if you train with heavy weights in basic movements like rows, squats and deadlifts, your waistline will balance up quickly. Besides, did you ever consider that your friends might actually be envious?

HOW MUCH PROTEIN?

Q. How much protein do you actually absorb at any one time? If I eat a steak with 100 grams of protein in it, how much do I really absorb and use? Is it better to take in slightly too much protein than not enough? What are the side effects of eating too much protein?

A. The amount of protein that you can digest and absorb (called bioavailability of the protein) is dependent on many factors, including the state of your digestive system and the type of protein eaten. For example, about 90 percent of high-grade animal protein is bioavailable; while some plant proteins, because they are poorly

digested and absorbed, may have a bioavailability of less than 50 percent. If you have diarrhea, then more of the protein will pass right through without being digested and absorbed.

By taking in a very large amount of protein all at once, you may overload your digestive system. It's best not to overdo protein consumption at any one meal. Most athletes who want to gain size will take their protein over several smaller meals rather than one or two larger ones – it's more efficient and you feel less bloated.

If you take 30 grams of a protein supplement, then you will likely digest and absorb about 25 grams. If you eat 100 grams of a high-protein food such as meat or fish then you are also getting 25 grams of protein. High-protein foods usually contain about 25 percent protein by weight.

MOTIVATION LEVELS

Q. What is the best way to motivate myself to lift weights? I can't go to a gym. Also – which amino acids are the best to take and when should I take them?

A. If you cannot find the reasons to motivate yourself to train, I can't do it for you. Set some goals for yourself and go after them. All bodybuilders are self-motivators. Something drives them into the gym, and makes them want to train harder. You have to get that "eye-of-the-tiger" desire.

The best amino acids are the complete amino-acid complexes. Taken with your meals and between meals they keep your blood-sugar levels elevated, keep you in a positive nitrogen balance, curb your craving for sweets, help build muscle, and burn fat. Try five with each meal and two every two hours between meals.

STICKING POINT

Q. I've come to a point where I just cannot seem to increase my workout poundages any more. I have been at a sticking point for over six months and my progress has stalled.

A. Adding weight is not the only method of adding resistance. Trying constantly to increase workout poundages leads to cheating, which limits muscle and strength growth. Try this trick. Do what I call one-and-a-halfs. Do a half rep followed by a full rep. This totals one rep. Do all your reps for every exercise in this manner. The secret is to do only 3 sets. Any more will lead to overtraining and a resulting loss of muscle tone and hormone depletion. I have found that bodybuilders always add exercises, sets, and reps when they stop improving. This never produces results. The real secret is to cut back on sets and use better form.

BETTER BICEPS

Q. I can't seem to make my biceps grow and respond. I haven't gained in six months. How can I make my biceps grow? I do barbell curls, dumbell curls and preacher curls, 3 sets of each of 10 reps.

A. Try doing 21s for increased arm size. Do 7 partial barbell curls, moving the bar halfway up. Next do 7 partial reps from the top, lowering halfway down. Next do 7 full reps. Your biceps should be pumped to the max and on fire! Try also to eat more – protein in particular. I recommend 30 grams of protein six times a day while on this biceps program. Also try taking five free-form amino acid tablets and five desiccated liver tabs every three hours. This will keep you in a positive nitrogen balance and your tissues will be saturated with protein.

OVERTONUS

Q. What exactly is overtonus? How is it caused?

A. Overtonus is a term rarely used these days, but in short it is a condition caused by too many sets, too many different exercises. The term used now is overtraining. This may cause muscle loss, hormone depletion, weakness, and a smoothed-out appearance. Other effects include an inability to produce a pump and general lassitude or weakness.

ENOUGH IS ENOUGH

Q. How do you tell when you have done enough sets, and how much of a pump should you aim for?

A. The right number of sets is the amount that produces maximum pump. To find out the right number of sets, exercise until you are pumped to the maximum. Then continue to exercise until you begin to lose some of your pump. At this point, refer to the number of sets, time tempo and repetitions required to achieve this effect. This is your personal exercise requirement level. When you lose your pump, you know you are doing too much. Next time do a little less.

EARLY-MORNING TRAINING

Q. The only time I can train is 6 a.m., before I go to work. How do I eat before this workout? A big meal is difficult at this time. Also, I wanted to know if my workouts can still be productive at this hour.

A. Better you than me, that's for sure! Seriously though, you're going to have to eat your large glycogen-loading meals the day before. These will fuel your early-morning workouts. Before your workout just eat something like fruit or an energy bar. You can also drink a couple of cups of coffee. You want energy to get through your workout, but not enough to make you puke after 3 sets.

As for productivity, sure your workouts can be productive at that hour. Whenever you can work out, do so.

JAZZING UP TUNA

Q. I hate tuna, but I want to eat it for its protein content. How do I get the stuff down?

A. Simple old bodybuilding trick, and I'm sure a lot of you out there have tried it: pineapple. Take a can of tuna and throw in a can of pineapple. (Make sure both are packed in water). The pineapple kills the dry tuna taste. Great protein, great carbs, no fat.

The best time
to train is
whatever
time you'll
actually go.

GOING FOR THE V

Q. Whenever I do T-bar rows and dumbell rows I can really feel my lats. When I do barbell rows, however, I can't seem to feel my lats at all. Do you have any idea what I'm doing wrong?

A. You might be using so much weight on your barbell rows that you're heaving and throwing the weight up rather than rowing it up strictly. Sometimes guys go so heavy that their bent-over rows look more like deadlifts. Try going lighter and concentrate on proper technique. Use a weight that allows at least 6 strict reps and then cheat out 2 or 3 extras at the end for more intensity.

LACKING LOWER TRICEPS

Q. I need to build more lower-triceps thickness, especially near the elbow. What's the best lower-triceps exercise you know of?

A. You should understand that you may have high triceps insertions and may be incapable of building much muscle mass near your elbows. Of course, you will never know unless you try. I think seated EZ-bar overhead extensions work the lower triceps more than the lying version; but one of the very best lower-triceps builders of all is the close-grip pushup. Place your hands together so they are almost touching and directly under your chest. For real lower-triceps work make your hands into fists. Now do as many pushups as you can. Do your reps slowly, feeling the lower-triceps work. Try 4 sets of max reps of close-grip "fist" pushups and see how much lower triceps you can build.

DIET – HOW IMPORTANT?

Q. Does diet play a big part in weight-training success? I'm asking this because I don't like taking all the supplements most bodybuilders take. Are they necessary? Also, what kind of diet should a beginner follow?

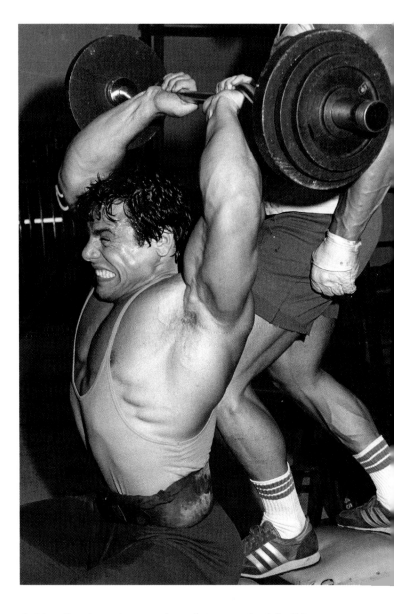

A. Yes, diet does play a major role in your bodybuilding program if you are trying for a muscular body. All experts agree that diet is responsible for at least 50 percent of your success in bodybuilding and most people who work in bodybuilding put the figure even higher. Jay Cutler and Larry Scott think it's more like 80 percent, especially when dieting for a contest.

Food supplements are not an absolute necessity, but most bodybuilders take supplements because results generally come a little faster and more easily with food supplements. This is especially true if you are underweight and need extra protein and calories in your diet. Then protein powders and weight-gain formulas really shine.

Generally speaking, you should try to eat low-fat protein sources such as fish, poultry, egg whites, skim or 1% milk, and some lean red meat. Fresh fruit and vegetables are a must. For starchy complex carbs try brown rice, yams, baked potatoes and some whole grains. Keep your fat intake as low as possible. If you wish to gain weight you will of course consume more calories daily than if you are overweight and needed to shed some pounds.

Most bodybuilders eat five or six small meals a day instead of three larger ones, as is traditionally done. This allows you to digest and assimilate your food better and keeps the blood sugar levels elevated throughout the day. Eating smaller, more frequent meals also keeps your muscles constantly supplied with nutrients.

TRAINING AROUND A LOWER-BACK INJURY

Q. I just received the bad news that I have to take a whole month off my weightlifting because of a minor lower-back injury. How much strength do you think I'll lose? How long it will take to regain that strength?

A. If you take a whole month off, you will probably lose about 30 percent of your strength, but you should regain most of that in a month or less. However, I do not suggest you take a complete layoff. With your doctor's okay, do some exercises that do not stress the lower back. This means mostly isolation exercises. For example, instead of shoulder presses for the delts, you might want to do light seated laterals, keeping the back straight and no cheating. For the arms, instead of the barbell curl, you might do seated dumbell curls with your back braced against a preacher bench or a wall. For legs, instead of squats, do light leg extensions and hack squats. For the chest, do light bench presses to the neck with no arch. For the lats, do lat pulldowns, which will help decompress the spine. For triceps, lying triceps extensions with an EZ-curl bar will not stress the lower back if you keep it flat. Use strict form with no cheating, arching, or throwing the weights around. You should

also do slightly higher reps than normal, say in the 15 to 20 range. If you follow these tips you shouldn't lose any of your muscle size or strength.

MUSCLE SIZE – HOW FAST?

Q. How fast can muscles grow? I want to get my body in shape as fast as possible. I do not want to wait 15 or 20 years to build up my body. How many pounds of muscle can I expect to gain each month?

A. The average bodybuilder, if he trains hard and eats well, can expect to average about one pound of weight gain per month (12 pounds a year). On the other hand, with a change up in training (change of diet, equipment, gym, atmosphere, training partner, etc.) some seemingly average bodybuilders have gained 12 pounds in a month! Needless to say, it all depends on whether you are a natural gainer, your training intensity, your diet, and your rest habits.

A bodybuilder with a positive attitude and personal goals who trains regularly and hard, eats five or six meals a day, takes the appropriate supplements and rests sufficiently between workouts is going to make far better gains than someone with infrequent workouts who misses breakfast, takes no supplements, plays tennis before his workout and goes to a club afterward.

ADDITIONAL ARM SIZE

Q. I weigh 225 pounds and have been weight training for about nine months. My best bench press is 300 pounds. My chest is 49 inches but my arms are only 17 inches. My triceps are good, but my biceps are flat. I work my arms hard, but I can't get them to grow beyond 17.

A. Eighteen-inch arms will come quickly for you with a "shock treatment." Do four alternating curls with 25-pound dumbells. Increase the weight five pounds each set until you can no longer curl. Now turn around, and work down the rack. No rest between sets, just shake your arms and take four deep breaths. Do no other biceps work, and work arms no more than three days a week. Also, no abdominal work of any kind. Take in some protein, amino acids or dessicated liver every two hours. In three weeks you will have that extra inch!

BREATHING

Q. I have heard varying opinions about whether or not to hold my breath during workouts. Should I or should I not? I'm confused.

A. It is impossible to give everything to the tough part of an exercise like squats without holding your breath. All heavy exercises involve holding the breath during the most difficult part of the movement, after which you immediately exhale.

There are many theories about breathing and exercises, but as long as you don't run into an oxygen debt there is no cause for alarm. In general, try to inhale and exhale for every rep of a given exercise. This is good for pacing and concentration, and ensures your body has adequate oxygen.

A DARKER, SAFER TAN

Q. What is the safest way to get a dark tan? I like the way I look with a dark tan, but with skin cancer and dry, aging skin, I'm concerned. How do bodybuilders always seem to have that dark glow, even in winter? I have seen ads on sprays, creams, and pills that you can take to give the skin color, but what's the story on these? What is safe and what is not?

A. First I should point out that most bodybuilders do not have year-round dark tans – they tan for shows and photo shoots. In the off-season and during the winter they have very little tan, if any. But you are right to be concerned about skin cancer from tanning in the sun.

While a little sun is okay, the safest way to achieve that dark look is to use tanning lotions. These allow you to get a tan without any exposure to ultraviolet rays.

Tanning beds are your next best bet, though their safety has also come into question. If you do tan in the sun, start slowly – say, 10 or 15 minutes a day – and then gradually build up. Make sure you use sunscreens to avoid burning.

WRIST PAIN

Q. I have recently started bodybuilding. After three months of workouts I have run into a problem with my wrists and forearms. It feels like my biceps can curl more than my wrists can hold. When I do any curling exercises, I get a pain in my wrists and in the tendons and ligaments of my forearms. This has forced me to stop curling.

A. The problem is that your wrists aren't able to take the strain while your biceps are. The solution is twofold. First, you can support your wrists with either a splint or supportive wraps, but only in your heavier sets. Next is to eventually become independent of any supports by concentrating on your wrist and forearm strength during every workout. Pick two or three exercises that give the wrists and forearms a good workout, such as wrist curls or reverse curls, but be sure that your wrists don't hurt regardless of which exercises you choose to do. If you feel pain, don't do that exercise – or modify it so that it still works the wrists and forearms but doesn't hurt.

SPLITTING THE PECS

Q. I want to know how to develop a split between my upper and lower pecs like some of the top bodybuilders have. Which exercises should I do?

A. A split between the pecs is not something that can be trained for. Just as some people cannot build peaked biceps or long, full calves, most people cannot build a deep split between the upper and lower pecs. The ability is strictly genetic. One of the best in this regard was former Mr. Olympia, Franco Columbu.

You will need to do specific exercises for the upper and

lower pecs – incline presses and flyes for upper pecs, and decline presses and flyes for lower pecs. Also, very important, you must have a low bodyfat level to show a split between the pecs. If you had this split it would be visible only without a layer of fat overtop. Build your pecs, lower your bodyfat and you may find that elusive split.

LACK OF ENDURANCE

Q. I like doing squats, but I get so out of breath after only a couple of reps that I'm unable to do a long enough set to work my legs. How can I train to improve my strength endurance?

A. You need to get into better cardiovascular shape. Besides running a few miles two or three times per week, try sprinting twice a week, either running or with a bicycle. Also, make sure that you breathe in and out with each repetition when you do your squats. Don't rush, but keep a steady rhythm when performing the exercise.

ABS – NOT EVERY DAY!

Q. If you work muscles hard and infrequently to build them up, and long, frequent workouts cause muscles to get smaller and tighter, then shouldn't I train abs every day for long sets?

A. As with any muscle, if you work abdominals every day you will lose them! They will smooth out and become bloated looking. Overtraining does not produce muscle tissue – it destroys it. Work your abdominals just as you would any other muscle.

FULL CANNONBALL-SIZED DELTS

Q. I want to build high deltoids that really look impressive when I do a double-biceps pose from the back. I have a friend with impressive shoulder width – his lateral deltoids stand out well from the side, but he doesn't have fully developed shoulders when viewed from the back. Please give me advice.

A. The exercises that contribute most to "high" deltoids when viewed from the back are the press behind the neck, the incline-bench press, and alternating front raises with dumbells. The muscle you admire is actually the frontal deltoid. Your friend must have spent more time on those deltoid exercises that give a longer look to the deltoid muscle.

TURNING CALVES INTO COWS!

Q. I don't have a calf machine at home, and I want to build really good lower legs. What do you advise? I live way out in the country, so I have to train at home.

A. Many bodybuilders train their calves without machines by doing such exercises as concentrated heel raises, single-leg calf raises and "burns." However, the greatest calf development has resulted from many, many sets of standing calf raises using a machine. The best non-apparatus exercise for building lower leg size is the donkey calf raise. Place your toes on a four-inch block of wood, bend over at the waist (supporting your body with your hands on a chair or bench), and have a heavy training partner sit on your lower back. Try to do no fewer than 20 reps and work up to the point where you are doing at least 8 sets three times a week.

FAT EMULSIFIERS

Q. I want to know if choline and inositol help the body lose fat. Also, I have heard that regular doses of cider vinegar, lecithin and kelp can help definition. Is this true?

A. This is a difficult question to answer. The medical profession tends to disagree with the usefulness of any of these ingredients as fat mobilizers. However, many bodybuilders swear by some or all of the above – especially when taken in conjunction with a low-calorie diet. The difficulty is in knowing which, if any, of the supplements work, and whether or not any increased definition is due to the supplements, or the low-calorie diet, or to both.

The answer would be more definite if some unbiased authority would arrange some strict controlled tests on bodybuilders.

TOO OLD!

Q. I am worried because I have just discovered the wonderful world of bodybuilding, but I think I may be too old to make progress. My doctor says I am fit and recommended that I take up weight training to gain bodyweight, but I am 26 years old.

A. Dear me! 26 years old! One foot in the grave … Now hear this, if you are in good physical health, you can make fine bodybuilding progress at twice your age! Granted the ideal age to start bodybuilding is the middle to late teens, but just because you're a touch older doesn't mean you can't make amazing progress. Just make sure you start right and don't waste your time on incorrect training methods.

TOO MUCH PROTEIN?

Q. I follow a high-protein diet, trying for 50 grams of protein, six times daily. My doctor tells me this is too much and that it will put a strain on my liver. How can I get the protein I need without harming my liver?

A. Try free-form amino acids, which go directly into the bloodstream. This places little or no strain on the liver, and you get all the protein you need.

CUTTING THE PECS

Q. I am a loyal reader of *MuscleMag International* and really enjoy it, and I hope you can help me. I have been working out for over a year and have a big chest but can't seem to get my pectoral muscles tight or cut. I do a lot of decline and incline presses and flyes, but to no avail. I am big, but not hard and tight. I would appreciate it if you could give me a few pointers.

A. If you are big but not cut, you are carrying too much bodyfat everywhere, not just in the pecs. You must lose some fat. Cut back on your calories. Your chest will be smaller, but cut and better shaped. Eat only good, nutritious foods, no junk. As for exercises, I recommend that you do more isolation exercises for your pecs, as well as trying supersets. For example, try decline presses superset with decline flyes, incline presses superset with incline flyes, or dips superset with dumbell pullovers.

STRETCH MARKS

Q. What is the cause of stretch marks and how can I get rid of them?

A. Stretch marks occur when your muscles grow faster than your skin. They also occur when individuals gain too much weight (usually fat), too quickly. It has also been suggested that poor nutrition causes the skin to lose its elasticity, and therefore it doesn't stretch when the underlying muscle grows. The most common spots are the chest and delts, particularly the pec-delt tie-in. Many authorities suggest that a lack of minerals, such as manganese, contribute to the condition. Once you get stretch marks it's virtually impossible to get rid of them. You can reduce the chances of developing new ones by supplementing your diet with manganese and a good vitamin-mineral tablet. Also, take extra vitamins A and E. Finally, some bodybuilders have found that vitamin E-rich creams help alleviate already existing stretch marks, but the effect is minimal.

HERNIA

Q. I think I am developing a hernia. It hurts when I do squats and other leg and ab exercises. Can I correct this problem through exercise? What should I do?

A. The first thing you should do is see your doctor and determine if you indeed have a hernia. You can prevent a hernia by strengthening the abdominal wall, but once you have one only surgery can correct it. The condition is aggravated by intrathoracic pressure (holding your breath and straining). Do all your leg work sitting or lying on your back. Make sure you have no downward pressure.

MASSIVE LEGS

Q. I would like to know how to get massive leg size like Jay Cutler. I was wondering if a person can diet, train hard and compete successfully without strong genetic potential?

A. Just as there's no real substitute for a "winning hand" dealt by genetics, there's no substitute for the basic squat when it comes to quad growth. Whatever exercises you do for thighs – and you should be doing at least two exercises for size and one for shape – base them around the squat. Work up to 6 to 8 sets of 10 to 20 reps in the squat before performing your shaping exercises. Treat the lower leg the same and do at least three exercises (with different foot placements) for the calves. Base your calf workout around the standing calf raise.

BUILDING THE INNERS

Q. I have two questions for you. One, how do you build up the inner-thigh area, and two, will leg extensions hamper my squat strength?

A. On the first question, all you have to do is perform all your squats, leg presses and hacks with your feet wide apart. Be sure to point your toes outward and go all the way down.

As for question number two, who knows for sure? I've always done both in my leg workout, whether on the same leg day or consecutive leg days. As a bodybuilder you should aim for total development, and this means hitting the muscles from all angles. Leg extensions might hinder achievement of a one-rep lift record on the squat, but is this what you're after? I advise going for the maximum effect, and hitting the muscle with as many different exercises as possible.

SIDE DELTS

Q. It seems that I can't get my side and rear delts to grow with regular standing laterals and rear laterals. Do you recommend any exercise that works not only the side and rear head, but also the tie-in between both heads?

A. I have just the exercise to meet your needs. It's the lying one-arm lateral. You can do it either lying on the floor or off a bench. The important thing is to lie on your side and to lift the dumbell smoothly and strictly with delt power alone. Keep a slight bend in your elbow as you lower the dumbell in front of your body. To take advantage of negative resistance, lower slowly and with great control. Never allow the dumbell to rest or touch the floor – keep constant tension on the delt. Keeping the little finger higher than the thumb at the top position will work the side head, the rear head and the tie-in. This was Serge Nubret's favorite delt exercise and he had superb side and rear delts. Keep the reps in the 10-to-15 range and do at least 4 sets every delt workout. And by the way, if you lower the dumbell along the body you work mostly the side head. Lower behind the body and you hit mostly the front head, with some side head and tie-in involvement.

UPSET STOMACH

Q. Every time I take vitamins I get an upset stomach. Help!

A. The cause could be the brand of vitamins, the time of day you take them, or whether or not you've eaten. Experiment with all of these variables and I'm sure you will find a plan that works. If not, you might want to see your doctor, especially if you have allergies or are taking prescription medicine.

MORE ON TRAINING TIME

Q. I've always wondered if there was a specific time of day to train for better and faster bodybuilding results. In all your years of experience have you found that any particular time of day is better than all others for fast and superior results?

A. From the time one rises in the morning, energy levels build. so that by midafternoon, between 3:30 and 6:00 p.m., they are supposed to be at their peak. This energy level depends on a person's habits, the amount of sleep he or she gets, and how well his or her diet meets the demands of the body.

However, not everyone is in a position to train at four in the afternoon, regardlees of energy levels. Besides, this energy peak can be disturbed by other frustrating or emotional factors, which exact their toll on a person during the day. Therefore, there is no particular hour better suited to training than the next. Make adjustments and fit your training schedule into whatever hours are available. By far the most important thing is that you train consistently, so the ideal time is whichever time you will actually go.

STARTING OVER

Q. My interest in training with weights started at age 17, and now that I'm finished having children I want to pursue bodybuilding. I need more information on fat-burning, supplements, and muscle-building.

Most of my mass is in the lower half, so I have to work harder to burn fat. Burning fat and building muscle at the same time seems contradictory. Could you please give me some advice? Thanks!

A. It is possible to burn fat and build muscle at the same time, but you must have a good solid plan that balances training with nutrition.

To burn fat you need to follow a low-fat, moderate-carbohydrate, high-protein diet. Try to eat at least every three hours, with your morning meals the largest, fol-

Serge Nubret performing his favorite delt exercise, the lying one-arm lateral.

lowed by decreasing meal sizes throughout the day. Take a multivitamin-mineral supplement with your meals. Also, drink at least eight glasses of water daily.

As for your training, work out with weights four or five times a week, training two bodyparts each session. Add some sort of aerobic exercise five or six times a week (45 minutes for maximum results). I recommend separating your weight training and aerobics because if your total exercise session goes over 90 minutes, you will probably start losing muscle instead of fat. All the best and good luck!

HOW MANY CALORIES?

Q. I'm a beginning (female) bodybuilder who needs to lose weight. Every article I've read says you need to eat 6,000 or even 7,000 calories to build muscle mass, but I need to lose fat. Is it possible to do both at the same time, or do I have to lose fat, then build the muscle mass?

A. Those articles do not apply to you or most any other women. To build muscle you do need to eat plenty of protein (approximately one to one-and-a-half grams per pound of bodyweight per day), but the number of calories should probably range from a minimum of 1,600 to a maximum of 2,500, depending on your current weight and metabolism.

Don't think in terms of just losing weight. Replace excess bodyfat with good solid muscle tissue. When this happens you are leaner, but your actual bodyweight may not go down because fat takes up far more volume than muscle, pound for pound. Finally, while you need cardio for health and to help lose bodyfat, don't make the common mistake of doing hour upon hour of cardio – especially if you aren't eating enough. This makes you lose weight but you may still appear fat, because you will have lost some muscle. Eat right and train right for sculpting a lean, tight body.

Photo of Lou Joseph by Jason Breeze

16 AND NEEDS HELP!

Q. I am a 16-year old beginner in bodybuilding. I have been training for four and a half weeks with no results. Please recommend a good training program for me, along with the max amount of time I should spend in the gym. I would appreciate it if you would recommend my daily calorie intake. Thank you very much for your help.

A. I'm going to answer this letter not just for the individual but for every beginning bodybuilder out there. You see, today's kids who are in the gym are not getting the right picture. They want it all, they want it now, and they don't want to sweat a drop to get it! Come on dude, I've taken longer layoffs than four weeks. In a month I might train a bodypart only four times. How can you expect anything to happen in a month?

Now let's get a grip on reality here. I want to see some honest blood, sweat and tears in the gym. Barbells, dumbells, clanging plates, rock and roll cranking loud, and sounds of pain and groans throughout the concrete walls. Do all that and then talk to me in a year.

HIGH REPS OR LOW REPS

Q. I am confused about how many repetitions I should do. Some guys at the gym say never do more than 10 reps on any given set, or you will be overtraining. What do you recommend?

A. So you are looking for the magic number of repetitions? I searched for years, and to be honest with you, I am not sure I have the answer. What I do know is this: Each muscle is composed of two different types of muscle fiber: fast twitch and slow twitch. Fast twitch is identified as the explosive type, and responds best to lower reps, while slow twitch are defined as the endurance muscles, which respond best to higher reps. Logically, what follows is that to thoroughly train the total muscle you should incorporate both high and low reps in your sets. The following is a good rep sequence based on a 4-sets-per-exercise routine.

Set 1 – 12 reps with a medium weight
Set 2 – 8 reps with a heavier weight
Set 3 – 4 to 6 reps with your heaviest weight
Set 4 – 15 to 20 reps with your lightest weight

LACKS DEFINITION

Q. I don't know what to do. I'm 16 years old, 5'9" and weigh 195 pounds. I train on a three-days-on/one-day-off routine. While I've built my share of mass, I lack definition. My problem areas are my abs, thighs, and obliques. Could you suggest a few exercises and a diet I could follow?

A. You likely need to lose 15 to 20 pounds. You didn't list your training routine, so I can't make any recommendations there. Keep your sets per bodypart to 12 or under for major muscle groups, and 8 or fewer for minor ones. Keep your reps from 6 to 12 for upper-body exercises, and 10 to 20 on lower-body exercises. Train abs, calves and forearms with higher reps.

I recommend that you start to do some cardio, such as jogging, biking, or classes. This will increase fat burning and also give your physique a harder appearance. As for your diet, cut down on your fat, salt, and sugar intake. Avoid packaged foods. Eat clean, five or six meals a day, and reduce your portions slightly. When you reach the point that your abs are hard and defined, no doubt the rest of your body will be the same.

JUST PLAIN SKINNY

Q. I am a just plain skinny 15-year-old. I cannot gain weight. I train like crazy, never missing workouts. My father says I am naturally skinny and that I'll never be really built. Please help me beat this thing.

A. If you are healthy, you will build up. You may never become a Mr. Olympia (few do!), but with hard, regular training you will get bigger and add muscle. At 15 years of age your male hormones are just kicking in. Look for good gains during the next few years. Train each bodypart twice weekly, three exercises per bodypart, 5 sets of 8 to 12 reps. Split your workout into two or three parts. Rest as much as possible when not training. Eat every couple of hours – meats, eggs, sweet potatoes, rice, fruit, yogurt, nuts, and don't forget the best gainer of all – milk!

STILL IN PAIN

Q. Two years ago I was really into lifting. I would exercise four days a week training different bodyparts but making sure I worked all major muscle groups.

I hurt my leg and had to have surgery. It has since healed and I have resumed training. Now my left elbow is giving me problems. No matter what the lift or weight it still gives me great pain. What do you suggest?

A. Any pain, whether from an old injury or from training, must be treated with care. Ease up on those exercises that cause pain in your elbow. If you find it still hurts after a good warmup, don't train. Rest that arm until the tendon or ligament is healed. If the pain continues to occur after six weeks, see your doctor. If you can train with slight pain, then applying ice packs to the elbow after workouts will help.

WHEN TO TRAIN

Q. I am wondering if training a different bodypart every day would be the answer to my problem of gaining muscle size. I have tried working the whole body on Mondays, Wednesdays, and Fridays, but I just didn't gain. I would appreciate your thoughts on this.

A. You are thinking about changing from training each bodypart three times a week to training each bodypart only once a week. Bodybuilding researchers have determined that in most cases our muscles grow best from two workouts a week. I suggest you split your routine in three parts and train three days on, one day off, or else split your workout in two and train four days a week. In both cases you will be exercising each bodypart twice a week.

BAREFOOT

Q. I heard that you recommend calf work be done barefoot. I have tried this on the standing calf machine at my gym, but my feet really hurt after the first few reps.

A. Yes I do recommend barefoot calf work, but only when the step of the calf machine is covered with a thick layer of hard rubber. You get more range and action when you train your lower legs with bare feet. In your case, however, wear proper exercise shoes; otherwise you could damage the arch of your foot. If you find that the stiffness of the sole hinders your range of motion, then undo the laces of your sneaker, and you will obtain both comfort and a full range of motion.

EXERCISE SEQUENCE

Q. Is it necessary follow a certain exercise sequence? I like to alternate my training routine, though I actually use just about the same exercises. On one day I may begin with a press, followed by a curl, etc. And the next day I will start by squatting or deadlifting, or even do some abdominal work first in the routine. In the end I still do all the exercises I am supposed to do, so what's the difference? A friend tells me that I would make better progress if I followed my exercises in a definite pattern every training day.

A. I personally do not subscribe to the idea that exercises must follow any specific pattern, although some do work better in a sequence. I am referring to leg exercises that should always be followed by some chest-expansion movements such as breathing pullovers. All other exercises can be used in whatever sequence you prefer.

The idea of proper exercise sequence, where you work the middle pecs before working the upper pecs or delts before the triceps has some popularity, but what if your upper pecs and triceps are the least responsive to training? Wouldn't it be better to work them early on?

Also, many bodybuilders find that training one group of muscles completely then moving on to another group has its limitations. The congestion associated with the first group often interferes with training the second. To get around this I do one or two exercises for one muscle group, and then work the antagonistic (opposite) muscles (i.e. biceps and triceps or chest and back).

Most bodybuilders find that training the small arm muscles first interferes with training the larger torso muscles. For this reason they leave the biceps, triceps, and forearms till last. Of course, if your arm muscles are woefully weak you will have to give them priority.

100 SETS

Q. I have a question that has been bothering me. From reading just about everything I can lay my hands on regarding bodybuilding, I have concluded that every exercise hits a muscle in a different way. Therefore, if someone did just one set of each exercise, but performed 60 to 100 different exercises, would this give more development all round?

A. Theoretically, yes. In practice, however, the first set doesn't seem to do the job of fully stimulating the deeper muscle fibers. Most bodybuilders find at least 3 sets of a given exercise is needed to fully work the muscle for overall size, and most prefer 5 sets (some even go to 8 sets). If anyone out there is using one set per exercise with a wide variety of movements, I would like to hear from them about their results. I will gladly print the information in *MuscleMag International.*

BODYBUILDING – BAD FOR THE BONES?

Q. I am 14 years old and have been bodybuilding for five months. My mother tells me weight training is bad for the bones and that it will stop my growth. Can you tell me if this is true?

A. There is no evidence to show that weight training, or indeed any form of vigorous exercise, adversely effects bone growth. This is a myth. Every time you pull or push yourself up on a piece of playground equipment, you are in effect training with weights.

Check with your doctor if you have any doubt. If you are in good health I am sure he or she will heartily approve your weight training.

FIVE-HOUR WORKOUT?

Q. I will be 15 soon. I have been lifting weights for just over a year, but I am not getting any bigger and I need help. I am trying a new method. I am lifting weights five hours every other day. I need to know what kind of foods I need to eat to gain weight.

A. Five hours' training every other day is too much. Cut it down to two hours. Eat a varied diet including fish, meat, vegetables, fruit, whole grains, nuts and milk. Many teenagers find difficulty gaining because their hormone levels don't kick in fully until their later teens.

NITROGEN BALANCE

Q. I keep reading the term nitrogen balance in the different magazines. What is this nitrogen balance?

A. When the body utilizes amino acids, nitrogen is liberated. Fat and carbohydrate contain no nitrogen. When amino acids are used for energy, nitrogen is passed in the urine. If you consumed no protein, 19 grams of protein each day could be catabolized from your muscles to supply your needs. Even if you were to consume 19 grams of protein, you would be in a negative nitrogen balance, because not every gram of protein has the necessary complement of amino acids. A large quantity of protein must be available to provide the body with the necessary balance of amino acids. Research has shown that the average person needs about 95 grams of protein a day to maintain a nitrogen balance. If enough protein is eaten to create a positive nitrogen balance, the excess will be deposited as new tissue (provided the body's muscles have been stimulated by some form of exercise). This will ensure that a growing muscle is well fed.

MILK INTOLERANCE

Q. I have been drinking a lot of milk to gain weight over the years, but in recent years it seems to cause loose bowels. I have tried milk that contains acidophilus, but it did not help. Is there anything I can buy to put in my milk to correct the problem?

A. A high percentage of people have this intolerance to milk. About 10 percent of the adult white population is lactose intolerant, and estimates run as high as 85 percent for other ethnic groups. The symptoms range from diarrhea, gas, distension, and abdominal pain to severe illness.

These individuals lack sufficient amounts of the enzyme in the small intestine that breaks down lactose, the disaccharide found in milk. Lactose cannot be absorbed into the bloodstream if it is not digested into simple sugars. As a consequence, the undigested milk sugar ferments, causing the previously mentioned problems.

Try a lactose-free milk. If this doesn't work, you may have to switch to rice, soy, hemp or almond milk. You may also find you have trouble with whey protein, but there are plenty of protein alternatives.

MORE THAN JUST THE BASICS

Q. I come from the old school of bodybuilding. I believe that to develop a top physique you just need the basics: squats, deadlifts, bench presses, etc. Why do you advocate so many isolation and sissy exercises, like sissy squats and side lateral raises?

A. As I glance through pages of various muscle magazines or look at the physiques of the competitors at the contests I attend, rarely do I see a body that I consider fully developed. Almost every bodypart has a weak area. This is because most bodybuilders don't know the proper exercise for bringing out the specific slow-developing portions of individual muscles (weak points). To be a good bodybuilder you must train for shape. The basics work only the belly of the muscle, but do nothing for the origins and insertions. If basics worked the entire muscle, we would have no need for exercises such as preacher curls for low biceps development, hack squats for lower thighs, lat pulldowns for lengthening the lats, dips for lower and outer pecs, cables for inner pecs, lateral raises for side delts, incline presses for high pecs, and incline side raises for rear delts. The point is, unless you do shaping exercises you will get big but you will not look good.

FAST OR SLOW?

Q. Should I do my reps at a fast pace (lighter weight, continued tension) or use heavy, paused reps? Personally, I feel that pausing between reps because the weight is too heavy is just another form of cheating. What's your opinion?

A. Both methods of performing reps have proved useful. Beginners should stick to one method for a few months until results slow or stop, at which point they should change it up.

The most important aspect of training is consistency, followed by constant efforts at making your training progressive (getting more reps or adding more weight without sacrificing style). Finally, you cannot expect to grow unless you are taking in plenty of wholesome food every day, plus getting adequate relaxation and sleep.

NEED MORE CHEST DEVELOPMENT

Q. I've got pretty good arms, which just seemed to arrive after six months of training. My delts, back, and legs are developing well too, but my chest is under par. I have a fairly deep rib cage, however. I do a lot of bench presses, especially with a wide grip. What am I doing wrong?

A. The bench press is a great chest exercise for some people, but it is not suitable for everyone. Although a deep ribcage is desirable, it is probably a factor in holding back your pectoral development. You are not getting the needed stretch in your pectorals because the bar cannot travel low enough to really work the chest muscles.

Fortunately, there are hundreds of chest exercises to choose from. Try narrowing your grip to a little more than shoulder width on presses. This will give your pectorals more stretch. If you have access to a cambered bar, give it a try. The bar's shape allows for a better stretch at the bottom of the bench-press movement.

Other fine chest exercises are: flat and incline dumbell presses and flyes, pec-deck machine flyes, and various cable-crossover movements. Do at least 10 sets for your pecs on chest day.

EGG WHITES

Q. Bodybuilders all seem to eat lots of egg whites in their diet. Why the whites and not the yolk?

A. For many years bodybuilders have realized that eggs are one of nature's most nearly perfect foods. They actually rate higher than any other food for protein bioavailability. In the past some bodybuilders have eaten as many as three-dozen eggs a day!

Egg whites are low in calories with zero fat but tons of protein. Egg whites have only 17 calories, compared to 75 calories for the whole egg. When attempting to get as ripped as possible you must reduce your consumption of fat, and eliminating the yolk is a quick and effective way to do so.

Egg whites may not appeal to you, but they are tasty scrambled with chopped onion and vegetables or eaten with salsa.

NATURAL SIZE

Q. I'm very skinny, and want to build big muscles without resorting to drugs. I am 19 years old and train hard on and off. I often feel tired after work and skip workouts, but I do like playing other sports like basketball. Can you help?

A. You have three main problems with your bodybuilding quest. One, you are young and probably have a fast metabolism, making it difficult for you to gain weight. Two, you skip workouts and do not train consistently. Three, you play other sports – they burn up precious calories, making it even harder for you to gain weight.

To get big you have to 1) Train big – that means hard, heavy, progressively and regularly on a proper routine. 2) Eat big – that means 5,000 to 6,000 calories a day, including at least one gram of protein per pound of bodyweight per day. 3) Limit the other sports you play unless you are willing to eat an additional 1,500 to 2,000 calories a day for all the calories you'll burn up.

A few key points: When I say 5,000 to 6,000 a day, I'm talking all good food – no junk food at all. You must eat: lean red meat, eggs, chicken, fish, baked potatoes, rice, beans, nuts, fruits, raw vegetables and milk. Eat no sugar, unhealthy fats, salt or processed food. You must eat this way every day until you obtain the size you desire.

As for training, lift two days on, one day off – half your body one day, the other half the next. Take a day off, and then repeat the cycle. Use two exercises per muscle group, doing 4 sets of 6 to 10 reps each.

LACK OF ENERGY

Q. Is there anything I can eat or take that will give me instant energy? I have the desire to train but lack the energy to do it. Should I go off junk food or cut down on my cigarettes? I drink heavily, but only on weekends. I am young (23) and need my fun!

Occasionally, I have a whole bunch of energy but when I train, this soon runs out. Any suggestions?

A. Some people simply have more energy than others. But in your case you are responsible for your own lack of energy. First, your weekend binges have got to stop. Heavy drinking for two or three days in a row can mess you up physically for several days. You will recover just in time to start partying again. Better to have one drink a day, every day of the week, than go crazy on the weekend. Junk foods will kill energy levels because most are loaded with refined sugar and other garbage your body has to work hard to remove. You need natural complex carbohydrates such as grains, fruits, and vegetables. They deliver a steady, long-lasting flow of energy-rich high-grade fuel to the system.

Finally, I'm shocked that you smoke. Few things kill energy more quickly and effectively than cigarettes. They leach your body of oxygen, vitamins and minerals. Cut them out completely – now. Don't even think about ever smoking again. It's old-fashioned, causes all sorts of diseases, and is a complete waste of money.

SHOULDER INJURY

Q. I had been doing straight-arm barbell pullovers (3 sets of 10 to 15 reps with 40 pounds) as part of my workout for about a month. While I was doing them recently I felt my shoulder pop out of place. It popped back, but I have stopped working out. Is this a common injury with this exercise? Is there some way I could avoid it in the future? How long should I wait until I start to work out again?

A. Your first step should be to get checked out by a sports physician to make sure the injury is not serious. If he gives you the okay to return to training, start back very light – say just an empty barbell. Do 2 sets of 25 to 30 reps and do the reps very slowly and smoothly. It's very important that you use no bouncing, jerking, or momentum in your reps. Add weight only when it is comfortable to do so. The way to avoid this injury in the future is to warm up well and avoid heavy weights. Instead of adding weight, try to do higher reps.

FOR SUPERIOR BACK DEVELOPMENT

Q. I've been bodybuilding for two years and have made great progress. I've studied anatomy and now have good knowledge about muscles. Even so, I can't figure out which exercise will benefit my back the most. I am big-boned and have naturally broad shoulders, so having a muscle-studded back would help my physique very much. I know how to develop the lats and the infraspinatus, but have held off developing the other muscles of my back. I would truly appreciate it if someone could help me.

A. If you have studied anatomy you should know that it's nearly impossible to work any of the back muscles independently. In fact, it's quite impossible for any muscle to function separately. Every muscle is dependent upon another in some way. Even biceps, which seem to be totally isolated, depend on the delts, forearms, and even the trapezius. The muscles of the back are even more closely associated and tied together, so it's impossi-

A back that stops traffic.

ble for you to work the rhomboids, teres muscles, lats, or infraspinatus separately. All back muscles work in unison when any back exercise is done, though you can emphasize one muscle over another.

In order to better work your back and obtain as much muscularity and size as you're capable of, include a variety of back exercises to activate all the muscles to varying degrees. As your back develops and improves, you will show greater mass and have the muscularity you desire. All this, however, takes time and patience.

FULL DELTS

Q. Recently I've gone on a deltoid binge. This makes me appear somewhat round-shouldered. My side and front delts are well built, but I need some magic advice to beef up the rear section.

A. The rear deltoid can be a little stubborn to build effectively, but with proper application you can bring about plenty of growth. The best exercise is the bent-over lateral raise. Sit on the edge of a bench with feet together. Lean forward so your chest and abdomen rest on your thighs. Raise two light dumbells out to the side, keeping this position. Try 4 sets of 10 repetitions. In addition, remember that all rowing movements work the rear delts to some extent.

HOW MANY EXERCISES PER BODYPART?

Q. How many exercises per bodypart do you suggest? I've been told that as many as five are necessary for full development. Can a bodypart be fully developed with only two or three exercises if you vary the exercises every few months?

Also, how do you avoid building the upper portion of the glutes? I think this gives a square, bulky look to the glutes. Is this a genetic factor, or from squatting? If it is from squats, can I avoid the problem by doing front squats or leg presses instead?

A. I think two or three exercises per muscle group can give a muscle good development. However, the longer you are in the sport the more quickly your body adapts to the stresses placed on it from training, and the more frequently you need to change exercises. In other words, the advanced bodybuilder needs more variety than the beginner or intermediate. Most top bodybuilders have a repertoire of five to seven exercises for each muscle group that they choose from – usually picking two to four exercises for each workout. The beginner should, of course, pick only one or two exercises per muscle group each workout, do 2 or 3 sets each, and not increase his

sets or number of exercises until his recuperative powers increase.

Now for your glute question. If you train naturally and your glutes are getting a square, blocky look from squats, the cause is probably genetic, although exercise style should be considered too. If you squat with a wide stance and/or in a bent-over powerlifter style, your glutes will get more stress than if you squat in a close-stanced, strict, upright style. Squatting on the Smith machine may help. And do leg exercises that don't stress the glutes: hack squats, sissy squats, lunges, and leg extensions.

LACKING THIGH SWEEP

Q. I have been doing all kinds of squats and leg presses for five years, but lack thigh sweep. Which exercise will stimulate outer-thigh growth?

A. Squats with the toes pointed straight ahead or even slightly in (and feet close together – 12 inches or less) are superior for thigh sweep. Leg presses with the feet close together and toes pointing straight are also very good. Probably the best exercise is the hack squat with toes pointed out. Also, try Smith-machine squats with the toes pointing both in and out – 3 to 5 sets each.

FOREARM

Q. My forearms are very skinny and weak. I just started bodybuilding three months ago and find that my grip is really poor. Sometimes my grip gives out before my biceps do. Is there any exercise that will improve my grip and build my forearms at the same time?

A. The best exercise you can use to improve your grip and build your forearms is the barbell wrist curl. Sit at the end of a flat bench holding a barbell as you would for a regular curl. Rest your forearms on your knees so your wrists and hands extend past the knees. Using wrist strength only, lower the barbell and then wrist curl it up. To build your grip even more, allow the barbell to roll

A bodybuilder doesn't look balanced without full leg development.

Photo of Erik Fankhouser by Alex Ardenti

Will Harris demonstrates his most-muscular pose – with a smile.

down so just your fingers hold it. Pull it back into the palm of your hand then wrist curl it up again. Wrist curls are a high-repetition exercise, so aim for 15 to 20 repetitions per set. This one really burns, but that's what you want. Four or 5 sets of 15 to 20 reps twice a week should improve your wrist strength and forearms greatly.

MUSCLE-BLASTING TECHNIQUES

Q. What muscle-blasting techniques do you advise during the off-season, and which ones should be used in the precontest phase?

A. Most top champs train heavy and basic in the off-season – straight, heavy sets on basic exercises, while always trying to handle heavier and heavier weights. The muscle-blasting techniques are saved for the precontest phase, or for specialization on a weak muscle group that isn't responding to regular training. Supersets, trisets, giant sets and other intensity techniques are too intense to be used year round and can lead to overtraining.

THE MOST-MUSCULAR POSE

Q. I'm 18 years old and have been training hard for two years. I have recently signed up for my first contest (a novice show, two months away), and have a question about posing. How do I do a most-muscular pose to look my best? I feel that I look good on most of the others. My double biceps from the front is the best, but I just don't feel right about the most muscular. It seems so awkward. Also, if it's not too much trouble – would you tell me what you consider to be the best color for posing trunks?

A. You should try to stay away from showing any weak areas. The same stage lighting that does wonders for a hard, well-prepared muscle will magnify faults. This is also true of facial expressions. A big smile and a confident look is a definite plus. However, you should learn to pose to display your physique to full advantage, so here

are some pointers on the most-muscular "crab" pose:

Start with one foot slightly forward. Flex your legs. Bring your arms out to your sides. Rolling your shoulders forward, flex your trapezius while rotating your wrists so your palms go downward. Flex your abdominals at the same time. Now bring both hands together in front of you, slowly flexing your pectorals, rippling your chest upward. Lock your fingers together and pull outwards, making your trapezius bulge. Hold your breath to bring out the veins. Don't lean too far forward or the shadow from the stage lights will darken the whole of your upper body. Common mistakes are to hold the hands too high or too low, or to have the elbows too close together. Remember to look forward and not down at yourself, and don't forget to smile. Check out photographs of the pros.

Remember the saying "practice makes perfect?" Get in front of the mirror every night between now and the contest. Rigging up two mirrors will help you see your back. A friend can help with the poses you cannot see – photos are also helpful.

As for the color of your trunks, who can say for sure? It depends on your skin, hair and eye color. High cut or low cut will depend on whether you have long or short legs in relation to your upper body. All I will say is get a good tan all over. Don't try any fancy carb-loading this first time out, and don't wear trunks that contrast too much with your skin color unless you have a small, well-muscled waist and great thighs. Good luck.

SHOULD I GO HEAVY?

Q. I have been bodybuilding for 18 months now, following a basic routine of presses, rows, bench presses, squats, curls, etc. My gains have recently come to a halt. I was wondering if I should train really heavy using 2 or 3 reps per set, or perhaps even do some singles. Thanks.

A. I guess every male bodybuilder has to have his fling using heavy weights, so you might as well get it out of

Photo of Will Harris by Jason Mathas

your system. But only use ultralow reps on multijoint exercises such as deadlifts, bench presses and squats. You will destroy your tendons and joints if you try to exceed your limit for poundages on lateral raises, dumbell curls, triceps extensions, and other single-joint, isolation exercises.

Injury often occurs when we use heavy weights, because in the effort to increase the poundage we move out of our normal exercise groove and bring about a tear or strain. Make sure to warm up thoroughly before making one- or two-rep attempts. Personally, when I performed singles in deadlifts, squats, presses behind the neck and bench presses, I found the practice greatly interfered with my recuperative powers. I was always totally drained the day after my workout. See how it goes for you.

FASTING TO CLEANSE

Q. I recently read an article on fasting, and I understand that fasting "cleanses" and "re-energizes" one's body. I'd like to try fasting, but I'm afraid of losing muscle mass! Do you think fasting is a bad idea for a "growing" bodybuilder? Have you ever tried it?

A. I've done a grapefruit fast for three days and I liked how I felt after the fast. I felt healthier and lighter, and my energy level increased. I did lose a few pounds from my weight, but I think it was just because I didn't have the usual amount of food in my stomach. I still have my muscles.

I wouldn't recommend any extreme fasting because you do need protein to keep your muscles, but a short two- or three-day vegetable juice or fruit fast is fine. Check at your local bookstore for books on fasting, and read how different fasts benefit your health.

DISTRACTIONS, DISTRACTIONS!

Q. I have a hard time keeping my concentration in the gym where I train, because all of my friends train there and we always end up talking. I don't feel like answering

them but that would be rude. How can I deal with this problem? Thanks.

A. I have run into the same problem at Gold's Gym in Venice. I love all the people there, but I have a hard time completing a set because someone always has to "tell me something quick." When your schedule is strict, as mine is, and your time is limited, it's important to get in and get out of the gym as quickly as possible while having a great workout. An iPod is great for such times. When they see your earbuds they will probably not try to talk to you. But if they do, the best thing is to be honest. Explain that you only have a little time to train and it's important that you get to finish your workout. Say: "You want me to win, don't you?" If you're not a competitor then just tell your friends you'll catch up with them later.

MORE ACHES AND PAINS

Q. I have been training for some time now, and continually have a problem with aches and pains in my elbow and knee areas. What do you think is the problem? Do you think I should lighten up my weights?

A. You have probably come to the correct conclusion that your pain is caused by heavy poundages. I have had similar pain in the past, especially around the time of a contest. My doctor explained to me the reason I have such pains is because the muscle surrounding the joint becomes very tense. Deep tissue massage is helpful because it releases the tension.

TORN PEC?

Q. I am a 16-year-old bodybuilder, and I have been training for about a year. When I started, I didn't have a clue which exercise builds which muscle. I soon found out that bench presses build the chest. Not knowing any different, I overtrained my chest, and now my left pec is developed nicely but my right pec has kind of a hole near the center, though the outside part is built.

Something I recently read gave me the impression that I have torn a tendon off the bone at the center of my chest. I also read that it can only be corrected through surgery. What do you think I should do?

A. It sure sounds as though you have torn your pectoral muscle. I'm not a doctor so I cannot say for sure, but I feel you should see a sports physician as soon as possible. It's important that you take care of it quickly, otherwise it will continue to develop in a deformed manner. Best of luck with fixing this.

TROUBLE WITH LEG CURLS

Q. I have trouble with leg curls because I have a weak back, and for some reason I just cannot avoid tension in that area when I use a regular leg-curl machine. I hope you can suggest something that would help me.

A. I'm glad you understand that it's wise to seek a change when an exercise feels awkward and causes the wrong kind of tension.

As you perform the exercise, make sure you hold on to the bench and keep your chest and shoulders on it to avoid excessive arching of the back. You could also see if the gym where you train has a seated or standing leg-curl machine. If nothing helps, try dumbell leg curls. Don't know what they are? Here's a description:

Have your partner place a light dumbell between your feet as you lie on a flat bench, with your knees at the end of the bench. Move your legs up and down slowly. Stop at the top of the movement as you feel the maximum contraction in your hamstrings, and squeeze your glutes, pressing your hips against the bench. Make sure the weight stays securely between your feet, and remain in complete control by holding the sides of the bench or extending your hands to the floor.

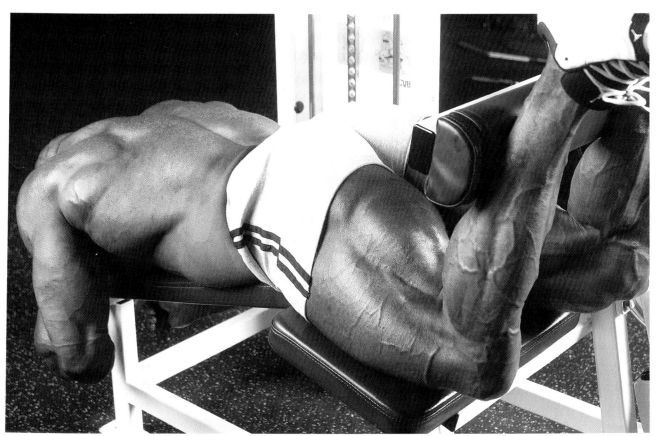

Photo of Bill Wilmore by Ralph DeHaan

Exercise Descriptions

Following are descriptions of the exercises I d[...]
throughout the book. Although I have tried t[...]
clear as possible, you may occasionally need [...]
with a more advanced bodybuilder or per[...]
er. Have him or her observe you for a coup[...]
to quickly correct any mistakes you might be [...]
ing. Finally, never perform an exercise if you are
unsure of the proper technique. Check its description in this book, a bodybuilding magazine, or with
someone at the gym.

near the center, though the outside part is built.

Something I recently read gave me the impression that I have torn a tendon off the bone at the center of my chest. I also read that it can only be corrected through surgery. What do you think I should do?

A. It sure sounds as though you have torn your pectoral muscle. I'm not a doctor so I cannot say for sure, but I feel you should see a sports physician as soon as possible. It's important that you take care of it quickly, otherwise it will continue to develop in a deformed manner. Best of luck with fixing this.

TROUBLE WITH LEG CURLS

Q. I have trouble with leg curls because I have a weak back, and for some reason I just cannot avoid tension in that area when I use a regular leg-curl machine. I hope you can suggest something that would help me.

A. I'm glad you understand that it's wise to seek a change when an exercise feels awkward and causes the wrong kind of tension.

As you perform the exercise, make sure you hold on to the bench and keep your chest and shoulders on it to avoid excessive arching of the back. You could also see if the gym where you train has a seated or standing leg-curl machine. If nothing helps, try dumbell leg curls. Don't know what they are? Here's a description:

Have your partner place a light dumbell between your feet as you lie on a flat bench, with your knees at the end of the bench. Move your legs up and down slowly. Stop at the top of the movement as you feel the maximum contraction in your hamstrings, and squeeze your glutes, pressing your hips against the bench. Make sure the weight stays securely between your feet, and remain in complete control by holding the sides of the bench or extending your hands to the floor.

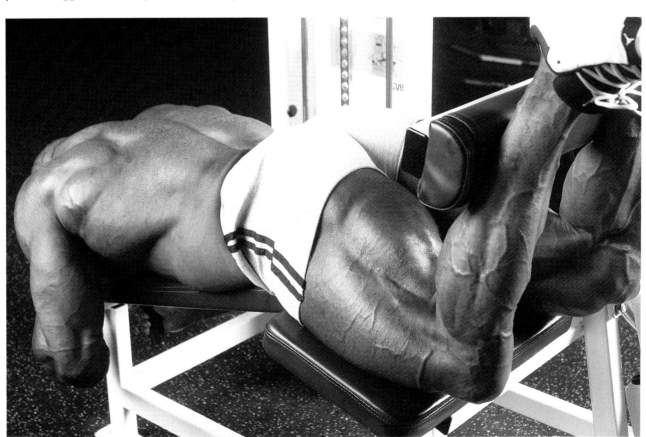

Photo of Bill Wilmore by Ralph DeHaan

APPENDIX II

Exercise Descriptions

ollowing are descriptions of the exercises I discuss throughout the book. Although I have tried to be as clear as possible, you may occasionally need to check with a more advanced bodybuilder or personal trainer. Have him or her observe you for a couple of sets to quickly correct any mistakes you might be making. Finally, never perform an exercise if you are unsure of the proper technique. Check its description in this book, a bodybuilding magazine, or with someone at the gym.

ABDOMINALS

Crunches

You will need a flat bench or chair to perform this exercise. Lie down on the floor and rest your calves on the bench. Adjust your distance from the bench so your thighs are perpendicular with the floor. Raise your shoulders, trying to bring your chest toward your knees. Face the ceiling throughout the movement.

Comments

Most bodybuilders consider crunches one of the best abdominal builders. At first you may want to perform the movement with your hands by your sides. As you get stronger, place your hands to the sides of your head – doing so adds the weight of the arms to your upper body, thus making the exercise more difficult.

Muscles Involved

Crunches primarily work the upper abs, but there is some lower-ab stimulation as well. The exercise also brings the hip flexors into play, although to a much lesser extent than sit-ups.

REVERSE CRUNCHES

Lie on your back, legs off the floor, legs up, toes at ceiling, knees bent. Keep your hands at your sides. Lift your butt off the floor, using only your abdominal muscles. Your pelvis should be aiming for your chest.

Comments

Make sure to use your abdominal muscles and not momentum from your legs. Keep legs bent.

Muscles Involved

Reverse crunches primarily work the lower abs, but the obliques, lower back, intercostals, and upper abs also come into play.

SWISS-BALL CRUNCHES

Sit down on the ball. Slowly walk your feet forward. Lie back so the ball is positioned in the natural curve of your

lower back. From here the movement is virtually identical to the floor crunch. With your hands behind your head, elbows pointing straight out and eyes focused on the ceiling, slowly crunch your torso toward your pelvis. Slowly return to the starting position so your torso is just below the horizontal.

Comments

The two primary advantages of ball crunches are that they allow you to exercise your abs through a slightly greater range of motion, and they force the other smaller muscles of the core to contract for stabilizing purposes.

Muscles Worked

Ball crunches primarily work the upper abs but the lower abs, obliques, lower back and intercostals are also active in this exercise.

BALL PASSES

Lie back on the floor and hold a small swiss or medicine ball between your feet. Slowly draw your knees toward your torso, and grab the ball with your hands. Bring the ball behind your head with straight arms and stretch the legs out to just short of lock out. Pass the ball back to your feet and repeat.

Comments

This is one of the toughest but most effective of all ab exercises. As with most abdominal exercises you'll want to watch your lower back as you stretch your legs out.

Muscles Worked

Ball passes work the entire abdominal area quite strongly.

MEDICINE-BALL TWISTS

Sit down on the floor with your legs out in front, a slight bend at the knees. Hold a medicine ball at your upper chest, and slowly lean back. Slowly twist to one side and then back to the center for a one-second pause. Twist to the other side and back to the center. Repeat.

Comments

To make this exercise more challenging, lift one foot off the ground. You could perform 15 to 20 reps and then switch legs, or you can alternate the feet every 4 or 5 reps. When lifting one foot becomes easy, try performing the exercise with both feet off the ground.

Muscles Worked

Medicine-ball twists work the upper and lower abs, as well as the intercostals and obliques.

LEG RAISES

For this exercise you can use the chin-up bar on the Universal multi-station or you can use a freestanding version. Jump up and grab the bar with both hands. Lift your legs up to the parallel position, keeping them slightly bent. Lower them slowly until they are once again in line with your upper body.

Comments

Some bodybuilders perform this movement with their knees locked. This places unwanted stress on the lower back. This can lead to problems down the road.

Don't swing your legs up and down. Doing so only defeats the purpose of the exercise. You want to lift the lower body using abdominal power, not momentum.

Muscles Worked

This exercise primarily works the lower abdominals, but the upper abdominals and hip flexors are also stimulated.

LYING LEG RAISES

Lie supine (face up) on a flat bench or slant board, and grab the bench or board behind your head. Lift your legs until they reach a vertical position, keeping your butt on the ground. Keep a slight bend in your knees. Pause a second and then slowly lower your legs. Try not to touch the board or bench at the bottom. This will keep the tension on the abdominals throughout the exercise.

Comments

Once again, don't perform the movement with straight legs. Also, resist the urge to use your upper body to pull your legs up. Use abdominal strength only. If using a slant board, start with it in the lowest position. As you get stronger you can increase the board's angle, thus making the exercise more difficult.

Muscles Worked

Upper abs and hip flexors are both active, but the primary muscle area is the lower abdominals.

ROMAN-CHAIR SIT-UPS

The Roman chair looks similar to a low incline bench, but it has a pair of foot supports at one end. Anchor your feet under the supports (they are usually round padded rollers) and lean back on the bench. Pause at the bottom and then return to the starting position. Try to use only your abdominals and not your hip flexors.

Comments

Roman-chair sit-ups are very effective for working the lower abdominal region. By bending and locking the legs, it's virtually impossible to cheat. If there's a disadvantage to this exercise it's the stress placed on the lower back. Many bodybuilders find arching the back in this manner very painful. Give these sit-ups a try and see how they feel. If you encounter any back pain, substitute one of the other abdominal exercises.

Muscles Worked

Roman-chair sit-ups primarily work the lower abdominal region, but the upper abs are also stimulated. Depending on your ratio of leg/upper-body length, you may find the hip flexors taking much of the strain. Only you can judge how effective the exercise is for the abdominals. If you feel your abs are doing little of the work, switch to another exercise.

ROPE CRUNCHES

Kneel down facing a pulldown machine and grab the attached rope. Bend forward so the rope is straddling your neck (i.e. one side of the rope touching each ear). With the knees and feet kept firmly on the ground, bend forward until your forehead is a couple of inches from the floor. Return to the starting position by raising the torso a foot to a foot-and-a-half from the floor.

Comments

This is one of the hardest exercises to master, because the body tries to cheat by rocking the torso up and down. Even with good technique, some individuals get nothing out of this exercise. Others find they have to tire the abs out first with another exercise before they derive any benefit from rope crunches.

Muscles Worked

Rope crunches work the entire abdominal region. The obliques, hip flexors, and serratus also come into play.

LEGS (QUADRICEPS)
SQUATS

Place the barbell on the squat rack, about shoulder height. Load with weight. Step under the bar and rest it across your traps and shoulders. Step back, away from the rack, and place your feet slightly less than shoulder width apart. Now in a slow and controlled manner bend your knees and descend toward the floor. Stop when your thighs are approximately parallel to the floor. Pause for a second and then return to the starting upright position.

Comments

Most trainers consider squats to be the king of the thigh builders. Done properly they will build you a phenomenal set of quadriceps. Done improperly they may put you in traction. Try to use a squat rack with "catchers." These are pins set to stop the bar if you get into trouble. If none are available, make sure you have one or two spotters watching you. In fact, spotters are always a good idea when squatting.

Always wear a belt when performing squats. Also, don't bounce at the top or bottom of the exercise. Remember you have a loaded barbell on your shoulders, which is putting a lot of stress on your spine. Keep control of the weight throughout the movement.

Rest the bar across your shoulders and traps, and not on the bony protrusion at the base of your skull. Rest the bar on the bones and you will need regular chiropractic visits.

Keep your stance shoulder width or less. The wider the stance the more glute involvement. (Powerlifters use a fairly wide stance because they need the tremendous power of the glutes to help in lifting such huge weights).

Muscles Worked

While primarily a quad builder, squats stimulate the whole leg region. Even with a narrow stance, the glutes do come into play. Also, your calves and hamstrings help stabilize your legs as you move up and down.

Though you may not think of them in regards to squats, the spinal erectors (lower-back muscles) are use to keep the body upright. In fact, they are often the weak link in the chain. Most injuries obtained while doing squats center around the lower-back region. This is why you must concentrate fully during this exercise.

SMITH-MACHINE SQUATS

Set the bar to a height just lower than your shoulders, and load it with the appropriate weight. Step underneath, release the catches at the side, and lower as you would for a barbell squat.

Comments

As with regular squats, don't bounce at the bottom of the exercise. Try experimenting with different foot positions – both wide and narrow and forward and back. The Smith machine allows foot positions that would be impossible with a regular barbell squat.

Muscles Worked

This exercise primarily works the quads and glutes, but the lower back, hamstrings, and calves also come into play.

LEG PRESSES

You will need a leg-press machine to perform this exercise. Sit in the seat and place your feet on the pressing board. The average foot placement is shoulder width, but you can vary this to focus the stimulation on different areas. Extend your legs until straight, pause, then bring them down until your knees touch your chest. Perform the movement in a slow, controlled manner.

Comments

Although leg presses don't offer the same degree of thigh development as squats do, they are a close second. Trainers with knee or back problems often find the leg press can adequately work the thighs without aggravating these areas.

As with squats, the wider the stance, the more glute involvement. By making a V with the feet (heels together, toes apart) you can do wonders for the difficult-to-reach teardrop area above the knee (vastus medialis).

Perhaps the greatest advantage of leg presses is the amount of weight you can use. Unlike squats, for which the lower back is a limiting factor, the leg press allows you to pile on hundreds of pounds of plates. It won't be long before you have six, seven, eight or more 45-pound plates on each side. Provided you do the exercise in good style, you can really let your ego go wild on this exercise. The lower back is virtually eliminated, and even the knees don't have huge stress placed on them.

One word of caution concerns hyperextending your legs. If you place your feet low on the pressing board, you risk locking the legs and forcing them into a hyperextended position at the knee joint. When performing the exercise, don't forcefully lock out your legs, as this may damage the knee's supporting connective tissues.

Muscles Worked

The design of the leg press means most of the stress is placed on the quads. There is very little glute involvement, and the spinal erectors are all but eliminated from the exercise. The calves and hamstrings play only a small role in stabilizing the legs.

HACK SQUATS

These days this exercise is almost always done on a hack-squat machine. Place your feet about shoulder width apart on the machine's inclined footboard. Place your shoulders under the pads, lift up and then slowly squat down until your thighs are parallel to the footboard. Using thigh power alone, return to the starting position.

Comments

As with the leg press and Smith-machine squat, you can play around with your foot placement to put stress on different parts of your thighs. With any type of squat, don't bounce at the bottom as this places tremendous strain on the knee ligaments.

Photo of Peter Putnam by Robert Reiff

This exercise can also be performed with a barbell. Stand with a loaded barbell behind you. Bend down, reach behind you, grasp the barbell and stand up.

Muscles Worked

Hack squats are commonly used to create the nice sweeping look to the outer-quad area (vastus lateralis). They also help you get that attractive "teardrop" (vastus medialis) just above the knee in the inner-quad area.

LEG EXTENSIONS

If you've ever had a sport's related knee injury, then this exercise should be familiar. Leg extensions are among the most common rehabilitation exercises. Sit on the machine's seat and place your feet under the padded rollers. Raise your legs to a locked position and squeeze your quads. Lower back to the starting position and repeat.

Comments

Many older gyms and home-gym apparatus have an area or separate machine that incorporates both the leg curl and leg extension. The same weight stack is used, but for leg extensions you sit on the end and use the lower rollers, while for leg curls you lie face down and use the upper rollers. Most modern gyms have separate machines for each exercise. If you have access to a leg extension that allows you to do the exercise lying on your back, take advantage of it You can't use the same amount of weight, but this is made up for by working the quads through a greater range of movement. The downside is that doing the exercise this way places some extra stress on your lower back.

Resist the tendency to drop the weight into the starting position. As with other exercises, at least 50 percent of the movement is the negative (lowering) phase of the exercise. For variety you can perform the exercise one leg at a time.

Muscles Worked

Extensions are great for building the muscles around the knee area. They're also a very effective physiotherapy exercise. Following knee surgery, most athletes are limited in the amount of direct leg exercise they can perform. Leg extensions are great for strengthening not only the muscles, but also the associated tendons and ligaments.

SISSY SQUATS

Place your feet in a V position. Leaning back, squat down until your thighs are at least parallel to the floor. If you have trouble holding your balance, grab a stationary upright for support. If you can do 15 to 20 reps with relative ease, hold a weight plate against the chest with your free hand. Don't let the name fool you! This one's tough.

Comments

You can also do this exercise with a dumbell held to your chest. Most bodybuilders find the plate more convenient, but it's personal preference. Don't get carried away with the amount of weight. Save the heavy poundages for your regular squats and leg presses.

Muscles Worked

Sissy squats are similar to hack squats, in that they will add a great sweep to your outer thighs. Although more isolated to quads than regular squats, sissy squats do involve the glutes to some degree.

LUNGES

Rest a barbell across your shoulders and slowly step far forward with your right leg, bending down until you have a 90-degree angle between the upper and lower legs. Try to keep a slight bend in the rear leg. Slowly return to the starting position and then step forward with your left leg. Repeat.

Comments

Adjust your stance so the knee of the forward leg doesn't go past the toes. Also, try not to bounce in and out of the exercise, as this places extra stress on the knees. For variety you can perform this exercise by holding two dumbells in your hands, but this limits the weight used.

Muscles Worked

As with squats, lunges primarily work the quads and glutes, but the hamstrings, lower back and calves play a stabilizing role.

LEGS (HAMSTRINGS)

LYING LEG CURLS

Lie down on the leg-curl machine with your feet placed under the round foot supports (often called rollers). Curl your foot toward your butt just as if you were curling your hand toward your shoulder. In fact, the hamstrings are referred to as the leg biceps. Pause at the top, and slowly lower the legs back to the starting position.

Comments

Three types of leg-curl machines are available. The most common is the lying leg curl, but your gym may also have a seated leg-curl machine – you sit and push the rollers down toward the floor. A third type of leg-curl machine allows you to stand up and work one leg at a time. This is similar to one-arm concentration curls for the biceps.

Just as you wouldn't do biceps curls in an awkward manner, leg curls must be performed in a slow, rhythmic style. No jerking or bouncing the weight, and try to avoid lifting your bum off the bench. If you have to raise your glutes, you're probably using too much weight.

Muscles Worked

Leg curls primarily work the hamstrings, although there is some calf involvement. The glutes and thighs come into play only to stabilize the legs during the exercise.

STANDING LEG CURLS

Position yourself in the machine with the knee of the working leg resting on the pad. With the supporting leg locked straight, curl the other leg upward to just short of the butt. Lower back until the leg is just short of lockout.

Comments

Standing leg curls can be considered the concentration curls of hamstring exercises. They offer the advantage of allowing you to devote full attention to each leg separately. The downside is that you have to support your bodyweight on one leg. For the average person this is no big deal, but for someone with knee or back problems it may be too stressful. Also, you have to feel comfortable with a substantial decrease in the weight you use.

Muscles Worked

Standing leg curls target all the muscles collectively known as the hamstrings. The glutes and calves play a secondary role.

SEATED LEG CURLS

Once again you'll need a special machine to do this exercise. Each seated leg-curl machine is different, and you may need to get some help from the staff of your gym to understand how yours works, but the basic movement is as follows: Adjust the weight stack pin to the desired place. Position your feet on top of the roller. You will likely have some knee pads to hold your upper legs in place. Lower these knee pads till your legs sit snug underneath. Curl your legs back until they are just short of touching the main frame underneath. Allow the legs to slowly return to the starting position just short of lockout.

Comments

The advantage of the seated over the lying leg curl is strictness. It's very easy to cheat on the lying leg curl, by throwing the butt up into the air or pulling with the arms. The seated leg curl, however, forces you to move the weight with just your hamstrings. As a word of caution, many seated leg curl machines allow the legs to go past the locked-out position, thus hyperextending at the knee joint. Always keep control of the weight on the way up, and don't let the legs straighten completely out.

Muscles Worked

Seated leg curls primarily work the hamstrings, but the glutes and calves also play a small role.

STIFF-LEG DEADLIFTS

Place an Olympic bar on the floor in front of a block of wood or on the end of a very sturdy flat bench. Stand on the block or bench and, with your legs slightly bent, grab the bar with a shoulder-width grip. Lift your torso to the standing position, pause for a second, and then bend forward until the plates are just short of touching the floor. Repeat.

Comments

Although the term "stiff-leg" is part of the name, keeping the legs completely locked can put excessive stress on the lower back. Always keep a slight bend at the knee. Also, never bounce, for the same reason. The lower-back ligaments receive enough abuse in life without you giving them another reason to act up.

Muscle Worked

Although the lower legs do not bend as in a traditional leg curl, the hamstring muscles do cross the hip joint and are thus stimulated by extension at the hip. The lower spinal erectors and glutes also come into play on this exercise.

CHEST
FLAT BARBELL BENCH PRESSES

Lie on your back on a bench and take the barbell from the supports, using a grip 6 to 8 inches wider than shoulder width. Lower the bar slowly to the nipple area and then press it back to the locked-out position.

Comments

King of the chest exercises, bench presses are performed by virtually every top bodybuilder. A few points to consider: Don't drop the bar and bounce it off the chest. Yes you can lift more weight this way, but you are robbing the exercise of its effectiveness. You also run the risk of breaking ribs or splitting your sternum. Then you have to worry about the pec-delt tie-in. Dropping the bar in a loose fashion increases the risk of tearing the area where your chest muscles connect to your shoulder muscles. To keep the exercise safe and effective, lower the weight in a slow, controlled manner, and then push it back to arms length.

Whether you lock the arms out or not is your

personal preference. Some bodybuilders find stopping just short of lockout keeps the tension on the muscles throughout the movement. Others find locking out feels more comfortable. There is no physiological reason to perform this exercise either one way or the other, so try both and see which one seems best for you.

Another point to consider: don't arch your back off the bench (called bridging). Once again you may increase your lift by a few pounds, but at what cost? Arching decreases the amount of pectoral stimulation, and it certainly is no benefit to your lower back.

If you have trouble keeping your back on the bench, perform the movement with your legs up in the air. You will not be able to use as much weight, but there is no way you can arch your back when in this position.

Muscles Worked

Flat bench presses primarily work the lower chest region, but the whole pectoral-deltoid area is stimulated. You will also find your triceps receiving a great deal of stimulation. Finally, the muscles of the back and forearm are indirectly used for stabilizing the upper body during the exercise.

INCLINE BARBELL PRESSES

If using an adjustable bench, set the bench to an angle of about 30 degrees. You perform incline benches in pretty much the same manner as flat benches. However, instead of lowering the bar to the nipple region, bring it down to the center of the chest, just under the chin.

Comments

Most bodybuilders find angles above 30 degrees place too much stress on the front delts and not enough on the upper pectorals, but whether this is the case for you depends on your own physiology. You may have to play around with the bench's angle to see what works best for you. If you don't have access to an adjustable bench, make do with the fixed version. In many cases these fixed benches are closer to 45 degrees, which is too steep for working the upper pecs. You may find that

slightly arching the back can shift most of the stress from the shoulders to the chest. But be careful; the lower back was not meant to be arched to any degree. A better solution is to raise one end of a flat bench. You can use a couple of pieces of wood, another bench, or a specially constructed wooden block (most gyms have these for performing bent-over rows) to prop up the flat bench.

Muscles Worked

The incline barbell press primarily works the upper pectorals. It also stresses the front delts and triceps. Most bodybuilders find inclines excellent for the pec-delt tie-ins. Remember, as you increase the angle, the stress shifts from the upper chest to the shoulders.

SMITH-MACHINE PRESSES

Flat, decline and incline Smith-machine presses are performed in much the same manner as regular barbell presses. They are great when you don't have a spotter.

Comments

For variety try lowering the bar to different areas of the chest, and different lifting tempos.

Muscles Worked

Depending on the angle, Smith presses work the lower, center and upper pecs, and the front shoulders and triceps.

FLAT DUMBELL PRESSES

This exercise is similar to the barbell version, but you use two dumbells instead. Start by sitting on a flat bench and cleaning (lifting) a pair of dumbells to your knees. Lie back on the bench, and with the dumbells pointing end to end (i.e. they form a straight line across your chest like a barbell) lower them to the sides of your chest. Pause at the bottom, and then press to arms' length.

Comments

One advantage of using dumbells is the greater range of motion at the bottom. A barbell can be lowered only to

the ribcage, whereas dumbells can be brought below the ribcage. This gives the chest muscles a greater stretch. But be careful not to stretch too far and stress your ligaments too much. Dumbell presses are helpful for times when you do not have a spotter, as you can drop them if you get into trouble.

Muscles Worked

Dumbell presses are great for developing the pec-delt tie-ins. If you squeeze the dumbells together at the top, you also work the inner pecs. And no matter how much you try to eliminate them, the triceps and shoulders will always be involved.

INCLINE DUMBELL PRESSES

This is the inclined version of the flat dumbell press. With the exception of the angle, the exercise is performed in the same manner.

Comments

Because you have to hoist the dumbells up higher to get them into starting position, it might be a good idea to obtain the help of a spotter for incline presses. Most bodybuilders lift one of the dumbells up, and have a partner pass the other one. If you can, have both dumbells passed to you.

Without sounding too repetitious, lower the dumbells slowly, and go for a full but controlled stretch at the bottom.

Muscles Worked

Incline dumbell presses are an excellent exercise for developing the upper chest. Because of the increased angle, they also hit the front deltoids. And like most chest exercises, there is some secondary triceps involvement. If your shoulders are taking too much of the weight, drop the bench angle a few degrees.

DIPS

One of the simplest but most effective of chest exercises. Most gyms have a set of parallel bars for doing dips. If your gym doesn't, you can make do with the Universal shoulder press. Start the exercise with your arms in a locked-out position. With your chin on your chest, lower your body down between the bars, pause, and push yourself back to arms' length.

Comments

Dips are considered by many to be one of the best chest exercises, if not *the* best. To keep the stress on the chest, lean forward and flare your elbows out to the side. If you keep your body vertical and your elbows in tight, the exercise becomes more of a triceps builder. As with other chest exercises, don't bounce at the bottom. Doing so places too much stress on the pec-delt tie-ins.

Muscles Worked

Dips primarily work the lower, outer chest. They produce that clean line under the pecs. They also stimulate the front delts and triceps. For this reason, dips are an excellent beginning exercise.

FLAT FLYES

Start this exercise in the same position as dumbell presses. Instead of holding the dumbells end to end, rotate your hands until the palms are facing and the dumbells are parallel with your body. With your elbows slightly bent, lower the dumbells out to your sides for a full stretch. Pause at the bottom, and then squeeze the dumbells up and together, over the center of the chest.

Comments

Flyes are more a stretching exercise than a mass-building movement. Still, with practice, you'll eventually be using considerable weight. Always lower the dumbells

in a controlled manner, no matter what the poundage. Drop them too fast and you'll rip the pec-delt tie-in. Treatment for such an injury is surgery and many months of rehabilitation.

Muscles Worked

Flyes work the whole chest region. Fully stretching at the bottom works the outer chest and squeezing together at the top develops the inner chest. This gives your chest that clean line up the middle. This exercise can strain the pec-delt tie-in area, so be careful at the bottom of the movement.

INCLINE FLYES

This is the same exercise as regular flyes, but you do them on an incline bench. Once again go for a full, slow stretch at the bottom.

Comments

As with incline dumbell presses, the incline bench dictates lifting the dumbells up higher, so you may need a partner to help you hoist the dumbells into position. In fact it's probably a good idea to have the dumbells passed to you, whether you can lift them or not. Jerking heavy dumbells from the floor puts a great deal of stress on the biceps and lower back. Better to be safe than macho.

Muscles Worked

Incline flyes put most of the stress on the upper pectorals. They also strongly affect your chest-delt tie-ins. Once again, squeezing the dumbells together at the top will work the inner, upper chest area.

DECLINE BARBELL PRESSES

Position a decline bench (you can also use the Roman chair) to bring the bar to the lower-chest area. Perform the reps in the same manner as flat and incline bench presses, bringing the bar to your lower chest.

Comments

Many gyms have decline benches with bar supports welded to the back of the bench. If the bench's angle is adjustable, vary the angle to get the maximum feel in your pectoral muscles. You can substitute dumbells for a barbell and get more stretch.

Muscles Worked

Decline presses are similar to dips in that they work the lower, outer chest region. They are a good substitute if you find your front delts doing most of the work during flat bench presses.

CABLE CROSSOVERS

Stand between the two cable uprights and grab an overhead pulley handle in each hand. Adopt a runner's stance (one leg forward and bent the other back and bent just slightly) and bring the handles forward and down so they meet about waist height. Return to the starting position, with your arms stretched out to the sides about head level. You can do this exercise from different cable heights to stress the muscle differently.

Comments

Proper technique is an absolute must. If you let your arms fly back too fast you run the risk of tearing the pec-delt tie-in. Also, to ease the stress on the shoulder joint, keep a slight bend in the elbows.

Muscles Worked

Cable crossovers are great for working the center of the chest. There is some front delt involvement as well.

PEC-DECK FLYES

Sit down on the machine's chair and grab the handles or rest your forearms on the pads, depending on the model of machine. Push your arms forward and together until the handles or pads are just about touching. Return to the starting position with the handles or pad positioned out to the sides or just behind the body.

Comments

Don't let your arms fly back too quickly. Doing so is a great way to tear your pectoral or deltoid muscles. Also, be concious of using as little arm power as possible. Think of the arms as nothing more than extensions of your chest muscles.

Muscles Worked

Pec-deck flyes are similar to cable crossovers in that they are great for hitting the inner chest. They also work the pec-deck tie-ins.

BACK EXERCISES
CHIN-UPS

You will need access to an overhead bar to perform this exercise. Most Universal multi-stations have one attached, but a wall-mounted version is just as good. For wide-grip chins, jump up and grab the bar with a grip about twice your shoulder width. Now pull yourself up and try to touch the bar with your chest. Lower back to the starting position in a controlled manner.

Comments

Chins are considered by most to be the best back-widening exercise. In fact bodybuilders of all levels make them the mainstay of their back routines. They give the individual that great V-shape. When doing the movement, try to pull with the large back muscles (latissimus dorsi), not the biceps and forearms. Don't drop back to the starting position in such a manner that you yank your arms out of the shoulder socket. Do the exercise nice and slow.

At first you will find it easier to do the exercise to the front. As you get stronger you can pull up so the bar is behind your head. There is little difference between the two. When you reach a point that you are doing 12 to 15 easy reps, attach a weight around your waist or hold a dumbell between your legs. This increases the resistance and keeps the muscles growing.

Muscles Worked

Chins primarily work the large latissimus muscles (lats). They also stress the smaller back muscles like the teres. Finally, the rear delts and biceps are brought into play.

Wide-grip chins are the most common and help the V-taper the most, however you should experiment with other grips to stress your muscles in different ways. Put a double-D grip over the chin bar and pull yourself up to stress the lower-lat area, though your biceps also do some extra work. Use Flex Straps on any chinning exercise to help take your biceps out of the equation.

LAT PULLDOWNS

All though not quite as effective as chins, pulldowns enable you to adjust the amount of weight. Chins force you to use your body weight, whereas the lat machine allows the user to select the desired poundage. Instead of pulling yourself up to an overhead bar, the bar is brought down to you. Take a wide grip (if doing wide-grip pulldowns) and sit on the attached seat, or kneel down on the floor. Now pull the bar down to the front, so the bar almost touches your chest. Pause at the bottom and squeeze your shoulder blades together. Return to the outstretched arm position.

Comments

Many people find chinning very difficult. Lat pulldowns help build up your chinning strength. Do as many chins as you can, and then finish the set with the heaviest pulldowns you can manage. Each back workout, try to get one more chin. Your lat pulldowns will build your strength and muscles, making chinning easier each time.

Again, a narrower grip places much of the stress on your biceps, and in fact many bodybuilders use narrow-grip pulldowns as a biceps exercise! As with chins, using Flex Straps is useful to help remove your biceps from the equation while still working lats from different angles.

Because you have to grip the bar, the muscles of the forearms get a good workout. In fact they may be the weak link in the chain, so keep them strong.

Muscles Worked

Lat pulldowns work the whole back region, from the large latissimus muscles, to the smaller teres, rhomboids, and rear deltoids. They also stress the biceps and forearms.

BENT-OVER BARBELL ROWS

Bend over at the waist so your upper body is just short of parallel to the floor. Grab a standard barbell and, using a wide grip, pull it up your abdomen. Keep an arch in your back. No rounding. Lower slowly and then repeat. Concentrate on using the upper back muscles and not your spinal erectors.

Comments

You must be especially careful on this exercise. First, make sure to keep a straight (arched) back. Second, any sudden bouncing or jerking will put great stress on your lower back. If you have to throw your lower back into it, you are using far too much weight. Not only is this dangerous, it's ineffective. Use a weight that allows strict style. The only part of the body that should move is the arms. Your upper body and legs should remain stationary. To get a full stretch, stand on some sort of low platform. Most gyms have specially constructed boxes for this purpose. The extra 10 to 12 inches of stretch will add greatly to the exercise's effectiveness.

As a final point, bend your knees slightly. This will help reduce the stress on your lower back.

Muscles Worked

This exercise is considered one of the best back-builders. It's particularly effective in producing thickness in the back. Besides the full array of back muscles, bent-over rows stress the biceps and forearms. Finally, because of the bent-over position, the exercise stresses the hamstrings and spinal erectors.

T-BAR ROWS

Your gym may have a T-bar machine in which you rest on a pad, leaning forward, and grab hold of a cross bar, or it may have a bar with one end bolted to the floor.

Either way, T-bars provide an effective alernative to barbell rows. Grab the cross bar and pull the plates up to the chest/abdominal region. Squeeze at the top and then lower back toward the floor. After your set, rest the bar on the floor or on its supports.

Comments

Once again don't bounce or jerk the weight up. Like barbell rows, T-bar rows place a great deal of stress on the lower back. Keep your upper body stationary, and lift the plates with only your back muscles and arms. If your gym does not have a specially designed T-bar, or machine, you can do the same movement with one end of a regular Olympic bar pinned in a corner. Check with the gym's management first, however. Rotating an Olympic bar on one end may damage the bar's sleeve/ball-bearing mechanism. If you are allowed to do the exercise, try to use an old bar. In fact your gym may have an old bar set aside just for this purpose.

Muscles Worked

T-bar rows work the same muscles as the regular barbell row. The lats, teres, rhomboids, rear delts, biceps, forearms, and lower back all come into play. Because of the assortment of muscles worked, both types of rows are excellent mass-builders.

Note: If you have lower back problems, you might want to avoid both barbell and T-bar rows. If you must do them, start off by using light weight. Gradually build up the poundage over time. Don't make the mistake of slapping on 45 pound plates from day one. This will come with time. Keep in mind that lower-back injuries often don't heal. You may have them for life. Therefore the emphasis should be on preventing them. In a manner of speaking, rows can be a double-edged sword. Done properly they will help strengthen the lower back, thus reducing the chances of future injuries. Done improperly they may be the cause of such an injury. So pay strict attention to your exercise style. Don't get carried away with the weight, and don't lift with the lower back.

SEATED PULLEY ROWS

You will need a cable machine to do this exercise. Grab the double-D pulley attachment, and sit down on the floor or associated board. With your legs slightly bent, pull your hands into your lower chest/upper abdomen. Pause for a second and squeeze the shoulder blades together. Now bend forward and stretch the arms out fully.

Comments

Experiment with the different attachments, and select the one that feels the most comfortable, or alternate different handles. Cable rows can also be performed on the lat pulldown machine. To get the full effect, lean back and pull the hands to the lower chest. The direction of force should be about 90 degrees to the body.

When doing the seated version, keep your legs slightly bent. Performing the exercise with straight legs won't do your lower back any good.

Bend forward slightly when pulling, to get a full stretch, but don't use your spinal erectors to do the work. Make sure to sit straight up and pull right into your abdomen. Many people use momentum and lower back for this exercise, and then wonder why they aren't seeing the results they desire. Of course, using the lower back also invites injury. This exercise creates interest in the back area if done correctly.

Muscles Worked

Like most back exercises, seated rows work the whole back region, and also stimulate the biceps and forearms. They are more a thickness movement than a width builder.

ONE-ARM DUMBELL ROWS

Instead of using a barbell or cable, you can do your rows using a dumbell. Bend over and grab a bench for support. Make sure your back is not rounded. Looking up helps. Place one leg behind the other, in a running-type stance. Grab a dumbell with the arm not being used for bracing. Stretch that arm down, pause at the bottom, and then pull the dumbell up until your arm is fully bent. The exercise is comparable to sawing wood.

Comments

One-arm rows are great because they allow you to brace your upper body. This is essential if you have a lower-back injury. Even though your biceps will be involved in the exercise, try to concentrate on using just your back muscles. Once again, no bouncing or jerking the weight. If you have to contort the body to lift the weight, the dumbell is too heavy.

STRAIGHT-ARM PUSHDOWNS

Stand two to three feet in front of the lat pulldown or triceps pushdown machine. Grab the attached bar with a shoulder-width grip. With your arms in a locked-out position, push the bar down to your thighs. Raise the bar back up until the moving plates are about an inch from the stationary plates.

Comments

Taller trainers may find the plates touch before they get a good stretch at the top of the exercise. One suggestion is to adopt a wide stance. The wider you spread your legs the lower you'll go to the floor. You can also try kneeling. Because of the virtual elimination of the biceps and forearms, you won't be able to use nearly as much weight as you can on a regular pulldown.

Muscles Worked

This is as pure a back exercise as you'll find. It is especially useful for hitting the upper and outer lats, just under the armpits. Straight-arm pushdowns make an excellent first exercise in a pre-exhaust superset.

DUMBELL PULLOVERS

Grab a dumbell and lie face up across a flat bench. With your hips dropped below bench height and arms kept nearly straight, lower the dumbell behind your head to a comfortable stretch. Return to the starting position with the dumbell positioned at arms' length above your chest.

Comments

Some people prefer doing this exercise while lying lengthways on the bench. Others prefer doing the movement with an EZ-curl bar. Try all three and see which works best for you.

Muscles Worked

Pullovers are one of those exercises that incorporate a large number of muscles. For some it's a great lat exercise, while others get a great chest stretch. The serratus and shoulders also play a role.

MACHINE PULLOVERS

Sit on the machine's chair and, depending on the model, either place your elbows behind the pad or grab the overhead bar. Push down in front of your body to the machine's maximum range of motion. Return to the overhead position.

Comments

At the risk of being hounded out of the bodybuilding hall of fame, I think machine pullovers are one of the few machine exercises that are actually better than the free-weight equivalent. With dumbells you get only about 90 degrees of motion before gravity starts interfering. But most pullover machines keep the tension on the lats for 150 degrees or more.

Muscles Worked

Machine pullovers are another great exercise to hit the back muscles without the biceps playing a major role. The serratus and shoulders play a minor role.

SHOULDER EXERCISES
BEHIND-THE-HEAD SHOULDER PRESSES

With a grip about six to eight inches wider than shoulder width, take a barbell from the rack. Lower the bar behind your head, stopping just short of your traps. Push the bar to arms' length and then repeat.

Comments

Don't bounce the bar off your neck. If you strike either of the top vertebrae (atlas and axis) you run the risk of nerve damage. Perform the exercise in a slow and controlled manner. You don't need a rack to position the bar, but cleaning a loaded bar to your shoulders, doing your reps, and then having to lower it back to the floor is very energy-consuming. After a few months it will be impossible. So use either the squat rack or, even better, the shoulder-press rack. Most gyms have a special seat with a vertical back support. Two long supports enable the user to position the bar behind the head. All you have to do is reach back and lift the bar from the racks. Once your reps are finished, it's a simple matter of placing the bar behind your head.

Finally, as with behind-the-head pulldowns, behind-the-head presses can play havoc with the rotator-cuff complex. At the first sign of shoulder problems, stop the movement and switch to the next exercise.

Muscles Worked

Behind-the-head presses work the entire shoulder region, particularly the front and side delts. They also stress, to a lesser degree, the rear delts and traps. Finally, as with most pressing movements, the triceps are brought into play.

FRONT MILITARY PRESSES

This exercise is performed in the same manner as behind-the-head presses, except instead of lowering the bar behind the head, you lower to the front. Bring the bar down until it just touches the upper chest. Once again, no bouncing, just smooth controlled reps.

Comments

Most bodybuilders find it more comfortable to lower the bar to the front. It also eliminates the risk of striking the head or neck. There is a tendency to arch when doing the exercise, so be careful. A slight arch to bring the bar to the upper chest is fine, but nothing excessive.

Photo of Jorge Bentancourt (Left) by Alex Ardenti and Leo Ingram (Right) by Paul Buceta

Muscles Worked

Front presses put most of the stress on the front and side delts. The rear delts and traps receive some stimulation, but not as they do with rear presses. The upper pectorals are worked if you lean back when doing the exercise.

DUMBELL PRESSES

Instead of performing your pressing movements with a barbell, grab two dumbells and hoist them to shoulder level. You can stand or sit when pressing the dumbells, but if standing, be careful not to excessively arch the lower back.

Comments

You can press both dumbells at the same time, or in an alternating fashion. As with the barbell version, be careful of the lower back. Try not to arch excessively, and don't drop the dumbells into the starting position.

Muscles Worked

This exercise stresses the whole deltoid region. Particular emphasis is placed on the front and side deltoids. There is some secondary trap and rear-deltoid involvement.

BARBELL SHRUGS

Grab a barbell using a shoulder-width grip. With your arms locked, lift the bar, trying to touch your shoulders against your ears. Squeeze at the top of the movement, and then lower the bar.

Comments

There are a number of variations to this exercise. Instead of lifting and lowering the bar in a straight line, you can lift the bar in a circular motion. Also, you're not limited to using a barbell for the exercise. Many bodybuilders find the Smith machine is more comfortable. Instead of taking the bar from the floor, you can have it set at any desired height, making it easier on your lower back. The Universal bench press can also be used for shrugs. (In fact serious body-builders are far more likley to use the machine for shrugs than bench presses.) Try to keep your arms, legs, and back straight throughout the movement. And watch the lower back!

Muscles Worked

Barbell shrugs are by far the best trapezius builder. Make them a regular part of your training and you will have traps that give the Incredible Hulk pause. Besides traps, your forearms, hamstrings, lower back and rear delts will be indirectly stimulated.

DUMBELL SHRUGS

This is simply a variation of the barbell version. Hold the dumbells about shoulder width apart and perform the movement like the barbell variety.

Comments

You can hold the dumbells parallel or pointed end to end. The choice is yours. If you hold them end to end, watch you don't bang them off your thighs. Try keeping them in front of the body and slide them up the front of the thighs.

Muscles Worked

Dumbell shrugs work the same muscles as the barbell version. Since you will be using less weight (you can generally lift more weight with one barbell than two dumbells) the lower back will not have the same strain placed on it. In fact I strongly recommend using dumbells if you have a pre-existing back problem.

UPRIGHT ROWS

Start the exercise by holding a barbell at arms' length in front of your thighs. Lift the bar up the front of the body, keeping your elbows flared to the sides. Squeeze the traps together at the top, and then lower into the starting position.

Comments

The muscles worked depends on the grip used. In general, any hand spacing five inches or less puts most of the stress on the traps. The wider the grip, the more the side deltoids come into play. In most of the routines throughout this book I suggest this as a trap-builder. But you can easily substitute for one of the delt exercises. Just remember to keep the grip wide when doing so.

If you have weak or injured wrists, you might want to think twice about performing this exercise. Upright rows place tremendous stress on the forearms and wrists. If you experience minor pain when doing the exercise, try wrapping the wrists with support bandages. This should enable you to complete your sets in comfort. Of course you're the only one who can determine if the pain is just a nuisance or representative of something more serious. If in doubt, skip the exercise.

As with barbell curls, upright rows give you the option of adding a few cheat reps at the end of the set. Limit such cheat reps to one or two. Don't make the mistake of cheating from rep one.

Muscles Worked

With a narrow grip, upright rows primarily work the traps, with some secondary deltoid stimulation. A wide grip (six inches or more) will shift the work to the side delts, with the traps now playing a secondary role. The forearms are worked no matter which grip you use.

DUMBELL LATERAL RAISES

You can perform this exercise seated or standing. Grab two dumbells and, with the elbows slightly bent, lift them to the sides of the body. As you lift the dumbells, gradually rotate the wrists so that the little finger points up – as if you are pouring a pitcher of milk.

Photo of Ahmad Ahmad by Alex Ardenti

Comments

To target the medial delts, keep your arms bent throughout this exercise. Lateral raises can be done to the front, side, or rear, to target the different deltoid heads. You can use a cable instead of dumbells, if you wish. Either version may be performed with one arm at a time, for some unilateral training.

Muscles Worked

You can use lateral raises to work any head of the deltoid muscle. Most intermediate bodybuilders use them for the side (medial) delts, as the front delts receive ample stimulation from various pressing movements. Side laterals will give your delts that half-melon look. There's not much you can do to widen the clavicles, but you can increase your shoulder width by adding inches to the side delts.

MACHINE SIDE RAISES

Sit down on the machine's chair and place your elbows on the inside of the rollers or pads and grab the handles (if applicable) with the palms facing inwards. Slowly raise the arms outward and upward until they are parallel with the floor. Slowly return to the starting position with the arms stopping a couple of inches from your sides.

Comments

Many bodybuilders prefer machine raises to dumbells, as dumbells place stress on the wrists and shoulder joints. Try not to raise the arms above parallel, as this only brings in the traps as well as adding extra stress to the rotator cuff.

Muscles Worked

Side machine raises primarily work the side shoulders but the front and rear shoulders as well as the traps, also come into play.

BENT-OVER LATERALS

This is the bent-over version of regular side laterals. By bending over, the stress is shifted from the side to the rear delts. You can do the exercise free standing, seated,

or with your head braced on a high bench. The latter is for those with lower back problems or individuals who have a tendency to swing the weight up.

Comments

Concentrate on lifting the dumbells with your rear delts and not your traps and lats. For variation try using a set of cables. You will have to grab the cable handles with your opposite hands, so the cables form an X in front of you. This exercise is popular with bodybuilders in the months leading up to a contest.

Muscles Worked

When performed properly, bent-over laterals primarily work the rear deltoids. There is, however, secondary triceps, trap and lat stimulation. If you're not sure what a fully developed rear deltoid looks like, take a look at a recent picture of Paul Dillett. His rear delts contain as much muscle mass as most bodybuilders' whole deltoid region.

FRONT DUMBELL RAISES

Grab two dumbells and with the palms facing the floor, and arms locked straight, slowly raise them to shoulder height (arms are parallel with the floor). Slowly return the dumbells to the hips.

Comments

There are a number of different variations of this exercise. Some people find it easier to keep the palms facing inwards or upwards. You can also lift the dumbells in an alternating fashion as opposed to both at the same time.

Muscles Worked

Front raises primarily work the front delts but the medial and rear delts and the biceps also receive secondary stimulation.

SMITH-MACHINE SHRUGS

With a shoulder-width grip, lift a bar from the support catches. Keeping your arms straight, lower the bar as far as the traps will allow. Shrug your shoulders as high as

Photo of Troy Brown by Ralph DeHaan

you can, trying to touch your ears with your shoulders. Pause, and then lower to the starting position.

Comments

Smith-machine shrugs are great for those with lower-back problems. Unlike a standard barbell, which has to be taken from the floor, the Smith machine allows you to start and finish the exercise at waist level.

Muscles Worked

As with barbell and dumbell shrugs, this exercise primarily works the trapezius muscle. It also places secondary stress on the delts and forearms.

REVERSE PEC-DECK FLYES

Sit down in the pec-deck machine, facing the backrest. Depending on the model, either grab the handles with your hands or place your elbows in front of the pads. Bring your arms back to a comfortable stretch, which for most people means having the elbows slightly behind the body, or the arms straight out to the sides (depending on the model). Return to the starting position.

Comments

The advantage of this exercise over bent-over laterals is that it puts little or no stress on the lower back. The machine also makes it a bit more difficult to swing and bounce the weight up with body momentum, something many people do on bent-over laterals.

Muscles Worked

Reverse pec-deck flyes primarily hit the rear delts, but the teres, rhomboids and traps also come into play.

TRICEPS EXERCISES
TRICEPS PUSHDOWNS

You will need to use the lat-pulldown machine for this exercise. Grab the bar with a narrow grip, anywhere from two to eight inches. With your elbows tight to your side, press the bar down to a locked-out position. Pause and squeeze the triceps at the bottom, and then return the bar to about chest height.

Comments

Take a false (thumbs above the bar) grip when performing triceps pushdowns, and resist the urge to flare the elbows out to the sides. If you have to swing to push the bar down, you are likely using too much weight.

Muscles Worked

Triceps pushdowns work the entire triceps region, especially the outer head.

ONE-ARM DUMBELL EXTENSIONS

Grasp a dumbell and extend it above your head. Keeping your upper arm stationary, lower the dumbell behind your head. Try to perform the movement in a slow rhythmic manner.

Comments

It's possible to work up to 75-pound dumbells or more, but keep in mind the elbow joints and associated tissues (ligaments, cartilage, and tendons) were not designed to support huge poundages. Never bounce the dumbell at the bottom (arms in the bent position) of the exercise. Try to place the emphasis on style rather than weight.

Muscles Worked

Although it works the whole triceps region, this exercise is great for the lower triceps.

TWO-ARM DUMBELL EXTENSIONS

Grab a single dumbell with both hands, thumbs forward, palms facing the ceiling. Slowly lower the dumbell behind your head to a comfortable stretch. Slowly return the dumbell to the starting position by locking the arms out straight.

Comments

As with the one-arm version, don't bounce the dumbell at the bottom of the exercise.

Muscles Worked

Two-arm dumbell extensions are virtually indentical to the one-arm version. They target the whole triceps muscle, particularly the long rear head.

LYING TRICEPS EXTENSIONS (SKULLCRUSHERS)

Place an EZ-curl bar on the end of a bench. Lie down on the bench so the bar is above your head. Now reach back and grab the bar and extend your arms. Keeping your elbows in close, lower the bar to your forehead. Extend the bar back to arms' length.

Comments

If you are wary about lowering the bar to your head, lower down behind your head and lightly touch the bench. Don't bounce the bar off the bench, but merely pause and then extend the arms. Try to keep the elbows in toward each other, tight to the body.

Muscles Worked

This is one of the main triceps mass-builders. It stresses the whole triceps, particularly the long rear head of the muscle. Lowering the bar behind your head brings the lower lats and upper chest into play. The exercise also works the intercostals, located just below the rib cage.

UPRIGHT DIPS

For this exercise, you use the same apparatus as when performing dips for the chest. With a few minor modifications, you can shift the strain from the chest to the triceps. For starters, keep the elbows tight against the body. Flaring them to the sides will work the chest. Also, unlike dips for the chest, where you bend forward, keep your body as vertical as possible. In fact some bodybuilders lean back slightly to get that extra degree of triceps stimulation.

Comments

As with most exercises that rely on lifting your bodyweight, you will eventually reach a point where you can bang out 12 to 15 reps with ease. To increase the resistance, hold a dumbell between your legs, or attach a plate to a special dipping chain. Before you know it you will be dipping with 50 to 100 extra pounds!

With regards to safety, be careful at the bottom of the movement. Although dips are an excellent triceps exercise, they also place much stress on the front delts, particular the pec-delt tie-in. Don't bounce at the bottom. Perform the exercise in a slow and controlled manner (you might want to write the phrase "in a slow and controlled manner" in black letters and post it to your bedroom wall.

Muscles Worked

Performed in an upright manner, dips place most of the strain on the long rear head of the triceps. Because of the weight used (minimum of your bodyweight) they also work the other two heads quite nicely. And even though you may attempt to eliminate other muscles from the exercise, the front delts and chest will take some of the stress. Once again this is fine. Compound exercises such as this help infinitely to add overall muscle mass.

BENCH DIPS

Place two benches about four feet apart. Rest the heels of the feet on one and the heels of the hands on another. Slowly lower your body down between the benches by bending at the elbows. Slowly return to the starting position so the arms are locked out straight.

Comments

As with upright bar dips, the key to this exercise is to keep the torso leaning back and elbows close to the sides. As soon as the torso tilts forward and the elbows flare out, the larger chest muscles take over. Also, be careful not to bounce at the bottom of the exercise, as this places excessive stress on the shoulder joint.

TRICEPS KICKBACKS

With your body braced on a bench and holding a dumbell, bend over and set your upper arm parallel with the floor. Extend your lower arm until your elbow is locked – in other words, your entire arm is parallel to the floor. Pause and squeeze at the top, and then lower back to the starting position.

Comments

Resist the urge to swing the dumbell up using body momentum. True, you can use more weight, but it won't give the same triceps development. Keep your upper arm locked against the side of your body. As with bent-over laterals, if you have trouble keeping stationary or have a weak lower back, place your free hand on a bench or other support.

Muscles Worked

Triceps kickbacks are great for giving the triceps that horseshoe look. They are especially useful for developing the long rear head of the triceps. They are a favourite exercise during the pre-contest months.

REVERSE PUSHDOWNS

This exercise is performed in the same manner as regular pushdowns. The main difference is that you grab the bar with your palms facing up. Keep your elbows locked against the side and extend (push) the bar downwards. Flex the triceps at the bottom, and then return to the starting position.

Comments

You won't be able to use as much weight in this version of pushdowns, so don't become alarmed if you have to drop the weight 20 to 30 pounds. This exercise is great for finishing the triceps off after a basic movement like lying triceps extensions or dips. Concentrate more on the feel than the weight used.

Muscles Worked

This is another great movement for the long rear head of the triceps. A couple of sets and you will feel your triceps burning from elbow to armpit!

ONE-ARM CABLE PUSHDOWNS

With your body in the standing, upright position, grab one of the upper cable handles. Push the handle down, lock out the arm at the bottom, and then return to the starting position.

Photo of Steve Fraiz Oer by Ralph DeHaan

Comments

You can do this exercise either palms up or palms down. You might want to reach across with your free hand and grab your shoulder on the same side that is being exercised. Besides the bracing effect, you have your free hand in a position to spot yourself on the last couple of reps. As with the reverse pushdowns, go for the burn rather than huge poundages.

Muscles Worked

This is another great finishing exercise for the triceps. A palms-up grip will place most of the stress on the rear triceps, whereas a palms-down grip will hit more of the side head.

NARROW PRESSES

Lie on your back on a flat bench with an Olympic bar or EZ-curl bar placed on the supports above you. Grab the bar with a narrow (shoulder-width or less) grip and lower it to mid chest. Push upwards as if doing a regular bench press.

Comments

You will need to experiment with different grip widths to find the one that maximizes triceps involvement and minimizes wrist stress. As with flat bench presses, don't bounce the bar off your chest or arch your back.

Muscles Worked

Narrow presses primarily work the triceps, but the front delts and pecs also come into play.

ROPE EXTENSIONS

Attach a rope to the pulldown machine and set the pulley wheel just slightly above your head. Grab the rope with both hands and twist around so your back is to the machine. Lean forward and adopt a runner's stance, or kneel with your upper arms on a bench. With your upper arms kept parallel to the floor and elbows in line with your ears, slowly extend your arms to a locked-out position. Slowly return to the starting position by bend-

Photo of Branch Warren by Ralph DeHaan

ing the elbows. Your hands should be just behind your head at the end.

Comments

Try not to throw the body into the movement,as this only reduces the amount of triceps stimulation. Always keep your legs bent to reduce the stress on the lower back. For variety some bodybuilders like to set the pulley wheel on the floor and extend their arms straight up.

Muscles Worked

Like most extension exercises, rope extensions target the whole triceps, particularly the long rear head.

BICEPS EXERCISES
STANDING BARBELL CURLS

Perhaps the most used (and abused!) exercise performed by bodybuilders. You can use the standard Olympic bar, a smaller straight bar, or an EZ-curl bar. Grab the bar with a grip slightly wider than shoulder width, and curl it up until the biceps are fully contracted. Try to keep your elbows close to your sides, and don't swing the weight up with your lower back. Lower the weight back to the starting position in good style. Don't simply let the thing drop! Not only does this make you lose half the movement, but you run the risk of tearing your biceps tendon.

Comments

Barbell curls are considered the ultimate in biceps exercises. However, many bodybuilders forget that the negative (lowering) part of the movement is just as important as the positive (hoisting) segment. Try to lower the bar with about the same speed as you curl it up.

Keep your back straight, and don't swing. If you want to cheat, save it for the last couple of reps. You could perform 8 to 10 reps in good style and then "cheat" one or two more. Don't abuse a good thing, however. One or two cheat reps is fine, but cheating from the start is counterproductive. Beginners and

intermediates will get all the stimulation they want from strict reps.

If you have weak wrists or forearms, you might want to give the EZ-curl bar a try. The bar's bent shape allows you to rotate your forearms slightly, thus reducing the tension on the wrists and forearms. Most bodybuilders use a straight bar, but play it by ear. Give both types a try and pick the one that is the most comfortable for you, and that produces the greatest biceps stimulation.

Muscles Worked

The barbell biceps curl works the entire biceps muscle. Also, because you have to forcibly grip the bar, the exercise will give you a great set of forearms. Finally, the front delts and lower back come into play for stabilizing purposes.

STANDING DUMBELL CURLS

Instead of using a barbell, grab two dumbells. Although it's possible to simultanously lift both dumbells, most bodybuilders do alternating dumbell curls. As the name implies, you curl the dumbells one at a time. Start with the dumbells by your sides, the ends pointing forward and back (i.e. the dumbells are parallel to one another). As you curl, rotate your palms from the facing-in position to a facing-up position. This is called supination. Many bodybuilders are not aware that the biceps has two main functions. Besides the better-known curling movement, the biceps also rotate the forearms. You can see this if you hold your arm by your side and rotate your hand back and forth. Notice the biceps flexing as the hand approaches the palms-up position. Take advantage of this physiological trait by rotating your arms as you use your dumbells. Arnold sure did!

Comments

Once again, limit any swinging to the last one or two reps. Do a complete set first and then use cheating to get a few more. Don't cheat to make it easier, rather cheat to get some additional stimulation. Try to put total concentration into each and every rep.

Besides the psychological aspect of curling one dumbell at a time, there may be a physiological basis. Neurologists suggest that when two arms are used simultaneously, the brain has to split the nerve impulses. By alternating the dumbells, you get full nerve transmission to each biceps.

However, although you have no control over nerve impulses, you do have control over exercise performance. So choose the version that feels most productive. As a final comment, Arnold favoured the alternating version. Need we say more?

Muscles Worked

Dumbell curls are great for working the belly of the biceps. They also reduce the stress on the wrists and forearms. In fact many bodybuilders suggest starting your biceps workout (this only applies to intermediate and advanced bodybuilders who are performing more than one exercise for each muscle) with dumbells so as not to overstress the weaker areas.

PREACHER CURLS

Also called Scott curls, for the first Mr. Olympia Larry Scott, who popularized it, this exercise is great for working the lower biceps region. Start by sitting on the stool or bench connected to the preacher board. Adjust yourself so that the padded board fits snugly under your armpits. Take the barbell from the supports and curl it until the biceps are fully contracted – a couple of inches from the shoulder. Lower to the starting position and repeat. You can also do this exercise on the opposite side of the preacher bench.

Comments

Although biceps length is genetic, you can create the illusion of length by building the lower regions. Some Scott benches are positioned fairly high and require you to stand up when doing the movement. If your gym has both, give them each a try and pick the one that suits you.

Of all the biceps exercises, this one is the most dangerous if not performed in good style. Under no circumstances drop the barbell to the bottom position. You can

easily rip the biceps tendon off from where it inserts on the forearm bone. The only option then is surgery and many months of inactivity. With a little attention paid to good style, you can avoid this aggravation.

Muscles Worked

Although they work the whole biceps muscle, Scott curls are primarily a lower-biceps exercise. Because you are braced by the padded board, it's virtually impossible to cheat and bring your lower back into the movement. Finally, you will notice a great deal of forearm stimulation. This is fine, as you will need a strong grip for many of your other exercises.

INCLINE CURLS

You will need an incline bench to perform this exercise. Unlike incline presses for your chest, use a bench with an angle of at least 45 degrees. Anything less will place too much strain on your front delts. Lie back on the bench and grab two dumbells. Curl the dumbells up until the biceps are fully flexed. All the tips suggested for standing dumbell curls apply here as well. (Rotate the hands from a facing-in to a facing-up position, don't swing the weight up, don't bounce at the bottom etc.)

Comments

Once again you have the option of curling both dumbells simultaniously or in an alternating manner. When you lower the dumbells, be careful not to hit the side of the incline bench. In fact, this is another reason for starting the dumbells in a forward-pointing position. If they were in the standard end-to-end position, they would have less clearance with the bench.

The advantage of using the incline bench is that it limits the amount of cheating you can do. Let's face it, you can't swing very much if you have your back braced against a rigid board.

Muscles Worked

Incline curls work the whole biceps region. Many bodybuilders find them are great for bringing out the biceps peak. Of course this is more genetic than anything else. The exercise does provide some forearm stimulation, but not to the same extent as the various barbell curls.

CONCENTRATION CURLS

Sit down on the end of a bench and grab a dumbell. With your elbow resting on your inner thigh, lower the dumbell and then curl it back up. Perform one set, and then switch arms.

Comments

Most bodybuilders perform concentration curls in the seated position. A few (including Arnold Schwarzenegger) like to do the movement in the standing, bent-over position. Instead of bracing the elbow against the thigh, they hold it down and away from the body. Keep the shoulder on the exercising side lower than on the free side.

Resist the urge to swing, and use only biceps power. As with all dumbell curls, you may want to supinate the hands when performing the exercise.

Muscles Worked

Most bodybuilders consider concentration curls more a shaping and peaking exercise than a mass-builder. Keep in mind that peak and shape are primarily due to genetics. Unless you have the genetics, you will never develop biceps peaks like Robby Robinson's. Still, you'll never know unless you try, and this is where concentration curls come in. The exercise cannot change your genetics, but it can maximize whatever potential you might have.

ONE-ARM PREACHER CURLS

Instead of using a barbell, try preacher curls with a single dumbell. Remember to lower slowly and not bounce the weight at the bottom.

Comments

By using a dumbell you can adjust your upper body to take some of the stress off the biceps tendon. Many bodybuilders find preacher curls hard on the forearms and elbows. Using a dumbell allows you more flexibility than the rigidity of a barbell. A barbell puts the force at 90 degrees to the upper body. A dumbell allows you to vary this angle, thus placing less stress on the forearms and elbows.

Muscles Worked

Dumbell preacher curls place most of the stress on the lower biceps. As discussed above, they treat your forearms and elbows with more kindness than the barbell version!

STANDING CABLE CURLS

For variety, try standing biceps curls with a set of cables. Whether you work one arm or both at the same time is up to you. If doing them one arm at a time, grab the machine with your free hand for support. It's extremely difficult to stay stationary when exercising one side of the body.

Comments

As with most cable exercises, go for the feel rather than the amount of weight. Cable curls are an excellent way to finish off the biceps after a basic movement such as standing barbell curls. Of course you can take the opposite approach and use them as a warm-up exercise.

Many bodybuilders suggest starting your biceps workout with cables or dumbells. This warms up the area and doesn't put the same stress on the elbows and forearms that barbell curls do.

Muscles Worked

Standing cable curls are another so-called peaking and shaping exercise. They work the whole biceps region, and if performed one arm at a time allow you to really concentrate. For a great pump, try finishing your biceps workout with a couple of high-rep (15-20) sets of cable curls.

NARROW-GRIP REVERSE CHINS

Grab an overhead chinning bar with a shoulder-width reverse grip. Pull your body up until the bar is touching your mid-chest. Lower back down until your arms are just short of a lockout.

Comments

Despite being a variation of the regular chin-up, one of the best back exercises, the narrow reverse grip puts much of the stress on the biceps. As with regular chins, avoid swinging the body when performing the reps. You may need to experiment with different grip widths to maximize biceps tension.

Muscles Worked

Narrow chins primarily work the biceps and lats, but the forearms, teres, and rhomboids also come into play.

CALF EXERCISES
STANDING CALF RAISES

You will need access to the appropriate machine to do this exercise. Rest your toes on the attached block and rest the pads on your shoulders. From here the exercise is straightforward. With your legs locked, rise up and down on your toes. Stretch all the way down and flex up on your toes as far as possible. Go for that intense burn!

Comments

Even though this is primarily a stretching exercise, don't be afraid to load the machine with hundreds of pounds of weight. Keep your back and legs straight. The only movement is at the ankle joint. Although calf injuries are extremely rare (the calf muscle is composed of extremely dense muscle fiber, which makes tearing very difficult), you still shouldn't bounce at the bottom of the movement, as you might strain your Achilles' tendon.

Muscles Worked

Standing calf raises work the entire calf muscle, with the primary focus on the upper (gastrocnemius) calf region.

TOE PRESSES ON THE LEG-PRESS MACHINE

This is another example of using a machine for an exercise it was not designed for. Instead of pressing the weight using your thighs, you push the weight platform using only your toes. As with the standing version, go for the maximum amount of stretch at the top and bottom.

Comments

The advantage of this exercise is that you don't have the entire weight pushing down on your spine. The disadvantage is that it will take a bit of practice to get the foot positioning correct. Still, the exercise is an adequate substitute if you don't have access to a standing calf machine, or if you find a calf machine hurts your shoulders.

Muscles Worked

This exercise hits the upper calf (gastrocnemius) and the lower calf (soleus). If you really want to get that extra burn in the lower calf, use less weight and bend your legs slightly as you perform the exercise. This will shift all the stress to the lower calf. After one set of these your calves will be burning like crazy.

DONKEY CALF RAISES

With your toes resting on a block of wood (at least four inches thick), bend over at the waist and have a willing training partner sit on your lower back. Flex up and down on your toes, going for maximum stretch. If you find one rider too light, try to fit a second on your back.

Comments

The bashful and shy might want to avoid this exercise. Also, many upper-class gyms (health spas) advise you not to do them. The general public is intimidated by people riding on top of one another, especially if they are doing so with an up-and-down motion.

Having said that, donkey calf raises are considered by many to be the best calf exercise. Such bodybuilders as Arnold, Larry Scott, Franco Columbu, and Frank Zane made extensive use of donkey calf raises. The exercise is seen less frequently in gyms today. Still, if you check out Gold's or World gyms in California, you will see numerous bodybuilders burning their calves with donkey calf raises. And one look at their lower legs gives testament to the exercise's effectiveness.

You may be lucky enough to have a donkey calf-raise machine in your gym, and if so, make good use of it.

Muscles Worked

Donkey calf raises work the whole calf region. If you keep your legs completely locked, most of the work is done by the gastrocnemius. Bend the legs slightly and the lower calves take most of the strain. For variety you might want to include both in your training. Remember, when doing the bent-leg variety, you will need to use less weight as the lower calf cannot handle the same weight as the upper calf. Nor can your knees.

SEATED CALF RAISES

You will need a special machine to do this exercise. (Or use a weight on a towel on your knees.) Sit down on the machine's chair and place the padded knee rests on your legs. With your toes on the block, stretch up and down as far as you can.

Comments

Because it works the lower calf, you will need to use less weight than for other calf exercises. Go for at least 20 reps and try to feel every one of them. No bouncing the weight on your legs. Even though the supports are padded, improper style can injure your knees.

Muscles Worked

Since the legs are bent, most of the stress is placed on the lower calf (soleus), but there is some secondary upper-calf involvement.

Photo of Craig Richardson by Jason Breeze

GLOSSARY

Glossary

Abdominals

The series of muscles located on the lower midsection of the torso. They are used to contract the body forward through a range of six to eight inches.

Acupuncture

The ancient Chinese practice whereby the body's well-being is controlled by pressure points. Acupuncture involves stimulating these points with long needles.

Aerobic Exercise

Any long-lasting exercise that can be carried on within the body's ability to replenish oxygen in working muscles.

AFWB

The American Federation of Women Bodybuilders. This organization is an affiliate of the IFBB, and is responsible for organizing and running women's bodybuilding contests in America.

AIDS – Short for Acquired Immune Deficiency Syndrome

AIDS is caused by a virus and is contracted by the exchange of bodily fluids. There have been some cases of bodybuilders contracting AIDS from the sharing of needles (used for anabolic steroid injections).

Amenorrhea

Absence of menstrual periods due to a low bodyfat percentage. This condition is not dangerous and is common in such sports as gymnastics, bodybuilding, and track and field.

Amino Acids

Called the "building blocks of life," amino acids are biochemical subunits linked together by chemical bonds to form polypeptide chains. Hundreds of polypeptides, in turn linked together, from a protein molecule.

Anabolic

Metabolic process whereby smaller units are assembled into larger units. For example, the combining of amino acids into protein strands is a form of anabolism.

Anaerobic Exercise

Any high-intensity exercise that outstrips the body's aerobic capacity and leads to an oxygen debt. Because of its intensity, anaerobic exercise can be maintained for only short periods of time.

APC

The American Physique Committee. This federation is responsible for organizing and running men's amateur bodybuilding contests in America. It is also an affiliate of the IFBB.

Arm Blaster

Short, curved metal training apparatus used for bracing the arms when performing exercises such as biceps curls.

Arthritis

Chronic condition marked by an inflammation of the tissue surrounding the joints.

Asymmetric Training

Any exercise that targets only one side of the body. One-arm dumbell curls, lateral raises and triceps extensions are all examples of asymmetric training.

Back

The series of muscles located on the dorsal region of the body. The back-muscle complex includes the latissimus dorsi, spinal erectors, trapezius, rhomboids and teres minor and major.

Barbell

One of the most basic pieces of bodybuilding equipment. Barbells consist of a long bar, collars, sleeves, and associated plates made of steel or iron. They may be either adjustable (allowing the changing of plates) or fixed (the plates are kept in place by welded collars). Barbells average between five and seven feet in length, and usually weigh between 25 and 45 pounds.

Basic Exercises

Exercises that work more than one muscle group simultaneously. Basic exercises form the mainstay of a bodybuilder's mass-gaining routine. Examples include: bench presses, shoulder presses, squats, deadlifts, and bent-over rows. Also called compound exercises.

Belt

Large leather support worn around the waist by bodybuilders. Weightlifting belts are usually four to six inches wide. They provide support to the lower-back muscles and spine.

Biceps

Flexor muscles located on the upper arm. The biceps are composed of two "heads," and are responsible for bending the lower arm towards the upper arm.

Biofeedback

Physiological or psychological symptom given off by the body. The best bodybuilders are those who recognize such biofeedback signals and use them to improve their training, eating, and competitive preparation.

BMR

Short for Basal Metabolic Rate, the BMR is the speed at which the resting body consumes energy (calories).

Bodybuilding

Competitive or noncompetitive sub-division of weight training in which the primary goal is the improvement of one's physique. For most, the objective is not competition but for those who do compete the final placings are determined by a panel of judges who look at such physical qualities as muscle size, shape, symmetry, bodyfat percentage, and presentation (posing).

Bodyfat Percentage

The ration of fat to bodyweight. For most bodybuilders, 8 to 10 percent is the off-season goal, while two to four percent is the competitive goal.

Breathing Pullovers

Specialized exercise important to a bodybuilder as it stretches the rib cartilage, producing a large rib cage and therefore a larger chest measurement.

Bulking Up

Bodybuilding term which refers to the gaining of 30 to 40 pounds of bodyweight over a short period of time. This practice has become less common, given the increased number of competitions and the demand for guest posers on a year-round basis.

Burn

Term unique to the sport of bodybuilding, describing the feeling a muscle gets as it's exercised. The term also refers to partial reps done at the end of a set once performing full reps is impossible.

Bursae

Flat sacks filled with fluid. They support and protect joints.

Buttocks

Another term referring to the gluteus maximus, medius and minimus, extensors and abductors of the thigh at the hip joint.

Cables

Long wire cords attached to weight stacks at one end and a hand grip at the other. Cable exercises keep tension on the working muscle throughout a full range of motion.

Calves

Also called "lowers" and "bodybuilding's diamonds," the calves consist of the soleus and gastrocnemius muscles, located on the backs of the lower leg bones. The calves are similar to the forearms in that they are composed of extremely dense muscle tissue. Their function is to flex the ankles.

Carbohydrate Loading

The practice of depleting and replenishing the body's glycogen levels in the weeks leading up to a bodybuilding contest. This technique allows bodybuilders to saturate their muscles with stored water, thus making the muscles appear fuller and harder.

Cartilage

Connective tissue that acts as a shock absorber between bones. It's found wherever two bones articulate over one another – for example, in the knees.

Chalk

White, fine-grained powder, used to improve the grip on a barbell or dumbell. Chalk is formed from the shells of dead marine microorganisms.

Cheating

An advanced training technique that consists of utilizing fresh muscles to assist in the completion of an exercise when the muscle being trained is nearing fatigue.

Chelation

The process by which protein molecules are bonded to inorganic minerals, making them easier to assimilate by the human body.

Chest

The large pectoral muscles located on the front of the upper torso, responsible for drawing the arms forward and in toward the center of the body.

Cholesterol

Naturally occurring steroid molecule involved in the formation of hormones, vitamins and bile salts, and in the transport of fats in the bloodstream to tissues throughout the body. Excessive cholesterol in the diet can lead to cardiovascular disease.

Circuit Training

A specialized form of weight training which combines strength training and aerobic conditioning. Circuit training consists of performing 10 to 20 different exercises, one after the other, with little rest between sets.

Clean

Weightlifting technique whereby the barbell is hoisted to shoulder level using the arms, legs, hips, and lower back. This is the first part of the competitive lift called the "clean and jerk," which finishes with the barbell held above the head, arms locked.

Collar

Small, round, iron or plastic clamp, used to anchor plates on a barbell or dumbell. In most cases collars are screwed on, but some versions are held in a spring-like manner.

Compound Exercises

Any exercise that works more than one muscle group. Popular compound movements include: bench presses, squats, shoulder presses, and bent-over rows.

Compulsory Poses

The seven poses used to compare contestants in a bodybuilding contest. These are the side chest, rear lat spread, front lat spread, front double biceps, rear double biceps, side triceps, and the abdominal and front thigh.

Cortisol

Catabolic hormone released by the body in response to stress (of which exercise is one form). Cortisol speeds up the rate at which large units are broken down into smaller units (catabolism), and increases fat storage.

Cut

Competitive term used to describe the physical appearance of a bodybuilder. To be "cut," implies that you are in great competitive shape, with extremely low bodyfat levels.

Cycle Training

Form of training in which high-intensity workouts are alternated with those of low intensity. The technique can be applied weekly or yearly.

Decline Bench

Bench used to work the lower and outer pectorals. Decline benches require the user to place his or her head at the low end and feet at the upper end of the bench.

Definition

Another term to describe the percentage of bodyfat carried by a competitive bodybuilder. A bodybuilder with good definition shows a great deal of vascularity and muscular separation.

Dehydration

Biological state in which the body has insufficient water levels for proper functioning. Since the human body is over 90 percent water, athletes must continuously replenish any water lost during intense exercise.

Deltoids

The deltoid muscles – anterior, medial and posterior – are located at the top of the torso. The deltoids are responsible for elevating and rotating the arms.

Density

Term used to describe the amount of muscle mass carried by a bodybuilder. It generally refers to muscle thickness and hardness.

Descending Sets

An advanced-training technique involving the removal of weight at the completion of a set, and the performing of additional reps with the lighter weight.

Diet

A term that refers to a fixed eating pattern. In general usage it usually means to try and lose weight.

Dislocation

Type of injury where the end of one bone (called a "ball") slips out of a hollow indentation (called the "socket") of another bone. It is usually accompanied by tearing of the joint ligaments, which makes the injury very painful.

Diuretics

Any natural or synthetic chemical that causes the body to excrete water. In most cases the drug interacts with aldosterone, the hormone responsible for water retention. Some bodybuilders use diuretics before a contest as it improves their muscularity. But diuretics also flush electrolytes from the body (one of their functions being the control of heart rate), therefore it is a dangerous practice and a few pro bodybuilders have died of diuretic-induced heart attacks.

Down-the-Rack Training

An advanced training technique involving the use of two or three successively lighter dumbells during the performance of one set.

Dumbell

Short bars on which plates are secured. Dumbells can be considered the one-arm version of a barbell. In most gyms, the weight plates are welded on, and the poundage is written on the dumbell.

Ectomorphs

Body type characterized by long thin bones, low bodyfat levels and difficulty in gaining muscle mass.

Endomorphs

Body type characterized by large bones and an excess of bodyfat.

Endorphins

Chemicals released by the brain in response to pain. Often called "natural opiates," endorphins decrease the individual's sensitivity to pain.

Epiphysis

Locations on bones at which growth takes place. They fuse by the late teens or early twenties, but they can prematurely close in young teens with anabolic steroid use.

Exercise

In general terms, any form of physical activity that increases the heart and respiratory rate. In bodybuilding terms, an exercise is one specific movement for one or more muscle groups (i.e. bench press, squat, curl, etc.).

Flexibility

The degree of muscle and connective tissue suppleness at a joint. The greater the flexibility, the greater the range of motion in an individual's limbs and torso.

EZ-Curl Bar

Short, S-shaped bar used for such exercises as biceps curls and lying triceps extensions. The bar's unique shape puts less stress on the wrists and forearms than a straight bar.

Fast-Twitch Muscle Fiber

Type of muscle fiber that is adapted for rapid but short duration contractions.

Fluid Retention

Bodybuilding term referring to the amount of water held between the skin and muscles. A bodybuilder "holding water" appears smooth, and his muscularity is blurred.

Forced Reps

An advanced training technique whereby a training partner helps you complete extra reps after the exercised muscles reach the point of fatigue.

Fractures

Complete or partial break of one of the body's bones.

Free Posing

Held in round three of a bodybuilding contest, free posing consists of individual poses set to the bodybuilder's personal choice of music.

Free Weights

Term given to barbells and dumbells. Free-weight exercises are the most popular types performed by bodybuilders.

Genetics

The study of how biological traits or characteristics are passed from one generation to the next. In bodybuilding terms it refers to the potential each individual has for developing his or her physique.

Giant Sets

An advanced training technique in which four or more exercises are performed consecutively. In most cases the term refers to exercises for one muscle group, but bodybuilders have been known to use exercises for four different muscle groups.

Gloves

Specialized hand apparel worn while working out. Gloves help prevent blisters and the build up of calluses.

Glycogen

Primary fuel source used by exercising muscles. Glycogen is one of the stored forms of carbohydrate.

Golgi Tendon Organ (GTO)

Stretch receptors located at the ends of muscles. They terminate muscular contraction when too much stress is placed on the muscle.

Gravity Boots

Specialized boots fitted with an attachment device that allows the user to perform various exercises while hanging upside down on an overhead bar.

Gym

Although this can apply to almost any exercising venue (eg. high-school gym), for bodybuilders the term refers to a weight-training club.

Gynecomastia

Condition characterized by a swelling of the nipple region in males. It may occur naturally at puberty, but in most cases the term applies to the condition brought on by anabolic steroid use. From a biological viewpoint, the condition occurs after excessive amounts of testosterone (or anabolic steroids), is broken down into estrogen (a feminizing hormone), which then stimulate estrogen receptors in the breast region. Gynecomastia is also known as "bitch tits."

Hamstrings

The leg biceps located on the back of the upper legs, responsible for curling the lower leg toward the upper leg. The hamstrings are analogous to the biceps in the upper arm.

Head Straps

Leather or nylon harness that is placed over the head allowing the user to attach weight and train the neck muscles.

Heavy Duty

Training style developed by former Mr. Universe, Mike Mentzer. Much of Mentzer's theory is based on the works of Dr. Arthur Jones, and involves performing just one or two high-intensity sets for each muscle group.

Hypertrophy

Biological term that means muscle growth. Muscles are believed to primarily grow by increasing the size of existing muscle fibers although there is some evidence to suggest that intense weight training can increase the actual number of muscle fibers.

IFBB

International Federation of Bodybuilders. First founded in 1946 by Joe Weider, the IFBB is the largest bodybuilding federation in the world.

Incline Bench

Bench where the body is tilted back in respect to the vertical. Incline benches are primarily used to work the upper-chest region.

Injuries

In bodybuilding terms, injuries are any damage to bone, muscle, or connective tissue. The most common bodybuilding injuries are muscle strains.

Instinctive Training

One of the most advanced training techniques, it means training according to how you and your respective muscles feel, rather than training according to a structured routine. It takes many years of experience to get to the point at which you are in tune enough with your body to train instinctively in an effective manner.

Intercostals

Small, finger-like muscles located along the sides of the lower abdomen, between the rib cage and obliques.

Isolation Exercises

Any exercise aimed at working only one muscle. In most cases, it's virtually impossible to totally isolate a muscle. Some common examples are: preacher curls, lateral raises, and triceps pushdowns.

Isometric

Type of muscle contraction where there is no shortening of the muscle's length. Isometric exercises were popularized by Charles Atlas.

Isotension

Exercise technique whereby continuous stress is placed on a given muscle. Extending the leg by contracting the quadriceps and holding the position for 10 to 20 seconds or more is an example of isotension. Bodybuilders make use of the technique during the precompetition phase as it improves muscle separation.

Isotonic

Type of muscle contraction where the contracting muscle shortens. The muscle may also be lengthening, as when doing a "negative." Most bodybuilding exercises are examples of isotonic contraction.

Joint

The point at which two bones meet. Most joints have a hinge-type structure which allows the bones to articulate over one another.

Lactic Acid

A product given off during aerobic respiration. Lactic acid was once thought to be strictly a waste product, however recent evidence suggests that a version of lactic acid called lactate is used by the liver to replenish glycogen supplies.

Latissimus Dorsi

Called the lats, these large fan shaped muscles are located on the back of the torso, and when properly developed give the bodybuilder the characteristic V-shape. The lats function to pull the arms down and back.

Layoff

Any time spent away from the gym is called a layoff. It can be referred to as a training vacation.

Ligament

Fibrous connective tissue that joins one bone to another.

Lymphatic System

Parallel system to the cardiovascular system, responsible for collecting and removing waste products from the body. The system's fluid is called lymph, and collects at nodes found in the neck, armpits, and groin.

Mass

Term used to describe the degree of muscle size. Hence an especially large bodybuilder is referred to as "massive."

Massage

Recovery technique that involves a forceful rubbing, pinching, or kneading, of the body's muscles. Massage speeds up the removal rate of exercise byproducts, helps athletes relax, and improves performance. The most popular forms of massage are Soviet and Swedish.

Mesomorphs

Body type characterized by large bones, low bodyfat levels and a greater-than-average rate of muscle growth.

Muscularity

Another term used to describe the degree of muscular definition. The lower the bodyfat percentage the greater the degree of muscularity.

Muscle

The series of tissue bellies located on the skeleton that serve to move and stabilize the body's various appendages.

Nautilus

Type of exercise equipment invented by Dr. Arthur Jones. Nautilus machines employ a wide assortment of cams, pulleys and weight stacks, to work the muscle over a wide range of movement.

Negatives

A portion of the rep movement which goes in the same direction as gravity, but the user concentrates on resisting it. In most cases negatives are the downward part of an exercise. For example, during barbell curls, the downward part of the exercise is the negative half of the movement (the upward, curling part, is the positive phase).

Neuromuscular System

The combination of nerves and muscles that interact to control body movement.

Nutrition

The art of combining foods in the right amounts so the human body receives all of its required nutrients. In bodybuilding terms, eating to gain muscle size and keep bodyfat levels low is considered proper nutrition.

Nutrients

The various minerals, vitamins, proteins, fats, and carbohydrates needed by the body for proper maintenance, health, and growth.

Off-Season

Competitive bodybuilding term used to describe the period of the year primarily devoted to gaining muscle mass.

Oil

Liquid used by bodybuilders to highlight the muscles while onstage. Most bodybuilders use vegetable oils, as they are absorbed by the skin and give a better sheen.

Olympia, Mr. and Ms.

The top professional contest in men's and women's bodybuilding. The Mr. Olympia was first held in 1965 (won by Larry Scott) and the first Ms. Olympia was held in 1980 (won by Rachel McLish).

Olympic Barbell

The most specialized barbell in weightlifting. Olympic barbells weigh 45 pounds and are made from spring steel.

Overload

Term used to describe the degree of stress placed on a muscle. To overload means to continuously increase the amount of resistance that a muscle has to work against. For bodybuilders the stress is in the form of weight.

Overtraining

The physiological state whereby the individual's recovery system is taxed to the limit. In many cases, insufficient time is allowed for recovery between workouts. Among the more common symptoms are: muscle loss, lack of motivation, insomnia, and reduced energy.

Peak

This can mean the degree of sharpness or shape held by a particular muscle (usually the biceps), or it may refer to the shape a bodybuilder holds on a given contest day. A bodybuilder who has "peaked" is in top condition (i.e. full, vascular muscles and a low bodyfat percentage).

Peliosis Hepatitis

Liver condition often associated with anabolic steroid use. As of yet no hard medical evidence exists to support the claims that steroids do in fact cause the disease.

PHA

Short for Peripheral Heart Action, PHA was first developed by 1966 Mr. America, Bob Gajda. The training style involves grouping sets of exercises into sequences, each one aimed at a different muscle group. PHA is one of the best methods of combining weight training and aerobics.

Plateau

A state of training during which no progress is being made. Plateaus usually occur after long periods of repetitious training. Breaking the condition involves shocking the muscles with new training techniques.

Plates

Varying-sized cast-iron weights that are placed on a barbell or dumbell. Plates range in size from 1-1/4 pounds to 100 pounds. The most common plates in bodybuilding gyms weigh 5, 10, 25, 35, and 45 pounds.

Posedown

Final round in a competitive bodybuilding contest. The top three to six contestants match poses in a posing free-for-all.

Posing

The art of displaying the physique in a bodybuilding contest. Posing consists of mandatory poses used to compare contestants and free posing, where the individual combines favorite poses to highlight strong points, deemphasize weak body parts and let their personality show through.

Posing Trunks

The small one- or two-piece suits worn by competitors in a bodybuilding contest. Posing trunks allow the competitor to show as much of his or her physique as possible.

Positives

Part of the rep movement that goes against gravity. In barbell biceps curls, the positive phase would occur during the curling of the barbell. The lowering of the bar is the negative phase.

Poundage

Another term used to describe the weight of a barbell, dumbell, or machine weight stack.

Powerlifting

The competitive sport that utilizes three lifts – the squat, deadlift, and bench press. The objective is to lift more than your opponent both in the three individual events, and in total.

Precontest

Period of the year devoted primarily to refining muscle size and shape. Bodybuilders, on average, devote the last three months before a contest to this type of training.

Pre-Exhaust

This advanced training technique involves fatiguing a desired muscle with an isolation movement, and then using a compound exercise to stress the muscle even further. Pre-exhaust is ideal for eliminating the "weakest link in the chain" effect often encountered when performing compound exercises.

Prejudging

Section of a bodybuilding contest where most of the actual judging takes place. Although the competitors may go through their free-posing routines, most of the emphasis is placed on the compulsory rounds.

Priapism

The persistent and often painful erection of the penis that sometimes occurs with steroid use.

Priority Training

Training strategy where an individual devotes most of his or her energy to targeting weak muscle groups.

Proportion

Term used to describe the size of one muscle with respect to the whole body. A bodybuilder with good "proportions" would have all his/her muscles in balance with regards to muscle size.

Protein

Nutrient composed of long chains of amino acids. Protein is primarily used in the production of muscle tissue, hormones, and enzymes.

Psychological Warfare

Any verbal or behavioral strategies employed by competitors to interfere with their opponents' preparation or competition.

Pump

Biological condition where an exercised muscle swells and becomes engorged with blood.

Pumping Iron

Term coined by bodybuilders to refer to their sport. The name was immortalized by George Gains and George Butler in their 1975 documentary, *Pumping Iron*.

Pyramiding

Training technique whereby weight is added for the first couple of sets and then decreased for the remaining sets. Bodybuilders may also perform a half-pyramid technique where the weight is only added or decreased for the given number of sets.

Quadriceps

The quadriceps, normally called the "quads," are the large, four-headed muscles located on the front and sides of the upper legs. They are analogous to the triceps, and are the extensors of the legs. Their primary function is to extend the lower leg forward (bringing the upper and lower legs to a lock-out configuration).

Repetition

Abbreviated "rep" in gyms, this simply refers to one full movement of a particular exercise.

Resistance

The amount of force being placed on a muscle. In bodybuilding circles it refers to the amount of weight being lifted.

Rest-Pause

A training technique in which the user completes one set, and then rests only about 10 seconds before starting the next set. The technique is based on the biological fact that a muscle recovers about 90 percent of its strength within 10 to 15 seconds. Rest-pause allows the bodybuilder to use heavy weight for every set.

Ripped

Another term to describe the percentage of bodyfat carried by a competitive bodybuilder. A ripped bodybuilder has a very low fat percentage (2 to 4 percent).

Routine

Another word for program, schedule, agenda, etc. It refers to the complete number of sets, reps, and exercises performed for a given muscle or muscles on a particular day.

Set

Term referring to a given number of consecutive reps. Ten non-stop reps would be called one set of 10 reps.

Shocking

Training strategy that involves training the muscle with a new form of exercise. Shocking techniques are used to "kick-start" muscles that have become accustomed to repetitious training routines.

Sleeve

Short, hollow, metal tube fitted over both ends of a barbell. The sleeve allows the plates to rotate on the bar, thus reducing the stress on the user's wrists.

Slow-Twitch Muscle Fiber

Type of muscle fiber adapted for slow, long-duration contraction. The spinal erectors of the lower back are primarily composed of slow-twitch muscle fiber.

Somatotype

Term referring to an individual's body characteristics including such things as muscle size, bone size, bodyfat level, and physical personality.

Soreness

The mild pain felt in muscles after a workout, it is primarily caused by a build-up of lactic acid, and usually appears 12 to 24 hours after exercising.

Spinal Erectors

Two long, snake-like muscles located at the center of the lower back. The spinal erectors help maintain posture by keeping the upper body perpendicular with the floor.

Split Routines

Any routine for which different muscle groups are worked on separate days. The most common bodybuilding split routines are four- and six-day splits.

Sponges

Sponges are used to protect the hands from blisters and callouses. Many bodybuilders find sponges more convenient to work with than gloves.

Spot

In short, a helping hand when performing a particular exercise. A spot is provided by a training partner when you fail during an exercise. In most cases it involves providing a few pounds of upward pressure to keep the barbell, dumbell, or machine handle moving.

Staggered Sets

An advanced training technique whereby the user adds sets for a weak muscle group between their regular training exercises. For example, many bodybuilders with weak calves add extra calf training between other muscle groups. In many cases, the calf exercise is performed instead of taking a rest.

Steroids

Synthetic derivatives of the hormone testosterone that allow the user to gain muscle mass and strength more rapidly. In addition to their muscle-building effects, steroids (anabolic) increase the oxidation rate of fat, thus giving the user a more "ripped" appearance.

Sticking Point

The point during an exercise where the user is in the weakest biomechanical position. In other words, this is the most difficult part of the movement. The sticking point is usually close to the bottom of the exercise.

Straps

Long, narrow pieces of material used to increase one's gripping power on an exercise. Straps are wrapped around the lower forearm and bar in such a manner that as the user grips the bar, the straps get tighter. They are used on such exercises as deadlifts, shrugs, and chins.

Stretching

Form of exercise where the primary goal is to increase flexibility. Stretching is also an excellent way to warm up the body and prepare it for more stressful forms of exercise.

Stretch Marks

Red or purple lines caused by thinning and loss of elasticity in the skin. In most cases the marks are the result of rapid muscle growth, but gaining large amounts of fat can also cause them. The most common site for stretch marks on bodybuilders is the pec-delt tie-in. There is no effective means of prevention or treatment.

Strict Form

Training technique which involves performing exercises in a slow, controlled manner, and through a full range of motion, without the aid of a partner or cheating techniques.

Stripping Method

An advanced training technique whereby the individual removes a few plates at the end of a set and forces out extra reps. The technique allows the user to force a muscle past the point of normal failure.

Supersets

Advanced training technique whereby two exercises are performed consecutively without any rest. Supersets may consist of exercises for the same muscle group (eg. dumb-ell curls and barbell curls) or exercises for different muscle groups (eg. triceps extensions and biceps curls). If performing supersets for different muscle groups, bodybuilders usually pick opposing muscle groups (triceps-biceps, quads-hamstrings, chest-back, etc).

Supination

Technique in which the palms start off facing the body during a dumbell curl and rotate outward as the dumbell is raised. In fact supination refers to any movement in which a limb rotates away from the center of the body.

Supplements

Any form of vitamin, mineral, protein, or other nutrient taken separate from, or in addition to, the regular diet. Supplements come in many forms, including tablet, capsule, power, oil, or plant material.

Sweat Bands

Small pieces of material, usually cloth, wrapped around the forehead to absorb sweat. Bandanas and "do-rags" are used far more commonly these days.

Symmetry

In bodybuilding terms this refers to the overall look to the body in addition to its true meaning of right-left similarity. Symmetry is closely related to proportion.

Tanning

Biochemical reaction where the skin releases pigment upon exposure to sunlight. Bodybuilders tan because a darker color improves skin appearance in a contest or photo shoot and highlights muscularity. Tanning is even done by bodybuilders of African descent.

Tendinitis

Form of inflammation involving tendons and the points at which they attach to muscles and bones. Tendinitis is usually caused by overstressing a particular area. Bodybuilders often get tendinitis in the biceps-tendon region.

Tendon

Tough cord of connective tissue that connects a muscle to a bone.

Testosterone

Androgenic/anabolic hormone responsible for such physiological effects as: increasing muscle size and strength, facial hair growth, scalp hair loss, decreasing sperm production (males), and increasing aggression levels. Although both sexes have circulating testosterone, males have it in greater concentrations.

Training Diary

Daily journal or record kept by bodybuilders. Diaries are useful for keeping track of such items as weight, exercises, sets, reps, calories and overall motivation levels.

Training Partner

Any individual who matches you set for set during your workout. A training partner allows you to go for that extra rep. He or she also acts as a spotter, and even a coach on days when you just don't feel like working out.

Training to Failure

Any time you refuse to terminate a set until the muscle simply cannot contract for additional reps, you are training to failure. Most bodybuilders train to positive failure and then have a training partner help them perform a few extra reps.

Triceps

Extensor muscles of the upper arm. The triceps are composed of three heads that work in opposition to the biceps – they extend the lower arm and straighten the elbow.

Trisets

Similar to supersets but involving the use of three different exercises for the same muscle group.

Twenty-ones

Advanced exercise technique where you perform 7 half-reps at the bottom of the movement, 7 half-reps at the top, and finish with 7 full reps.

Universal Machine

The most common type of training apparatus (not counting free weights) found in home and bodybuilding gyms. The machines may train one muscle group, or have numerous stations to train the whole body.

Vascularity

The degree of vein and artery visibility. In order to be "highly" vascular, a bodybuilder must have an extremely low bodyfat percentage.

Visualization

Relaxation technique performed by clearing the mind and then concentrating and focusing on particular goals. For bodybuilders, common visualization goals include an upcoming contest, workout, or a new training strategy.

Warmup

Any form of light, short duration exercise that prepares the body for more intense exercise. Warming up should involve increasing the heart and respiratory rate, and stretching to prepare the muscles for exercise. A good warmup helps prevent injury.

Weight

This term refers to the plates or weight stacks themselves, or it can be used to describe the actual poundage on the bar.

Weight Class

Generally speaking, men's bodybuilding competitions are subdivided into four categories called weight classes: light, medium, light heavyweight, and heavyweight. Women's events have two divisions, lightweight and heavyweight.

Weightlifting

A general term used to describe the exercise form involving the use of weights, or an Olympic event. The competitive version involves two lifts: the snatch and the clean and jerk.

Workout

The program or schedule of exercises performed on any given day. Bodybuilders refer to exercise as "going for a workout."

Wraps

Long pieces of material (usually a first-aid bandage) that bodybuilders wrap around weak or injured bodyparts. Wraps keep the area warm and provide extra security. Many bodybuilders wrap the knees during squats and the wrists during bench presses.

Index